A Riverman's Lexicon

A Riverman's Lexicon

In Lehman's Terms

**Christened and Launched at JEFFBOAT
December 1972**

**Sponsor – Sally L. Lehman
Maid of Honor – Katrina A. Lehman**

A Riverman's Lexicon

© 2009 Charles F. Lehman

No portion of this book may be reproduced
in any form without permission in writing
from the publisher, except by a
reviewer, who is permitted to
quote brief passages in a review.

Pubished by
J. R. Simpson & Associates, Inc
Florissant, Missouri

Produced by Little River Books, a
division of J. R. Simpson & Associates, Inc.

Printed in the United States

ISBN-13 978-0-9841503-0-4

Library of Congress Card No. 2009938670

Price: $29.95 + $5 S&H
For additional copies contact author: Cflehman@aol.com or at:

P.O. Box 803
Crestwood, KY 40014

Dedication

To my wife Sally, my partner in the pilothouse of life, where we have navigated over many miles of river, both deep and shallow, but mostly calm and serene. My loving thanks for joining me on the voyage.

CFL

Introduction

Rivermen of the Mississippi River and its tributaries speak a unique and beguiling language melded of Elizabethan sailor talk, practical carpentry and the barnyard. It grew naturally in a state of induced isolation, where a riverman could throw a lump of coal from boat to shore, but could not go there. Despite its humble origins, the language of the rivers is an exact argot. The words, phrases and syntax are perfectly clear to those who use it, for very often a clear understanding between pilothouse and deck is vital.

A number of attempts have been made to organize lexicons of this speech. The earliest was an annex to *Pilotin' Comes Natural*, by Captain Frederick Way, Jr. in 1943. Soon this was followed by a booklet called *Language of the Western Rivers*, compiled by the United States Coast Guard, which had replaced the Steamboat Inspection Service. But, with their educations, lore and experience gained at sea, Coast Guard officers found themselves unable to talk with the brown-water mariners in their charge. Captain Alan L. Bates provided a very brief glossary in his book *Belle of Louisville* in 1964, and followed that with a more extensive one in *The Western Rivers Steamboat Cyclopoedium*, in 1966, but even this was limited to structural terms. Captain Jack Ross, a marine surveyor, made another dictionary titled *As They Say on the River* in 1996, primarily aimed at defining terms, including some slang, for use in the courts when he found that attorneys and judges could not comprehend the testimony of riverman witnesses.

Now Captain Charles F. Lehman has compiled a truly comprehensive lexicon combining excerpts from all of the above with the language he learned and loved during a long and varied river career. His experience ranged from deckhand through masterpilot to the board room of a huge towing firm. Geographically he ranged from the mouth of the Mississippi to such far-flung ports as Houston, Kansas City, Minneapolis, Chicago, and Pittsburgh and all the rivers between them. This enabled him to absorb the entire gamut of the river speech. The pity is that the twang of West Virginia, the French-tinted drawl of the Cajuns and the brisk tones of the Midwest cannot be transferred to paper, for he has heard and understood all of those dialects.

The book is more than a drab listing of definitions. Yes, indeed! In this witty book the reader will find opinions frankly stated, puns without apology, poetry and slang, and even a sentimental entry now and then. These derelictions of academic duty give Lehman's Lexicon a rare combination of warmth, personality and unexpected delight that may never be duplicated.

—Alan Bates

Acknowledgements

First, my gratitude goes to Al Winholt, who was the River Marine Manager for Socony-Vacuum (now Exxon Mobil) for giving me my first employment on the river in 1950. It started as a job, became a career, and a love. Most of all, I want to thank Captain William "Sambo" Dean, under whom I first went as a river Pilot. He made this book possible by teaching me how the river reacted a various stages, how to find the slack currents, what to avoid, how to work with nature when handling a boat and its tow, as well as all the other things a Pilot needs to do if one is to become a success in the trade of riverboating. He chewed me out almost every watch, but it was his way of teaching. He made me a better man and Pilot than I would have become if the tutelage was under another Captain.

Then, I am grateful to Barbara Huffman (author of Beatty's Navy) for the hard job of making a first proof-reading edit of what was put to print. It was a grammar and hyphen placement lesson that was supposed to be taught in the eighth grade, but I guess I was absent that day. If there are mistakes in the following text it is because of my reworking some of the terms, or it will be in one of the couple of hundred entries that were added after she finished her given chore.

And, of course, my esteem and fraternal kinship is extended to Alan Bates, writer and columnist extraordinaire, who wrote the INTRODUCTION to this volume, but also he was most helpful with comments and advice. The books he has written and his knowledge of steamboats and their equipment was extremely beneficial, but also his editing for content and a final reading to check for errors is most appreciated. I will always be grateful for his advice, assistance and friendship.

Finally, the utmost appreciation must be extended to my wife Sally who patiently puts up with my foibles, but who also drew a couple of pictorial renderings for this volume. She continually asked, "How's the book coming along", when she knew I was procrastinating in getting image results to my patient, but prodding publisher, Jack Simpson, who also rendered sound encouragement.

As indicated in the FORWARD to this LEXICON the terms listed have been derived from personal experience and from many other sources. The most helpful were the histories of the mid-continent Corps of Engineers Districts and the S & D Reflectors for past historical usage. Many of the definitions were written from researching more than one, sometimes many sources. At times it was found that they were in conflict, so "what others said" was occasionally added. It has been pointed out to me that "it would be nice to have a list of the sources for each term", but if I listed all the books in my maritime library of over 7000 volumes, plus other places where answers were sought, the lexicon would have to be two or three times its current size.

Many of the pictures and images at the end of each lettered section are from U.S. government sources, i.e. USACE, USCG, USN, and a few other technical or historical documents. Some are archival and in the public domain. Some others I do not know who to acknowledge, but where they are known I have tried to give proper recognition. Hopefully, the author won't be chastised too badly for failure to give credit where it was due. Notes from old files of stuff did not have all the necessary documentation as it was not believed the old clippings would ever be a part of a volume such as this one.

Different regions of the country have used the same term with a dissimilar meaning or employ another word or phrase entirely to describe an object or action. And, of course, on the river one Captain or Mate passes on how or what he or she learned when first being on the river to the new green deckhand who later becomes a Pilot whether the original meaning was absolutely correct or not. Then, however it was done on the *STEAMER ATLAS* is how they are supposed to do it on M/V *PODUNK*. So the terms, and their meanings, go from one generation of rivermen to another, with those in the upper reaches of the Ohio Valley having some terminology akin only to their region, as do the localized Upper Mississippi expressions, and the language of the Gulf Coast mariners is sometimes different from the upriver operations. All have been pretty much been put in this large pot of stew, burgoo, gumbo, or what have you, and is called a Riverman's Lexicon. It was stirred all up, a large dash of spice was added, and hopefully you will enjoy the feast.

USING THIS VOLUME

When perusing a term and viewing another word in the definition that is in all capitalized letters (not bold), means that word is also defined separately and may add additional meaning or information regarding the term being described. The exceptions to this are names of vessels which are always in capitalized and italicized form. Other terms which are defined in the book may or may not be capitalized if they are only descriptive and do not particularly add to the meaning of the word being defined.

The volume contains many legal and regulatory terms; however, it is not to be considered a legal dictionary. If one needs a term defined before a Judge, it is more appropriate to consult a proctor of admiralty, or at least an attorney that is familiar with language used in marine affairs.

This book was written to provide the reader that may have a fondness for river history and wanting to learn and understand riverboating terminology with a source for our unique words. As a Lexicon the information included has the purpose of preserving some of the heritage of the river community of crewmen and shore personnel who have grown up with the river, spent most of their working days (and nights) in constant appreciation, and sometimes fear, of what blessings we have for being a part of the Western Rivers culture.

It is hoped that this reference may increase one's comprehension of what and why we may speak a somewhat different language than do others employed in shore side occupations. The comments used at the end of some definitions are those of the author alone. A few of them may add to some lifted eyebrows, but they are heartfelt from a lengthy career involved in river affairs.

Have as much fun reading this volume as I did in the writing.

PILOTHOUSE INTERIOR OF GREAT REPUBLIC
From *Scribner's Monthly* (October 1874)

Lagniappe

After reading about and watching the TV coverage of the heroic efforts of the local people and their friends, neighbors, and others from surrounding states, and far off additional places that came to help fight the ever increasing inundating waters that descended on those living in the basin of the RED RIVER OF THE NORTH this 2009 year, these couple pages are added to this tome in regard to their struggle. Since the pages of this Lexicon had already been written and numbered by the publisher these following few included paragraphs are added here as a sort of additional *"lagniappe"* (which you can look up in this volume) addition of what happens when you weren't expecting it, or perhaps looking for something that may have been very nice, or conversely could have been an unfortunate incident. However, in future years one finds some little things to appreciate along with the catastrophic acts that occurred. The Red River flood certainly brought the stream into prominence with the nation's public who previously may never have heard of it, knew of its source, the area in which it flowed, or commented, "I thought that river was way down in Louisiana".

The following *lagniappe* was heard many years ago in a much more abbreviated form at a meeting with the Corps of Engineers discussing flooding and efforts being undertaken in an attempt to contain devastating waters that may descend on an area located in the confines of a floodplain. The speaker was attempting to put a little perspective on what was occurring at that particular time in rampaging flood flows of a section of the Upper Mississippi.

Although the tale is about FLOODing, and you should visit the various entries in that section, the best place to put this yarn probably would have been at the end of the "L" section as the "little extra" that might well be the something that was related to those in hearing distance that were lounging on the LAZY BENCH expounding on the topics of the day. Enjoy…..

FLOODS
(A YARN FROM THE LAZY BENCH)

There have been many floods throughout the world and on the river systems – some of them of disastrous proportions, probably long before natives settled on the many different river banks and had to escape to higher ground when the rains came and a river rose above the normal sloping confines of its flow. Each river has many smaller tributary streams which in aggregate can rise until the main stem also overflows its limit of containment.

It is said that at a gathering of different generations in the celestial body called "heaven" that a group of persons who had been displaced, and in some cases, lost their lives, by rising flood waters, were discussing the what, why, and when the worst floods had occurred. Each thought the flood they experienced was unique and without a doubt was the worst calamity to strike the world.

One from China said the Yellow River flood of 1887 couldn't be topped as at least 800,000 persons lost their lives. A woman from the Netherlands claimed that their county has had many floods that inundated their homes and lands and displaced and drowned many of their people, but they had preserved and built dikes to hold back the surges. Collectively she believed the amount of flooding was the worst in the world.

Then a caveman from the bronze age (which was about 2500 B.C.) said he sure didn't know where the rest of the people in the crowd were from as he only knew of the world as one day's walk from where his cave was located, but that he was in a flood that came up to the opening of his place halfway up a mountain side and almost all the rest of his tribe living in caves below him had drowned. What, he asked, could be a greater disaster than that?

Then a group of angels from the United States started arguing about the floods they had experienced or knew about. One person that apparently perished in the 1889 Johnstown Flood said it was undoubtedly the worst one in the U.S. Some of the others in the group, probably most were ex-Western River pilots said, "Well, we can understand you lost your life in that flood but you don't know what flooding is all about".

The first old grey beard pilot opined, "Yep, the flood of 1927 on the Lower Miss was assuredly the grandfather of all of them, changed channels, swallowed islands, drowned people, livestock, wild animals, and floated away homes".

Then a slim fellow from the upper Ohio River said, "I beg to differ with you Cap, but the 1937 flood on the Ohio River was undoubtedly worse in the scope of both human misery and economic loss". To that a Missouri River pilot from Nebraska piped up that the 1952 flood on the Missouri River was the most devastating the area up there had ever seen. An Upper Mississippi river pilot put forth his ideas stating, "The 1993 flood on Upper stopped navigation for a couple of months. "We've never have seen anything as bad as that one".

About that time another angel who had been listening to all the conversation he had heard, opined, "Damn, you old has-been pilots don't know what a flood is", and walked slowly away. The pilot group was offended and went to St. Peter and asked him who that know-it-all guy was and what flood he had experienced. St. Peter just smiled and replied, "Well, he's been here longer than most everybody and at times gets a little crotchety. Don't bother him with flooding tales, he's heard them all. His name is Noah, and he does know a tad about rising waters".

Foreword

The S.S. BENNESTVET BROVIG, a Norwegian flag cargo ship, introduced me to a maritime life when I shipped aboard her in 1950 as a deckhand. She was a small freighter engaged in shipping between ports in the United States and Mexico. My prior experience with life on the water was reading Moby Dick and swimming in a few lakes and Missouri's Meramec River. My experience at sea was thoroughly enjoyable. Although I was the only American of the crew on board, employed as a temporary during good weather to do chipping, scraping, painting and other deck work, they wanted me to stay on as a regular hand, but the pay, only being $50 a month, with 20%, or $10, of that deducted for the Norwegian tax man, left me with the feeling that it probably wasn't the best career path to follow. So that fall I left, but apparently the attraction to nautical life was somewhat addictive as the thought occurred to me that perhaps working on riverboats might be interesting. My first job was a deckhand aboard the M/V ST. PAUL SOCONY that was pushing refined oil product barges on the Lower and Upper Mississippi. Later the company sent me to take a test at the then Second District Coast Guard office and I became a Tankerman. However, with the Korean War going full blast the local draft board was casting its eye in my direction. With a merchant vessel-based background and skills gained working in the marine industry, my thought process decided that employment by the government might be best served in naval service, so I joined the USN and spent most of my four year tour on the second USS JUNEAU (CLAA 119), a light cruiser.

Upon discharge in the spring of 1955, and having visited my folks, various relatives and friends, and running short with my mustering-out pay I went to work for Commercial Petroleum and Transport Co., the predecessor of the "C" in ACBL, American Commercial Barge Line. At that time it was to be a temporary job prior to attending college in the fall on the G.I. bill with the thought of becoming a history teacher.

So much for career planning. When my time came to leave, the Captain recommended me for a job as Steersman, to learn the river and become a Pilot. At the time I didn't know much about what a "Steersman" did, and knew only a few of the words that are included in this Lexicon. However, having worn out my pair of work boots, they were thrown overboard, and I decided to give a shot at what became both my vocation and my avocation, the river industry.

When first aboard the M/V ST. PAUL SOCONY, there was a new language to learn that was not used, and was not familiar to, most of those living and employed ashore. There were no texts of river lingo that I knew of, and when asking a question of, "Why do you call it that?" the answer invariably was, "Well son, it's always been called that."

Apparently, a lot of persons in the U.S. Coast Guard didn't understand much of the river terminology either, so someone in the Second Coast Guard District, which has since been deep-sixed (see text), in the 1950s put together a listing of river words, with an explanation of their understanding of the meaning of the terms, some wrong, some mostly right. They then published it in a pamphlet entitled, *Language of the Western Rivers*. It somewhat filled in part of the gaps in my learning curve, but still left me wondering about the background of where and why we river persons were using the terms, with many of the "river-speak" expressions far different from definitions told to me in my previous stints on the Norwegian freighter and in the Navy.

A few books about the river have had brief glossaries with "some" of the river lingo explained, but none had any detailed listings. Other dictionary descriptions of river words have mostly been a reprinting in somewhat expanded form of the Coast Guard's *"Language"* publication, with some local interpretations added. The printed deep sea and the sailing terminology books define actions and gear in what at times is a foreign language to rivermen and isn't used on our Western Rivers. Many terms we do use are not even mentioned in their tomes.

The Western Rivers industry has been my career for over half a century, first as a Deckhand, then a Tankerman, Pilot and Master. The latter two-thirds of my profession was spent on shore in charge of the construction and maintenance of barging equipment, as well as being intimately involved in the legislative and regulatory affairs of our industry, all of which has required a lot of new terminology learning. The terms we use often in our everyday language then had to be explained to others who were drafting legislation and crafting regulations that could have profound effects on the persons who make their livelihood from river transportation. Some of our unique words had to be explained to others, including their history and the what's and why's of events that have occurred on the Western Rivers, from the explorations of Lewis and Clark, the westward migration across the Alleghenies to the Ohio Valley (which WAS the "west" of our country) and then beyond up the Missouri, the first steamboat out of Pittsburgh, and all that has followed on our river system.

Some volumes describing early river life and steamboating used words that I had not heard of in the modern post-WW II age. It required some research to discover what an author was writing about. The inquiry invariably would turn up a few more unfamiliar words that put me back to more digging, or paddling, if you will. So quite a few years ago I started putting river terms with an explanation of them in some file folders which has evolved into this *Lexicon*. It is called a lexicon as it really isn't just a glossary or dictionary, even though it has a bit of background of where the words originated. It isn't an encyclopedia, albeit in some cases it may have as much verbiage for one term as one might contain. It is not an almanac, even though it uses some explanations, dates, and statistics that a reader might encounter when perusing one. It is not a history dissertation; however, you will find a degree of historic happenings about our rivers as they meander downstream and pick up new expressions not used in other areas of work. And, of course, you will find a few personal inclusions of observations, comments, and even poems, etc. to which you have my permission to exclude from your own vocabulary; but perhaps the explanations will lighten the load of delving into this extensive catalog of wordings. As the old bard said, it's not work when you're having fun while learning, and it is hoped you also will have some enjoyment as you navigate this volume.

A number of readers may be disappointed if one of their favorite streams is missing from this text. One must remember that when flatboats and then steamers plied the small tributary rivers there were no roads linking together the pioneer settlements, and a vessel that only drafted a foot or so could stem and float out of most streams, at least in some periods of the year. To list them all with background would take another volume. Therefore, only those rivers with a general historic interest connected to the Western Rivers system are listed. It is hoped that some of what is included in this *Lexicon* will whet the appetite of its readers so they may become inclined to read more about our waterways, the rivermen and equipment they used in the past, and now use in the present, to transport vital national commerce on our inland river navigation system.

Therefore, the best term seems to be "lexicon", as it embodies some of "all of the above" and was suggested by my son-in-law to be called, *A RIVERMAN'S LEXICON IN LEHMAN'S TERMS*. "Riverman" is not used here in a generic sense as there are many women who have made a career of working on riverboats, from deck, to cook, to pilot and master, but in my mind if you have worked on a river vessel, you are, or were, a riverman. "River person" just doesn't work for me. The "term" language describes and tries to delineate the way the words were spoken of, and told to me, or what I read about in the many river books, articles, magazines, dictionaries from Falconer's *Dictionary of the Marine* published in the 1700s, Admiral W.H. Smyth's 1867 edition of *The Sailor's Word-Book,* to modern-day maritime wordbooks and word histories, and to numerous texts, especially histories of the Corps of Engineers Districts, the writings of Captain Fred Way and the other writers of articles in the *Sons & Daughters Reflector*, the books and articles of Alan Bates in the *Waterways Journal*, and to many others that have been great contributors to our Western River language heritage. Thanks to all.

Some of the terms and their explanations may only have a local or regional flavor to them and are not used in all places of the many miles of our inland Western Rivers commercial waterway system. It was fortunate that my own broad riverboat career included piloting nearly six thousand miles of different inland rivers and canals, and working with a variety of crew members from different parts of our great country who had been employed on a variety of different vessels under a diversity of Captains. Perhaps you may take umbrage with some of my explanations, or may believe they are not adequately described; or, worse yet, some words familiar to you may not even be included in this text. If so, please feel free to pass on new words and their descriptions, or amplifications and different particulars of those that are, or are not, included. If there is ever a second edition your meaningful suggestions will be sent on to whoever is around to edit a revised text.

The parlance of our rivers has evolved as equipment has been modernized with old vessels going to the boneyard; new generations of rivermen are taking up the occupation and bringing to the waterways new or different ideas or learning. A case in point is WW II. After the conflict was over many ex-Navy personnel migrated to the river, as I did after the Korean War, bringing along with them some of the seagoing terms which became commonplace, and which remain current in river-speak, that were not heard in steamboat days. An example is the use of "galley" for the old term of "cookhouse" or "kitchen" on the steamers. Another is that of "bulkhead", used in the deep-sea trade, where I have been told that only the term "wall" was used on steamboats. Also the names of the decks have changed. One now never hears of a "boiler deck" or "hurricane deck" except on the few steamers still operating.

Another change in language is the migration of people. As persons who operated tugs and small towboats on the Gulf Intracoastal Waterway migrated to the rivers, the term "Pilothouse", that venerable place where piloting is done, has often been called a "wheelhouse", as it was in more common usage on the Canal, where Pilots of canal boats were often termed "wheelmen". The background and language of those from Cajun country was different from those that grew up in snake country, and even more so from the loggers of the Upper Mississippi.

In the new age of government, from staffers on Capitol Hill to those running our regulatory agencies, the inevitable result has been the addition of more new terms and meanings to our vocabularies every day. In some respects all the eloquent, intelligent, and expressive books of terms and their meanings are out of date the day they are sent to a publisher. This lexicon, however, is an attempt to bridge past usage to the present. There will always be a postscript by others. Acronyms have been kept to a minimum except where widely used by river personnel. They are constantly being added and updated, or becoming outdated and often duplicated. At one time when researching for a paper on electronic charts I put together over ten pages of acronyms on this one topic. As it was a while ago, probably five of those pages have been superseded, but also, perhaps a dozen new pages could be added on the same subject. The last Homeland Security list I saw in 2005 had over 650 acronyms on it.

So words and speech change, for better or worse, but evolving, nevertheless. This volume attempts to put most of the words we now use, and have used in the past, into a little better perspective. Hopefully, when one may read and study a river-related work written during the 19th or 20th Century and wonder what the author was writing about, perhaps this lexicon will help explain how we rivermen accomplished our trade of moving steamboats, towboats, tugs, and barges on the Western Rivers, and those waterways connected to it, while at the same time have enjoyment reading the words and their definitions as well as learning from where they were derived.

A

ABAFT
Something that is in back of another object or place, or toward the stern of a vessel. Not a commonly used word on the rivers. More often one would use or speak the term AFT. The term *abaft* has usually only been employed in the past in describing characteristics of some of the navigation lights, such as when giving the characteristics of one of the side lights *"...so fixed as to throw the light from right ahead to two points abaft the beam..."*. Although the term is still used in the current collision regulations, points are not. The rules now use degrees. For use of the word *abaft* in the Navigation Rules see Rule 13(b), when overtaking another vessel; and Rule 21 that lists Definitions. The origin is of Middle English *baft*, meaning behind.

ABANDON SHIP
If some accident occurs this is the phrase no one wants to hear. It usually means the vessel is in imminent danger of sinking or a fire is out of control. When the term is announced all persons aboard are to leave in the most able and orderly manner they can. It is the only time an inland river vessel is called a "ship".

ABANDONMENT
The act of surrendering, relinquishing, or giving up ownership in a vessel. It usually occurs when a vessel has suffered damages so severe, due to allision, collision, fire, grounding, sinking, or other such casualty, that it is determined the vessel is considered a total constructive loss. The owner(s) *abandon* the vessel to their insurers or the government for salvage. The *abandonment* does not, however, absolve the owner(s) of certain legal obligations if the *abandoned* vessel is considered a hazard to navigation or the environment.

ABEAM
Something that is perpendicular to the fore and aft centerline of a vessel. Usually used in reference to an object such as, navigation light, buoy, bridge, point of land, or a dock off to the side, or anything at a right angle to the keel line.

ABOARD
Someone, or something, that is upon, or in a vessel, such as cargo, supplies, crew, or guests. The "a" implies the movement of going someplace, and the "board" comes from the Old English word *bord*, that refers to a timber or plank such as the wooden deck of a vessel, or the "steering board" as a RUDDER.

ABOUT
Used when changing the rotation of the vessel, i.e. turning the towboat, the tow, or barge around; i.e. "The Pilot brought the boat *about*". The term is from sailing ship practice and is now not often used in river terminology. More frequently used would be "around".

ABOVE
Used to describe a position of a vessel or of an object; i.e. "The downbound vessel is *above* the point"; or "Store the line *above* deck". Also, to go *above* from where one is located. A landsman term would be to go upstairs, whereas the riverman would say, "I am going up *above.*"

ABRASION
1. The act of rubbing, wearing, or grinding away. Used in relation to a wire or line that is chafing against a rough fitting or the side of a dock. When this is apparent, chafing gear is placed around the section that is being abraded to protect it from wear.
2. The act of materials in a river grinding against each other as they are transported along and wearing down the stream bed.

ABREAST

Used in referring to vessels laying side by side of one another at a dock, in a moored barge fleet, or in tow. Also used in relation to another object, i.e. "I am *abreast* of the old coal dock at Uniontown". However, the term ABEAM also can be used.

ABS

See: AMERICAN BUREAU OF SHIPPING.

ABUT

Where two timbers, planks or steel plates are placed end to end and joined, they are said to *abut* one another. The term seems to come from a combination of Anglo, French, and Latin to mean "at the end".

ABUTMENT

1. The shoreward side of the structure where a dam is constructed that supports the lateral pressure of the earthen shore.
2. A pier or other support between the shore and a gated structure of a spillway can also be called an *abutment*.
3. It can be considered a retaining wall for a bridge where the earthen shore ends and a bridge begins.

ACCESS HOLE

An opening, usually small, in the vessel allowing entrance to a space or to another compartment. Can be bolted closed with a flange, or kept closed with a manhole or hatch cover. It is referenced most often when referring to an entrance to the void spaces through a manhole or hatch on a barge.

ACCIDENT

Some unforeseen or unfortunate incident or mishap that causes injury, loss, or death. If an *accident* occurs on board a vessel, the U.S. Coast Guard requires the vessel Master to complete a form 2692 describing the details of the action, and forwarding it to them. The word originally simply meant a happening or and event from whatever cause. It later (19th Century) evolved into a type of mishap. See: ALLISION, CASUALTY, COLLISION, FATALITY, and INJURY.

ACCOMMODATION LADDER

On a ship it is the portable steps that are lowered over the side to disembark persons and stores. On a riverboat it is termed a GANGWAY from the towboat or barge to the shore used for the same purpose. On passenger vessels it is called a STAGE.

ACCOMMODATION SPACE

The compartments, STATEROOM, or living quarters on a towboat or tug for the crew or guests they may have aboard. At times, it is also referred to as a CABIN. Although a contract for building a vessel, or the blueprints of a towboat or tug may state *accommodation space*, no crew member ever says, "I am going to my *accommodation space* to rest".

ACCRETION

An accumulation or build-up of silt, forming a sandbar.

ACCUMULATOR

A pressure tank that is used to start diesel engines. It is commonly located on the engines that drive the barge pumps aboard tank barges.

ACORN

A decorative adornment attached to the top or end of booms, spars, masts, and some support beams that were exposed to the weather on steamboats. They were often painted in gilded or bright colors. The acorns also served a useful purpose in protecting the grain end of the pole to which they were attached. They took on the name, not only for their shape, but also for the staunchness of the oak tree.

ACRE FOOT

The amount of water necessary to cover one acre of land one foot deep. The term is used in the containment and release of water from reservoirs, and during times of flooding. An acre foot equals 43,560 cubic feet, or 326,851 gallons of water.

ACT OF GOD

A legal term, used in insurance investigations or other inquiries, in which fault is trying to be determined. It means a happening or event in a disaster, accident, or PERIL AT SEA or RIVER which is caused by some extraordinary force, such as a violence in nature uncontrolled or uninfluenced by the power of intervention by man. The *act* must be one that could not have been prevented by any foresight and care that would be reasonably expected from the vessel crew, meaning that they were not negligent in their duties.

Some examples might be tornado-like winds which blow a tow into a dock causing damage, an unforeseeable or unexpected cross-current against a bridge pier which drafts a tow into an allision with the bridge sinking a barge; or a sudden driving rainstorm which blocks the Pilot's vision as well as their ability to observe anything on the vessel's radar screen, resulting in a tow running aground causing damage and/or cargo loss. The courts will determine if it existed or if the accident could have been reasonably prevented.

AD VALOREM

A tax or duty imposed on a vessel computed as a percentage of the value of the cargo.

ADMEASUREMENT

To calculate, measure and certify the dimensions of a vessel for the purpose of documentation to determine the gross and net carrying capacity of a vessel. A type of measuring estimate of a vessel that is only in the eyes of the official taking down the dimensions that often defies the application of a reasonable degree of logic. See: TONNAGE, NET TONNAGE, and GROSS TONNAGE.

ADMINISTRATIVE LAW JUDGE

A person who represents the government to conduct hearings, take testimony, examine witnesses and render decisions in cases brought by the U.S. Coast Guard against persons or corporations for alleged misconduct, violations of law or regulations, or even judgments as to the actions of what would be considered prudent seamanship. Although ALJs are employees of a government administrative agency, in mariner cases of the USCG, they are to adjudicate independently of any agency influence. Decisions by the ALJ may be appealed by those being charged or by the prosecutor (USCG). If a case is appealed it goes to the Commandant of the USCG for review and decision. The second level of appeal is to the National Transportation Board (NTSB) for its review. If the decision is not resolved at that level it may be further appealed in the federal court system.

ADMIRAL

The term refers to high-ranking flag officers of a country's naval service, or as in the U.S., the Navy, the USCG and NOAA. It comes from a Moorish title *amir-al-bahr*, meaning commander of the sea. Except in the War Between the States, when *Admirals* from the North and South commanded fleets of vessels on our nation's rivers, steamboats and towboats did not have to contend with *Admirals*. Then in World War II the U.S. Coast Guard took control of the old Steamboat Inspection Service, but they never relinquished their authority over it after the war. Now we have *Admirals*, other military

4 ADMIRALTY

personnel, and their staffs, that oversee the safety regulations that govern the crews and vessels operating on the rivers.

ADMIRALTY

Refers to the practice of law governing maritime cases as well as to the courts that have jurisdiction in particular cases involving seamen and the vessels on which they serve. Some examples would be: Pilotage, crew wages, cargo damage, collisions, allisions, salvage, and charter parties.

Although *admiralty* is a system of laws going back to ancient times of customs from peoples who went to sea, the jurisdiction of the *Admiralty* Courts did not reach our inland waters until 1851 when the Supreme Court extended the dominion and administration of *Admiralty* for vessels that were seagoing to also include those on navigable lakes and rivers.

ADRIFT

To drift with the current, tide, or wind with no control over a vessel or any other object's movements or actions. A barge that has broken away from a fleet, a vessel underway that has lost power, or a buoy no longer secured to its sinker, moving downstream with the current, is said to be *adrift*. Also, gear aboard a vessel that is not secured and is moving about is termed to be *adrift*.

ADVANCE

The forward distance gained toward the direction of an original course while a vessel or tow is in the action of turning. This is not a term that is normally used by Pilots. It is more often involved in investigations when attempting to determine fault in a collision or other accident. See: TRANSFER.

ADVECTION FOG

The type of fog that forms when moist warm air moves over a cold surface and the air temperature falls to below its dew point. See: STEAM FOG.

ADVISORY COMMITTEES (to the USCG)

There are a number of committees that give counsel to the USCG that are either sanctioned by them or by Congress. They are made up of interested persons who have expertise in the subjects that the committees discuss. Some of them are national in scope and others are more localized to certain areas. The national committees and their acronyms of interest to mariners on the rivers and canals are as follows (see each for a description):

Chemical Transportation Advisory Committee (CTAC)
Merchant Marine Personnel Advisory Committee (MERPAC)
National Offshore Safety Advisory Committee (NOSAC)
Navigation Safety Advisory Council (NAVSAC)
Towing Safety Advisory Committee (TSAC)

ADZE

A tool used by loggers and shipwrights that is shaped like a farmer's mattock with its cutting edge set at a right angle, but sometimes instead of a pick on the other end it would have a peg to drive spikes. It is used to shape and smooth timbers by dubbing. The tool came in various models such as the "the scarphing, the spoon, the box, and the lipped", each for different jobs or at the preference of the shipwright.

AFFREIGHTMENT

An agreement or contract by a water carrier to provide cargo space (a barge) at a specified time and for a specified price to a cargo owner or shipper who is neither the operator nor the charterer of the vessel.

AFLOAT
A vessel supported, or borne up in the water, not aground. A condition all rivermen desire to be in while aboard their towboats, tugs, or barges.

A-FRAME
A type of DERRICK that is commonly used in river salvage and for heavy lifting. It most often consists of two heavy legs mounted on each side of the end of a barge, joined together at their apex, forming an "A". The legs can be fixed or movable by raising or lowering the backstay with a winch.

AFT
Toward the stern (back or rear end) of the vessel. *Aft* derives and is a contraction of ABAFT, and is a more commonly used term than the latter. A person goes *aft*, finds something *aft*, is *aft*, etc.

AFTER WATCH
The after watch is after noon or after midnight. Riverboat crews have historically stood SQUARE WATCHES. The Master stands the forward watch, 6 to 12, and the Pilot stands the *after watch,* 12 to 6, both a.m. and p.m.

AFTERMOST
The position of object(s) nearest the stern. Sometimes used in place of AFT, i.e. "Put the line on the *aftermost* cavel on the port side".

AFTERPEAK
The last, or most aft, watertight compartment in the stern of a vessel.

AGAINST THE SUN
Coiling line counter-clockwise, or in a left-handed manner. Since nearly all line used on the river is wound with a right-hand lay, to coil it *against the sun* could cause it to kink, as well as making it difficult to coil it very well; so, unless specifically ordered, always coil "with the sun".

AGGRADATION
The building or filling up of sediment in a watercourse, especially a navigable channel, usually due to low water flows and the gradual disposition of a stream's bed load.

AGROUND
The unfortunate position of any vessel(s), towboat, tug, barge(s), or tow, resting on the bottom of a waterway, unable to move. The opposite of being afloat. In the sandy, silting alluvial river bottom of much of the Western Rivers, many times a Pilot can work the grounded vessel(s) off, as opposed to being "hard aground" when it may take assistance from another towboat or a rise in the river to become safely afloat again.

AHEAD
1. In the front of the tug, towboat or tow, used to denote an object or place toward which one's vessel is moving.
2. To be in visual sight, as in "see that buoy *ahead* on the port bow", or it may be a broad statement, such as, "the motor vessel *SUNNYDALE* is 10 miles *ahead* of us".
3. Used in describing the throttle position of the engine(s), "we are going half *ahead*", or "full speed *ahead*".
4. On steamers it referred to the throttle setting of "full head" or "half head" of steam.

AHOY
In a formal sense, mostly used by a naval coxswain, or at the gangway of a naval vessel hailing an approaching vessel. Additionally it is used to attract attention between vessels, a vessel to a dock, or from the shore to a vessel. Various origins have been given. It has been said that it was the dreaded war cry of the Vikings when they raided another vessel or a village. Others have said it is derived from the French word *ohe* used when

hailing another vessel, but some say it comes from the German word *hue*. Also mentioned is the Dutch word *hui*, meaning "come". The gondoliers of Venice call out *hoi* when they are about to go around a blind corner. Still others state the hail came from the coasting vessel called a *hoy*. The call is seldom used by towboat men, but is more often shouted by yachtsmen and recreational boaters on our rivers to call to another person.

AHP

This is an acronym to denote Above the Head of the Passes of the Mississippi River where it starts to enter the delta of the river. The head of the passes is mile zero of the Lower Mississippi which is approximately 20 miles north of the Gulf of Mexico. As a vessel travels upriver from that point, each mile is AHP as shown on the river charts, or in the Light List for the mile boards maintained by the USCG, until the vessel reaches the juncture of the confluence of the Ohio and Upper Mississippi rivers, mile 953.8 (even though the city of Cairo, IL, is shown two miles above the confluence as mile 955.8).

AID(S) TO NAVIGATION

Any signal or mark used by a pilot to assist in the safe navigation of a vessel and tow. It could be a fixed or flashing light, signboard, a large tree, a tall building, electronic device, GPS, or any other object or signal that helps determine one's position relative to dangers or obstructions. Generally, however, on the river system the term is used for buoys, light beacons, and daymarks placed by the U.S. Coast Guard to mark the channel and give reference points to the mariner.

AIR BUBBLERS
See: BUBBLER SYSTEM.

AIR CONDITIONING

Perhaps after the use of diesel engines for towboats, *air conditioning* is perhaps the finest improvement that has been made in vessel livability. It first arrived on river boats in the mid-twentieth century shortly after radar was introduced to the inland towing industry in 1947. Instead of restlessly sleeping on the open deck in summer, or in a bed soaked with sweat, crew members could finally lie back and enjoy their slumber.

AIR DRAFT

The height of the highest protrusion of a vessel above the water. It is used to determine what the AIR GAP clearance may be.

AIR GAP

The distance between the highest protrusion on a vessel to an obstruction above the vessel, such as the lower framing on a fixed span of a bridge, or the clearance in high water to the sag of a power line or other object crossing the river.

AIR SCOOP

A rotating sheet metal device located on the weather deck above the engine room used to catch the wind and direct it into hot engine room spaces. The *scoop* is curved at the top to prevent rain from entering. It can be rotated and face, or face away from, the wind depending upon the weather circumstances. It also may be called a COWL, *wind catcher* or a *wind scoop*.

AIS
See: AUTOMATIC IDENTIFICATION SYSTEM

ALABAMA RIVER

The Coosa and Tallapoosa rivers join together north of the city of Montgomery, AL, and form the Alabama River, which flows in a west and southwesterly direction for about 315 miles until it joins the Tombigbee River to form the Mobile River, which then flows into Mobile Bay and mixes with the Gulf of Mexico. It is named for an Indian tribe called the Alabamas, which apparently is derived from the Choctaw word *alba,* meaning "vegetation", and *amo,* meaning "cutters or gatherers".

Steamboats arrived in the 1820s hauling cotton to market, as well as carrying numerous passengers. Later, railroads captured a majority of the traffic on the river, but between the early 1960s and through the 1970s a system of three locks and dams, namely Claiborne on the lower end, Millers Ferry in the middle, and Robert F. Henry on the upper reaches, were built on the river as regional development projects which also had a capability to generate hydroelectric power as well as provide for river transportation.

ALL CLEAR

When a vessel is entering or leaving a lock, going through a narrow bridge, maneuvering in a fleet, or whenever a Pilot needs a crewman to signal in a close situation for the vessel or tow, the person signaling will shout *All Clear* to signify the obstruction has been cleared if the Pilot is within hearing distance. If not, he will move his arm rapidly up and down on the side where the obstruction may lay, which conveys the same meaning.

ALL FAST

When a vessel and/or tow has been securely tied off.

ALL GONE

The call, most often including an arm signal, used by a Deckhand to the Pilot after he has completed the order to turn the boat, barge, or tow loose.

ALL HANDS

The term means everyone aboard the vessel. It is used at times as an order when there is an emergency that requires the attention or assistance of the entire crew. It is also used to express a policy or safety requirement, such as, "all hands are required to wear life jackets" (now called PFDs).

ALL STOP

When the propulsion gear is in neutral and the towboat is drifting. Also used as a signal the Mate or Lead Deckhand makes when he wants the Pilot to stop by facing forward and makes a repetitive up and down motion. See: SIGNALS, HAND.

ALLEGHENY RIVER

The river starts its journey in north central Pennsylvania from the Allegheny mountain range, flowing northwest into New York. Then it meanders southwest and returns to PA for a total of about 325 miles before it joins the Monongahela River at Pittsburgh to form the Ohio River.

The origin of the river's name is a bit murky. Some believe it came from an early Indian tribe, the Alleghewi, while others think the Iroquois Indians believed that the river we call the Allegheny was part of what is now the Ohio River, since it contributes over 80 percent of the Ohio's annual flow. When the Delaware tribe displaced the Iroquois they translated "Ohio" into their native tongue which became "wielding-heny", which meant "most beautiful stream". When new European settlers arrived, it was anglicized to Allegheny.

Flatboats and keelboats were on the river before the American Revolution. Early cargoes on the river were salt, lumber, and pig iron. A scheme to link the Allegheny to Lake Erie by canal was contemplated in the early 1800s, but nothing of utility came of it. The mid-1800s was the heyday of the river when oil was found. FLATBOATS, KEELBOATS,

8 ALLISION

BULKBOATS, FRENCH CREEKERS, and STEAMBOATS (see all) were numerous.

By the late 1800s Congressional funds were authorized to make channel improvements from Pittsburgh upstream. Lock & Dam #1, named Herr's Island Lock, was built in 1903, located at Pittsburgh. It was later removed when Emsworth L & D was built on the Ohio River. The last lock and dam, #9, was completed in 1938, allowing navigation to East Brady, PA, but by the time of completion of canalization little tonnage was moved on the river since the timber had been harvested and the oil had basically stopped flowing. All the locks, #2 through #9, are 56 feet wide by 360 feet long. Now, some sand and gravel is dredged and moved on the river and there are some commercial docks for more incoming and outgoing commerce on the river in the pools of dams #2 and #3. The peak glory days of river traffic had started to decrease before the building of the lock and dam system.

ALLISION

The act of a moving object, such as a vessel, running into a fixed object such as a bridge pier. The moving object (vessel) may run into another vessel that was anchored or moored at a dock and it would be an allision. When two or more vessels are underway and run into one another it is called a COLLISION.

ALL-ROUND LIGHT

A navigational light showing an unbroken light over an arc of the horizon of 360 degrees.

ALLUVIAL RIVER or STREAM

A *river or stream* where the bottom consists mainly of the erosion sediments from run-off of the floodplain, the caving or cutting of its banks along its shoreline, all of which are deposited into the river as it meanders downstream. As its current slows down when elevations flatten out it can no longer transport the load of sand, silt, clay or gravel. This settling sediment allows the river to build up some areas by its deposits, as well as washing out others, making a new channel, and can even cut through the throat or neck of a bend and reduce the mileage of the river, leaving a horseshoe backwater lake as it travels to the sea. Most of the Mississippi River and its tributaries are of the *alluvial* type. The word comes from the Latin, *alluvium,* meaning material deposited by running water. See: SAND WAVE.

ALOFT

Refers to something above the uppermost deck. Used mostly with sailing vessels. Not in common usage on river vessels.

ALONGSIDE

The side of one's vessel being moored next to another vessel, or an object such as a dock, or pier. Also used when maneuvering as in, "We are going *alongside* the M/V SUNNYDALE".

ALPHA FLAG

Rule 27 of the Navigation Rules requires a vessel engaged in diving operations to display a rigid replica of the International Code flag "A" not less than one meter in height.

ALTERNATING LIGHT

A lighted aid to navigation that shows flashes of light at regular intervals and may change colors. Seldom seen on the river system.

AMBER LIGHT

Under the old Western River Rules of the Road a towboat pushing other vessels ahead was required to show two *amber lights* in a vertical line at its stern (W/R Rule 3), and a flashing *amber light* on the centerline of the head of the tow (W/R Pilot Rule 95.29; and similarly in the Inland Rules 3, and Pilot Rule 80.16). When drafting the 72 COLREGS the "experts in chromaticity" decided that amber was not a color but a resin. Therefore, all *amber lights* suddenly became yellow ones when our Unified Rules went into effect. One must wonder what Katherine Lee Bates was thinking when she wrote, "O' beautiful for spacious skies, for amber waves of grain", in perhaps her most inspired bit of poetry, "America the Beautiful".

The U.S. Army Corps of Engineers (USACE) continues to describe caution when entering their locks with the use of *amber lights* on top of their lock walls. They probably still revere the song.

AMERICAN BUREAU OF SHIPPING

This organization is recognized as the official vessel classification society in the U.S. Its main function is to inspect vessels while they are being built in accordance with a set of standards that they publish called Rules for Building and Classing Steel Vessels for Service on Rivers and Intracoastal Waterways, generally referred to as the "River Rules".

Periodically after being put into service an ABS surveyor will re-inspect a vessel if the owner intends to keep it in class. Very few inland towboats are classed. Some are originally built to class, but are subsequently self-inspected and maintained by the operator of the vessel. Some inland barges, principally tankers, are built and maintained in class, especially those that may require a LOADLINE to go into Lake Michigan or the Gulf of Mexico.

AMIDSHIPS

The approximate middle area of a vessel between the bow and the stern as well as the halfway distance between the port and starboard side of the vessel, or centerline. It is also used in reference to rudder movement of the helm, i.e. "steering rudder(s) are *amidships*" (on the centerline).

AN EASY DISTANCE OFF

See: EASY DISTANCE OFF.

ANCHOR (ING)

A device, so designed to grab or bite, the bottom of a waterway and hold a vessel in place when attached to it by a chain, wire, or line. They were carried on packetboats and were useful on shallow streams where the *anchor* and gear might be carried upstream by a yawl and planted to assist the boat to CORDELLE through a shallow channel. They were also used to moor the vessel at shallow landings where there was little to secure the vessel, as well as to moor in inclement weather. Although tugs may carry *anchors*, towboats do not. The word comes from the Latin *ancora,* which came first from a Greek word meaning "bent". *Anchors* come in various designs for use in different types of bottom, as well as the desired holding power of the device. Even though *anchors* are not carried aboard towboats, the term is often heard in river lingo. For instance, a navigational buoy is attached to a chain or wire that in turn is attached to concrete sinkers *anchoring* the buoy. In addition the word *anchor* can be used to mean the act of safely and securely stowing gear or objects on board a vessel so they will not come loose. The term is often used in connection with other words, see below: ANCHOR AWEIGH, BARGE, BELL, BUOY, CHAIN, FLEET, LIGHT, and WATCH.

ANCHORAGE

An area in a river or harbor that is specifically set aside to hold vessels under permit from the U.S. Army Corps of Engineers as to the conditions and the size of the area. The term is more associated with areas frequented by deep-draft vessels that are equipped with anchors, such as in the harbor of New Orleans. Holding areas on the rivers are called *barge fleeting areas*.

ANCHOR AWEIGH
Marks the time when the *anchor* has pulled loose, and is loose, from the bottom, but not hauled out of the water and housed. See: AWEIGH.

ANCHOR BARGE
A barge which is either fastened to an *anchor* in the river or the barge is made fast to a DEADMAN on the bank. It is more or less permanently moored and used to hold fleets of barges.

ANCHOR BELL
A bell located in the fore part of the towboat, usually located just under the pilothouse. The bell is to be constructed and have the necessary intensity as described in Subpart B, Annex III of the Navigation Rules. It is to be sounded in restricted visibility in accordance with Rule 35(f) if at *anchor*, and in accordance with Rule 35(g) if aground.

ANCHOR BUOY
A large floating *buoy anchored* to the bottom of the river or to a shoreline that is used to hold a fleet of barges. It is also called a *mooring buoy*. It should not be confused with the term *anchorage* buoy which is a *buoy* used to mark the limits of an *anchorage* area in some ports.

ANCHOR CHAIN
An *anchor* is usually attached with a heavy linked *chain* that leads to the vessel. In some cases where an *anchor* is not holding a large or heavy object, like a vessel, a wire may be used, such as in the case of holding a navigation buoy in place that marks the channel.

ANCHOR FLEET
An area in a river that has an *anchor* barge(s) suitable to safely moor a large number of barges, commonly used in such ports as St. Louis, MO; Cairo, IL; and New Orleans, LA.

ANCHOR LIGHT
A vessel that is at *anchor* must display the *light(s)* required in Rule 30 of the Inland Navigation Rules. Since towboats usually do not carry *anchors*, nor do they *anchor*, they would seldom, if ever, show these lights.

ANCHOR WATCH
The precaution taken, especially in inclement weather, where a crew member is assigned to keep watch to insure the vessel(s) at *anchor* do not start dragging *anchor* or break away.

ANCIENT MARINER
In sailing and whaling days this was the name given to the albatross, since it was believed the souls of dead sailors went to that largest of sea birds and that bad luck would come to anyone who tried to catch or kill it. Since Western River towboats do not roam the South Seas, there should not be any towboat crews with this title. However, towboat crews do have many dealings with the U.S. Coast Guard, and rivermen have to be careful of not catching or killing (heaven forbid) their "Ancient Mariner", the designation given to the Coast Guardsman on active duty with the most time in that service.

ANEMOMETER
An instrument mounted at a high place on some towboats that measures the velocity of the wind. It may have a vane to also measure the wind direction. It is a useful device, especially if you have a long tow of empties and are navigating in a narrow channel.

ANGLE

The common name given to steel construction pieces in the shape of an "L" that are used as stiffeners to the steel plate and framing of a vessel. They are more officially known as *angle*-irons or *angle*-bars.

ANGLE OF HEEL

The measured angle at which a vessel may lean from the vertical in an athwartship inclination, i.e. "She seems to be heeling (or angling) a couple degrees to starboard (or port)". Usually referred to as LIST.

ANGLE OF REPOSE

The greatest angle, or gradient, that granular bulk cargoes will stay at rest before a shifting or sliding will take place. Different types of materials will come to rest at differing angles. Size, shape, density, moisture content, and other features will also cause similar substances to have differing sloping attitudes. This *angle*, or slope, is especially important regarding deck barge cargoes. If water is in the void of a vessel and a list develops, a deck cargo, such as gravel, may shift, and as the *angle* of the gravel changes, it can cause the barge to dump its cargo, or even capsize.

ANNUNCIATOR

See: ENGINE ORDER TELEGRAPH.

ANODES

Small blocks of zinc or magnesium attached to the underwater hull plate and rudders or other appendages to allow them to be sacrificed, especially in brackish or salt water, rather than causing rapid corrosion to the steel hull itself and/or its appendages. See: CATHODIC PROTECTION.

ANPRM

An acronym used in the Federal Register meaning, Advanced Notice of Proposed Rule Making. Used by Federal Agencies to give notice to interested parties that they are seeking information on possible future regulatory action and requesting advice on the impacts, both adverse and beneficial, that may occur. After the comments are received, if the agency decides to go ahead with action they issue a "NPRM" which is a Notice of Proposed Rule Making.

ANSWER

The turning movement of a vessel when rudder angle is applied. When the towboat or tow starts to turn it is said to *answer* its helm, or rudder; or "It's not *answering* its rudder!" Then it's probably time to start backing full astern.

ANTEBELLUM

In U.S. steamboating days, or in an architectural time frame, it refers to the period before the Civil War. The term comes to us from Latin, *ante*, meaning before, and *bellum*, to mean war.

ANTENNA

The structure(s) or appendage(s) that receive electronic impulses. These might include radar, radio, GPS, etc.

ANTLERS

The symbol of the horns from an elk or large rack of a deer was displayed on a steamboat that has won a race with another steamer to show all other vessels and people that it was the fastest in that particular service. Usually they were gilded to make them stand out. It was said of the winning vessel that "she takes the horns". On the Upper Mississippi River with smaller vessels a broom was often fastened between the stacks to denote a clean sweep with the same bragging rights.

APALACHICOLA, CHATTAHOOCHEE, FLINT RIVER SYSTEM (A-C-F)

The three rivers are considered by the USACE as a single system of navigation since the Chattahoochee and the Flint merge together at the southwest corner of Georgia and the panhandle of Florida, in the Lake Seminole Reservoir formed at the Jim Woodruff L & D. They then become the start of the Apalachicola River which continues to flow to the Gulf Intracoastal Waterway (GIWW) and on to the Gulf of Mexico. The whole of the A-C-F system serves multiple purposes of hydropower, water supply to the area, flood control, recreation, and other functions, as well as navigation.

Although the navigation component has a nine-foot authorized depth, low flows in the drier summer and fall periods often results in less than the controlling amount of water. Maintenance dredging has met with environmental concerns, as well. Only a limited amount of tonnage now moves on the system.

The total navigational system is about 285 miles in length. The Apalachicola is a little over 106 miles up to Lake Seminole, and the Chattahoochee is navigable up to Columbus, GA, a total of about 154 miles. A section of Lake Seminole allows for navigation of the Flint River to the city of Bainbridge, GA, about 25 miles.

1. APALACHICOLA – The French and Spanish used the name when referring to the Creek Indian tribes that lived in the area. It is said it may have meant "people on the other side". Most of the land the river flows through is swamp and forest land.

2. CHATTAHOOCHEE – The longest of the three arms of the A-C-F system, this river starts its flow as seepage in Atlanta, GA. Along with some other streams it forms Lake Lanier, the main source of water for the city and surrounding area. Its total distance is about 430 miles. Most of the dams on the upper end are to provide hydroelectric power and water supply. Three L & D's are on the lower end for the navigational aspects of the system. The locks are 82 feet wide by 450 feet long. When steamboat traffic started in 1828 the most prominent cargoes were cotton and passengers. The name of the river is derived from the Creek Indian, *chatu-hachi,* meaning "marked" or "pictured rock" which was found in the area.

3. FLINT – The River has a total length of about 200 plus miles. It is, however, a fairly short segment of the A-C-F at present, but one that had more than 26 steamboat landings in 1860 that mostly were in the cotton trade. The building of the railroads pretty well decimated the river traffic. The original name of the river comes from a Creek Indian village called Thronateeska, which in their language meant a place where flint could be picked up. I guess it was easier for settlers to use a one syllable word than the longer initial one of the Indian site.

APPENDAGES
Those additions to the exterior of a vessel's hull that protrude into the watercourse such as its rudders and propellers.

APPORTIONMENT OF FAULT
A legal term used when a judge awards damages in a case in proportion to what he believes the degree of culpability was for each of the parties involved. So if you are involved in a casualty a court could decide your degree of fault was only two percent or even zero percent, or maybe fifty to one hundred percent.

APPRENTICE MATE
A recent term now used by the USCG in their regulations for a STEERSMAN that pertains to a mariner in training in order to become a MATE (PILOT) on towing vessels, and who has met the time

requirements and passed all required examinations for an applicable towing license. See: MASTER, MATE and CUB.

APPROACH POINT
A point above or below a lock that a tow should not pass if there is another tow coming out of a lock in the opposite direction and cannot safely pass. Any vessel intending to lock should contact the Lock Master to seek permission to proceed beyond this point. See: ARRIVAL POINT.

APPROVED
Used for certain equipment required by the U.S. Coast Guard to be carried aboard vessels. The USCG tests, or has approved testing societies, to evaluate the equipment. It then certifies and labels such gear or devices as *approved* to be carried aboard vessels.

APRON
1. An extension on the deck of a ferry flat that will reach the bank of a shore to permit loading when the hull of the flat strikes ground in the river near the ferry landing.
2. A pad or structure built at the base of a dam to prevent erosion from swift water running through the dam opening.

AQUEDUCT
1. A structure built in a CANAL that was used to supply the canal with water from a FEEDER CANAL, a reservoir, or a river. The word derives from the Latin *aquae ductus*, meaning *aquae* for water, and *ductus* for conveying or carrying.
2. A part of a CANAL itself and was used as a sort of portage or trough to span across an obstruction in the canal's path or to bridge a stream. They were usually narrower than the canal itself and only provided for one-way transit of boats.

ARBITRATION
The use of a supposedly unbiased third party to attempt to settle contractual differences between two existing interested factions, such as a shipper and a carrier, or a shipyard and a vessel owner. It is sometimes required to be used in contract arrangements and is often preferred rather than entering into a lawsuit and court action to resolve a dispute.

ARC (OF LIGHT)
The distance in degrees a navigation light shall show over a continuous portion of a curved line of the horizon. It is used in Navigation Rule 21, Definitions, to give the parameters of how each navigational light is to be placed and the degrees over which it is to be displayed.

ARC LIGHT
See: CARBON ARC LIGHT.

ARCHIMEDES (PRINCIPLE)
A mathematician who lived a couple of hundred years B.C. who expostulated the theory that an object partially submerged in a body of water (fluid) is subject to an upward force equal to the weight of the amount of water that it displaces. That is why a heavy steel vessel is able to stay afloat in the river.

ARKANSAS RIVER
The river flows from its source in Colorado to its mouth in the Mississippi River for a distance of 1450 miles, making it next to the Missouri River the longest tributary of the Mississippi watershed. In the 1500s the explorer Coronado forded the river in the vicinity of Kansas and DeSoto was on its lower reaches. Then in the latter quarter of the 1600s LaSalle claimed all of its lands for the King of France. After the Treaty of Paris in 1763 that ended the French and Indian War the Louisiana Territory was transferred to Spain;

then France again won it back when Napoleon was doing his battles in Europe. He then needed money and the U.S. wanted to expand. After the U.S. made the Louisiana Purchase in 1803 of the new western territories, Zebulon Pike explored the river's basin. Most of the trade was of fur trappers.

In 1820 the first steamboat, the *COMET* stemmed the river for about 60 miles up to the Arkansas Post. Two years later the *Str. EAGLE* made it past Little Rock. However, little work was done except for some snagging. In 1832 the Rivers and Harbors Act provided for the federal government to maintain a channel for 465 miles of the river wide enough for "heavy boats". Some dipper dredging was done, as well as bank stabilization and construction of training dikes. More extensive work on the river did not occur until the late 1870s with greater dredging and dike placement. After the 1927 flood on the Mississippi, including the Arkansas River, a more comprehensive look at water resources and management was starting to be made. It was reinforced by the 1937 flood on the Ohio River and local flooding, so the focus was on flood control, not particularly navigation development. After WW II there were renewed efforts for flood protection and local interest in development of the river system. Former Governor Kerr of Oklahoma became a Senator and teamed up with Senator McClellan of Arkansas to eventually authorize projects to make Tulsa, OK, a seaport. Thus was born the McCLELLAN-KERR ARKANSAS RIVER NAVIGATION SYSTEM (see).

ARM

1. The spokes in a paddlewheel that are attached to the flange and carry the bucket planks that propel the boat. See: STERNWHEEL.

2. The section of a steamboat anchor between the crown (bottom end) and the bill (holding fluke).

ARM (THE LEAD)

Before the days of depth recorders and when there were extremely changeable and unstable channels, a Pilot would have the Mate or other crewman take a leadline out on the tow to sound, or to find out, the depth of the river. If the Pilot also wanted to know the type of river bottom that was being navigated he would tell the crewman to *arm the lead*. At the end of the leadline was a lead weight that had a hollowed-out section at its lowest extremity. The leadsman would put tallow in the hollow, thus *arming the lead*. This would cause some of the river bottom material to stick to the tallow, giving an indication of its consistency. Few, if any, riverboats carry LEADLINES anymore.

ARMORING

1. The placement of rock, revetment mats, or other material on cutting or washing river banks to prevent or retard further erosion.

2. The addition of cast steel plate strips in a lock wall surface that are embedded in the concrete to help prevent damage by the constant sliding of barge hulls along the walls.

ARREST

The seizure and detention of a vessel when a federal marshal has served a writ against it in order to secure its value during a suit of an alleged breach of the law by its owner. See: SEIZURE.

ARRIVAL POINT

A place, marked by a signboard, both above and below a lock that is the point used to designate the *arrival* of a vessel at the lock. When a towboat and tow arrive at the board the Pilot will blow a locking whistle, thus establishing the vessel's turn to lock. Currently, with radio-telephone communications between the Lockmaster and the Pilot the use of lock whistle signals are basically obsolete. See: APPROACH POINT.

ARRIVAL TIME or NOTICE
The time when the vessel arrives or expects to arrive at a given place such as a lock, bridge, mile post, dock or other point on the river (or canal). Sometimes in "security" or "safety" situations it is required by the USCG that they be notified when a vessel arrives in certain areas.

ARTICULATED TUG-BARGE (ATB)
A combined unit consisting of a tug that fits into a relatively deep notch recessed into the stern transom of a barge whereby the two pieces are physically locked together, usually by a set of large retractable pins extending out from the tug into the barge hull that allows vertical movement of the tug. This allows the two vessels to operate as a single unit in rough seas at greater efficiency and maneuverability than when the tug would be towing the barge astern. As a *composite unit* it is regarded under the interpretative rules of the Inland Navigation Rules as a single vessel and is to show the lights prescribed in Rule 23. Examples of ATB system connections used in the U.S. are the "Artubar", the "Bludworth", and the "Intercon".

AS IS, WHERE IS
The contracting or sale of a vessel wherein a seller offers a vessel for contract or sale in its present condition where the vessel is located at the time of signing an agreement, and the buyer, or person contracting for it, agrees to the terms.

ASCENDING
The old *Western Rivers Rules of the Road* used the word *ascending* to mean a vessel that was proceeding upstream against the current, and conversely when the vessel was going downstream with the current it was termed the DESCENDING vessel. The Navigation Rules now use the term, "proceeding upstream against the current".

ASH CHUTE or PIPE or WELL
An opening formed by a piece of pipe about eight inches in diameter leading from the ash pan of a furnace of a boiler on a steamboat to the river used to discard hot coals and ashes into the water.

ASH PAN or PIT
The collection area for burnt cinders under the grates of the fire box of the boiler on a steamboat.

ASHORE
Someone or some object off the vessel. For instance, a crewman leaves the vessel and goes *ashore*, or takes *ashore* for repair the old broken ratchets. It is the opposite of *aboard* or *on board*.

ASSHOLE
A colloquial term used to describe a kink, or a short tight twist in a wire or line, which could cause problems when using it as well as weakening it and shortening its useful life. One may have to let the imagination work to rationalize the origins of this term. Perhaps when it was used to address a scornful person it became translated into a bad or malignant action in a length of line or wire.

ASSISTANCE TOWING
A vessel that gives assistance to a disabled vessel for monetary consideration.

ASSIST TOWING
On the river the term is used when a tow is too large to go though a lock and a smaller towboat is contracted to take a portion of the tow, usually one or two strings, through

the lock independently, where it waits for the line boat to lock through with the rest of the tow. The assist boat will then place the barge strings back in the mainline tow so that it may continue up or downstream. Sometimes referred to as a HELPER BOAT, but that term is more often used and limited to assistance getting into a lock and pulling lock cuts.

ASSOCIATIONS

Over the many years since the development of the inland rivers and canals there have been various regional and sometimes national in scope, organizations that have sought to promote and secure improvements for the navigability of our nation's internal waterways. They start up, sometimes merge, or leave the scene as their objectives are accomplished or their efforts fail. In the past 50 years the most important ones were the Ohio Valley Improvement Association (OVIA) which later became DINAMO, the Mississippi Valley Association (MVA) which later became the Water Resources Congress (WRC) and was later resurrected as the Midwest Area River Coalition (MARC 2000). They have all faded into wherever old *associations* go. There are still a large group of organizations educating people about the value of particular river systems as well as those national in promotional activities. Not all will be listed here, but some of the current main ones are:

American Waterways Operators (AWO)
Gulf Intracoastal Canal Association (GICA)
National Waterways Council (NWC)
Waterways Council, Inc. (WCI)

ASSUME (THE WATCH)

When one Pilot relieves another standing a navigation watch, he/she *assumes the watch*. It has been inferred that the "assumption" was when no one was previously in control and the person who took control had "assumed" it. However, in most cases when a Pilot enters the pilothouse to relieve the watch, the vessel's position, traffic, and other pertinent data are exchanged and the relieving Pilot takes over the pilotage duties. On towboats and tugs it isn't the formal declaration of, "I assume the watch". It is usually an informal, "OK, I got it, Cap".

ASTERN

1. Toward the stern, in the back of, or aft of the vessel, i.e. "The towboat *astern* of us is the M/V *LANDLUBBER*".
2. Used when referring to motion, i.e. "I will drop *astern* of the dock", or "we will fall *astern* of the lower piling", or "move the starboard lead barge *astern* of the lead barge now on the port side of the tow".
3. Used when referring to the propulsion force of the engine(s) and the direction of the propellers, such as "I am going full *astern*". *Astern* propulsion is the opposite of "ahead".

ASTRONOMY

A technology which involves the observations of celestial bodies in space. It is what Pilots do at night when they aren't looking for where a buoy is supposed to be, but isn't. *Astronomy* is a captivating science that most ancient cultures studied and developed legends of the different celestial bodies. A most interesting book in this regard is *THE ROMANCE OF ASTRONOMY* (originally published as *THE MUSIC OF THE SPHERES*) by Florence Arm-strong Grondal. The word comes from the Greek *astronomos*, meaning "star arranging".

ATB

An acronym meaning ARTICULATED TUG BARGE.

ATCHAFALAYA RIVER

The river is a distributary of the Mississippi River, its source mainly flowing from its larger parent the Father of Waters. At one time the RED RIVER flowed into the Mississippi at the upper bight part of an oxbow bend in the river called Turnbull's Bend. The *Atchafalaya* was clogged with logs and not a lot of water went through it, but it was located at the lower end of the bight of Turnbull's Bend. In 1831, Henry Shreve (see: SHREVE, HENRY), made a dredging cut across the neck of Turnbull's Bend in order to shorten the Mississippi. The upper loop filled in and the lower part of the loop became known as the OLD RIVER. The Red River then flowed into the Old River and the *Atchafalaya* received its waters from it and the Mississippi.

To allow navigation on the *Atchafalaya*, the State of Louisiana removed the log jam and the river started receiving more water from the Mississippi, causing it to deepen and widen. Hydrological engineers predicted that if the flow trend continued the *Atchafalaya* would capture the main amount of the Mississippi's flow and if it reached 45 percent it would become irreversible. This would eventually make the mouth of the *Atchafalaya* the new delta of the Mississippi, causing the existing Lower Mississippi below that point (about mile 300) to silt in and making the Port of New Orleans incapable of being a seaport for ocean freighters.

The Mississippi River Commission recommended that a structure be built to control the flow to an approximate 70 to 30 ratio, with the *Atchafalaya* receiving the latter amount. Building of the OLD RIVER CONTROL PROJECT to accomplish this task started in 1954 and was completed in 1962. With the control structure in place a rock fill dam was put in the Old River, and a canal with a navigation lock was constructed from the Mississippi River to the *Atchafalaya*. The distance of the waterway from the lock to the mouth below the GIWW is about 170 miles. The river's name comes from the Attakapas Indian tribe, *hacha falaia*, meaning Long River. The word is pronounced on the river as "Shaf – ah – lie". Leave off the "At" and "yah".

ATHWART

Transverse or cross movement, usually meaning at, or close to, a right angle. It can be something lying across, or moving across.

ATHWARTSHIPS

From one side of the vessel to the other, i.e. "Take that line *athwartships* at the stern quarter over to the cavel on barge 5555".

ATON

An acronym used by the USCG meaning, "Aid to Navigation".

AUTOMATIC DEPENDENT SURVEILLANCE (ADS)

A radio transceiver that sends a signal indicating a vessel's identity, position, course, speed, and other information to another receiver that can plot the course of the sending vessel.

AUTOMATIC IDENTIFICATION SYSTEM (AIS)

A type of communications system that shows on an electronic chart screen the position of vessels in the vicinity, what type of vessel each is, the size or number of barges it has in tow, their cargo, their heading and course, speed through the water, and their destination. It is basically done by GPS signals sent to and from vessels to a base station through the use of VHF transmitters. AIS equipment will eventually be required on most commercial vessels. It is the maritime "black box" that knows all, records all, and saves all. The USCG will be able to detect, identify, and monitor the operations of all vessels in U.S. waters that are required to be so-equipped.

AUTOMOBILE BARGES AND CARRIERS

The transportation of automobiles by inland waterways goes back a long ways. When cars first became common in the early part of the 1900s some were transported on steamboats. Later barge loads were carried to various destinations. Even double-decker barges were in use in the 1930s. However, production in WW II was limited to the war effort and this type traffic halted. After WW II the demand for automobiles revived, and potential buyers would take any model, any color, and at most any price. Transportation by water of autos also revived, with special loading and unloading ramps at various river locations. Car carriers with three decks and flat-deck tank barges, some with double decks, were in demand.

By 1960, the selling of autos had changed, with consumers wanting a particular color, type of radio installed, type of seat covering, etc. and they wanted it "now". Also, the railroads implemented new rail cars and ways of loading them so the practice of water carriage of automobiles died out. Some barges became office landings, shop barges, and CATTLE BARGES.

AUTO-PILOT

A steering device connected to a gyroscope to allow a vessel to automatically maintain a given course. Although of some use on the long stretches on the Lower Mississippi when upbound, it is not too useful when proceeding downbound due to the need to constantly change one's heading in the bends of a river.

AUXILIARIES

The various types of motorized machinery aboard a vessel used to power many pieces of non-propulsion equipment such as the capstans, winches, various pumps, other motors, etc.

AUXILIARY LOCK or CHAMBER

At a dam where there is more than one lock, the main lock is the largest one and the other adjacent *lock*, usually smaller, is the called the *auxiliary*. Often the *chamber* is used to lock small tows, LIGHT BOAT, and recreational craft, as well as to provide lockage service when the main chamber is shut down for any reason.

AVAST

A command that is given sometimes to order someone to stop heaving or pulling on a line, usually as, "*avast heaving*", but the expression is seldom used on the river. The term is said to come from the Dutch *houdvast,* meaning "hold fast".

AVULSION

1. The rapid erosion of a shoreline by current or wave action.
2. An action by a flooding river where the current breaks through a section of land separating it from its existing shoreline and basically changing the river's course and channel line.

AWASH

1. The condition when river or canal water is coming over the deck of a towboat, tug, or barge. It could either be a temporary wave or swell action due to low freeboard, or the vessel may be in sinking condition as the decks become *awash*.
2. Used to describe water just covering something, i.e., "At this river gauge the bar abreast the White River is just barely *awash*".

AWAY

The term used to denote when the lines from a vessel or tow are turned loose and it is departing from a fleet, dock, mooring, lock, or pier.

AWEIGH

When an anchor is being raised, it is said to be *aweigh* when it first clears the bottom of a waterway, but not necessarily hauled up. A vessel is then considered underway even though it may not be making way (movement) through the water. Since towboats do not use anchors, one never hears the call of the Mate, "Anchor *Aweigh*!"

AWO

The acronym for the American Waterway Operators, an association of owners and operators of vessels in the tug, towboat and barge industry. The association consists of members from the shallow draft river industry, those who operate in the harbors of the East Coast, Gulf Coast, West Coast, the Great Lakes, as well as the Rivers and Canals of the United States. They represent the interests of their members in Congressional and governmental regulatory affairs. Their headquarters office is in Washington, DC.

AXE

Like the ADZE, the *axes* used by loggers and shipwrights came in various sizes and head designs. The most common was the Shipwright's, or Broad *Axe*, with a blade about 10 inches long. The term is Old English for *aex*. It is often simply spelled "ax".

AXE KNOT

A *knot* that has been pulled so tight, or is under such strain, that it cannot be readily undone to turn the line loose and has to be cut with an *axe* or a knife. Other terms are often used to describe such a knot, not often complimentary to the person who tied it.

AYE-AYE

A universal maritime phrase (naval, seagoing, and on the rivers) used to acknowledge a given order that it is understood and will be carried out. All deck, engine room, and galley crew personnel always have the last word when serving aboard a vessel, for when they reply, it usually is: "Aye, aye, sir". The response phrase has the meaning, "*I* do understand and *I* will comply".

One time, long ago, way down on the Mississippi, two tugboat Captains who had been friends for years would always sound their whistles when they met port to port and then cry out *AYE* to each other from their respective pilothouses when they passed. A new young deckhand asked the Mate, "Why do they do that?" The Mate looking surprised at the deckhand's question, replied, "Well son, you mean to tell me that you haven't heard, ...A toot for a toot, and an *aye* for an *aye*?"

20 ILLUSTRATIONS

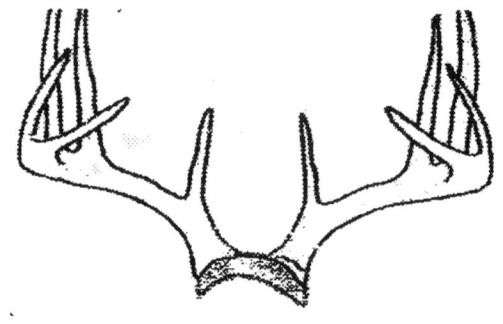

THE GILDED ANTLERS
"SHE TAKES THE HORNS"

Indicating the vessel is the fastest in her trade

**THE BROOM
(UPPER MISSISSIPPI)
"A CLEAN SWEEP"**

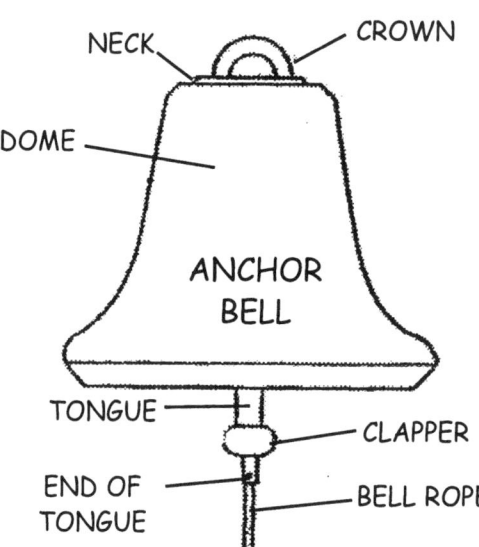

ANCHOR BELL — NECK, CROWN, DOME, TONGUE, CLAPPER, END OF TONGUE, BELL ROPE

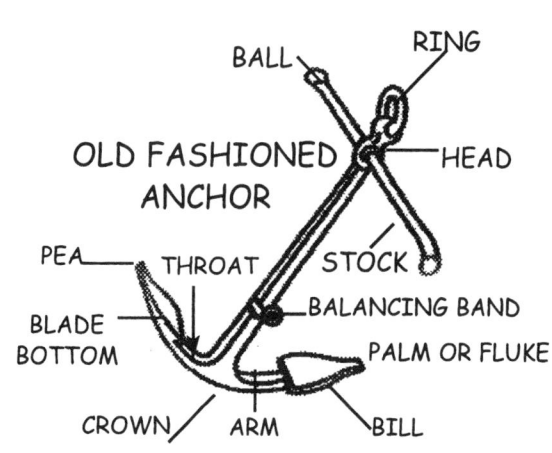

OLD FASHIONED ANCHOR — BALL, RING, HEAD, PEA, THROAT, STOCK, BALANCING BAND, BLADE BOTTOM, PALM OR FLUKE, CROWN, ARM, BILL

B

BABBLING BROOK

Those pretty little streams of poetry that flow from the heights and feed enough water into the tributaries of our river system to make steamboat and riverboat navigation possible throughout the Western Rivers.

BACK

1. Refers to the action of moving a vessel astern or reversing the movement of the propeller(s) to go astern. A Mate or Lead Deckhand in signaling the Pilot into a lock or landing, will call out as the boat gets closer in order to stop the headway of the tow, "*Back* 'er down Cap". The Pilot will reply, "Backin' down". See: BACKING DOWN.

2. The term is mostly used as a verb, i.e. *backing* as in *backing* slow, *backing* easy, *backing* full astern, or *backing* to port (starboard), or "I'll *back* her into the tie off spot above the dock".

3. The forward side of a propeller when mounted on the tail shaft.

BACK CHANNEL OR CHUTE

A passage navigating through an old cut-off, or formerly used section of the river, or behind an island. It is most often used during high water to find slacker current rather than bucking the faster current in the main channel. It may also contain a dock or a fleeting area.

BACK HAUL

Barging companies usually have a towing trade from an origination area to a destination area which is their main source of revenue from these cargoes they are contracted to transport. After a barge, or a tow of barges, unload at destination there sometimes becomes an opportunity to reload them with a different cargo and transport it to a destination near the region where their prime source of cargo and income revenue are located. This new opportunity is called a *back haul*. When the *back haul* barges are unloaded they then return to the primary trade. Usually the rates for these movements are less than what towage rates are charged for the prime movement.

For example, when the grain harvest season is at its peak, and demand for barging equipment is high, carriers will dedicate their barges to grain haulage, taking loads south to the Gulf area and often return with empty barges to be reloaded. However, when the grain trade slacks off and rates for haulage of grain are greatly reduced, these same carriers will seek *back haul* cargoes to offset some of their operating costs.

There are times when the usual prime trade is going for such a low towage rate, usually because of an oversupply of barging equipment, while at the same time there is a demand for equipment to be loaded at the usual destination area that the *back haul* becomes the prime business. It is, of course, the simple matter of supply and demand. Also see: TRIANGULATION.

BACK OFF

1. To gradually slack, or pay out (loosen), a line or wire.

2. To reverse a capstan, windlass, winch, or a ratchet in order to slacken the attached wire or line.

BACK SCATTER

1. The reflection of light, whether it is from navigation lights, deck lights, or searchlights which results in an impairment of night vision to a Pilot that can occur during times of rain, fog, snow, or mist.

2. Reflections on the radar screen that cloud the images, usually from weather conditions such as heavy rain or snow.

3. Static or multiple transmissions on a radio channel that make it difficult to understand what is being said.

BACK SPLICE
Usually done on the BITTER END of a small line. The strands of the end of a line are made into a crown knot and then each strand in turn is tucked back into the bight. This is done to keep the line from unlaying or unraveling.

BACK UP
1. Propelling astern.
2. The act of reducing a vessel's headway with astern propulsion. The term is used when a Pilot is going to flank his tow in a tight bend or other close place in the waterway. The Pilot may say, "I'm going to *back up* at Craighead".

BACK WATCH
The watch that is stood on a river vessel from midnight to 6:00 a.m. and from noon to 6:00 p.m. Generally, it is referred to as the AFTER WATCH.

BACKING DOWN
A vessel going with astern propulsion to retard or stop the forward motion of a vessel. The call of the Mate as a tow enters a lock and wants the tow to stop, "*Back* 'er down Cap," or from one Pilot to another on the radio, "I'm *backing 'er down*, see ya on two whistles".

BACKING LINE or WIRE
1. A line or wire that is laid so that it is leading forward from a barge being pushed to a barge being towed or dragged alongside in order to keep barges from moving ahead in a tow when the towboat is backing astern. The *backing line* is laid in the opposite direction of a TOW LINE.
2. A line used in a lock chamber to keep the tow in place when using a towing line lead at the head and a *backing line* at the stern to keep the tow from moving into the lock gates. A similar situation occurs when tying a tow to the shore or a dock, only in reverse. The line used at the head of the barge, or tow, would have the weight of the vessel(s) on it from the current in the river and leads forward from the barge to the dock. It would be called the *head line*, while the stern line would be leading aft to the dock in order keep the barge(s) from running forward in the event of an eddy, wind, or surge.

BACKING RUDDERS
Another name for FLANKING RUDDERS. They are used to assist towboats in directing their movement when going astern. The rudders are located forward of the propeller(s) so that when the engines are reversed the wheel wash thrust is going forward, allowing the *backing* or *flanking rudders* to control the steering direction of the vessel.

BACKLASH
1. The extreme slingshot action occurring when a wire or line breaks under a heavy strain. This is especially true of some of the synthetic fiber lines that have an ability to stretch to a greater degree than do natural fiber lines. It can be quite dangerous to be in the area of the whipping action that takes place when a line or wire parts after it has reached its breaking point.
2. The action of water on the lower side of a dam that can cause a tow to move out from the guide wall toward the dam, an eddy effect.

BACKWASH
1. The action of the propellers moving in the astern direction, or the astern rotation of a paddlewheel vessel.
2. To wash out the silt at a landing.
3. Most often refers to the action of clearing the wheels or kort nozzles of drift or ice by using astern propulsion.

BACKWATER

1. The result of a large rise on a river that causes its flow to back up into a confluent or tributary stream. When there is a high flow coming out of the Ohio River and correspondingly low water on the Upper Mississippi River, the *backwater* from the Ohio can be 50 miles or better upstream on the Upper from where the rivers merge at Cairo Point. Conversely, when the Missouri and Upper Mississippi rivers are at flood stage and the Ohio is at low gauge the *backwater* will be upstream on the Ohio River.

2. An area of navigable water off the main channel.

BACKYARD BOAT

A towboat or tug not built in a shipyard. Usually only rudimentary plans are drawn and no particular specifications are made. These vessels are usually small in size and will vary greatly in ability of the builder. In some areas called a "Cornfield Boat".

BAFFLE DIKE

1. A dike built shoreward and above a REVETMENT that supports the revetment and tends to protect the bank and its revetment in case high water overtops the bank.

2. A tie-in dike from the shore to a LONGITUDINAL DIKE that adds support.

BAFFLE PLATE

The plate structure installed in a tank or barge carrying liquid products to reduce the free surface force effect of liquids flowing either in a fore and aft movement or athwartship causing an unstable condition to the vessel. The separate cargo compartments in a tank barge or in the bunkers of a towboat or tug are in reality a *baffle* type of marine engineering design.

The term may have come from the French *bafouer,* meaning "to deceive", or the Scottish *bauchle,* expressing "to revile or discredit", probably in an attempt to discourage the adverse actions of another. This is what a *baffling plate* does to the possible forces that can be exerted by the flowing or the sloshing of liquid in a tank or barge.

BAGGED BOILER

A *boiler* that has a bulge in its skin. It is caused by a buildup of too much silt and scale that tends to insulate the water on the inside of the *boiler*, causing the casing to become as hot as in a forge thus weakening the steel. The pressure in the *boiler* then will find this weak spot. If it is too high, the sediment will break loose and cooler water will rush to the spot of the hot casing that will cause a bulge, or *bag*. The bulge will have to be cut out and new casing welded in to it. If the pressure is high and the cooler water cannot adequately cool the steel, the *boiler* will explode, which is called a "bad day on the river".

BAIL

The action of removing water from a small boat such as a yawl or skiff by means of a scoop, can or bucket. Comes from the French *baille,* (bucket) that was derived from the Latin *baiulus,* (carrier). For other interpretive terminology of the term if one may have been arrested for a dastardly deed can only be found in a legal dictionary.

BAILMENT

The placing of goods or equipment, such as a barge, into the care, custody, and control of another, such as a dock or a fleet. The person (facility) receiving the goods or equipment, the bailee, must use due diligence to properly care for such equipment and return it in similar condition to its owner/operator (bailor).

BALANCED RUDDER

A rudder with approximately 15 to 30 percent of its blade forward of the axis of rotation, or rudder shaft. This allows the water pressure on the main section of the rudder blade to be partially counterbalanced, resulting in ease of rudder movement as well as increase in the area of blade surface exposed to the thrust action of current or propeller producing more efficient steering performance.

BALK

A straight timber cut from a small tree and is then squared. It is about five inches to no more than eight inches square.

BALL

Ball(s) are shapes to be displayed in certain situations by vessels as prescribed in Rule 27, 29, 30 and 31 of the Navigation Rules. Some of these requirements are mandated when a vessel is not under command or restricted in its ability to maneuver, a vessel engaged in mineclearance operations, pilot vessels, anchored vessels and vessels aground, and seaplanes (if possible). The *ball* shape shall be black and not less than 0.6 meters in diameter as delineated in NAVRULES Annex I, 84.11.

BALLAST

Extra weight added to a vessel, usually to increase stability. Although towing vessels do not normally carry *ballast* in the same manner that seagoing vessels do, they will pump water into, or out of, tanks on the towboat to provide better economy of fuel, less vibration, to insure a water seal for the propellers, or to allow a towboat to better headlog with its tow. Barges are sometimes *ballasted* down by pumping water into void compartments because their air height, especially with stacked lift covers, when they are too high to clear some fixed bridges, such as in the Chicago area. The word *ballast* in days gone by appears to have meant "bare load", or a cargo load that was taken on only for the weight it provided to better weather the rolling seas, and had no commercial value for the ship.

BALLAST TANK

A watertight void compartment on a vessel that can be filled with water to trim a vessel if it is down on one end or side. Often void tanks of barges are ballasted to make them HEADLOG with another barge, or to clear low bridges in some areas of the inland waterways.

BANK

The shoreline of the river. Used in conjunction with other phrases, i.e. "tying off to the *bank*", "running the *bank* close", "going up the *bank*", "I wish I was on the *bank* at Christmas time". The word is derived from the German. It originally took on the meaning of a "ridge or slope" and sailors used the term for a shallow place in the sea floor, but of sufficient depth for navigation, such as Grand Bank or Georges Bank. It apparently took further meaning as the shore slope of a river coming from sea. At any rate, it is used in a number of ways by rivermen, even as a place to put one's paycheck.

BANK EFFECT or SUCTION or CUSHION

The countering effects on a tow when it is in a narrow constricted channel and navigates too close to one of the banks. The bow wave tends to build up water on the near bank at the head of the tow causing it to want to sheer away. At the same time water is being displaced from the stern of the tow on the near bank, creating a suction force on it. The hydraulic effect is to apply a twisting movement on the tow with its head veering away from the bank and its stern moving into it. If the sheer effect is too severe the vessel will become unmanageable and may veer to the opposite side of the channel.

BANK FULL
When the water level in a river rises to the point where it overflows the top of its bank. This is usually the point where a river is at flood stage. However, with levees and other flood management structures in many river valleys, it is *bank full* when what is called the bottom land becomes flooded.

BAR
The result of a buildup of silt or sand at the mouth of a tributary stream, or on the point side of a bend. It can also build in the navigable channel, obstructing it, and requiring dredging to remove the bar in order to maintain required project depth. The word appears to come from the Latin *barra,* meaning "a barrier", which a sandbar is to navigation. It is not known how the other use of the word came into a riverman's vocabulary as a place to partake of alcoholic beverages, where at one time there were a lot of them at small towns all along the river bank. See: CROSSING THE BAR.

BAR BOOK
A set of notes, or a book, kept by Pilots to indicate high water marks, obstructions in a waterway at various stages of a river, unusual currents, eddies, and any other information on a channel that can be useful in finding the best water for efficient and safe navigation. See: GAUGE or GAGE, GAUGE WATER, and HIGH WATER MARKS.

BAR PILOT
A ship *pilot*, licensed by the State of the waters being piloted, that brings in seagoing vessels from approximately the sea buoy into a harbor. In Louisiana, the *Bar Pilot* takes a vessel from the sea buoy to the HEAD OF PASSES or mile 0 of the Mississippi River, where pilotage will be given to a Crescent River PILOT. In New Orleans, if the ship is going further upriver, it is piloted by a New Orleans to Baton Rouge, or NOBRA PILOT.

BAR SCALE
A line or series of lines at the bottom of a chart or map of the river that can be used to determine distances on the display; also referred to as a "legend".

BAR SIDE
The inner curvature of a river bend, the shallow cross-sectional part of a river course, as opposed to the bend side of the channel. The term is used between vessels when arranging their positions to meet, i.e. "I'll be on the *bar side* and you can have the bend and will meet you on one whistle".

BAR TAUT
A wire that is stretched almost to a rigid breaking point, to become like a steel bar.

BARE BOAT CHARTER
The hire or lease of a barge or towboat by an owner (charter party) to a charterer, without crew, and less fuel or stores (unless inventoried), and with minimum restrictions as to the employment of the vessel. A survey is usually conducted at the commencement of the charter and again when the vessel goes off charter. A *bareboat charter* is termed a "demise" charter wherein the charterer in effect assumes total responsibility and control for the vessel and its crew and in effect becomes, in legal terms, the "owner pro hac vice". When the vessel goes off-charter any discrepancies between the surveys, less normal wear and tear, will be repaired from the account of the charterer.

BARE STEERAGEWAY
See: STEERAGEWAY

BARGE

The term *barge,* used for a vessel that is the most economical, fuel efficient, environmentally friendly means of transporting bulk commodities, is derived from the Latin *barca,* which in turn comes from the Greek *baris,* for an Egyptian boat that used to haul Cleopatra around on the Nile River. Navy personnel use the word to designate a boat for a flag officer (Admiral) to attend ceremonial affairs or meetings, or just to go ashore from one's ship. They are very well painted and decorated, and kept in spic and span condition. Woe be to the coxswain who doesn't keep it so. River people have found a much more utilitarian use for *barges* by filling them with cargo. They may not be as pretty as the Admiral's Barge, but they serve the nation better.

Barges come in a variety of different descriptions and in numerous sizes from small work flats to large ocean-going vessels. Some are manned on the coastal waters and the Great Lakes, but the majority of them are unmanned, especially the great numbers which are operated on the inland river and canal systems of the United States. A few are self-propelled, but most are not. A basic generic definition to cover most *barges* used on our river system is: A non-powered, unmanned, steel hulled, flat-bottomed cargo carrying vessel used to transport various types of bulk cargo.

TYPES OF BARGES are: Hopper, deck, tanker, and miscellaneous.

HOPPER barges come in two types: "Open", for such commodities that do not generally have to be protected from the elements, such as coal, coke, steel plates, scrap, pulpwood, and iron ore.

COVERED hoppers are used for products that require protection from the weather, including grains, paper products, alumina, lime, cements, and manufactured goods.

DECK barges are used for a variety of products, including sand and gravel, marine shells, rock, logs, large construction machines, and military equipment. They are also used as work barges, carrying cranes or winches or other gear for their intended purpose.

TANK or liquid product barges transport petroleum products, chemicals, liquid fertilizers, and wastewater. Many tank barges have auxiliary engines to power pumps used to off-load their cargoes.

MISCELLANOUS barges include the rest of the field of barging equipment, some of which are self-unloaders of cement, garbage scows, spud barges, LASH (Lighter Aboard Ship) and other such special purpose barges.

PRODUCTS CARRIED

The products listed in types of barges above may at times be carried interchangeably in the different categories of barge types. For instance, cement may be transported in covered hoppers. Salt may be in covered or open hoppers. Logs could be loaded in hoppers or deck barges. Even corn (grain), which is normally always carried in covered hoppers, has been transported in open hoppers when equipment is in short supply, sometimes with a plastic covering, sometimes not.

BARGE SIZES

There is a general standardization of barge sizes used on the inland waterways of the United States. It basically is a multiple of the size of the piece of equipment times a number of barges that are of the same size that are able to economically fit into the dimensions of the locks on the river system. Most of the river barging equipment today fits into one of the following categories:

STANDARD BARGE, 175' x 26' — There is a deviation from this size when operators want additional lock space usage and build what are termed

"Slim Jims" or "Stumbos", which are the same width as the standard but the length of a jumbo, 195' long.

JUMBO BARGE, 195' or 200' x 35' — This is currently the most popular-sized barge now in use for general cargo.

TANK BARGES – River tank barges can be much larger than standard or jumbo barges as many of them are in UNIT TOWS. Their widths are 50' and over, and their lengths are up to 300'.

BARGE BUILDING BLOCKS

Many towboats have a set of toy blocks that are scaled to size for barges. When a Pilot is going to build a tow, or rearrange one by adding or taking out barges at a fleeting area, he/she will arrange the block barges on a desk to show the Deck Mate how, where, and what and will happen in the fleet by rearranging the blocks for each intended sequence of occurrences while at the fleeting area. With computers the blocks may float off into barge heaven.

BARGE-CARRYING SHIP

See: LASH

BARGE COVERS

A roof covering for a hopper barge that keeps the cargo contained in it from becoming wet. Types of terms describing barge covers are: Roll – telescoping or non-telescoping, Lift-off, Stack, Weather-Tight, Water-Tight, and Fiberglass (sometimes called Plastic).

BARGE-LINE BUZZARD

The crew is having chicken for dinner, Wednesday or Sunday.

BARGE-LINE SUITCASE

A cardboard box tied together with an old clothes line that a crewmember brings aboard as a suitcase holding most of his worldly belongings.

BARGE MOVER

A winch mounted on a dock (floating or fixed) that is capable of moving a barge up or down the dock to facilitate the loading or unloading of the barge.

BARGE PUMP

1. A portable electric, gas, or diesel pump that is used to remove water from the void tanks and cargo box of a barge. It is also is used to hose down and clean decks.

2. A permanently installed electric-motor or diesel-driven pump on a tank barge used to discharge cargo.

BARGE RATES

The *barge rates* for towing different commodities on the mid-continental river system varies with the type of product, the equipment necessary to move it, supply and demand, distance, and other factors. Some rates are established in stable long-term contracts, others are made on a trip-by-trip basis that are based on a percentage of a benchmark tariff rate which was established in about 1976 when the last official general commodity TARIFF was published.

BARGE WINCH

A *winch* permanently installed on the end(s) of barges to facilitate the coupling of barges together instead of using ratchets. They are most frequently seen on unit tows of tank barges, but are also installed on some dry cargo barges.

BARNACLE

A shellfish that attaches itself to the bottoms and sides of vessels or other submerged objects. River vessels never encountered *barnacles* that are common on the hulls of all seagoing vessels until the 1980s when it was found that freshwater ZEBRA MUSSELS had invaded the lakes and rivers of the United States. So the nemesis of the seas now is ours to cope with also. The word comes from the Latin *bernaca,* which in legend was a goose which attached itself to a tree with its bill until it finally dropped off and swam merrily away. The English changed it somewhat and gave it a "le" ending, so now we have to live with the critters as they now stay fastened.

BARN DOOR RUDDER

Said of a vessel that may have a large steering *rudder(s)* that gives maximum steering power in a minimum amount of time.

BAROMETER

An instrument used aboard vessels to measure the changes in atmospheric pressure. Generally a rising *barometer* indicates fairer and drier weather while one that is falling is an indication that there will be a change to wet and stormy weather.

BARRATRY

A legal term that is the fraudulent act undertaken by the master or crew of a towboat or a tug which might be detrimental to the interests of the owner(s), such as deliberately damaging her, deserting her, smuggling illegal goods, stealing cargo, or other harmful acts. The word comes from the French *baraterie,* meaning "to combat", or "deceit".

BARREL

1. A liquid unit of measurement used in the petroleum industry. Each *barrel* equals 42 gallons. Tank barges are measured in *barrels* of capacity, i.e. a typical 195' x 35' barge has a capacity of about 10,000 *barrels*. The viscosity of the product determines the number of *barrels* contained in the barge at a given displacement. The capacity of a whiskey *barrel* is about 31 gallons. Unfortunately, river barges do not transport very much of this cargo.

2. The drum of a winch or CAPSTAN that rotates on a spindle. Also called a *gypsy drum* or a *cathead.*

3. The term comes from the Latin *barriclus,* meaning "small cask".

BARREL SLING

A steel center "O" ring with two short chains, wires, lines, or rods fitted with a can or chine hook on their ends that fit over and grasp the lips of a barrel when loading same aboard a vessel with a crane or davit. Also called a "can hook".

BARRIER ISLAND

An offshore wave-induced island of deposited sand which can be found along the Gulf Coast, particularly in the Mississippi Sound. Except during severe storms the islands tend to protect the main shore from erosion, and the waters between the islands and shore tend to be more calm with less wave height.

BASCULE BRIDGE

A type of lift bridge that is required to be opened to permit navigation. It operates on the principle wherein one end is counterbalanced by the other similar to a seesaw effect. It can be either a single-span lift or of double-span design with the leaves meeting in the center. The word comes from the French *bacule,* meaning "seesaw".

BASE FLOOD

A standard of an area in floodplain management wherein there would be a one percent chance of that area flooding over the base height of the standard; the odds of it flooding over that height would be once in 100 years.

BASIN

1. Our rivers and their tributaries lie in a drainage area, trying to find the fastest way for their waters to reach the sea. These drainage areas are called *basins*. Most of the U.S.

Corps of Engineers Divisions are divided on the basis of the river *basins* they must oversee.

2. A fairly large pool of water in a semi-enclosed area above a dam, such as that above Keokuk L&D and McAlpine L&D.

BASKET

The term refers to the optional day shape(s) which vessels engaged in fishing may display in accordance with the Navigation Rules. Seldom ever seen on the rivers and canals.

BASTARD REPAIR

The use of a fitting or attachment that doesn't have standard threads, holes, diameter, etc, and is not the correct size or shape to properly repair some item. Oftentimes a competent Engineer, Deckhand, and even a Captain will *bastardize* a repair and have it "make do" until the proper fittings or gear can be obtained at the next available place or shipyard. Sometimes it is called by inspectors an illegitimate repair.

BASTARD TOW

A tow that is made up of barges of different lengths and widths which leave notches at various places along the side of the tow. This unevenness can allow the corner of a notched barge to catch in the recess of a lock or along a protective sheer fence of a bridge, causing damage to one or the other or both.

BATEAU (plural *BATEUX*)

A French term for "boat". In North America it usually is meant to describe a fairly good-sized double-ender that is a flat-bottomed craft. It carried over into river terms since many of the French Acadians (Cajuns) who settled in Louisiana called any vessel larger than a PIROGUE a *bateau*, which is pronounced: baa – toe. The pirogue was originally a hollowed out log, but as times change it became the French name for a canoe, and may now even be flat-bottomed.

BATON ROUGE

The head of navigation on the Mississippi River for most oceangoing vessels due to the restriction of bridge clearance height across the river, as well as no maintenance of a deep enough navigation channel. Also the city is the capitol of the State of Louisiana with the highest, 450 feet, state capitol building in the United States.

BATON ROUGE TO NEW ORLEANS PILOT

See: NEW ORLEANS TO BATON ROUGE PILOT (NOBRA)

BATTEN

1. A thin strip of wood, usually tapered, that may be used to temporarily stop a leak. More often on the river referred to as a SHINGLE.

2. A backup piece of wood attached with the STIRRUP to the BUCKET of a paddle wheel to hold it in place.

3. See below: BATTEN DOWN.

BATTEN DOWN

1. Battens can be wedged strips of wood used to secure hatch covers, tarpaulins, or other coverings when protecting gear or cargo spaces from weather elements.

2. The order to the crew to *batten down* is to tell them to secure all loose gear because of weather conditions.

BATTURE

The area of land lying between the edge of the river and the foot of the levees along the Lower Mississippi River.

BATWING BOAT

A small sidewheel boat that operated mostly on shallow tributaries of the Ohio River, such as the Big Sandy River. The sidewheels had no housings on them, sacrificing their weight to reduce the draft of the vessel while carrying freight or passengers. Probably called *batwings* because they might have looked to some wag like bats beating their wings as the little vessels paddled along; or maybe they thought they looked like the flapping or swinging doors of the old-time saloons that were usually on the riverfront in the days when and where these boats operated.

BAY

The term denotes a body of water, usually seawater, formed by an indentation of the coastline. They are found in many areas along our Gulf Coast where riverboats operate, such as Galveston *Bay* and Mobile *Bay*. They are, of course, also found along the East and West Coasts, such as Chesapeake *Bay*, and San Francisco *Bay*. The word comes from the Spanish *baia*, used to describe an opening or a wide indentation in the land which was surrounded by the sea.

BAYOU

Local areas define the term with different interpretations. It is most often described as either an inlet flowing into a larger stream or bay, or as a minor river. It has little current and can be affected by tidal influences. The term is used frequently in Louisiana when describing small streams. It is thought to come from the Choctaw Indian word *bayuk*, which was then corrupted into Cajun French *bayou*.

B/C RATIO

See: BENEFIT TO COST RATIO.

BEACH

To run a vessel aground on a bar or bank, either intentionally to keep it from sinking, or to simply hold a barge tow temporarily against the bank or bar while changing barges in tow with the help of a SHIFT BOAT, or simply waiting turn at a lock or for a channel to be cleared, etc. If the act was unintentional, the vessel aground is said to be *beached* or hard aground. The term is also used to mean going ashore, i.e. "I'm going to hit the *beach*".

BEACON

Term used by the U.S. Coast Guard in reference to both lighted and unlighted navigation marks. Both lights and daymarks are called *beacons*. They are both guides and warnings for mariners. *Beacon* is from an old English word *beacen*, which simply meant "a sign".

Besides the lights of city fronts or landings along the river, the first *beacon* on the Western Rivers is thought to be one shown on the riverfront at Madison, IN, which was put up in the 1840s that was meant to be an aid to steamboat Pilots. (S&D Reflector) In 1869, the Louisville Pilots Association set up a group of lights at the Grand Chain on the Lower Ohio, miles 955 to 965. See: GOVERNMENT LIGHT, LIGHTS (NAVIGATION), and LIGHT LIST.

BEAM

1. The widest breadth of a vessel. In old English the term referred to a tree. Probably since stout timber was the structural material athwartship on which the deck was laid, the term *beam* was used to mean the widest part of the vessel.

2. The name for large timbers that are laid transversely on a steamer to support the deck.

3. *Half-beams* were used at openings to support the deck where there was no framing.

4. Sometimes used as a direction, i.e. "It's on the *beam*", as in the term ABEAM.

5. The focused rays of a searchlight, i.e. "Put the *beam* off the starboard head Cap, I think I saw something floating there".

BEAM ENDS

A vessel that is heavily listed over so that all, or almost all, of her side plating or planking is showing, is said to be "on her *beam ends*"; or in a most unfortunate circumstance with the possibility of capsizing, unless it was purposely undertaken to make a repair.

BEAM ENGINES

The first steamboats built for use on the eastern waters had their engines and boilers placed down in the hull near the bottom of the vessel with the connecting rod moving upward. The boiler was in a vertical position powering what was sometimes termed a STEEPLE ENGINE. Some version of this type of arrangement may have been on the first steamboat on the Ohio River, the *Str. NEW ORLEANS*, but no one knows for certain, not even what she looked like.

In 1816, with Shreve's (see: SHREVE, CAPT. HENRY MILLER) arrangement of the horizontal boiler and placement of it on the main deck eventually lead to the reduction in hull draft of steamers, even though the *Str. WASHINGTON* (Shreve's steamer) had a keel and housed the engine in the lower hull. However, the old boiler and engine position soon disappeared on the river system as flat bottomed shallow draft craft became the accepted construction method with the engine and boiler on the main deck The placement of *beam engines* in their deeper hulls continued to be the practice on the East and West coasts.

BEAR

Used in relation to observing an object or point. Also used in relation to movement, i.e. "*Bear* a little closer to the right bank", or "*Bear* away from the eddy under the point", or "The tow that *bears* off the port bow is going into the bank to tie off, and the one *bearing* off the starboard bow has agreed to meet on two whistles".

BEAR A HAND

A command to assist someone who is doing work and requires some help.

BEAR OFF

A directive to steer one's vessel heading away from the current course, as in, "*Bear off* to starboard when abreast of the ABC dock".

BEAR TRAP

A so-called gate in a section of movable dam between concrete piers that are approximately 100 feet apart. There may be one or more of this type gate at a dam, which may be raised or lowered to control the amount of water flowing through the dam. The gate consists of two sections. The lower part is hinged to the dam sill on the downstream side and the upper part is hinged to the upstream side of the dam sill. When there is high flow the *bear trap* is opened to allow excess water to pass through, and when it is necessary to maintain the pool above the dam at sufficient project depth the *bear trap* gate is closed to hold the river's water back. There are still some of these type gates in use, but they are no longer deemed suitable for construction due to high maintenance caused by silt, sand and debris deposits making them difficult to raise and lower.

This type of gate derives its name from the hinged effect of the two overlapping leaves of the gate, which resembles a gigantic hunter's trap used to catch bears. If a bear that large was caught maybe they could revisit the movie *King Kong* with a bear instead of an ape. See: TRAP WATER.

BEARING

1. In open waters where plotting on a chart is necessary, the term is a direction taken by a compass, i.e. "the

crossing vessel *bears* at 42 degrees". Since most towboats do not carry compasses, nor do they plot courses, *bearings* given are usually in relation to one's vessel with the bow always being zero degrees, i.e. "The crossing vessel is *bearing* 20 degrees off the starboard (or port) bow".

2. The machinery on steamboats, towboat and tugboats has a variety of different types of *bearings*. Generally these can be considered to be a lubricated sleeve that supports a revolving shaft and confines its sliding or oscillating movements either horizontally or vertically, such as the propeller shaft, the rudder stock, or the pitman, etc.

BEAUFORT WIND SCALE

Created by British Admiral Francis Beaufort in the early 1800s, from notations taken from ship logs as to the observations of the wind's effect on sails. The scale assigns a number to the strength of the wind ranging from Force 0, (meaning Calm, less than 1 knot, with a ship being able to be at full sail), to Force 12 (meaning Hurricane, more than 64 knots, or 74 MPH), at which time the sails would be carried away. The scale is still used today for land, sea, and rivers.

BEBOUT or BOULE WEIR

The *Boule weir* was named for its inventor in France. A Wheeling District engineer in the employ of the U.S. Corps of Engineers revised the design which was then named for him, Bebout. The *Bebout* design of the weir consisted of steel plates, five feet wide, which were smooth on the upstream side. On the downstream they were fitted with flanges that were used to guide the plates into a slotted A-frame structure that collapsed to the side when the weir section of a dam could become navigable. The individual frames were loosely chained together which allowed them to be raised in sections of about five at a time. The raising and lowering of the *weirs* or *wickets* as they are commonly called, was accomplished by a crew on a MANEUVER BOAT, or sometimes called a *Wicket Boat*.

BECKET

1. The holding ring on the end of a block used to secure it to the standing part of a fall.

2. The eye in a small-diameter line used to tie down a steering wheel for a short period of time.

3. A small piece of line used with a TOGGLE to secure gear such as oars, tarps, awnings, etc.

BED

See: RIVER BED.

BED LOAD

The portion of a sediment load in a river that is carried along the stream bed without being permanently suspended in the flowing water of the river. See: SAND WAVE, STREAM LOAD and SUSPENDED LOAD.

BED PLATE

The structure upon which the main engine of a vessel is supported, as well as the foundation for any auxiliary engines within the vessel or on barging equipment.

BEETLE

The largest of the mallets employed in CAULKING was the *beetle*. It was used for the heaviest work of REEMING, or opening seams between planking to remove old oakum, and in HORSING, or hardening a seam after caulking. The other mallets were used with the various CAULKING IRONS, depending on the location being caulked. The *beetle* was sometimes called a "bittle". Also it is used to drive in TREENAILS, PEGS, or WEDGES.

BELAY

To stop off a line or wire, as in, "*Belay* the line on the mid cavel on the lead port barge". Also used as a command to cease or stop doing a present action, or the cancellation of an order, i.e., "*Belay* that". The term comes from the old English *belecgam*.

BELL

All towboats carry a *bell* to comply with the Navigation Rules and it must be in accordance with the dictates of Annex III regarding its construction and the intensity of its sound. It is to be sounded in restricted visibility when at anchor or aground as required in Rule 35(g) or (h). It is believed the term comes from the Dutch *bel*, which was the sound of a stag in rut; however, it may be related to the Latin *bella*, meaning "beautiful" for the sound of its ringing on a vessel or in a church.

Originally steamboats used the *bell* to signal their intent as to passing using the same one or two strikes of the *bell* to indicate the side on which they wanted to meet one another, the same as the current whistle signals. Three strikes meant a signal to make a landing. More than three strikes would indicate danger. With the passage of the 1852 Steamboat Act, the *bell* signals were done away with and replaced with whistle signals.

The *bell* was also used to announce an arrival at a landing as well as a signal for everyone to come back on board for departure. Rapid and repeated ringing of the bell was also used to arouse everyone to a danger, such as fire. Additionally, the bell was employed when the Pilot had the LEADSMAN take SOUNDINGS. When the Pilot gave one tap of the bell it meant to sound on the starboard side of the vessel, and if he wanted soundings on the port side he would tap the bell twice. When soundings were no longer needed the Pilot would give one tap.

When a towboat was originally christened, its name was usually inscribed on the *bell* along with the christening date. It was considered a bad omen in some places to transfer a roof *bell* from one boat to another, especially from a sunken vessel. Then, one should always beware of the Coast Guard Inspector that comes aboard and says, "It ain't a *bell* if its got no clapper and if it ain't got no clapper it's a dumbbell". See: SUCTION BELL.

BELL CORDS or ROPES

1. These were wires in the pilothouse of a steamboat that were attached from a BELL PULL in a BELL STAND to a signal bell located in the engine room. They were pulled as BELL SIGNALS to alert or signal the engine room crew for a change in speed.

2. The short rope connected to the clapper or striker of the bell to be pulled in certain situations required during restricted visibility or when aground. It is the only piece of "rope" aboard a river vessel. All other cordage, either natural fiber or synthetic, is called "line".

BELL PULLS

A brass or wooden ring attached to a BELL CORD used to signal the engine room from the pilothouse.

BELL SIGNALS

A steamboat usually had four types of bells on it that were used by the Pilot to signal the Engineer on watch as to what was wanted. The largest, and deepest in tone, was the STOPPING bell. The next largest was the BACKING BELL. Then came the SHIP-UP GONG, the clapper of which was designed to ring only once with each pull. The last and smallest is the JINGLE BELL, sometimes called the Chestnut Bell. Not all steamboats

BELL SIGNALS (CONT.)

had the same signals, or the same bells. The JINGLE was used mostly by steamers on the upper Ohio and Kanawha rivers. Vessels on the Upper Mississippi didn't usually have a GONG. From Alan Bates we have these typical signals:

1. CALL the engineer to his post —- Ring three or four GONGS.
2. COME AHEAD —- Ring the STOPPING BELL.
3. STOP, from either direction —- Ring the STOPPING BELL.
4. HALF HEAD, in either direction —- Ring one GONG after establishing the direction with either the STOPPING or the BACKING BELL.
5. DEAD SLOW, in either direction —- Ring one GONG and the JINGLE after establishing the direction with either the STOPPING or the BACKING BELL.
6. From HALF HEAD to FULL HEAD, in either direction —- Ring one GONG.
7. From HALF HEAD to DEAD SLOW —- Ring the JINGLE BELL.
8. From DEAD SLOW to HALF HEAD, in either direction —- Ring the JINGLE BELL.
9. From DEAD SLOW to FULL HEAD, in either direction —- Ring the JINGLE BELL and the GONG.
10. FULL STROKE, in either direction —- Ring the GONG twice.
11. To SHIP UP the engines from AHEAD to BACK, or from BACK to AHEAD, when the engines are stopped —- Ring one GONG.
12. FINISHED with engines —- Ring three or four GONGS.

Now if you have that down pat and promptly answer all the Pilot's signals you may qualify as an Engineer. However, if you can't answer the bells in timely fashion, consider this: There once was a Pilot that was continually gonging and jingling so fast when going into a landing one time that the Mate had the steamboat tied off while the Engineer was still answering the bells a half hour later. Alan Bates further explains the system as follows (from the March 1977, S & D Reflector):

ENGINEROOM BELLS

ONE TIME
I went cub pilot on a sternwheel boat,
'bout the biggest old-timer that was still afloat,
LOCKWALL BUSTER was the steamer's name,
And movin' black diamonds was always her game.

SHE HAD THEM OLD-TIME BELLS,
So I asks the pilot, "Just what do they mean?
There ain't no sense to 'em I ever seen.
You sometimes ring that and you sometimes ring this,
The whole dang set-up just looks hit-or-miss."

AND HE SAYS
"It's the simplest thing that ever has been,
The man who can't learn 'em is dumber than sin.
Now, to come ahead full you ring the stoppin' bell,
And to make her go slow you ring backing, as well."

I THINKS TO MYSELF
"This ol' fellow is a-pullin' my leg,
He thinks I ain't got the sense of an egg,
Saying, "Come ahead full on the stopping bell,"
Why that ol' boob can go straight to hell!

SO I ASKS THE CHIEF
"Tell me just what do them three bells mean,
I know you use them to run this machine,
You turn this valve and you lift that rod,
And you jump for them bells like the pilot was God."

AND HE SAYS
"Well to back half-head you ring the backing bell,
Then you tap the gong once, as you surely can tell,
If you watch the pilot when he checks her down slow,
In a lock or a landing when he's making up tow."

I THINKS TO MYSELF
"That ornery old pilot's put him up to this,
Or he's listened too long to the engine's hiss.
For how in the Worl' can you back half-ahead?
That'd break the boat and we'd all be dead.

SO I WENT TO THE OLD MAN
"Cap'n tell me what these bells do mean,
For I'm new on the river and I know I'm green,
But the chief and the pilot don't make it quite clear,
And I want to get license by the end of next year."

AND HE SAYS
When the water's swift and the wind is strong,
That's when we ring up a double gong,
And after we're through that scary place,
We ring the gong twice to resume our pace."

SO I GIVE UP
There ain't no sense to stayin' on here,
They won't tell me nothing for maybe a year.
I'll pilot a desk or a Greyhound bus,
And them engineroom bells can just rot down to rust!

BELL SUCTION
The flared device fitted at the end of a suction line in a tank barge. It is in close tolerance to the bottom of the tank, which allows a greater degree of liquid to enter the discharge line without sucking air and losing suction resulting in a better stripping action of product from the tank.

BELL STAND
An upright stanchion in the pilothouse of a steamboat on which are located the BELL PULLS and BELL CORD which are used to signal the engine room crew on a steamboat for a change of speed.

BELL TIME
Although bells are not sounded on towboats to indicate the time of day or night, the lingo of *bell time* is used by some members. Basically, starting after 12:01 the bells for either a.m. or p.m. are struck as follows:

Bells	Times	Pattern
1 bell at	12:30 – 4:30 – 8:30	*
2 bells	1:00 – 5:00 – 9:00	**
3 bells	1:30 – 5:30 – 9:30	** *
4 bells	2:00 – 6:00 – 10:00	** **
5 bells	2:30 – 6:30 – 10:30	** ** *
6 bells	3:00 – 7:00 – 11:00	** ** **
7 bells	3:30 – 7:30 – 11:30	** ** ** *
8 bells	4:00 – 8:00 – 12:00	** ** ** **

Some vessels observe the custom of striking 16 bells at midnight on New Years Eve to greet and ring in the New Year for happy and prosperous riverboating.

BELLE OF LOUISVILLE
The oldest commercial steamer on the U.S. river system. She was built by the James Rees & Sons Company in 1914, with its birthday on 18 October, the day of its launching on the Allegheny River in the Pittsburgh area. The vessel's owner, the West Memphis Packet Company, christened her the *IDLEWILD* and basically used her as a passenger ferry between Memphis, TN, and West Memphis, AR. Later she entered the "tramping trade" doing excursions at various river towns until WW II. She was then outfitted to push oil barges as well as used as a floating USO night club for troops at military bases along the river system.

In 1947 she was sold and the following year her name was changed to the *AVALON*. For a number of years under that name the vessel traveled over much of the Western Rivers system making excursion trips to many large and small river towns. In 1962 the steamer was in sorry shape and went on the auction block. She was acquired by Jefferson County, KY, and home-ported in Louisville. A lot of restoration was undertaken which continues to this day, and the steamboat took on her present name, the *BELLE OF LOUISVILLE*.

BELLY ROBBER

An extremely poor cook. Other similar terms might be "Bull Roaster, Bean Burner, Stew Hand," and some not printable. Oftentimes used with a few other more descriptive words. An inferior cook usually means an unhappy crew.

BELOW

1. Used to describe a position of a vessel or object, i.e. "The upbound vessel is just *below* the point", or "Store the line *below* deck"
2. To go down from where one is located. A landsman's term would be to go downstairs, whereas a riverman would say, "I am going *below*".
3. A downstream movement, i.e. "We'll move the boat *below* the DBC barge", or "We'll be taking this tow *below* Baton Rouge before we meet the turn boat".
4. Used as a warning from someone located higher up, as in, "Look out *below*", if an object might be falling their way.

BENCHMARK

An observation made by a Pilot in judging a gauge or level of water which he/she has noted that certain high water marks can be run, i.e. "My *benchmarks* to run the chute is when the Helena gauge is 15 feet and rising or 18 feet when falling", or "The *benchmark* down there for throwing the dam for open river is when the water on that old cottonwood tree about a mile above the dam on the right bank is just lapping at its trunk".

BEND

1. A long curving section of the river given a name, such as "Deadman's *Bend*".
2. A section of the river that changes direction, and if long enough it can result in a loop of almost 360 degrees.
3. The correct term, rather than "knot", for tying the ends of two lines or ropes together or one rope to an object such as a block, or to attach a wire to a shackle.
4. When used as "to *bend* to" it can mean the tying of two lines to one another, not necessarily the ends; or to tie a line to an anchor or spar pole.
5. The old English word was *bendan*, meaning "to tie up" as well as for "curve", from the tightening of a line tied to an archer's bow that resulted in a curved weapon.

BEND SIDE

The concave outside or longest track of a *bend*, as opposed to the "bar side", or the shortest curvature line of the *bend*. The *bend side* is usually where the deepest water and the channel are located. Often used when pilots are discussing who will be on which side when they meet, i.e. "I'll be on the *bend side*, you take the bar, and I'll see you on two whistles".

BEND SIGNAL

The one prolonged blast required by Inland Navigation Rule 34(e) to be sounded by vessels when "nearing a bend or an area of a channel or fairway where other vessels may be obscured by an intervening obstruction".

BENDER BLUES

On October 1, 1976, the newly authorized polyester blue uniforms the USCG members were required to wear came into effect as conceived by Admiral Chester Bender, the Commandant of the USCG at the time.

BENDING MOMENT
An engineering term describing the action that occurs when a vessel, particularly a barge or a wooden-hulled steamboat, when undue stress is induced on the framing of the vessel due to a concentrated loading of cargo in the center or at the ends of a vessel that causes it to HOG or BUCKLE.

BENDWAY WEIR
An under water rock *weir*(s) that is placed in the THALWEG of a bend where the current is cutting the channel deeper and at the same time narrowing the channel width by depositing its sediment on the bar opposite the bend. *Bendway weirs* are located from the shore side angled upstream toward the flow of the river current, and are placed deep enough to allow a tow to pass safely over them. The *weirs* tend to slow the current in the bend, allowing secondary currents to cut more into the bar side of the channel, thus widening it and preventing the further deepening of it on the shore side.

BENEFIT TO COST RATIO
Most often referred to as the B/C Ratio, a management pricing efficiency tool that Congress requires for all water resource projects to meet prior to authorizing a project to be constructed. It measures the national benefits the project will net to the nation over the economic life expectancy of the project against its cost. The project, in order to receive authorization, must meet at least a one-to-one ratio or better. Of all the programs in the national budget, only water resource projects are required to meet this rigorous test.

BERM
1. In coastal areas it is an embankment along a shore that is caused by wave action.
2. On the river it refers to a deposit from a dredging operation.
3. A rock-filled dike-type structure that protects a marina.
4. From the French *berme,* meaning "narrow space".

BERTH
1. The place where a crewman sleeps, a bed. A double *berth* means the cabin has BUNK beds installed.
2. The designated space to be occupied by a vessel and/or its tow at a dock, pier, or wharf.
3. A job on a vessel.
4. To stay well away from a danger or "to give adequate sea room", that is, to give "wide *berth*" in a situation where safety for the vessel and crew is required. The term appears to have originated from the use of BEAR and BEAR OFF in the sense of avoiding risk of some peril.

BEVEL
1. Having a slope from the horizontal or vertical surface as in the end or side of a piece of wood or steel, or a type of cogged gear wheel.
2. A tool used to measure a degree of angle.

BIBLE
1. The Old and New Testament.
2. The Operations Manual for the Vessel.
3. The Rules of the Road (Inland Navigation Rules).
4. WATERWAYS JOURNAL.

BIFURCATE
The division of the main flow of a river into two or more branches in its delta area such as at the HEAD OF THE PASSES in the Mississippi River.

BIG MAMA
A term that was affectionately used when referring to the largest

steamboat ever built on the river system, the *SPRAGUE*. The expression is now often used when commenting on an extremely large towboat.

BIG SANDY RIVER

This river is formed by the Levisa Fork and the Tug Fork streams coming out of the mountains of Kentucky, West Virginia, and Virginia. It eventually enters the Ohio River near Catlettsburg, KY, and is navigable for about 29 miles. In 1819 Kentucky declared the river navigable from the Ohio, "up as high as the forks and the Louisa (Levisa) from its mouth up as high as the mouth of Russell's Fork". Fur trading was the first main river commerce. Early traffic was by flatboat or keelboat. Steamboat traffic did not arrive until the 1830s. Little money was spent for improvement, and then the Civil War played havoc with commerce and navigability of the river.

In the 1870s a plan was devised to canalize the river system with three locks and dams on the Big Sandy, 13 on the Levisa up to Pikeville, and six on the Tug Fork up to Warfield. Work on the plan commenced in the 1890s. The first L & D, number 3, at Louisa, was completed in 1897. It was the first NEEDLE or movable dam built in the U.S., since the logging industry opposed any fixed dam, which would not allow the river to be used for rafting logs. L & D number 1 and 2 were opened in the early 1900s, but only two of the upper river locks were ever built since by this time there were rail lines to the upper coal fields. The lower two locks were 160' x 55', while number 3 was a few feet shorter and narrower. Some small amount of traffic moved through the locks until all were finally closed in 1952. After Greenup Dam on the Ohio River was built in the early 1960s, L & D #1 was demolished. Presently the lower reaches of the river contain some coal-loading facilities. The river was called different names by the Indian tribes, such as *Chatteroi, Tatteroa, and Chatterwha,* all of which mostly meant, "a river with many sand bars". The Big Sandy was noted for its BATWING boats.

BIG-TOW PILOT

A Pilot who has the ability and experience of handling and navigating tows of 30 or more jumbo (195 or 200 by 35 feet) barges.

BIGHT

On the river it refers to any part of a length of line between the eye and the end, which some refer to as the "standing part". However, it often refers to a loop in a line lying on deck. A crewman is always given the safety warning to "stay out of the *bight*" of a line when it may be paying out since one's leg or arm could become entangled in it and be crushed against a timberhead or cavel, or thrown over the side into the river. The word comes from the Old English *byht,* meaning a "bend" or "angle".

BIGHT OF A BEND

The deepest section, in terms of distance (not the depth) of a bend in the river.

BILGE

The lowest part of the interior of a vessel. The place where slight leakages from the shaft or engine will collect in a towboat. These drippings are called BILGE SLOPS. In years past the deepest bottom curvature was the "bulge", which evolved into *bilge*.

BILGE BLOCKS

Built-up blocks or cribbing on which a vessel rests while it is in drydock. Sometimes called *keel blocks*.

BILGE KNUCKLE

The curvature where the side plate meets the bottom plate of a vessel. Since this is often an extreme wear area it is usually made of heavier plate thickness.

BILGE PUMP

A pump used aboard tugs and towboats to remove accumulations of water from the bilge. Originally *bilge pumps* were piped so the discharge went directly overboard. Since the engine(s) and shaft(s) are just above the bilge a residue of oil is usually present, it is now a violation to pump it overboard. *Bilge pumps* are now piped to a separate holding tank.

BILGE WATER or SLOPS

1. The accumulation of oil from the engine(s), water, and any other material that collects in the area at the lowest part of a vessel's hull. It is the place where Samuel Clemens said, "only the dead can enjoy life".
2. An expression used when someone is suspected of elaborating the truth to the point where it might be termed an outright lie, "That's *bilge slop* he's spouting!"

BILL

1. The extremities of the flukes of an anchor.
2. The opening across the mouth of a HOOK.
3. The posting of a general notice such as a STATION BILL or a safety notice.

BILL HOOK

A term used to describe what happens when navigating a downbound tow off a sharp point in a crossing. In making the turn the head of the tow gets caught in the slack water under the point while the stern is in the swift current. The force of water on the stern may cause the tow to completely turn around, or go aground on the bar side of the crossing, or cause the tow to break up. The word is probably so used and named as the navigating action resembles the curvature of the blade of a *bill hook* which is a metal brush cutting tool. See: OVER STEER and TOP AROUND.

BILL OF LADING

A shipping document that lists the terms and condition of carriage between shipper and carrier. It serves as a receipt for the cargo and lists the owner of record.

BILLBOARD

A large board at various locations along the river, especially at navigation locks, where the USACE posts the current river gauge for that particular place. Also called a BULLETIN BOARD. With the use of good radio communication and the use of computers on board towboats these information boards are being terminated.

BIN

An enclosure structure around part of, or all, the deck of a deck barge. It serves to keep cargo, such as sand and gravel or other material, from washing overboard. Sometimes referred to as a CARGO BOX.

BINDER

1. A type of fastening sometimes used to hold together the rolling covers of a barge.
2. A pole used by loggers to tighten a BINDER CHAIN.

BINDER CHAIN

A chain used by loggers to hold the logs in a raft together. Also called a *wrapper chain*.

BINNACLE

A casing which holds the compass, mounted on a stand. Seldom seen on a river towboat, but used on tugs.

BINOCULARS

A short handheld instrument that has two adjustable magnification chambers in it, one for each eye, equipped with lenses and prisms, that allows Pilots to more easily locate and identify objects in or on water or land. They are sometimes called "field glasses". Although handheld telescopes had been in use since the 17th century on ships and later steamboats, practical *binoculars* were not common until the late 1800s. The word comes from the Latin *bina*, meaning "two together", and *oculas*, meaning "eyes".

BIN SIDES

The coaming used on a deck barge in the sand and gravel trade. The area enclosed is sometimes called the "box" or "pen".

BIRTH MARKS

See: PLIMSOL MARKS.

BITCH BOX

The powered megaphone or intercom system used by the Pilot to communicate with the deckhands.

BITE

Used to describe what an anchor does when it is LET GO or dropped and its flukes take hold in the bed of a water course.

BITT(S)

In the days of wooden ships *bitts* were made of wood. Now made as steel castings, they are securely welded to the deck of vessels. They can be single posts, or used in pairs, and called TIMBERHEADS on the river. Two upright posts with a cross bar and horns are sometimes called H-BITTS. B*itts* are used to secure lines or wires. Most of the time H-BITTS are located between the towknees in the center of the bow of a towboat. If a towboat or tug is rigged for towing astern they will also be located athwartship on the stern, preferably forward of the steering rudder(s).

BITTER END

On ships it was referred to as the end of an anchor chain. On the river it refers to the extreme end of a line, wire, or chain. Sometimes a crewman aboard a river vessel feels he has reached the *bitter end* when a relief doesn't show up. The term comes from the use of "bitter", meaning the last turn around the bitts, or the post(s) on deck to fasten cables or lines.

BIXBY, CAPT. HORACE

The steamboat Pilot who is credited with teaching the cub, Samuel Langhorne Clemens, all about the necessaries to become a steamboat Pilot starting in 1857. Bixby was born in 1826 and kept piloting until shortly before his death in 1912.

BLACK BOX

A device that combines a VOYAGE DATA RECORDER (VDR) and an AUTOMATIC IDENTIFICATION SYSTEM on board a vessel that can be retrieved to evaluate an incident.

BLACK BUOY

No longer used; replaced by green buoys. See: BUOY.

BLACK DIAMONDS

The nickname sometimes given to coal, one of the major commodities transported on the river system, mostly to provide energy to electric generating plants that allow citizens to flip a switch in their homes and have light.

BLACK GANG

Originally used to describe the engine room crew on a coal-burning steamboat. After standing their watch the crew usually emerged from the engine space in pretty dirty condition. On modern diesel towboats and tugs the term is no longer used as generally there are at most only one or two engineers aboard, and the engine spaces are pretty clean except when overhauling the engines.

BLACK ICE
Clear, smooth, unbroken and undisturbed hard ice.

BLACK STACKING
If a diesel engine is not properly adjusted and receives too much fuel it can result in heavy smoke conditions, hence the term.

BLACK WARRIOR RIVER
The river's two principle streams, the Mulberry Fork and the Locust Fork, come together just west of Birmingham, AL. It is over 400 navigable river miles from Birmingham to Mobile Bay after the *Black Warrior* links up with the Tombigbee River just north of Demopolis, AL. This rich region of fertile cotton land, and later coal, had its principle products floated out on flatboats until steamboats of very shallow draft arrived. In 1888 construction started on the river to canalize it with 17 locks and dams. The project was completed in 1925 with a channel depth of six feet. After WW II the system was modernized, replacing the existing 17 structures with six new L & Ds that provided a channel depth of nine feet. The locks are 600' by 110'.

The *Black Warrior* carried various different names by its Indian inhabitants. When European explorers first came to the area they indicated the tribes called it *Pafallaya,* which meant "long hair", used when they referred to the Choctaw Indians.

BLADE
1. The flat part of an oar used in a skiff that enters and is pulled against the water to propel the boat forward.
2. The part of the arm of a stock anchor that receives the palm, or holding piece.
3. The driving force of the propeller attached to the propeller hub, or BOSS. The number of *blades* on a propeller varies, but usually there are three, four, or five. The curvature of the *blades* cuts through the water causing a thrusting motion, moving the vessel.

BLAST
1. The signals used on the whistle of a vessel. Inland Navigation Rule 32 provides for two types of *blasts* to be given. A "short *blast*" means one of about one seconds' duration, and a "prolonged *blast*" is of from four to six seconds' duration.
2. When not in a situation where a *blast* could be mistaken for a navigational signal, a very short *blast* when a tow is tied to the bank or a structure means to turn the tow or vessel loose.
3. As with "2" above, if a vessel is underway a <u>very</u> short *blast* is to call the Mate or lead man to the pilothouse for instructions.

BLEEDERS
Plugs that are placed in the hull of vessels that can be removed when placed on drydock to allow for easy drainage of water accumulation. Sometimes called *drydock plugs*.

BLIND-BEND SIGNAL
When in an area of the river or channel where, due to curvature or a junction with another channel, or because of an obstruction a vessel may not be able to see or detect another vessel, NavRule 34(e) requires one prolonged blast of the whistle to be sounded.

BLIND or BLANK FLANGE
A heavy round steel covering that can be bolted with a gasket to the end of a pipeline on a tank barge. All loading and discharge lines on tank barges that are not being used are required to be fitted with a *blind or blank flange*.

BLIND SPOT or ZONE
An area surrounding a vessel or tow that is out of the Pilot's normal range of vision.

BLIP

A target showing up on a vessel's radar screen.

BLOCK

1. A mechanical device used to assist in lifting heavy items. *Blocks* come with different names; generally they are called by the number of sheaves, or roller pulleys, they may have, i.e. one, two, three, or more. The *block* consists of a shell made of wood or steel containing the pulleys with a pin allowing them to roll. A single *block* with a line rove through it can be used, but for greater purchase (lifting or pulling) power *blocks* are most often used in tandem. Those rigged together are called "*blocks and tackle*". The use of the term *block* derives from what a log or stump was called, so when making a pulley from a piece, or *block* of wood it took on the name as all parts of it were made of wood. See: SNATCH BLOCK and TACKLE.

2. The term *block* has various other nautical meanings, such as, to *block* a channel (disrupting navigation), a cylinder *block* (of an engine), the engine *block* itself, to *block* a rupture in the hull (to prevent the ingress of water), and probably others.

BLOCK AND TACKLE

See: BLOCK (above) and TACKLE.

BLOCKING

A system of keel blocks or cribbing on which a vessel rests when it is on drydock or on shore when being built or for repair.

BLOW

1. The sounding of the towboat's or tug's whistle, i.e. "I'll *blow* her two whistles".

2. Used on a steamboat in "blowing off steam" is the act of the engineer opening a valve to reduce the pressure in the boiler.

3. It is further used as a description of persons getting rid of something they are mad about such as the Mate getting rid of the unkind thoughts on his mind by "*blowing* his stack". It is also combined to become "*blowhard*" describing a person on a riverboat who likes to talk a lot in a bragging fashion. It might be said he was "*blowing* his own horn".

4. The word came into use from German, then to old English *blawan* meaning "to send out air". See: BLOW HER DOWN.

BLOW DOWN

The operation of cleaning the MUD DRUM, located at the base of the boilers on a steamboat, of silt from river water by blowing live steam through the drum into a fitted pipe leading through the hull to the river.

BLOW HER DOWN

A term directed at another vessel as soon as there is doubt or danger as to understanding another vessel's intentions or actions, or a Pilot believes there is not sufficient action being taken by the other vessel to avoid a collision, a Pilot must sound the danger signal consisting of at least five short and rapid blasts on his whistle as required by Rule 34(d).

BLUE SUITER

A term used to refer to U.S. Coast Guard personnel by vessel crew members. Also sometimes called "Coasties".

BLUE WATER

Refers to vessels and personnel who work on ocean waters, as opposed to vessels and persons who work on the river, i.e. BROWN WATER trades.

BLUFF BAR

A sandbar that is being cut by the channel current and has deep water on its cutting side. Usually occurs where the channel is realigning itself in a crossing. On the Lower Mississippi the term sometimes refers to a steep bank along the shore and may be called a "bluff bank". See: CAVING BANK or BAR.

BOARD
To go onto, or embark upon, a vessel.

BOARDING PARTY
A group of officials, such as from the USCG, OSHA, or other official, or semi-official organizations *boarding* a vessel to inspect it or to interview the crew. Some of the members of the group might be called, *Boarding Inspector*, or *Boarding Officer*.

BOAST(S)
All Pilots have an ego and believe they are just as good as about any other Pilot on the river or canal, and better than most. A few with the greatest egos are used to inflating how they might respond to the SHORE BOSS when given an order:
  1. When told to pick up more barges on a pretty large and heavy tow, "Don't mind this old mule, just load the cart with as many as gotta go".
  2. Even in high water with an extremely large tow, "Ain't been any bridge built that I can't run with as many as they can hang on me".
  3. When fog comes up, "I can run from New Orleans to St. Louis without stopping in the worst pea soup out there". The rest would fill a separate book.

BOAT
Short for TOWBOAT. Used by river persons when talking about "their" *boat*, and by shore personnel in referring to the equipment they have, i.e. "We've got five *boats* working the Upper and three on the Illinois. Then, we're short a *boat* on the Lower, but have two more *boats* than we currently need on the Ohio".

BOAT DRILL
Drills that are conducted aboard towboats and tugs to train personnel what to do in an emergency, such as fire, man overboard, or other critical circumstances.

BOAT HOOK
A long pole used by the crew to pick up lines or mooring wires which are out of reach. It is more often called a SPIKE or PIKE POLE. The pole has a hook in the end. At times the pole will be painted in stripes, each one foot in length and of alternating colors so it can be used to easily measure the depth of water.

BOAT SLING
A sling attached to a small auxiliary boat so it can be attached to a boom and lowered to the water on an even keel.

BOAT STATION
An assigned position where a crew member is to go in the case of an emergency, such as fire, man overboard, etc.

BOAT STORE
A store that delivers groceries and supplies to a towboat, either at a dock, or midstream by a small boat, or by a fuel service flat. Sometimes called a chandler. See: STORE BOATS.

BOAT TRIALS
The trying out, or testing, of a vessel before acceptance of it from a ship builder or repairer by the owner/operator of the vessel; or a trial after a vessel has been in for a major overhaul. It may be called a SHAKEDOWN CRUISE, although these trials are usually of longer duration after the initial acceptance of the vessel.

BOATMAN
A favorable term which migrated to the river from those who work on

the GULF INTRA-COASTAL WATERWAY (GIWW) where it at times might be said, "He's a damn good *Boatman"*, meaning he is a fine boat handler and Pilot. The term may come from the bayou country where many of the Canal personnel originally grew up and first learned about boating while catching fish in their pirogues; or perhaps the term migrated from over the pond in Great Britain where the Pilots for the narrow boats used on their canals were called *Boatmen.*

BOBTAIL

A steamboat in which the CABIN did not extend over the full length of the CABIN DECK towards the stern, but had a shortened structure like the docked tail of a dog, cat, or horse.

BOIL

Turbulence in the river current that causes water to bubble violently up from the riverbed. This happens frequently where there is a dike, pier, or other obstruction when current rushes against it causing a boiling appearance to occur. Large rushing *boils* on a crossing mean deepest water; slick *boils* fanning out as they surface mean shallow water.

BOILER

The purpose of a *boiler* on a steamboat is to heat water within the *boiler* to generate steam by a series of tubes enclosed in its body. A boiler whose tubes contain gaseous heat from the *boiler* furnace is called a "fire tube *boiler."* The *boiler* water then becomes hot enough to produce steam pressure that is used by an engine to push a piston rod in a cylinder of an engine which in turn through use of a connecting rod turns the shaft of the steamboat's wheel. Small steamers may only have had one *boiler,* but most had multiple *boilers,* with as many as eight on the larger ones.

Although most Western River steamers were of the fire tube construction the other type *boiler* that is used is called a "water tube *boiler,"* wherein the tubes contained water and the flames and gases are on the outside of the tubes in the body of the *boiler*. The *boilers* on steamboats are sometimes referred to as "kettles" by the crew. The word comes from the Latin *bullire,* meaning "to bubble".

BOILER DECK

The second deck of a packet or steamboat where cabins were located. It was not the deck where the *boilers* were located, as they were installed on the main deck, below the *boiler deck.*

BOLD REEF

A steep and prominent sandbar. Also called a BLUFF REEF.

BOLLARD

Usually a single strong, heavy mooring post, similar to BITTS on a barge. It is used on a pier, wharf, lock wall, or dock to hold or secure a tie-off line to moor a vessel, or tow. Sometimes *bollards* are set in pairs, usually slanting away from one another. A *bollard* may have a pin protruding from it on its shore side, or a pin all the way through on its fore and aft sides parallel to the pier. This is called a NORMAN PIN and assists in keeping a line from slipping off the *bollard* when the lead is too acute.

BOLLARD PULL

A static measurement of the amount of force a tug or towboat is capable of exerting or applying to a tow in a given set of circumstances. It is probably a better measurement of the towing vessel's ability than is horsepower since it measures the thrust of the propeller, taking into account its diameter, the pitch of the blades, and the revolutions of the shaft.

BONDING

The act of electrical *bonding*, or grounding, a vessel to protect it from a possible electrical charge, especially on tank barges loading or discharging cargo. This is done by attaching a grounding wire from a steel fitting on the vessel to the shore side piping. Some new cargo hoses have built-in grounding capability.

BONE (IN HER TEETH)

The turbulence and foam at the bow of a vessel or tow that is going at a fairly fast speed through the water. The froth looks like a large, happy dog salivating over a meaty bone. Hence, the use of the phrase "Looks like that tow has a *bone in her teeth*".

BONEYARD

A location where old vessels, out of navigation, are moored or laid up for a long time, or where they may be sent to be dismantled, scrapped, or otherwise disposed of. Sometimes it is used to refer to a shipyard if a vessel will be in for a lengthy period for extensive work and some of the crew will be retained on board.

BOOBY HATCH

Any large horizontal hatch door on a vessel that leads down into a storage area, or into a machinery compartment. It is unknown how a useful access received its name. The term *booby* is usually given to a somewhat dim-witted person who is unable to correctly follow directions. It took its name from slow moving sea bird that sailors sometime caught. Perhaps a deckhand not watching what he was doing fell down into the *hatch* which then later was given that name.

BOOKING

1. An arrangement between a customer of water transport service and a barge company for the carriage of the customer's shipment of freight. In effect, it is a reservation of the space, or the loading, of a barge.
2. Reservations for passengers that buy tickets when taking a cruise.

BOOM

1. A crane-like spar sometimes used on a towboat to raise and lower a small yawl on and off the vessel. The word is related to the Dutch *boom,* meaning "beam, pole, or "tree".
2. Used on some tank barges to assist in hooking up hoses and fittings between pipelines on a barge and the dock, or between barges.
3. Used on a steamer to swing out a GANGWAY or STAGE.
4. Logs or timbers fastened together end to end and used to hold floating logs together.
5. A floating device used to contain oil or other pollutants that have spilled into the water.
6. A floating device used to deflect drift from the head of a dock or fleet.
7. The sound of a buoy that had been inadvertently run over and is bouncing along the bottom of the hull making a *boom, boom, boom* clanking sound with the Pilot hoping it doesn't get caught in the propeller or kort nozzle.

BOOM BOAT

A boat used by loggers to push a BOOM, pull out logs, assemble logs, or brails, etc.

BOOM CRADLE

See: CRADLE.

BOOM OFF

The action of keeping a tied-off vessel(s) a distance away from the shore so it will not go aground on a falling river.

BOONDOCKS

An out-of-the-way place with not much going on. Not a good place to catch or get off a boat.

BOOTJACK STERN

A hull with a recess in the stern of a sternwheel vessel that would surround the paddlewheel on three sides and extend aft, leaving the end open to allow the wheelwash to emerge. The design apparently allowed extra deck area, especially when used as a ferry. It also gave some protection to the paddlewheel from damage by driftwood and when operating close to the shore. See: RECESSED WHEEL.

BOOT TOP

The area of a towboat or tug from the water line usually up to the deck, most often painted in black. It is sort of like keeping the top of one's boots shined even though one has to wade through a muddy river bank.

BOSS

The hub of a propeller where the propeller blades are attached.

BOTTOM

1. The keel of the vessel out to the bilge knuckles.
2. Sometimes referred to as the keel to the water line of a tug or towboat.
3. A term used to describe the RIVER BED, i.e. "We hit *bottom*".

BOTTOM CLEARANCE

The measured amount of water between the river bed and the bottom of a towboat, tug, barge, or tow. Most often it is used when referring to the *bottom clearance* of the deepest draft barge in tow.

BOTTOM DROPPED OUT

A saying used when there is a sudden fall in the river stage resulting in a low depth of water in the channel.

BOTTOM LAND

Shore land along a riverbank that is subject to being inundated by rising flood waters. Sometimes the land is referred to by the crop that may be grown there, as in "corn *bottom*" or "bean *bottom*" for soybeans.

BOTTOMS

The residue cargo left in a tank barge that has been pumped off and can be stripped no further.

BOUND

The condition or attitude of a vessel and/or tow, i.e. "down*bound*", "up*bound*", "wind*bound*", "fog*bound*", or "ice*bound*".

BOUNDARY

1. The area of a USCG District or that of its District sub-commands.
2. The area of a USACE Division or its Districts.
3. The line between where the U.S. Inland Navigation Rules apply and on the other side where the International Navigation Rules apply. Also called the DEMARCATION LINE.
4. When referring to barges, the area where the sides of the cargo box meets the floor deck of the cargo box.

BOW

The very forward end of a vessel or its tow. Can be used when referring to the forward "starboard *bow*" or the forward "port *bow*" when using the term. If an object, such as a buoy, a dayboard, or another vessel, is sighted off the forward part of a vessel, up to 45 degrees from centerline, it is said to be so many points or degrees off the *bow*. The term is pronounced as the "ow" in "wow" or "how." The nautical term, as opposed to the bow (with a long "o") used to shoot arrows, comes from the Dutch word *boeg,* or the German *boog,* meaning "shoulder" or "ship's *bow*".

BOW LINE

A line leading forward off the head of a vessel or tow. When used to tie off a fleet of barges it can be referred to as a HEAD LINE.

BOW-LINES

Line drawings of a naval architect that fashion the longitudinal vertical curvature of the bow of a vessel if it so designed. Also see: BUTTOCK-LINES.

BOW PIECE

1. The lead barge in a UNIT TOW. It usually has a long streamlined rake to overcome resistance through the water.
2. Sometimes refers to a single barge pushed ahead that is used by a towboat to cover its bow allowing the boat to make better speed without taking water over the head if it is required to go some distance running light boat.

BOW STEERING UNIT

A small barge with propelling power placed on the head of a tow, activated by remote controls in the pilothouse of the towing vessel. These units are used to assist in steering long tows around bends by added sideways thrust on the bow. Some of these units have the capability of operating independently and are then used to assist a line haul towboat in dropping and picking up barges at docks and fleets. They have mostly gone out of service at present.

BOW THRUSTER

A propulsion unit placed in the bow of a vessel, particularly a passenger vessel to assist it in turning around or docking. This type of unit also can be installed in the lead barge of a tow with a tunnel-type design to allow the barge to have lateral or side movement. It is remote-controlled from the towing vessel's pilothouse and assists in steering long tows around close bends. When the tow is empty they are very useful in high winds in narrow channels and when docking or going into a navigation lock.

BOW WAVE

An undulation of water thrown off by the bow of a vessel or a tow. A large *bow wave* at the head of a tow is deemed to be moving with "a bone in her teeth".

BOWBOATS

At different times in river history the term has been used to describe different jobs that these vessels performed. Generally, however, *bowboats* have been used to assist another vessel to control the head of its tow. The first ones were used on log rafts that usually drifted with the current. The *bowboat* would be lashed across the head of the raft, steering the raft by use of either forward or backing propulsion as directed by signals from the pushing vessel. In today's navigation a *bowboat* is hired to assist a tow into lock facilities by pushing its head in when there is a strong outdraft current across the upstream guidewall toward the dam, and it sometimes assists around bridges and other places. See: BOW STEERING UNIT and BOW THRUSTER.

BOWLINE

Pronounced *boe – lin*. Probably the most useful knot a riverman knows. It makes a tight loop that will not slip and does not pull down too hard to make it difficult to undo. Sometimes it is called "the king of knots". It is most used as a temporary eye in a line if one does not have time to splice one. The knot was first used in sailing days, as lines made fast to the leeches, or sides of the sail, to pull them forward. *Bowline* comes from the German *boline,* or the Dutch *boechline,* meaning "the line from the ship's bow".

BOWSPRITTING

River vessels do not, of course, have a bowsprit, which is a long spar protruding forward of the bow of a sailing ship. Its main function is to attach forestays to support the main mast in order that it may carry more sail. However, the history of *bowspritting* may be of interest to those on the river when contemplating the travails of our nautical brethren.

Associated with the bowsprit was a practice of punishment imposed on seamen that was described by Eugene Burdick many years ago. Since I have never seen a prior mention of the practice in other maritime stories, it is described here simply so history is retained and to show how far we have come as a civilized society.

Although there was much flogging of sailors with a cat-o'-nine-tails for rule infractions and an occasional KEELHAULING for more major violations, the worst punishment that could be imposed at a Captain's Mast, besides hanging or walking the plank, was *bowspritting*. A guilty seaman upon receiving this sentence was taken to the bowsprit where his body was tied to it with rope, leaving his arms free. At the base of the sprit he was left a jug of water or ale and a half loaf of bread. He was also given a rope knife. None of his shipmates were allowed to render any assistance lest they suffer the same fate. He was never again to set foot on the main deck of the ship. In the log of the vessel it was written the transgressor "died at sea".

A seaman thus sentenced had only three alternatives upon consuming the bread as he slowly starved and drinking the last sip of the sweet water with a parched throat burnt by the hot sun while gulls pecked at his weakened body. First he could stay at the bowsprit and finally starve to death. Eventually, his body fluids would dry up causing his body to slip out of the rope that bonded him to the sprit, or the rope would rot and break sending what was left of the body into the sea below. The second alternative was to use the knife to slash his wrists or throat to quickly end his misery. The only other choice left would be to cut his bonds with the knife and fall into the seas below, then taking a chance of swimming perhaps hundreds of miles in the ocean to the nearest land with sharks always present. Whatever his decision, he was a dead man.

A century ago the worst punishment of a riverman would suffer was to be fired and put off on the nearest bank. In the 21st Century even that would probably result in a lawsuit.

BOX
See: CONTAINER

BOX BARGE
A barge that has a square end on both its bow and its stern. Ideally the barge is put in tow between two SEMI-INTEGRATED BARGES with their square ends made up to the squares of the *box barge,* making an efficient unit. A loaded *box barge* is hard to handle at docks and in fleets as the square end puts a lot of pressure on mooring lines when there is a swift current, as well as being hard to push. They do, however, carry about 200 tons more cargo at a given draft than does a similar-sized semi-integrated barge.

BOXING THE COMPASS
Although most towboats do not have compasses on board, the old Rules of the Road used points of the compass to designate the visibility area that navigation lights were required to be seen. There are 32 points in the compass and each point is 11 1/4 degrees. The term comes from the Spanish *boxar,* meaning "to sail around".

BRACES
The heavy timber posts which supported the HOG CHAIN system that provided a degree of stiffness for the limber, shallow draft-steamboats.

BRACKET
Any small steel plate, usually triangular in shape, used for reinforcement between two or more connecting parts, such as a vertical frame attached to a horizontal one, or to a deck, etc. It is used to stiffen a structure.

BRACKISH WATER
Water that is to some degree moderately salty. This is the case when tugs, towboats, and barges are operated along the Gulf Coast area of the Intracoastal Waterway and the harbors and ports that it intersects. Tidal flows mix the sea water with the fresh water flowing into the sea.

BRAIDING (CHANNEL)
As a river flows downstream it picks up sediment. When picking up more than it can carry it drops some, especially the heavier bits, to the riverbed. These gravelly parts build up into a bar that may split the existing channel in two or more parts, or *braid* it, similar to the strands of interwoven hair of a young girl, or some male pony-tailed country singer.

BRAIL
A large rectangular arranged group of logs held together by a floating frame of the largest linked logs. A single *brail* was about 600' long by about 40' wide. Three *brails* made a "piece", or a half raft. Two "pieces" made a RAFT. The term is from the Latin *bracale*, meaning "girdle".

BRAIL BOAT
A boat rigged to harvest mussels from the river, not a "brail" of logs. These vessels are mostly seen on the Tennessee River and are so-called from the numerous small lines with brailing hooks attached that are put down both sides of a small flat deck pontoon boat to snag the mussels. Some spell the word "Braille" which is a system of raised dots used by blind persons. Perhaps the name is attached to these mussel boats because the mussel fishermen can't see what they are catching, nor can the mussels see what they are closing on.

BRAILING HOOK
A miniature grappling hook without the sharp ends that are placed on the ends of brail lines used when harvesting mussels. When the *brailing hooks* are drug across the river bottom and they hit an open mussel shell, the mussel's reflexes automatically close their shell in response to the intrusion, allowing the mussel fisherman to haul up the brail with a mussel attached.

BRAIN BOX
One of many slang words sometimes used when referring to the pilothouse. This term could be used out of respect or disparagement depending upon the user of the term. See: KNOWLEDGE BOX, LAZY BENCH, and LIAR'S BENCH.

BRAKE
1. A device used to slow down the spin of a large pilotwheel or to hold it stationary. It was operated by a foot pedal that had leather pads which, when applied, came against the sides of the steering wheel, retarding its movement. The *brake* was especially important when backing full astern on a sternwheel steamboat since the wash would immediately turn the rudders causing the wheel to rotate violently.
2. A mechanism that can be screwed down on a winch to safely hold it insuring that if the holding dog comes loose the winch drum will not pay out.

BRAKE HORSE POWER (BHP)
The power at the crankshaft to a wheel determined by use of a brake.

BRANCH PILOT
A Pilot, licensed by the State of Louisiana, who generally directs the

steerage of vessels from the vicinity of the sea buoy in the Gulf of Mexico at the entrance to the Mississippi River. They guide vessels across the bar upriver about 20 miles to Pilot Town where they will turn over their pilotage duties to a Crescent River Pilot who guides the vessel to New Orleans. The pilot organization was formed in Louisiana in 1870. Also known as BAR PILOTS (see).

BRASH ICE
An accumulation of floating broken pieces of ice, not too large in size.

BRASS
1. An alloy material made mostly of copper and zinc.
2. Was used extensively on vessels since it doesn't corrode in the same manner as steel, especially in fittings; however, newer materials are now in use, such as stainless steel and polymers. This replacement is a joy to crew members who were required to polish *brass* daily.
3. A term used to describe USCG officers, or senior corporate officials.

BREACH
1. A gap or break in a levee or dam caused by erosion or other failure in the structure allowing water to pour through, usually only happening in flood conditions.
2. Damage to the hull of a vessel with the result of an inflow of water.
3. A violation of law or agreement resulting in a *breach* of contract.

BREADTH
1. Generally, on the river the term refers to the greatest overall width of a vessel.
2. "Molded *breadth*" refers to the distance measured between the outer faces of the frames.
3. "Registered *breadth*" refers to the distance measured between the outer faces of the shell plating of a vessel at the widest frame.

BREAK
1. A situation where the surface of the water is disturbed by something in the river. The *break* could be over a sandbar, a diving buoy, a sunken vessel, or other obstruction.
2. When a line or wire under severe strain parts.

BREAKAWAY
Refers to moored barges or vessels which have become adrift from a dock, pier, wharf, or fleeting area.

BREAK BULK CARGO
General cargo that is handled as separate units of goods. This can be a single unit such as large machinery, rolls of paper, sheets of steel, or boxes on a pallet. If grains such as wheat or rice are packaged in sacks, it is considered *break bulk*. Generally, it is units of cargo that is able to be counted. The *break* part of the term refers to the act of taking apart the unity of cargo within the hold of a ship or the hopper of a barge when unloading it. See: BULK CARGO.

BREAK COUPLING
The area of a tow where the rigging must be detached on the barges in order to make a double locking or a jack knife single lockage.

BREAK OUT
1. To get gear ready for use, i.e. "*Break out* the coil of line from the locker".
2. To turn loose from a tow, i.e. "We'll tie the tow off and *break out* to go to the dock".
3. A term used to call the crew, "*Break out* the forward watch".

BREAK UP – ICE
The time when solid sheets of ice are breaking up and start flowing with the current.

BREAK UP TOW
The action, when voluntary, means to take the barges apart from

the tow and drop them at a fleet or a dock. However, when it is involuntary, the term refers to when the tow hits a sandbar or other object and the wires pop and cause the tow to come apart.

BREAKDOWN BAR
A piece of pipe about four feet long and of large enough diameter to fit over the pelican hook of a ratchet to give additional leverage to close the pelican and fasten it with a keeper ring when wiring barges together. Then the *bar* can be used to fit over the ratchet handle to give additional leverage when tightening the ratchet screws. More often called a CHEATER BAR.

BREAKING
A term used in the maritime world to indicate the cutting up or dismantling of vessels. On the river this term is seldom used. More often it is called SCRAPPING.

BREAKING POINT
When a line or wire is under extreme tension and with any additional strain it will part.

BREAKWATER
A structure that protects a shore area from wave action. Usually, the term is used to describe a structure that protects a shore area from the massive sea waves generated by storms; however, it is also used on the river to describe structures that protect small boat marinas from vessel wake or wind waves. It is similar to the word BERM.

BREAST BOARD
In old steamboat days there were no glass windows that were effective to see through to steer the vessel. The front of the pilothouse consisted of a lower *breast board* that would close off the bottom portion of the pilothouse center front that was met above by an adjustable BROW BOARD.

BREAST LINE or WIRE
A line or wire that leads directly abeam from a vessel to an adjacent vessel or structure, used to keep a vessel from moving out, or away, from what it is fastened to.

BREASTED or BREASTING
Vessels that are tied alongside one another. The connection itself is termed a "breast coupling". See: BREAST LINE or WIRE (above).

BRIDGE
1. The area of a propelled vessel from which it is navigated. Not often used on the rivers. The term most generally used is PILOTHOUSE, or WHEELHOUSE.
2. A structure that spans a waterway to allow people, other animals, vehicles, rail cars, etc. to get to one side of a river or canal without using a ferry. There are various types, i.e. fixed, suspension, etc. See the following, BASCULE, DRAWBRIDGE, FLOATING, LIFT, PONTOON, SWING, and WAGON BRIDGE.
3. An obstruction to navigation. See: *EFFIE AFTON* and WHEELING BRIDGE CASE.
4. Famous quote by a bridge designer, "If you build it, they will hit it".
5. Famous song, "Bridge Over Troubled Waters", if you hit it.

BRIDGE ADMINISTRATION PROGRAM
A program administered by the USCG. The Administration issues permits and regulations for bridges over navigable waters as well as overseeing their lighting requirements. It also administers the TRUMAN-HOBBS studies of obstructive bridges to navigation.

BRIDGE CLEARANCE
1. Vertical: Measured from the underside structure of the bridge, where lights are located, to the sur-

face of the water. Most bridges have channel span piers painted with clearance numbers in feet to give a Pilot an approximation of the vertical clearance distance. On the underside of some bridges there is an arched structure, such as used on the Eads Bridge in St. Louis. The clearance shown on the piers is only for the center of the span and not the lower end of the arched section. The vertical clearances are sometimes referred to as AIR DRAFT and AIR GAP.

2. Horizontal: Measured distance between the channel piers supporting the bridge. Navigational charts show both the vertical and horizontal clearances.

BRIDGE LIGHTS

The channel span(s) of bridges at the center of the river channel are marked with green light(s), sometimes in an array with white lights. The piers will be marked with red lights. Some piers may have reflective tape on them to assist in nighttime navigation.

BRIDGE-TO-BRIDGE RADIO

All commercial tugs and towboats are required to carry, and have in operational condition, and on which to transmit as necessary and required, a radiotelephone in accordance with the regulations stated in 33 CFR 26. Basically, a towing vessel (26 feet and over in length) is required to maintain a listening watch on the safety and calling channel then, after initial contact, use another channel to communicate. Most towboats carry at least two radiotelephones at present. If a vessel "reaches agreement with another vessel in a head-on, crossing, or overtaking situation" by radiotelephone the Pilots are not obliged to sound whistle signals prescribed by the Inland Navigation Rules.

BRIDGE WINGS

The open deck on both the port and starboard sides of the pilothouse on most towboats. More often called pilothouse wings.

BRIDLE (a)

Used when towing astern. Although not much towing of barges astern occurs on the river or canals anymore, it is undertaken at times when there is heavy ice on the Illinois or Upper Mississippi Rivers, or in strong winds on the GIWW. When the operation occurs it is usually in restricted waters and the barge(s) towed astern will be trailing fairly close to the towing vessel; therefore, to maintain steerage control a single towing line would not be used but, rather, a *bridle* arrangement.

The *bridle* looks like a "Y" with the wire or line of one arm going to a port timberhead on the barge, and another wire or line going to the starboard timberhead. Where they meet they will be attached to a shackle, or a FLOUNDER PLATE, with another single line leading to the stern deck fitting on the towing tug or towboat.

BRIDLE (b)

A device used to hold the large pilotwheel of a steamboat in place temporarily if a Pilot wanted to get a hot cup of coffee and no one was in the pilothouse.

BRIG

See: JAIL.

BRIGHT WORK

Refers to metal that needs cleaning or polishing, such as brass. It is the scourge of all who are required to clean and rub it to a shiny finish. Most modern vessels have little brass used in outfitting, preferring to use composite materials.

BROACH

1. Broadside to the current or wind.
2. An action that can occur in a fast current when a vessel gets broad-

side to the current and a barge or tow hits a pier or other object, exposing the vessel to the danger of taking on water or even capsizing. This can happen when a towboat attempts to make a DOWNSTREAM LANDING on a barge in high water. If the Pilot is not extremely careful, and the deckhands are not too experienced in quickly catching a line, or if drift gets caught in the wheel, or if an engine may happen to fail, the vessel could get broadside and very possibly may *broach*.

BROAD
Used as a directional reference, such as: "*Broad* on the (port or starboard) bow", which would be about 45 degrees off the bow; or "*Broad* on the (port or starboard) quarter", which would be about 45 degrees off the stern, or "*Broad* on the (port or starboard) beam", which would be directly off to the side of the vessel.

BROADHORN
A beamy flat-bottomed scow that floated with the current, once used to carry cargo in the early days of navigation on the Western Rivers. They had long SWEEPS to assist in guiding the vessel that resembled "horns". When these boats reached New Orleans they were dismantled and used for lumber to build houses. Similar to a FLATBOAT.

BROADSIDE
The entire side of a vessel or of a tow. Used mostly when describing an action that is somewhat sideways to the current or wind, i.e. "I'm going to land the tow *broadside* to the upper tier in the fleet", or "Watch out, the wind is taking the tow *broadside* into the dock".

BROKEN-BACKED
The term that is sometimes used in referring to a vessel, such as a steamboat, and particularly a barge, that has a loss of longitudinal strength. It is called SAGGING or BUCKLING if the mid-section of the vessel is settling down in the water with its ends at a higher level. However, if the bow and stern of the barge are settling down with the mid-section appearing to be at a higher elevation the vessel is said to be HOGGING.

BROKE-UP
A tow that has hit the ground or the bank and has broken the wires that hold the tow together which may be set adrift.

BROOM
See: ANTLERS

BROW BOARD
Since there were no effective glass windows for a Pilot to see through and navigate in the old steamboat days, the center section of the pilothouse consisted of two parts. The lower was called the BREAST BOARD, and the upper part was called the *brow board*, which was an adjustable visor to be raised and lowered partially to shed some driving rain or snow. Most of the time the *brow board* was in the fully raised position.

BROWN BAG BOAT
Refers to a harbor or fleet boat that works in a very limited area. The crew does not live aboard the vessel that usually has no, or a very limited amount, of food on board. Hence, each crew member brings with them a bag or lunch pail before reporting aboard to stand watch.

BROWN-WATER SEAMAN
A term used by "salties" or those in deep water ocean or Great Lakes trades, to refer to seamen employed in the river trades. Although it was never used by those employed on the inland western rivers, the term has been adopted by the USCG and others

as a more or less descriptive term. Uninformed "salties" utilize the term in a degrading fashion while rivermen wear it with pride. "Salties" sometimes deride those that are employed on the so-called "small river vessels" thinking they have lesser competency. In reality, some tows are longer and wider than the largest supertankers on the oceans. They just do not have as deep a hull draft, but river tows continually navigate closer to the bottom and in waters with constant congestion of vessels than do their ocean and lakes cousins.

BTU
An acronym for British Thermal Unit. A measurement of a unit of energy defined as the degree of heat required to raise the temperature of one pound of water one degree Fahrenheit. The term is used to measure the efficiency of fuels in providing mechanical power.

BUBBLER SYSTEM
A system used at some navigation locks to pipe compressed air into the water of the recess and around the lock gates to effectively clear them of debris or broken ice that may have floated in behind them in order that the gates can be fully recessed.

BUCK FRAME
A vertical transverse truss in a wing void of a barge, or other vessel, tying the side-framed inner shell plate of the cargo hold to the outer shell framing.

BUCKET
1. The wooden plank or board of a paddlewheel that propels a vessel as the wheel turns and each *bucket* is dipped into the water. See: BUCKET PLANK.
2. A clamshell, grabber, drag, or backhoe device used to move material or to dredge.
3. The devices on a dredge ladder or a material unloader that move in a continuous chain.
4. The pail a deckhand uses to soogee the bulkheads or when swabbing the deck with a mop. See: FIRE BUCKET.

BUCKET DREDGE
1. A type of dredge used in the sand and gravel business that has a series of small *buckets* on a belt or chain that run continuously around a rigid frame that supports them, called a ladder. The ladder is lowered into the water to the river bottom and the *buckets* bring up material, which is either then dumped on the dredge or into an adjacent barge. Also called a "ladder dredge".
2. Basically a deck barge that is equipped with a crane that has a clamshell *bucket* used in dredge work.

BUCKET PLANK
The thwartship planks on the paddlewheel of a sidewheel or sternwheel boat. The *bucket planks* of the wheel, driven by the vessel's engine, dip into the water to move the boat either ahead or astern. Sometimes shortened and simply called "buckets".

BUCKLE
The permanent damaging distortion of the plating of a barge, usually toward the center or in a diagonal, causing the center of the barge to sag downward. It is usually a condition caused by improper loading of tonnage in the center while leaving voids in the bow or stern, or both ends. The action starts with a SAGGING of the vessel. When the stress becomes too great the plating and framing give way with the *buckling* structural deformation occurring. It is the opposite of HOGGING.

BUGGY
1. The name given to the wheelbarrow used by a coal passer to move

coal from a fuel flat to the bunker where it is used to feed the boiler furnace.

2. A rolling set of support blocks similar to bilge blocks, cribbing or keel blocks that are used in a shipyard that has assembly line type of construction. Sections of barges, or even towboats or tug hulls are rolled to different positions as they are being constructed, and eventually to the final position at the launch ways.

BULB LIGHT

A searchlight that uses an incandescent or xenon *bulb* for its light source. On larger towboats these lights are much more powerful for their size than the old type CARBON ARC LIGHTS that they are gradually replacing.

BULKBOATS

Timber barges that carried oil in an open hopper space of vessels on the Allegheny River in the latter half of the 1800s. They were floated downstream like a flatboat, but were often under tow of a steamer going back upstream after being unloaded. This type of craft was generally unstable due to the free surface effect of the oil, causing much loss of cargo when going aground, hitting bridge piers, or overturning. See: ALLEGHENY RIVER and FRENCH CREEKERS.

BULK CARG0

A cargo which is not packaged, nor can it be counted. It is a product that is stowed in the cargo space and not enclosed in any bag, box, bale, or container of any kind. It can be dry cargo such as grains, ore, coal, salt, sand or gravel; or it can be liquid such as molasses, petroleum, or chemical products; however these are usually referred to a liquid cargo. See: BREAK BULK CARGO.

BULKHEAD

1. An upright or vertical partition that separates compartments in a tug, towboat, or a barge. They can be constructed either transversely or longitudinally and can be of oil tight, or watertight, or non-watertight construction. It can be a full dividing partition from one deck to another, or it can be a partial partition. See: COLLISION, CORRUGATED, LONGITUDINAL, and TRANVERSE BULKHEAD, all of which are synonymous with the term "wall" as used by land lubbers.

2. A retaining wall of stone, piles, concrete, or other materials to protect a shore or dock from erosion.

BULL BOAT

A bowl-shaped vessel used by Indian Tribes on the Missouri River and other rivers. It was made of buffalo hides stretched over a sapling frame. They no longer exist, but were still in use when Captains Meriwether Lewis and William Clark embarked from St. Louis up the Missouri River on their journey to explore the Louisiana Purchase over 200 years ago in 1804.

BULL CHAIN

A short, strong, looped piece of chain with both ends attached to an oval ring, used to go over a barge deck fitting. Its oval ring is attached to one end of a ratchet, which in turn is attached to a barge wire used to couple barges together. Not many in use today as it has been largely supplanted by the CHAIN SLING or HULA HOOP.

BULL RAILS

Wooden planks set in slots in the STATIONARIES on the outboard sides of the main deck on steamboats, used to hold in cargo and/or to fence in livestock. They could be easily removed or added as necessary.

BULLETIN BOARD

An information board that at one time was used at some locks, maintained on certain bridges, and at a few landings along the rivers listing the gauge reading for that day. The practice has mostly been replaced by clear radio communication and computers used on towboats. See: BILLBOARD and RIVER INDUSTRY BULLETIN BOARD (R.I.B.B.).

BULLHORN
Refers to either a large fixed loudspeaker outside the pilothouse directed forward for the Pilot to call out directives to the crew on the tow; or it can be a portable powered megaphone. See: BITCH BOX.

BULLNOSE
The massive concrete structure which is rounded and slanted outward at the end of the intermediate lock wall where double locks are located. It is painted with alternate yellow and black stripes. See: BULLNOSE DIKE (below).

BULLNOSE DIKE
This type of dike is U-shaped and is placed on the upstream end of an island to protect it from excessive erosion. It is sometimes called a *horseshoe dike* and is usually used in conjunction with other types of dikes.

BULL'S EYE
A thimble in the end of a wire used to take a shackle, or to bend in a line to keep the wire from cutting into it.

BULWARK
The framed steel plating around a portion of the deck to prevent water from coming on the deck and to provide safety to the crew. Used a lot on tugs but is not very common on towboats.

BUMBOAT
A small grocery store supply boat that delivers groceries and supplies to a towboat. The name was originally applied by sailors to small boats filled with various goods and operated by peddlers who visited foreign vessels as they pulled into port. It is from the Dutch *bom,* meaning bluff. More often called a BOAT STORE or a MIDSTREAM FUELER on the rivers. See: STORE BOAT as used 150 or so years ago.

BUMP
Refers to a vessel, a barge, or a tow that is swinging into another object and will make fairly hard contact. It is used when one calls out, "Watch the *BUMP!*" It alerts crew members to brace themselves in order not to lose their balance and fall.

BUMP AND GO
A minor grounding that the USCG defines as "the touching of the bottom on the Western Rivers by uninspected towing vessels and uninspected barges in the navigational channel with no damage, no pollution, no personnel injuries, and no unintentional breaking apart of the tow". Hopefully, with the inspection of towboats, this definition will still be utilized.

BUMPER
A type of FENDER that is made of old knotted line, used tires, or similar material to place over the side of a barge when going alongside another tow, a dock, or into a lock. The bumper will absorb the shock of the blow and not cause damage to the barge or the other object. It is also called a POSSUM or *a poor man's fender.*

BUNK
A built-in bed that can be a single or double *bunk* (one over the other). Believed to come from the Dutch word *bank,* meaning "bench". See: BERTH.

BUNKER C FUEL
A heavy viscous fuel oil mostly used in steam-powered vessels. Some large diesel engines used on towboats

can burn some types of number 6 oil or Navy Special, but it is not common on most tugs and towboats.

BUNKERING
The act of a vessel taking on fuel.

BUNKERS
A name occasionally given to the tanks that hold the fuel used by a vessel's engine(s). Sometimes refers to the fuel itself. The term comes from where coal was stored on steamers for use in the boiler furnace. It originally came from the Scandinavian word *banke*, which means "to hold".

BUNTING
A material to make small colorful flags that may be strung on vessels to mark a festive occasion such as a boat launching or christening. The flags themselves when displayed take on the name *bunting*.

BUOY
A floating object secured to an anchoring device that is mostly used to mark a navigation channel. Other *buoys* are used to warn of an obstruction, to designate a quarantine area, an anchorage, fish nets, dredging, or other special purposes. Generally *buoys* are of two shapes on the inland river system: the CAN which is shaped like one, or the NUN, which has a conical top. There are some areas where a SPAR type (long and slender) is used, but these are generally private aids. If a *buoy* carries a light it is called a LIGHTED *buoy*.

River *buoys* are mostly set with a chain or wire leading to a heavy concrete block termed a SINKER which serves as an anchor. In fast-moving alluvial rivers, such as the Missouri, *buoys* were set with a small anchor that was jetted down into the river bottom. In the packet days sometimes the Pilot would send out the Mate in a dinghy to sound a channel. It would be marked with a chip of wood tied to a string with a heavy rock on the other end. When finished marking, the Pilot would head the steamer over the *buoyed* channel. At night, a little larger piece of wood with a lighted candle would be used to mark the channel. See: EATING UP THE LIGHTS.

It is thought the word *buoy* comes from either the German *boye*, and earlier was spelled and pronounced "boy". Some say it comes from old English *boye*, which meant "float". Others think it came from the French, *boie*, which means "to chain", and is pronounced *boo-ee*. That is how most river people now pronounce the word. See the following types of buoys: ANCHOR, MOORING, QUARANTINE, SPECIAL PURPOSE, DREDGE, and LIGHTED.

BUOY LINE
A group of two or more *buoys* marking the contour of the channel's apparent limiting project depth.

BUOY TENDER
A vessel operated by the USCG designed to service the aids to navigation, its *buoys* and lights. The first *buoy tender* built for the (then) Lighthouse Board was constructed in 1857 and was used on the Pacific Coast. The Lighthouse Board in 1910 became the Lighthouse Service, which became a part of the USCG in 1939. On the river these *tenders* are usually referred to as *Buoy* Boats. See: LIGHTHOUSE TENDER.

BUOYAGE
The term refers to setting of buoys or other channel markers. Although the use of buoys goes back many centuries, the first system of *buoyage* was established in England by the Trinity House in 1514. Since that time many different systems of channel markings have evolved throughout the world. The early history of *buoyage* in the U.S. was no different and adhered

to no set standard. Various types, shapes, sizes, and colors of buoys marking channels were used in different ports by local governments. It was estimated in the 1970s there were 30 different systems worldwide. Numerous efforts over the years had taken place by international committees to develop a uniform *buoyage* system for all countries but they were not successful.

Finally in 1980 at a conference organized by the International Association of Lighthouse Authorities (IALA), the International Maritime Consultative Organization (IMCO), the International Hydrographic Organization (IHO), and other national and international organizations agreed to recognize a *buoyage* system that divided the world into Region A and Region B for LATERAL SYSTEM marks, and agreed to a standard for CARDINAL MARKS that can be used in combination where appropriate. Cardinal marks indicate dangers by one or more buoys and/or beacons that are laid out in quadrants of the compass to denote where a particular danger lies in relation to the mark.

North and South America (including the U.S.), the Philippines, Japan, and Korea are in Region B of the Lateral system that use red buoys on the starboard hand, as in RED – RIGHT – RETURNING from the sea, and with green buoys on the port hand indicating GREEN – GOING – GONE (to sea). The rest of the world uses red buoys on the port hand and green buoys on the starboard hand.

The devices used to mark a channel or obstruction may have been used before the Christian Era (B.C.). However, the first known recorded use of a fixed floating marking device was used in the approaches to Sevilla, Spain, in the 13th Century. In United States waters, the use of buoys was first recorded in the latter part of the 1700s on the Delaware River, as well as marking channels leading into some eastern seaports.

On the Western Rivers the Corps of Engineers, which is charged with maintaining the navigability depth of the federally authorized channel, for many years set the buoys in the rivers. After the channel became more stable with construction of training works (revetments, dikes, etc.) the U.S. Coast Guard took over the day-to-day responsibility of channel marking. See: LIGHTHOUSE BOARD & SERVICE.

BUOYANCY

The ability of a vessel or object to stay afloat by upward pressure of the water in which the vessel or object, such as a buoy, is immersed, equaling the weight of the water it has displaced. If the vessel or object is heavier than the water being displaced, that vessel or object will sink to the bottom of the river. It is called the ARCHIMEDES PRINCIPLE, who is said to have discovered it while bathing.

BURDENED VESSEL

The vessel that is required to stay out of the way of another vessel. This was a term that was used in reference to the old RULES OF THE ROAD. The term now used since the Inland Navigation Rules went into effect is the GIVE WAY VESSEL. See: STAND-ON VESSEL.

BUREAU OF LIGHTHOUSES

The name given to the LIGHTHOUSE BOARD in 1910 when it was stationed in the Department of Commerce and Labor until transferred in 1939 to the USCG.

BUREAU OF MARINE INSPECTION & NAVIGATION (BMIN)

The successor agency of the Bureau of Navigation and Steamboat Inspection Service in 1936 by an Act of Congress which stated: "An Act to provide for a change in the designation of the Bureau of Navigation and Steamboat Inspection, to create a marine casualty investigation board, and increase efficiency in administration of the steamboat inspection laws, and for other purposes".

In 1942, soon after the start of WWII, by Presidential Executive Order No. 9083 the duties and functions of BMIN were transferred to the Coast Guard. Such transfer was to "remain in force only during the continuance of the present war and for six months after the termination thereof, unless the Congress by concurrent resolution or the President shall designate an earlier time". After WWII ended, the USCG reverted from being a part of the US Navy and was returned to the Treasury Department. There was later a governmental reorganization with the USCG being transferred to the Commerce Department. The BMIN was abolished with its former functions being absorbed by the USCG. See: BUREAU OF NAVIGATION and STEAMBOAT INSPECTION SERVICE.

BUREAU OF NAVIGATION

As navigation and its regulations became more complex and enforcement became more confusing, Congress in 1884 passed legislation that set up the *Bureau of Navigation* in the Treasury Department. Its functions were mostly promotional and aimed more at seagoing commerce. It provided for the documentation of vessels and listed them, gave tonnage statistics, supervised the shipping and discharge of seamen, and collected tonnage dues. In 1936 the *Bureau*, and the Steamboat Inspection Service, were merged to form the BUREAU OF MARINE INSPECTION & NAVIGATION.

BURGOO

A sort of thick soup or stew made with meats of all kinds (whatever one could shoot or catch), potatoes, and various vegetables, and throw in the spices to suit your taste, slow cooked for a goodly time. Then guard the recipe with your life (if it's any good). The food some years ago was dished out a lot on the Ohio River, particularly in Kentucky, which owns about half the Ohio River. The name is said to come from the Arabic *burgegul,* which was a type of mid-eastern wheat, but none of the recipes we've seen for Burgoo called for wheat, nor have there ever been but few in Kentucky who knew the Arabic language. It's the upriver version of gumbo.

BURN BARREL

A barrel that is placed on the deck of a barge and used to burn trash. This act of burning was declared illegal and *burn barrels* have gone the way of the passenger pigeon.

BUSHEL

Contains 2,150 cubic inches or 1 1/4 cubic feet. Although cargo moved on the river is measured in tons of capacity at a given draft, grains are measured by *bushel* in the agricultural business. Therefore, it is also important to know both the amount of *bushels* a barge will contain at a given draft, as well as the cubic capacity of the barge. Generally the rule of thumb is 60 pounds per *bushel* for wheat and soybeans, 56 pounds for corn, and 32 pounds for oats.

On steamboats, the use of coal was sometimes measured in the amount of *bushels* of coal it took to keep them running and how many *bushels* would be needed at each coaling station. The general number was about 75 pounds to a *bushel* of coal, and about 26 2/3 *bushels* to the ton.

BUSHWHACKING

When moving upriver, especially in high water, part of the crew of a keelboat would pull on the overhanging branches of trees and willows along the shoreline to assist in moving the vessel upstream, while the rest of the crew worked the poles on the river side of the vessel.

BUSTLE STERN
When steamboats were built with rudders in the slope at the stern of the hull there was only a slight clearance between the top of the rudder and the skin of the vessel when the rudder was amidships. When the rudder was moved to the right or to the left the clearance increased allowing a considerable opening between the bottom of the hull and the top surface of the rudder, which was subject to large pieces of drift becoming jammed between the rudder and the hull, causing a loss of steering. To overcome this variance of clearance, blocks of wood were added to the wood hull and molded to conform to the rudder as it turned which was called, "building a *bustle on*". Later on when building new hulls the framing was built to accommodate the *bustle*.

BUSY PILOT
A Pilot that is always moving the rudder controls. See: ZIG-ZAG PILOT.

BUTT JOINT
1. Where two steel plates are placed side to side, and not lapped are then welded together. Also termed a *butt weld*.
2. In wooden vessels it is referred to as the *butt end* of a plank that is placed against another plank and then fastened. Often the *butt ends* of the planks are SCARFED together.
3. If full length timbers were not used in the hull framing then *butt joints* of adjacent strakes were to be at least five feet apart.

BUTT LINE
A fiber or synthetic line spliced into a thimble of a face wire used to couple a towboat to the tow. The *butt line* can then be quickly put on a capstan and tightened, or slacked off, as needed.

BUTT STRAP
A strip that is laid across and attached to pieces that are joined together in a BUTT JOINT.

BUTTERFLY
A small section added to the topside of the rudder on a sternwheel vessel to increase the rudder's bearing area against the current, thus adding to its rudder efficiency.

BUTTERWORTH
A method of cleaning tanks, especially tank barges, by a system of two nozzles rotating in a right-angle plane capable of reaching all sections of a barge tank with hot water and cleaning solutions. Most tank barges have a hole on deck fitted with a *butterworth* plate through which the system is inserted.

BUTTING BLOCK
A king-sized log chained to the middle of the upstream end of a log raft that a steamboat would push against when rafting logs or lumber. It is probably where the term HEAD-LOG came into being.

BUTTOCK-LINES
The lines drawn by a naval architect to lay off on a print or template to reconcile the shape and sheer of a vessel stern that is to be constructed. The lines fashion the longitudinal curvature of the stern as it rises upward depending on its shape to accommodate the appendages that will be mounted there. It is hazy as to how the term came into being. It apparently comes from the rounded rear end of an animal and from its base of "butt" meaning "to join flush one to another", and the lines that made it possible. Similar lines are used at the bow if there is a curvature. They are termed BOW-LINES.

BUTTON

A short mushroom-shaped deck fitting of various circumferences used for leading lines or to secure wires on tows. See: ROLLER CHOCKS.

BUTTON UP

1. Finishing up on an assigned job or task.
2. The closing of all covers or hatches.

BY THE HEAD or STERN

If a vessel is not running on an even keel, she is said to be down *by the head or the stern*. This is usually the case when it is either heavy or light on fuel in some of its bunkers, or the hull could have a leak and a void tank would be flooded.

BY THE MARK

The call of the leadsman while taking a sounding of the river depth with a leadline, as in: *"By the mark, twain"*, or, *"By the mark, a quarter less tyree"*. Use of a LEADLINE (see for terms when sounding) is seldom, if ever, used today. If sounding is required it is now usually done with a SOUNDING POLE, painted at foot marks with alternating colors of red/white, or red/black with a distinctive mark at nine feet, or the vessel is equipped with a mechanical sounder.

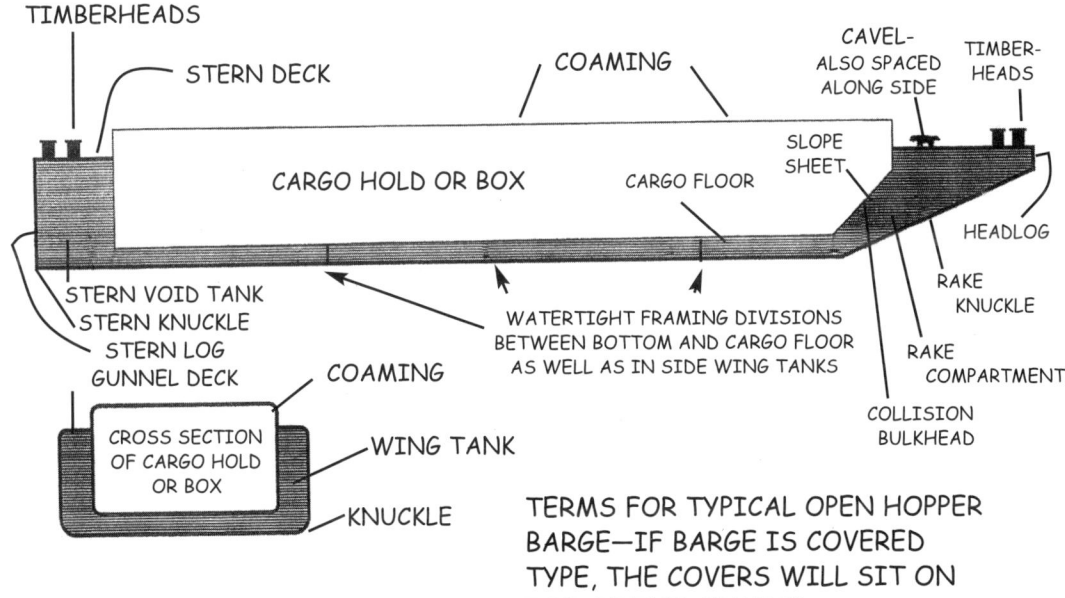

TERMS FOR TYPICAL OPEN HOPPER BARGE—IF BARGE IS COVERED TYPE, THE COVERS WILL SIT ON TOP OF THE COMING.

BRIDGE TYPES ON WESTERN RIVERS

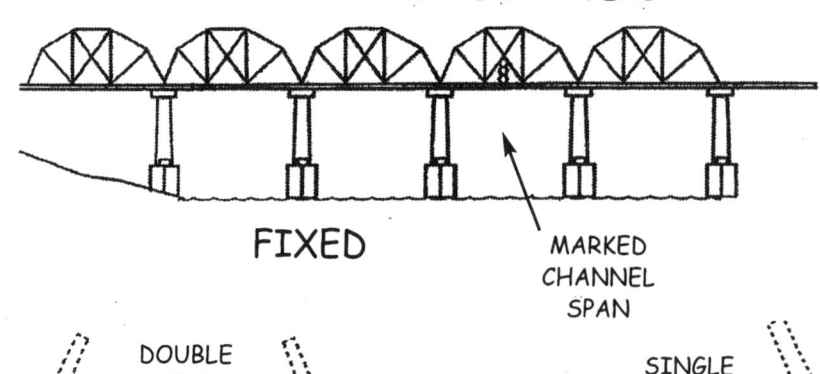

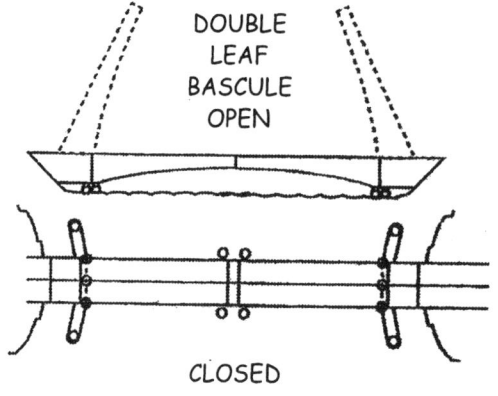

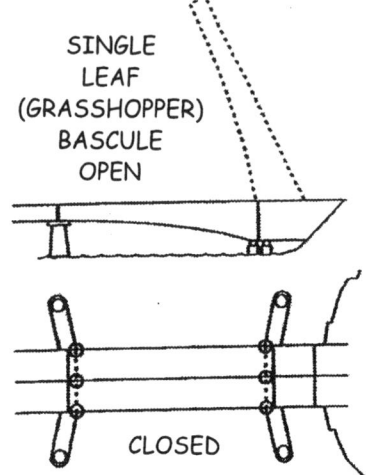

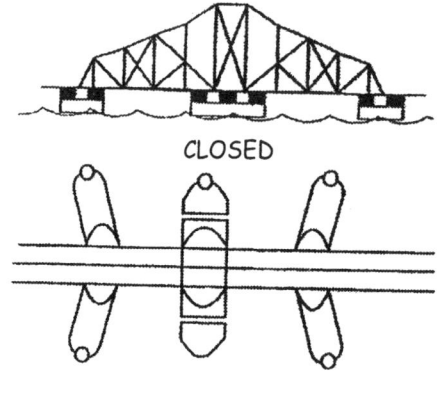

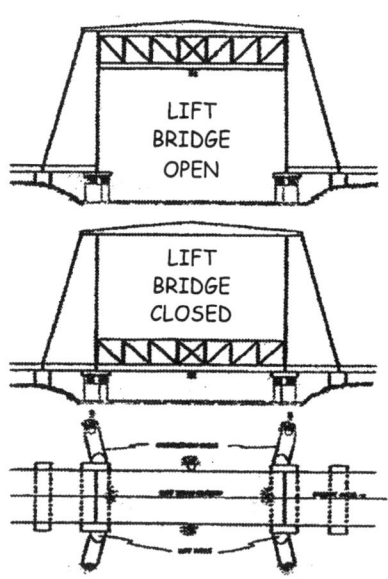

CAN BUOY

OF CYLINDRICAL SHAPE AND IS GENERALLY GREEN WHEN MARKING THE LEFT HAND SIDE OF A NAVIGATIONAL CHANNEL WHEN PROCEEDING UPSTREAM.

GREEN - GOING - GONE
(TO SEA)

NUN BUOY

OF CYLINDRICAL SHAPE AND IS GENERALLY RED WHEN MARKING THE RIGHTHAND SIDE OF A NAVIGATIONAL CHANNEL WHEN PROCEEDING UPSTREAM.

RED - RIGHT - RETURNING
(FROM SEA)

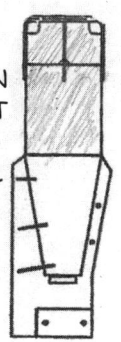

BLOCK

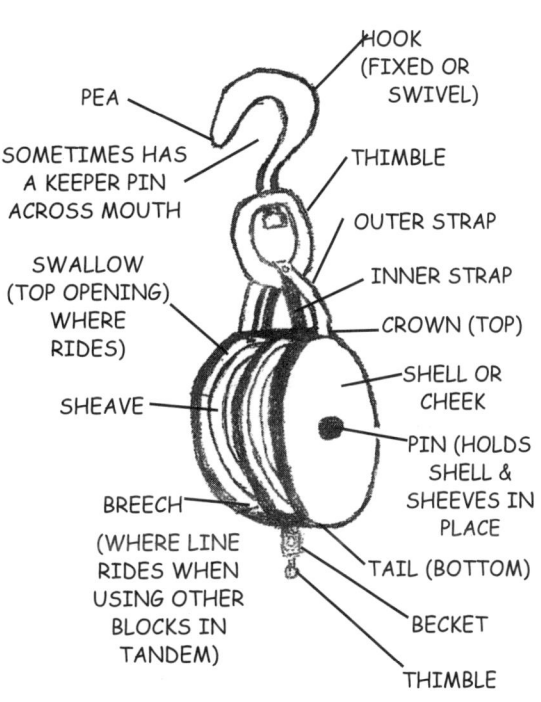

- HOOK (FIXED OR SWIVEL)
- PEA — SOMETIMES HAS A KEEPER PIN ACROSS MOUTH
- THIMBLE
- OUTER STRAP
- INNER STRAP
- SWALLOW (TOP OPENING) WHERE RIDES)
- CROWN (TOP)
- SHEAVE
- SHELL OR CHEEK
- PIN (HOLDS SHELL & SHEEVES IN PLACE)
- BREECH (WHERE LINE RIDES WHEN USING OTHER BLOCKS IN TANDEM)
- TAIL (BOTTOM)
- BECKET
- THIMBLE

THE CROWN OF THE BLOCK IS HINGED ON ONE SIDE, WHICH DOES NOT REQUIRE A LINE TO BE REEVED THROUGH IT, BUT CAN BE ATTACHED QUICKLY TO THE BIGHT OF A LINE.

C

CABIN
On the packet steamers the cabin was the center-space lounging area on the boiler deck superstructure outside of the staterooms which were to its sides. It did not refer to the actual sleeping spaces as it may on ocean-going passenger vessels. The forward part was the men's section of the cabin, where the bar was located. The ladies cabin section was at the after end where single men were not allowed at night. On the river the term *cabin* may now at times be used to refer to the living space or quarters for crew members, or for the rooms of any guests that may be aboard.

CABIN ARCH
Ornately carved arch pieces that decorated the cabins of some of the finer steamboats giving rise to the decorative term, STEAMBOAT GOTHIC.

CABIN DECK
Usually the second deck of a towboat where most of the living quarters of the officers are located.

CABLE
1. A heavy wire used in the rigging aboard barges to tie them together or to fasten the tug or towboat to its tow. In old sea terms it could have been a heavy fiber or wire rope that was used as a hawser.
2. Also used as a MOORING WIRE.
3. The wire attached to a buoy and its anchor.
4. Electrical wire for lights on the tow, or for a depth recorder.
5. A length equal to 100 fathoms, or about 600 feet. A *cable's* length in deep sea language was approximately one-tenth of a nautical mile.
6. The word comes from the Latin *capulum,* meaning "a halter for catching cattle", which later came to basically mean wire.

CABLE CLAMP
See: WIRE CLIP or CLAMP.

CABLE FERRY
A ferry that is pulled from one bank to another across a stream or one that propels itself across the stream while attached to a cable. This type of ferry is seen on the Intracoastal Canal and on the Illinois River as well as on other narrow waterways.

CABLE-LAID LINE
A line that is laid up left-handed. It is seldom, if ever, seen on riverboats.

CABLE STOPPER
The use of a chain or piece of line to hold a cable or wire taut while moving it from a deck fitting, or a winch, in order to make it fast to some other deck fitting.

CABOTAGE
Laws which require cargo shipped by water between points within a country to be carried in vessels owned and registered or documented in that country. In the United States our *cabotage* law is called the JONES ACT, which requires that all cargo loaded and shipped in the U.S. and destined for another port in the U.S. must be carried in vessels built in the U.S., owned and operated by U.S. companies, and the crews must consist of citizens of the U.S. It is believed the term came from the French *caboter,* meaning "to sail along a coast"; or perhaps the Spanish word, *cabo,* meaning "the cape" or "headland".

CAHABA RIVER
Flows from the Appalachian foothills area northeast of Birmingham, AL, for about 191 miles to its confluence with the Alabama River. It had some steamboat traffic, however dangerous, and perhaps would have been dammed and made navigable except

for the Civil War and the development of the railroads. The river takes its name from the Choctaw Indian words, meaning "water above." It was the territorial division between the Choctaw and the Creek tribes. Its name is phonetically, kuh – HUH – buh. See: DROP 'EM THROUGH for an incident involving the M/V CAHABA.

CAIRO POINT

The juncture where the Ohio River at Mile 981, and the Upper Mississippi River at Mile 0, meet to form the Lower Mississippi River, Mile 964. Cairo is pronounced, *Kay* – Roe, unlike in Egypt, which is *Ki* – Roe.

CAISSON

1. A structure used similar to a COFFERDAM.
2. The gates of a GRAVING DOCK.
3. Watertight tanks that are filled with water and placed alongside a sunken vessel. They are then rigged to the sunken craft; air is pumped in to displace the water to accomplish a lifting capacity. The word comes from Italian *cassone*, to mean "a chest of large size". In the Army it was considered a wagon for carrying ammunition. See: CAMEL.

CAJUN

A corruption of the word "Acadian" or person of French descent who came from Acadia, Canada, which is now Nova Scotia. They were driven out by the English in the 1700s and migrated south with many finding homes and living in what is now the State of Louisiana. Many riverboat persons come from this heritage.

CAJUN RATCHET

When barges are made up with doubled up lines between them a bar is inserted between the bights. Then the bar is twisted around numerous times to tighten the lines. At times the bar lets go and becomes a flying missal if it isn't tied down. An unsafe practice that is no longer used. A colloquial term used with different names in different ethnic cultures, such as a *Kanawha River ratchet* on the upper Ohio River, and additional local names in other parts of the river system. In deep-sea trades it is often called a *Spanish Windlass*.

CALLING & DISTRESS FREQUENCY

The VHF radio frequency Channel 16, designated by the Federal Communications Commission (FCC) that is reserved to be used for distress calls or for vessels to make an initial contact to another vessel or station. With contact the vessel or station will go to a "working channel" to continue conversation. The *calling frequency* is required to be monitored by all vessels underway unless they are operating in a VESSEL TRAFFIC SYSTEM (VTS) and are monitoring that particular VTS radio frequency signal, which they will then use for their initial contact between vessels.

CALLING THE LEAD

When sounding with a LEADLINE the Leadsman would *call* out the depth, as in "a quarter less twain" or "no bottom", etc. See: ARM (THE LEAD), BY THE MARK, and LEADLINE.

CALLIOPE

A piano-like musical instrument originally powered by steam, which was furnished by the main boiler or by a small separate DONKEY BOILER. Modern ones are powered by air. It was, and is, used on showboats and excursion vessels and was considered a necessity to play it prior to making a landing at a small (or large) town. It would sound out loud and lively tunes to notify the populace that a showboat had arrived. A *calliope* consists of a set of 24 to 42 whistles, each having a different pitch. The instrument was invented in the mid-1800s by Joshua Stoddard who named it after the Greek mythological Muse of Beautiful Sound. The word comes from Greek *Kalliope,* one of nine sister Goddesses who oversaw the arts. It means "having a beautiful voice or sound". If any person on the river bank doesn't think this is true, they better talk to a STEAMBOAT BUFF.

The first *calliope* was installed on the steamer *AMAZON* in 1856 when it operated on the Ohio River. The word is pronounced *CA-LIE*-O-PEE, at least by river people. As Doc Hawley is fond of reciting:
  Full of joy, full of hope,
  Some folks call me cally – ope.
  Sounds of joy, sounds of glee,
  Others say cal – lie – o – pee.

CALL LETTERS or SIGN
Each tug or towboat is assigned a set of letters by the FCC that it is required to use when making any radiotelephone transmission.

CALL WATCH
Crew members who do not stand a regular watch but are subject to work when required as needed. This can be the case on small vessels with limited crew, when a vessel is shorthanded, when one or two of the deckhands only make locks, or when picking up and dropping barges.

CALM
A period when the river surface is almost smooth and there is an absence of wind to less than a couple of miles per hour.

CAMBER
A slight slope of the deck from the centerline transversely, or athwartship, to the port and starboard sides of a vessel. This adds strength to a vessel and allows any water that might accumulate to rapidly run overboard. Sometimes, especially on steamers, it was referred to as the *crown*. The word comes from Latin *camurus,* meaning curved inwards.

CAMEL
1. A float, usually wooden, that is placed between a vessel and a wharf or pier, or another vessel, to cushion and protect the vessel (and pier) from any damage due to wave or wake action causing the vessel to continually bump the pier.

2. A lifting device, most often used in pairs, wherein an airtight container is filled with water and attached to the side of a damaged or sunken vessel. The water is then evacuated from the *camel* thereby obtaining lift for the damaged vessel. See: CASSION.

CAN BUOY
A *buoy* in the shape of a cylinder with a flat top end. Usually painted green to mark the left-hand side of the channel to denote the 3-G system of Green—Going—Gone (to sea). *Can buoys* may be painted other colors to denote other specific purposes. In early English a drinking container or jug was termed a "canne" which apparently was similar to the cylindrical "cans" that contain many products in our grocery stores, so the shape of our formerly black, now green, buoys took on the name. See: NUN BUOY.

CANAL
An artificial, or manmade, waterway used for navigation. Although not the first *canal*, the canal era began in the United States with the building of the Erie Canal in New York to connect the Hudson River with the Great Lakes. It was completed in 1825. Its success led to the building of over 3300 miles of inland canals by 1840, and over 5000 miles of them in 1850. Very few of them are still in existence, or only partially survive due to historical preservation associations. During their heyday these crisscrossing

arteries going north-south and east-west were important connectors carrying freight to the internal Western Rivers steamboats. A few of them are included in this Lexicon: the OHIO AND ERIE CANAL, the MIAMI AND ERIE CANAL, and the WABASH AND ERIE CANAL. *Canal* building in the U.S. provided the training for engineering competence and innovation that eventually went into construction of railroads, highways, and industrial America.

Most often *canals* were built near or alongside a natural waterway in order to utilize the available flows it possessed to supply a *canal* with sufficient water. If the *canal* could not parallel a river, or was being excavated between two rivers, feeder *canals* from reservoirs would be constructed to supply the needed water. AQUEDUCTS often had to be constructed to either provide additional water or to float canal boats across streams or obstructions. Almost never were mechanically powered vessels allowed on a canal. Power to propel a vessel along a *canal* was by horses or mules. Early experience found that vessels propelled by steam caused washing of the banks of the narrow *canal* with resulting siltation of its bed reducing the already shallow channel's depth. Although some *canals* remained in use until the end of the century the era of canal traffic started phasing out after 1850. Flooding damage with cost of repairs, and the rail "iron horse" spelled their doom.

Many persons do not realize that the mid-continent waterways utilized by towboats and barges presently contain many miles of productive *canals*. Some include the Cal-Sag Canal on the south side of Chicago, as well as the Chicago Canal, the *canal* at L&D 27 on the Mississippi River above St. Louis, the *canal* at Louisville on the Ohio River above McAlpine L&D, the Tenn-Tom Waterway, the Industrial Canal in New Orleans, and most of the GIWW along the Gulf of Mexico. The word apparently traces back to Latin *canalis*, which basically meant "channel".

CANAL BOAT

The term that was given in a bygone era to vessels that plied the many thousands of miles of canals in the interior of our nation. They were mostly powered by mules or horses walking along a tow path. Very few were ever propelled by engines. If fact, on some canals powered vessels were forbidden as their wake would erode the banks and wash into the already shallow channel of the *canal* increasing the cost of maintenance. Nowadays the term *canal boat* is usually employed in reference to tugs or towboats which operate basically on the GIWW.

CANALIZE

The modification of a river stream to make it suitable for navigation by utilizing such techniques as dredging to deepen or widen the channel, dikes or other training works to manage the direction of flow and scour the channel, revetment of shore banks to keep the river from cutting and eroding the shoreline, building dams with lock chambers to provide transportation service, etc.

CANDELA

A unit of luminous intensity (candle power) to measure the range of visibility of required navigation lights. The required intensity range can be found in the Navigation Rules, Annex I, section 84.15(b).

CANNIBALIZE

The removal of parts from one unit and inserted in another piece of equipment whose parts had failed, but were of a compatible type or model. It is not a particularly good operating practice but at times a necessary one to prevent a shutdown while awaiting replacement parts.

CANOE BARGE

A *barge* 109 feet long by 29 feet in width, with a hull of 12 feet built with a high coaming and fitted with covers. The coaming had doors in the side, which allowed for ease of loading some cargoes. Basically, they were made for less than barge-load service of small or mixed shipments in the days of regulated freight. They didn't make up well in a tow (similar to the LASH barge today), were unstable, and unsafe in tow as they created DUCKPONDS when made up wherever they were placed in a tow. The *canoe* designation came from the ease at which they could tip over. They were basically operated by the former Mississippi Valley Barge Line Company. Others called them *point* barges, or *sheepnose* barges. Still others had a lot more words and titles for them that cannot be put in a Riverman's Lexicon that may be read by his/her children. An idea that should have been given the deep-six treatment before it even came to pass. The barges were phased out of service by 1950. Sometimes small favors are granted to rivermen.

CANT

When loggers moved rafts on the river they sometimes took the logs to mills where they were made into lumber. *Cant* logs were those that had pieces (called slabs) cut off a round log. The squaring up of these logs formed a *cant* lumber raft.

CANT FRAMES or TIMBERS

Frames or beams that rise obliquely, or at an angle, from the keel line. The term is used for most support members that do not stand square, i.e. they are on a *cant*.

CANT HOOK

A type of hook on a wooden handle about four feet long with a swiveled hook on the end that is used by loggers to move logs around to place them in position in a raft. See: PEAVY.

CAPACITY

It is difficult to measure the *capacity* of a vessel and its tow because apples are not oranges; however, to put it in perspective as to single barges and tows compared to other forms of transportation see CAPACITY COMPARISON CHARTS at the end of the chapter. Barge transportation is the most cost effective, energy efficient and environmentally friendly mode of transportation for products available in the market place.

CAPSIZE

To overturn a vessel, or to have it overturned by the elements. This usually results in a vessel sinking. However, deck barges have *capsized*, losing their cargo load, and do not usually sink. Tank barges that *capsize*, but have not been damaged by a collision or allision also are capable of remaining afloat, although bottom side up.

CAPSTAN

A vertical drum or barrel that rotates on a shaft used to apply mechanical purchase to a line or wire to draw it taut. The drum has ribs, called whelps, which help to keep a line from slipping on the *capstan* drum. Similar to a windlass except the drum is mounted vertically. On towboats, the *capstan(s)* is located on the forward main deck. Some older or larger vessels also have *capstans* mounted on the side main deck. Usually powered electrically. If used manually the *capstan* has holes in the drumhead (top) called PIGEON HOLES that allows a CAPSTAN BAR to be inserted to give additional leverage to the crew member turning it. The base of the *capstan* is fitted with PAWLS that drop into slots or notches of the base plate to prevent the barrel from any backward movement in case of loss of power. Pawls will not be used for a reversing *capstan*. The term *capstan* is from the Latin *capistrum,* meaning "to seize or fasten".

CAPSTAN BAR
A round length of wood which is placed in the PIGEON HOLES of the drumhead of a mechanical capstan that gives a person leverage or purchase to turn the capstan and tighten the line leading to it.

CAPSTAN PIN
A short stout piece of wood that is inserted in one of the pigeon holes of a CAPSTAN on which a line can be made fast with a reverse hitch to keep it from slipping on the capstan barrel.

CAPTAIN
On riverboats, it is the title given to a licensed person who is in overall command of a vessel, or MASTER, as well as the licensed person who is in command of a navigation watch, who is normally called the Pilot, or Watch Captain and now MATE (PILOT). The term comes from the Latin *caput,* which means "the head".

CAPTAIN OF THE PORT (COTP)
A Coast Guard officer, not necessarily holding the rank of Captain, in charge of a Coast Guard-designated zone that provides the immediate overall law enforcement and safety activities within their assigned area. In the USCG chain of command they report to their District Commander. Different from a private company's PORT CAPTAIN.

CAPTIVE SHIPPER
A company or shipper that is located in an area where it has limited access to competing forms of transportation; therefore, its freight rates for haulage into or out of its facilities are high. Plants located where access to river transportation is available receive the most competitive freight rates available, as all forms of bulk commodity transit are available: truck, railroads, or by any barging company.

CAR FLOAT
As used on the river system these vessels were steam-powered rail-transfer boats or deck barges that ferried rail cars across a river, usually just a short distance. Both types of vessel were equipped with tracks. Bridges have replaced these vessels today. The last on the river was the steamer *GENEVIEVE* on the Upper Mississippi.

CARBON ARC LIGHT
A searchlight used on towboats to locate buoys, daymarks, other objects on shore, assist in transiting a bridge or entering a lock chamber, or any other purpose to aid the person on watch. It consists of two carbon electrodes that arc together to make a powerful light in its cylindrical casing, with a reflector to intensify the beam. They are being phased out and being replaced by XENON lights.

CARDINAL MARKS
A system that uses navigational marks (such as buoys) to indicate that the deepest water in the area lies to the named side of the mark. In the U.S. river system CARDINAL MARKS are not used; rather the LATERAL SYSTEM of BUOYAGE is employed.

CARDINAL POINTS
The four main points of the compass, i.e. North, South, East, West. The intermediate points are called sub-cardinal points, or inter-cardinal points.

CAREEN
To severely list a vessel to one side. Sometimes it is done purposely

in order for an owner to make repairs, or replate a damaged area of a vessel's side or bottom. See: HEEL.

CARGO
Freight carried by a vessel. In the case of river freight, cargo is carried in a barge. There are generally three kinds of cargo:

1. BULK CARGO – Commodities such as coal, grain, salt, dry fertilizer, sand and gravel, etc.

2. GENERAL CARGO – Various countable products such as steel, manufactured goods, containers, sacks of sugar, paper, etc.

3. LIQUID CARGO – Petroleum, chemicals, liquid fertilizer, molasses, etc., that must be pumped to off-load.

4. The term comes from the Latin *carga,* meaning load; also the Spanish *cargar,* meaning "to carry".

CARGO BOX
1. The interior compartment, or hold, of a dry cargo barge where cargo is carried. A *high box* is a term referring to barges with very high COAMINGS built to carry light cargoes, such as paper or soybean meal, that need more cubic space to reach the minimum tonnage called for in a contract of afreightment.

2. On a deck barge, in the sand a gravel trade, it is the area inside the coaming on the sides and sometimes the ends of the barge.

CARGO COVER
The covers, or hatches, over the cargo-carrying space of a dry cargo barge. Although the covers on barges are not watertight, they are weathertight in that they will shed rain. They can be LIFT COVERS, which require a crane to lift them off to unload cargo, or ROLL COVERS, which usually telescope to some degree to allow a different portion of the barge hold to be open at any time in order that cargo can be loaded or unloaded.

CARGO CRANE
A mechanical handling device used to lift and move various types of products out of, or into, a barge. These cranes can be either on a dock or on a floating deck barge. They can be rigged in various ways: with a bucket for bulk commodities, a magnet, hook, or slings for general cargo, or used to handle heavy hoses for liquid transfers.

CARGO DOOR
A door, or set of doors, built in the cover of a dry cargo barge. Cargo doors can be in either lift-off covers or rolling covers, but are generally constructed only in the former. When the lift covers are spread over the cargo hold these doors can easily be opened and bulk cargo, mainly grains, can be loaded through them with a directional loading spout.

CARGO IDENTIFICATION CARD
A card which is to be displayed at or on the WARNING SIGN of any barge that has a hazardous cargo aboard. It lists the generic name of the cargo, as well as the dangers associated with it.

CARGO TANK
A compartment in a tank barge that holds liquid cargo.

CARGO TON
1. Short ton (2000 pounds), used in river commerce for the weight of cargo shipped and in the displacement of tonnage of barges at a specific draft.

2. Long ton (2240 pounds), more readily used in international trade. See: TONNAGE.

CARGO TON MILE(S)
One *ton of cargo* transported one *mile*. It can be used in pricing, or as a method of measuring efficiency. The USACE records both *tons of cargo transported* and the *ton miles* of

generic movements on specific waterway segments.

CARGO TRANSFER SYSTEM
All the components of a tank barge, including the piping, the cargo hoses, the pump, pump engine, drip pans, and any other gear necessary for the efficient and safe transfer of liquid products to or from a vessel.

CARGO VOID SPACE
Any empty tanks surrounding the cargo space. On barges they are the bow void tank, the stern void tank, and the port and starboard wing void tanks.

CARLINES or CARLINGS
Short beams running fore and aft between the transverse framing binding them together and also serve to support the deck above.

CARRIER
Any company that transports freight on the river. There are COMMON CARIERS, that transport freight at a set published rate, and there are CONTRACT CARRIERS, that enter into an agreement as to price and conditions to transport goods. Nearly all transportation business now conducted on the river is done by contract.

CARRY AWAY
1. To wash overboard.
2. Sometimes used when a line breaks under a heavy strain, but the terms to part or parting are the more common terminology.

CARRY WAY
A vessel that is moving through the water.

CARRYING CAPACITY
The estimated space (area) or amount of tonnage that a lock, a port, or a segment of a waterway can safely and efficiently accommodate. See: CAPACITY and Efficiency of water transport.

CAST OFF
To untie, or let go, of a line or wire from a vessel to a dock, a lock wall, a shore, or to another vessel. It comes to us from the Norse *kasta,* meaning "to throw".

CAST THE LEAD
One of the terms used when SOUNDING; to throw the LEADLINE out to take a sounding in a shallow channel. Also, "heave the lead" was used. See: BY THE MARK.

CASTING FIELDS
Located at various areas along the Lower Mississippi, a *casting field* is where the USACE casts concrete blocks that are made into a large MATTRESS that is laid on the riverbed up a graded bank shoreline by a MAT-PLANT to protect it from erosion by the river current. Each individual block is 4' by 25'. They are held together by cables in the mattress.

CASTLE
The use of the *castle* or "turreted *castle*" insignia by the U.S. Corps of Engineers goes back to 1839 when it was first worn on the new uniform of the Cadets at the academy of West Point. It was designed by its Superintendent, Colonel Delafield, and approved by General Totten, the Chief Engineer at the time. It has undergone some design change over time, but essentially the *castle* is still intact as a symbol of the Corps' stature and fortitude.

CASUALTY (MARINE)
Title 46 CFR definition: "The term marine casualty or accident includes any accidental grounding, or any occurrence involving a vessel which results in damage by or to the vessel, its apparel, gear, or cargo, or injury or

loss of life of any person; and includes among other things, collisions, strandings, groundings, foundering, heavy weather damage, fires, explosions, failure of gear and equipment and any other damage which might affect or impair the seaworthiness of the vessel". See: CASUALTY REPORT.

CASUALTY REPORT

Any time there is a *casualty* or accident, an immediate notification must be made to the nearest USCG Marine Safety Office. Then it must be followed up by a written report on form CG-2692, Report of Marine Accident, Injury or Death, and sent to the Coast Guard.

CATAMARAN

A twin-hulled vessel. The word comes from the Indian Ocean, *kattumaran,* meaning "tied wood", referring to a sailing vessel of logs tied together to make a raft. The first SNAGBOAT built by Capt. Henry Shreve was of this basic type construction.

CATCH A TURN

A directive for a deckhand to take a turn, or another turn, with a line or wire on a timberhead or cavel, usually given when a line is paying out too fast and is needed to be snubbed down.

CATENARY

1. A weight put on a hawser to dampen any sudden strain on it while towing astern.
2. Sometimes applied to the curvature of a chain, wire, or line between two points. The term traces to the Latin *catena,* meaning "chain".

CATFISH NAVY

During WW II many inland river shipyards built vessels for the U.S. Navy, which had to be piloted down river to a seaport. This task was accomplished by licensed river pilots who were commissioned into the U.S. Coast Guard. The men became known as the *Catfish Navy.*

CATHEAD

Used occasionally as the name for an auxiliary small drum on a winch that is more correctly called a GYPSY or other colloquial terms. It is sometimes used incorrectly as a name for the barrel of a CAPSTAN.

CATHODIC PROTECTION

A sacrificial material attached to the immersed steel hull plating, kort nozzles, and other underwater appendages that will then waste away before brackish or salt water can attack the steel. Zinc anodes are most commonly used. From the Greek *kathodos,* meaning "way down", probably because if the steel is eaten away your vessel will go "way down" to the bottom. See: ANODES.

CATTLE BARGE

Shipping cattle on the river is nothing new since there were reports of hauling them on steamboats back in the 1800s. In modern times only a few shipments have been made. In the 1960s the King Ranch of Texas bought, or chartered, a laid-up TRIPLE-DECKER barge which previously had been used for hauling cars. They outfitted it with pens, water troughs, plenty of feed, and took it to Texas. There they loaded her up with cattle from the ranch and had the barge towed to Kansas City on the Missouri River. The trip was successful and it is believed they made two trips. The King Ranch said it was the only time they moved cattle to market that gained weight instead of losing it. The problem, however, was that they arrived at the stockyards with so many pounds of meat on the hoof that the market price for beef plummeted. So there apparently wasn't much profit made and they terminated the movement.

CAUGHT or CATCH OUT

When a vessel, usually a barge, goes aground on a falling river gauge, or the barge is not properly attended to in a fleet and it goes hard aground on the sloping shore. See: STRANDED.

CAULK or CAULKING

Although *caulk* was associated with wooden-hulled vessels, the term has carried over to steel-hulled ones. Originally meaning "to fill the cracks between wooden timbers or planks", the term still means "to stop the ingression of water". Some of the same materials and types of tools are used. SHINGLES and OAKUM or other fibrous materials are driven into a cracked or holed area to stop or slow down the water inflow. Sometimes a CEMENT BOX will have to be installed. The term comes from the Latin *calcare,* meaning "to tread or force". See: CAULKING IRON, CREASE, MAKING IRON, PAY POT, PITCH, PITCH POT, REAMING or RAMMING IRON, and REEFING IRON.

CAULKED BOOTS

The type of boots worn by log raftsmen that had long sharp spikes to allow the men to walk and run across the logs in a raft without slipping and falling. The spikes on the boots were usually called *corks*.

CAULKER

The person who does the caulking. However, his profession is not pronounced as it is spelled, rather it is more like *Corker*. To call a man who can make the "iron" ring (or sing) when he swings his caulking mallet a *Caulker* would be an insult to his craft. It is said the "boss man" can tell who is working and who is not by the ringing sound of each man's iron as it is hit by his mallet.

CAULKING IRONS and TOOLS

The *irons* were various types and sizes of chisels used to drive OAKUM into a crack or hole. They were generally made and sold by the size of the CREASE which was the thickness of the blade head. There were different names for various irons depending on the area to be caulked. Some were:

1. Caulking, Making, or Dumb Irons were the most commonly used ones, coming in different crease sizes.
2. Clearing or Reeming Irons cleared out old oakum.
3. Crooked or Bent Irons were for driving oakum into angles.
4. Sharp or Butt Irons helped at joints.
5. Spike Irons got into corners and tight places.
6. Horse Irons used on thick planking on deck. They had a large CREASE that was grooved to allow the oakum to better receive the pine tar from the PAY POT.
7. A Caulking Wheel was a hand-held device with a rolling wheel at the end grooved to receive the oakum and roll it into the space to be caulked prior to using the irons to harden it down.

CAULKING MALLET & CAULKING HAMMER

A hammer-like tool fitted with a tapered iron ring on the striking end, which caused the ringing sound when it struck an iron. The largest of the *mallets* was called a BEETLE which was used for the heaviest work of REAMING, or opening seams, and to HORSE UP, or harden a seam after caulking. The other *caulking mallets and hammers* were used with the various CAULKING IRONS to fill seams with OAKUM depending upon the location being *caulked*.

CAVE-IN-ROCK

The cavern, about 55 feet wide, was first reported by a Frenchman who called it "caverne dans Le Roc" in the early 1700s. It is at about river mile 881 on the Ohio. When flatboatmen started traveling the Ohio River it became an infamous haunt for outlaws and river pirates who preyed on travelers as they floated down the river. There were numerous gangs, including those of Samuel Mason, the Harpe Brothers, and others, who sold whiskey, conducted gambling, and committed robbery and murder. By the late 1830s most of the gangs had been driven away. The place is now part of the Illinois State Park System.

CAVEL
A large cast steel cleat-like fitting with two long prongs protruding from its center, called horns. Used to tie lines to, or other rigging. Can be solid or have an opening in its base to allow a line or wire to pass through, or have the horns open. Sometimes it is spelled, *caval* or *cavil*, however *caval* has no meaning, and *cavil* means the making of petty or unnecessary objections, which is something the dispatcher does while the *cavel* serves a useful purpose. It is not a *kevel,* a fitting that is similar, but much smaller, than a *cavel,* which is used to tie off small lines on sailing or recreational vessels. It also is not a *cleat* which is what the Navy calls *cavels*, but maybe we'll learn 'em yet. One can buy a *cleat* in the hardware store which is used to tie off things like window blinds or awnings. See: KEVELHEAD.

CAVING BANK or BAR
A bluff unprotected shoreline (without revetment or dikes), or sandbar that is breaking off into the channel. Occurs often when there is high water that falls out rapidly, leaving the inundated soil in a weakened and collapsing condition, or when the shore or bar are subject to swift currents continually eroding the soil or sand. See: BLUFF BAR.

CAVITATION
The action which occurs during certain conditions when air pockets are formed in the thrust area of a vessel's propeller, causing the propeller to run away (increase RPMs) and resulting in excessive vibration and wear as well as the loss of thrust efficiency. From the French *cavite,* to mean "a hole", as when the water has a section of air or a "hole" in it. See: LOSE THE SEAL.

CELESTIAL OCCURANCES
The prime ones that occur on the river and the rest of the world are:
   VERNAL EQUINOX Marks the beginning of Spring
   SUMMER SOLSTICE Signifies the start of Summer
   AUTUMNAL EQUINOX When Autumn begins
   WINTER SOLSTICE Marking the start of Winter

CELL
A large-diameter structure built of steel sheet piling that is filled with rock, gravel, or sand and oftentimes capped with concrete. It is commonly used at docks for moorings, having tie-off rings at various locations on the *cell*. Also used at times for protection of bridge piers, or other structures, and for building cofferdams. It is from the Latin *cella,* meaning "chamber".

CEMENT BOX
When a crack or hole develops in the hull of a vessel it is stopped as much as possible by driving SHINGLES and OAKUM into the leaking area. In order to make the repair semi-permanent in case the shingles are rubbed off in some manner, a box is built over the area where the leaking occurred and filled with quick-drying *cement*. The size of the box is generally six to eight inches deep and of sufficient length and width to amply cover the area of damage. If the shingled area is still slowly leaking and cannot be completely stopped, a

length of pipe is placed at the damaged area leading outside the box. The pipe is threaded on the end. When the *cement* cures a cap is screwed onto the pipe thereby stopping all leakage.

CENTEGRADE
See: FAHRENHEIT.

CENTERLINE
An imaginary straight line that runs from the extreme forward end of the bow to the stern that marks the equal amidships distance between the port and starboard sides of a vessel.

CENTERLINE BULKHEAD
A solid vertical partition running fore and aft that is used in some tank barges for the compartmentation of the cargo tanks.

CENTER-WHEEL STEAMBOAT
Essentially a catamaran-type vessel with two hulls, with the wheel between them about two-thirds of the way back from the bow. Not too many were built.

CENTIGRADE
A measurement of water graduated in degrees from the solidification (freezing) of water at 0 degrees to when it boils at 100 degrees. The term is from the Latin *centum,* which is "a hundred". Often called the Celsius Scale, it was invented by a Swedish astronomer in the 1700s and named for him, Anders Celsius. See: FAHRENHEIT.

CENTRIFUGAL PUMP
A type of pump commonly used on tank barges to pump off cargo. These consist of an impeller mounted on a shaft in a casing which spins at high velocity, forcing the liquid to the outer edge of the casing and up into a pipeline. The word derives from the Latin, *centrifugus,* to mean "fleeing from the center".

CERCLA
An acronym for Comprehensive Environmental Response, Compensation and Liability Act. It is the federal statute establishing the legal and financial responsibilities of persons and/or corporations that discharge or otherwise dispose of hazardous substances on or into land, air and the navigable waters of the U.S. It is more often called the Superfund Program. The law and its regulations are primarily administered by the Environmental Protection Agency.

CERTIFICATE OF ENROLLMENT
See: DOCUMENTATION.

CERTIFICATE OF FINANCIAL RESPONSIBILTY (COFR)
A certificate issued by the Federal Maritime Commission attesting that the owner of a tank barge has sufficient financial coverage to pay for any obligations which might be imposed on the barge in case of a spillage of oil or hazardous liquid cargo. It is required to have a copy of this certificate aboard the tank barge.

CERTIFICATE OF INSPECTION
Issued by the USCG and required to be on board all passenger vessels, as well as all tank barges subjected to inspection. The Coast Guard inspects these vessels when they are being constructed and then yearly for defects that must be repaired. Regulations also require that all inspected vessels be drydocked periodically, depending upon their areas of operation. The certificate must be renewed every year for passenger vessels listing the number of persons that it may carry. On tank barges the certificates must be renewed every two years and lists the cargoes the vessel is allowed to carry as well as the date of its last drydocking, and other information.

CERTIFICATION
A statement from a manufacturer that the product it makes is designed and constructed in accordance with Federal regulations that apply to the product.

CETANE NUMBER
A measurement of a diesel fuel's volatility. The higher the *cetane number* the easier the fuel is to ignite. It is similar to the use of the term octane in measuring the volatility of gasoline.

CFR
An acronym for Code of Federal Regulations. The Federal Codes, or regulations, applying to towing vessel operations and crews are mostly found in Titles 33 and 46.

CFS
An acronym for Cubic Feet Per Second. It is a measurement of one cubic foot of water, equaling 7.48 gallons, that moves by any given point in one second. One cubic foot per second equals approximately two acre-feet per day. The USACE measures the flows and current speed by this term in thousands of feet per second, as well as at dam sites to state how much release of water is going through the dam.

CHAFE or CHAFING
The action of constant rubbing of a line or wire on a fitting, the side of a vessel, or other object, resulting in wear or fraying. To reduce excessive wear a doubler plate will sometimes be added on a vessel in a wear area, or chafing gear (consisting of mats, pieces of wood tied to the line, or old canvas wrapped around the line where wear might occur), or the WORMING, PARCELLING AND SERVING of a wire can stop or reduce the chafing. The word is given to us from the Latin *calefacere,* meaning "to make hot", such as the friction of excessive rubbing often does.

CHAIN
1. A series of rocks or rock ledges in the navigable channel.
2. Stiffening rods with turnbuckles to tighten or loosen them. See: CROSS CHAINS, HOG CHAINS, and KNUCKLE CHAINS.
3. A holding line attached to an anchor, or a buoy.
4. To add protection. See: GUARD CHAIN.
5. Used as barge rigging. See: BULL CHAIN, and CHAIN LINKS.

CHAIN DOGS
A small chain fitted with metal spikes used in some river areas by log rafters to hold the floating logs together.

CHAIN LINKS
Short sections of heavy linked *chain* (each link about six inches long) used in rigging when wiring barges together. The *links* are shackled to a barge wire on one end, while the other end of the *chain* is engaged by the PELICAN HOOK of a barge RATCHET, making it easier to take up the slack in the wire when tightening the ratchet by using the appropriate link when hooking up.

CHAIN OF ROCKS CANAL
The *Chain of Rocks* in the Upper Mississippi River was upstream of the city of St. Louis and caused much damage to vessels navigating the region during low water. Just after World War II the USACE started construction of a canal to by-pass the *chain,* which was completed in 1953, consisting of two locks and an 8.4 mile-long canal. A fixed rock dam was constructed across the Mississippi in the vicinity of the *chain.*

CHAIN REACTION
A series of events that are caused to occur usually referring to an initial accident, such as a barge hitting a pier causing a tow breakup with free

floating barges hitting fleeted equipment that break away and damage other vessels in a harbor area; or a small fire that starts at a dock igniting other material and spreading to a tank barge which catches on fire, breaking away to set other equipment ablaze; etc.

CHAIN SLING or STRAP

A short piece of wire containing an eye in one end, with the other end spliced into a set of chain links. Used as part of the rigging when wiring barges together. A particular type of *chain sling* often used on the river is called a HULA HOOP, which is a short piece of wire made into a total loop with its two bitter ends held together with an aluminum swage fitting. The "hula hoop" usually includes a set of chain links.

CHAMBER (LOCK)

The space between the two sets of gates (upstream and downstream), where water is raised or lowered in a LOCK.

CHANDLER

See: BOAT STORE and STORE BOAT.

CHANGE

Like death and taxes it is inevitable, whether it is the weather, barging orders, bosses, or vessels. It makes life interesting and taken as a whole, better.

CHANNEL

1. The bottom, or riverbed, of a navigable stream where the principle amount of water flows. It is the section of a waterway used by vessels to navigate. It can be a natural evolving streambed or one that is artificial, or trained by dikes or other means. If the *channel* has AID(S) TO NAVIGATION defining the limits of project depth or lights to give direction it is called a "marked *channel*". The term derives from the Latin *canalis,* for "channel". See the following terms for *channel*: NARROW, PROJECT, and STABILIZED. Also refer to CANAL and CANALIZE.

2. The radio frequency or station(s) to which a vessel is standing by and monitoring or possibly calling and transmitting with another vessel or shore station. See: RADIO CALL SIGNAL.

CHANNEL BUOY

A buoy(s) that marks the side(s) of a navigable channel. They are usually set at the limit of its project depth width in normal or low water conditions. In high water they are removed or set way out to just act as a guide in crossings or mark the point of a bar.

CHANNEL IMPROVEMENTS

1. The placement of dikes or weirs in a navigable stream to direct the flow of current.
2. The armoring of river or canal banks with revetments to protect the bank from erosion or cutting away.
3. Dredging the navigable channel to maintain project depth.
4. The placement of aids to navigation.

CHANNEL REPORT

A report written, broadcast, or posted on internet sites by a channel inspector of the USCG, and in some cases by the USACE on non-pooled rivers, such as the Missouri R. and the Lower Mississippi R., where channel conditions sometimes rapidly change. They include marks to be steered, soundings in crossings at a particular river gauge, and other information that is pertinent to Pilots. See: RIVER GUIDES.

CHANNEL SPAN

The particular section of a bridge across a waterway that is used for navigation. It is usually the widest span of the bridge as well as having the deepest depth of water. See: BRIDGE LIGHTS for markings.

CHANOINE WEIR

A hinged WEIR or WICKET, three feet, nine inches in width; the length depends on the height of the water to be maintained in the pool of the dam. The weir or wicket is hinged to a concrete foundation on the riverbed. The wicket itself is wooden with a metal frame that is called a HORSE that has a long metal PROP fastened to the middle of the HORSE to hold it in place when upright to stop the flow of water. When the wicket is in the down position and lying on the river bottom and it has to be raised, a MANEUVER BOAT goes out and uses a grapple hook on a cable to catch the top or upper part of the wicket and pull it up. As it does so the PROP also comes up, sliding in a slot or groove in the concrete bed called a HURTER. When the wicket is raised high enough the PROP sliding in the HURTER goes into a niche that allows the wicket to stay upright.

When lowering the wicket, it is pulled forward by the MANUEVER BOAT and the PROP slides out of the niche allowing the wicket to be lowered to the bed of the river. The distance between wickets is about 3 inches. During extreme low flow of the river when more water has to be restrained in the pool, the space between wickets is closed up using long narrow pieces of wood called NEEDLES. The name *chanoine weir* is named after Jacques Chanoine, a Frenchman, who first designed the weir.

CHARACTERISTIC

1. The Navigation Rules define lights and shapes with their *characteristics* in Rule 21, and the Annexes to the Rules. They state visibility, range, color, placement, scope of degrees to be seen, and intervals of flash if required.

2. Aids to navigation *characteristics* generally are color, shape, sound, and flash phases.

CHART

A map of the river. Before 2000 each USACE District published its own version of maps in various formats and sizes. Some were not to scale, some were actual aerial photographs, some were detailed, while others were not. At the turn of the century, the use of GPS, ELECTRONIC CHARTS, and requirements for AIS, enabled the Corps to standardize their *chart* system nationwide.

Early in steamboat days there were few to no *charts* of the river systems as are known today. The USACE had made some surveys but, if available, contained little operative data or information suitable for use by a Pilot. Some private river guides were somewhat useful (see: CRAMER, ZADOK), however, they were mostly just for the Ohio and Lower Mississippi rivers and had little detail. River Pilots during the early days of steamboating had to memorize every detail of the water course as there was little written material in which to refer. The term *chart* comes from the Latin *charta,* meaning "paper".

CHARTER

A contract to hire or lease a vessel for a voyage, or for a period of time. The conditions agreed to appear in a document known as a CHARTER PARTY. The person who charters a vessel is called a "Charterer." Also see: BAREBOAT CHARTER, CHARTER PARTY, and DEMISE CHARTER.

CHARTER PARTY

A contractual document between a vessel owner and a charterer, who is hiring or leasing the vessel. The terms and conditions are set forth in the document. The term comes from the Latin *charta*, meaning paper, then down to the French *charta partie,* meaning "a divided paper agreement". See: BARE BOAT CHARTER and TIME CHARTER.

CHATTAHOOCHEE RIVER

The river starts from a spring in the Appalachian Mountains and creates Lake Lanier, a major water supply for the city of Atlanta. It forms the southern half of the state boundary line between Georgia and Alabama. The river, having run over 400 miles, merges with the Flint River in Florida's panhandle to form the Apalachicola River, which flows into the Gulf of Mexico. After the Civil War steamboat traffic flourished on the river, but by WW I, with the competition from railroads, traffic had drastically declined. The last steamboat left the river in 1921. The stream is a part of the A-C-F navigational system consisting of the Apalachicola, Chattahoochee, and Flint rivers. There is some seasonal river traffic of limited drafts. It derives its name from a Creek Indian word meaning "painted rock". See: APALACHICOLA, CHATTAHOOCHEE, FLINT RIVER SYSTEM.

CHEATER BAR

A piece of pipe about four (plus) feet long of sufficient diameter to fit over the pelican hook of a ratchet or a ratchet handle. It is used to apply increased leverage in hooking up the ratchet's pelican hook and breaking it down over an eye in a barge wire or a chain link. After hooking up it is then placed over the short handle of the ratchet to increase the power advantage when tightening it. It is also sometimes referred to as a "breakdown bar".

CHECK or CHECKING

To reduce, or gradually stop, the forward movement or swing of a vessel. This can be done in a variety of ways, i.e. to back one's engines to "*check* the speed", or to apply opposite rudder "to *check* the vessel's swing", or to slack a line or wire slowly that is in tension while movement is in progress.

CHECK LINE

A line specifically used to slow down or stop a vessel or tow when going into a navigation lock or landing at a dock.

CHECK-LINE LANDING

When a steamboat or towboat does not have enough power to fully stop the tow from continuing to move downstream, or has lost power, the tow is maneuvered as close as possible to the shore and deckhands are sent ashore in a yawl with a line to tie it to a suitable tree or any other object for mooring. The crew aboard the tow then attempts to slow and stop the tow's unrestrained drift in the current by the action of *checking* with the other end of the line. The process of any *checking* is termed *checking her down*.

CHECK PIN

A short "L" shaped, very heavy steel pin inset at various locations inset on a lock wall's side. Used to check movement and to tie off to when locking. Should only be used for tying off as the forces of a large tow can bend, break, or pull out a pin.

CHECK POST

1. The mooring bollard, or bitt, on the top of the lock wall.
2. Vertical braced timbers buried in the coal of a COALBOAT with the head of the timber showing. Used to tie off or used with a CHECK LINE. Different from TIMBERHEADS, which were bolted or welded inside or on the deck of the gunwale of a barge.

CHECK VALVE

A valve contained in a piping system that allows fluid to flow in one direction, but will close automatically if the fluid attempts to return or flow in the opposite direction of its original motional force.

CHEEKS
The side pieces of a BLOCK.

CHEMICAL TRANSPORTATION ADVISORY COMMITTEE (CTAC)
An advisory panel to the USCG, consisting of ship and tank barge operators, and shippers of chemicals by water. CTAC makes recommendations regarding the safe transportation of hazardous products in tank barges, ships, and at vessel-loading facilities.

CHEVRON DIKE
A dike shaped like the rating given to a Private in the Army or somewhat in a "U" or "V" shape; can be pointed upstream or inverted, pointing downstream and used in place of traditional dikes. Sometimes forms a small island outside the dike with a scour hole in the inverted part that attracts certain kinds of fish. It is used generally in side channels of an island to divert stream flow to the main channel, as well as providing environmental benefits to habitat.

CHICAGO RIVER
The river starts from some small streams north of the city of Chicago that join into what is called the North Branch. The whole system of the river consists of the North Branch, the South Branch, the Main Stem, the Sanitary Ship Canal, and the Cal-Sag Channel.

Originally the river flowed into Lake Michigan and was a dumping ground for untreated sewage waste of the populace of the city. Typhoid fever, cholera, and dysentery plagued the citizens. In 1852, over five percent of the people in Chicago died from cholera. In 1887 a scheme was devised to change the flow from the river's terminus at Lake Michigan and route its flow through the Des Plaines and Illinois rivers and on to the Mississippi. To accomplish this task a 28-mile canal was built and completed in 1900 with locks at Lake Michigan and Lockport, IL. In 1910, another eight mile canal was built to divert the wastes from suburban Evanston that discharged into Lake Michigan and divert them to flow to the new "sanitary canal". In 1922, on the south side of Chicago, the Little Calumet River's flow was also reversed from its natural discharge into the Lake and into the new 16-mile long Cal-Sag Channel.

The untreated effluent and its discharges earned the waterway its nickname as "the stinking river". In the 1930 some primary sewage treatment started, but it wasn't until the 1990s that all sewage was properly treated. River Pilots can tell stories of having to enter "Bubbly Creek" to deliver barges when rats ran across the top of the sludge in the slough and the crew could not keep their dinner down because of the smell.

On St. Patrick's Day dye is dumped into the river downtown to paint it green where some of the 45 movable bridges of its courses are located, but are seldom opened. The towboats that operate in this area are RETRACTABLE PILOTHOUSE vessels.

CHICKEN PLAY
The unintelligent actions by WEEKEND CAPTAINS of small boats, especially recreational craft, veering across the bow of a tow, or riding close astern the discharge wake of a towboat's propeller, or water skiing anywhere close to a tow.

CHIEF (ENGINEER)
The short title given to the Chief Engineer on a tug or towboat is *Chief*, who is responsible for the upkeep of the vessel's engines and auxiliary equipment. As with the name for "cap-

tain" the word comes from the Latin *caput,* meaning head. The *Chief* was an indispensable officer aboard a steamboat. The training, for a good one, had to be as extensive, or more so, than for the other officers aboard the vessel, but at a lesser rate of pay. The job didn't require a starched uniform since the engineers were usually sweaty, smudged with oil or grease, and mostly unappreciated by passengers and the owners. The *Chief* had to be a jack of all trades to keep a vessel running. He had to know what every rattle, squeak, or knock meant. He also had to answer a series of BELLS sent by the Pilot, quickly, accurately, and without question. At times the *Chief* was called upon, when racing, for more steam pressure on the boilers than he deemed prudent. If something happened to the boiler or engine he was considered at fault, especially by the Steamboat Boiler Inspector. See: ENGINEER.

On diesel vessels the engine room used to be manned by a *Chief,* assistant engineers (STRIKER), and oilers. Due to technology and the placement of redundant systems on modern towboats, many of the smaller-powered ones have no engineers. A deckhand checks the oil and takes some basic readings letting the Captain know if something is out of set parameters. The larger diesel-powered vessels often have only one engineer. There is a series of monitors on the engine(s) that will set off an alarm if something goes wrong. If minor, the engineer will correct it. If major the home office will send out a crew with parts to fix it.

CHIEF OF ENGINEERS
The General who heads up the USACE in Washington, D.C. The first Chief Engineer, appointed by General Washington in 1775, was Richard Gridley; an ex-British Colonel who's first task was to build the fortification to protect the American Revolutionary soldiers who fought in the Battle of Bunker Hill.

CHIMNEY
The name given to the smokestack(s) on a steamboat. It was where they were required to carry their sidelights after 1852. Sometimes used when referring to the stack(s) of a diesel towboat that is putting out black smoke. The word comes down to us from the Greek *kaminos,* which means "oven".

CHINE
The line on a vessel's hull where the sides and the bottom meet. When the side plating meets at a rather sharp angle as on a tugboat, it is described as *hard-chined.* If the angle is not very sharp, somewhat rounded, it termed *soft-chined.* If the plates are rounded to a flat bottom, as on towboats at this juncture, it is called a *bilge knuckle.* From French *eschine,* meaning "the spine".

CHINSE IRON
A narrow caulking iron blade used to force caulking material into a seam between the planks of a wooden-hulled vessel where the opening, or space, is too narrow to use a regular CAULKING IRON.

CHIPPEWA RIVER
The *Chippewa* is formed by two forks which merge together in north-central Wisconsin forming Lake Chippewa, then from it the river flows out for over 180 miles where it enters the Upper Mississippi River at mile 763, opposite Read's Landing, MN. The river deposited a great deal of sediment at its mouth which formed a delta into the Mississippi which caused the formation of Lake Pepin. At one time the river was an active area of logging. Huge rafts were gathered together at Read's Landing prior to being rafted down river to the lumber mills. No logging

or commercial barging is done presently on the river.

CHIPPING HAMMER
A hammer with a chisel face on one side of the head and a blunt point on the other side, used to remove old paint, rust, or slag when welding. Sometimes called a *slag* or *scale hammer*. A pneumatic *chipping hammer* is used for large jobs. See: NEEDLE GUN.

CHOCK
1. A heavy steel fitting on the deck of a vessel which serves as a fair lead for a line or wire to reduce chafing. A closed *chock* is a totally enclosed oval. An open *chock* has two horns leading up from its base and allows a line or wire to be set in the *chock*. A rolling *chock* has a rolling sheave in its center to further reduce chafing.
2. It can be a stop, such as to prevent a rudder from moving beyond a certain limit. It then takes on the name of what it is used for, i.e. *rudder chock*.
3. It may be of block shape (see: GLUT) or an elongated piece of wood in a "V" shape placed under anything to keep it from shifting due to heavy weather, to brace it, or to stop or reduce vibration in machinery parts. The term is believed to have come from the French *choque,* referring to "a block of wood".

CHOCK-A-BLOCK
When two blocks of a TACKLE come together. Sometimes called *two-block*. Also, both terms are used as slang when referring to something that is extremely tight or fixed right, and also when a tank may be filled to capacity, i.e., "The drinking water tanks are chock-a-block full and running over on the deck."

CHOKE
The act of fouling a set of blocks and tackle by jamming them together. The term probably comes from the artichoke fruit, which is not very tasteful and could cause someone to gag on it.

CHOKE A STUMP or TREE or WILLOW
To tie off or moor a vessel or tow to a tree on the bank.

CHRISTMAS ON THE RIVER
As with sailors overseas on ships or troops in the field, it is a lonely time on the river to be away from loved ones, family and friends. Even though the crew would rather be home than on a towboat, there is usually a spirit of comradeship that prevails when Christmas Day arrives. The following poem tries to capture that spirit. With all apologies to W. Clement Moore who wrote the original poem, 'Twas The Night Before Christmas" in the early 1800s. Also see: SANTA CLAUS.

'Twas the watch just before Christmas on our towboat,
When the Pilot came up to relieve in his overcoat.
The channel report said to proceed with great care,
Because of a most eerie feeling in the air.

The crew changed watches, the forward going to bed,
With sweet dreams of home dancing around in their heads.
Thoughts of wives, preparing the holiday dinner,
If they could be home, it would be a real winner.

The kids would be opening presents with great glee,
Torn paper wrappings as far as the eye could see.
The dog and cat would sniff boxes to find their toy,
A big rawhide bone and a catnip mouse, what joy!

Suddenly, on the tow arose such a clatter,
Turned on the searchlight to see what was the matter.
It flickered, and fluttered, and it wavered, then flashed,
At what I was seeing, the tow I almost crashed.

Light shone on barges covered with new fallen snow,
Gave a bright shining glow to objects on the tow.
And, then, what to my wondering eyes should appear,
But a yawl being pulled by eight little swamp deer.

The yawl's Pilot, he was lively, and he was quick,
And looked like images I'd seen of Old Saint Nick.
But how could that be way out here on this river?
My mind was blank, but up my back ran a shiver.

That yawl's old Pilot was totally in command,
As he shouted orders to the pulling deer band.
They pranced and they tramped to his every beck and call.
I wished my own deckhands were as much on the ball.

"Now BALLAST, now CAVEL, now CAPSTAN and STARBOARD,
On DRYDOCK, on SHACKLE, on BARGE, and you LARBOARD;
Then to the boiler deck, and up over the stack,
Now on with you," as he cracked his whip with a thwack!

It was off with those swamp deer as they rose on high,
Like a flash of lighting as they flew through the sky.
Up over the rigging, and the bank top they flew,
Their yawl full of goodies and that old Pilot, too.

Then in a twinkling heard on the pilothouse roof,
Was a prancing and pawing of each little hoof.
I spilled my coffee on the deck and turned around,
In came that bearded Pilot with a mighty bound.

The old codger was dressed in red, with lots of moss;
How did he get in? I was at a total loss.
He had a big bundle of stuff flung o'er his back.
He was like a peddler just opening his pack.

His eyes – how they twinkled, one was red and one green;
On a woman, or a man, never had I seen.
Perhaps reminding him of the Rule of the Sky,
To prevent collision risks was the reason why.

Cheeks as roses, his nose like red cherries, but large,
The color of the flag on a tank cargo barge.
His mouth had a smile that lit up the whole space,
Shining through the white beard covering all his face.

He had an old ivory pipe held between his lips,
With blue smoke bellowing forth like fog over ships.
I warned him the pilothouse was to be smoke-free.
He laughed, said "Government regs don't apply to me".

He went to the galley and poured himself a cup,
And looked to see where the stockings might be hung up.
The engine room he then went, and saw hanging there,
Were crew skivvies strung up to dry,

many a pair.

Laughing, wondering what the world was coming to,
He filled those skivvies full, and now who could argue.
He put in work gloves, rope knives, a couple of books,
Socks, candy bars, and other stuff, but no fishhooks.

When finished he then climbed the aft ladder to where,
His team of swamp deer, waited to take to the air.
In his yawl he jumped and gave his whistle a toot,
And with a quick kick to the brake with his red boot.

Off that old yawl went into the dark starry night,
To visit some more towboats, giving them delight.
Then I heard a clear voice as he faded from sight,
HAPPY CHRISTMAS TO ALL, AND TO ALL A GOOD NIGHT!

The crew was now up, the 6 to 12 watch to stand,
When the Chief came in saying, "Now ain't this life grand"?
To the engine room the entire boat crew now went,
Seeing their skivvies filled, much like a circus tent.

There was an oil can for Chief, can opener for Cook;
I wondered why he left the Pilot a prayer book.
For the Mate he left a warm woolen stocking hat,
All crew members got a little of this and that.

Then I got to the stuff that said was marked for me.
There was a gift-wrapped package which I opened to see.
It was the best present of all that it could ever be,
Jim Swift's mighty *Backing Hard Into History*.

So now all you men and women on river tows,
Who have to be there whether it rains, hails, or snows,
And Christmas comes around and there is no relief,
Remember the entire day need not end in grief.

Go down to the galley for pie and a drumstick,
Wolf all the good food down, without becoming sick.
Turn in to your bunk and dream of happy sweet things,
And all of the bestowed blessings that our life brings.

You may wish you could be in some other far place,
But on this Christmas Day it will not be the case.
However, if you all believe in Old Saint Nick,
Your life has probably had more than one free kick.

May all who receive this most humble little verse,
Remember that there are others whose times are worse.
Be happy you're here in the good old U.S.A.
We'd rather be here than elsewhere any old day.

CHRISTMAS TREE
1. A term used in reference to a section of electrical wire with three or more outlets on it to allow various lights or other power requirements to be plugged into it. Since the running lights are green, red, and yellow, some wag probably coined the term to reflect the colored lighting arrangement.

2. Also used when referring to a pipe junction with three or more inlets or outlets.

CHROMATICITY
See: COLOR SPECIFICATIONS

CHUTE
1. Usually a narrow, swift, short section of a river that is a CUT-OFF of the river. Sometimes the *chute* captures the major flow of the river and becomes the main channel. If a *chute* is unrestricted by a dike or other obstruction and the current is not too swift, Pilots may use it rather than the main channel in high water to shorten the distance to travel.

2. A backwater off the main channel where a dock or tie-off mooring for barges might be located.

3. A narrow opening in a mill dam to allow flatboats to pass through.
See: NAVIGABLE CHUTES and SLOPES.

CIF
An acronym used for "Cost, Insurance, and Freight", that indicates the insurance and freight charges are included in the cost of the goods being shipped.

CIRCUS BOATS
Besides transporting cargoes and people efficiently, riverboats have been used for a variety of other purposes such as excursion trips, showboats, hospitals, and even for traveling circuses. Although circus performers might travel on different packetboats to various cities on a tour, in the latter half of the 1800s some circus owners bought their own steamers, and eventually barges, to carry their animals and performers to the different cities they visited. Samuel Clemens wrote of these in his novel *Huckleberry Finn*.

CITY BOATS
The term given to a series of Lower Mississippi River propeller-driven steam towboats named for cities. They were operated by the old Inland Waterways Corporation, then later Federal Barge Line. They were built by the Marietta Mfg. Co. in 1921 with a stern tunnel and had both flanking and steering rudders, making a significant change from the traditional sternwheelers. Their hulls measured 200 x 40 x 8, and had 1800 hp. The STATE BOATS were operated on the Upper Mississippi.

CITY CLASS (CIVIL WAR)
In the Civil War these were a group of seven Union ironclad gunboats named for cities along the Upper Mississippi and Ohio rivers; namely the *ST. LOUIS, CAIRO, CRONDELET, CINCINNATI, MOUND CITY and PITTSBURG* (no "H"). They were built by James B. Eads and designed by Samuel M. Pook, and became known as "Pook's Turtles". The most well known one is the *U.S.S. CAIRO* which saw little duty, but was sunk by an electrically detonated torpedo on the Yazoo River about seven miles above Vicksburg. The hulk was discovered about 1960. It was salvaged and partly reconstructed; now residing in the Vicksburg National Military Park.
See: IRONCLADS.

CLAIM
A submission for payment by a shipper to a carrier for alleged loss or damage to their cargo while in the custody and care of the carrier.

CLAM-SHELL BUCKET
A type of grab bucket which, when attached to a crane, is used to move bulk material such as coal, salt, sand, gravel, grain, and other products. It is hinged to open and close, resembling the action of a clam as it opens and closes its shell.

CLAPPER
1. The striker piece of a vessel's BELL (see).

2. The leather closure flap valve on a SPRING POLE PUMP box.

CLARK, CAPT. WILLIAM

A co-captain of the Lewis and Clark expedition which went up the Missouri River of the new Louisiana Purchase and on to the west coast. Born in 1770, he was the brother of George Rogers Clark, who was a leader in the French and Indian war, and who resided in the areas of Louisville, KY, and Clarksville, IN. Clark met Meriwether Lewis, who served under him when he was building forts along the east bank of the Mississippi River.

In October 1803 Lewis brought a flatboat constructed in the Pittsburgh area down to Louisville, shook hands with Clark and shortly thereafter commenced their trip of "Discovery". Lewis and Clark started up the Missouri River in May of 1804. The expedition returned to St. Louis in 1806. Clark married in 1808 and was a businessman in St. Louis arranging the trading of furs. In 1813 he was named Governor of the Missouri Territory. He died of natural causes in 1838.

CLASS or CLASSIFICATION

1. A vessel built to *class* is one that is built to rules set by a classification society and is inspected while being constructed, as well as on a periodic basis while in operation in order to maintain its classification. Riverboats and barges built to *class* are usually inspected by the American Bureau of Shipping (ABS).
2. A grouping of vessels with similar characteristics, such as size, horsepower, design, etc. and usually constructed in the same shipyard.

CLASS or TYPE OF FIRE

See: FIRE EXTINGUISHMENT.

CLEAR

1. To remove an obstruction, as in "*Clear* the timberhead of that fouled line".
2. To remove gear from a place, i.e. "*Clear* the stern deck of loose rigging as the store boat will tie up there", or "*Clear* those barrels out of the engine room and get ready to put them on the fuel flat".
3. The state of the weather, as opposed to hazy, misty, rainy, foggy, etc.
4. To be by or past a place, i.e. to *clear* a point of land, or to depart and be *clear* of a lock, or to *clear* the fender works of a bridge. As example, "I'm *clear* of the turn buoy, you can come ahead and I'll see you on two"; or a deckhand saying to the Pilot, "You're *clear* of the bullnose on the port side", meaning that the tow is past the end of the bullnose.

CLEARANCE

1. The horizontal distance between two structures, such as bridge piers.
2. The vertical distance between a bridge span or a power line crossing and the surface of the river at a given gauge.
3. The horizontal distance between a vessel and/or its tow and an object it is close to, such as a bridge pier, a dock, or another vessel.
4. The vertical distance between the deepest draft of a vessel and the sill of a lock chamber or the bed of a river.
5. The AIR GAP between the highest projection of a vessel and an object above it.
6. Permission to proceed by a regulatory body such as the USCG or the USACE, if a hold had been imposed for a safety or security reason.

CLEAT

1. A small KEVEL or a very miniature CAVEL. Used for the same purpose in securing a line on a small recreational craft or sailboat. Used on towboats and tugs only to make fast

the halyard on the flag staff. It is a Navy term for what rivermen call a CAVEL.

2. A strip of wood nailed transversely on a sloping gangplank to keep a person from slipping when embarking or leaving a vessel.

CLEMENS, SAMUEL LANGHORNE

Born in 1835. Clemens said he came in with Halley's Comet and would be disappointed if he didn't go out with it. The comet fulfilled his expectations as it came again in 1910 when he died. A writer of many stories and novels and *Life on the Mississippi* which recounts his learning to become a river pilot. It is widely quoted and probably the best descriptive account of steamboating before the Civil War. He appropriated the sobriquet MARK TWAIN (see) from Capt. Isaiah Sellers who used it when writing occasional articles for a New Orleans newspaper on river conditions. Clemens wrote a biting parody of Sellers' writings when he was still a "cub", signing it "Sergeant Fathom." The proud Capt. Sellers never wrote another article and never forgave Clemens

In today's regulatory procedures, Clemens probably would not be able to get a Pilot's license as he was color blind. Some steamboat pilots disparaged his ability (probably through jealousy), but Capt. Horace Bixby, who taught Clemens the art of piloting, is reported to have said he was a fine pilot, having run some of the largest steamers of the period, and never had a bad accident.

CLERK (STEAMBOAT)

The *clerk* was a sort of business agent who took care of the needs of passengers and kept track of the freight and expenses aboard a steamer. His authority varied but he was on board to look out for the interests of the owner. He was assisted by a MUD CLERK.

CLINCH

To turn over the end of a nail driven through planking so it will not work out; or to burr down the end of a bolt or rivet to keep it permanently in place. The word is a variant of "clench" and means "to hold something firmly or securely".

CLINCH RIVER

The Clinch rises in the Appalachians of southwest Virginia. It is joined by the Powell River in the TVA Norris Dam reservoir north of Knoxville, TN, and continues for a total of about 300 miles before joining the Tennessee River just north of Kingston, TN (TN River mile 568), about 80 miles downriver from Knoxville, TN, in the Watts Bar Pool. The dam provides limited navigational depths up the river for about 20 miles. The river took its name from a hunter named Clinche, since people in area had taken to calling it Clinche's River when he lived and hunted there. In its early settlement days, timber rafting was a main source of commerce.

CLINGAGE

Any liquid residue of cargo that adheres to the inside of a tank or is left in the cargo tanks of a barge after the product has been discharged, usually referring to heavy oils or asphalt. The word is related to the Dutch *klingen,* which meant "to adhere".

CLINOMETER

A device that indicates the degree of list in a vessel. Not seen much on the river, but there are sure some towboats that could use them.

CLOGGED PIPELINE

1. A pipe with an obstruction in it, such as a sounding tube or sump well pipe.

2. The movement of a company's barge fleet is compared to the smooth

flow of an efficient pipeline. When the fleet is out of synchronization with too many barges at one end of a river and not enough at the other end due to weather (hurricanes, floods, etc.) or an accident, or lock outage, the *barge pipeline becomes clogged*. See: LOGISTICAL BALANCE.

CLOSE

1. A very narrow or tight channel.
2. The setting of buoys in a narrow crossing.
3. To come nearer to an object, dock, or another vessel, as in, "We are *closing* on the *M/V NEVERSINK*".

CLOSE ABOARD

Something that is near, almost alongside, i.e. "That damn water skier is *close aboard*".

CLOSED CHOCK

A chock that is not open at the top.

CLOSED GAUGING

A system on a tank barge where the amount of cargo in its tanks can be measured without opening an ULLAGE HATCH to take soundings or readings. These systems are required for carriage of certain hazardous cargoes.

CLOSURE or CHUTE DIKES

A dike structure that reaches from the upper end of an island to the main shore, thus blocking the flow of water through a chute or back channel, which allows an increase of the flow into the main channel of a stream. These were the first training works used on the Upper Mississippi River to provide for a navigable channel. They were basically alternate layers of brush mats called FASCINES and rock which would capture sand and sediment. By laying them on opposite sides of the channel, thereby restricting the river's width, they allowed the main flow to scour and increase the channel's depth.

CLOUD(S)

A collection of vapor in the air which a Pilot enjoys looking at on a bright sunny day, or dreads when the sky darkens with them indicating a storm, or when they lie close to the surface of the water as a heavy mist or fog. In general the types are:

1. Highest or Upper Type – Cirrus group, appears wispy or fibrous, given the name by seamen as *mare's tails*. When cumulus-type clouds are high they form what is termed a *mackerel sky*.
2. Middle-Height Type – Alto group, can form a sort of veil, or be of the cumulus type, which is then called a *woolpack* by seamen.
3. Low-Height Type – Strata group, appears as heavy white or gray masses and can even lay on the water as mist or fog. The cumulonimbus cloud is the storm or thunder cloud which has a rising vertical mass and is very dark.

CLUTTER

Interference with a clear picture on the radar scope from a variety of causes, such as snow or rain, or other atmospheric conditions. Heavy *clutter* can totally obscure small objects such as a buoy, or recreational craft.

COAL

A combustible carbonized rock, usually brown-grey to shiny black. It can be high BTU or low BTU; *coal* can be called soft, high or low sulfur; can have high or low ash content; can be deep-mined underground or strip-mined by removing a soil overburden and digging out the exposed *coal* layers. When used as fuel on steamboats it was estimated that one ton of coal was equal to two cords of wood.

Coal is one of the important commodities moved by barges on our inland waters in terms of tonnage. Huge barge fleets move coal to electric generating plants to allow people and industries to flip a switch and be able to turn on their electric lights. The term comes from old English *col* meaning "glowing embers", which was derived from the Dutch *kool* and the German *kohle*.

COAL BUSHEL
At one time in the 1800s the movement of coal was dug, measured, sold, and transported by the bushel. Each bushel weighed about 75 pounds. It took 26 2/3 bushels to make a ton.

COAL FLEETS
Areas where large numbers of *coal* barges are tied off, either awaiting movement to a dock or to be placed in tow to transit to another destination. Oftentimes these fleets are seen near electric generating plants.

COAL PASSERS & WOOD CARRIERS
In the days of steamboats when the fuel used was coal, the *passers* were the men who wheeled the coal from where it might be stored on the steamer, such as on the head of the boat, or from the coal fuel flat alongside the steamer, taking it to where the firemen could easily get to it to fire the furnace. If the steamboat burned wood it was the job of the *wood carriers* to bring it aboard from a wood lot when WOODING UP, or to go on the bank and cut wood and bring it on board.

COAL RIVER
The *Coal River* is formed by two streams called Big and Little Coal River that merge together and eventually empty into the KANAWHA RIVER at St. Albans, WV, at mile 45. The river is almost unknown today to navigation interests, however, in the mid-1700s a settler discovered that the valley through which the river flowed contained a great deposits of a type of bituminous cannel coal that could be made into coal oil to provide illumination giving the river its present name. Channel improvements by local mining companies started in 1748 to keep the river navigable most of the time to a depth of four feet to Peytona, a distance of 30 miles. Eight crib and lumber locks (24 feet wide by 125 feet long) and dams were built in this short area with lifts from eight to 15 feet. Seasonal flooding often damaged the structures. Then in the late 1870s a disastrous flood destroyed most of the dams and it was estimated that it would cost a million and a half dollars to rebuild and replace them which was deemed uneconomical. By that time the development of kerosene negated the need for coal oil and many of the mines closed.

COAL SPREADERS
Those persons employed by a coal tipple operator to make sure the coal which was loaded into COALBOAT barges in steamboat days was spread evenly throughout the barge. Sometimes called a *coal trimmer*.

COALBOAT
1. A boat, and tow, that operates exclusively in transporting coal. Used in the past to refer to the tows that operated mainly above Cincinnati, Ohio, but since there are so many different areas where coal tows now operate it has a more generic flavor.

2. A wooden barge used in the 1800s, fairly large, but built for usually only one trip south from the Pittsburgh, PA area to New Orleans, where the coal was off-loaded and the barge was broken up and used for lumber. The practice was phased out in the early 1900s. In the early days of the coal industry on the Monongahela River these barges were floated out and steered by long sweep oars like the ones used on log rafts.

COALBOAT WATER
Before canalization of the Ohio

River, when the river was at a low stage, fleets of barges loaded with coal would sit in the local harbor, particularly in the vicinity of Pittsburgh, waiting for rain runoff and a rise in the river to occur. When there was a sufficient gauge of water it became *coalboat water* and all the waiting steamboats with coal barges in tow would head downriver. The term was also used when there was sufficient water at Louisville and the steamers could run the FALLS OF THE OHIO. Sometimes it was also referred to as the "coal rise".

COALING

As timber became hard to get and more expensive steamboat owners and private entities set up yards at various points along the river where the steamers could get coal fuel for the boiler furnaces on their vessels. See: WOODING UP.

COAMING

1. The raised border around the edge of a hatch to keep water from running into the opening.
2. Raised steel side framework above the deck line around the hold or hopper of a barge. If it is a covered barge the covers sit on the *coaming*. See: CUBIC CAPACITY for "high cube" barge *coamings*.
3. On a deck barge, the framework at sides and sometimes the ends of the CARGO BOX.

COAST AND GEODETIC SURVEY

This is the name formerly used, but is still given, by the agency now named the National Ocean Survey which is part of the NATIONAL OCEANIC and ATMOSPHERIC ADMINISTRATION (NOAA), that is one of the principal agencies to provide charts for coastal and ocean areas. They also publish the COAST PILOT volumes.

COAST GUARD

See: U.S. COAST GUARD

COAST GUARD DAY

The day, 4 August 1790, in which the USCG officially recognizes the founding of its service from the "Revenue Cutter" days.

COAST PILOT

A series of volumes published by the NATIONAL OCEAN SURVEY that gives guidance to the coastal waters of the U.S. including sailing directions on near coastal areas and information data on ports and structures therein.

COASTWISE

The *coastwise* movement of cargo is generally thought by many to be traffic between the coastal ports of our country. In reality the trade applies to cargo moving between any two ports in the United States, including that between Pittsburgh and Paducah, Minneapolis and Memphis, Sioux City and St. Louis, or Helena and Houston, etc. In reality, all cargo moving on our inland waterway system is trading *coastwise*.

COATINGS

A material that is applied to the components of a vessel to protect them from deterioration. This was termed painting until the development of synthetic primers and finish substances that give greater protection and last longer. They come in various generic names such as vinyl, epoxies, zincs, etc.

C.O.B.

An acronym for Container-On-Barge. See: CONTAINER.

COCKED HAT

A triangular shaped wooden block that was used at the flange of a paddle wheel to brace the wheel's arms. It also refers to a triangular wooden reinforcement piece that was used to brace the futtocks and floor timbers where they met at the side of a wooden hull. The term derives from the appearance of the piece like a conical hat set to side of one's head.

CODE OF FEDERAL REGULATIONS (CFR)

The general and permanent rules that have been promulgated by federal agencies to implement and interpret the statutes enacted by Congress by which citizens and corporations are required to follow. The Federal Code is divided into 50 parts, called Titles, each of which represents a broad range of issues. The two that most affect navigational operations are Title 33 and Title 46. See: UNITED STATES CODE.

CODGER

Mostly used with the prefix "old". Describes an aging, or aged riverman who is somewhat eccentric when using or describing the various terms of the river, steamboats, tugs, or riverboats.

COFFEE

The exquisite nectar of the gods which most Pilots could not do without while standing a watch, whether it be regular roast, dark roast, or chicory blend.

COFFERDAM

1. A space between two bulkheads to keep cargo in one compartment from contaminating an adjacent compartment's cargo in case there is a leak. Sometimes used in tank barges that carry certain products that can stand no pollutants.
2. A temporary, mostly watertight, enclosure that is constructed in a waterway, usually of interlocking sheet piling. The existing water is then pumped out, allowing men to work on a construction project in the dry below the existing water level. Most navigation locks are built in this manner, and many bridge piers. When the construction is completed the *cofferdam* is removed.
3. Sometimes small enclosures are made around a vessel to make repairs below the waterline, especially when involved in salvage work.

COIL

1. Line that is neatly laid down, or wound, in ring-like concentric circles usually in a tier, one circle on top of another, in order that it can be fed, or payed out without becoming tangled and possibly kink. The word comes from the Latin *colligere,* meaning "to gather together".
2. The act of *coiling* a line in concentric circles. Nearly all line used on the river is right-hand laid and must be coiled in a clockwise direction, in other words, from left to right or "with the sun". If not, it will not coil properly and tend to kink when used.
3. Types of *coiling* actions are FAKE and FLEMISH.
4. Line or rope is sold and bought by the *coil,* usually in lengths of 600' or 1200'.
5. The tubes used in tank barges to heat cargoes that tend to solidify when cooled. The tubes, or *coils,* may be of serpentine pipe construction, or of inverted angles or channels welded to the inner deck tank floor connected to a supply header. This latter type allows for easier cleaning of internal tanks. Steam injected into the *coils* is most frequently used as the heating agent when at docks, but if the cargo must be under continuous heat a special oil or liquid is used as the heating substance.

COLD WELL

A tank on a steamboat that receives water from the SEA CHEST and is pumped through the feed water system to the heater and eventually to the boilers.

COLLAR

A term used for a closure plate placed around an opening in a watertight bulkhead or decking where piping or other structures have to go through. It insures there will be no leakage to compromise the integrity of compartments. The plate is used where necessary in both vertical and horizontal plating. The word is from the Latin *collare,* relating to "the neck". The name was possibly adapted as the plate is fitted "around" the protrusion through the plating.

COLLISION

The striking together of two underway vessels, with or without a tow, resulting in some degree of reportable damage. If a vessel strikes a fixed bridge, a dock, a lock wall, a moored vessel, or similar such fixed object it is termed an ALLISION. The term is from the Latin *collidere,* meaning "to strike together".

THE POSSIBLE COLLISION

The crossing vessel was burdened I did say;
So I kept my course and speed coming what may,
To the starboard side I continued to lay,
But the crossing vessel was steering over my way.

The tow came on as a single blast I blew,
The vessel crossing answered not, then I knew,
His knowledge of the Rules was mostly askew;
This day was one I most certainly would rue.

On he did come, so I started backing full,
The whistle cord, I did grab and five times pull;
Whether we could stop in time was most doubtful,
Engine screaming, vessel shaking, most fearful.

Only barely did he miss our bow ahead,
As he slid on by and upriver he fled.
On radio I called to that Pilot and said,
"What do you think you were doing, you knucklehead"?

He answered apologetically, and pled,
On the phone with wife before she went to bed.
Told him if he didn't want to see barges spread,
All over the river, keep sharp lookout ahead.

I watched him pass and fade into the night,
Gave thanks to the Pilot at a greater height.
The Rules must be followed both by day and night,
So to prevent a collision, do what's right.

"A collision at sea can ruin your entire day." This famous quote is attributed to Thucyides who said it about 2500 years ago. The same reaction can be said of vessels coming into collision on the rivers. Another is, "The best place to know the rules and the worst place to study them is in a collision approach".

COLLISION BEARING

A bearing where two vessels are converging with one another and the risk of collision is apparent if appropriate action is not taken. Navigation Rule 7(d)(i) states: "such risk shall be deemed to exist if the compass bearing of an approaching vessel does not appreciably change". River vessels do not take bearings as they are always in curving channels and constantly changing course. However, the relative bearings in all vessel encounters must be closely watched to avoid the risk of collision.

COLLISION BULKHEAD

The foremost transverse watertight bulkhead in a vessel's hull. It is designed so the vessel will remain afloat if its bow is damaged and becomes flooded. The *collision bulkhead* limits the flooding from the rest of the vessel and keeps it contained in the bow void.

COLLISION COURSE

The course of one or more vessels, that if maintained without change of course or speed will result in a collision. See: COLLISION BEARING.

COLLISION MAT

A heavy piece of canvas or other suitable material lowered over the side of a vessel that has been holed, or has some other aperture in the hull. After placement, the flooded compartment of the vessel is pumped and the *collision mat* is sucked against the hull by the exterior pressure allowing temporary repairs to be made. See: FOTHERING.

COLOR SPECIFICATIONS or CHROMATICITY

The standard for the color of navigation lights required under the Navigation Rules, as determined by the International Commission on Illumination and found in Annex I of the NAVRULES in section 84.13.

COLREGS

An acronym for the International Regulations for Prevention of Collisions at Sea, that were enacted in 1972, but which have had numerous amendments to update them since they went into effect. They are the Navigation Rules required to be used by vessels when they leave the waters governed by the U.S. Inland Navigation Rules. See: INLAND RULES and NAVIGATION RULES.

COLUMBIA-SNAKE RIVER SYSTEM

Although the *Columbia-Snake river system* is not a part of the Western Rivers, it must be mentioned here as our brethren of the West Coast share a commonality of steamboats, towboats, tugs, and barges with those that ply the rivers of the Mississippi Basin. This dates from the time when Lewis and Clark floated down the Ohio, keeled up the Mississippi and Missouri rivers, crossed our continental divide, paddled down the Clearwater River (a tributary of the Snake River), and then entered the Lower Snake River until it joined the Columbia before finally concluding their trip on its waters as they flowed down to the Pacific Ocean. They were the pathfinders that linked our nation's lands from the early settlers on the Atlantic coast to the Pacific by river travel.

The Columbia River starts its journey from a lake in the mountains of British Columbia, Canada, about 2650 feet above sea level. Its waters flow north from the Rocky Mountains and then its path turns south to the State of Washington before turning west along the boundary line with Oregon, and finally into the Pacific Ocean. It travels about 1200 miles (465 in Canada) from its source to the sea and its basin drains more acrefeet of water at its mouth than any other river in the U.S. except the Mississippi River.

Some of the first explorers entering the mouth of the Columbia believed it could be the entrance to the possible Northwest Passage leading from the Pacific across the inland seas to the Atlantic Ocean. It was called the "River of the West". Its official name, Columbia, as we know it today was given to it by a Captain Robert Gray of a sailing trading vessel which was named the *COLUMBIA*. Early trade on the river was by bateaux carrying bales of furs downriver by trappers.

The first steamboat trade was started in the mid-1800s from Astoria

COLUMBIA-SNAKE CONT.

near the mouth of the Columbia up to Portland, OR, and later the trade was extended about 160 miles upriver from its mouth to the Cascade area which presented the first obstacle to navigation. Another impediment a little further upstream was the *dalles,* which in French means "stones". To overcome these problems locks were built over a period of almost 20 years in the last quarter of the 19th Century. In 1937 during the Depression, the Bonneville Lock & Dam was built at the foot of the Cascades reach that inundated the former locks and provided an improved channel depth. Later three more locks were built upsteam (The Dalles, John Day, and McNary) to provide a reliable channel to the SNAKE RIVER.

The *Columbia-Snake* system is not only an important navigation artery but also has great hydroelectric development. The system's generating capacity exceeds 21,000,000 KW. The Columbia River has ten main tributaries in her total system. The major one is the Snake River which provides about half of its entire final discharge.

The Snake River starts off the continental divide in Wyoming from the Grand Teton mountain range and flows over a thousand miles until it joins the Columbia in its travel to the sea. In the early days of the white man's intrusion into the area trapping was the main source of harvest. Settlement mainly came from families who gradually moved into the area from along the west coast. Timber and then farming became the main trades. Today, multi-purpose dams on the Snake provide for the generation of power as well as navigation through four dams up to Lewiston, Idaho, about 140 miles above where it enters the Columbia River.

The other major tributary, the Willamette River, flows northward from its source in the coastal area of the Cascade Mountains of Oregon for about 187 miles, entering the Columbia system at the city of Portland. Agriculture was the early commerce from its fertile valley of farms which made its way downriver to San Francisco. In the last quarter of the 1800s the USACE made a survey of the river and Congress appropriated monies for wing dams to somewhat develop a navigational channel. Private operators, wanting better utilization of the river, built a series of locks to move wheat out of the valley. Later, in 1915, they sold the structures to the U.S. government, which after rehabilitation are still in service.

COLUMBUS DAY

Celebrated each October "to commemorate the landing of Christopher Columbus on an unidentified island in the Caribbean" over 500 years ago. Columbus did not keep good records of his port call. On Christmas Eve 1492 his flagship *SANTA MARIA* grounded at Hispaniola and sank the next day. No marine casualty report was filed. On the return voyage, he landed first in Lisbon, Portugal, rather than in Palos, Spain (his official destination), and failed to file an advance notice of arrival. It was events like this that resulted in the Port State Control program. (Taken from the Haight Gardner Report)

COMBINE

"The former Monongahela River Consolidated Coal & Coke Company of Pittsburgh which, formed in 1901, operated more than sixty steamers in its twenty years of existence;" (Fred Way). The *Combine* set near-monopoly pricing of coal during its existence. All its vessels had the letters R.C. painted on each side of the pilothouse which stood for "River Coal".

COMBUSTIBLE

1. Any material that can catch fire and burn easily.

2. Any liquid having a flash point above 80 degrees Fahrenheit. See: FLAMMABLE LIQUID which is divided into classes of "A", "B" and "C".

3. Combustible liquid is divided into class "D" which has a flashpoint above 80 degrees and below 150 degrees F (kerosene, etc.) and class "E" which has a flashpoint of 150 degrees and above (diesel fuel, bunker C, asphalt, etc.).

COMBUSTIBLE GAS INDICATOR

An instrument that is used to detect and measure the explosive or hazardous atmosphere in a tank or enclosed space.

COME ABOARD

A greeting extended to a visitor to come on board one's vessel.

COME AHEAD ON HER

A phrase used by a Deck Mate to the Pilot to indicate that the tow needs to move forward. Also used when slowly moving through a bridge or at a lock and the tow has cleared the last obstruction to indicate that any danger is over.

COME HELL OR HIGH WATER

A phrase to mean that a person can overcome all obstacles in order to accomplish a task. It might be the confident expression used by a Pilot (or others) when a dispatcher on the shore calls the Pilot and asks if he can handle 40 loads from Cairo Fleet to New Orleans. Sometimes he wishes he had high water and then at other times he might find out what *Hell* is like in flooding conditions. Another phrase for the situation is, "Just load up the old mule, she can carry anything".

No one knows just when and where the phrase originated, but it would seem logical that it was uttered by people striving to make a go of it along the banks of a rising river believing they could make it into the next year *come hell or high water*. Numerous authors have taken on the expression and have used it in the title of their writings or music. Regarding river subjects there is a book by Michael Gillespie on steamboat history, one by Mike Jacobs on the 1997 Red River flood, and one by Michael Dyson regarding hurricane Katrina in 2005.

COME-ALONG

A portable cable or chain hand-operated hoist used for pulling or lifting objects.

COME-AND-GO-BOAT

Any towboat that makes good time in a fairly steady run, going up- and down-stream, and seldom has any lay-up time for repairs or delays.

COME-BACK LINE

A line or wire used to moor a vessel or tow where the tie-off line eye is taken ashore, then put around the object used to hold the vessel and brought back on board and placed on a fitting. The standing part of the line is then made fast. This method facilitates casting off when the vessel is departing without having to send a crew member ashore to unfasten the line, as well as adding strength to the tie-off by having it two-parted. Occasionally, if not put out properly, it can pull or saw down a lot of small timber. It is sometimes called a *high-water tie* or a *running tie*.

COME 'ROUND

Term used for direction for steering, as in, "*Come 'round* to starboard and hold on the daymark on the right bank", or, "*Come round* to port and hold on that saddle in the trees".

COMMANDANT

The Officer, appointed by the

President, confirmed by the Senate, who is the director of the U.S. Coast Guard, a four-star Admiral.

COMMERCE
There are a lot of activities involved in *commerce,* such as buying, selling, trading, labor, agreements, etc, but for the riverman it is the transportation of commodities or products by barge from one place to another. The word is from the Latin *commercium,* with *com* meaning "together" and with *merx* meaning merchandise or trade.

COMMON CARRIER
Although the term has a broad interpretation in law, in the river trade it is considered a regulated carrier of freight that is available to all shippers at a published TARIFF, or rate. The last published general commodity tariff was in 1976, but almost all freight moving on the rivers is now by contract.

COMPANIONWAY
Generally, any internal passageway on a tug or towboat, including the stairs leading to another deck.

COMPANY NOTCH
Running the engine(s) at normal full speed ahead, but not at overload speed.

COMPARTMENT
Any separate room or space on a tug or towboat, or a void space on a barge, which is divided by bulkheads.

COMPARTMENTATION
A partitioning of a vessel's hull by watertight transverse, and sometimes longitudinal, bulkheads. A damage control design to ensure the vessel stays afloat if one or more (depending upon the design) hull compartments are damaged and flooded.

COMPASS
An instrument that gives the heading of a vessel based on the magnetic North Pole. Most towboats do not carry a *compass* unless it is associated with a GYROCOMPASS, however, tugs generally are equipped with one. Riverboats often are equipped with what is called a SWING METER that works on the gyro principle and indicates when the vessel is starting to move in one direction or the other off course. The word *compass* appears to have been developed from the lodestone in the days when the Vikings traveled the seas. It comes originally from the Latin *compassare,* meaning "to pace out", and then to the French, meaning "to measure"; however, there is no definitive agreement as to why this device to direct the course of vessels obtained its name. *Com* is Latin for "together" with passus as "pace or step out", so perhaps it is for taking a step in a trip together in the right direction.

COMPASS ROSE
The circular graduation from 0 degrees to 360 degrees showing the points of a compass. It is shown on nautical charts to lay out and measure distances, but is seldom ever seen on the maps or charts of inland river. River and canal boatmen always know which way they are headed and how far it is to the next destination.

COMPETENT PERSON
Defined by OSHA in 29 CFR 1923.32(f) as: "one who is capable of identifying existing and predictable hazards in the surroundings or working conditions which are unsanitary, hazardous, or dangerous to employees, and who has authorization to take prompt corrective measures to eliminate them".

COMPETITION
The main *competition* to river transportation is the railroads. Other competing modes are pipelines and trucking. Although transportation

modal *competition* is real it is also complementary to each other. Rail, pipeline, and trucks bring cargo to river terminals to be loaded into barges, as well as pick up and further distribute the cargoes that are brought to the terminal by barge.

COMPOSITE UNIT

The Inland Navigation Rules state: "A *composite unit* is interpreted to be the combination of a pushing vessel and the vessel being pushed ahead that are rigidly connected by mechanical means so they react to sea and swell as one vessel. Mechanical means does not include lines, wires, hawsers, or chains." Therefore, a river towboat connected to a tow is NOT a *composite unit*. See: DEEP-NOTCH TUG-BARGE.

CONDENSING ENGINE

A steam engine that sends the spent or exhausted steam into a cooling tank in order that it may be reused in the boiler. The steam flows around a set of boiler tubes that are fed cooling water. The tubes absorb the heat of the steam, *condensing* it.

CONE SHAPE

A *cone shape* is described in the Inland Navigation Rules, Annex I, as a black day shape that "shall have a base diameter of not less than 0.6 meter and a height equal to its diameter". The *cone shape(s)* shall indicate a condition of navigation and shall be displayed how, when and where required as found in the Navigation Regulations, Part C.

CONFINED SPACE

Defined by NIOSH as: "A space which by design has limited openings for entry and exit, unfavorable natural ventilation which could contain or produce dangerous air contaminants, and which is not intended for continuous employee occupancy". The document goes on to state: "The standard is designed not only to make the confined space safe for the worker, but also to make the worker cognizant of the hazards associated with this work area and the safe work practices necessary to deal with these hazards".

CONFLUENCE

The point where two rivers flow and join one another, such as where the Upper Mississippi River and the Ohio River join to form the Lower Mississippi River, or the Allegheny and the Monongahela rivers meet to form the Ohio, or where one river joins another, such as the Illinois River entering the Mississippi. The term comes from the Latin *confluere,* meaning "to come or flow together".

CONN

The responsibility taken to navigate or take control of a vessel. Used in a formal sense in military and some merchant ships when an officer relieves the watch and says, "I've got the *conn*". On the river it is much more informal. When a Pilot relieves another he usually says, "Okay, I've got her, Cap". The word comes from the Latin *conducere,* meaning "to lead".

CONSIGNEE

One to whom a consignment of goods is shipped and then received.

CONSIGNOR

One who sends or ships a consignment of goods.

CONSOLE

The housing where the Pilot stands (or sits) that contains all the indicators and controls that are needed to safely navigate the vessel. These include all electronic and radio equipment, gauges, engine speed controls, rudder control, searchlights, etc.

CONSOLIDATOR

A firm, or agent, that combines

different shippers' cargo, such as steel, and now containers, to load into a single barge for delivery. The cargo may have more than one customer destination.

CONSTRUCTIVE TOTAL LOSS

A vessel that has been damaged to the extent that the cost of salvage and repair would exceed its insured value. After such determination the owner of the vessel usually abandons the vessel to its insurer, who pays the owner the insured value and sells the damaged vessel to the highest bidder.

CONTACT

A target that is picked up on radar and shows on the screen.

CONTACT PILOT

In the days before improved stabilization of the channel on the Lower Mississippi when there were no dikes, many cutting banks with not much of the shoreline having revetments, the USACE had *Contact Pilots* who had intimate knowledge of the river who were assigned to the various Lower River District offices. They not only talked to towboat Pilots about the conditions in their area, but also rode the tows to find out where there might be problem areas that needed attention or buoy or navigational light placement changes were required.

Presently, a *Contact Pilot* is most often a towing company Pilot that is stationed on a vessel or a lock facility where there might be a congested or dangerous channel conditions. He/she gives traffic information and controls movement through the area. They may be stationed aboard USACE vessels, or directed by them, especially when a dredging operation is underway.

CONTAINER

Large boxes used for shipping a wide variety of goods. Usually they measure nine feet high by eight feet wide, and come in various lengths; however, the standards are usually expressed as a TEU (Twenty foot Equivalent Unit), or a FEU (Forty foot Equivalent Unit). Ocean ships and terminals are sized by the amount of TEUs or FEUs they can accommodate. Sometimes they are simply referred to as *boxes*.

Containers of different types and products have been carried by inland vessels for many years, but transportation of ocean going boxes started sporadically in the early 1960s. It wasn't until the turn of the century that regular continuous service started to take hold. It is called C.O.B. for Container-On-Barge service.

CONTRACT CARRIER

A water transportation company that offers its service for hire on a negotiated and agreed-to price to transport goods from one place to another. See: COMMON CARRIER and TARRIF.

CONTROL VESSEL

A vessel stationed on a temporary basis to direct traffic in an emergency. Usually a Corps of Engineers vessel, or contracted by them, when dredging is being conducted, or at a construction site where there is a very close channel or people are working in dangerous conditions.

CONTROLLABLE-PITCH PROPELLER

A propeller whose blade angle or pitch can be changed by an hydraulic system working through the prop shaft to accommodate the most efficient thrust for the conditions to which the vessel is being subjected at the time. The speed of the vessel is controlled by the pitch of the blades while the engine is turning at constant rpm's. Very few are presently being used on the river system as the initial cost is expensive and subsequent repair due to heavy drift in the river at times has made use of them unprofitable.

CONTROLLING DEPTH
1. The least *depth* within a channel in which a vessel can navigate.
2. The depth at a dock, fleet, or other place a vessel may be required to go.
3. The draft to which a barge can be loaded in order to navigate in a channel. See: DEPTH.

CONVECTION
See: FOG

CONVOY
See: MULETRAINING

COOK
An important crew member. A good cook on a vessel usually provides for a contented crew, whereas a BELLY ROBBER can result in a disgruntled one.

COOKHOUSE
The place on the steamboats where food was prepared for the crew and passengers or guests. It was a place where the cook ruled supreme, and had an assistant cook and a handful of messmen. It was the locality that shore people call a "kitchen". With the demise of steamers and the changing crew types and sizes after WW II, it obtained the designation of GALLEY which is what most crew members call it today.

COONASS
A slang word for a Cajun, who is a person descended from the French Acadians forced out of Canada by the British in the 1700s. Considered by Cajuns as a somewhat defaming term if used in an address by a non-Cajun, but used in an affectionate or kidding sense by two Cajuns conversing with one another.

COOSA RIVER
The river makes its start from the Oostanaula and Etowah streams flowing out of the Blue Ridge Mountains. It flows for 286 miles through Alabama until it joins with the Tallapoosa River to form the Alabama River. Its name comes from an Indian word, *coosha,* meaning "reed".

Flatboats in early days carried cotton, tobacco, and other products down to Mobile. The first steamboat on the Coosa was named for the river. It was built at Cincinnati, came down the Western Rivers and across the shoreward passages of the Gulf over to Mobile Bay and headed upriver. It was stopped by a set of rapids on the Coosa called the "Devil's Staircase", which was the extent of navigation on the lower part of the river. The steamer was dismantled and reassembled above the series of rapids. Most of the commerce on the Coosa in the early years was on the upper portion between Greensport, AL, and Rome, GA (the town of Greensport became an underwater city after a hydro dam was built in the 20th Century).

In 1870, a survey was made to extend navigation down over the rapids to Wetumpka, Al, with a channel depth of four feet, with five L & Ds. Four of them were completed in 1890. The fifth, which was to be located near Wetumpka, wasn't completed and was later abandoned. In 1931 the USACE recommended abandonment of the whole navigation project. Later efforts to revive navigation after WW II died aborning due to lack of funding by Congress and protests by environmental groups.

CORDAGE
In a total sense, it refers to all lines, ropes, and wires used aboard a towboat, however, on the river it is used to mean the line, from small diameter to hawser size. The term comes to us from the French *corde,* which means "rope".

CORDELLE
A term used by boatmen in the

1800s to describe a method of moving keelboats upstream. When the river was too deep to pole a keelboat it would be *cordelled*. The *cordelle* was a very long line, of about 1000 feet, that was fastened to the top of the mast. The other end of the *cordelle* was taken upstream by the boat crew, who then pulled the boat along. If there was not a suitable bank to walk along, a skiff was sent upstream and the line was tied to a stump or other object. It was then pulled in, or warped, on a capstan if available, or hand-over-hand if none was outfitted on the boat. Packet steamers in shallow channels also would *cordelle* by taking a line out to a tree upstream and hauling it in on a capstan or winch, or taking their anchor upstream and planting it attached to the *cordelle* line. The word *cordelle,* comes from the French, meaning "to take out a rope". See: WARP.

CORE
The center of a wire rope around which the other strands of wire are laid. The *core* can be either rope (usual on the river) or wire.

CORNFIELD YARDS
The term used by the U.S. Navy for the shipyards on the inland waterways used by the Navy to build Landing Craft during WW II. Over 500 LST vessels, and other types, were built in the yards located in Pittsburgh, PA; Jeffersonville, IN; Evansville, IN; and Seneca, IL, for the war effort in the 1940s. These vessels were taken from the inland shipyards down to New Orleans to be delivered to the USN by the CATFISH NAVY.

CORPS OF ENGINEERS
See: U.S. ARMY CORPS OF ENGINEERS

CORROSION
The gradual deterioration of material by chemical process, such as oxidation or attack by chemicals. It is common on steel barges with weathering from the atmosphere and sometimes from the types of cargoes they transport. It occurs more rapidly when operating in a brackish or a salt-water environment. The word derives from the Latin *corrodere,* "to gnaw through".

COST (RUNNING A TOWBOAT or TUG)
The cost of operating a vessel, like any business, includes both fixed and variable costs. Different companies will break them down differently, having more or less categories or groupings. The following covers the basic tabulation of where they fall:
1. Fixed
    a. Administrative
    b. Interest on debt
    c. Depreciation
    d. Insurance
2. Variable
    a. Crew travel and wages (fringe benefits, taxes, etc)
    b. Fuel and lubricants
    c. Food
    d. Repairs and maintenance
    e. Stores and supplies (including line and rigging)
    f. Shifting and assist expense (including fleeting)

COST-BENEFIT RATIO
See: BENEFIT TO COST RATIO.

COST & FREIGHT (C&F)
The quoted price of goods shipped by water, including the transportation cost.

COST-INSURANCE-FREIGHT (CIF)
The quoted price of goods shipped by water that includes not only the initial price of the product but also the cost of marine insurance, freight charges, and other associated charges until the goods are delivered at a stated destination. Similar to F.O.B. (see)

quotes except the seller arranges for the transportation and insurance.

COTTON BALE
The white gold of the South in the mid-1800s. A bale was approximately 5 1/2 x 4 1/2 x 2 1/2 feet, but they could vary in size depending on how tightly the cotton may be packed in the bale. However, all *cotton bales* weighed approximately 500 pounds. These were covered with burlap and strapped originally with cordage and, later, steel strapping. Steamers loaded their guards from bottom to top, transporting the bales to coastal ports. The word *cotton* is traced back to an Arabic term, *kutn*. The word *bale* derives from the Old Norse *bollr*, to mean "something bundled".

COTTONCLADS
A steamboat running during the Civil War that used cotton bales to serve as protection from rifle fire during the conflict. See: IRONCLADS, TIMBERCLADS and TINCLADS.

COUPLING
1. The connection between the ends of two barges, or a side-to-side connection between them. It is normally used meaning a "hard *coupling*" of wire, using ratchets to take up any slack. If line is used it is called a "soft *coupling*".
2. Used extensively with machinery and piping to join parts together. It can be a straight *coupling* with the ends flanged together, or a screwed fitting, or used with a reducer fitting, or with a flexible joint.

COURSE
The direction being steered in a channel, or the intended direction to be steered from one place to another. It does not mean a compass course, as riverboats do not usually have a compass mounted on board, but rather a track to take which may involve many directions to steer over the time on watch as the river is a meandering waterway with many bends or curving channels. The term comes from a Latin base, *curus*, meaning "to run", and then to the French *cours*, on to our current usage of a directional movement.

COVERED BARGE or HOPPER
See: BARGE. A hopper barge that has its cargo space enclosed with a weather-tight covering for protection from weather related damage.
1. Roll Cover – The cargo space coaming is fitted with rails to accommodate covers that are fitted with wheels to open and close them. This type of cover is usually of the telescoping type. Used in any trade where the cargo is required to be protected from the elements.
2. Lift Cover – This type cover requires a crane to lift and stack them on one end of the cargo space when unloading cargo. When they are spread they usually have doors installed in the covers to provide ease in loading when utilizing a loading spout. Mainly employed in the grain trade.
3. Fiberglass Covers – A type of cover, usually a lift type with a rounded crown, made of fiberglass. Most other covers are made of steel. It is lighter than steel, weighing 30 to 40 tons less per set of covers. Sometimes called "plastic covers".
4. Temporary Cover – A covering of the cargo, usually grain, in an open hopper barge with sheets of heavy mil plastic sheeting that is weighted down with old tires or other means to keep the plastic from being blown off in a storm (sometimes not very successfully).

COWBOY
A reckless Pilot who is going full ahead when he/she should be observing Rule 6 (Safe Speed) of the Navigation Rules, or one who is mak-

ing careless maneuvers. There is a fish that is named *cockeye pilot*. It may be related to a *cowboy*.

COWL
A movable covered elbow shaped funnel located on a weather deck that directs fresh air to lower compartments. See: AIR SCOOP.

COWTAIL
The fraying bitter end of a line, or a short section of line that is unraveled into strands that a deckhand uses in tying up rigging or for a variety of other jobs, similar to a length of heavy string. The name derives from looking like the end of a cow's tail used to flick flies away.

CRAB
1. To move a vessel or tow in a somewhat sideways motion, similar to the crustacean of the sea, proceeding at an angle to the current or the wind in order to maintain one's desired course in the channel.
2. When rowing, an oarsman is said to "catch a *crab*" if his oar splashes into or out of the water.

CRABBING THROUGH
The act of a steamboat backing through a shallow channel by thrusting water up under a steamer's hull with the reverse paddlewheel action. The washing procedure basically results in dragging the boat over the shoal area.

CRABS
Lines used on a rafting steamer to pull the stern around and change the shoving position and direction.

CRACKER BOX
A small wharfboat.

CRADLE
1. A sturdy elongated triangular frame on a LAUNCH-WAYS or a HAULING-WAYS in a shipyard that a vessel is placed upon in order to be level when launching or hauling on a marine railway. Sometimes called a *bilge-ways, launching-ways, sleds, or sliding-ways*. The term is believed to come from the Old English *cradol* and perhaps going back to the German *kartte*, both meaning "basket" to hold a baby. The shipyard name and use of *cradle* is for how it gently supports the "infant" vessel as it makes its debut in the world when sliding down the ways to begin its life in the water. Also see: SIDE-LAUNCHING and SKIDS.
2. The heavy supports on the bed of a drydock to support a vessel and make hull bottom repairs. See: CRIB.
3. The framework on the deck of a vessel that may support a small work boat.
4. A yoked stanchion used to hold and secure a BOOM when it is lowered and secured when not in use.

CRAMER, ZADOK
A printer from Pittsburgh who began publishing in 1801 early river guides called *The Navigator*. It became the river bible to the early flatboatmen and keelboaters. Cramer took the reports of those who traveled the Ohio River Valley, wrote them in his book, and cited the best channels as well as describing the towns and settlements along its shores. He later expanded the guide to include the Lower Mississippi river. In 1806 the fifth edition contained woodcut drawings of the river, showing islands, back channels, obstructions, and other information. See: RIVER GUIDES.

CRANE
A mechanism designed to lift and move things or material. When used on a barge or towing vessel it is usually referred to for the task it was primarily designed, i.e. *hose crane* on a tank barge, or *boat crane* used to lift off the skiff and put in the water from

a towboat. This term derives from the long-necked bird of the same name. The mechanical device takes its name from the resemblance of its long arm to the bird's neck.

CRANE BARGE
A barge that has a crane on it, either as a portable mobile unit such as one with crawler treads or wheels, or one that is permanently installed such as a heavy lift derrick or one with an installed A-FRAME. This equipment is used for a variety of jobs, including lifting barge covers to stack or spread them, to lighter or transfer cargo in a barge, handle equipment at a shipyard, for salvage work, etc.

CRANK
1. A device attached to an object that receives the fore and aft oscillating movement of a shaft such as a PITMAN and converts the thrusting action into a movement that rotates, such as that of a PADDLEWHEEL.
2. A handle used to apply manual force to work a gear such as employed on a small winch to a boat crane. The term appears to come from the German *krank*, that meant a sick person, or someone bent in pain.
3. A vessel that tends to roll easily in even the slightest of waves is said to be *cranky*.
4. An eccentric person who speaks and writes about nautical river terms.
5. An ill-tempered or grouchy person who doesn't understand or even care about nautical or river terms.

CREASE
The thickness of the blade end of a CAULKING IRON. A #0 crease was 1/16 inch wide, #1 was 1/8 inch wide, #2 was 3/16 inches wide, and #3 was 1/4 inches wide. The name probably comes from the French *creste,* meaning "wrinkled".

CREEK BAR
The buildup of material, sand and gravel that is deposited from a current's effluent deposited at the mouth of a small stream flowing into the main stream of a larger navigable river.

CRESCENT RIVER PILOTS
Those Pilots who board ocean going ships and bring them upriver from Pilottown, LA, at the Head of the Passes of the Mississippi River and guide the ships to the city of New Orleans. If the vessel is destined above New Orleans the pilotage duties are taken over by a NOBRA Pilot.

CREST
1. When a river is rising, it is the highest stage or gauge reading of the rise. It then is on a STAND until it starts to fall. See: FALLING RIVER or GAUGE.
2. The top of a fixed dam.
3. The top of a breaking wave.
4. A record of flooding heights on an annual basis at gauging sites.

CREST DAMS
These were dams that had types of temporary FLASHBOARDS attached to the upper extent of the dam to allow extra depth in a pool during low water. These boards could be three to six feet high across the dam structure.

CREVASSE
Used on the river to mean a breach or break in a levee during flood conditions. The word comes from Old French *crevace,* meaning a "crack, opening, crevice, or fissure".

CREW
On the river it means the entire complement of persons who man and operate the vessel and its tow. The word is from the Latin *crescare,* meaning an increase in force, probably used in a military sense.

CREW CHANGE
On tugs and linehaul riverboats the crew members work on a rotating schedule of so many days aboard the vessel and so many days of earned time off, i.e. 30 days on, 20 days off, or day for day, 30 on 30 off, etc. When a crew member has put in a period of time he/she is relieved by another crew member. Each company has different schedules.

CREW ENDURANCE MANAGEMENT
A program developed by the industry and the USCG to promote safety by supporting initiatives to be used aboard vessels to manage the factors that may increase fatigue, reduce endurance and possibly contribute to casualties. These elements can include, but are not limited to, diet and exercise, light management while sleeping, change of watch hour time periods, and the continuing education in ways to change crew members' culturally instilled habits to ones that could provide for a more healthful work and lifestyle environment.

CRIB
1. A section of a log raft, made up about 16' by 32'. *Crib* logs were those that would surround floating lumber logs as a boom. However, few, if any log rafts move on the Western Rivers anymore.
2. The blocking used on a drydock to support a vessel without a flat bottom.
3. A square box-like structure made of heavy timbers and then filled with rocks for a support or retaining structure. Some of the first locks and dam structures were made out of rock-filled *cribs*.

CRITICAL (IN ENGINE)
The term used when some vessel engines at a certain low rpm, will vibrate excessively and are said to be in its *critical*. Usually somewhere between idle speed and low speed.

CROP(PING)
The action taken in a shipyard to remove by cutting out with an acetylene torch a damaged section of a vessel in order to prepare it for replacement with new steel.

CROSS CHAINS
Similar to HOG CHAINS, but like KNUCKLE CHAINS, instead of running longitudinally over the length of a steamer, they were rigged athwartship over a SAMPSON POST to support the side paddlewheeler's housing and the wide guards that overhung the sides on the hulls of some steamboats in order to carry extra cargo, especially bales of cotton.

CROSS CURRENTS
The point where two different sources of currents intersect resulting in strong turbulence, sometimes to the extent wires on a tow can part. It occurs in many different situations, such as at the junction of two streams, or a where strong current is flowing off a dike and meets a current running off a point of land, or a stream flowing to the Gulf of Mexico flowing across the GIWW especially when there are strong tidal currents.

CROSS RUDDERS
The placement of the rudders on a twin-screw riverboat where the steering rudders are placed hard over (or mostly so) in one direction and the FLANKING RUDDERS are placed hard over in the opposite direction. The Pilot comes ahead on one engine and goes astern on the other. If the Pilot wants to turn to port, the steering rudders are put hard over to port. The flanking rudders are placed to starboard. Then the Pilot comes ahead on the starboard engine and backs on the port engine. If he/she wants to turn to starboard the rud-

ders are hard over in the opposite direction and the engine settings are reversed. This allows the Pilot to quickly turn the vessel around. See: WALKING THE TOWBOAT.

CROSS SIGNALS

The old (pre-1980) Inland Rules and the Western River Rules specifically prohibited what is termed *cross signals,* that is, "answering one whistle with two, or answering two whistles with one". Although there is not a specific written prohibition in the new Inland Rules, a careful reading of all the rules, especially Rule 2 (Responsibility), still prohibits the action of *cross signals*.

CROSSBOARD

A type of daymark that was used in the past, probably last used on the Missouri River. It consisted of two crisscrossed boards painted white and nailed to a tree, although can still be used as a temporary marking on all rivers.

CROSSHEAD

In mechanical appliances it converts the action of the piston to the action of the connecting rod. On a paddlewheel boat the PITMAN is attached to the piston rod of the steam engine with a wrist pin. The fore and aft movement of the piston is controlled in a set of guides. The other end of the pitman is attached with a crank pin to a CRANK that is on the paddlewheel shaft. In other words, the fore and aft piston motion is converted to rotation of the paddlewheel.

CROSSING

In navigating a meandering river the channel will flow down one bank side for a time and then cross over to the other side in a bend, which is called a *crossing*.

CROSSING DAYMARK

A diamond-shaped board with reflective tape which is placed at the approximate head and/or foot of a river crossing that a Pilot can sight as an aid to keep the head of the tow in proper alignment with the channel when navigating a crossing, i.e. "Hold about 100 yards below the *daymark* at the next crossing as the channel has moved down a bit".

CROSSING LIGHT

A light on the bank placed at the approximate head and/or foot of a river crossing that a pilot can sight on to aid in navigating, i.e. "When you make the XYZ *crossing* have her well out and hold about 200 yards open on BCD *light* which will clear the dredge working there".

CROSSING THE BAR

The final crossing. Refers to one who spent a long time on the river or who was involved in river affairs and has passed away. As with the three-gun salute of the military to one who has honorably served our country and died, it is appropriate to salute one who has dedicated his career and honorably served the river industry, with the salute being three longer than prolonged blasts of a towboat's whistle. See: WHISTLE SALUTE.

CROSSING THE BAR
By Alfred Lord Tennyson

Sunset and evening star,
And one clear call for me.
And may there be no moaning of the bar,
When I put out to sea.

But such a tide as moving seems asleep,
Too full for sound and foam,
When that which drew from out the boundless deep
Turns again home.

> Twilight and evening bell,
> And after that the dark;
> And may there be no sadness of farewell,
> When I embark.
>
> For tho' from out our bourne of Time and Place
> The flood may bear me far,
> I hope to see my pilot face to face,
> When I have crost the bar.

CROSSING SITUATION

Rule 15 of the Navigation Rules states:

"(a) When two power-driven vessels are crossing so as to involve risk of collision, the vessel which has the other on her starboard side shall keep out of the way and shall, if the circumstances of the case admit, avoid crossing ahead of the other vessel".

"(b) Notwithstanding paragraph (a), on the Great Lakes, Western Rivers, or water specified by the Secretary, a power-driven vessel crossing a river shall keep out of the way of a power-driven vessel ascending or descending the river".

CROWN

See: CAMBER.

CRUISING

Just uneventfully moving along the river in the company notch at full speed, with a good depth of water under your tow, a wide channel, all the buoys in place, the weather is clear and sunny, no squares on the bow of the towboat, not much tow traffic, no recreational boats in sight, no narrow bridges to run during the watch, nor any locks to make, the coffee is hot, and life is good, except you're not home.

CUB

The term used to denote a person serving under the tutelage of a licensed Pilot when learning the intricacies, foibles, and ficklenesses of river currents and the vessels which traverse them, as well as to the laws and rules which govern river navigators. When the person serves the required time and the licensed Pilot attests to the knowledge and proficiency of the person, he/she will be able to apply for a USCG license.

In the old steamboat days, one paid the Pilot a fee to teach a person the river and its ways, as well as how to handle a packet or a steamboat. It is best described in Samuel Clemens' *Life On the Mississippi*. Though the rivers have been transformed, and the vessels have changed, the principles of "learning the river" and handling a boat, and working with nature are the same. The term *cub* is seldom used at present on the river. The more prevalent term is STEERSMAN, while the USCG uses the term APPRENTICE MATE.

CUBIC CAPACITY

The internal measurement of the cargo space of a barge, without considering the deadweight displacement of cargo. Some barges are built with extra high coamings to accommodate less dense or light weight commodities. When such cargoes are loaded in a barge with a normal sized coaming, of about four feet, when filled the barge would not reach the normal project draft of approximately nine feet. Cargoes that fall into this category are wood chips, soybean meal, paper, etc. Barges with high coamings, seven to eight feet in height, are usually referred to as "high cube".

CUBIC FEET PER SECOND (cfs)

A term used to describe the amount of water, or volume, flowing past a gauging point in the river. One cubic foot of water equals 7.48 gallons. One *cfs* equals about two acre-feet per day. A cross section of the river is first measured; then the velocity of the current in that section is determined. The product of the two assessments will determine the amount of *cubic feet per second* are flowing which can then be converted into predictions of flooding on the rising end, and possible shoaling conditions when falling.

CULVERT

The filling and dewatering tunnels of a lock that are utilized to receive or add water to and from the intake and outlet ports of the chamber.

CUMBERLAND RIVER

The *Cumberland River* rises in Harlan in southeastern Kentucky with the merging of three forks, and winds down 667 miles until it enters the Ohio River at Smithland, KY (mile 920 on the Ohio), about 15 miles above Paducah, KY. Presently navigation is maintained to Carthage, TN (mile 308). The river had various names given it by the Indians of the region and the traders, but in 1760 an Englishman gave it the present name which he used to honor King George II, naming it after his son, the Duke of Cumberland.

Flatboats started travel on the *Cumberland* as soon as it was settled in the late 1700s, which were built from the region's abundant timber stands. Crops and other products were floated to New Orleans. Even Ludlow's touring showboat went to Nashville in 1817. Keelboats started a two-way traffic on the river in the early 1800s. The first steamboat on the river was the Str. *GENERAL JACKSON* which navigated the stream in 1819 up to Nashville (mile 191). The heritage of that venture lives on in the name of an excursion showboat, the *GENERAL JACKSON*, based in Nashville.

When the GENERAL SURVEY ACT passed in 1824, some river improvements were undertaken by the USACE including the removal of snags and rocks from the shoals, or shallowest, sections of the channel. Various surveys were made in the 1800s for other channel improvements, but it wasn't until the latter two decades of the 18th century that canalization was finalized. Fifteen timber-cribbed and stone-filled lock-and-dam structures were built to allow for a six-foot channel. The locks were 52 feet wide by 280 feet long. However, by 1924 steamboat traffic had essentially died out.

After WWII a nine-foot channel was proposed and adopted by Congress, with mostly multi-purpose dams with modern locks. The modernization was undertaken and completed by the early 1970s. The two locks furthest upstream are 400' by 84' and the two at the lower end of the river are 800' by 110'.

CUMSHAW (or KUMSHAW)

A Chinese dialect saying that means "grateful thanks" for a gift or handout received. It is a carryover from the deep sea or persons that were formally in the Navy. The meaning basically deteriorated into the inappropriate acquisition of gear, material, parts, or supplies that might be obtained without permission from a fleet, shipyard, another vessel or place by crew personnel to be used on their own vessel.

CURRENT

1. The downstream movement of a river's flow of water from its elevation source en route to the sea. A cross section of a river channel shows that generally the swiftest *current* is in the bend and the slacker water is on the bar side.

2. In a tidal situation, the flow and ebb speed and direction of the water. The term derives from the Latin *currere,* meaning "to run". See: CROSS CURRENT.

CURSOR

A movable pointer on radar that

can be used to note on the screen the bearings or distances from one's own vessel to other vessels or targets.

CURTAIN DIKE

A dike that has piles driven in pairs, six feet or so apart, that were crossed at the top and fastened securely together. Each pair in a dike's length was spaced apart approximately 12 feet apart. They were joined at the top and at about mid-level with a cross horizontal board or timber. A *curtain* was made of wire mesh with willows, sticks, branches and similar material from along the bank inserted in the mesh which was then lowered into the water along the dike fence and attached to the pilings. Weights of rocks or gunny sacks filled with sand or gravel held the ends of the *curtain* mesh to the river bottom. See: MATTRESS REVETMENT.

CUSPIDOR

A receptacle in the pilothouse where Pilots and those who were jawing on the LAZY BENCH could relieve themselves of old chewing tobacco-enriched saliva as they were expanding on the "truth" as they knew it. It is also called a "spittoon". The word comes from the Portuguese word *cuspir*, meaning "to spit". The *cuspidor* was usually made of brass, but some less affluent vessels might have an enameled steel one.

CUSTOM

1. Duties that may be imposed on certain cargoes by a Customs Officer.
2. A traditional and widely accepted way of performing an action. It may be a procedure that is not spelled out, nor required, by the Navigation Rules, but if it is a commonly accepted practice known to mariners it could be interpreted by courts to have the force of law.

CUT

1. A DREDGE excavating material from the river usually makes several passes through the area being dredged. Each pass that widens the channel width is called a *cut*.
2. When a tow makes a DOUBLE LOCKAGE, the tow must be broken in two separate sections with each part of the tow being called a *cut*.
3. If a tow has to DOUBLE TRIP and must take part of the tow a distance up or downstream while tying off the other part of the tow, each part is called a *cut*.
4. To pass very close by to an object, i.e. a buoy, a bridge pier, or other action while navigating.
5. `A wash or erosion in the bank. If severe it is called a *cutting* bank.

CUT HER LOOSE

When the Pilot or Mate tells a crewman standing by a line to cast it off.

CUTLESS BEARING

A propeller shaft with a rubber bearing that is lubricated by water.

CUTOFF

When the river seeks a shorter path to the sea and breaks through a narrow neck of a horseshoe or oxbow bend. It has sometimes been helped along by the Corps of Engineers in attempting to make the river more efficient (see: PILOT CANAL), and at other times the Corps has gone to great efforts to protect the place where the river, left to its own desires, would have *cut* through. *Cutoffs* have been controversial since steamboat navigation commenced on the Lower Mississippi. Henry Shreve created some, including the one at Turnbull's Bend where the Red River entered the Mississippi and formed the Old River. This did not prove to be beneficial, as time later demonstrated.

The Mississippi River Commis-sion did not care for the program of creating *cutoffs*, other than natural ones, and stopped the practice in 1884. Then after the 1927 flood other studies were made to reduce flood stages, and in the 1930s a series of new *cutoffs* were made. New Madrid Bend, sometimes known as Slough Landing Neck, is the longest meandering bend on the Lower Mississippi wandering from its head almost 20 miles to its foot. Across its neck it is only two miles wide. Pro and con arguments were made as to whether a *cutoff* should be made. The Corps studied it numerous times and concluded if undertaken; the increased stream flow would lead to the possible reduction in channel depth upriver. Some thought it might cause a severe drop on the Ohio below Lock 53 (some said as much as 14 inches) and also at a rock bed reach between Commerce, MO, and Thebes, IL, on the Upper Mississippi, (at about mile 43) during low flow periods, but others believed the problems could be overcome. The citizens of the town of New Madrid however, were violently opposed as the *cutoff* would have left their town "high and dry" so the project was never undertaken.

The USACE now usually actively tries to stop a river from eroding out the neck of a looping bend by protecting the bank with revetments or dikes. On the Ohio, at a bend near Evansville, IN, the river keeps trying to shorten its course, and the Corps just as adamantly keeps dropping rock in the river to prevent it from doing so.

Samuel Clemens in his *Life on the Mississippi* calculated that the Mississippi River was 1215 miles long 176 years ago. When writing the book he said the river was then 973 miles long, indicating the Lower Mississippi had lost 242 miles of its length, or about one and one-third miles per year. Then he figured at that rate of loss, New Orleans and Cairo would be joining their streets together in about the year 2600.

CUT-OFF VALVE

A device used to control or stop the flow of liquid or gas. On a steamboat it referred to the valve that stopped the admission of steam into the cylinder of an engine.

CUTTER

`The term that was adopted by the REVENUE CUTTER SERVICE, the predecessor of the USCG, and is now applied to all vessels in their service over 65 feet in length. A "W" for some reason is used to denote a Coast Guard vessel. Apparently it was given to differentiate similar type Navy vessels from those operated by the Coast Guard, but why "W" is only speculation, however many urban legends abound. Some of the types you may see on the rivers or canals are:

WLI   Inland Buoy Tender
WLIC Inland Construction Tender
WLM   Coastal Buoy Tender
WLR   River Buoy Tender
WPG   Patrol Boat

CUTTERHEAD DREDGE

A hydraulic dredge that has a *cutterhead* on its suction end, which is a mechanical device that has rotating blades to break up hard-pan clay or other material that can then be sucked up and pumped out through a pipeline to a disposal site.

CYCLOIDAL PROP

A type of propulsion system where the propeller blades are arranged vertically on a horizontal disc. The system acts as both the motion driver (propeller) and the direction executer (rudder). Though they are installed on a number of harbor tugs, they have so far not proven suitable for use in most river environments where the bottom of a vessel's hull is at times close to the bed of a river and damage to the propeller blades can be caused by drift, groundings, etc.

CYLINDER

1. A black day shape to be displayed by a vessel that is constrained by its draft. Used only under the International Rules. This term is not used in the Inland Navigation Rules, since most river vessels are always "constrained".

2. The chamber in an engine that is fitted with a piston whose movement is impelled by pressure either from a fluid or gas. The movement of the piston provides the propelling force that allows steamboats and diesel vessels to turn their paddle wheels or propellers.

CAJUN RATCHET

1. A bar is inserted into the bights of a line.
2. The bar is then twisted between the bights numerous times until the line is tight.
3. The bar is then tied off to the twisted line with small stuff.

STEAM CALLIOPE
"Beautiful Music"

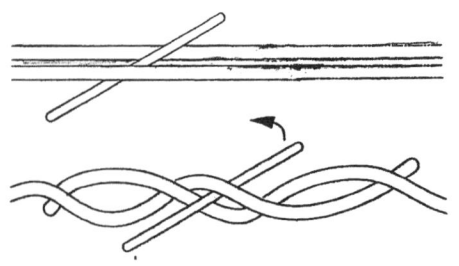

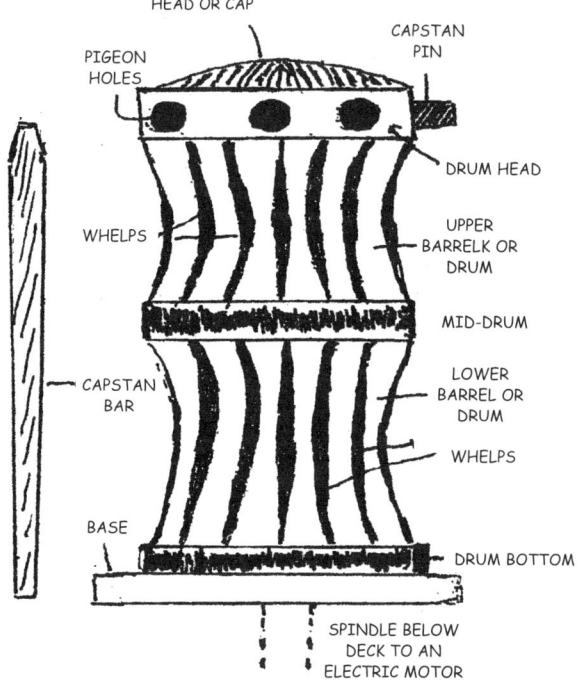

CAPSTAN

Most capstans in use aboard towboats are electrically driven. Some smaller type may be used on barges that are mechanically operated. These usually have a single barrel with pawls mounted on the drum bottom. The base of the capstan will have slots in it to engage the pawls as the barrel is turned by a crew member using a capstan bar fitted into one of the pigeon holes in the drum head. The capstan shown is a 2-barrel type. While usually only one line is used on it, this type can be utilized to haul in 2 different lines at the same time, one on the top barrel, and one on the bottom. When hauling in, one line is allowed to slip while the other is becoming taut. When both lines have an even strain they hold until fully taken up and dogged off.

CAR CARRIERS
(See: AUTOMOBILE BARGES)

Flat deck empty petroleum barges loaded with cars- from stem to stern and stsrboard to port and a triple deck specially designed vessel withree decks to carry auyomobiles and pickup trucks.

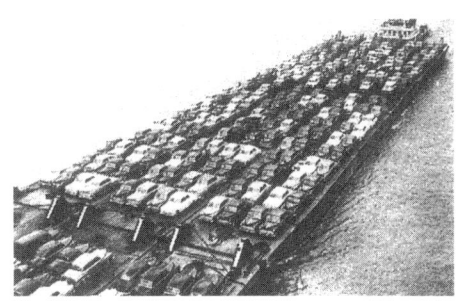

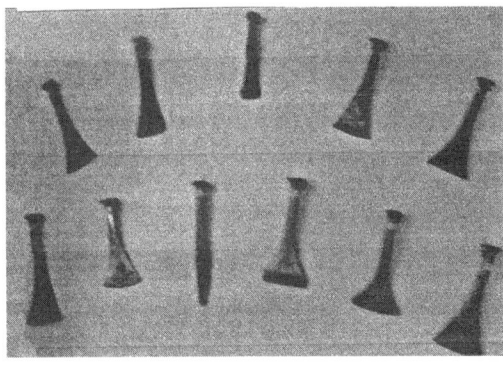

TOOLS OF THE CAULKING TRADE
(On display at the Howard Steamboat Museum)

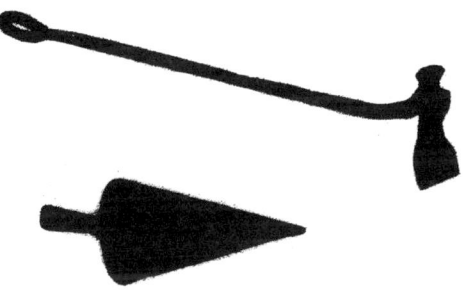

The picture shown in the upper left shows various caulking irons of different creases and angles that had specific names, i.e. bent, dumb, butt, reefing (for clearing), spike, etc.

The picture at the lower left displays cauking mallets and a beetle.

The picture above shows a pay pot, which was filled with hot pitch to pour over a caulked seam and then spread with a pitch mop. Also shown is a hauling or hawsing iron, which was a two man job. One held the iron while another hit its head with his mallet. It was used to insure the oakum caulk was solidly in place.

112   ILLUSTRATIONS

COILING A LINE
(Also see: FAKE and FLEMISH)

The reason for properly coiling a line is so it wil not take up much deck space and will be out of the way of the working crew. When line is correctly coiled it can be readily and safely payed out when needed at docks, locks, to another vessel, etc. without its loops, or coils, becoming tangled in the process.

COIL

FLEMISH

FAKE

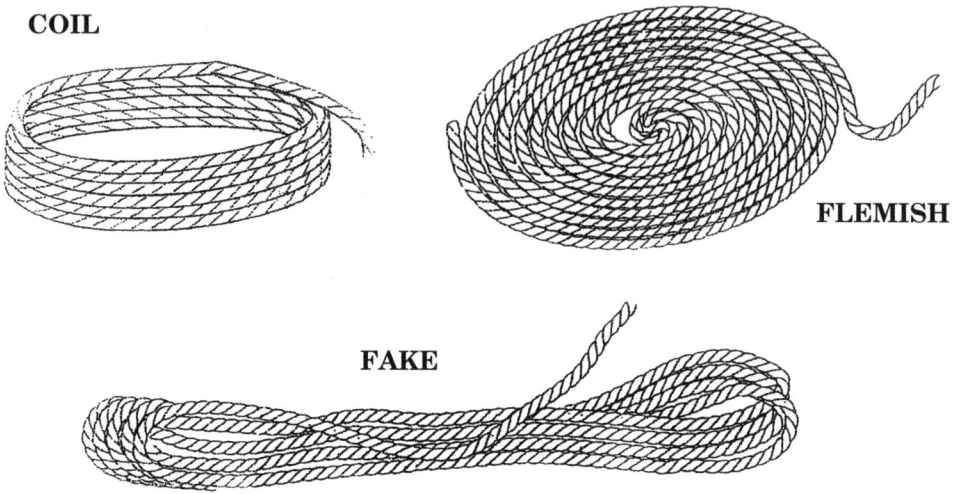

A typical facsimile of a USCG Certificate of Inspection that is currently issued to inspected vessels, such as tank barges that carry cargoes that are hazardous and/or flammable. The certificate is carried at all times aboard the vessel, unless it has a gas free or a permit to proceed authorization on board.

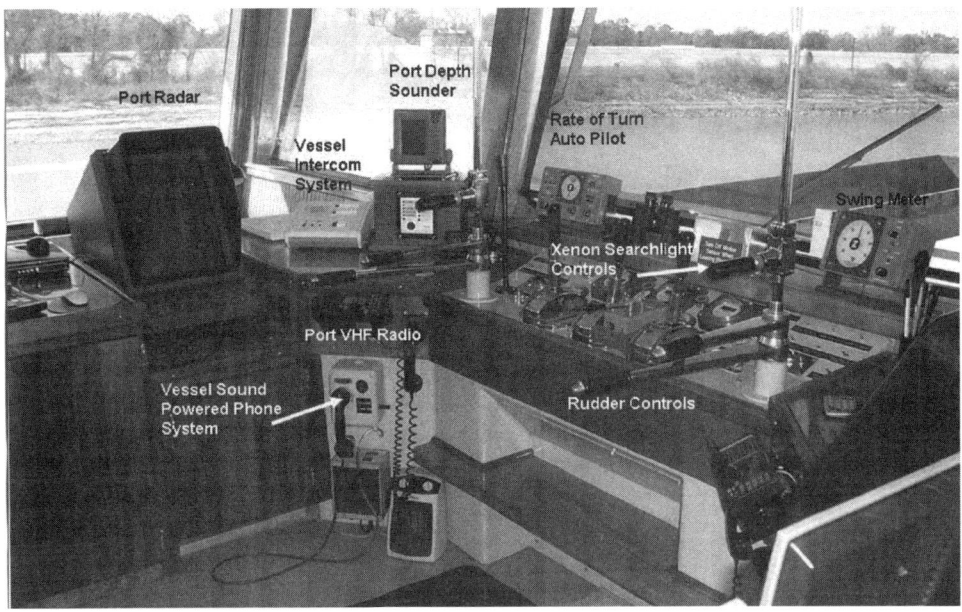

CONSOLE IN PILOTHOUSE OF TOWBOAT (Ingram Barge Company)

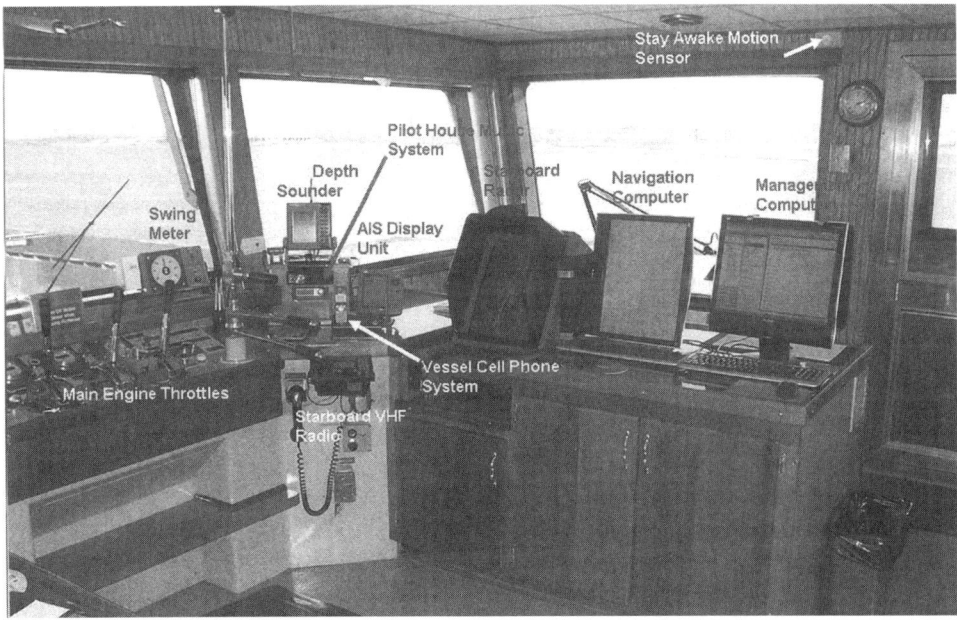

From the days steamboats first started navigating on Western Rivers when the only aids to piloting were a steering wheel, rudimentary way to communicate with the engineer, and a leadsman sounding the depth of the river, the modern pilothouse has evolved into a virtual multiple assemblage of electrical and electronic aids. Some are shown here with a port and starboard view of the modern navigating post of a pilot.

D

DAGGER BOARD
See: SKEG

DAGGER PIN or WEDGE
A wedge-like steel pin used to latch or keep the roll covers on a barge from moving when a barge might not be in a fore-and-aft trim while loading or unloading. Also, when the covers have been spread over the cargo hold, the *pin* or *wedge* secures the covers so they will not move while underway and expose the cargo to weather damage. Sometimes called *cargo cover wedges*.

DAM
A fixed physical barrier that is constructed across a river. It can be a solid weir or it can be built with gates and/or wickets to control the flow of water. A *dam* raises the level, or depth, of water behind it, which then can provide for navigation on the waterway. Most *dams* on our Inland Waterways System have locks to permit the passage of vessels.

The word *dam* apparently comes from the Swedish and the German *damm,* which is a further corruption of the Gothic German word *faurdammjan,* meaning "to block up". A derivative, the curse word "damn," was to stop persons from entering the Pearly Gates. To rivermen *dams* are fine structures, as long as they have a lock in them, since they provide many public benefits, and it is painful to hear one say, "I don't give a damn". However, this meaning derives from India's currency, the rupee, and its coinage of the *dam* which was only worth about one-fortieth of the rupee, or not of much value. For various *dam* structures see: GATED NON-NAVIGABLE SPILLWAY DAMS (with various types of gates), GATED NAVIGABLE SPILLWAY DAMS (with various types of weirs) for some further description. Remember, this is a Lexicon, not an engineering manual.

A *dam* is also an assemblage of limbs, twigs, and other forest products made by beavers. They build them without engineering degrees from prestigious universities, but with an innate sense of how to increase the productive use of a waterway. Their structures are illegal since they never obtain the required governmental permits, nor do they conduct any type of environmental assessment studies, or even evaluate the benefits to the cost of the edifice prior to construction. However, the gross failure in their design efforts is to <u>not</u> provide for adequate-sized locks in the structures they create.

DAM BUOY
A warning buoy, particularly to recreational boaters warning of "danger ahead". Usually painted with alternating horizontal black and red stripes. Sometimes a warning sign is also posted indicating danger.

DAM OPEN
1. The dam has its ROLLERS wide open.
2. The wickets are down. See: WICKET and WICKET DAM.

DAMAGE CONTROL
The measure(s) taken by the crew of a vessel that has been damaged in some fashion, i.e., preventing or stopping leakage or listing; controlling fire; preventing, stopping, or cleaning up after spillage of liquid cargo; or any other mishap that affects the crew's and vessel's safety. The word *damage* comes to us from the Latin *damnum,* meaning "loss", while *control* is from the Latin *contra,* to mean "against".

DAMAGE STABILITY
The ability of a vessel to maintain positive buoyancy and remain afloat after having a breach in its outer hull. See: STABILITY.

DAMAGE SURVEY

An inspection conducted by the owner's representatives and any other parties who may have an interest in the vessel. The survey consists of noting the extent of damage to the vessel and what will be necessary to accomplish a seaworthy repair at what cost; or damage to the vessel's cargo. A detailed report is usually made listing the damage and including the cost of repair.

DANGER

1. Any possible peril or hazard in the river's course, such as a sandbar, rock outcropping, snag, etc. that could cause damage to the vessel or tow.
2. Any occurrence when vessels are encountering one another in a close situation or narrow channel when those piloting each of their vessels must be extra alert in the event that a mishap to one's own vessel or the other vessel could occur such a failed engine, hitting ground, etc.
3. Any material condition from lack of maintenance or deficiency of attention to safe work areas that could result in injury to vessel personnel.
4. A condition when a Pilot is not "shaped up" to make a navigational movement into a lock, through a bridge, flanking a bend, etc.
5. When total safe seamanship is not a priority.

DANGER or DOUBT SIGNAL

An audio signal sounded on a vessel's whistle of at least five short blasts as required under Rule 34(d) of the Navigation Rules whenever a vessel fails to understand the intentions or actions of an approaching vessel, or is in doubt as to whether sufficient action is being taken by the other vessel to avoid collision. Also may be sounded to alert crew members to an impending danger.

DANGER OF COLLISION

See: RISK OF COLLISION.

DARKEN BOAT

The act of turning out all deck lights and shielding others in order to have more acute night visibility, especially when surface fog or other atmospheric conditions may exist causing reflections that retard a Pilot's vision.

DATUM POINT

A base point of reference from which a numerical change is measured. As examples, a river gauge of zero feet at St. Louis is calculated from a baseline established many years ago. Every change is recorded as a stand, rise, or fall from that baseline. The *datum point* of clearance available to navigate through the channel span of a bridge is measured from the bottom of the bridge floor support guiders to the current level of water underneath the bridge. In coastal area waters the tidal *datum* is given on the chart.

DAVIS ISLAND LOCK & DAM

The first lock and dam built on the Ohio River by the USACE. After much controversy and different proposals, construction was started in 1878 and Davis Lock and Dam finally opened in late 1885. It was 110 feet wide and 600 feet long with *roller lock gates* (see: LOCK GATE(S) – 2. SLIDING or ROLLING). The 110 feet width was to accommodate the width of four STANDARD barges wide. The dam had a navigable pass with CHANOINE WEIR wickets. There were problems with both the lock's roller gates, scouring at the dam, and operating the wickets, but the structure lasted until it was replaced by Emsworth Lock and Dam in the 1920s.

As an interesting factoid, the Panama Canal locks were built 110 feet wide as a model from the *Davis Island Lock*. Could it have been that President Teddy Roosevelt was thinking we ought to send barge tows down the Atlantic Ocean and through the new canal to the Pacific?

DAVIT

A type of small crane or boom, usually straight-armed, or slightly curved, used on riverboats to hoist and lower a skiff over the side of a vessel. *Davits* can also be used to hoist barrels or other gear to the second deck or to swing it to the engine room space. The term is believed to have come from someone named David who may have invented the device. In Welsh, the name David is pronounced *Davit*.

DAVY JONES'S LOCKER

Although viewed as a spirit who presides over the evil of the deep sea, he also has a "locker" in every reach of the rivers that flow to the sea. He gathers up that which is cast overboard, and when a riverman dies, he is sometimes said to have gone, "to *Davy Jones's Locker*" and is required to clean up whatever mess he may have made.

DAY or DAILY RATE

Used in reference to a contract, either written or verbal, to hire for an agreed-upon fee, such as for a vessel (crewed or not crewed), or a salvage rig, for a fixed amount per day.

DAY BOAT

A term sometimes used for a fleet boat that works at a dock or in a harbor usually only during daylight hours. The crew does not live on the boat, but ashore. Used interchangeably with the description of a Fleet Boat, Harbor Boat, Lunch-Bucket Boat, or Dinner Bucket Boat.

DAY SIGNAL or SHAPE

The distinctive marks to be shown by certain vessels during daylight to indicate a particular type of work in which they are engaged. They shall be black in color and are either in the shape of a ball, a cone, or a diamond (two cones having a common base). The Navigation Rules describe when and how they are to be shown in Part C, Lights and Shapes, Rules 20 through 31. Annex I, part 84.11 describes the size and color of the shapes. They are most often seen on vessels at anchor, dredges, a vessel restricted in its ability to maneuver (a USCG buoy tender setting an aid to navigation), and occasionally on fishing vessels.

DAY TANK

A small tank located above the engine(s) which receives diesel fuel oil pumped from the bunkering tank after it is filtered. It feeds fuel to the engine by gravity to the fuel injection pumps. It is sometimes called a *ready tank*.

DAYBOARD

See: DAYMARK

DAYMAN

A person who only works day watches from 6 a.m. to 6 p.m. Usually it refers to an extra person working in the engine room. With automation and more efficient engines the term is seldom used any more.

DAYMARK

An unlighted aid to navigation, however, it may have reflective tape added to more easily be seen with a source of illumination such as a searchlight. On the river, they are usually mounted on shore or at the end of a dike in a diamond shape, but they also may be square or triangular. Pilots use them to steer on when in a river crossing. It is also referred to as a *dayboard*.

DAYS of the WEEK (on the river)

Even without a calendar, crew members on towboats can keep track of what day it is simply by their daily noon meal. Of course, it depends on the Master and the Cook and some boats may have variations of this weekly fare.

SUN	Chicken Day
MON	Day after Chicken Day
TUE	Day before second Chicken Day
WED	Second Chicken Day
THU	Day after Second Chicken Day or day before Fish Day
FRI	Fish Day
SAT	Steak Day

DEAD AHEAD

Something that is directly in front of a vessel, such as another vessel, a point of land, or an object. If it is not directly *ahead,* but is off to port or starboard, one should use only *ahead*, saying, "A small boat is *ahead* off to starboard (port)".

DEAD ASTERN

Something that is directly *astern* of a vessel. If it is not directly *astern,* but is off to port or starboard, one should use only *astern*, saying, "A small boat is *astern* off to starboard (port)".

DEAD BOAT

1. A towboat or tug that is tied off, without power, and without crew, at a dock, fleet, or shipyard.

2. A towboat or tug in tow with another vessel, but which is not providing any power assistance in propulsion.

DEAD END

Sometimes used to refer to the end of a line that is fastened to something such as a BLOCK, however, the end of a line is usually referred to as the BITTER END.

DEAD IN THE WATER

A vessel that is stopped in the water, but is not anchored, or moored, but could be moving with the current only.

DEAD LOW

When the water in a channel is as low as it can get and still permit navigation.

DEAD RECKONING

The determination of where one's vessel will be from the present position to where it will be at some specific time. The term is not used on the river since it usually means a point on a chart and advancing a course plot line to some future point. Since river vessels do not navigate for any distance in straight course lines, Pilots figure vessel and tow speed through the water to make an educated determination of time as to where they will be at another specific place, i.e. "We're only making 2 MPH in this swift current so we won't reach Memphis until 9:30 p.m. Wednesday".

DEAD SLOW

A vessel that is proceeding at idle speed, the slowest speed possible with the engines engaged and the propeller(s) barely turning.

DEADEYE

A small loop, or eye, in the end of a wire fitted with a THIMBLE. Also, the socket terminating in the end of a wire that is closed with a splice to be used to receive a SHACKLE.

DEADHEADING

1. A Pilot who is posting up, but is not standing, a watch.

2. A person who is a guest and is not paying any fare.

3. Cargo which is shipped at no charge.

4. The name log rafters gave to a log that had more sap in one end, which would make it tend to sink toward the bottom with one end floating up creating havoc with steamer paddlewheels. Also called, sinkers, sleepers, sawyers, and hull inspectors.

5. A towboat running without a tow. See: LIGHT BOAT.

DEADMAN

An anchoring device that is buried on the shore, and held in place with heavy timbers, steel channels, concrete, or some other type of weight. Attached to the *deadman* is a heavy wire or chain with a ring at its end that is used to receive a line when tying off tows. Often the *deadman* has a SHORE WIRE attached to it that can be easily reached by the tow's crew with a SPIKE POLE and then used to make a tie off for barges. It was probably termed *deadman* as when it is secured in the ground it doesn't move.

DEADRISE

An upward slope from the centerline of the keel to the sides of the vessel. It is designed on vessels so built that any water in the hull will drain toward the center to be easily pumped out. However, the term is often used indiscriminately to describe any slight rise on a vessel.

DEADWEIGHT CAPACITY or TONNAGE

The total weight a tug or towboat will carry at its designed, fully-loaded operating draft. This includes the crew and their gear, all galley stores, other vessel stores, fuel and lube oil, fresh water, any ballast water, etc. This tonnage is the difference between the light displacement (prior to being placed in service) and the vessel's loaded displacement.

DEATH HOOK

A hook on the end of the lever of the safety valve to a boiler. When in a steamboat race the engineer could hang on some extra weight on it to build up the pressure so a steamer could run faster. If too much weight was added the safety valve couldn't pop open, but would continue to increase pressure and perhaps cause the boiler to explode with great loss of life, which is how the *hook* got its name.

DECIBLE

A unit of sound intensity measurement, or a degree of loudness and audibility. In tables of intensity and range it is abbreviated as dB or dB(A) that denotes the level has been adjusted (A) to the sensibility of a human's ear. The term *decibel* from *dec* meaning "a tenth" and *bel* which is a power level named after Alexander Graham Bell. The use of the word on our rivers is found in the Inland Navigation Rules, Annex III, in regard to whistles and bells. See: HERTZ.

DECK

The horizontal structure on a vessel that would correspond to a floor by those who do not live on a tug, towboat, or barge. Originally the term meant a covering and came from the Dutch *dec*, meaning a "roof". Apparently some of the structures were covered and became something that was walked upon, so it became a *deck*. The *decks* of vessels are given various names, some being: main, second, third, pilothouse, upper, cargo, forward, stern, boat, boiler, hurricane, lower, etc.

DECK BARGE

A barge with a flat deck that can be used as a crane barge, or used to carry equipment. Sometimes it may be equipped with a coaming to more easily contain its cargo, such as shells, sand or gravel.

DECK CARGO

Cargo that can be carried on an open deck exposed to the elements.

DECK ENGINEER

A person on a towboat, usually with a small crew, who works as a deckhand but also does some routine maintenance on the engine, checking gauges, necessary oil work, etc.

DECK GEAR

A general term for most of the working equipment used on deck to work the towboat and the tow, including line, barge wires, ratchets, slings, chain links, etc.

DECK LIGHT(S)

The exterior lights on the main deck of a tug or towboat.

DECK LOG

A rough record of all navigational information that takes place on a Pilot's watch. Includes such things as the mile point when the watch starts, the times of any barge pickups or drops with the names and numbers of the barges, the times of locking, any unusual weather conditions such as fog, any damages or accidents, crew changes, or any other incident that may occur on watch. See: OFFICIAL LOG.

DECK PASSAGE

Persons who made a trip on a packetboat who did not pay for the glorified opulence of the cabin or staterooms; but probably more persons traveled in *deck passage* than were booked in cabin passage. Sometimes a cot would be provided, but mostly these passengers rode wherever they could find space: on the cargo, a wood pile, or space on the deck. They were not allowed on the upper decks or in the cabin. Usually no food was provided. They ate what food they brought, or attempted to buy some at a landing. The sanitary facility was simply a bucket. Most of these passengers were emigrants heading to start a new life in the West. Outbreaks of disease, especially cholera, were often rampant. When the Steamboat Inspection Service came into existence in 1852, it did little except require a means of escape for these passengers if the vessel was on fire or was sinking.

DECK STORES

The spare material or stores that a vessel might carry for its upkeep, such as paint, extra line, flashlight batteries, ladders, swabs, brooms, etc.

DECKED OVER

An area that is usually open, but a covering has been built over the area.

DECKHAND

A member of a vessel's crew who works on deck whose duties include making up tow, picking up and dropping barges, making locks, chipping paint, painting, cleaning the vessel, or anything else the Mate or the Captain believe is required to keep the vessel shipshape and operating properly.

DECKHOUSE

1. A small house, usually portable and movable, sometimes placed on board a tank barge for a watchman or tankerman to get out of the weather.
2. Sometimes used to refer to a storage room for rain gear, work vests, and other gear, located at the bow. Also called a deck locker, gear locker, or DOGHOUSE.

DECKING

The act of carrying out the duties to be performed by a deckhand.

DECLARATION OF INSPECTION (D.O.I.)

Prior to the transfer of a cargo of oil or hazardous material to or from a vessel the designated person-in-charge is required to fill out an inspection form that requires information as to time, place, cargo, etc. and has a checklist of requirements to be undertaken prior to any commencement of cargo transfer.

DEDICATED TOW

A tow, including the boat and its barges, that moves only one type of cargo from origin to destination. Only in rare instances will the tow pick up or drop other barges en route. It is a common practice in the movement of coal and liquid products.

DEEP-NOTCH TUG-BARGE

A rounded "V"-shaped recess built into a barge to accommodate the bow shape of a tug that will be rigidly connected to it, forming a COMPOSITE UNIT.

DEEP SIX

An expression carried over from sea going vessels. In old sailing days when the LEADSMAN heaved the lead sounding *deep six* it meant six fathoms, or 36 feet of water depth. It was usually enough safe water in which to navigate, or nearly a "no bottom" sounding. The term took on the meaning that if one wanted to get rid of something no longer of use, or if gear washed over the side in rough water, it had been *deep-sixed*, or never again to be seen. It was also a custom that when a person died aboard a vessel their body would only be committed to the deep in over six fathoms of water. There have been instances when river deckhands have taken old steamboat ratchets which weighed about 125 lbs and *deep-sixed* them rather than carry them back to the steamboat; however, since the 1899 Refuse Act has been interpreted by the courts to mean that putting or throwing anything in our rivers is illegal, no one throws anything into it anymore.

DEEP-WELL PUMP

A centrifugal-type pump commonly used on tank barges carrying refined petroleum or chemical products. The pump is mounted on a long shaft with its impeller on the end. It sits in a sealed well that has cargo piping from the cargo tanks to the well, and then from the pump to the discharge line.

DEFENSE PLANT CORPORATION (DPC)

A government agency that came into being at the start of WW II to allocate resources and supply capital where it was not available in the private sector to produce things to help the war effort. On the rivers the *DPC* built 21 towboats, 180 feet long, 52 feet wide, with an 11-foot hull and nine-foot twin screws. These vessels were originally specified to be diesel-powered, but the need for engines for war equipment was more pressing so steam engines were installed instead. The boats, as well as barges the *DPC* had built, were run by private companies. The steamboats were generally named after battles that took place early in WW II. After the war was over, the boats were gradually phased out since they became too expensive to run, requiring large crews. Some were converted to dredges; others to floating harbor offices, one or two became restaurants, while others became landing fleet boats.

DEFERRED MAINTENANCE

Needed normal planned maintenance of navigation facilities that is postponed due to lack of budgeted funds, usually leading to unscheduled shutdowns and increased costs. See: OUTAGES and FIX-AS-FAILS.

DEGRADATION

When used in reference to a river it is the erosion of sediment from the stream bed when flows are diminished from higher levels of water flow with a lessening of silt material washing into the stream as well as reduction in the gradient slope of the river causing more flow activity along its bed. The term is the opposite of AGGRADATION.

DEGREE

1. A unit of temperature, either in Fahrenheit or Celsius measurement. The term goes back to Latin, with *de* meaning "down", and *gradus*, meaning "a step", or "rise"; therefore, as used in measurement it can be an increase or decrease.

2. A unit of angular distance, or $1/360^{th}$ part of a circle.

DELAY TIME

The time in hours and minutes that a vessel and tow have to wait for lockage after arriving at a lock site.

DELTA

An alluvial deposit formed at the mouth of a stream or river. These can be as small as what is termed a "creek bar", or if a large amount of sediment is deposited it may be termed a "river bar", such as the *delta* at the mouth of the Chippewa River on the Upper Mississippi that formed Lake Pepin. They also can be as great as the deposit of the Mississippi River formed at its mouth before it enters the Gulf of Mexico. *Deltas* are generally formed in a fan-type triangular shape as the effluent from the river stream drops its sediment when reaching the end of its journey at a slower moving or standing body of water. The term comes from the fourth letter of the Greek alphabet, which is shaped like a triangle.

DELTA QUEEN

One of the few overnight passenger steamboats operating on our river system.

She, along with her sister ship, the *DELTA KING*, were built in 1926 to carry passengers on the Sacramento River in California. The USN took over the vessels at the start of WW II and used them in ferrying operations. They fell into disrepair after the war, but in 1947 the Greene Line of Cincinnati, bought the *DELTA QUEEN* and brought her from San Francisco, through the Panama Canal, on to New Orleans and up to Pittsburgh to be refurbished and put into service on our inland waterways. The whole story has been written in numerous books. She was granted various exemptions to continue to carry passengers after the Safety Of Life At Sea (SOLAS) Act requirements went into effect in the 1960s that vessels with wooden superstructures carrying over 50 passengers on overnight trips would no longer be allowed to operate, but as this is written the *DELTA QUEEN's* last exemption expired in 2008 and may not be renewed.

DEMARCATION LINE

An imaginary line that is drawn in coastal areas that determines when a vessel must operate in compliance with the International Navigation Rules when leaving waters that are determined to be under the jurisdiction of the Inland Navigation Rules. Generally, the line is short and direct from headland to headland, with distinct marks usually visible to the naked eye, but which are also marked on navigation charts. A general list of the *Demarcation Lines* designating COLREGS waters along U.S. shores are listed in 33 CFR 80, and the USCG book on the Navigation Rules. Few towboats ever pass the *line of demarcation* as they are not capable to operate in sea conditions, but tugs are frequent visitors beyond the line and have to adapt to the changing rules when they do.

DEMISE CHARTER

The charter of a vessel without crew or stores. See: BAREBOAT CHARTER.

DEMURRAGE

The days a barge, or other vessel, is delayed through no fault of the vessel owner, after being placed for loading or unloading at a dock, beyond agreed to LAY DAYS. A monetary penalty or charge is assessed on the shipper for the delay, either in hours or days. The word comes to us from the French *demur,* meaning "delay".

DEPARTMENT OF HOMELAND SECURITY

After the 9/11/01 terrorist attack on our country, Congress enacted legislation that created the Department in 2003. Its mission is to lead the unified national effort to secure America. Its intent is to prevent and deter terrorist attacks, protect against and respond to threats and hazards to the nation, ensure safe and secure borders, welcome lawful immigrants and visitors, and promote the free-flow of commerce. The U.S. Coast Guard is one key component of the Department, with the Commandant reporting directly to the Secretary.

DEPARTURE

The logged place and time of leaving a particular port, lock, or other location, en route to another destination.

DEPOT

In the Eighth Coast Guard District it usually refers to the home base for a USCG buoy tender station where the crew and boat is based. Buoys, lights and all the appendages of gear that are used by the buoy boats is stored at the *depot.*

DEPRECIATION

An accounting measure of the reduction in value of an asset, be it a tug, towboat, or barge, due to age with normal wear and tear based on an average life from acquisition to a time it is believed the asset will no longer have an economic value. Therefore, it will have to be retired from service. The word source is the Latin *de,* to mean "down", and *pretium,* which is "price". The term "to depreciate" originally meant "to disparage" or to marry someone of inferior ranking. Later in mercantile trade it took on the meaning of a lessening of market value. Tell that to your spouse.

DEPTH
1. The vertical distance from the water surface of a river to its bed or bottom. See: PROJECT DEPTH and CONTROLLING DEPTH.

2. The depth of a vessel's hull submerged in a body of water. More often termed the DRAFT of a vessel.

3. In vessel construction it a measurement of different scantling proportions, i.e. the size of a floor frame, or the vertical height of the hull from its keel plates to the deck structures at various locations, etc.

DEPTH SOUNDER or RECORDER
An electronic device that is used to determine the depth of water in which a tow or vessel is operating. It receives a signal from a TRANSDUCER that is mounted on the head of a tow, usually in the center, that sends an audio signal to the bottom of the riverbed. When it receives an echo back it electronically measures the depth of water and sends the signal to a monitor in the pilothouse of a towboat or tug. Some vessels are equipped with two *depth sounders* and will have a transducer mounted on both the starboard and port sides of the tow. The sounder is sometimes called an *acoustical depth finder*, *echo sounder*, or an *ultrasonic depth sounder*. A "Fathometer" is a trade name for one type of *depth sounder* and should not be used in a generic sense. If the signal is printed out the device is called a *depth recorder*.

DERELICT
A vessel that is entirely deserted or abandoned in that the owner has made no intention to recover or return to the vessel, whether the status was the result of a casualty, adverse weather, deterioration, or some other cause, and was done out of necessity, or was a voluntary act of abandonment. If the vessel is an impediment to navigation the government can require its removal by the owner, or if the owner fails to remove it, the government may take steps to have it removed and bill the cost to the owner. The word comes from the Latin *derelictus,* meaning "abandoned".

DERRICK
A type of crane that is a boom anchored at the foot of a TOPPING LIFT that provides support of the *derrick boom*. The topping lift gives the boom the necessary angle for the lift, while guy lines control the lateral movement of the boom. Like DAVIT, the word is named for a person. Ominously, it was named after a famous executioner in England and was a gallows that resembled the crane that was used to carry out his trade; it took on the name of the hangman called *Derrick*. See: A-FRAME.

DERRICK BOAT
Either a self-propelled vessel or a barge that is pushed by a tug or towboat that has a *derrick* mounted on the deck. Very large *derrick boats* are used for heavy lifts in river construction or salvage work and are often called A-FRAME barges. Others, with varying lifting capacities, are employed by shipyards and docks to do a variety of work. The USACE uses, and used them at all the dams that had movable wickets that had to be tripped and lowered when there was open river, and then when the wickets had to be raised when the river flows subsided.

DESCENDING VESSEL
The old *Western River Rules of the Road* used the word *descending* to mean a vessel that was going downstream with the current, and conversely when the vessel was going upstream against the current it was termed the ASCENDING vessel. The Navigation Rules now use the term, "proceeding downbound with a following current".

DESIGN FLOOD
Refers to the maximum amount of water a flood-control project is designed and engineered to withstand and offer protection.

DESIGNATED EXAMINER (DE)
A Master/Mate(Pilot) who is qualified to supervise, train, assess, and certify the ability and performance of an Apprentice Mate (Pilot), or steersman, who is qualifying to become a Mate(Pilot) of towing vessels. The apprentice will work under the direct supervision of the Master learning towboat/tug navigational skills along with the knowledge and application of required safety practices and regulations.

There is an extensive checklist of tasks required to be accomplished. After satisfactory evaluation the DE will sign and date the TOWING OFFICER ASSESSMENT RECORD (TOAR) of the candidate. When all tasks are completed and time in service requirements has been met the candidate may apply to the USCG to receive a Mate (Pilot) license.

DESTINATION
The place to which a cargo, barge, or tow is consigned.

DETENTION
An event or act that occurs causing the delay of a vessel that is the result of an action or another party depriving the owner or charterer of the vessel's use.

DEVIATION
The term refers to a magnetic compass and the amount of error its needle may show from true magnetic North. Very few riverboats carry a magnetic compass on board since Pilots don't set their course or steer by compass.

DEVIL
Wooden-hulled vessels had to have their hull seams caulked, usually a hard and dirty job. A seam in a particularly hard place to work, just above the waterline, was called a *devil* (to caulk). From this we inherit the phrase from the old seagoing ships, "between the devil and the deep blue sea", because caulking the *devil* put one in a very precarious position. Also, caulked seams were coated with pitch or tar spread from a PAYPOT to seal them, called "to pay". From that we get the expression, "the devil to pay".

DEVIL'S BACKBONE
A description of a rock ridge that runs along the Upper Mississippi River in the area of Grand Tower, IL. The area claimed many a steamboat, including the Steamer *GOLDEN EAGLE* in 1947.

DEVIL'S COFFIN
A small, shallow-draft, decked-over boat with very little freeboard that was subject to capsizing. See: SNEAK BOX.

DEW POINT
The air can only hold a certain amount of moisture at a given temperature. That amount is its relative humidity. The *dew point* is reached when moisture in the air exceeds the relative humidity, or 100% of saturation, causing condensation or fog to possibly occur.

dGPS
An acronym for Differential Global Positioning System, which is a more accurate form of GPS, using radio signals to more precisely correct the satellite GPS signal.

DIAMOND-SHAPED
1. The usual shape of a DAYMARK aid to navigation on the river.
2. A black day signal required by certain vessels to display indicating their employment such as dredges,

DIESEL ELECTRIC

certain vessels being towed astern, inconspicuous partly submerged vessels, and a vessel restricted in its ability to maneuver or deviate from its course. The description and where they are to be displayed are listed in the Navigation Rules.

DIESEL ELECTRIC

A diesel engine that drives an electric generator that in turn is coupled to the propeller shaft to provide propulsion power. Not frequently used on towboats.

DIESEL ENGINE

An internal combustion engine that uses diesel fuel to power it, rather than burning gasoline. Injectors in the engine spray diesel fuel into the engine combustion chambers, which is then ignited, resulting in the compression stroke providing power. Nearly all towboats and tugs on the river and canals of the U.S. are diesel-powered. Diesel fuel and engines acquire their name from Rudolf Diesel, who developed the first prototype engine in 1893 which was designed to run on vegetable oil.

DIFFERENTIAL

A negotiation that occurs if a vessel owner has a contract to deliver barges between an origin and a destination point for a shipper at a certain rate. If, during the contract the shipper wants some barges or tonnage to go to a different destination, the resolution of an adjustment in the cost of the shipping rate is then mutually arbitrated and a new rate is resolved and agreed to by both parties. It is also termed EQUALIZATION.

DIKE

A type of construction used by the USACE on rivers to manage the current flow in order to stabilize the channel by a predictable scouring action of the river bottom and to protect the shore bank from erosion. *Dikes* were originally constructed by driving piling more or less perpendicular to the shore and current, except for trail *dikes* which ran parallel to the shore. Now nearly all new *dikes* are of rock construction and can be not only perpendicular, but also in other shapes. The names of some types of constructed *dikes* varies in different Corps Districts and in publications. Although *dikes* can usually be seen during low or normal flows of water, they may be covered at high stages and can present a danger to vessels not operating in the channel. The USACE publishes the elevation of *dikes* on river charts and/or in river bulletins. The word *dike* comes from the old Norse word *dik,* related to "ditch".

See: BAFFLE, BENDWAY WEIR, BULLNOSE, CHEVRON, CLOSURE, CURTAIN, DIKE FIELD, HARD POINT, KICKER, LONGITUDINAL, L – SHAPED, MULTIPLE ROUND POINT, NOTCHED, PERMABLE, PILE, SPUR, TOE, TRAIL, VANE, and WING DAM. Other names given to various types include contracting dikes, cross dikes, cross dams, GROINS or groynes, JETTY, submerged sills, and transverse dikes. There are probably others, since when one type doesn't fit an exact description of those listed the potamologist will invent a new one.

DIKE FIELD

A group or series of dikes along a shoreline in a single area constructed to manage the channel flow. The *dike field* is carefully engineered according to dike height, the space between the dikes, whether notches are included, the level of the dikes, either all level or sloped from the bank, or step-crested from the bank, depending upon what the hydrology of the locality indicates to most appropriately scour the channel without creating sandbars in inappropriate areas.

DIKE MARKER

An aid to navigation in the form of a light or daymark placed on the riverward end of the dike. It is usually called a *dike light* or a *dike daymark*.

DINGHY

A small rowboat carried aboard a towboat. Also called a *yawl, skiff,* or a *pirogue* (though incorrectly). It is believed to come from the Hindu *dinhi,* which means "small boat".

DINNER BUCKET BOAT

A harbor or fleet towboat where the crew lives on shore and has to bring anything they wish to eat while on duty from home in a lunch pail or bag. The boat they work on does not have living quarters and usually has only limited or no facilities for food storage or preparation.

DIP

The distance a PADDLEWHEEL enters the water with its buckets. Generally, the rule for the design of a paddlewheel that was built for power when pushing heavy loads was to use a small wheel and deep buckets. When speed was desired, the rule was to increase the diameter of the wheel and reduce its dip in the water. The term *dip* comes to us from Old English, *dyppan,* and possibly traces back to the German *taufen,* that meant "to baptize", or in other words "to douse, immerse, or *dip*" an infant (or a paddlewheel) in the water.

DIPPER DREDGE

A dredge fitted with a boom and an excavating shovel mounted on a barge. Also called a DRAGLINE DREDGE. Sometimes incorrectly referred to as a crane with a clamshell bucket that is used for dredging.

DIPPING THE EYE

When tying off a vessel at a dock and it is necessary to put the eye of a line on the same bollard or timberhead that already has one leading from some other vessel, it is prudent to put your line's eye up through the eye of the line already placed and then put it over the fitting. In this manner either line can be easily removed independent of each other.

DIRECT DRIVE

The coupling of steam-reciprocating or diesel-propulsion drive to a propeller shaft without the use of an intermediate gearbox. Requires the engine to be disengaged when operating in the forward or ahead position, and then restarted in the reverse position to go astern.

DISABLED

A vessel that is unable to safely navigate, because either its engine or steering gear is not properly functioning, or it is aground. In the Navigation Rules such a vessel is defined in Rule 3(f), ".....a vessel which through some exceptional circumstance is unable to maneuver as required by these Rules and is therefore unable to keep out of the way of another vessel".

DISCHARGE

1. The unloading of cargo from a barge.
2. Any release that may be emitted from a vessel by spilling, leaking, emptying, or other like causes.
3. The amount, or volume, of water flowing through a dam in cubic feet per second.
4. The river flow in CUBIC FEET PER SECOND at certain monitoring stations along the river.
5. The flow of water or ice from a river at a given time.
6. The flow of current away from the propeller.
7. The outward flow of suction material from a dredge's pipeline to an area away from the channel.
8. The release or firing of crew personnel.

DISCHARGE BOOK

The book used by steamboat clerks to list all items of cargo that were unloaded at each landing the vessel made.

DISCIPLINE

Back in the days of keelboats and flatboats if the crew members didn't do what the Mike Finks of the river required of them, they would be lucky if they were only heaved overboard to fend for themselves. Perhaps a little less stressful was steamboating since the Captain might only put a person who didn't do what he was told, or was disrespectful, off on the nearest bank, even if it happened to be an island. Now-a-days, with laws, regulations, grievance committees, arbitration, and what have you, the Captain of a towboat is lucky if he can make a firing stick of a lazy, unsafe, filthy, malcontent crewmember.

But even the keelboaters had it good. In a seagoing sailor's day prior to the 1800s, routine punishment might be cuts from the lashes of a cat-o'-nine tails. More serious offenses could result in a keelhauling where a seaman was lashed and hauled up to the yardarm on one side of a vessel. His legs were tied with weights attached and another line. The seaman was then pulled under the vessel and pulled up on the other side. This punishment was conceived by the Dutch but was adopted by other seafaring countries as well. The worst offense by a seaman might call for BOWSPRITTING. So, things have come a long way in the maritime world, including the conditions when working on our rivers.

DISCONTINUED

The term used by the USCG to indicate the removal from operation, either permanent or temporarily, of a previously authorized aid to navigation.

DISCOUNT RATE

A percentage interest *rate* assigned to the present valuation of a navigation project in an attempt to measure the return in benefits to the public over the estimated economic life of a structure. It is not precise as many of the probable benefits to the public are not accrued, nor included, when studies are made. Additionally, the *discount rate* often used is higher than the cost to the public for the investment.

DISCREPENCY

The failure of an aid to navigation to be in its prescribed position. It may be damaged, unlit, or is missing, such as a light, daymark, or channel buoy.

DISEMBARK

Persons leaving a vessel, either temporarily or permanently. The term was used more frequently on packetboats, passenger vessels, and excursion boats, than on towboats or tugs. The term is the opposite of EMBARK, or to go aboard a vessel.

DISMANTLE

1. To strip, or take off, all the stores, equipment, and gear from a vessel.
2. To take apart, such as an engine, to overhaul it.

DISPATCHER

The person in an office of a vessel-operating company who sends, or *dispatches*, orders to a vessel as to what barges to pick up or drop, and where. Also refers to the person who schedules crew changes.

DISPLACEMENT

The number of tons of water displaced by a vessel, which gives the actual weight of the vessel at the given time of measurement. On the river it is, one ton = 2000 pounds. Of course, when the USCG requires naval architects to calculate tonnage for admeasurements, it must be done in tons of 2240 pounds.

DISPLACEMENT LIGHT
The weight of a vessel without stores and cargo.

DISPLACEMENT LOADED
The weight of a vessel fully loaded with cargo, stores, and fuel.

DISPLACEMENT TONNAGE TABLE or SCALE
A chart that gives the tonnage in a barge at a given average draft. When taking drafts to estimate cargo tonnage it should be remembered that each inch of water in the voids or cargo box of a jumbo barge weighs approximately 17 tons. Most barging companies have a set of tables prepared by the shipyard where a barge may be constructed that calibrates the amount of tonnage in the barge for each inch of immersion in the water.

DISPLAY
The image shown on a radar scope or an electronic chart.

DISTANCE MADE GOOD
The amount of river miles traveled in a measured amount of time, such as a watch, or a day. It is used to estimate the miles per hour the towboat and tow are making and to calculate the time it will take to get to a dock, landing, lock, etc.

DISTINCT BLAST
The term was used in the pre-1980 Rules of the Road which described the *blast* as: "When applied to whistle signals shall mean a clearly audible blast of any length". The new Navigation Rules do not include the term, but does require in Rule 32 that a "short blast" be about one second, and a "prolonged blast" be from four to six seconds. The Rules also require the blast to be within certain Hz frequencies, depending upon the length of the vessel. These requirements are in Annex III of the Rules.

DISTRESS CALL
In case of emergency any *distress call* should be made on Channel 16 (156.80), the VHF radio telephone stand-by channel required to be monitored by all towboats and tugboats. To get the needed attention, voice communication should be initiated using, "MAYDAY, MAYDAY, MAYDAY", followed by a position and the nature of the emergency.

DISTRESS SIGNAL
In Rule 37 of the Navigation Rules numerous signals are given which can be used to indicate that a vessel is in distress and needs assistance.

DISTRICT COMMANDER
The officer, usually flag or flag select, of the USCG, in command of all Coast Guard activities within his designated area. In 2003, all of the Western Rivers were placed in the 8th Coast Guard District, headquartered in New Orleans, LA. This probably makes the 8th Commander the overseer of the largest fleet of vessels in the world.

DITCH
A term that is used to affectionately, or disparagingly, when describing the Gulf Intracoastal Waterway (GIWW).

DIVE
1. What occurs at times when a tow navigating upriver, running slack water in an eddy and enters the swift water coming off a point causing the lead barges in the tow take water over the bow.

2. To veer off course due to shallow water, especially when MOUNTING A REEF.

3. The action of a channel buoy in swift water that submerges and reappears.

DIVER'S FLAG

Rule 27 of the Navigation Rules states the requirements for lights and a flag to be displayed when a vessel is engaged in diving operations. The *diver's flag* is to be "A rigid replica of the International Code flag "A" not less than 1 meter in height. Measures shall be taken to insure its all-round visibility". Many recreational vessels engaging in scuba diving, however, use a small red flag with a white diagonal stripe through it.

DOCK

1. On the river it is a wharf, pier, landing, or quay where a vessel, particularly a barge, is moored in order to discharge or receive cargo.

2. To land, or bring a vessel or tow alongside a place designated, particularly a wharf or pier where cargo is handled. The term is of Dutch origin *docke,* meaning the "water space between piers", where a vessel can be taken out for repair.

DOCK TRIALS

The testing of a vessel's equipment without leaving the dock. Usually it is performed during or after an overhaul or prior to making RIVER TRIALS.

DOCKAGE

A fee, charge, or tax imposed on a vessel that is moored at a dock or is loading or unloading cargo at a dock.

DOCKING

The act of navigating a vessel or tow alongside a dock and tying off; i.e., "We'll drop the tow at the ABC Fleet and then go upstream and *dock* at the EFG wharf".

DOCKING PLAN

A schematic of the underwater hull lines given to the docking master in charge of a drydock in order to determine how the blocking is to be set to accommodate and safely support the particular hull bottom shape of a vessel intending to be drydocked and repaired. Since nearly all inland barges and towboats have flat bottoms, there is usually not much need for a detailed *docking plan*.

DOCKING TUG

A tugboat in a seaport area that assists a ship in maneuvering to berth or leave from a wharf, dock, or anchorage.

DOCTOR

A type of pump used on river steamboats that feeds the water into the vessel's boilers when a steamer is stopped temporarily at a landing or dock. In the early steamboating days auxiliary pumps were coupled to the propulsion engine, so in effect when the boat was not underway, and the engines were stopped, no water was being fed to the boilers. If the fire heating the boiler was not radically reduced and adequate water was not in the boiler, pressure could build up to catastrophic ranges and possibly explode.

An independent pump for feeding water to the boiler basically solved the problem and took on the name of *doctor* as it was supposed to cure the ills of boiler explosions. The pump was also used to do auxiliary work, such as running the fire-fighting system, pumping bilges, washing down decks, etc. It has been reported that Henry Shreve was the first to use a *doctor* on his snagboats; however, others have claimed the first one put in service was on the *Str. ORLEANS* in 1839. Others state the first was on the *Str. MISSOURI* in 1841. Whoever was first is unimportant since they soon were placed on all steamers if their owners wanted to reduce the danger of their boilers exploding.

DOCUMENT

1. The certificate a mariner receives after qualifying to perform

certain duties by the USCG, such as a Tankerman endorsement on the MERCHANT MARINE DOCUMENT. See: LICENSE for other personnel *documents*.

2. A vessel's CERTIFICATE OF ENROLLMENT.

3. A vessel's CERTIFICATE OF FINANCIAL RESPONSIBILITY.

4. A vessel's CERTIFICATE OF INSPECTION.

5. The bill of lading, manifest, or shipping papers on each tank barge in a tow carrying liquid products regulated by 46 CFR 35 and 151

DOCUMENT HOLDER or TUBE

Certificated tank barges usually have a small piece of pipe, two or three inches in diameter, with a screwed cap located on or near the warning sign that carries the barge's Certificate of Inspection, and other information required. Others have a rural mailbox placed on the barge.

DOCUMENTATION

The process of showing proof of ownership by obtaining a CERTIFICATE OF ENROLLMENT for a vessel from the U.S. government (USCG) that means the vessel is enrolled under the laws of the United States and is therefore considered "a vessel of the United States". The *certificate* lists the owner of the vessel who is required to be a U.S. citizen, shows the trade in which the vessel is allowed to engage, as well as the designated homeport of the vessel. A *documented* vessel is subject to a preferred mortgage which will be recorded on the *certificate* which gives the mortgage a superior ranking in filing claims against the vessel.

DOG

1. A handle or lever used to tighten down and secure a door or hatch.

2. The act of securing something, i.e. *dog it down,* or *dog it off.*

3. Sometimes used incorrectly to refer to a HOLD FAST or PAWL.

4. A member of the canine species of dubious parentage that has been somewhat domesticated, but like Pilots, has a mind of its own. Often seen on lock walls, it will follow a tow into the chamber positioning itself opposite the door to the galley. If not noticed it will let out a low bark or two until the cook or a crewman offers it a treat.

DOG STEPS

Short pieces of inverted angle iron welded on the slope sheet of the hopper space of some barges to create a foot hold. They are used by anyone to climb in or out of the hopper when loading or unloading cargo or when cleaning the barge.

DOG WATCH

On Naval vessels with a traditional three-watch system of four hours each, in order to change the monotony of being required to stand the same period of watch day after day, there was developed a system of breaking up the period of the 1600 to 2000 (4 p.m. to 8 p.m.) watch into two watches, one from 1600 to 1800 and the other from 1800 to 2000.

No verifiable information of origin is known. Some say "dog" is a corruption of "dodge" meaning that the *dog watch* was meant to dodge the routine schedule. Others have opined that it was a watch that was "cur-tailed" hence the word "dog". This was mentioned in Admiral Smyth's work, *The Sailor's Word-Book,* in 1867. Some have said it comes from the French, and others the Germans. However, no one seems to know.

Given that history, there were *dog watches* practiced on some of the steamboats, although the period of time for the watch was different. Starting at midnight they ran thusly:

12 a.m. to 3 a.m.
3 a.m. to 6 a.m.
6 a.m. to 12 p.m. (noon)
12 p.m. to 6 p.m.
6 p.m. to 12 p.m. (midnight)

There were different variations of this schedule, but *dog watches* broke up the time that Pilots said was the hardest for them to continually stay alert: from late at night to 6 a.m. Under present law this arrangement would be considered illegal since a Pilot is not allowed to stand more than 12 hours of watch during a 24-hour period. However, during any 48-hour period they would not violate the 12-hour-per-day watch rule. It seems like it could be worth a try.

DOGHOUSE
1. Small temporary cabins or tents where the crews on log rafts slept.
2. Somewhat portable metal sheds that were on some tank barges to shelter a tankerman or watchman when keeping watch on one or more tank barges.
3. Sometimes used to refer to the space just off the forward main deck where the crew stores their work-vest life jackets, rain gear, work tools, and other equipment. It is also called a DECKHOUSE.

DOGLEG
A crook, or sharp turn, in a channel crossing. At times, especially in low water, there can be more than one.

DOLLAR HOLE
Used as a term in the galley where scraps or unused food was thrown in a chute to be disposed of. In steamboat days it was a chute or pipe that led directly to the river. Termed a *dollar hole* since some owners believed the waste disposal was their money going into the river. No scrap food is thrown in the river nowadays, therefore, the dollar hole has gone by the waterside and is as extinct as the Dodo bird.

DOLPHIN
1. A cluster of wooden pilings cabled together, or a round structure made of interlocking sheet piles and filled with rock and/or sand; used as moorings at a dock or as protection at a bridge or other structure.
2. A single wood pile or steel structure often used by the USCG to display an aid to navigation, especially in lakes and bays.

DOMINANT MIND DOCTRINE
A legal term in which the courts long ago decided when a vessel that has other vessels in tow, the entire tow is in the control of the vessel under power, and operates as if it is a single vessel. Therefore, a towboat or tug is the *dominant mind* of its barge tow, and is the responsible party for damages in any casualty if it is found negligent.

DONKEY BOILER
A small auxiliary steam boiler for non-propulsion use to run winches, cranes, siphons, provide heat, etc.

"DON'T STEP ON A SHADOW"
A warning given to all persons when walking on a barge tow. The blinding beam from a searchlight or the bright lights on a dock might give the impression of a shadow, but may actually be the river since it is difficult at times to determine the end or side of a barge or of a pier.

DOUBLE BITTS
Two single bitts close together on a dock, usually on a single base. Sometimes called a *double bollard* when used ashore or in deep sea language. On a river barge they are called TIMBERHEADS.

DOUBLE BOTTOM
A watertight compartment between a hull's bottom skin and a cargo or working space above it. Many of today's towboats are built with *double bottoms*. Also most hopper and tank barges are DOUBLE SKIN and the term is used to denote the void space under the cargo space

DOUBLE-ENDER
1. A ferryboat that can be operated in either direction without being required to be turned around. Both the bow and the stern have the same hull lines.
2. A person who is licensed to serve as a river Engineer and as a Pilot.

DOUBLE GONG
The signal or action to go ahead full power with all the rpm's the engine is capable of producing. It was a signal from the pilothouse to the engine room on the steamboat bell system, but the term is used on diesel-powered vessels to denote overload propulsion through a difficult area. See: BELLS.

DOUBLE-HEADER
The action of log rafters at narrow bridges to move the towboat and bow boat to one side of the raft, break loose the lines on half the width of the tow and let it drift down until it could be swung under the half being held by the towboat, then tying the ends together to go through the bridge. After completion of transit the bow section would be swung back alongside the other half of the raft. The towboat and bow boat moved into original positions while the raft proceeded downriver. See: DOUBLE TRIP, SADDLEBAG, and SPLITTING THE PIER.

DOUBLE LOCKAGE
When a tow is of dimensions that are longer than the size of a lock chamber, the towboat enters the lock, separates the tow at the BREAK COUPLING, then backs out of the lock chamber and ties off on the lock wall while the first part of the tow is locked through. The first part of the tow is next pulled out of the lock by a winch and tied off on the lock wall outside of the chamber. Then the lock is TURNED AROUND to lock the second half of the tow. After locking the second part, the towboat shoves it out of the chamber and reattaches it to the first part and departs the lock.

DOUBLE-PLATE or DOUBLING
The covering over of a vessel's hull skin, either wood or steel, without removing the existing shell covering. It was sometimes performed on old hulls that needed frequent repair to give them a few more years of life. The act of *double-plating* a hull is also called *half-sole*, or *putting on a band-aid*.

DOUBLE SKIN
A vessel, especially a barge, with an outer hull skin over a watertight inner skin that encloses the cargo space, with a void between the enclosures. All hopper and tank barges on the Western Rivers presently being built are *double- skinned*.

DOUBLE-STACK
The stacking of containers, one on top of another, in a barge. It can be more than two high, i.e. "I've got 'em three (or more) high this trip".

DOUBLE-TRIP
To tie off a tow, take a portion of it to another location, and then return to get the rest of the tow. This is usually done when the current in a section of river is extremely swift and the towboat does not have sufficient power to stem the current and push the tow through it; or if the Pilot of a vessel with a large tow, while proceeding downriver, deemed it unsafe to navigate into a lock chamber or through a narrow bridge.

A similar action was taken by log rafters at narrow bridges by splitting a large raft into two sections and taking one part through at a time. For other actions of rafters at bridges see: DOUBLE HEADER, SADDLEBAG, and SPLITTING THE PIER.

DOUBLE-UP
1. The act of doubling, or making a mooring line lead into two parts for greater strength with less chance of

132 DOUBLER

parting, or breaking.

2. The action of putting on two sets of rigging on the fore and aft couplings on a tow. It is most often done on the outside couplings of the tow where the greatest leverage is exerted when steering.

DOUBLER

1. A steel plate that is welded to an existing hull plate to add reinforcing strength spread over a greater area. It is often done where mooring fittings, such as bitts, cavels or chocks, are welded to the deck of a vessel.

2. The process of welding a steel plate over a holed or cracked area to make repair to a damaged area.

DOWN (BY THE HEAD or STERN)

A vessel that is not on an even keel, or not having the same measurement both fore and aft, but is of greater draft at the bow, or the stern. Although this condition occasionally occurs on a towboat or tug due to fuel tank usage, or a leaking void tank, it is uncommon as most Engineers and Masters want their vessels running on an even keel as they were designed to operate at greatest efficiency and with less vibration. The action more often occurs in barges that are often sloppily loaded or could possibly have a flooded void compartment. Sometimes barges have to have an end ballasted in order for it to adequately HEADLOG with another barge.

DOWN THE SHAPE

To proceed with a vessel and/or tow an easy distance off the shape of the shore, dikes, revetment, docks, etc.

DOWN TIME

1. A period of inactivity when a vessel is not able to be productive.

2. A period when a piece of equipment on a vessel, such as an engine, generator, or other machinery, is out of service for repair or other reasons.

DOWNBOUND

A vessel or tow that is proceeding with the flow of a downstream current.

DOWNDRAFT

When the current is drawing a vessel in a particular direction, i.e. "There is a strong *downdraft* on the lower green buoy", or "There is a strong *downdraft* running across ABC Point", or "There's a pretty good *downdraft* on the shore at the lower guidewall of McAlpine Lock".

DOWNSTREAM

1. The direction in which a vessel or tow is proceeding with the current.

2. A point, place, or direction that is further down the river than where one is presently located.

3. The opposite of UPRIVER or UPSTREAM

DOWNSTREAM LANDING

1. A maneuver undertaken by a towboat of going upstream from a barge or tow, turning around, and then proceeding downstream to land on the head of the tow. In heavy flowing current a maneuver such as this should only be undertaken by an experienced Pilot since it can be risky, especially if the towboat does not handle well under these circumstances.

2. The action taken of a downbound tow being backed into, or alongside, a landing, dock, wharf, or another tow with the towboat's direction still heading downstream.

DPC

See: DEFENSE PLANT CORPORATION

DRAFT

1. The depth of water in which a vessel floats, measured from the surface of the water to the lowest or

deepest part of the vessel's hull. See: DRAFT MARKS, DYNAMIC DRAFT, LIGHT DRAFT, LOADED DRAFT, MEAN DRAFT, and STATIC DRAFT.

2. A current that draws a vessel or object in a particular direction, i.e. "There is a right-hand *draft* on the right channel pier of the ABC Bridge", or "There is a DOWNDRAFT on the lower red buoy in this crossing".

DRAFT MARKS

Numerals, usually Arabic on the river, which are painted, and usually bead-welded, on fore and aft places of towboats and barges to indicate the depth of water in which the vessel is immersed. The numerals are six inches in height to make it easier to read, or GAUGE, the *draft*. The measurement is taken from the bottom edge of the number. For instance, if the water is exactly at the bottom of the "9", the *draft* is nine feet; at the top of the "9" it would be nine feet and six inches.

DRAFT SURVEY

To take the draft measurements of a barge at the port bow and stern, and starboard bow and stern, both when empty and then when loaded. The results can then be averaged to find the MEAN DRAFT from which the loaded cargo tonnage can be determined from a DISPLACEMENT TONNAGE TABLE.

DRAFT TABLES

See: DISPLACEMENT TONNAGE TABLE.

DRAG

1. The resistance or friction of a vessel's hull being moved through water.

2. A tow that has heavier loads on one side may cause some slight extra rudder to the opposite side in order to keep on course, i.e. "The tow *drags* to starboard".

3. The friction and turbulence caused by a barge's square end, i.e. "We've lost some time because we're *dragging* three boxes".

4. Said of an anchor that has lost its bite, or hold, on the bottom.

DRAG STRING

A STRING of barges that are tied, usually on lines, to the barges that are being pushed by a towboat. Also see: PUSH STRING.

DRAGLINE DREDGE

A large evacuator crane boom with a bucket attached that is pulled in to remove material or smooth out a river bottom or a shoreline. See: DIPPER DREDGE.

DRAINAGE AREA

The total land area from which rainwater or snowmelt drains, into a stream or river. For a major river such as the Ohio or Missouri, all tributaries are included. The total *drainage area* of the Mississippi River before it enters the Gulf of Mexico comprises 41% of the land area of the contiguous United States.

DRAW

1. A navigable span of a movable bridge; on a SWING SPAN a Pilot might say, "I'm going to take the right-hand *draw*".

2. The DRAFT of a vessel, i.e. "She *draws* eight feet on the bow and nine on the stern".

3. The action of current towards an object, i.e. "There is a *draw* (of current) toward the left-hand pier of the bridge".

4. The process a First Class Pilot had to perform in sketching the river over the stretch for which he wanted to obtain a license.

DRAWBRIDGE

A bridge crossing a waterway that is too low to provide for the passage of vessels and must be opened to allow for navigation through it. See: BAS-

CULE BRIDGE, FLOATING BRIDGE, LIFT BRIDGE, PONTOON BRIDGE and SWING BRIDGE.

DRAWDOWN

The upstream lowering of a pool created by a navigation dam in order to increase the dam's holding capacity in anticipation of flooding conditions. Also, a *drawdown* of a pool is done for environmental considerations in some areas at certain times of the year.

DREDGE

1. A vessel that is designed to remove sediment or hard river-bottom material from the channel to maintain navigational project depth, or from around docks to maintain access to load and unload vessels. Different versions of the origination of the term have been postulated. Some say it comes from the Dutch *dregghe,* that is a sort of grappling hook that one uses when dragging the bottom of a stream trying to catch or hook on to something; others seem to believe it was from the Anglo-Saxon *drecq,* meaning "to pull or to draw". See: BUCKET DREDGE, CUT, CUTTERHEAD DREDGE, DIPPER DREDGE, DUSTPAN DREDGE, and HOPPER DREDGE.

2. The act of removing material from the bed of a waterway maintain a desired depth. A *dredge cut* is one pass, or line, of the *dredge* through an area in which it is evacuating DREDGE MATERIAL.

DREDGE MATERIAL or SPOIL

The substances that are excavated or removed from a riverbed channel, or other area. In the past, this was referred to as *dredge spoil,* or waste to be disposed of. *Spoil* came from the Latin *spoliare,* meaning "to plunder". However, it was found that oftentimes the material that was dredged had value and benefits to be used for other purposes, so the term *spoil* has been dropped and replaced with *material* which refers to a product that is employed to make something useful.

DREDGE TENDER

1. A vessel that moves a non-self-propelled dredge from place to place as needed.

2. A small vessel that provides support to a dredge in moving sections of a pipeline, setting anchors, sometimes placing buoys to mark a change in the channel, transporting personnel, etc.

DRESSED

A riverboat or tug is *dressed* when it is decked out in bunting and flags for some ceremonial event, such as when launched, or christened, or for some holiday open house. So, in reality a riverboat always sails nude except when the PR people get involved. They do, however, paint her up a bit.

DRIFT

1. The horizontal movement of a vessel or object under no power floating with, and in the direction of, the current. See: DRAFT.

2. A vessel or object that is floating in the direction of the wind.

3. The speed of the current.

4. Any debris that is floating in the current or left on the shore from a falling river.

5. The motion of a vessel that moves off its intended course due to current or wind. Sometimes used in place of SET, i.e. "Check the *drift* line on that buoy", or "Did you notice the *drift* on the left pier at the ABC Bridge?"

6. Used in conjunction with other floating objects that are floating with the current, i.e. *drift* ice, *drift*wood, etc.

DRIFT BOLT

A long heavy bolt that was used in bolting together timbers of a steamboat.

DRIFTWOOD

The limbs from trees, or the trees themselves, that are floating free in the river, usually washed off the riverbanks on a rising river. They can cause havoc with paddlewheels and propellers, especially those ensconced in a kort nozzle. *Driftwood*, or *drift*, can also build up on the heads of fleets of barges to the extent of breaking them loose if not securely tied off and watched closely. When a river stage starts falling some of the *drift* will go ashore only to become waterborne again on the next rise. "A river always comes back to claim its *drift*" (unknown).

DRINKING WATER

See POTABLE WATER.

DRIP PAN

A container that is placed under a liquid tank transfer hose at the connection to a vessel pipeline header in order to catch any drippage when hooking up or uncoupling the hose, and during cargo transfer.

DRIVE

To come full speed ahead on the engines of a tug or towboat. The term is most often used after a Pilot has slowed down to line up prior to making a narrow bridge, or other navigational situation. Similar to slowing down and backing for a FLANKING maneuver and then, when lined up or completing the desired action, to proceed ahead at full speed, i.e. "I'm coming ahead to *drive* her home".

DROP or DROP OUT

1. To leave a barge in tow at a dock, fleet, or give to a harbor boat. The plural, *drops* means that a group of barges will be left at a facility.
2. A lower gauge reading due to a sudden, rapid fall, or *drop,* after a stage of high-water.
3. The maneuvering of a barge out of its place in tow, "*Drop* the starboard head barge back into the notch."
4. To move down, or behind, i.e. "*Drop* below me and come up on my port side".
5. To lose or remove something, i.e. "I *dropped* a rudder last trip".

DROP 'EM THROUGH

Before the Old River Control Structure, and the Old River Lock with its rock-filled dike was built, tugs and towboats used to transit the open waterway of the Old River and then down the Atchafalaya River with its swift current en route to the GIWW. Since tugs were single-screw with limited control when backing full astern (since they had no flanking rudders), making the Simmsport Bridge was not a simple safe maneuver. Therefore they often employed what was called, *Drop 'em through.*

Heading downriver, the tug would put its tow of barges under one of the fixed spans next to the open swing span of the drawbridge. Just before the tug got to the fixed span the face wires to the tow would be knocked off, freeing the barges. Since the dynamics of a single-screw tug, when backing, would move its stern to port, the Pilot would simply flip the tug around and go down though the right span (looking downstream) stern first. Then the tug would again turn around and go down and catch his free-floating tow.

This was done on other rivers of narrow bridges as well. On the Internet in 2002 there was a series of pictures of an incident that occurred on the Warrior River some years before at the old Rooster Bridge (since demolished), which displayed the *M/V CAHABA* of being unable to get free from its tow in time. The towboat was caught on the bridge structure and completely capsized under the bridge before popping up, righting itself, and then catching its tow downriver. It is not recommended that this maneuver be attempted.

DROUGHT
An abnormal period of lack of precipitation in a river basin area resulting in low flows and possibly reduced channel depths. The term comes from Old English *drugath,* meaning "dryness".

DRUM
1. The cylinder of a capstan, winch or windlass where a line or wire is wound to take up slack, or reel it in to the vessel.
2. A steel barrel that holds 55 gallons.
3. The hub of a pilotwheel around which the TILLER LINE is wound.

DRY CARGO
Bulk cargo that is generally free-flowing, such as grains, ores, coal, limestone, etc. that cannot be counted, like packaged goods or sheets of steel; nor is it liquid cargo.

DRY ROT
A type of fungus that attacks the timbers of wooden vessels. It is not often visible to the eye. Though it may soften the inside of the hull, the outside portion may still be leak-free. When the Steamboat Hull Inspector eventually came around for his annual inspection of a steamer, however, an ice pick was used to poke into random places in the hull. If the pick went easily into a timber, it was marked up to be removed and replaced before he would approve the vessel's current license.

DRY SIDE
Refers to the inner edges of the barges in a tow, two strings or more wide, where a crew member is protected from falling overboard. Conversely, the extreme port and starboard edges of the tow are called the WET SIDE. A crew member does well to remember which is which.

DRY TIE
A vessel's mooring line that is tied off to a place on the bank at as high an angle to the water as possible in order to prevent it from drooping or sagging into the water. This is especially important in the winter to keep the line from getting wet and freezing stiff.

DRYDOCK
1. A floating structure with wing walls on both port and starboard sides, while open on both ends, in a squared-off "U" shape. The floor section and wing walls can be flooded by ballasting or lowering the dock in the water, in order to receive a vessel that may require repairs, or an inspection. The vessel is floated in between the *drydock's* walls. The dock is then pumped out, raising the vessel on it, and repair work can be accomplished in the "dry".
2. In the days of wooden-hulled steamboats the Steamboat Hull Inspector carried with him a pick to stab the hull timbers to see if any of them were rotting. If so, they had to be replaced. Since there were few drydocks or hauling ways in those days some operators, especially those far from shipyards, would build a large timber box, with a sort of "L" shape. Lengths of old firehose would be run across its open top and along the lower wall. Then the box would be sunk, the steamboat floated onto it, then winched or ratcheted as tightly as possible to the box with the old firehoses acting as gaskets. The box would then be pumped out and workers would go into the box under the steamer, chisel out the rotten timber, fit in a new one, caulk it in tight, then again sink the "drydock box" and float the wooden steamer off as good as new, or at least to the satisfaction of the Inspector. See: DOCK for background on origin of the term. Also see: GRAVING DOCK, LIFTING WAYS, and SYNCROLIFT DOCK.

DUBB(ING)

The act of cutting, shaping or smoothing a timber with an ADZE by loggers and raftsmen.

DUCK POND

An open space of water directly forward of the head of a towboat and its tow. The concept of this towing arrangement evolved because the old time wooden coalboat barges loaded with coal were relatively lightly built and a large horsepowered steamer working against the end of a barge could severely weaken its structure causing disastrous leakage. This type of tow makeup distributed the steering pressure over a wider area between the barges. Sometimes barges, called "drivers" or "steering barges", were lashed alongside the towing vessel and into the other barges in tow in order to add to the tow rigidity. Since the days of steel hulled barges this type of *duck pond* is seldom, if ever, seen. Sternwheel steamers had relatively poor steering power when moving ahead and the steerage of bends were mostly made by backing down and flanking..

However, the term *duck pond* has since evolved to mean any open water space that creates a hazard between barges in a tow into which a person could fall and drown, especially at night when shadows might appear to be a solid surface. It is an extremely dangerous area when people are walking or working on a tow and which should be covered and marked. Called a *duck pond* since it was an enclosed area in which any competent and responsible duck would feel comfortable floating in unless the cook saw it paddling around.

DUCK WATER

An area of water with almost no current that is generally found on the bar side of a bend or underneath a sharp point of land. Also said of pools when the navigation dams are releasing very little water and the current is negligible.

DUMB BARGE

Refers to a barge that is unmanned and without power, as opposed to barges which are powered and commonly used in European waters, as well as on some small work flats, i.e., rigging barges, pump flats, etc. Nearly all cargo barges utilized on the Western Rivers fit the description of *dumb barge*; however, barges carrying cargo are the producers of revenue for towing companies while the propulsion mechanism, the towboat or tug, is the high-cost vessel that generates no profit, so it seems inappropriate to term barges *dumb*.

DUMBBELL

See: BELL.

DUNNAGE

1. Loose wood or pallets used in the cargo space for blocking, shoring, and stacking, to secure and protect the cargo carried. *Dunnage* serves to protect it from any moisture that might accumulate on the floor of a hopper, either from rain or condensate, as well as to provide air passage. It also keeps the cargo from shifting.

2. The term is sometimes used to refer to the unused space in a tank, though the word more often used is ULLAGE.

3. Some engineers designate the space between the piston and cylinder head at the end of its stroke as the *dunnage*.

4. An old term that referred to the personal belongings that a crew member brought with him when he boarded the boat. The term derives from the Dutch *dunne,* meaning "light material".

DUSTPAN DREDGE

A suction-type dredge that is extremely efficient in the alluvial area of the Mississippi Valley. The suction pipe is lowered and raised by a winch

138 DYNAMIC DRAFT

and the dredge is pulled forward by winches. It swings over a wide cutting line of riverbed. The *dustpan* on the end of the suction pipe has water jets fitted along the leading edge of the structure that stirs up the bottom material; then it sucks up fine silt, sand, and mud from the riverbed. The slurry mixture is piped to an out-of-channel area and discharged. The oldest steam *dustpan dredge*, the Corps of Engineers' *POTTER*, presently in use on the river, received diesel-electric power in 2002. At that time she was about 70 years old.

DYNAMIC DRAFT
The distance from the water's surface to the lowest point on a vessel's bottom while the vessel is in motion through the water. Opposite of STATIC DRAFT.

DYNAMOMETER
A machine that is hooked up to a diesel engine to test the power output.

DAY SHAPES or SIGNALS

● **BALL**
Not less than 0.6 meters in diameter

◆ **DIAMOND SHAPE**
Or 2 cones with bases together

▲ **CONE (or conical shape)**
Apex up

▼ **CONE (or conical shape)**
Apex down

◆ **2 CONES**
Apexes together

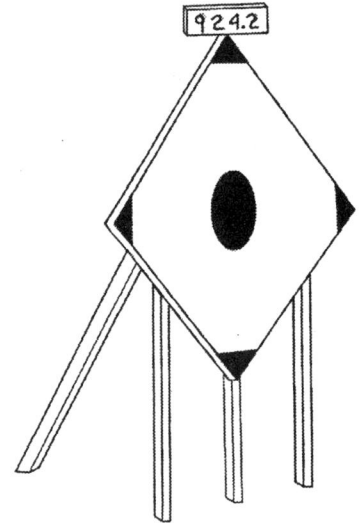

DAYMARK
OLD TIME WOODEN DAYMARK USED EXTENSIVELY ON THE LOWER MISSISSIPPI AND OTHER RIVERS. IN LATER YEARS IT HAD REFLECTIVE TAPE (AS SHOWN) ON ITS CORNERS AND THE CENTER OF THE BOARD. USUALLY MADE 4' X 4'.

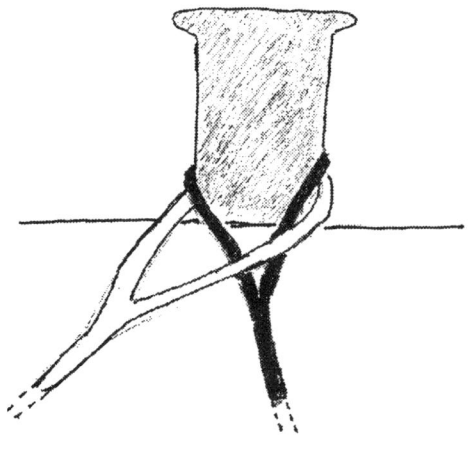

DIPPING THE EYE

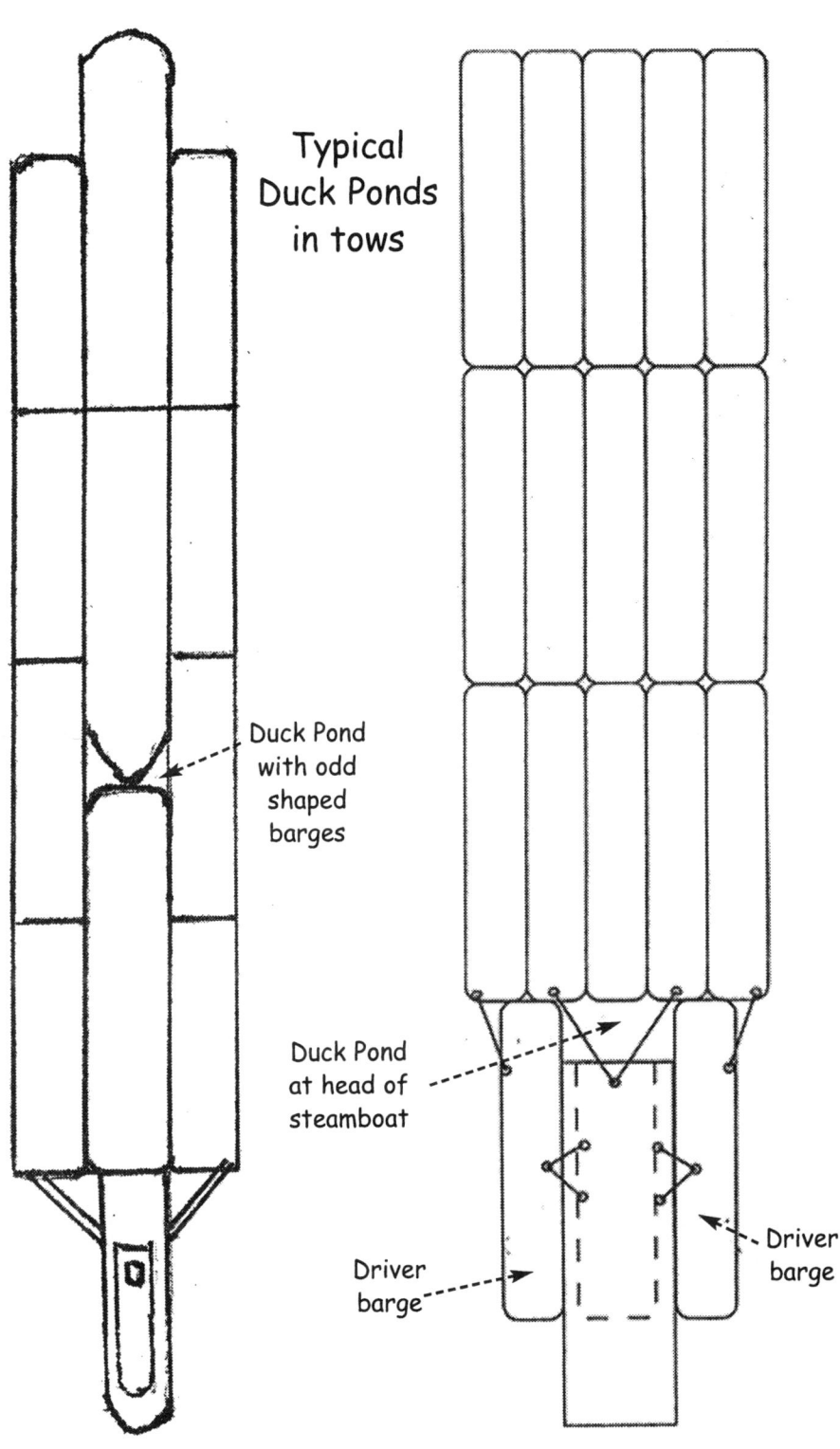

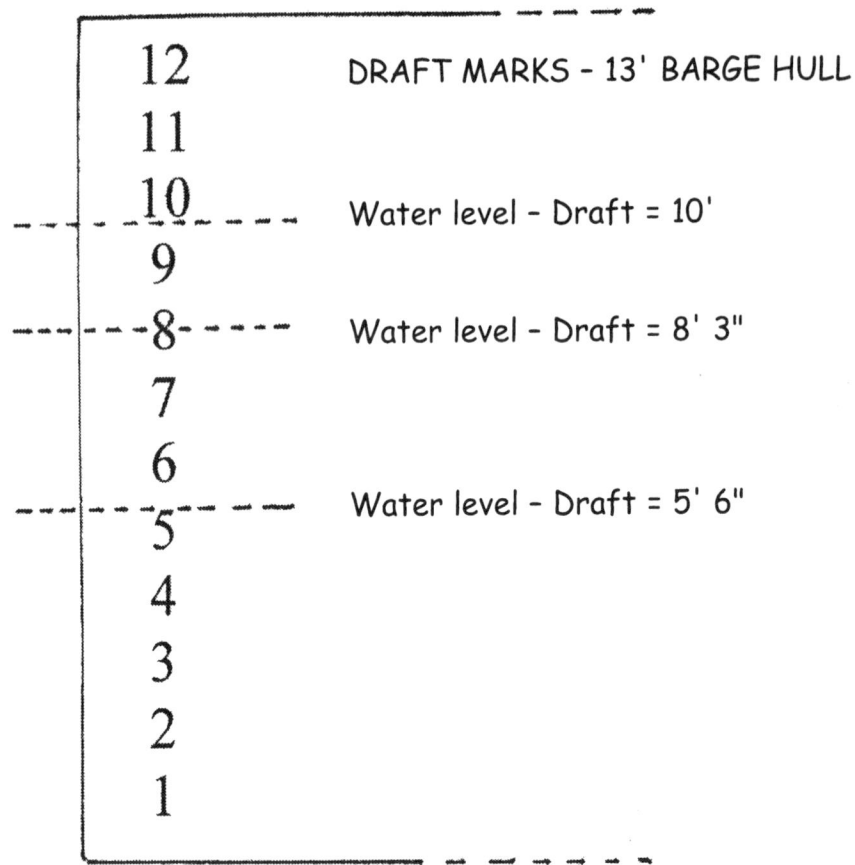

DRAFT MARKS – 13' BARGE HULL

Water level – Draft = 10'

Water level – Draft = 8' 3"

Water level – Draft = 5' 6"

DIKE

Typical dikes used by the USACE for training the river. Pile-driven dikes were once built extensively on the Lower Mississippi and the Missouri Rivers, but now most docks are the rock fill type.

PILE DIKE

STONE OR ROCK FILLED DIKE

E

EADS, JAMES BUCHANAN, THE EADS BRIDGE, and New Orleans as a seaport

Engineer, inventor and builder, *James Eads* is hailed as one of the greatest engineers of all time. Some of his accomplishments were the building of the bridge across the Mississippi at St. Louis which bears his name. He was told it couldn't be done, but it opened on July 4, 1874. Eads also developed a diving bell to go down on wrecks for salvage. These were called "bell boats". Eads built two of the snagboats for Henry Shreve, and designed and built gunboats for the Union in the Civil War. He designed and built the system of jetties in the Mississippi River delta to keep it navigable to ocean shipping with access to the Port of New Orleans. The USACE said it wouldn't work but Eads took the job on a "no cure, no pay" basis using his own funds to build the jetties in the South Pass of the delta, creating a 30-foot channel by 1879. He was appointed as a first member of the Mississippi River Commission when it was formed.

EAR BOBS

Long oval-shaped wooden buoys, used on the old steamers that handled log rafts to determine the speed of the raft in the current. They were similar to the FLANKING BUOYS used by Pilots today when flanking a sharp bend.

EARTHQUAKE

See: NEW MADRID EARTHQUAKE.

EASE

1. To slack or pay out a line that is in strain, i.e., "*Ease* off on the port spring line".
2. To fall off from holding a vessel's course on an object, i.e., "*Ease* off ABC point and let her fall down into the bend".
3. To reduce the amount of rudder, i.e., "*Ease* off the rudder, she's coming around fine".
4. To go slow, i.e. "*Ease* off the RPM and let the current put her into the dock".

EAST OF HARVEY LOCK (EHL)

Mileage on the Gulf Intracoastal Waterway is measured both east and west from the Harvey Lock, located on the west bank of the Mississippi River in New Orleans, with the lock being at "O" miles. See: WEST OF HARVEY LOCK (WHL).

EASY

Similar to EASE. It means to not push or press an action, to be moderate in applying any force, such as the helm, speed, or any other action.

EASY DISTANCE OFF

A subjective pilotage term known only to those who navigate towboats. It depends upon the particular river, the width of the channel, the speed of the current, the curvature of the bend, the size of the tow, the tonnage and draft of the tow in relation to all before mentioned, plus whatever peculiar attributes a certain stretch of river might contain. So when two vessels meet and one says, "I'll run the shore an *easy distance off* and see you on two", both Pilots know what it means in that area of that river, for that situation, at that particular time. It is not close, nor far off, but rather an experienced judgment of a Pilot who believes it is sufficient and safe for the tows to navigate in relation to the factors involved.

EATING UP THE BUOYS

The term comes from action by a COWBOY Pilot who will run over a series of buoys in a narrow channel, which is illegal. It derives from the time when there were no buoys to mark the channel, so when there was low water of unknown depth, especially when going into a landing, a Pilot would sometimes send a yawl with a leadsman to sound out the water ahead. The yawl crewmen would use a lead line or sounding pole to find good water and would mark it with a piece of wood with a COWTAIL tied to a rock for an anchor; at night they would put a candle on the piece of wood. The Pilot would steer his vessel directly over the lights which became known as "eating up the lights".

EBB

To fall back, reduce, or recede, such as the current in a river, or of a tide that is receding from shore. The word comes from the Old English *ebba,* meaning "to flow back" or "move away from".

ECDIS

An acronym. See: ELECTRONIC CHART DISPLAY AND INFORMATION SYSTEM.

ECHO

The return of an electronic signal from a target to the signaling device, such as radar, a depth recorder, GPS, etc.

ECHO SOUNDER

See: DEPTH SOUNDER.

ECLIPSE

1. The darkness phase of a flashing or occulting lighted navigational aid.
2. A celestial body that is obscured from sight by a larger one on its path through the sky.

ECOLOGY and ECOSYSTEMS

The study or science of organisms in the environment. On our rivers it is all the relationships occurring between the living and those non-living factors which affect them. The term ecology derives from the Greek words *oikos* and *logy,* meaning "house" and "study", or in other words the study of the "house" (environment) in which we live.

EDDY

1. Water that is flowing counter to the main current. Often occurs under a point of land at the foot of a bend.
2. Small whirlpool turbulences that occur along indents in the shore, a revetment, at dikes, under a pier of a bridge or dock, at the lower end of a lock wall, or some other obstruction to the current flow.
3. An *eddy* can extend "well out", as noted in channel reports, and can have a cause and effect sequence reaching as far as half the width of a river.
4. The term is probably from the old English *ed,* meaning "back".

EDUCTOR

A pump that works on the siphon principle, used to remove water or liquid product from a tank. The term comes from the Latin *educere,* meaning "to lead out".

EFFICIENCY OF WATER TRANSPORT

There is a chart that depicts the greater energy efficiency of water transport compared to moving cargo tonnage by rail or truck. It shows one typical bargeload having the same equivalent tonnage as 15 jumbo rail hopper cars, and the same as 58 large semi-trucks. Even more mind-boggling figures depict a typical 15-barge tow equaling 2.25 unit trains of 100 cars each, or 870 semi-trucks. See: CAPACITY.

This is not the first such chart to compare the different modes of moving cargo in this country. Before steel wheels moved on steel rails with the invention of the railroads, or after trucks started congestion on our roadways, the canal boat industry had a poster with pictures:

To move 50 tons of freight,
you could hire
1 CANAL BOAT with 2 CREW
and 2 HORSES
OR
25 WAGONS with
25 DRIVERS and 100 HORSES

Just imagine the increase in cost of putting those drivers up for the night and feeding them during their long trip; and what about the horse feed and perhaps stabling? Talk about efficiency!

EFFIE AFTON (Steamer)
The Mississippi and Missouri Railroad Company built a bridge across the Mississippi River at Rock Island, Illinois, much to disconcertion of the steamboat companies. The bridge had a swing span with a horizontal clearance of 116 feet when opened. On May 6, 1856, the steamboat *EFFIE AFTON* hit the pier of the bridge, became afire resulting in a total loss. The owners sued the railroad for damages claiming the bridge was "...unconstitutional, an obstruction to navigation, dangerous..."

It was a celebrated case in river and railroad history. For the river people it was the issue of free and unobstructed navigation on all the inland rivers of the nation. For the railroaders it was ability to move commerce east and west, not just north and south, to open up trade across the country. In the end, the jury didn't agree one way or the other. The case died and the railroads kept building more bridges. Abraham Lincoln was the lawyer for the railroads. All the official records of the case were destroyed in the great Chicago fire of 1871.

EFFLUENT
1. The outflow of a waste product entering the river from a storm sewer, sewage plant, industrial discharge line, etc. The term is from the Latin *effluent,* meaning "flowing out". There are possibly more oil slicks and sheens from roadways running through storm sewers to the river than that which comes from any spills of products escaping from barges.

2. A term used to describe any stream whose source is the flowing out of a lake or another river, which makes all tributary rivers *effluent* to the main stem.

EKING
When building or repairing a vessel, to add on a wooden piece to a timber that is too short or combining it with another structural member. The term seems to come from *eke,* meaning "to barely make it", or "making it out of not much", as in to *eke* out a living.

ELASTICITY
Refers to the level of sensitivity and responsiveness to marketplace changes. A fairly modern term being used in river terminology, which is a fancy way of saying that one should be aware of supply and demand in the industry, both short and long term, to anticipate it and to plan for its effects.

ELBOW
1. A sharp change in the direction of a channel. Similar to DOGLEG.
2. The deep part of a bend.
3. A pipe fitting usually bent at either 90 or 45 degrees, but could have other curvatures.

ELECTRIC DRIVE
See: DIESEL-ELECTRIC DRIVE.

ELECTROLYSIS
The chemical decomposition by an electric current set up between two dissimilar metals in brackish or sea water, causing metal wastage or corrosion. ANODES, such as zinc are placed at critical points under the hulls of tugs and some towboats to sacrifice themselves and prevent

wasting of the steel hull and its appendages.

ELECTRONIC CHART DISPLAY AND INFORMATION SYSTEMS (ECDIS)

A format developed by the International Maritime Organization (IMO) that is used by ships in the deep-sea international trades. It displays a vector chart that has all the symbols and required information set out by IMO, as well as the up-to-date changes and corrections that are available. Other electronic charts that are available are usually called *raster charts* which are basically an electronic version of an existing printed chart. A third alternative is the USACE effort to format and make available on the internet Inland Electronic Navigation Charts (see below).

ELECTRONIC NAVIGATION CHARTS for INLAND (ENC)

Navigation charts that are being developed for all the inland commercial navigable waters in the United States by the USACE. They are not considered true ECDIS charts, but have been developed in concert with the Pilots of companies that utilize the Western Rivers and are more compatible with the needs of the navigators of inland waters, as well as using the terminology familiar to river persons. They adhere to the IMO so-called S-57 standard as closely as possible, but some of the things we do in the U.S. are unknown in most of the rest of the world. The new ENCs of the Corps will be available on the internet.

ELEVATION

The vertical distance above or below some reference point. Most elevations on the river are measured relative to mean sea level, or zero. For instance, the city of St. Louis is about 413 feet above sea level; Minneapolis is about 695 feet above sea level; Pittsburgh is 710 feet above sea level; and New Orleans is about minus 4 feet below sea level in some areas.

EMBANKMENT

An earthen, and sometimes rock-filled or lined, structure that creates a dam with sloping sides to keep water in or out of an area. See: LEVEE.

EMBARGO

1. An order by a government prohibiting the departure of vessels or cargoes from a port to some other port that is hostile to it.
2. In a commercial sense an *embargo* can be an order by an official prohibiting the movement or handling of cargoes at specific points or port areas, or on certain waterway areas, due to weather (floods), emergencies, or other unusual conditions.
3. A term derived from the Spanish *embargar,* "to arrest".

EMBARK

To go on board a vessel. The term is mostly used regarding persons on packetboats, passenger vessels, ferry boats, and excursion boats. The word comes from the French *embarquer,* "to leave", or "put in" a ship.

EMBARRASSMENT TO NAVIGATION

The action taken by one vessel, or the failure to take proper action, that results in the cause of another vessel to have an accident.

EMBAYMENT

A large area in a flood plain maintained by the USACE that can be allowed to flood during high-water conditions in order to reduce the pressure and possible breaching of a LEVEE. See: FLOODWAY.

EMD

A division of General Motors called Electromotive Diesel, which provides many engines that power diesel towboats in the USA.

EMERGENCY
1. An unexpected, serious occurrence that is a deviation from normal operation that could cause personnel, property, or environmental damage, such as fire, cargo spillage, etc.
2. A severe weather incident, such as tornado, hurricane, ice gorge, flood, etc.

EMERGENCY DRILL
A training exercise to alert crew members regarding the proper procedures that must take place as to manning stations and the actions required if an actual emergency did occur, such as fire, loss of steering, collision, man overboard, etc.

EMERGENCY PROCEDURES
During transfer of cargo to/from tank barges carrying oil or hazardous materials it is required for persons conducting the transfer to have a means of communication to manage any *emergency*. This may be by an approved 2-way radio system. The *procedures* must be an effective means to shut down the pumping of cargo by remotely shutting off a pump engine, valves, or other sequence of events to alleviate any possible spillage or danger. See: FIRE EXTINGUISHMENT and TRANSFER PROCEDURES.

EMPTY
A term for a barge in a tow that has no cargo, or is in a fleet to be cleaned from a previous cargo, or is cleaned and waiting to be placed at a dock to be loaded. After it receives cargo it will be termed a LOAD.

EN ROUTE
A vessel and/or its cargo are moving from one place to another.

ENDORSEMENT
An amendment to a license or document noting additional training, or limiting the use of the license or document.

ENGINE
The machinery that provides power to propel a vessel or to drive generators or pumps. It can be powered by steam or diesel fuel. Only very small *engines* use gasoline.
Early engine operation on river steamers was mostly a matter of trial and error attempting to improve on the design of others. Most of them that were employed were a sort of BEAM or CROSSHEAD type. With the first usage of the horizontal cylinder designed by SHREVE on the *Str. WASHINGTON*, standardization of placement and usage became the norm on the Western Rivers.

ENGINE FOUNDATION
The heavy, built-up box-like structure that supports the main engine(s), distributing its weight to the framing and plates of the hull and reducing vibration.

ENGINE ROOM
The space aboard a tug or towboat where the propelling machinery that powers a vessel is located. Also positioned here are generators, gear boxes, shaft couplings to the propeller, pumps, air compressors, other machinery, tools, spare parts, etc. It is also the castle, fortress, realm, and domain of the Chief Engineer who minds his engines as a doctor tends to babies in his care.

ENGINE ROOM BELLS or SIGNALS
Before the ENGINE-ORDER TELEGRAPH was invented there had to be a system where the Pilot could signal the Engineer on watch to change speeds. This was done with BELL PULLS; one pull rang a gong, and

one rang a jingle. There was no specific signal by regulation. On some rivers the custom was different, some companies had the signals to be used on their vessels, and some Captains specified what signals they wanted. Sometimes *bell signals* even differed on the same boat depending upon who was doing the piloting; it was a case of "different strokes for different folks". Also see: BELL SIGNALS. The example below was reported to be used by some steamers on the Cumberland River, as follows:

When engine is stopped
1 bell means slow ahead

Running full ahead
1 bell means slow

Running slow ahead
1 bell means stop

Running slow ahead
jingle means full ahead
When engine is stopped
2 bells mean slow astern

Running astern
jingle means full astern

Running full ahead
4 bells mean full astern

Running slow astern
3 bells mean full astern

ENGINE-ORDER TELEGRAPH
A device used in steamboats and diesels that do not have direct control of the speed of the vessel but must signal the engine room for the Engineer on watch to alter speed. In the pilothouse the device was on a stand with a lever on each side for port and starboard engines. If one moved the lever forward it was for different rates of speed ahead, slow, half, full, etc. If the lever was pulled back, it was to signal to go astern at the rate indicated. When moving the levers, bells would ring in the engine room. The engine room personnel on duty would signal back to the pilothouse the same signal that had been given them and like bells would ring in the pilothouse. When the levers were straight up it was "stop". See: FINISHED WITH ENGINES.

With the advent of direct pilothouse control over the starting and stopping of engines and their speed, few tugs or towboats have engine-order telegraphs installed on them anymore. They have become a "talk-about item" for nautical collectors and now can mostly be seen in their recreation rooms.

ENGINE-SPEED INDICATOR
A gauge in the pilothouse that indicates the engine RPMs from the relay of a signal sent from the engine room.

ENGINEER
The person who maintains the machinery on board a vessel. See: CHIEF and CHIEF OF ENGINEERS. The engineer as they see themselves, written in the USACE dredge JADWIN's paper in the 1930s:

A Pilot is a man who knows a great deal about very little and who goes along knowing more and more about less and less until finally he knows practically everything about nothing.

A Captain on the other hand is a man who knows very little about a great deal and keeps on knowing less and less about more and more until finally he knows practically nothing about everything.

An Engineer starts out knowing practically everything about everything and ends up knowing nothing about nothing, due to his association with Pilots and Captains.

ENROLLMENT
A document issued to United

States riverboats (and some barges) engaged in the domestic coastal trade. It differs from a Register that is required for vessels engaged in foreign trade. See: DOCUMENTATION.

ENSIGN
The United States national flag of 50 stars on a background of blue, with alternating seven red and six white stripes flown near the stern of a riverboat. When it is at half-mast it is a sign of mourning. If it is flown upside down it is a sign of distress. The term derives from the Latin *insignia,* which was a symbol of office.

ENVIRONMENTAL IMPACT STATEMENT (EIS)
A study outlining the effects that might occur to the current habitat and ecology of an area by human induced changes, along with alternative actions that might be undertaken to minimize, alleviate, or otherwise alter the impacts in as positive manner as may be possible.

EPA
An acronym for the Environmental Protection Agency. A governmental office that is charged with safeguarding our land, water, and air.

EQUALIZATION
A monetary allowance paid to a carrier for delivery of a cargo to a location different from the contracted destination. See: DIFFERENTIAL.

EROSION
1. The wearing away of soil by natural causes, mainly by water moving against a shoreline or sand bar, or over the riverbed. There is no net loss since the material flows in the water course to another place, such as the soil of Iowa becoming the land of Louisiana.
2. The deterioration or corrosion of metal surfaces due to rusting, electrolysis, or simply mechanical wear.
3. The word is from the Latin *erodere,* meaning "to wear away".

ERROR IN NAVIGATION
A charge that can be levied on a Pilot in a navigational accident, such as making an incorrect interpretation of the Navigation Rules, displaying improper lights, or light(s) not burning, posting no lookout where needed, navigating out of the channel, etc.

ESCORT TUG or BOAT
A vessel that is required or requested to follow along the course of a towboat with a tow or some other type vessel. In certain waterway areas that are restricted or deemed dangerous, the *escort* in theory would be able to render assistance if required.

ESSAYONS
The motto of the U.S. Corps of Engineers, which was taken from French, meaning "*Let Us Try* ", and in "trying" they built an inland navigation system that is the envy of the world. It is hoped they will keep on trying throughout the 21st Century. The saying is inscribed on the buttons of the Corps uniforms, with an eagle holding in its beak a scroll or streamer with the word *Essayons* written across it.

ESTABLISH (ATON)
The adding of a navigation mark (light, buoy, daymark) by the USCG.

ETA
An acronym for Estimated Time of Arrival.

ETD
An acronym for Estimated Time of Departure.

EVEN KEEL
When a vessel is trimmed and drawing approximately the same amount of water fore and aft, as well as to port and starboard.

EVEN STRAIN
When all lines and/or wires leading from a vessel or tow are under equal tension.

EXCEPTION
When a carrier receives a cargo, it may survey the shipment and if detected it will note any damage or discrepancies on the bill of lading for which it will assume no responsibility.

EXCESSIVE SPEED
A speed that is considered unreasonable for the condition of navigation, i.e., in fog, or restricted visibility, that leads to an accident; speed that could cause wake damage to a shoreline or a levee; speed that breaks loose vessels at a fleet or dock; etc.

EXCURSION VESSEL
On the inland waterways it usually refers to a vessel that makes short trips with passengers aboard for sight-seeing or other social affairs. They are inspected by the USCG and upon its completion to the inspector's satisfaction with all regulatory requirements a certificate of inspection will be issued listing number and positions of crew, route, and other pertinent data.

EXEMPT CARRIER
A riverboat company that is not considered a regulated common carrier. The term is not used much anymore as almost no freight moving on the rivers at the present time is regulated as to a TARIFF.

EXEMPTION
The granting by a government agency of a permanent or temporary suspension of a rule, regulation, or other provision of law to which it administers.

EXHAUST
1. The emission of steam or gases through the chimney or stack from the engine of a steamboat, towboat or tug. See: 'SCAPE PIPE.
2. The ventilation system of fans or blowers to expel or displace stagnant or contaminated air or fumes from a hold, tank, or compartment of a vessel, replacing it with fresh air.
3. Steam that escapes from a cylinder.

EXPANSION TANK or TRUNK
A small raised cylindrical chamber or reservoir above the cargo deck of a tank barge, about three feet in diameter to allow some degree of expansion of liquid without overflowing in warm or hot weather. The tank is fitted with a hinged, dogged-down vapor-tight hatch for access. It also sometimes has a small ULLAGE hatch fitted into it which is used for gauging the tank.

EXPERT
A term given to many who come on riverboats thinking they know all there is to know about the vessels that ply the inland rivers. The word consists of two parts, *ex* and *spurt*. The first, *ex,* is defined as "a has-been", and the second, *spurt,* means "a drip under pressure". They come, they go, what they do, nobody knows. The term originates from the Latin *expertus,* meaning "try". Perhaps experience would be more appropriate, if one has it.

EXPLOSIMETER
A device that is used to detect the explosive range of the atmosphere in a compartment or tank that is not gas-free.

EXTINGUISHED (ATON)
When a lighted aid to navigation is not burning.

EYE
A fixed loop at the end of a line that is spliced or knotted in a BOWLINE, or a loop at the end of a wire that is spliced, swaged, or permanently clamped.

EYE BOLT

1. A threaded bolt that has a circular eye at its head.

2. A shackle pin that is usually threaded with an eye in the end. It is inserted through the eyes of the shackle and the threaded pin is tightened to make a secure connection.

EYE LEVEL

The vertical elevation of a Pilot's eye above the surface of the water.

EYE SPLICE

A loop spliced in the end of a line or wire, used to put over a fitting on a barge, lock wall, dock, or other appendage.

THE EYE SPLICE

1. The end strands of a length of line are unlaid for a couple of feet to be used to make the eye splice. The yarns of each strand are whipped or otherwise prevented from fraying apart.

2. The middle unlaid strand is tucked under and through one of the laid up strands in the bight of the line depending upon the size loop or eye required.

3. Then the left strand is tucked under and through the adjacent strand of the line's bight to where the first tuck was made.

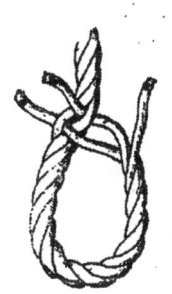

4. The remaining right strand is then tucked into the last untucked strand in the bight of the line at the same level as the other two strand tucks.

5. Finally, alternative tucks are made with each of the remaining strands until at least three are completed on all strands.

6. If the strands left over after completing the eye splice are too long they can be cut and the yarns rewhipped, but do not cut them too short as they may pull out of a tuck if great strain is placed on the eye of the line when in serice.

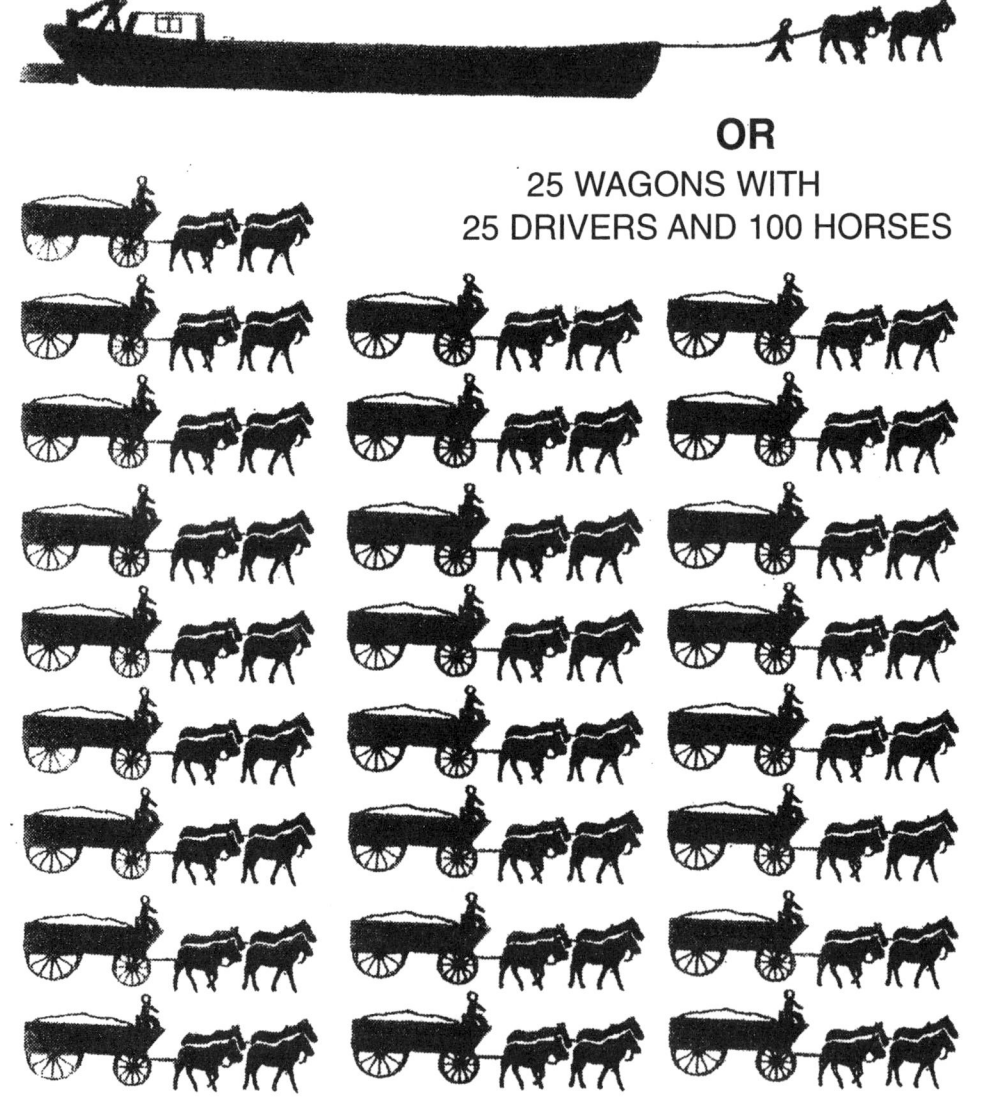

Courtesy *NATIONAL CANAL MUSEUM*

ILLUSTRATIONS 151

Increasing Cargo Capacity

A typical cargo barge moves much more cargo than a single truck or rail car.

Modal Freight Use	Standard Capacity
Barge - Liquid Bulk	27,500 Barrels
Barge - Dry Bulk	1,750 Tons
Rail - Bulk Car	110 Tons
Highway Tractor-Trailer	25 Tons

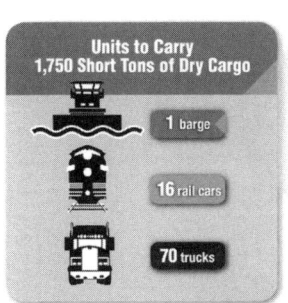

One loaded covered hopper barge carries 58,333 bushels of wheat, enough to make almost 2.5 million loaves of bread.

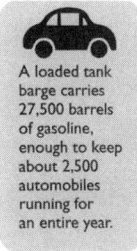

A loaded tank barge carries 27,500 barrels of gasoline, enough to keep about 2,500 automobiles running for an entire year.

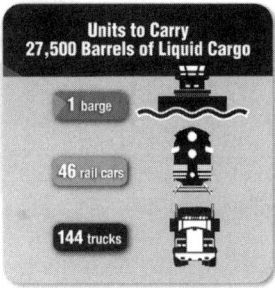

Courtesy of Waterways Council, Inc.

TOW OPERATING SIZE

The chart shows a freight tonnage comparison for tows operating on locking rivers, normally pushing 15 barges. However, on the Lower Mississippi River where there are no locks much larger tows navigate that are double, or even triple, the size of those running on rivers that require locking.

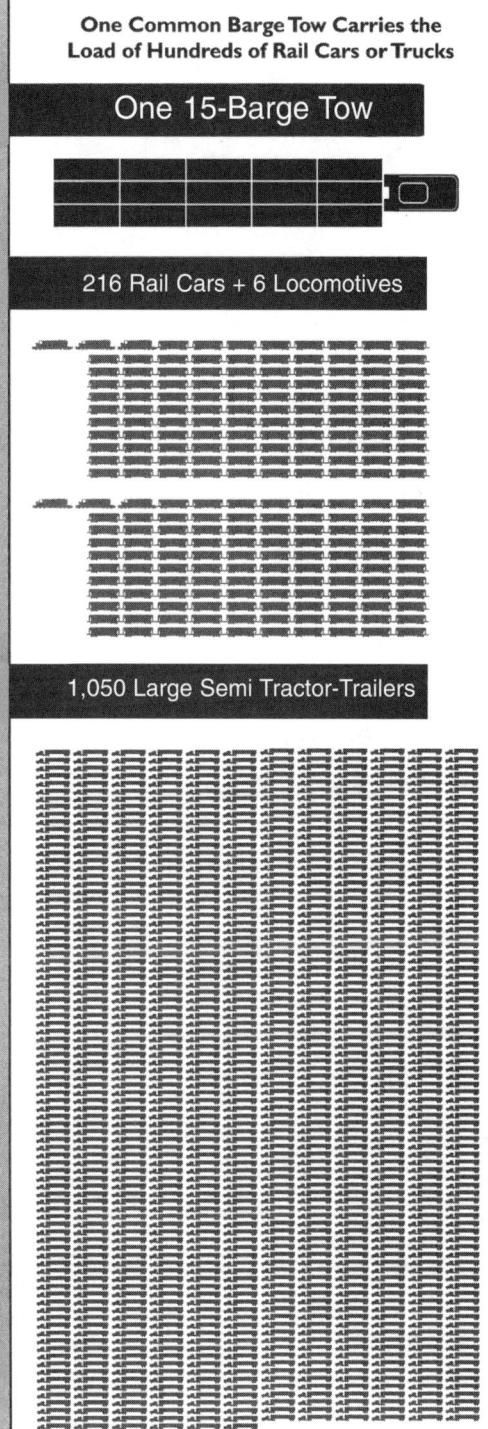

EFFICIENCY IN MARINE TRANSPORTATION

The major difference between surface size of large ocean carriers and river tows is that vessels in sea service have deeper hulls and are loaded to greater depth. However, river tows constantly have their hulls operating closer to the bottom than where their deep sea brethren are navigating. Inland barges are normally loaded between 9 and 12 feet depending on river conditions while ocean vessels may carry a draft of four times that.

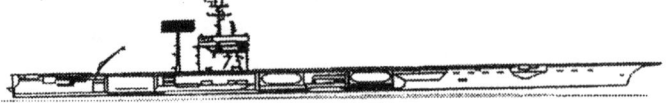

USS GEORGE WASHINGTON CVN 73
1092' IN LENGTH X 134' WIDE
FLIGHT DECK COVERS 4.5 ACRES

VERY LARGE CRUDE CARRIER
1100' in length x 230' wide
Takes up about 4.8 acres

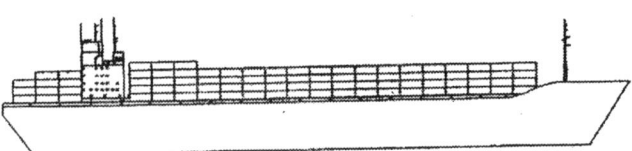

LARGE CONTAINER VESSEL
1200' IN LENGTH X 150' WIDE
Surface area 4.14 acres

LOCKING RIVER TOW (maximum)
5 barges long + towboat – 1170'
3 barges wide – 105'
Covers about 2.36 acres

LOWER MISSISSIPPI RIVER TOW

Upbound
7 barges long + towboat – 1570'
9 barges wide – 315'
Takes up over 10 acres

Downbound
5 barges long + towboat – 1170'
8 barges wide – 280'
Covers over 7.5 acres

ENROLLMENT CERTIFICATE OF DOCUMENTATION

EXCURSION VESSEL Str. BELLE OF LOUISVILLE

154 ILLUSTRATIONS

ENGINE ORDER TELEGRAPH

TANK BARGE EXPANSION TANK

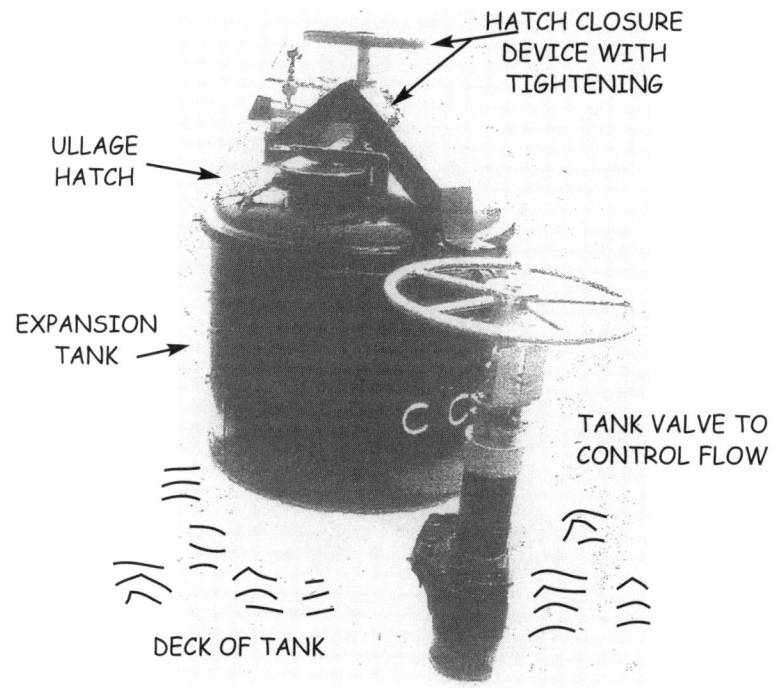

- HATCH CLOSURE DEVICE WITH TIGHTENING
- ULLAGE HATCH
- EXPANSION TANK
- TANK VALVE TO CONTROL FLOW
- DECK OF TANK

USACE ESSAYONS MILITARY BUTTON

F

FACE (of PROPELLER)
When standing at the stern of a vessel looking forward it is the aft, or driving, surface of the propeller, which moves the vessel forward.

FACE PIECE
When a towboat has to run LIGHT BOAT (without tow) for any great distance, the vessel will usually take a single barge, most often an empty, to couple to the head of the boat. To run a towboat at any graduated speed without a tow would cause water to run over the boat's bow and could even swamp it. The barge on the head of a towboat is the *face piece* since it is covering the head or *face* of the towboat.

FACE-UP
The act of maneuvering a towboat up against the end of a barge or tow from which it will navigate in the river, and attaching FACE WIRES to it. Usually refers to the stern end of a tow, but can mean either bow or stern, especially when shifting barges.

FACE WIRES or LINES
Wire cables leading from the bow of a towboat to a barge or tow and back again to a winch or capstan on the towboat in order to make a secure connection. Some vessels utilize extremely strong types of synthetic line, which is much lighter and also has a higher breaking strength than wire.

FAG END
The frayed or unraveled end of a line.

FAHRENHEIT
Temperature degrees used in a thermometer, with 32 degrees being the freezing point of fresh water, and 212 degrees being the boiling point. It is based on a scale developed by a German physicist, G.D. Fahrenheit, in the early 18th Century, and was named for him. See: CENTIGRADE.

FAIR
1. To correct and make even the original designed structural lines of a vessel's plates and framing when repairs are required.
2. A favorable weather condition, i.e. "*fair* weather", "*fair* wind", or "*fair* current".

FAIRLEAD
Any fitting or device (either stationary or with a roller) that serves to lead or guide a line or wire with a minimum of abrasion in a proper direction from or to a vessel.

FAIRLY CLOSE
To navigate a vessel and/or a tow as short a distance a possible away from a shore, fleet, buoy line, dike, or other object without compromising safety. It is a directive given between Pilots or in a channel report as to how best to navigate a certain section of a channel when some change might have occurred, such as a bar that has built up or other modification that requires attention. For another such directive of advice, see: EASY DISTANCE OFF.

FAIRWAY
Technically the navigable area or channel of a waterway, particularly a marked channel for larger vessels. Not used much in river terminology except when the term is marked on charts for use in some areas for coastal navigation into a harbor.

FAKE
A manner of coiling down a line with a loop at one end, then laying the bight of the line out for a length of 12 or more feet, then looping it at the opposite end bringing it back and forth in close and snug formation on the deck, with each succeeding loop laid over the preceding loop so that when the line is run out it will not foul or kink. It is sometimes called a

"flake". Different nautical writers say flake is proper, others say it is out dated and that *fake* is correct. Only those that have debates on *po-tae-toe* and *pa-tah-toe* can find time for pronunciation discussions while crewmen are on a tow handling lines. See: COIL and FLEMISH.

FALL

1. A line that is rove through one or more blocks. The standing part is where the line is permanently secured and the other is called the working part, which may also be called the *"fall* part".

2. An entire set of tackle that is used in hoisting and lowering a small boat or skiff from a towboat or tug into or out of the water.

FALL ASTERN

See: DROP.

FALL OFF

To move or deviate away from a given course, i.e., "Hold on the point until abreast of the lower dike, then let her *fall off* until you see the bridge come into view". The movement of *fall(ing) off* is usually done as a result of current when making a steer with the slide of lateral direction, but it can also be induced by steering to direct the course of the vessel or tow to gradually move in a down stream direction.

FALLING RIVER or GAUGE

After there has been a rise in the level of a river, the term is used to describe the condition of a decreasing flow. It is usually stated in feet, or tenths of feet, i.e., "The river at Vicksburg is dropping (or *falling*) two feet a day", or "The gauge at McAlpine Lock is dropping (or *falling*) at the rate of a tenth an hour". See: GAUGE or GAGE and GAUGE WATER.

FALLS OF THE OHIO

The *Falls* are located at approximately mile 604 on the Ohio River. They are not really a *falls* but a run of rapids that originally fell about 26 feet over a course of a couple of miles prior to the building of the dam, now called McAlpine Lock and Dam. Navigation on the Ohio at the *Falls* was not possible during low water and prior to the building of the Louisville and Portland Canal in 1830 with the first locks that were built there. Vessels had to tie off and wait for high enough water to safely navigate the *falls* area using a FALLS PILOT.

In 1930 with the canalization of the Ohio, Lock and Dam #41 was completed with a modern (at that time) lock. The dam structure was built along with a fixed and a wicket dam that in moderately high water could be lowered to allow vessels to by-pass the lock during open water periods. The wicket dam was replaced with a concrete navigable weir in the 1960s, but there must be extremely high water to be able to navigate a vessel or tow over it.

The *Falls* area is a region of fossils dating back to the Devonian Period 400 million years ago. There is a fine State Park and Museum located there, on the Indiana side of the river at Clarksville, IN, that is well worth a visit. See: LOUISVILLE AND PORTLAND CANAL.

FALLS PILOT

An experienced Pilot who was hired to navigate the FALLS OF THE OHIO at Jeffersonville, IN, across the river from Louisville, KY, when there was sufficient water to do so. The *Falls* channel was extremely swift and treacherous and required different sets of marks to navigate a steamboat through the channel depending on the gauge level, and especially when there was barely *falls* water to run.

FALSE

Not according to facts, truth, or in

compliance with laws and regulations. From the Latin *falsum,* meaning "fraud". Some examples of *false* as used on the river are:

1. *Alarm* – something that did not happen, i.e., a hot engine alarm goes off but all is normal.
2. *Echo* – a target showing on the radar which is not there.
3. *Point* – an illusory, deceptive protrusion along the shore. It can cause a set in the current and may have an eddy just below where it juts out from the bank.
4. *Reef* – action of wind waves appearing to be water breaking on a reef.

FANCY WORK
The use of small cord or line wrapped or woven into decorative knots to adorn rails, lanyards for bells, attachments for rope knives, etc. A somewhat forgotten skill today on the rivers.

FANTAIL
The open part of the furthest aft rounded section of the deck on a tug. Also sometimes referred to as the stern section of a towboat even though its stern is not rounded. On a sternwheel vessel, the *fantail* is the length of the port and starboard GUARDS that extend beyond the stern splash wall.

FAREWELL SALUTE
See: WHISTLE SALUTE.

FASCINE
These were bundles of willow branches which went into the bank stabilization program to hold the banks from the cutting currents that would wash them away. Used from the late 1800s on to the 1900s, they were held in place with wooden stakes of varying lengths driven through the material into the bank, called "dead stakes". The word comes from the Latin *facis,* meaning "bundle".

FAST
1. To securely tie off a line or wire, i.e., "Make that line *fast* to the lead barge midship cavel", or "Take another wrap on the head wire to insure it stays *fast*".
2. Speed, i.e., "I've got a *fast* moving tow", or "This current is sure moving *fast*".
3. Ice – ice that is frozen *fast* to the shore, as opposed to floating ice.

'FAT IN THE FIRE'
The term used when steamboats were in a close race and the Chief Engineer would add fat or rosin to the fire box to quickly increase the heat and boiler pressure to get more speed.

FATALITY
The loss of life, from whatsoever cause on board a vessel, either from an accident or from natural causes. It is termed a marine casualty under 46 CFR 4.03.

FATHER OF WATERS
An honorary and affectionate title given to the MISSISSIPPI RIVER as it drains the entire system of Western Rivers leading to the Gulf of Mexico.

FATHOM
A measurement equal to six feet. Often used in measuring out lengths of line and in taking SOUNDINGS on the depth of water. The term comes from the old English *faethm,* meaning "embracing", so if the outstretched arms from tip to tip of the average man equals approximately six feet in length we have a *fathom*. Not used too often on the river since most visual measurements and estimates are made in feet and yards, although a deck mate will measure off about 17 *fathoms* from a coil of line by using his arms spread to get a 100-foot lock line and enough to splice in an eye. Occasionally, a deckhand will stretch his arms in despair at a command to carry out some order, which might

mean he is unable to *fathom* what the Mate wants him to do.

There may have been a time or two a Pilot may have commented to another Pilot, "I can't *fathom* how you made that bridge without hitting the right-hand pier". Probably it was said because if the Pilot had hit it, a barge or two may have been a *fathom* or two below the surface of the river.

FATHOMETER
A trademark name for a type of DEPTH SOUNDER.

FATIGUE FAILURE
A weakening, perhaps a cracking or splitting of material, in some piece of machinery or gear due to continuous movement and strain that are above the yield strength of the material.

FAULT
A fissure in a geological rock structure, or overlapping of rock formations, such as the New Madrid *Fault*, which, when it shifted in 1811-1812, caused a series of the worst earthquakes in the history of not only the Mississippi Valley, but in the entire United States.

FAVOR
To take advantage of a condition, i.e., "*Favor* the red buoys in the next crossing since it is kind of shallow on the green buoys", or "Below ABC Point *favor* the right shore since the current is a lot more slack on that side".

FAVORABLE
Used in describing an advantageous wind or current, i.e. "When you get to the lock with this empty tow you should have a *favorable* wind to land on the GUIDE WALL", or "At this stage the current should be *favorable* at XYZ Point".

FAY
The closely laying of two planks or of a plank and timber joined together so that no space can be perceived between them. The term is carried over to steel construction where two plates are united together by welding or riveting. A "*faying* surface" is the surface contact between two adjoining parts.

FEATHER
1. The tapering down of the edge of a plank, timber, or piece of steel. Sometimes done to make it fit, or at times to allow it to SCARF to another member.
2. When efficiently rowing, it is the act of turning the oar blade on the return of a stroke in order that there will be little resistance to wind or water until it again enters the water for another pulling stroke.

FEATHERING WHEEL
1. An arrangement on the sternwheel bucket attachments that allowed the bucket to commence its dip into the water at an almost perpendicular angle to the surface as with a conventional bucket, but after its thrust it would drop its water load and not carry it upward. This, in effect, made the boiler on the steamer more efficient; however, the complex design of cams and rods made it expensive and time-consuming when repairing broken buckets. The idea found little favor in the river trades.
2. The action of a propeller to rotate freely when the engine is not engaged, such as when it may be under tow. This reduces resistance and possible damage of floating debris.
3. The action of changing the pitch of a CONTROLLABLE PITCH PROPELLER.

FEATHERS
1. Wedges that are used to tighten a paddlewheel to its hexagonal shaft.
2. Decorations on the top of a steamer chimney. See: FLUTES or FLUTING.

FEDERAL AID TO NAVIGATION

President James Monroe signed the first waterways improvement Act in 1824. It was to remove snags obstructing navigation on the Ohio and Mississippi rivers and experiment on how to best deal with sandbars. The U.S. Army Corps of Engineers was tasked with the effort. There have been up and down Federal appropriations for navigational improvements from that time down to the present day.

FEDERAL BARGE LINE

In 1918, during WW I, the government, in order to meet the need for logistical support for the war effort, commandeered privately owned barges and steamboats on the river. After the war the government maintained the vessels under control of the War Department, and expanded its operation in an attempt to show the value of the river system for transportation. At that time the barge operation was called the Inland and Coastwise Waterways Service, but was commonly called the Inland Waterways Corporation, a name that was made official in 1924.

After WW II, there was a movement to get the government out of the barge line business as it was continually losing money. In 1953, Herman Pott of the St. Louis Shipbuilding & Steel Co. bought the corporation assets renamed it *Federal Barge Line* (FBL), and it was successfully operated for many years. In 1985 FBL was sold to Midland Enterprises, Inc., a division of Eastern Gas and Fuel Corp. which also owned The Ohio River Company, at the time one of the largest operating barge lines. Then in 2001, Midland Enterprises was sold to the Ingram Corporation, based in Nashville, TN, which took over the remnants of the old government-run barge line.

FEDERAL REGISTER

A U.S. government publication that lists notices of proposed and final regulations that are issued by the federal government departmental agencies, as well as notices of hearings and other information of concern to the public. Especially important to the river industry are those notices issued by the USCG and the USACE.

FEDERAL WATER POLLUTION CONTROL ACT (FWPCA)

The U.S. *Federal Water Pollution Control Act* enacted in 1972 established legal and financial responsibilities, including enforcement and penalties for persons or corporations who spill, discharge, or dispose of oil or hazardous substances into or on the navigable waters of the United States. After several amendments in 1977 it became known as the "Clean Water Act". It is primarily administered by the Environmental Protection Agency; however, on navigable waters the USCG plays a big role in investigation of spills and overseeing their cleanup.

FEED WATER

Water that is added to the boiler to replace that which is used through the steam process when operating the engine. Initially, on steamboats the water was supplied to the boilers by a pump driven by the engine itself. Later, about the 1850s, an independent pump was added in the engine room called a DOCTOR, which would continually supply water to the boilers regardless of whether the engine was propelling the boat or not.

FEELING

When *feeling* is used with another word on the river it describes a consciousness of what may be happening to the vessel or an action being undertaken:

1. The *Bottom* – see: SMELLING THE BOTTOM.
2. The *Current* – the vessel or tow isn't steering the way the Pilot wants it to.

3. The *Helm* – the vessel or tow is starting to turn after the rudder is moved.

4. The *Way* – to move the vessel or tow slowly in an unknown or unmarked channel or in restricted visibility.

FEMALE

The part of a fitting that receives a corresponding MALE part inserted into it to make a connection.

FENDER

1. On the river *fenders* are usually referred to as hand woven shock absorbers. These consist of a series of knots tied around straight lengths of line (four to six pieces about two feet long), one containing a loop to form an eye. They are used to absorb the impact of a vessel coming in contact with another vessel, a lock wall, dock, or other object. See: BUMPER and POSSUM, a makeshift *fender*.

2. On a tug, especially one used in docking ships, heavy woven rope is placed across the bow to protect both the tug and the ship from damage. Sometimes, woven rope, rubber tires, or other protection is placed on the sides and across the stern of the tug. These are called *fenders*.

3. On steamboats *fenders* were heavy timbers, usually about eight inches square. They were hung from the boiler deck to just below the main deck and fastened to the STATIONARIES with loose light line, which gave them flexibility when landing by absorbing the blow, keeping them from breaking.

FEND OFF

To push off or away from a dock or piling, or another object.

FERRULE

1. A type of bushing used to make a water or steam connection leak proof.

2. Sometimes refers to a metal reinforcement band around the handle of a caulking mallet, axe, hammer, or other tool to protect it from splitting or other damage if it might miss its mark when swung.

3. Another name for a SWAGE fitting that clamps a wire together to make an eye or hold a thimble in a wire.

FERRY or FERRYBOAT

A vessel used to transport passengers, vehicles, and sometimes cargo a short distance. On the inland river system these usually simply traverse a river. The term comes from the Norse *ferja,* meaning *ferryboat.* They were an important component in the early days of travel as there were few bridges crossing the streams. At times of low water a wagon and horses could ford at a shallow reach and in the winter rivers were often iced over. Originally *ferries* were propelled by manpower, similar to moving a keelboat. Later horse or mule power provided the propulsion on a turnstile; then came steam and on to diesel power, but only a few are left from the hundreds that propelled persons, livestock, wagons, and also cars, trucks, and railcars across the Western Rivers. See: CABLE FERRY, CAR FLOAT, HORSE FERRY, and TRANSFER BOAT FERRY.

FEU

An abbreviation for a "Forty Foot Equivalent Unit", referring to a container standard size. The other standard for container sizes is a TEU, which refers to a container that is twenty feet long.

FIBERGLASS COVERS

See: COVERED BARGE.

FIBER ROPE

Sometimes used to distinguish LINE from WIRE ROPE. Cordage on the river is usually made of manila, sisal, or synthetic fiber, although the latter is usually referred to as SYNTHETIC LINE, and sometimes "plastic line."

FID

A heavy round piece of hardwood tapered to a blunt point, used when splicing line to ease apart the lay of the line to tuck in the separate strands. Fids are made in various sizes to accommodate the various circumferences of line. When splicing wire rope, a steel-pointed shaft is used, called a MARLINE-SPIKE. It is unknown as to the origination of the word. One might speculate it was a shortened version of one meaning of "fiddle", which was to tinker with something to make adjustments, compromises, or improvements, such as adding an eye to a line, making it more useful.

FIDDLE

Removable bars around the galley stove to keep the pots and pans from rolling or vibrating off and burning someone. Similar wooden bars, ropes, or slats surrounding shelves. Also, a raised edge around a table for the same purpose, to keep things from sliding off.

FIDLEY

A framework built around the deck of a hatch opening leading to a lower compartment.

FIDLEY DECK

The deck around the engine room that is above the lower structure where the base of the engine is located.

FIELD DAY

A Naval term to mean a general cleaning of all spaces on a towboat. Not too often used on the river except by ex-Navy persons.

FIGUREHEADS

Steamboats and towboats do not have *figureheads* as did some of the old sailing vessels and some of the first East Coast steamers who imitated existing sailing craft. However, there was on occasion a display between the stacks, or the mounting of a wooden eagle or other ornamentation, or the winning and display of the GUILDED ANTLERS. About the only display on modern towboats and tugs is the owner's company emblem on the side of the stack or funnel.

FILL

1. To load fuel, water or cargo into a tank or hold of a vessel.
2. The deposition of dredge material to another location. It may be put to various beneficial uses, such as to build up a bank area for a dock or a levee, or to make a park area, or to be deposited in an eroding area to rejuvenate it, etc.
3. To add one or more barges to *fill* out a tow

FILTER

A device that removes particles or impurities in air or from a liquid before it can reach critical components of a mechanical apparatus. It comes from words relating to "felt" and derived from the Latin *filtrum*.

FIN

A small thin protrusion that gives directional stability to an object such as a buoy to keep it from spinning or a weather vane to correctly gage the direction of the wind.

FINISHED WITH ENGINES

For vessels that were equipped with an ENGINE ORDER TELEGRAPH it was a signal from the pilothouse to the engine room after making a landing that no more signals would be given and that the engineer on duty could shut down the engines and boilers. The signal consisted of the movement on the handle(s) of the annunciator from the "stop" position quickly to the "full ahead" position, then immediately reversing to "full astern", moving back to "full ahead" and finally bringing the handle up to the "stop" placement.

FIRE

1. To light off a boiler.
2. The Fire Triangle consists of heat, fuel and oxygen, the three essential components to support a fire. Actual fires that may occur on towboats fall into three categories:

   a. *Class A* – material such as wood, paper, bedding, or rags. See: FIRE EXTINGUISHER.

   b. *Class B* – flammable or combustible liquids such as cooking oil, gasoline or diesel fuel. See: FLAMMABLE LIQUID and COMBUSTIBLE LIQUID.

   c. *Class C* – live electrical equipment.

   3. *Alarm* – A continuous ringing of the tug or towboat's bell for not less than 10 seconds, and also a sounding the vessel's general alarm for not less than 10 seconds.

   4. *Station* – The place a crewman is assigned to man in case of a fire on the vessel.

   5. *Watch* – A crewman with proper equipment, including a portable fire extinguisher, at a space where welding or other hot work is taking place.

FIRE BOAT
A vessel operating in a harbor equipped with fire-fighting equipment, with the capability to fight fires on other vessels and shore-side facilities.

FIRE BOX
On a steamboat the area or space the fireman occupied when shoveling coal or adding wood to provide fuel to the furnace.

FIRE BRICK
A type of brick, similar to that used in kilns that protected the boiler casing and the deck from the direct fire process and more evenly distributed the heat. The boiler shell or skin itself was directly in the flames and hot gases.

FIRE BUCKETS
Buckets that were placed in racks and so marked, located at various intervals on the decks of the old packetboats and steamboats carrying passengers. They were kept full of water and ready at all times to be used in case of fire on board. The buckets had a rope lanyard attached of sufficient length of twice the depth of distance from the lower deck to the water surface. They also had rounded dome bottoms that had to be in the racks in order to stay upright and could not be used for any other purpose. If a Steamboat Inspector came aboard and the bottom of a bucket had been mashed down so it could be used for soogeeing the Inspector would discard it.

FIRE DOOR
A hinged closure to the furnace where the fireman on watch on a steamboat would shovel in coal or pitch in wood to keep the boiler fire burning.

FIRE DRILL
A training exercise or practice undertaken periodically by the crew on vessels to insure a readiness of all members as to their fire stations and how to safely fight fires.

FIRE EXTINGUISHER
A self-contained portable device with a hose and nozzle that holds an *extinguishing* agent that can be expelled to put out a fire, such as a foam type, carbon dioxide gas or a dry chemical powder.

FIRE MAIN
A system of piping and valves to various locations on the decks of riverboats and tugs. Each station is equipped with fire hoses, spanner wrenches, hose nozzles, and fire axes to use in case of an emergency.

FIRE TUBE BOILER
A number of metal tubes in a boil-

er that are covered with water. The heat and gas of the furnace fire under the boiler also goes through the *fire tubes* adding heat to the boiler water, making the boiler more fuel efficient. See: WATER TUBE BOILER.

FIREMAN

The person(s) who tended the fires for heating the boilers on a steamboat. Considered one of the hardest jobs on a steamer, *firemen* worked two shifts of four hours, one during the day and one at night, unless there was an emergency or a task where all crew members were required to help. They also had to assist when wooding up was required. Prior to the Civil War most *firemen* were slaves.

FIRST WATCH
See: FORWARD WATCH

FISH

The act of using a spike pole or grappling hook on a handy line to find a tie-off wire or line in a fleeting area used to moor vessels or tows to the shore.

FISH HOOK

A broken strand in a wire rope that curls up, especially where a hand eye splice was made. It can result in a bad cut or tear for a person if the wire is not handled carefully.

FISH PLATE
See: FLOUNDER PLATE

FIT FOR DUTY

A term which is defined in different ways depending upon the circumstances, whether it is a quarterback playing on a football field, a soldier's readiness to do battle, or an employee who was injured on a towboat. Generally, it means whether a person is suffering from some impairment, injury, illness, medications, etc. that may limit his or her ability to perform their assigned duties which might have an effect on the safety of a vessel and/or its crew and would not be *fit for duty*.

FITCH, JOHN

Although many persons experimented with steam to propel vessels the inventor of the first practical and successful (although not monetarily) steamboat probably should be considered *John Fitch*. He lacked backers with funding for his ideas, as well as other problems. Even though he built and operated a steamboat on the East Coast in 1787-90, he became discouraged and finally went bankrupt. Fitch went to Kentucky in the mid-1890s where he had previously done survey work for Virginia between the Green and Kentucky rivers. He became despondent and committed suicide in 1798. Although Robert Fulton didn't build a steamboat until after the death of Fitch it is ironic that Fulton is given the credit by many historians as the man who introduced steam navigation in the United States.

FITTING OUT

Insuring that a vessel has all the needed operational and safety supplies necessary to carry out the tasks assigned to it, whether it is a new vessel or one that has previously been in operation but has been laid up for a period of time.

FITTINGS

1. In reference to the engine room the term is used for various components used on machinery and piping.
2. On deck structures the term can refer to planking, but is more often used in reference to deck equipment that is used to guide and/or fasten lines or wires, such as timberheads, cavels, chocks, etc.

FIX

Determining and noting a tug's or towboat's position. On riverboats a *fix* is not done by taking bearings visually, or by a radar plot, as is undertaken on seagoing vessels, rather a *fix* is simply visually observing where the vessel and tow are at a given point. It can also be noted by observing the radar, or now by GPS.

FIX-AS-FAILS
An unsatisfactory, but accurate, term for a maintenance program that does not keep up with a normal planned overhaul of infrastructure, but only makes repairs after a component of a system breaks down, leading to unscheduled shutdowns and delays. See: DEFERRED MAINTENANCE and OUTAGES.

FIXED COSTS
Those costs a towing company will have regardless of its activity of towage. These basically non-varying costs cannot be readily reduced in the short term and include administration, interest on debt, depreciation of equipment, insurance, and certain taxes. See: COST.

FIXED CREST DAM
A dam that is stationary and simply allows excess water in the upper pooled area to flow over it when a run-off of rising waters occurs.

FIXED DAM
A rock fill or concrete barrier or weir across a river to retain water.

FIXED LIGHT
An aid to navigation light that shows a steady, continuous, lighting phase.

FLAG
1. The National *Flag* of the United States, flown from the flagstaff of a vessel.
2. House *Flag* – A *flag* displaying the company emblem flown from a jackstaff on the head of a tow. Sometimes it is a smaller pennant version flown on a short staff on a towknee.

FLAG OFFICER
A flag that may be displayed by an Admiral in the U.S. Coast Guard. Gold stars on a field of blue will denote the rank: Two stars for Rear Admiral, three stars for Vice Admiral, and four stars for the Commandant.

FLAG SALUTE
Not often practiced on the river. It is a friendly greeting to another vessel by briefly lowering one's flag from the flagstaff about one-third of the way until the other vessel responds in a like manner, and then fully raising, or two-blocking the flag. Since traffic is so heavy and crews are so busy, this greeting is almost non-existent today.

FLAGSHIP
Some river companies designate one of their vessels as their *flagship*, usually their newest and most powerful towboat or tug, and put in command their most senior Master.

FLAGSTAFF
The *flagstaff* on most riverboats is located at the aft end of the second deck. It is the place where the U.S. National ensign is flown during daylight hours.

FLAKE
A variation of the term FAKE.

FLAME SCREEN
A fine mesh stainless steel or copper screening fitted to a removable frame covering a liquid product cargo opening or ULLAGE HATCH that is used to prevent fire or explosion. Also used in vapor return lines.

FLAMMABLE LIQUID
1. Any liquid with a flash point of 80 degrees Fahrenheit or below. See: COMBUSTIBLE LIQUID, FIRE,

FLASH POINT and REID VAPOR PRESSURE.

2. *Grade A* – Any *flammable liquid* having a Reid vapor pressure of 14 pounds or more (casing head, light napthas, etc.).

3. *Grade B* – Any *flammable liquid* having a Reid vapor pressure under 14 pounds and more than 8 1/2 pounds (most commercial gasolines).

4. *Grade C* – Any *flammable liquid* having a Reid vapor pressure of 8 1/2 pounds or less and a flash point of 80 degrees Fahrenheit or below (most crudes, benzene, alcohol, etc.).

FLANGE

1. A steel plate used with a gasket to cover a liquid pipe header of product and is securely bolted to prevent any liquid or vapors to escape. See: BLIND FLANGE.

2. The part of a steel shape that provides strength and stiffness to a structural member, usually bent at a right angle, and can be used to attach to another member.

3. The hub of a sternwheel from which the arms to support and hold the buckets radiate.

FLANGED

The collar fitted on the end of a pipeline on a tank barge that has holes bored in it to receive a cargo hose that couples up to the *flange* with a gasket between the two, and is securely bolted to it in order to prevent leakage. See: BLIND FLANGE.

FLANK(ING)

The term *flank* as used on the Western Rivers is unique to Pilots who navigate our river systems. Most dictionaries define the word as basically a portion of beef, or to go to the side of something, or in a military sense, to move laterality around an opposing force, i.e., to *flank* them. The only place in nautical language that the word is referred to is in *"flank* speed", mainly used by the Navy, meaning more than full ahead, or at maximum speed. Perhaps the term in Navy lingo was to pursue an enemy vessel at top speed by going around it and surprise it, or, in other words, to out-*flank* the enemy.

It is unknown how it became used as a term for a maneuver of a downbound vessel to safely navigate a loaded barge tow around a sharp bend without sliding into the bank when maneuvering downstream. Perhaps it was because the tow in a *flank* is moving somewhat obliquely as it proceeds downbound, so going to the "side" as used militarily probably transfers to our Western Rivers as a "sideways" movement and became called a *flank*. Tows of empty barges are not normally *flanked*, since they usually can be steered though a bend. With the draft on an empty barge tow only about 15 inches, current does not have much effect on the barges as it does on a loaded tow.

The process of a <u>perfect</u> *flank* is to position a tow with its head pointing into the bend, where the current is fastest, and keeping the stern of the tow on the bar, or buoy, side of the channel where the flow is slacker. Then proceeding at a speed slightly faster than the progress of the water on the bar side, the Pilot controls and steers the stern by backing and maneuvering the FLANKING RUDDERS as the swifter current in the bend directs the head of the tow downstream. At the start of the *flank* the tow's stern will be more or less straight with the slower flows on the bar, while the bow will be at some degree of an angle to the stream velocity in the bend, depending on the width of the channel, size of tow, and speed of current. The tow will be positioned in a somewhat broadside motion, but also moving down the shape of the bend, as measured by the Pilot observing the drift, or by watching a FLANKING BUOY, off the stern of the tow. Since the bow of the tow is in swifter water and at a greater angle to the flow than the tow's stern which is in slacker water, the force of the current against the bow will swing the head of the tow in a greater and faster arc than at the stern where the Pilot is controlling its movement.

At all times, however, the tow is moving in a semi-sideways motion as well as in a downstream direction at a greater rate than a "cross sectional average" of the current speed. When the Pilot decides the head of the tow is coming out, or being pushed out, of the bend sufficiently by the swifter bend current, and any slide toward the bank has been alleviated, he sets the rudders straight, comes full ahead, and the *flank* is completed.

The perfect *flank* only occurs when a Pilot makes an exacting judgment decision on how fast the tow is moving through the water, the angle at which the head of the tow will engage the side force of the current along the shore, and how much that force will be if the tow appears to be moving more forward into the shore than the side force of the current is swinging the head of the tow. Not all *flanks* are perfect. Most require some degree of adjustment.

Making corrections to a *flank* maneuver may require the Pilot to keep backing full astern to go slower than the current on the bar to give the head more time to start swinging. This is sometimes necessary when the current on the bar side is fairly swift, or the bend current is not of very strong velocity, or perhaps the Pilot headed down into the bend at too fast a speed. The Pilot, while backing, can also steer the stern down toward the bend to start the head swinging faster. If the Pilot holds the *flank* too long, the tow will be pushed to the bar by the current, causing it to go aground or even top the stern of the towboat into the bank possibly causing much damage and breakup of the tow. This is termed an "over*flank*". If the Pilot does not hold the *flank* long enough there is a danger that the tow will slide into the shore.

It is a lot easier to read a definition of the dynamics of *flanking* than it is to put 50,000-plus tons of cargo that is the length of four football fields in front of you into a well-executed *flank*. It takes skill and experience. It can be a thing of wonder and beauty that is not readily understood by the uninitiated, but appreciated warmly by other fellow Pilots when it is well accomplished. Therefore, one has to understand the *flank* is an attack by a "tow" on the wiles of a devious enemy opponent called "current", by going around a bend holding the "stern reserves" in readiness, while at the same time, making a frontal attack with the "bow". When the "bow forces" succeed in the battle, then the "stern reserves" do the mop-up of what remains, heading down into the bend, and the *flanking* maneuver is successful with the "dynamics of the bend enemy" raising the white flag of surrender. The "tow" of the "bow and stern brigades" continues their advance downstream joined up and ready for the next "attack". Also see: RUNNING FLANK.

FLANKING (2)

The course of a stream flow around a training structure, or other type of construction, into a bank, perhaps causing eddy action of erosion that may lead to a failure of the structure.

FLANKING BUOY

A small float or buoy, or usually an empty gallon bleach bottle, tied to each outboard corner of the stern of a tow in order for the Pilot to judge the speed of the tow through the water when entering into a flanking maneuver. See: FLANK and EAR BOB.

FLANKING RUDDERS

Rudder(s) that are installed forward of the propeller(s) that assist a Pilot in controlling a vessel's movement when backing. The force of the propeller wash goes under the towing vessel and against the *flanking rudders* rather than against the steering rudder.

FLARE

1. An upward and outward curvature of the bow of a vessel.
2. A rocket *flare* set off to indicate distress.
3. A smoke *flare* set off to indicate distress.

FLASH FLOOD

An extremely rapid rise in the river. Usually the rise carries a lot of drift. Most of the time this type of rise falls out as quickly as it rose, sometimes causing damage to the channel, by moving sandbars around.

FLASH POINT

The lowest temperature, in Fahrenheit degrees, that a liquid gives off flammable vapors.

FLASHBOARD DAMS

Before canalization of the Ohio River a system was used by vessels during extremely low water periods where a small dam in the channel was built with boards or timber to temporarily build up the water level. Then with a vessel in place, a key section was knocked out allowing the vessel to float down over the shallow area.

A similar system was used by keelboats, both when going downstream and when keeling upriver over shallow reaches. The keelers would drive stakes at an angle to the vessel on the upriver side of the vessel and attach boards to them. The process would divert current under the keelboat to help wash a bar away and provide an extra amount of water to assist in moving through the channel.

FLASHING LIGHT

1. As an aid to navigation, a *flashing light* means one that shows one or more flashes at certain intervals.
2. As defined for lights to be shown on vessels, Navigation Rule 21(f) states a *"Flashing Light* means a light flashing at regular intervals at a frequency of 120 flashes or more per minute". See: SPECIAL FLASHING LIGHT.

FLAT

1. Having an even horizontal surface without camber or bevel.
2. A small work barge used at a shipyard, fleet, or around floating vessels to make repairs, do painting, or used to move rigging to or from a tow.

FLAT BOTTOMED

A vessel that has no centerline keel, nor any upward inclination of its bottom from the centerline toward its sides. Nearly all towboats are of this type design and construction as well as all inland barges.

FLAT POOL

A navigation pool between dams which is at normal height with the dam running practically "no flow", hence, there is very little, or almost no, current.

FLATBOAT

Flatboats, described as "Noah's Arks", were classed as lightly built Kentucky boats or New Orleans boats for those more heavily constructed with a roof completely covering the cargo area. The latter were used for long distance travel most often to the city for which they were named. These vessels were used in early navigation on the Ohio and Mississippi rivers and their tributaries. They had no power and simply floated with the currents downstream. They were fairly large rectangular box-like structures without a keel. They could be put together cheaply and when at their destination in New Orleans, could be broken up and sold for the lumber in them. *Flatboats* were of various sizes, mostly 20 to 60 feet long, with the largest reaching about 90 feet. Their widths varied from 10 to 25 feet. They carried 25 to 100 tons of freight, generally at a draft of about two feet when loaded.

Flatboats were fitted with oars and long SWEEPS, one at the stern and one out to each side in order to give the crew some degree of control of the vessel in the current. The sweeps that extended well out from the sides of the boat gave it the look of having horns, so the term "Broadhorns" was coined which became the popular name for *flatboats*. The use of *flatboats* pretty well died out after the Civil War except in the reaches of small tributary streams, mainly due to the competition of steamboats. Two famous historical *flatboat* personages were Davy Crockett and Abe Lincoln.

FLATTEN OUT
To come alongside a dock, fleet, lock wall, another tow, or other place in a parallel or almost parallel fashion, or when coming into one of the foregoing areas, catching a bow line and then *flatten out* along the space by bringing a vessel's and/or tow's stern in parallel.

FLEET
1. A group of vessels, usually just barges, moored in a group or groups in one area.

2. The tugs, towboats, or barges that belong to particular company, i.e., "Those barges are a part of the ABC *fleet*".

3. Derived from the old English *floet,* meaning "ship" or "shipping".

FLEET BOAT
Usually a small towboat that is assigned to a fleet or a dock area that primarily keeps watch over it and shifts barges in and out of a fleet to tows or docks in the immediate vicinity. See: SHIFT BOAT.

FLEETING
1. The act of placing a barge in a fleet area.

2. The holding of barges in a fleet area until they are called by a dock for loading or unloading, or picked up by another towboat.

3. A place for the assembly or disassembly of barges and the make-up of tows going to different destinations by different towboats.

FLEMISH
The act of coiling a line flat on deck in only one tier starting in the center with its bitter end and continuously increasing the size of the concentric circle. This is sometimes done on excursion vessels and ferryboats for decorative purposes, usually with short lengths of line, but is seldom seen on working towboats or tugs. See: COIL and FAKE.

FLINT RIVER
See: APALACHICOLA, CHATTAHOOCHEE, and FLINT.

FLOAT
Any device that will stay above water when immersed, such as a life preserver, buoy or a raft. The word is from Old English *flotian,* with a Germanic base from the word "fleet", meaning "to pass quickly".

FLOAT GAUGE
A type of gauge that indicates the level of liquid in a tank by use of a device that *floats* at the surface of the liquid.

FLOATING
1. A vessel in the condition of being afloat in a body of water, not sunk or sinking, or being aground, or hauled out on a drydock, or on the shore.

2. Any vessel or object that is moving and not moored, tethered, or otherwise attached to anything, but subject to wind or current action.

3. A vessel that has no power engaged for forward or astern movement, but may use idle speed to hold or maintain a vessel's position in a stream.

FLOATING AIDS
Buoys placed by the USCG to mark the channel, designate anchorages, quarantine, fishing, dredging, danger, wrecks, or other special purposes.

FLOATING BRIDGE
There have been various bridges at times that have been floating, especially on small streams and canals. They principally were operated by a pivot on one end and when opened they loosened on the opposite end and either allowed to float with a current into the open position or were pulled open by a line or wire. After a vessel transited the area the *floating bridge* was pulled back into position. See: PONTOON BRIDGE.

FLOATING DECKHOUSE
See: VIBRATION ISOLATER.

FLOATING DOCK
A dock that rises and falls when the river level goes up or down. Usually the dock is between piers or pile cells, especially where liquid products are handled and where the pipeline connections are located.

FLOATING DRYDOCK
See: DRYDOCK.

FLOATING PALACES
The name given to the ornately decorated and appointed passenger steam packets from the middle to the latter 1800s on the Ohio and Mississippi rivers. One of the first was the *Str. ECLIPSE* in 1852, however many have said the second *Str. J.M. WHITE* was the finest steamboat ever built.

FLOATING PIPELINE
A *pipeline* for a dredge that has each section of the line mounted on a pontoon. The pontoons are coupled together and lead to an appropriate disposal area. The dredged material is then pumped through the *floating pipeline* and discharged.

FLOATING PLANT
A group of work vessels in an area undertaking construction work along a shore, such as a USACE MAT LAYING PLANT, or barge equipment of contractors building a bridge or a dam in mid-river, or a dredge and tenders clearing a channel, etc.

FLOATING TIMBERHEAD, PIN, or BOLLARD
A watertight floating cylinder recessed in a lock wall with a *timberhead, pin, or bollard* mounted on its top that is used to secure a vessel and/or tow in a lock chamber. There is no need for a lock tender to handle lines on and off the lock wall since the deck crew can easily attach a short line to the fitting on the *floating timberhead*. The floating cylinder, with its tie-off fitting, rises, as do the barges, when the lock is filling with water so there is no need to constantly take up slack in the lock line. The same occurs when the lock is turned around and the next tow is lowered along with the *floating timberhead*, etc.

FLOG
To punish by striking one with a rope whip, a club, a cat-o'-nine tails, or other object. Formerly the punishment was administered by both Navy and merchant vessels to crewmen who were deemed guilty of violating some rule or command of the vessel's Captain. In 1898, the U.S. Congress passed a law prohibiting *flogging* and all forms of corporal punishment on merchant vessels. For a more severe form of punishment, see BOWSPRITTING, but as far as is known that was

never practiced on steamboats or their successors in the river trades.

FLOOD

1. Filled with water because of a leak or a damaged hull, i.e., "The No. 1 starboard wing tank is *flooded*".

2. In coastal areas when the tide is rising, or moving into a harbor or shore area.

3. As one writer described the term, "Floods result from abnormal distribution of rainfall".

4. When the river reaches FLOOD STAGE in an area. Generally, this is when a river overflows its banks, which can be a devastating disaster in the area where it occurs. Some of the worst *floods* in the last century were the 1927 flood on the Lower Mississippi, the 1937 flood on the Ohio River, the 1993 flood on the Upper Mississippi, and the devastation to New Orleans in 2005 as a result of hurricane Katrina. The word comes from the Old English *flod,* apparently of Germanic origin, but perhaps can be traced back to the biblical Noah, who first started all this stuff. At least he had a sound vessel in which to ride it out.

FLOOD CONTROL

A program under the direction of the U.S. Corps of Engineers. The term itself is a misnomer as *control* is in the eyes of the beholder and *floods* still wreck havoc in many river valleys and cost the nation billions of dollars. Perhaps *Flood Management* would be a better term for this work. Even though damaging floods still occur, the USACE has done a magnificent job in taming some of their worst effects. Since 1928, when they began in earnest to address the problem of *floods,* to the end of the 20th century, the program has saved almost a trillion dollars in damages, approximately 6.5 times the cost of their *control* efforts. The Corps does it by a variety of approaches, including building levees, floodwalls in cities, reservoirs in upper reaches of headwaters and tributary streams, operating floodways when necessary, and studying new methods to minimize the effects of flooding.

FLOOD CREST

The highest stage of a *flood* incident, from which the *flood* will subside. In some flooding events the water level will *crest*, then subside, but with additional inflow will rise again to reach a higher *crest*.

FLOOD OF RECORD

The highest recorded height of water level observed at a given location since records have been kept; however, it may not be the highest known stage of water.

FLOOD STAGE

The time when the river rises to a predetermined gauge level set by the USACE in a particular area. It is generally when some part of the main riverbank overflows, but not necessarily all of it. *Flood stage* usually indicates that some form of damage will occur.

FLOOD TIDE

The shoreward movement of water in a tidal area.

FLOODGATE

An opening in a floodwall that is secured when the river rises to a level that may go through the opening.

FLOODPLAIN

Low-lying areas along the shore of a river's course that are subject to flooding when the river rises and overflows its banks.

FLOODWALL

A structure, usually of concrete, constructed to protect an area from the damage caused by floods. It is built mostly in urban areas to exceed the height of record historic flooding gauges.

FLOODWAY

In order to reduce flood heights which might overtop the LEVEE system, the USACE created a system of relief valves called *floodways*, sometimes referred to as *spillways*. These structures create a large basin that is able to retain or divert the flow of a flood from the main stem of the river. Each structure has a "fuse plug" that allows the water to enter the *floodway*. Sometimes it is a low spot in a levee that when overtopped will rapidly wash away; other times the fuse may be dynamited, or go over a fixed concrete structure at a fixed gauge level, and in other cases it will have a controlled section with stop logs and/or gates. The three main *floodways* on the Mississippi River system are:

Birds Point – On the Missouri side of the river opposite Cairo, IL, where floodwater enters, fills the basin area, and then makes its re-entry to the Mississippi just above New Madrid. It was dynamited open in 1936 when its fuse plug failed to wash out. It can be opened when the gauge at Cairo is 58 feet and predicted to exceed 60 feet.

Morganza-West Atchafalaya – This system opens at Old River and follows down through the Old River outlet in equal amounts through levee-protected spillways on both sides of the Atchafalaya River until they eventually merge and flow into Wax Lake and the Lower Atchafalaya River. It was opened in the 1973 flood when there was a danger of the Old River control structure collapsing.

Bonnet Carre Spillway – This is a controlled *floodway* and has been opened numerous times to protect the city of New Orleans from disastrous floods. It is located about 60 miles north of New Orleans and, when opened, it flows into Lake Pontchartrain. The *spillway* is usually opened when the Carrollton gauge is expected to reach 20 feet.

FLOOR FRAME

The transverse frames that are attached to the bottom plate of a vessel providing a foundation for the structures above it, whether it be an engine or a cargo space of a barge. It is one of the few times in nautical language that the term *floor* is used.

FLOP AROUND

The act of turning a barge, or a tow, completely around and heading it in the opposite direction. It is another term for ROUND TO.

FLOTATION

When a person wonders why steel vessels, or any other vessel, floats in water, always remember Archimedes' Law: The weight of a floating body is equal to the weight of the fluid displaced.

FLOTILLA

A fleet of vessels. Used on the river to refer to a group of recreational vessels either in a marina or operating in a waterway. Comes from the Spanish *flota*, meaning "fleet".

FLOTSAM

Cargo that may be cast overboard or floats away from a vessel that is in peril. The cargo that is lost is to be appraised at its fair value and the shipper/owner of the goods compensated for the loss. The term goes back to, and prior to, one of the tenets of the LAWS OF OLERON. This loss of cargo becomes known as part of a legal term, entitled "general average" of maritime perils; whereby the value of the cargo is combined with the vessel, its cargo, and freight (which is the vessel owner's charges for transportation), and all parties share in the loss and any restitution. However, legal freight documents may modify this arrangement. Usually the general average rule only comes into action when there is a total loss, as in a vessel sinking. The courts will adjudicate as usual. See: LAGAN and JETSAM.

FLOUNDER PLATE
A triangular steel plate with a hole drilled or burned in each corner. Used by a tug or towboat that is towing on a bridle. Two legs of the *flounder plate* are shackled to equal lengths of wire leading from opposite side corners of the object being towed, while the other leg is shackled to a pendant leading to the towing hawser or wire from the tug or towboat. Sometimes called a "fish plate", probably so named as it resembles a type of flat fish, the *Flounder*.

FLOW (of water)
The volume of water going past a particular point per unit of time. It is usually given in cubic feet per second (CFS).

FLUCTUATION
The word *fluctuation* has various meanings as used in different disciplines whether it refers to commercial markets, cyberspace circuits, air currents, etc. To the Riverman it usually means the range level between the rise and fall of a river stage or gauge. A potamologist studies the different *fluctuation* measurements of the river when devising engineering solutions to control what the various flows in a stream do at high and low levels along with different speeds of the current.

FLUES
On a steamboat, piping that took advantage of the hot gasses from the FIREBOX beneath the boiler. This piping ran from the firebox through the boiler to provide additional heat to make steam. The gases were then vented into the chimneys and exhausted to the outside. See: SUPERHEATER.

FLUSH
To be even with something, as "The two new planks fitted into the hull were *flush*", or "The tow we picked up at Cairo didn't have a *flush* coupling in it and we were either pushing squares or dragging them".

FLUSHING
The act at a lock and dam structure to remove ice or drift from the upper lock entrance, or the lowering of a dam gate to let ice or drift run out of the upper pool.

FLUTES or FLUTING
A decorative addition to the exit of a steamboat chimney. The splaying appendages were supposed to disperse embers that might be emitted from the furnace of the boilers, however many steamers did not have any fluting. Sometimes called "feathers," "bonnets," "or petticoat tops." See: PUDDINGS.

FLUVIAL
The geological characteristics and actions of a river as it flows and carries its sediment load from its source(s) to the lower slopes of its course where it meets the sea. The term comes from the Latin *fluvius,* meaning "river".

FOAM
1. A chemical or mechanical agent used to smother a fire.
2. A type of polyurethane used at one time to fill the voids of barges to extend their useful life cycle. Also used in buoys to keep them afloat even if they suffer damage and are holed.

F.O.B.
An abbreviation for a shipping term meaning, "Free On Board," or the point from which transportation charges are determined after a cargo has been loaded. See: COST-INSURANCE-FREIGHT.

FOG

Condensed water vapor in the air that has reached DEW POINT. It can basically be called a cloud that is lying close to the water. If the wind is more than about 15 mph fog usually will not form. It is the weather situation most frequently occurring that is of great concern to the river industry. Even with the continually improving state of electronic navigational instruments, safe navigation requires a special alertness by the crew of any vessel during fog conditions. There are basically three types of fog conditions affecting river Pilots on towboats and tugs. They are:

1. Advection Fog – Occurs when warm air blows over the surface of colder water or land causing the air to cool and reach dew point, resulting in fog. It is of the least of the types of fog of concern to river Pilots since this weather formation mostly occurs in the ocean environment rather than where rivers run through valleys of land masses. However, along the Gulf Coast and the Lower Mississippi Valley, the surface temperature of water is lowered when cold northern river water reaches the Bayou Country with its warm gentle breezes. Under these conditions this type of fog can form and last for days at a time.

2. Radiation Fog – Occurs more often over land than over wide expanses of water such as an ocean, but the waters that riverboats operate in are the highways running through the land where this type of fog readily occurs. Since colder air is in the lower reaches of valleys, absent a stiff breeze this type of fog is at its thickest where towboats push barges, while the surrounding hills may be above the fog line. This fog most often forms in late evening when the sun has set. With a high relative humidity level in the air and the heat from the sun going over the horizon to the next time zone, it doesn't take too much cooling for the air to reach dew point to have a fog event. The season for fog on a river is usually fall and winter. When first forming and rising from the river it seems to appear like "smoke rising from the water".

3. Steam Fog – This type of fog develops when the temperature of the air is very cold and it moves across a relatively warm body of water. In some areas where there is an incidence of thermal pollution of a river or canal due to the release of warm water from power plants and other industrial entities, the combination of warm water and cold nights allows *steam fog* to readily develop, especially in such areas as the upper reaches of the Illinois Waterway where the only place there is fog may be in the immediate area of the river. The adjacent land masses will be clear. Of course, when it dissipates the Pilot on watch can revel in the beauty of the branches of trees lining the bank with their many-layered coats of glass-like fog frozen moisture.

FOG SIGNALS

The audible *signals* a vessel is required to sound when conditions of "restricted visibility" exist. Such signals are found in Rule 35 of the Navigation Rules, "Sound Signals in Restricted Visibility" which are to be sounded whether by whistle, gong, or bell.

FOGBANK

A dense mass of fog next to a clear area. The vessel in the *fogbank* operates under the dictates of Rule 19 in the Navigation Rules. A vessel in the cleared area, if there is a risk of collision also operates under Rule 19, "Conduct of Vessels in Restricted Visibility", as they are "near an area of restricted visibility". Only when both vessels are in sight of one another do the other navigation rules come into effect.

FOGBOUND

A vessel that is delayed, holding up, tied off, or pushed into the bank due to RESTRICTED VISIBILITY because the Pilot is of the opinion that it is unsafe to navigate. There are various conditions of fog that are described in different unofficial and subjective terms such as, "wispy", "steam", "heavy", "pea soup", "shutout", and probably other local variations.

FOLLOWING EDGE

The edge of a propeller blade opposite the leading or cutting edge of the propeller when it is in the ahead rotation.

FOLLOWING WAKE

A wave along the shore given off by a vessel or tow moving fairly fast through the water. The wake travels out behind the vessel or tow and may hit shallow water, causing it to build up and become a fairly large swell when hitting the shore area.

FOLLOW UP

A device that indicates the actual position of the steering and/or flanking rudders as the Pilot moves the rudder levers in the pilothouse to steer the vessel. It is usually an arrow marker that moves at the same rate that the rudder is actually moving.

FOOT (of BEND or ISLAND)

The lower or downstream end.

FOOTBOARD

A low raised platform at the throttle in the engine room of a steamboat where the engineer on watch was stationed. All the main controls of the engine were nearby.

FORCE MAJEURE

An unplanned, unforeseeable event or set of compelling circumstances, such as overwhelming weather (flood, ice conditions, hurricane, etc.), strikes, lock closure, etc., that causes a party to a contract to notify the other party(s) that they are negating their contractual obligations. The event causing the action must be for a period of longer than 24 hours, and any "Acts of God" that would trigger the execution has to be declared in writing within 72 hours of the event. The term comes from the French, meaning "superior strength".

FORE

Used in conjunction with other terms to indicate something or some structure that is toward, near or adjacent to the bow.

FORE AND AFT

From the bow to the stern.

FORE AND AFT WIRES or LINES

A hard coupling makeup of wire cables between the ends of two barges in the same string. See: JOCKEY WIRES or LINES.

FOREBAY

The area of water immediately above some lock structures between the guide wall and a guard wall or other structure around the upstream area of entrances to the lock chamber(s).

FOREPEAK

The most forward compartment or space of a tug or towboat. On a barge it is referred to as the bow void or compartment.

"FOREVER FREE"

The rallying voice against the proponents of user charges on inland waterways navigation structures when their future was being debated prior to 1980. The term derived from the 1787 Ordinance outlining the freedoms to be enjoyed by governing the new Northwest Territory that now includes the states of Ohio, Michigan, Indiana, Illinois, Wisconsin, and part of Minnesota. In Article IV it stated:

"The navigable waters leading into the Mississippi and St. Lawrence, and the carrying places between the same, shall be common highways and *forever free*, as well to the inhabitants of said States that may be admitted into the confederacy, without any tax, impost, or duty therefore".

This compact was negated in 1978 when a user tax on fuel was imposed on inland waterway carriers for construction and rehabilitation of waterway improvement structures. However, the States involved did not secede from the Union when the compact under which they joined was violated. See: USER TAX or CHARGE.

FORK

1. A junction where two rivers meet and join together to form one stream.

2. A place where a stream branches off from the main channel.

FORWARD

Near, at, or toward the bow of the vessel, unless a location is *forward* or ahead of the bow.

FORWARD WATCH

The watch from 6 a.m. to 12, and 6 p.m. to 12, the *watches forward* of noon and midnight. This is the traditional watch stood by the Captain of a towboat. The Pilot stands the AFTER (or AFT) WATCH. These traditional descriptions of watches are changing as companies are experimenting with different lengths of watches in an attempt to alleviate any effects of fatigue.

FOTHERING

A method used in an attempt to stop severe leakage in the bottom or side of a vessel. A loose canvas or burlap type bag is filled with material such as ashes, sawdust, oakum, torn rags or other suitable debris with some heavier material such as cinders or rocks to give it some weight. Small limbs or pieces of boards are fastened on the outside length of the bag to somewhat stiffen it. Then it is lowered over the side as close as possible to where the breach is located. While still pumping water from the compartment that is flooding it is hoped the bag will be sucked into the fracture, but that the limb or board stiffeners will keep it from going all the way through. If successful the crew can then enter the compartment and make better temporary repairs on the inside of the hull that will hold until they can get the vessel to a repair yard. Except for salvors this is seldom done on the river today, and they use collisions mats for large holed areas. However, there have been many sunken barges raised, or kept from sinking, by simply sucking a canvas over the holed section of a hull. It is believed the word comes from *fodder*, as in animal feed, to infer that one is feeding the hole where the pigs are lapping up the food. See: COLLISION MAT.

FOUL(ED)

1. A wire or line that becomes kinked, snarled, or tangled and cannot run free. The word comes to us from the Latin *putere*, meaning "to stink". It evolved into various languages with variations of dirty, filthy, rotten, lazy, etc. Anything that is *foul* is one or more, or all of these terms.

2. A wire or line that has become jammed tight on a vessel or shoreside fitting, or on a winch or capstan, and cannot be worked free.

3. To be entangled with an obstruction, such as, sucking up a cable in the wheel, a floating buoy stuck between the wheel and the kort nozzle housing, or a floating log jammed in the rudders making them immovable.

4. Unfavorable weather.

5. A hull encrusted with barnacles on a tug, or zebra mussels on a freshwater operating towboat.

FOUND

1. To fit properly and firmly. See: FULLY FOUND.

FOUNDATION

The heavy plating and framing in a hull that supports the engine, generators, boilers, reduction gears, and other machinery.

FOUNDER

A vessel that fills with water, loses buoyancy, and is in a sinking condition, but still afloat.

FRACTURE

The failure of a steel plate or weld causing a crack or break in a structure. It usually is due to a severe pressure strain, or a heavy striking force, such as may occur in an allision or a collision. In some cases brittle *fractures* may occur over time due to some error in calculation of the ductile strength of the steel when manufactured. At other times a fatigue *fracture* may occur after a long period of service in which a plate or weld may be under continual on again, off again, stress levels.

FRAME(S)

The structural members, both horizontal and vertical, that comprises the skeleton of a vessel to which the skin plate is attached. Various modifiers are attached to these members, such as bow *frames*, buck frames, cant *frames*, floor *frames*, etc. The word derives from old English *framian*, meaning "to make ready for use", and the *frames* of a vessel are as important to it as skeletal parts are to mankind.

FRAME TIP WEAR

On older vessels, especially those of thinner plate skin, the sides may become somewhat washboarded. This condition creates a hard spot on the vertical internal framing along the side of the vessel, in particular the lower part above the knuckle of a barge, which is subject to increasing wear as it rubs against other barges, docks, and lock walls and can eventually wear a hole in the side of the hull.

FRAPPING LINE

A small line placed around the tackle of a hoist to guide the object being lifted or lowered. The term comes from French *fraper*, meaning "to bind".

FRAY

Heavy wear on a line, with some outer strands broken. The word comes from Latin *fricare*, meaning "to rub".

FREE

Something that is not secured, tied down, running loose, or is adrift. The antecedent use of the word goes back to ancient times to mean a loving relationship or closeness to family members that were united together. How it evolved to mean something that was detached, or no longer connected is unknown. Maybe there was a black sheep that left the flock.

FREE DAYS or TIME

The amount of time a vessel owner or operator will allow for the loading or unloading of cargo prior to charging demurrage or a detention fee. Usually only holidays are excluded.

FREE SURFACE

The surface area of liquid in a tank or cargo space that can move unrestricted from side to side or fore and aft. The greater the quantity of liquid and the greater the amount of surface, the more unstable a vessel may become. This is why liquid tank barges have various compartments that can act as baffles to reduce the *free surface* effect.

FREEBOARD

1. The vertical distance from the

waterline to the main deck of a vessel, or the place where water would put the deck awash. See: DRAFT MARKS.

2. The vertical difference between the predictions of a maximum flooding event and the structure designed for protection. For instance, with 100-year flood estimation, it is the design height of a floodwall, levee, or dam, to withstand waves and other surface movements from overtopping it. The *freeboard* becomes the actual vertical distance from the top of the structure to the surface of the flooding water.

FREEING PORT
See: SCUPPER.

FREIGHT
1. Cargo being transported in a barge.
2. The charge paid to the owner or operator of a barge for the transportation of the cargo.

FREIGHT RATES
Those rates published in a tariff. The last official general tariff for the rivers was published in 1976. Nearly all rates now are by contract, verbal or written.
2. With certain commodities, such as grain, barging rates change daily and are based on a supply and demand basis. They are based on a percentage of the 1976 common carrier barge tariff rate, which reflects the cost in cents per bushel from and to listed locations.

FRENCH CREEKERS
A type of open-hopper wooden barge used to transport oil out of the Allegheny River in the mid-1800s. They carried over 1000 barrels in either bulk or in barrels, and were about twice as large as the BULKBOATS. They were called that name as the French Creek, a fairly large tributary, enters the Allegheny River at the town of Franklin, PA, just below Oil City where the oil boom was in full swing and many barges bearing that designation were built in Meadville, PA, about 30 some miles up French Creek. See: ALLEGHENY RIVER.

FRENCH LANDING
A term sometimes used by steamboats to describe basically a downstream landing at a wharf, or other place, with the stern facing upstream.

FREQUENCY
1. The estimated evaluation of stages of water in the river over a period of years, i.e. the height and recurrence of a 100 year flood in disaster planning and the construction of protection structures.
2. The amount, time length and repitition of flashes for navigation lights.
3. Vessel whistle audibility and ranges.
4. Radio channels to monitor and on which to communicate.

FRESHET
A sudden flood in a stream. They rise fast and usually fall just as fast. Mostly used in reference to a tributary to a main navigable river, i.e. "There's a *freshet* coming out of XYZ Creek".

FRESNEL LENS
Named after Augustin Jean Fresnel (1788—1827), a French physicist and civil engineer who developed the theory of light refraction waves that led to producing the lenses that are used in lighthouses, vessel navigation lights, and other places.

FUEL FLAT
1. A small tank barge for diesel fuel, usually operated by a MIDSTREAM BOAT STORE to service a towboat while it is underway. It delivers fuel and potable water, sometimes groceries, mail, and supplies.
2. A small flat deck barge towed alongside a steamboat to supply coal to fire the furnaces of the boiler.

FUEL OIL
Refers to diesel petroleum products used in most towboats and tugs to power their engines and generators.

FUEL TAX
See: INLAND WATERWAYS TRUST FUND.

FULCRUM
A post or device that acts as a point on which a lever will operate to perform a task more efficiently, such as a THOLE PIN for an oar, or a prop for a SPRINPOLE PUMP. The term comes to us from the Latin *fulcire*, which has the meaning of "to prop up".

FULL AHEAD
Said of a vessel that has its engine(s) running at maximum speed.

FULL DOUBLE
The full utilization of the surface space of a lock chamber with two sections (cuts) of a tow. Usually refers to locking through a 600-foot lock. With all jumbo (195' x 35') barges it would amount to 17 barges and the towboat, or in effect, a tow of almost 1200 feet long.

FULL EFFICIENT FUNDING
A term used to indicate the degree of capability in the USACE to support a level of funding to construct, rehabilitate, or repair project infrastructure.

FULL RUDDER
A rudder that is placed as far to its maximum position to port or starboard, to allow it to move all the way to its stops. See: HARD (DOWN).

FULL TOW
A tow of the maximum size to fit into the locks on the river, or one that is considered by a company to be the most that a particular towboat can safely handle with regard to the existing river conditions at the time.

FULLY FOUND
This term is usually associated with a charter agreement. It means that an owner will lease or charter a vessel to another entity that is completely and legally equipped, with the owner providing crew, insurance, routine repair and maintenance costs, any fees required, and fuel to run the vessel. At times fuel costs are negotiable. The agreement will set the contractual fee for use of the vessel and a time period for its availability.

FULTON, ROBERT
Born in Pennsylvania in 1765. Although he did not invent the steamboat, he was the person who put in place the workable design for a practicable one. His first steamboat was the *NORTH RIVER* which people called the *CLERMONT*. Wealthy and influential Robert Livingston, an ex-Ambassador to France, was his partner. They obtained monopoly rights to run steamboats in New York. Then they built the *Str. NEW ORLEANS* in Pittsburgh in 1811, the first steamboat (at least of any size) on the Western Rivers. Fulton was an artist, an engineer, gunsmith, inventor, and he had many other talents, too numerous to mention. He invented the submarine and also designed underwater torpedoes, and even a steam warship. He also was involved in canal engineering. Fulton died in 1815.

FUNNEL
The smokestack on a vessel. Not often used on the river. It is more often called a "stack", or on the old steamboats, a "chimney". The term *funnel* is said to have been given to the place on vessels where the furnace emissions were exhausted, since the early stacks looked like inverted *funnels*. Since the term

comes from Latin *infundere,* meaning "to pour in", the use of the word is appropriate since the furnace smoke was pouring into the sky.

FURNACE

The boxed area under the boiler where a fire is made to heat water in the boiler to provide power to a steamboat. The word is from the Latin *fornus,* meaning "oven".

FURRING

1. The double planking of a wooden hull.
2. The cleaning off of the sediment and buildup of incrustations on the inside of a boiler, a most unfavorable job.

FURROW

The action of the wave coming off a stern paddlewheel. Used when a steamer is making good time through the water by saying, "She's plowing a *furrow*".

FUSE PLUG

A place in a fixed FLOODWAY control structure where it can be crevassed allowing flood waters to be drained away from a river and into a basin in order to reduce pressure on a levee system. If the floodway is landlocked, a *fuse plug* will also be placed at its lower end elevation to allow drainage once the danger of flooding has subsided.

FUSIBLE PLUG

A safety device in a boiler. If the boiler does not receive enough water to cool the plug in the skin of the boiler, the plug's core would melt and the pressure in the boiler would be relieved through the hole, keeping the boiler from bursting. All plugs were required to be replaced at each annual inspection.

FUTTOCKS

Upright curved ribs that rise up from the keel in a vessel. The name derives from "foot" plus "hook", which in essence is what they are, with "foot" being a support and "hook" being a somewhat curved piece of material. Various names are given to different particular *futtocks*.

FACING UP THE TOWBOAT TO A TOW

The location, type and amount of fittings, winches and capstans vary on towboats, tugs, and barges depending upon the size of the vessel, the trade in which it is engaged, owner preference, etc. The illustrations below will give the reader a general sense of what is involved when the crew is engaged in "facing up" to a tow.

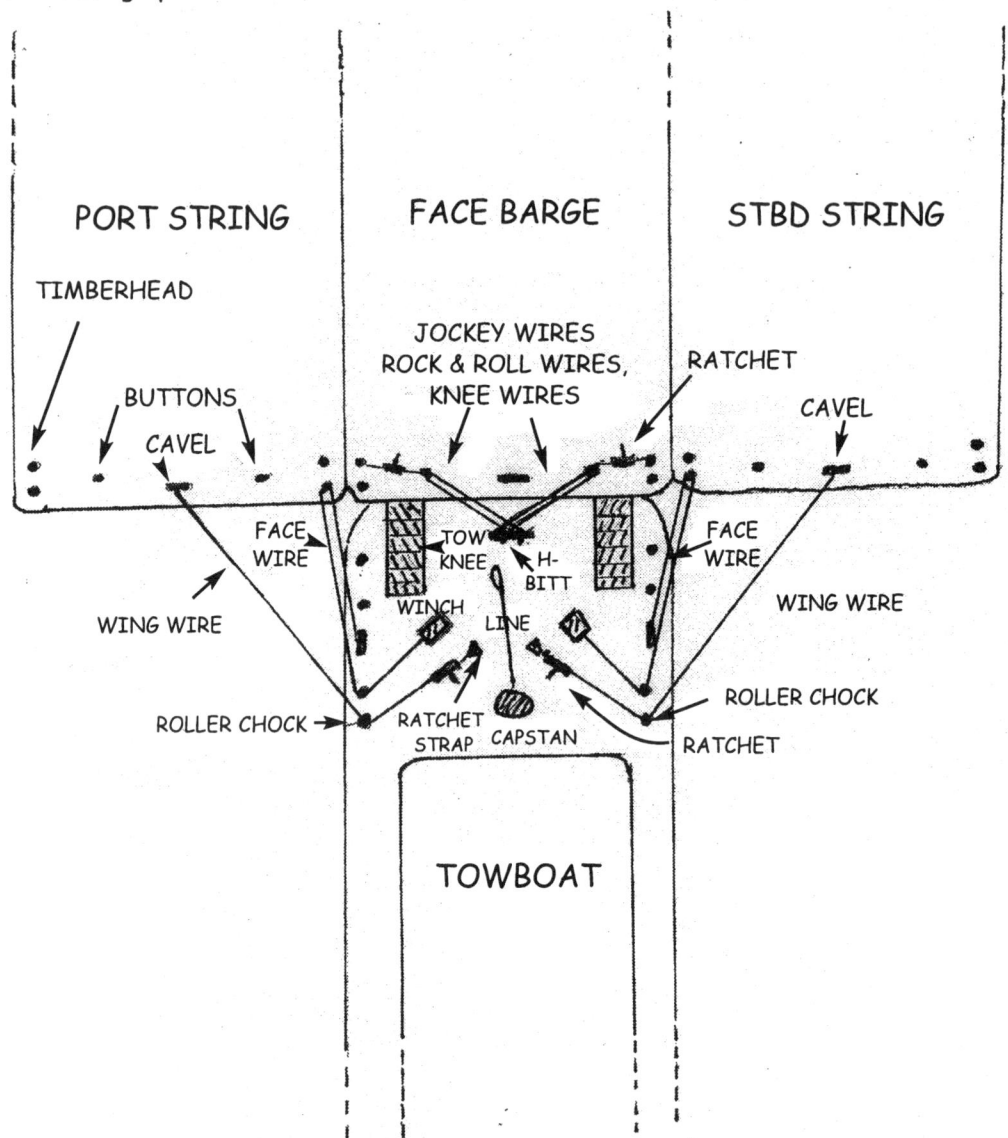

- A – Towboat comes up to barge(s) where Pilot wants the towboat positioned. It is usually at the downstream end of the tow, but at times the towboat will will make a downstream landing on the head of the tow, depending upon how the tow is situated.
- B – The deckhands place a doubled up capstan line between the H-bits of the towboat (at the center of the bow) to deck a fitting on the tow and take up (tighten) the line.
- C – Then the "face" wires from the towboat are placed on the tow (both to port and starboard) and tightened by the deck winches.
- D – The towboat with tow may turn loose at this time if the tow is small, or if the tow is large, wing wires may be added prior to getting underway.
- E – When underway the centerline capstan may be removed and replaced with jockey wires(rock & roll or knee wires) that lead from the H-bits to the barge the towboat is faced up to.

FLANKING MANEUVER

The art and the principle of flanking when proceeding downstream is simiar whether it is with 35 or 40 barges on the Lower Mississippi, or with only one or a few barges in a narrow, shallow, close and twisting turn of a small but navigable stream

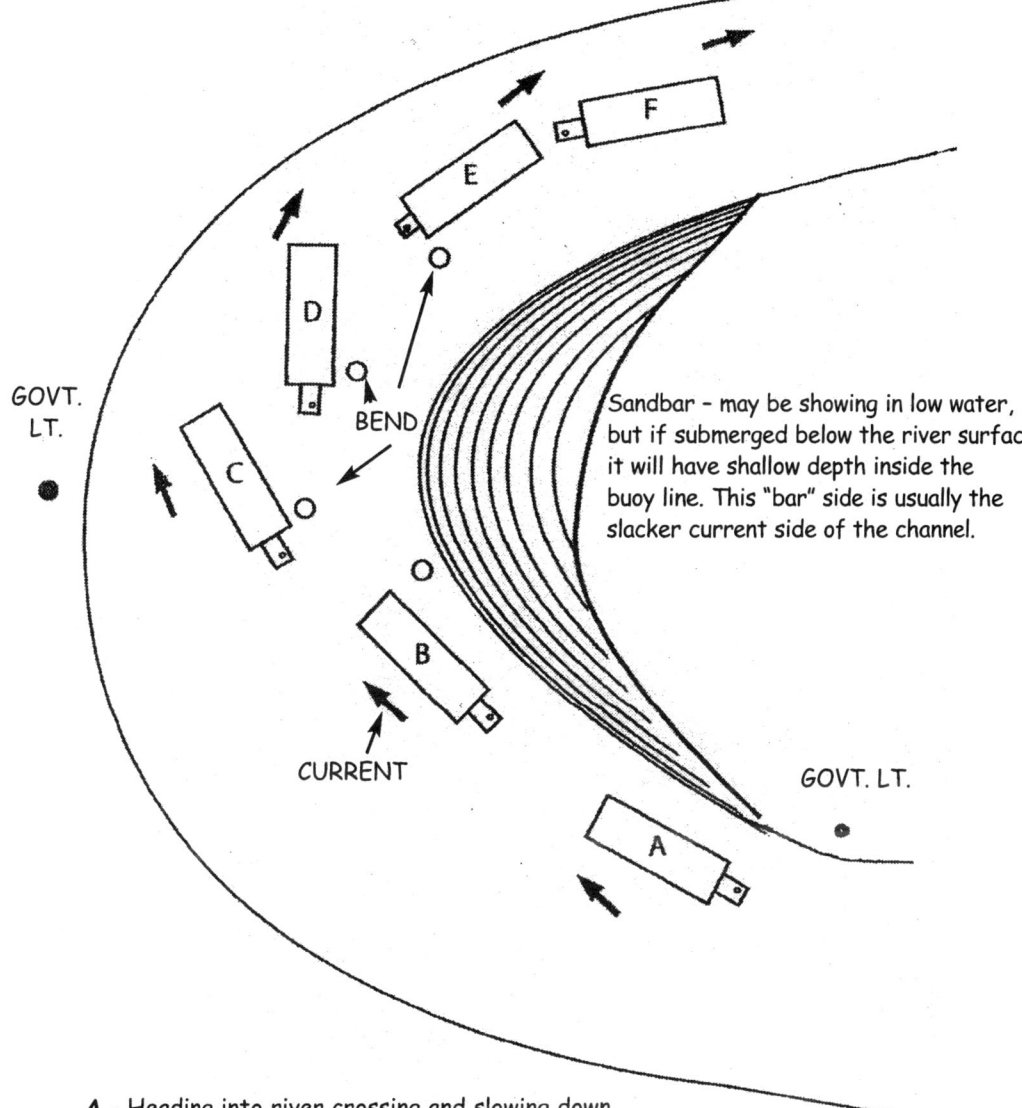

Sandbar - may be showing in low water, but if submerged below the river surface it will have shallow depth inside the buoy line. This "bar" side is usually the slacker current side of the channel.

A - Heading into river crossing and slowing down
B - Backing astern to take off headway
C - Backing full astern holding stern on buoy line, moving downstream with swifter current in bend steering head of tow while stern in slacker water on the bar side is controlled by towboat with flanking rudders
D - Still moving downstream, but at slower rate than the current in the bend
E - Current still setting tow away from the bank
F - All lateral slide out of tow, coming full ahead, with straight rudder, proceeding downstream

FITTINGS
that are commonly used on Western Rivers vessels and docks to guide or secure lines, wires or gear.

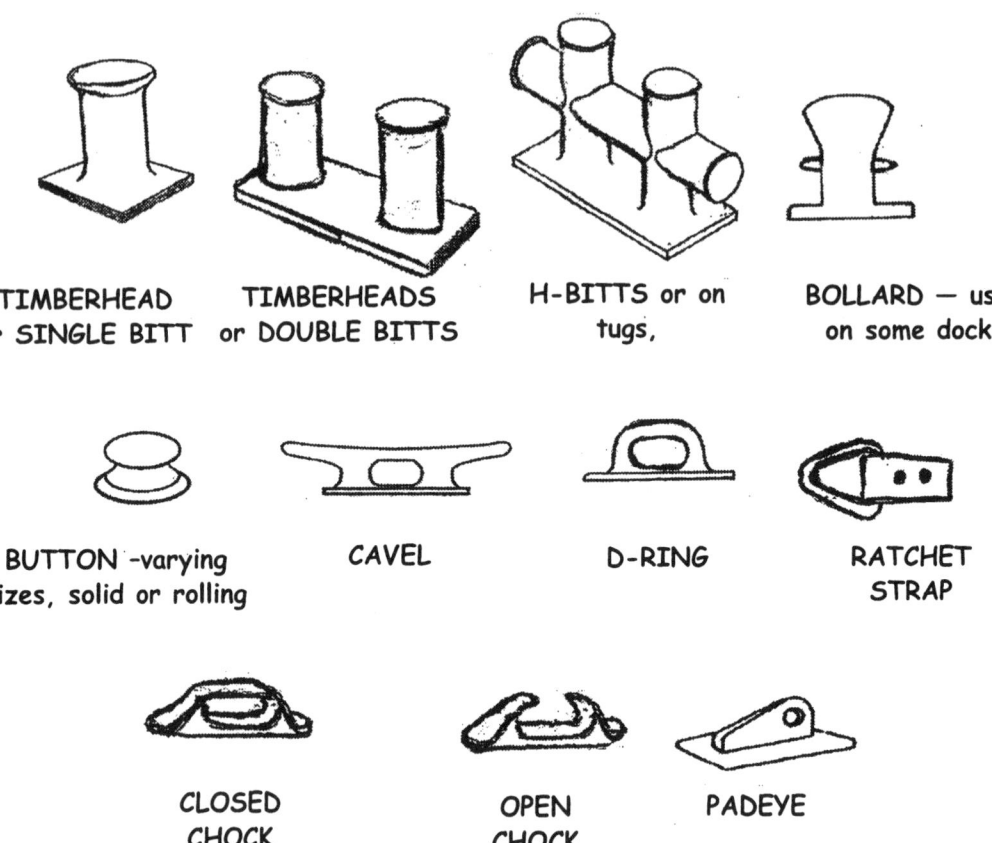

TIMBERHEAD or SINGLE BITT

TIMBERHEADS or DOUBLE BITTS

H-BITTS or on tugs,

BOLLARD — used on some docks

BUTTON — varying sizes, solid or rolling

CAVEL

D-RING

RATCHET STRAP

CLOSED CHOCK

OPEN CHOCK

PADEYE

FIRE FIGHTING

Placed at various locations on towboats and tugs for use in case of emergency

HAND HELD FIRE EXTINGUISHER

FIRE BUCKETS
Shown at Howard S/B Museum

G

GAFF
On the river the term is sometimes used to refer to the small spar on and abaft the mainmast where the U.S. Ensign is flown.

GALE
A very stiff wind with a force of approximately 32 to 60 mph. See: WEATHER WARNINGS.

GALLEY
The place on board a tug or towboat where food is prepared and served. Those that live on shore call it a kitchen. The word comes from Greek. There are differing theories as to its origin; one speculation was that it is a misuse of the word "gallery", which was a stone platform on ancient vessels where the cooking of meals was done. Another is that (also in ancient times), a vessel, called a *galley* which, besides the force of the wind filling its sails; it was additionally propelled by slaves pulling on oars. Since the cooks (also slaves) working on the *galley*, survived in their existing type of job after the abolition of slavery, their workplace became stuck with the name *galley* from the type of ship. In steamboat days, and probably up to WW II, most river crewmen still called it a kitchen or cookhouse, but with the influx of servicemen migrating to the river it became the *galley* on most boats running today.

GALLEY GOSSIP
Often the crews of towboats and tugs gather in the *galley*. Their talk often leads to what is going to occur on the vessel, or with the company operations. With much of the talk being strictly rumors; the term has become another word for SCUTTLEBUTT.

GALLON
1. A measurement of liquid volume equal to 3.79 liters. Used on the river when referring to the amount of POTABLE WATER the drinking tanks hold, or those that hold diesel fuel and how much they would currently have on board, as well as the amount to order at the next fueling location. The term derives from the Latin galleta, to mean "a pail or bucket".
2. The measurement of liquid cargo on board barges in tow is usually referred to in the amount of barrel capacity of each barge. A barrel contains 42 gallons of product.

GALVANIC ACTION
See: ELECTROLYSIS. The term *galvanic* comes from the French, who used it crediting an Italian scientist, Luigi Galvani.

GAMBLERS & GAMBLING BOATS
In years past *gamblers* would ride some packet boats, but on others were banned by the owners or the Master. There were boats that operated excursions for more than sightseeing where *gambling* and games of chance were undertaken. There were jurisdictional disputes as to who was to exercise policing authority when the vessels were midstream, so it was difficult for the different States to stop the practice.
Presently there are CASINO BOATS in States where it is legal to gamble. When first licensed by the States where they dock, *gambling* was only allowed when the boat was underway, but since that caused the operators of owning firms some problems, most of this type of vessel are allowed to conduct *gambling* while moored.

GANGPLANK
A portable temporary ramp used to provide a walkway for persons to embark upon or disembark from a tug or towboat, from or to a dock or other place. It often has cleats or strips

nailed at intervals across it in order to help prevent persons using it from slipping. Sometimes, if the ramp is of a more elaborate form, it is named a GANGWAY. However, an opening in side of a ship or its bulwarks used to load cargo or people is more properly called a gangway. This also provides an opening for the accommodation ladder which can be lowered from a ship's side to a dock or to where launches can be accommodated for persons coming to and going from the ship. A more proper term for a boarding ramp is STAGE. The word *gang* comes from the Norse, meaning "a going" or "passage"; and *plank* derives from the Latin *planca,* meaning "board". It is also referred to as a gangboard.

GANGWAY
See: ACCOMODATION LADDER.

GANTRY CRANE
A large crane that travels on tracks; however, there are now some in service that roll on tires. Extensively used at shipyards to hoist steel, propellers, other material, etc., from one place to another. It is also used on wharfs to transfer cargo to and from vessels.

GAS FREE
A procedure undertaken to clean a tank or cargo compartment that previously contained products capable of giving off flammable vapors. After cleaning, the vessel, or compartment, is inspected by a licensed gas chemist who will test the compartment and issue a *gas-free* certificate citing the conditions of work, i.e., safe for men and/or safe for fire, in case welding has to be performed.

GASKET
1. A fiber material used to seal the space or joint between two flanged fittings.
2. Material used to make a watertight fitting to a hatch or door.

GATE RECESS
That area in a lock wall where the GUDGEONS that hold the PINTELS of the GATES for the lock are located, and where the gate rests when it is open and flush with the horizontal length of the lock wall.

GATE VALVE
A valve with a disk for its closure device, called a *gate,* that is raised to open and lowered to close by either a handle at the top of the valve or by the handle turning a reach rod if the valve is in a tank. The valve is extensively used in the operation of tank vessel pipelines as this type allows for the full cross-sectional pipeline diameter flow of product when fully opened.

GATED NAVIGABLE SPILLWAY DAM
A dam that has WICKETS that can be lowered to the bed of the river to allow vessels to go over the dam when the water is high enough to allow safe navigation. The dam may also have other types of GATES in it to control the flow when the wickets are in the raised position.

GATED NON-NAVIGABLE SPILLWAY DAM
A dam that has fixed control gates to regulate the flow of water through the dam, but that does not generally allow for navigation at the dam location except where a lock is located. A few dams have fixed concrete weirs that can allow vessels to pass over them in extremely high water. Also see the types of gates to control flow in GATES.

GATES
1. *Lock* – The upstream and downstream closures that control the ability of a lock to lift or lower a vessel or tow. See: LOCK GATES.
2. *Graving Dock* – This type of structure, when its *gates* are closed,

allows the dock to be pumped out, permitting a shipyard to, in effect, drydock a vessel by holding back the water outside the dock area. See: GRAVING DOCK.

3. Dam – The movable structures that control the amount of water that is allowed to flow through a dam. These *gates* are either overhead or submersible. A Lockmaster will inform a Pilot as to how many feet "are running", meaning the height the *gates* are open. Various types of dam *gates* have been employed at different structures over the years such as BEAR TRAP, ROLLER, TAINTER, and WICKET, as well as Drum, Hinged Crest, and Vertical Lift.

4. The surname of William Henry *Gates* (b. 1955), who sold "Windows" to the world, a type of communications *gate* now used on towboats.

GATHER WAY

When a vessel begins movement to gain headway or sternway through the water.

GATHERING RANGE or AREA

The distance from a river port that cargo will have a cost advantage to be loaded in a barge and moved to its destination by water rather than by some other mode of transportation, particularly by rail. The term usually refers to grain movements, but pertains to all freight. The distance from the river varies with the cargo and with the area, as well as availability of competing modes.

GAUGE or GAGE

A device that can indicate, record, or is used as a reference. It can measure distance, pressure, vacuum, height, length, atmosphere, size, position, capacity, temperature, thickness, weather, altitude, diameter, depth or draft, increases or decreases, and probably anything the senses are able to perceive. A *gauge or gage* can change by the second or be considered a master record for long time evaluation and used as a reference. Certain instruments used on vessels that are described include STEAM GAUGES, FLOAT GAUGE, PRESSURE GAUGE, and P/V VALVE. Also see: BAR BOOK, GAUGE WATER and HIGH WATER MARKS. The term apparently derives from the French *jauge*, with a lot of speculation as to its further origin.

Originally the word was used in the maritime trades as a measure of the wind when observing another sailing vessel. If meeting and another vessel to windward the vessel was said to be on a "weather *gage*", but if it was to leeward it was said to be on a "lee *gage*".

Most often it is used on the river in reference to measuring the draft of a vessel. After being constructed, barges are issued a set of DISPLACEMENT TONNAGE TABLE or SCALE papers. When a barge is empty the draft is *gauged*, and then again when it is loaded. From the two measurements a surveyor can determine from the draft tables how much cargo was loaded into the barge.

It is a reading taken at a Lock and at certain points along the rivers, particularly major port areas, indicating the rise and fall of the river level. These river *gauges* were set in a bygone year, long ago establishing a zero *gauge* number as the mean low-water level known to those living in the area or port. All subsequent readings are relative to the initial zero *gauge*, either plus or minus. For instance, in the year 2000 a zero *gauge* at St. Louis might mean low, but navigable water for a vessel with a nine foot draft. In the 1800s however, it might have meant there was only enough water for those steamboats with a very shallow draft. Over time, the channels cut and deepen their beds, and there may be conditions when a minus six reading on the *gauge* at St. Louis can provide a narrow, but navigable, channel. The

FLOOD STAGE *gauge* at St. Louis is 30 feet. All dams on the river have two *gauge* readings, that of the Upper Pool, and the Lower Pool. Although the USACE has many sites where *gauges* are maintained they do not make predictions of future rises or falls of river levels. All predictions are made by NOAA's National Weather Service who has not only the Corps-supplied information, but also data of rainfall, snow melt, run-off, etc. to add to the equation of predictability. See: STAGE.

At times on towboats and tugs the term is used to evaluate the disposition, feelings, or the comments of a fellow crew member, i.e. "I can't *gauge* how the old man is feeling today. He didn't make me swab the deck as he usually does". To which a fellow deckhand might reply, "Yeah, I can't FATHOM him either."

GAUGE COCK

Small valves that indicate if there is a safe amount of water in a boiler. These are usually three in number. When the upper one emits steam and the lower one gives off water, with the middle one spurting water and steam, the system is operating properly. These *gauge cocks* are sometimes called "try cocks", i.e. to "try and see" if there is enough water to keep the boiler from exploding.

GAUGE WATER

A term that was/is used in reference to one of the many gauge boards that were posted at various places along the Lower Mississippi and other rivers. A Pilot would base his HIGH WATER MARKS in a BAR BOOK to note when there was sufficient water to run in certain places, behind islands, through certain CHUTES, and in POINTWAYS across or behind mid-bars.

Some *gauge* readings would relate to the same depth of water in some areas. For instance, if a *gauge* read 15 feet, it might also mean there was about 15 feet of water depth in a chute or pointway, but the regular channel might have 30 feet of water. Or at other gauges one Pilot might note, "At l2 feet on the XYZ gauge the water is just covering the bar behind DEF Island. Not safe to run unless it is a rising river showing 25 or more on the gauge".

Since the placement of rock dikes on the Lower Mississippi River with many of them closing off channel chutes, as well as increases in the size of tows, there is much less ability to utilize back or off channels to take advantage of slacker water, especially if the marks posited by a Pilot weren't quite accurate and a mishap occurs, the USCG is likely to take dim view of the action. High water running presently is now basically navigating wide in the bend on the bar side, crowding it as much as the Pilot's Bar Book believes he is able to chance.

GEAR

Refers collectively to all the equipment used to work a vessel in its trade, i.e. lines, wires, shackles, ratchets, ladders, life vests, rain suits, etc. See: REDUCTION GEAR for a *gear* used in conjunction with the engine.

GEAR BOX

The housing that encompasses the REDUCTION GEAR that governs the speed of the engine and its eventual transmission to the speed of the drive shaft to the propeller.

GENERAL

The person in overall command of the U.S. Army (four stars). The General in charge of the USACE is usually a Lieutenant General (three stars) or a Major General (two stars). Those Generals who are in command of the different Divisions will usually be Major Generals, and those who are in command of the Districts are usually Brigadier Generals (one star).

GENERAL ALARM

An alarm system on board towboats and tugs that loudly rings throughout the vessel whenever there is an imminent danger to the vessel, its tow, or persons on board. When rung by the person on watch, every crew member on board is to go on deck at any assigned station and await further orders.

GENERAL ARRANGEMENT DRAWING

A blueprint or plan showing the general layout of a vessel, the arrangement and size of its spaces, the engine room design, its watertight compartmentation, fuel and water tanks, and other features.

GENERAL AVERAGE

An insurance term that is applied when a vessel encounters a peril and must sacrifice a portion of the cargo in order to save the vessel or limit its damage. The owners of the saved cargo value is averaged into the total value with the "saved cargo owners" being apportioned" and sharing with the owner whose cargo is lost.

GENERAL PRECAUTIONARY RULE

See: GOOD SEAMANSHIP RULE.

GENERAL PRUDENTIAL RULE

This gospel was in the old Western Rivers Rule 25 and the Inland Rule 27 that is now incorporated in the current Inland Rule entitled "Responsibility" in part 2(b), which states: "In construing and complying with these Rules due regard shall be had to all dangers of navigation and collision and to any special circumstances, including the limitations of the vessels involved, which may make a departure from these Rules necessary to avoid immediate danger." It is sometimes also called the "Rule of Special Circumstances".

GENERAL SURVEY ACT

An Act of Congress passed in 1824 to allow for surveys to be made of routes for roads and canals of national importance, in a commercial or military point of view, or is necessary to improve a route for the transportation of public mail. Rivers were not specifically included, but later that year Congress appropriated $75,000 to improve navigation on the Ohio and Mississippi rivers by removing sandbars, snags, and other obstacles. The initial thrust of a national system became a political log-rolling exercise and the Act was repealed six years later.

GENERATOR

A machine that converts mechanical energy into electrical energy, either direct or alternating current. On a tug or towboat it provides all the electric power for lights, radio and radar, air conditioning, searchlights, and other equipment requiring electrical power on board the vessel.

GENSET

A slang term used in referring to the generator on a towboat or tug.

GEOGRAPHIC INFORMATION SYSTEM (GIS)

A *system* of storing *geographical information* on a computer to evaluate the data in order to develop various predictive possibilities of what may or could occur. It is an important development in implementing electronic charting and navigation.

GETTING IN SHAPE

See: IN SHAPE.

GETTING THE LONG LINE

Tying up a vessel for an extended period and laying off the crew.

GHOST

A manifestation that occurs on the

screen of the radar that is not actually there in the water; a false echo that has reflected off a flock of ducks, a high wire crossing, or some other anomaly.

GIB

A notched piece of wood that fits over an end of one of the blocks in the WOOD CIRCLE of a paddlewheel. It is utilized to protect the grain end of a block piece to keep it from deterioration and absorption of water. The *gib* is held in place between it and the paddlewheel ARM by a WEDGE KEY which is driven in to tighten and hold the blocks firmly in place in the "circle".

GIBBONS v. OGDEN

An important case in river history that went before the Supreme Court in 1816. The Court sanctioned federal control over interstate commerce and they stated that its ruling was based in the Commerce Clause of the Constitution. A group, headed by Robert Fulton (designer of the first successful steamboat on the Hudson River) and his partner and financial backer (Robert Livingston) had obtained exclusive rights from the State of New York to operate steamboats. They also held a franchise from Louisiana. Although the so-called Fulton monopoly of the steamboat design was already in a morbid state from other competing interests, they believed their licenses gave them exclusivity to operate steamboats on waterways. The Supreme Court decision tolled the "exclusivity's" death. It was upon this decision that Congress based the GENERAL SURVEY ACT.

GILDED or GOLDEN ANTLERS

A racing tradition of steamboats in the same trade was to attempt to better the trip time of a rival boat between two main river cities. If accomplished it would be symbolized by the display of a set of deer horns or ANTLERS that had been gilded with gold paint. They were only to be displayed, in some prominent place, until some other steamer beat the former holder's time. Then the cry would be, "She takes the horns". The antlers replaced the use of displaying a BROOM indicating a "clean sweep".

GIMBALS

A set of rings that pivot at right angles to one another to hold a compass or other equipment in a horizontal position, even if a vessel is rolling or pitching. They are often used to house a compass aboard a tug, but seldom seen on river equipment.

GIN POLE

A temporary boom or spar fitted with a block and tackle to lift gear.

GINGERBREAD

The use of ornate wooden scrollwork to decorate (internally and externally) the packetboats of the mid-1800's. To many it made them look fancy. To others it was considered gaudy. The term probably originated from the decorative icing that trims baked *gingerbread* houses at Christmas.

GIRDER

A single large beam, either wooden or steel, or a compound structure of two or more parts, that provides longitudinal strength and stiffness to a hull supporting the engine bed. Lesser *girders* are used to support decks that are in turn supported by vertical pillars or stanchions.

GIRDING

An action that can occur while towing astern. If a vessel being towed astern comes abreast of the towing vessel at approximately at a 90-degree angle, with the towline perpendicular to both vessels, it can cause a transverse force against the towing vessel by the pulling effect of the vessel being towed. This may cause the towing vessel to heel over, either flooding and/or capsizing it, unless the towing line is slacked or cut. Sometimes referred to as "tripping".

GIVE
As used on the rivers in a nautical sense:
1. The stretch of a new line, especially a synthetic one and, more specifically, one of nylon.
2. To keep clear of another vessel, or GIVE WAY.
3. To apply more rudder angle, i.e., "*Give* her more port rudder".
4. To increase power, i.e., "*Give* her a kick ahead".

GIVE-WAY VESSEL
A vessel that is required by Navigation Rule 16, "...to keep out of the way of another vessel (and) shall, so far as possible, take early and substantial action to keep well clear". In the old Rules of the Road it was termed the BURDENED VESSEL. See: STAND-ON VESSEL.

GIWW
See: GULF INTRACOASTAL WATERWAY.

GLASS COVERS
See: COVERS, FIBERGLASS.

GLASSES
A slang term used when referring to binoculars, i.e., "Let me take a look-see with the *glasses*".

GLOBAL POSITIONING SYSTEM (GPS)
A satellite-based navigation system that can give the positioning coordinates of a vessel within less than five meters of the actual position. With the use of electronic charts and requirements for AUTOMATIC INFORMATION SYSTEMS it becomes the radar of the future on the river. See: dGPS.

GLUT
Refers to a stout wooden peg used as a blunt wedge to keep a cylinder timber from sliding on a deck due to the action of a PITMAN arm. Its dimensions, as well as the amount of *gluts* used depended upon the size and force exerted by the pitman. An interesting word as used in steamboating. The word apparently comes from the Latin *gluttire,* meaning "to swallow". How it became used to define a wooden square wedge piece is unknown. In Admiral Smyth's 1867 book it is "a piece of wood applied as a fulcrum to a lever power", and then goes on to describe an eyelet in a piece of canvas for a line used to prevent slippage. Perhaps the term *glut* was appropriate to steamboaters as it was used to prevent framing timbers from moving by the pitman lever power.

GO
As used on the rivers in a nautical sense:
1. *Aboard* – to enter or go on board a vessel.
2. *About* – to turn around.
3. *Adrift* – to break loose, or away.
4. *Aground* – (see)
5. *Alongside* – to go up to the side or abreast another vessel, dock, or pier.
6. *Astern* – to shift the engine to the astern position and back up.
7. *Below* – to proceed to a deck(s) down from where one is currently.
8. *By the Board* – gear or material that is washed or carried over the side.
9. *By the Head* (or Stern) – loading or sinking faster at one end of a vessel.
10. *Down* – to sink or be swamped.
11. *Well Over* – navigating advice noted on a channel report to mean

190 GOLD-BRAID

when making a crossing, to go close to the shore before going down the shape of the bend.

12. Crazy – when one's relief doesn't show up after 100 days on the vessel.

GOLD-BRAID

In the days of steam packets, many of the Captains and Pilots wore uniforms. In modern times, especially after WW II, more informal wear became the norm. Those that continued to wear uniforms were somewhat disparaged, and their vessels became known as *gold-braid boats*. Few towboat or tug officers wear uniforms now, except for those on passenger-carrying vessels.

GONG BUOY

A set of gongs mounted in a tower framework that emits a series of ringing *gongs*. Not seen on the Western Rivers but not uncommon in coastal areas that may have severe fog conditions.

GOOD SEAMANSHIP RULE

This is the old Western Rivers Rule 26 and Inland Rules 29 that are now incorporated in the current Inland Rule entitled "Responsibility" in part 2(a), "Nothing in these rules shall exonerate any vessel, or the owner, master or crew thereof, from the consequences of any neglect to comply with these Rules or of the neglect of any precaution which may be required by the ordinary practice of seamen, or by the special circumstances of the case". It is also sometimes called the *General Precautionary Rule*.

GOOSENECK VENT

A 180-degree elbow-shaped pipe vent with a screen over the end, commonly used to vent void spaces, water tanks, and diesel fuel tanks.

GORGE

See: ICE.

GOUGER

When flatboating and drifting downstream with the current the crewmen manned long SWEEPS to assist in steering and keeping the boat in the current and off the rocks and sandbars. The sweeps were manned on the stern and both the port and starboard sides as well as on the bow. The person controlling the bow sweep was called a *gouger*. The word "gouge" comes from the Welsh to mean a pointed piece. Perhaps the *gouger* being on the head, or point, of a flatboat, he was given the name because if he dipped his sweep too deep in the water it might stick in the bottom of a shallow reach *gouging* it and either breaking the sweep or throwing the man in the river.

GOVERNER

A device that limits the maximum speed of an engine.

GOVERNMENT LIGHT

The name given to the navigational lights, lanterns, or beacons along riverbanks, originally maintained by the Lighthouse Board. This later became the Bureau of Lighthouses in the Commerce Department, until the Bureau was transferred to the U.S. Coast Guard in July 1939. After the river Pilots of that generation retired they simply have become *lighted aids to navigation*.

There were no navigational shore lights, nor river navigational lights, in the golden age of the packet steamers of the 1800s. Sam Clemens in writing about it said, "…vast streams like the Mississippi and the Missouri, whose alluvial banks cave and change constantly, whose snags are always hunting up new quarters, whose sand bars are never at rest, whose channels are forever dodging and shirking, and whose obstructions must be confronted in all nights and all weathers without the aid of a single lighthouse or a single buoy, for there is neither light nor buoy to be found anywhere in all these thousands of miles of villainous river".

In 1874, Congress extended the jurisdiction of the Lighthouse Board over the Mississippi, Missouri, and Ohio rivers. The first lights to be maintained by the U.S. Government were lights at Jefferson Barracks, just below the city of St. Louis, in December 1874. Later that month the first light on the Ohio River was established at the foot of the Grand Chain, about 16 miles above Cairo, Illinois.

When Clemens wrote the book *Life on the Mississippi* in 1883 and had gone back to ride on the river again, he wrote: ".....the national government has turned the Mississippi into a sort of two-thousand-mile torchlight procession. In the head of every crossing, and in the foot of every crossing, the government has set up a clear-burning lamp. You are never entirely in the dark, now; there is always a beacon in sight, either before you, or behind you, or abreast". See: BEACON, LIGHT LIST, LIGHTHOUSE BOARD & SERVICE, LIGHTHOUSE TENDER, and LIGHTKEEPERS.

GPM

An abbreviation for gallons per minute.

GPS

See: GLOBAL POSITIONING SYSTEM.

GRAB BAR or RODS

Bent rods in an elongated U-shape that are welded on a coaming above a manhole or other opening to assist a person going into or coming out of a void space on a barge. Also used in some voids as a ladder.

GRAB BUCKET

See: CLAM SHELL BUCKET.

GRADUAL

To navigate in a moderate fashion, i.e. to *gradually* pull down in a crossing from one side of a river to the other shoreline, or to *gradually* come ahead on the engine while leaving a lock, or to *gradually* apply more rudder when making a bend, etc.

GRANDFATHER

An action taken in new regulatory initiatives when requirements are changed which allow certain persons who have obtained licenses in the past to not have to be retested for the new obligations; or, if useful equipment is in good repair, permission is given to continue to use it for a period of time, even though it may be forbidden to be installed on new construction; or other similar type circumstances where a *grandfather* clause is prudent.

GRANNY KNOT

The *knot* a green, or new, deckhand ties instead of a SQUARE KNOT. The square knot is two overhand knots. They are tied first right over left followed by one that is left over right. The granny has both overhand knots tied right over left.

GRAPNEL or GRAPPLING HOOK and GRAPPLING IRON

A device with three or more hooks that is attached to a small line. It is used to drag the river bottom to recover a line or wire, especially a mooring wire attached to a DEADMAN on the shore. The *iron* was a stiff pole with a *grappling hook* on the end that is used when attaching to the end of a NEEDLE at a movable dam when raising it. A *grapnel* was used originally in medieval times by the crews of vessels in combat. When one vessel would go alongside another, the *grapnel* would be thrown over to the rigging or gunnels and made fast in order to board the enemy vessel. The term is of German origin *grapa,* meaning "hook".

GRASS LINE
A line made from natural fiber such as manila, sisal, or other fibers. Even though most of the lines used on towboats and tugs at present are of synthetic fiber they are usually referred to as *grass*, however, sometimes the multi-colored polypropylene lines are called *plastic lines*.

GRASSHOPPER BRIDGE
A bascule-type bridge that hinges from one side of the bridge only.

GRASSHOPPERING
The method employed when going aground in a shallow channel and lifting the vessel across it in a series of sparring actions. It was used a extensively on the Missouri River in the old steamboat days. The process required two heavy spars set off the forward sides of the steamer into the river bottom, tilted somewhat forward. To each spar was attached to tackle with the other end fastened to the gunwale of the vessel, with the running line going to the capstan on each side. When the capstan was tightened the Pilot would signal the engine room to come full ahead. With the lifting action of the spars and the thrust of the paddlewheel the steamer would move further through the bar. On occasion the process had to be done numerous times. The wheelwash would also start moving the alluvial soil of the bar, and eventually the vessel would again head upriver, at least to the next shallow crossing. See: SANGAMON RIVER for the patent of an invention that Abe Lincoln took out to assist vessels over shoal waters.

GRATE
A metal frame of iron bars at the base of a steamboat furnace where the fire received its draft, and the wood or coal would burn with its ashes falling between the bars. The word comes from a Latin base *cratis*, meaning "hurdle".

GRATING
A skeletal lattice, steel-deck framework often used in the engine room as a support platform to walk on that allows air to circulate as well as providing visibility to observe working parts and the bilges. They are usually in a framework and are removable, being lighter and stronger than steel plating for the same area covered.

GRAVEYARD WATCH
A term sometimes given to the traditional nighttime after watch, that is from midnight to 6 a.m. which is the time it is hardest to stay alert.

GRAVING DOCK
A type of drydock in a water basin. The entrance to the dock is at water level. After a vessel is floated in, the gate(s) to the entrance are closed, the water in the dock is pumped out and the vessel remains "in the dry" for its work to be accomplished. When completed the dock is allowed to flood by gravity, the vessel becomes afloat, the entrance gate(s) are opened and the vessel is removed. The term comes from the French *greve,* meaning "shore". Vessels in olden days were run up on a gravel or coarse sand beach at high tide to clean their bottoms of barnacles and sea growth. The cleaning process took on the name, "to grave", or to clean a ship's hull.

The only *graving docks* on the river were operated by the USACE at Louisville, Kentucky, at old Lock 41, on the Ohio River, and one at Keokuk, Iowa, at old Lock 19, on the Upper Mississippi River. There are, however, these types of docks on the Gulf Coast.

GRAVY TRAIN PILOTING
Having a short run between two points on the river, piloting on a well-kept and supplied towboat, working for a good company, and operating in an area where most of the crew lives.

GRAY WATER
Relatively clean water that is dis-

charged from washing, showering, washbasins, and galley sinks, as opposed to human waste material that must go into a holding tank for discharge to a disposal system.

GREAT LAKES

The Inland Navigation Rules define the term as, "the Great Lakes and their connecting and tributary waters including the Calumet River as far as the Thomas J. O'Brien Lock and Controlling Works (between mile 321 and 322), and the Saint Lawrence River as far east as the lower exit of Saint Lambert Lock". This, of course, includes lakes Michigan, Superior, Huron, Erie, and Ontario. Western River towboats and their barges have limited involvement with traffic on the *Great Lakes,* except for short runs on the lower part of Lake Michigan in fair weather only.

GREAT RAFT, THE

See: RED RIVER RAFT

GREEN RIVER

The *Green River* rises in the foothills of the southern Kentucky mountains and flows northward across the state for over 300 miles until it reaches the Ohio River at mile 784. Settlers in the region moved their crops on the river to market in flatboats and keelboats. When steamboat fever came in the early 1800s, promoters wanted them to be able to navigate up to the area of the city of Bowling Green. Beginning in 1833 five timber and masonry locks (140' by 36') were built by the State and completed in 1842, bringing steamboats to the region. The structures were not well engineered and had high maintenance costs, often exceeding the tolls charged.

The Civil War also led to deterioration of the system, and since the State didn't have money, the locks were then leased to a private company. Most of the early traffic included farm products, animals and passengers; saw logs were floated out. Later some coal started moving down the river. Certain interests saw the privatization of the locks as rampant with favoritism toward the lease owners. After a few big political battles, and further deterioration of the locks with one falling in the river, the private company sold their lease rights to the Federal Government in 1888. The USACE began repairing the locks in 1890 and built two new ones in 1901 to allow navigation to Mammoth Cave. These two stayed open until 1950 when a National Park was established, after which they were shut down. Later, in 1965, Dam #4 failed; its lock had previously allowed traffic to reach Bowling Green.

In the 1930s with the use of asphalt rock and coal from the region in abundance, Congress authorized two new locks, which were completed in 1934, that were 56' by 360'; however, these were not of sufficient size to compete with coal being transported from other regions. When the use of coal rejuvenated the prospects of *Green River* navigation, interest revived and the citizens in the basin convinced Congress in 1954 to authorize two modern 84' by 600' locks on the lower end of the Green to provide improved navigation to mile 103. They were opened in 1956.

GREENHORN

A new inexperienced crewman aboard a riverboat for the first time. Considered a LANDLUBBER until one "learns the ropes". Somewhat naive or gullible and might be prone to being the butt of ridicule for lack of river knowledge. Where the term comes from is unknown. "Green" has been described as the condition of a person that becomes seasick (due to the rolling of a vessel at sea) and whose complexion turns extremely pale, and is useless when work needs to be accmplished. The "horn" part may be from the hard bone-like outgrowth of a ram or bull which has to be subdued to be controlled. Sometimes *greenhorns* stay long enough to make good hands; others soon leave to pursue other types of endeavors and become "landlubbers" again.

GRID COOLER
See: SKIN COOLER

GRIPE
1. On wooden-hulled steamboats it was a curved knee timber used to strengthen and tie together the stem and the keel where they met.
2. What deckhands do when the Master tells them to soogee, or what the Pilot does when the office dispatcher changes orders on the tow for the third (seems like the tenth) time after the tow was finally made up and you were just going to depart the fleet.

GROIN
Another word for DIKE. The term is more often used when a DIKE or JETTY is extended from the seashore to protect it from wave erosion and to capture sand for the beach, or to control the flow of water to scour a channel.

GROMMET
A small metal eye fastened into tarpaulins, or canvas awnings, or other pieces of material to be able to put a section of line through to make it secure to a framework.

GROSS TONNAGE
The *gross tonnage,* or *gross registered tonnage,* is not a measurement of weight, but rather a measurement of a vessel's enclosed cubic foot capacity divided by 100 to determine the tons. *Gross tonnage* is the overall cubic capacity of a vessel as determined by an admeasurements formula before deducting for certain exemptions. See: NET TONNAGE, TON and TONNAGE.

GROUND
As used by those on the rivers in a nautical sense:
1. The bed of the river.
2. To touch or hit bottom, or to go AGROUND.
3. *Tackle* – the gear used in dropping and raising an anchor. Not used on towboats.
4. *Ways* – the timbers used at a shipyard for launching a vessel.
5. *Swell* – a return swell or wave of water that moves off a vessel toward the shore, caused by the displacement suction action of a vessel or tow as it moves through the channel in a shoal area.
6. *Fog* – a condition where the fog does not rise off the water much higher than the height of the barges in tow.

GROUP FLASHING LIGHT
A light that shows two or more flashes in succession at regular intervals.

GUARD
As used on the rivers in a nautical sense:
1. The port and starboard fore and aft main deck on the outside of the cabin structure of a towboat.
2. On a steamboat, the overhang on the hull of the main deck. This allowed for a greater carrying capacity of cargo, especially cotton bales.
3. A shield over moving machinery, such as a propeller shaft, etc.
4. *Chains* or *wires* – safety protection around the main deck of a towboat to protect a person from falling overboard.
5. *Rails* – safety railing around the upper decks of a towboat. These *guard rails* are usually prefixed by the deck they surround, i.e., on the second deck they would be second deck *rails*, or on top of the pilothouse they would be roof *railing*, etc. On the main deck of a steamboat the *guard rails* were called BULL RAILS.

6. *Lights* – Illumination on the main deck of a towboat.

GUARD WALL

An extension of the riverward lock wall on the upstream end of the lock chamber to create a larger forebay area of slacker water to keep a tow from being drawn toward the dam by a cross current at the upper end of the lock wall. These are usually located only at dam sites that have two lock chambers. See: PORTED GUARD WALL.

GUDGEON

1. A metallic eye fastened to the sternpost on which the pintles (pivot pins) of the rudder rest, providing support and allowing the rudder to swing.
2. The same terms apply to the hinged gates of a lock chamber.
3. The term is from the French *gougen,* to mean a type of "pivoting". In olden days this type of holding and pivoting was called *googings*, but apparently the word has faded from use and dictionaries.

GUIDE WALL

The upstream and downstream extension of the landward lock wall from the lock chamber that towboats with tows use to line up and land on as they navigate into a lock chamber. Also used in DOUBLE LOCKING when the first cut of a tow is pulled out and tied off in order to turn the lock to receive the second cut.

GULF INTRACOASTAL WATERWAY (GIWW)

The *GIWW* stretches from near our Texas border with Mexico on the western terminus to Carrabelle, Florida, on the eastern end. Total distance is 1046 miles. Mileage starts at "O" in Harvey Lock on the west bank of the Mississippi River in New Orleans and is measured from that point going both east and west on the *GIWW*. The canal is heralded as the 1000 mile miracle. It has returned over twenty-five dollars to the economy for every dollar invested in it.

In the early 1800s a route along our eastern Gulf Coast was described by engineers, however, it was but a vision. Then in the early 1900s, proposals by Texas businessmen suggested that a canal on the western Gulf Coast should be built. In 1925 Congress authorized the building of the western section from New Orleans to Galveston, and two years later extended it to Corpus Christi, TX. The canal was to be 100 feet wide with a project depth of nine feet. Ten years later, in 1935, Congress passed legislation to fund the canal route on the eastern section between New Orleans and Apalachicola, FL.

In 1942, with German submarines sinking our ships off the Gulf Coast, Congress authorized extending the canal to Carrabelle on the east and almost to our border with Mexico at Brownsville, TX. They also authorized that the canal channel be widened to 125 feet, with a project depth of 12 feet. During WW II the shipment of petroleum along the canal was vital to our national war effort. The *GIWW* continues to be essential to the economy today.

GUN TACKLE

A tackle consisting of two single blocks. Double or triple force is gained, depending on which block is moving.

GUNWALE OR GUNNEL

On the river the term is used to refer to the walkway on the side of a hopper barge between the COAMING and the outer edge of the barge; or, on a typical open hopper with no coaming, it is the walkway deck on the barge hopper side. Also used on a tank barge if it is built with a tank coaming. The term comes from the old English with *wale* coming from the Norse word

196 GUSSET PLATE

vala, meaning "knuckle", therefore, it refers to timber that supports the *guns* (or cannons) of a navy vessel. The word is pronounced *gun – ell.*

GUSSET PLATE
A bracket or tie plate that is usually triangular, but sometimes square in shape, that is fitted and welded to connect frame members and distribute the strength forces between them.

GUST
A sudden short increase in the velocity of the wind. Sometimes it can cause havoc when maneuvering a tow of empty barges.

GUY
1. A wire, chain, or line that is used to support a smokestack or mast.
2. Used as a guide to swing a spar or boom. The term comes from old French *guie,* to mean a "guide".

GYPSY or GIPSY
A small horizontal winch usually attached to the main powered winch. Used for taking up a small line.

GYRO
Short for gyroscope, or for GYROCOMPASS.

GYROCOMPASS
An electrically driven instrument with a gyroscope that points to true north rather than magnetic north. Not a lot of towboats have them installed unless they have an operating automatic piloting device.

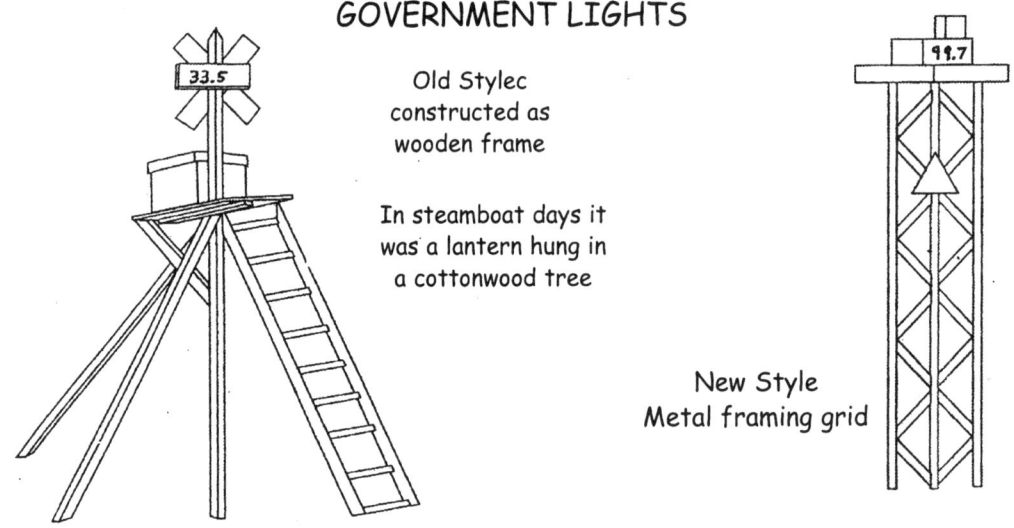

GOVERNMENT LIGHTS

Old Stylec constructed as wooden frame

In steamboat days it was a lantern hung in a cottonwood tree

New Style Metal framing grid

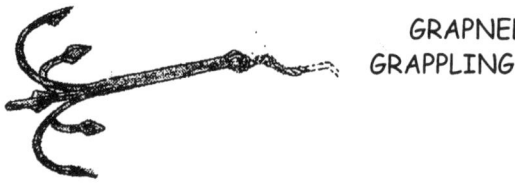

GRAPNEL or GRAPPLING HOOK

H

HAGESTEPS

A type of modification to the traditional TOWKNEE that was designed by Walter Hagestad of Canal Barge Company. Instead of steps in the angled end of the conventional towknee leading forward and up to a higher deck of an empty or light loaded barge, a separate angled set of steps are installed on the inside of each existing towknee perpendicular to the forward end of it. This arrangement allows for a crewman to easily get on or off a tow without jumping regardless of the difference between the elevations of the towboat and barge decks.

HAIL

During the era of the steam packets, landings were numerous along both shores of a navigable river. Prior to the forms of communication available today, a passenger needing transportation, or a shipper needing to move goods by water, would give a signal to a passing steamer that they wanted the boat to come to shore. The signal, called a *hail,* consisted of a simple wave during the day, often made more visible by adding a white handkerchief or rag. Nighttime *hails* were indicated by swinging a lighted lantern. A packet would use a LANDING WHISTLE distinctive of the line or company the vessel worked for to acknowledge a *hail* and signaling the landing that the vessel would stop.

Nowadays the *hail* for commerce has gone overboard and a *hail* is only used as a salute, a greeting, or attention-getter sounded on the vessel's whistle. Most Pilots still use the company signal of the old days, if their company had one. However, there are so many new firms that there isn't any standard company *hail,* so a sort of universal one now seems to be a prolonged blast followed by two short blasts. Since this is a signal to be used by Rule 35(d) of the Inland Rules in certain situations it probably should not be sounded as a *hail,* especially in the fog; but then who would be sounding a *hail* in the fog? The word comes from the English "healthy", as used in a salute or toast when downing a ha' pint of stout. Not allowed on towboats or tugs, so pilots will just have to "wet the whistle".

HAILING PORT

1. The port (city and state) where a vessel is officially documented, and from which it receives its certificate of DOCUMENTATION in accordance with Title 46 CFR.

2. The port designated by the owner of the vessel to be displayed on the stern of a vessel. Also see: HOME PORT.

HALF-COCKED

To undertake an action when a person doesn't know how to properly perform it, or doesn't take the necessary precautions and preparation to correctly undertake the task. The term comes from the use of a firearm which might be improperly cocked before pulling the trigger resulting in the gun firing prematurely. So it is with beginning any job *half-cocked* which will usually result in delay, possible failure, and a very mad Captain.

HALF HITCH

A single *half-hitch* knot, or *hitch*, is seldom used alone except sometimes when slacking CHECK LINE. However, it is one of the basic hitches from which many other knots are made. Basically, it is an underhanded loop around an object and back to the bight. Some crew persons adopt the use of a double *half hitch* knot too readily when securing a tie-off line. If it pulls down under severe stain it is almost impossible to untie without the help of a ROPE KNIFE or an axe.

HALF MAST

1. About half the distance in

height of an object being hoisted or lowered from the apex to the surface.

2. The height, or distance, on a staff a U.S. flag is flown when displayed as a symbol of mourning. The flag should first be raised to full staff and then lowered to *half mast*.

3. The ancient tale of the *half mast* custom is that at sea, when a sailor was killed in battle, the flag was lowered to allow space above it for the flag of the "Angel of Death".

HALF MILE RULE

The Navigation Rule 34(a) stating, "When power-driven vessels are in sight of one another and meeting or crossing at a distance within *half a mile* of each other, each vessel underway, when maneuvering as authorized or required by the Rules":..... (Type and number of required blasts are then given).

HALYARD

A small line run through a small pulley used to raise and lower a flag or other object, usually at the end of a staff. The term comes from "haul (to the) yard" with "haul" being a derivative of "hale" (from the Norse *hala,* meaning "to drag or draw"). *Yard* came from the Old English *gerd,* which was a "short stick or rod" and became a unit of measurement.

HAMPERED

The term refers to a vessel that is impeded in its ability to take normal and proper action in a navigational encounter. In accordance with the Navigation Rules it becomes a vessel RESTRICTED IN ITS ABILITY TO MANEUVER due to the nature of its work.

HAND

As used on the river in a nautical sense:

1. The side of a tug or towboat, i.e.. the starboard (port) *hand.*

2. To bear, lend, or give a *hand,* to someone needing help in the work required.

3. *Good* – A person who does a well performed job.

4. *Grab* – An elongated "U"-shaped rod welded in a hold with a narrow hatch for a person to hold onto when lowering into a compartment. Also used as a ladder into some voids or tanks.

5. *Lead* – Used in shallow water to measure water depth. See: LEADLINE.

6. *Rail* – Fitted along the guard to hold onto when necessary.

7. *Rope* – A line from a skiff used in tying it off.

8. *Signals* – The signals given by the deck mate on the tow indicating distances and direction to the Pilot, or indicating what he wants the Pilot to do, i.e., Come ahead, go astern, head to starboard (port), all stop, etc.

HAND LEAD

See: LEAD and LEADLINE.

HAND PUMP

On the river it is usually a small pump which is activated by a manual crank turned by hand. It is often used to remove or transfer fluids from barrels and occasionally from tanks of vessels.

HANDLE

1. To operate a vessel or tow by maneuvering it.

2. Refers to how a vessel is operating, i.e., "She sure is *handling* well", or "I don't like the way she *handles*; must have a bent rudder".

HANDSOMELY

Deliberately, with care. Although the term does not necessarily mean slowly, it can require one to take time to accomplish an action properly. The expression is not usually as advice given to do something *handsomely,* but rather as a reflection on how an act was carried out, i.e. "Man, you made that Vicksburg Bridge *handsomely*". It certainly doesn't have anything to do with the looks of the Pilot.

HANDY BILLY

A small portable pump, either manually operated or gasoline powered. Used for a variety of purposes aboard tugs and towboats, its main use is to dewater void spaces in barges. It is also called a JIGGER PUMP.

HANDY LINE

Cordage of small circumference used for multi-purposes aboard a vessel. See: HEAVING LINE.

HARBOR

On the river the term refers to an area, usually around a city within the confines of commercial activity involving maritime commerce, i.e., St. Louis *Harbor*, Louisville *Harbor*, New Orleans *Harbor*, Galveston *Harbor*, etc. A *harbor* may encompass many miles of waterway.

HARBOR ASSIST

The use of a towing vessel to help another vessel in its maneuvers in docking, undocking, locking, mooring, etc.

HARBOR BOAT

A small towboat or tug that provides service in a harbor at barge fleets, breaking up and assembling tows, shifting barges to and from docks, and assisting towboats in making drops and pickups of barges. Sometimes called *Shift Boats*, *Helper Boats*, *Day Boats*, or *Fleet Boats*.

HARD

As used on the river in a nautical sense:

1. *Aground* – Firmly on ground in that a towboat will either require assistance to work a tow off or the tow will have to be broken apart to get it afloat again.
2. *And Fast* – Same as "Aground".
3. *Down* – In reference to the helm or rudder position, i.e., all the way, full rudder to port or starboard.
4. *Over* – Same as "Down".
5. *Rigging* – The wires, chain slings, shackles, and ratchets used to stiffly wire a tow together. See: SOFT LASHINGS.

HARD-HAT DIVER

A salvage diver that wears a heavy metal helmet attached to a diving suit that is watertight, along with heavy diving shoes and a lead belt at his waist. Air is supplied by a compressor and attended by an assistant on a work flat or vessel. Although once in common usage on the Western Rivers, most divers now use scuba gear when engaged in salvage work.

HARDPAN

The term refers to an area of riverbed that consists of heavy clay or other material that is hard to dredge; if a tow goes aground on it, it is tough to get it off.

HARDPOINT DIKE

A short dike perpendicular to the shore. Used in groups, mostly to stabilize the banks of side- or back-channel chutes or to provide improved habitat.

HARVEST MOON

The full moon closest to the autumnal equinox. A beautiful time of year, especially on the Upper Mississippi River, as the leaves of trees change their color.

HARVEY CANAL & LOCK

Located at mile point 98.5 AHP on the Mississippi River, on the west bank across from New Orleans, LA. The Canal was originally built as a private waterway for drainage in the early 1800s. In the mid-1800s one of the original owner's daughters married a man named J.H. Harvey, who built a large house overlooking the canal. River Pilots called it Harvey's Castle and dubbed the waterway the *Harvey Canal*. Eventually, the canal and the lands around it were sold to the U.S. government. The house was torn down and the old lock gate was replaced. The center of the *Harvey Lock* chamber is mile 0 on the GIWW going either east to St. Marks, FL, or west to Brownsville, TX.

HATCH

1. A restricted opening from one place to another or through the deck of a vessel to a tank, void space, cargo area, etc.

2. An opening in a barge cover used for loading cargo, i.e. a grain *hatch* door.

3. A cover over the hopper of a covered barge, i.e. "Open the #3 *hatch* in order that the inspector can take a grain sample".

4. The *hatch* opening can be square, rectangular, round, or oval. It can be fitted with hinges, rollers, or twisted open and closed. *Hatch* is usually preceded by the name of what it is covering, i.e., ullage *hatch*, or #3 port wing tank *hatch*, or stern cargo *hatch*, etc.

HATCH COVER

A protection to secure entrance, or provide for it, through an opening on a tug, towboat, or barge that leads to a vessel supply tank, a cargo hold or tank, a void space, a storage compartment, etc. Depending on the space being covered, the *hatch cover* can be watertight, weather tight, oil tight, or vapor tight. There is a lip, or coaming around the opening that engages the *hatch cover*. See: CARGO COVER and COVERED BARGE.

HAUL

The term *haul* originates from the 16th Century when sailors pulled on sails "*hauled* close to the wind". As used on the river in a nautical sense:

1. In – To pull on a line or wire to take up slack or bring aboard.

2. Down – To lower, or take down the U.S. flag.

3. Off – To steer away from an object or place.

4. Out – To go on a LIFTING WAYS or DRYDOCK.

5. Together – To work in unison to pull in a line or wire.

HAUL OUT

See: DRYDOCK and LIFTING WAYS

HAUL-OUT WIRE

The small diameter wire used for pulling when a tow requires double locking. It leads from a winch on a lock wall to the first half of a barge tow that is disconnected from the towboat when locking. When the section of unattached tow has completed its lockage the lock tender will reel in the *haul-out wire* on the winch in order to pull the barge section out of the lock chamber.

HAULING PART

The part of the falls of a tackle to which power is applied.

HAULING WAYS

Another name for LAUNCHING WAYS, but instead of launching a vessel it is being used to *haul* or lift a vessel out of the water. See: CRADLE.

HAWSE

That part of a tug's bow that has the *hawse-pipe* openings for the anchor chain to ride in. Towboats do not have *hawse-pipes* since they do not carry anchors. However, the phrase, "coming up through the *hawse-pipe*, meaning to work up from a deckhand to become a Pilot, or an engine room oiler or striker to become an Engineer, is sometimes used on the inland waterways to describe a career path as it is at sea.

HAWSER

Although a towing *hawser* can be of any rational length and of any circumference, its size will depend upon the power of the tug and the size of what it is towing. Some tomes on seamanship state that a *hawser* is a line over five inches in circumference, but since most mooring and lock lines used daily on the rivers and canals are this size or larger, to a riverman a *hawser* is normally thought of as a larger heavy fiber or synthetic line of more than six inches, used when tugs are towing other vessels astern. The term derives from the French *haucier*, meaning "to hoist".

HAZARD TO NAVIGATION

An obstruction, usually sunken, that presents sufficient danger to navigation so as to require expeditious, affirmative action, such as marking and/or removal to provide for navigational safety.

HAZARDOUS SUBSTANCE

In regard to the liquid cargoes carried in barges that are defined and covered in Title 46 CFR 151 (Subchapter O), they would all fall under the definition of a *hazardous substance* subject to the carriage, spill, reporting, cleanup, and penalty provision provided in law.

HAZMAT

An acronym or abbreviation for *hazardous material*.

H-BITTS

One of the most important fittings on board tugs. The *H-bitt* is looks like a squat letter H. The upper portions above the crossbar are called posts. The crossbars that stick out from the "posts" are called "horns". On tugs you will find them located athwartship on the stern deck well forward of the steering rudder. Sometimes, especially on docking tugs, they also are also placed on the bow. Some of the older towboats operating had aft *H-bitts* located in the same position as tugs and would occasionally engage in towing, especially in ice. Most all towboats today have *H-bitts* located forward at the center of the main deck bow between the towknees. The normal use is for a fairlead of a line leading to the capstan. Also used with crosswires to prevent sliding when made up to a tow.

HEAD

As used on the rivers in a nautical sense:

1. The forward or upper end of a landing, pier, lock wall, bends, etc.
2. The bow end of a tug, towboat, barge, or tow.
3. A latrine and washroom.
4. Pressure in a pipeline of steam, water, or liquid cargo.
5. A vessel with a deeper draft on the bow than the stern is termed, "down by the *head*".
6. The difference at a dam between the water level of the upper pool and the height of the tail water.
7. *Block* – A cargo block at the end of a boom.
8. *Boards* – Planks that are fitted in channels between the towknees of a towboat to keep water from coming on deck over the bow when running light boat.
9. *Down* – To go downstream.
10. *Light* – Short for a navigational masthead light.
11. *Line* – A line that is used to tie off the bow of a vessel or tow and usually takes the main holding strain.
12. *Off* – Steer away from a place or object.
13. *On* – A situation where two vessels are meeting on reciprocal, or nearly reciprocal, courses so as to involve the risk of collision. Covered by Rule 14 of the Navigation Rules.
14. *Pressure* – Keeping up a good *head* of steam in a boiler.
15. *Up* – To go upstream.
16. *Way* – The forward movement

of a vessel. It does not just mean that a vessel has ahead propulsion; it must be making progress through the water.

17. Wind – The vessel is going directly into the wind.

HEAD DECKHAND

A term that developed around the 1950s when some towing companies and vessels eliminated the position of MATE. Instead, the most experienced deckhand on a watch was given the new title of *Head Deckhand*, and was placed in charge of the deck crew on his watch.

HEAD OF NAVIGATION

The point or place furthest upriver where the channel is deep enough for commercial towboat and barge navigation.

HEAD OF PASSES

The point in the Mississippi River delta where the river diverges into separate waterways, called *Passes* that make their way to the Gulf of Mexico. The three main *passes* are the Southwest *Pass* to the West, the *Pass* A Loutre to the East, and the South *Pass* in the center. The *Head* is where the water separates, in essence the mouth and mile 0 of the Lower Mississippi River where it starts its mileage going north, until it reaches the convergence of the Upper Mississippi and Ohio rivers at mile 964.

HEAD OF STEAM

When a vessel is coming full ahead and making maximum speed through the water. Even though most towboats and tugs are diesel-powered today, the *steam* in this maxim is a carryover from when steam was king.

HEAD-ON (or IN) LANDING

A landing where only the bow will be made fast to a dock, piling, or other object.

HEAD-ON SITUATION

As defined in Navigation Rule 14, it is "When two power-driven vessels are meeting on reciprocal or nearly reciprocal courses so as to involve risk of collision..." and states the action and responsibility of each vessel.

HEADER

1. The end of a pipeline on a tank barge that serves as the connection place for hooking up the pipeline hoses.
2. The supply line to HEATING COILS.

HEADING

The direction in which a vessel's bow or tow is pointing and the course it is taking at any particular time.

HEADING FLASHER

An illuminating line that shows up on each sweep of a radar screen to indicate the direction of a towboat's heading.

HEADLIGHT

A tug's or towboat's searchlight. Most towboats that push tows of any size use either a carbon arc light or, since the 1980s, a Xenon light. Smaller harbor boats use a high-wattage incandescent bulb.

HEADLOG

The term *headlog* is unique to riverboating and comes from the time when barges were made of wood with a heavy timber across the bow (the log) for reinforcement. The expression also may have some nexus to logging terms, dating from the time when a BUTTING BLOCK, which was a very large log, was placed at the *head* of a raft for a rafting boat to push against. Since it was the "head" log, the term may have carried over to when steamers started pushing against barges. It is still used on the river even though all barges are now of steel construction, but the term as a structural component usually refers to the heavy plating and framing across the head of a RAKE barge.

Headlog or *headlogging* as an action in making up tows refers to the ability of two vessels to come together with one not overriding the other. For example, towboats have TOWKNEES on their bows which usually can be made up to a barge that is riding low in the water, or to an empty RAKE-ended barge whose bow end sits high above the waterline. A tug, with its somewhat pointed bow would be able to *headlog*, or make up to most loaded barges, but probably not be able to *headlog* to an empty RAKE barge. In the case of barges there is no problem with square ends MAKING UP or COUPLING to one another; however a lightly loaded raked barge probably would not be able to *headlog* with the stern end of a loaded barge since it would override it.

HEADPIECE

When a towboat has to run some distance without a tow it will, at times, face up to a barge which will usually be an empty one, and use it as a *headpiece* in order to run at maximum speed without water coming over the foredeck of the vessel.

HEADQUARTERS

The place from which all orders, directives, rules, instructions, advice, judgments, decisions, etc. are rendered. However, the ultimate determination of action regarding the safety of the vessel and its crew rests with Captain.

HEADWATERS

Where all rivers begin, whether it is from a spring, lake, or tributary rivers joining together.

HEATING COILS

They are made from either inverted angle irons or channels that are welded to the cargo floor of a tank barge connected to a header, or a run of serpentine piping throughout the bottom of a tank barge cargo compartment. They are used to heat viscous cargoes such as molasses or asphalt in order that they may be pumped ashore. The medium for heating is usually shore-supplied steam hooked up to a pipe header. Some barges have heating systems on board and the heating medium is an oil product.

HEAVE

As used on the river in a nautical sense:

1. To throw, i.e., throwing an object, "*Heave* me the line".
2. To pull in a line on the capstan or a winch is to "*heave* round".
3. When a vessel is underway and stops it is said to, "*heave* to".
4. When an order is given to start a capstan or winch to bring in a line or wire the command is "*heave* away".
5. When a LEADSMAN throws the leadline to sound the depth or water, he either "casts" or *heaves* it.
6. When a tug brings up an anchor it is said to "*heave* up" the anchor.
7. To *heave* up the anchor to a point just short of breaking ground is to "*heave* short".
8. The word comes from the German *heben*, meaning "to lift up", and came to the nautical world as a command to haul in on a rope or line.

HEAVING LINE

A small line, usually a HANDY LINE that has a weight or MONKEY FIST attached at its end. It is used to heave to or from the shore, dock, pier, another vessel, or other place to bend on a heavier line or wire to be hauled in.

HEEL

1. A temporary transverse inclination of a vessel when it makes a quick turn or runs up on a sandbar.

2. The product left in a tank barge cargo compartment after discharging its cargo.

3. To move a vessel or tow out from a dock, alongside a fleet, or a lock wall by twisting the stern end against the object using hard-over rudder to swing the vessel or tow away from the object.

4. To turn a vessel in a very short space, to heel around.

5. The lower end or foot of a place, such as an island, or pier.

6. The boat end of a landing stage.

7. The base of a mast or spar.

8. Sometimes used interchangeably with LIST when a vessel takes on an inclination to one side. See: STIFF and TENDER.

HEIGHT

The measurement of vertical distance from a base line to a more elevated place, such as the distance from the water's edge to the bottom of a bridge span to figure out a vessel's clearance when navigating under it, or the depth of a river back-channel at a certain gauge reading, or how high the rocks are in a certain place at pool stage, the vertical measurement between two decks, etc.

HEIGHT OF EYE

The measurement of distance between the water surface and that of a Pilot's eye when navigating from the pilothouse.

HELIOPOLIS

The first SNAGBOAT. Designed and built by HENRY SHREVE in 1829. It was first used successfully at the Ohio River's Great Chain of Rocks about 20 miles above Cairo, IL, to clear the area of snags and other impediments to navigation.

HELM

The term originally applied to the tiller or wheel of a vessel. Technically the *helm* includes all of the steering mechanism from the steering wheel or levers at the steering station to the rudders that control the direction of the vessel. On river towboats the term *helm* is seldom used and when it may be applied, it refers to the act of taking control of the navigation of the vessel, i.e., "I've got the *helm*, but usually just, "I got 'er". The word derives from old English *helma,* which is related to "helve", to mean the "handle of a weapon or tool". This makes sense in that a vessel in combat was used as a "weapon" when it was steered into another vessel to ram it, or to board it to affect its capture. At other times, however, the vessel was used as a "tool" when being in commerce carrying cargo from port to port.

HELMSMAN

Refers to a person who may be steering a vessel; however, it is not in general usage on the inland waterways, since on the rivers the person navigating is the PILOT, but now termed MATE (PILOT) by the USCG.

HELPER BOAT

A small vessel, similar to a HARBOR BOAT which is how it is usually employed. *Helper boats* assist vessels with tows at locks (such as helping a towboat moving downstream with an all-empty tow land on the guide wall in adverse wind conditions), assist a downstream tow land when there is a severe outdraft across the head of the lock wall, or other similar unusual conditions. They are also used at times to pull the first cut of barges out from a lock when double locking in order to speed up the procedure when there is a queue of tows waiting to lock. At times the *helper boat* will take what is called OVERAGE BARGES from the towing vessel and lock them through separately, then place them back into the tow when the towboat with the rest of its tow completes the lockage. The term is also used synonymously with vessels used in HARBOR ASSIST work and other support activities.

HEMP
Cordage made from a plant called Cannabis. It is not very strong relative to other cordage, but during WW I when it was difficult to obtain alternative fibers to make rope it was extensively cultivated in the Midwest of the U.S., especially in Kentucky. Presently, if you grow it the government will frown on you as it can be smoked as marijuana.

HENNEPIN CANAL
The canal was originally called the Illinois and Mississippi Canal. The idea for constructing it started in 1834 to connect the two rivers and shorten the distance to and from the area of the Upper Mississippi to Chicago. Due to state financial problems nothing was done until 1892, which saw the start of construction; the first boat, the *MARION*, cruised on it in 1907. It shortened the distance to the mid-Upper by 419 miles, with its 33 locks, and nine aqueducts. However, it was deemed obsolete by the time it was completed and was little used except for recreational purposes. The canal starts at its junction with the Illinois River at mile 223, and ends in the Upper Mississippi at Rock Island, IL, or the mouth of the Rock River, mile 479. The canal itself was 155 miles in length. Originally the canal was conceived in 1870 to be built 160 feet wide with locks sized 350 by 75 feet. When finally authorized the canal was 80 feet wide with locks 170 by 35 feet. It had been originally estimated that the canal would have seasonal theoretical capacity of over 18 million tons; but in reality when opened for traffic it only averaged carrying about 10 thousand tons per year. The Illinois and Mississippi Canal was closed in 1951 and turned over to the State of Illinois. The canal is now named for Father Hennepin, a missionary who traveled the Illinois River with the explorer LaSalle.

HERRINGBONE WHEEL
A STERNWHEEL design plan that had its wheel boards in a wide V-shape. When propelling forward the "V" was at the apex of the turn. It was claimed by the designers that the arrangement would increase efficiency in movement, both ahead and astern and reduce vibration and eliminate cracked shafting. However, the vessel when backing astern was very contrary in the way it would want to go. The idea and design of the wheel did not catch on with many owners. Also, perhaps the intricacy of fitting up buckets for repairs to the wheel was not worth the efficiency, if any, that was gained.

HERTZ (Hz)
A measurement of sound frequency, equal to one cycle per second. It is used in setting standards for sound signaling devices employed on vessels which are stated in Annex III of the Inland Navigation Rules regarding intensity and range of audibility. The term is named for Heinrich Rudolf Hertz, a physicist who was a pioneer in radio communications in the late 1800s.

HIGH AND DRY
A stranded vessel, completely, or almost completely out of the water due to a grounding, or from becoming stuck in a fast-falling river. Often happens to fleeted barges that have been left untended for a period of time. Also used for the placement of gear or material in an area where it won't get wet, i.e. "Make sure it is placed *high and dry*".

HIGH IN CROSSING
A directive or advice to a Pilot to favor the upstream side of the channel, either because the downriver side

HIGH-INTEREST VESSEL

A vessel designated as such is one that the USCG has reason to suspect could be a security threat and a danger to homeland security.

HIGHLINE

Any electrical-type wire strung across a river. It can cause a false echo on a radar screen that might appear to be a small vessel or aid to navigation.

HIGH-PRESSURE SYSTEM

A weather pattern that usually brings fair conditions as it moves in on a LOW-PRESSURE SYSTEM. The front moves in a clockwise rotation with increased pressure nearer to the center. The usual movement is from west to east. It most often is a welcome change from a low-pressure front.

HIGH-SPEED CRAFT (HSC)

An INTERNATIONAL MARITIME ORGANIZATION (IMO) designation of a vessel built to a formula that in general terms means it can achieve speeds in excess of 30 knots. The acronym is HSC. The formula for the craft is in Annex I of the NAVIGATION RULES under Parts 84.01 and 84.24.

HIGH-SPEED VESSEL

A working designation given by the USCG to a vessel that is not designed to the international standards of an HIGH SPEED CRAFT, but is capable of speeds exceeding 30 knots, or about 35 MPH plus.

HIGH-WATER

A relative term, however, to a Pilot it means well above normal river stages. Where dams are (and were) located that had WICKETS *high water* is/was the time when the wickets were thrown and the towboat and tow could go up or down over the dam in open river. When a river is flooding it is *high water*, but is referred to as *flood stage* or exceeding it.

HIGH-WATER BUOY

1. An unlighted buoy which is permanently fastened to the end of lock walls, bear traps of dams, prominent dikes in a DIKE FIELD, mooring cells, etc., that will go afloat to mark the structure when the water rises high enough to cover them.
2. Buoys that are moved well out from the normal channel in high water to give the Pilot guidance of a wider channel and to protect the buoys from being run over and lost.

HIGH-WATER MARKS

1. In some city areas there is a prominent marker that shows the highest recorded level the river reached in a flood.
2. The record Pilots keep during low and rising rivers of when sandbars, back chutes, dikes, and other places have water in them or over them at what particular river stage, in order that when the stage of water is high enough they can take a short cut over or through them, particularly if the water is slacker than in the main channel. See: BAR BOOK, GAUGE or GAGE, and GAUGE WATER.

HIGH-WATER TIE

When the water is high and there is a need to tie a tow off on shore, the Pilot will nose a corner of the lead bow barge into the bank and the deck crew will run the eye of a line around a suitable tree back to the bow corner timberheads then slack out the line as the tow is flattened along the shore line. When a sufficient scope of line is out it is made fast. If unable to reach a suitable tree, a skiff is employed to run the line out to the tree and back to the tow. When it is time to cast off the line and get the tow underway, the eye can be taken off the timberhead while the vessel moves out into the river, pulling the line from around the tree and the crew bringing it on board the tow. This is sometimes called a *running headline*, or a *quick un-tie line*.

HILL

A colloquial river term used to mean the shore, regardless of the elevation, although from a river's edge almost all land once you leave a vessel is elevated. It is used most often when someone is going ashore, i.e., "I'm going up the *hill* to make a phone call". At the foot of a *hill* is the place where a boat most often makes a landing to insure that tired crew members will have something to climb in order to get them in shape when going home.

HINGE POINT

The *hinge point* in a HINGED POOL is at approximately the midpoint between two navigation dams. The pool operates on a gradient between the dams, and the lockmaster controls the level, or gauge, at the point. The dams on the Upper Mississippi use this method of pool control.

HINGED POOL

The pools of water created by a navigational dam, such as those on the Upper Mississippi, operate on the control of the gradient between dams by the amount of water to be released in order to maintain the authorized project depth at the HINGE POINT of the pool.

HINTERLAND

A term used to describe the gathering area within the proximity of an inland port which is, or might be, susceptible to use water transportation for the products generated from a specific area. The term is used more by persons who study markets than those who navigate rivers. The word comes from the German *hinter*, meaning "behind" or "away from".

HIP and HIPPING

The process of a *hip* arrangement requires a tug or towboat making up or attaching itself to the stern quarter of a barge, usually with the stern of the tug or towboat a ways aft of the barge's stern to provide better control and steerage. *Hipping* is the movement of a barge from one place to another, usually for fairly short distances.

HITCH

1. A type of knot, usually referring to turns of a line to secure the *hitch* to an object, such as a clove *hitch*, or two half *hitches*. See: BEND and KNOT.

2. To do a period of time on a job, i.e., "I'm going over on the tug MARY JANE to do a *hitch* as Pilot", or "I'm only going to do a 20 day *hitch* this time on the boat as my wife is expecting".

HIWASSEE RIVER

The river starts its flow in north Georgia, on into North Carolina, and finally into the State of Tennessee. It enters the Tennessee River in the Chickamauga Pool at mile 499.4 and is navigable for 18.8 miles above its mouth to Charleston, TN. The Cherokee Indians called the river *Tlanusi-yi,* for the "leech place", since the Indians believed it was the home of a large leech which could consume persons who were not careful in its waters.

Keelboating was accomplished on the river in the early 1800s when the boats and people would go up the *Hiwassee*, unload and travel cross a relatively short land journey, and then they floated down the Coosa and Alabama rivers to the Gulf of Mexico. In the 1850s steamboats traveled on the river and much activity took place on it during the Civil War.

HOG

See: HOGGING.

HOG CHAINS

On steamboats the need for their ability to run with shallow draft of hull and increase the vessel's speed caused the ratio of length to depth to reach, and even be over, 30 to 1. This made for a very limber hull in longitudinal strength that could cause SAGGING or HOGGING. To overcome the problem, the design of a truss structure called *hog chains* was developed to stiffen the hull. They were not *chains* as such, but consisted of iron rods ranging from 1 to $1^1/_2$ inches in diameter that were bolted fast at the end to timbers in the hull. They were then run up over a series of posts above the superstructure on both the port and starboard sides of the vessel. The *hog chains* could be tightened or loosened by the turnbuckles that fastened them together. See: CROSS CHAINS and KNUCKLE CHAINS.

HOGGING

The bending or breaking movement of a vessel in a stressed condition with the forward and aft portions of the vessel bending down and the center section arching upwards. This occurs when cargo is loaded or unloaded improperly and the vessel does not have the longitudinal strength in its framing to overcome the stresses imposed on the hull. If a barge of pig iron is loaded only in the bow and stern sections of a barge, or is unloaded only from the center, it puts great strain on the middle section; or if a tank barge has different cargoes in different tanks and the bow tanks are filled with one cargo, and the stern tanks with another, while the midship tanks are left empty while being moved to another dock or port and the towing vessel goes aground or experiences a heavy wave action from the wake of a ship, it could cause a bending stress resulting in *hogging*. It is the opposite of SAGGING. The result of *hogging* becomes a vessel that is *hogged*. See: BUCKLE, HOG CHAINS and KNUCKLE CHAINS. The term appears to have its origin in the shape of the back of a swine, or *hog*, with its rear end and head lower when it is eating at the trough, and showing a hump in the *hog's* back.

HOIST

To lift, raise, or elevate some object or cargo, usually with a single block or pulley, i.e., to *hoist* the flag, to *hoist* the yawl on board, or to *hoist* cargo out of the hold of a vessel. Believed to come from the Dutch *hijsen,* or the German *hissen,* both essentially the same as *hoist*.

HOIST AWAY

A command to continue *hoisting* on a winch, chain fall, or other gear making a vertical lift until given another order.

HOLD

1. The cargo space of a barge.
2. An interior compartment of a towboat or tug where gear may be stored, usually termed the HOLE.
3. To keep a course, i.e., "*Hold* on ABC Light in the crossing", or "*Hold* about 100 yards above (or below) ABC Light", or "*Hold* about 200 yards open on the point below ABC light".
4. To stop, as in when slacking off a wire or line, i.e., "*Hold* the line".

HOLD FAST

Any device that acts as a keeper brace to not allow slippage or movement of gear or cargo. It is sometimes used somewhat incorrectly in place of other terms such as DOG or PAWL.

HOLDING TANK

A *tank* installed on a tug or towboat to receive the waste material from the toilets on board the vessel

HOLE
Can mean many things, but on a riverboat it usually refers to the forward bow compartment where gear is stored, i.e., "Put those coils of line down in the *hole*".

HOLED
A vessel that has received damage that will allow the ingress of water, i.e., in reference to a barge, "She's *holed* in the #2 starboard wing tank Cap, but we're pumping her and I think we can shingle her ok."

HOLIDAY
An imperfection, a spot, area or space that was missed or overlooked while painting, cleaning, chipping, or some other maintenance duty.

HOLSTON RIVER
The river rises from the streams of three forks in southwest Virginia flowing downstream into Tennessee. Officially it presently joins with the French Broad River above Knoxville, TN, at mile 652 to form the Tennessee River. Actually, the French Broad prior to the 1930s was a tributary of the *Holston* on whose banks the city of Knoxville was sited. The *Holston* flowed on past the city until it met the Little Tennessee River (mile 601) at the city of Lenoir, TN, where it at that time merged to start the Tennessee River. But, the creation of TVA in 1933 stipulated that the headquarters of the organization would be required to be on the banks of the Tennessee River. Since the bureaucrats wanted their offices to be in Knoxville they conveniently redirected the Tennessee River's source to be some 50 miles upstream to where the French Broad met the Holston.

The river was called the Hogoheegee by the Indian tribes. It took its Anglican name from an early settler and trader by the name of Stephen Holston who had explored much of the reaches of the river. In the early days of U.S. territory furnaces for iron making were established in the area of the *Holston* which manufactured nails. These and agricultural produce were floated downriver for trade at Knoxville. In 1828 a steamer came up the Tennessee and the *Holston* rivers to the mouth of the French Broad. Later, regular steamboat traffic (at least when adequate water was available) was between Decatur, AL (mile 305), and Knoxville, TN (mile 647). During high water periods vessels could continue up the *Holston* to Kingsport.

HOME
1. To bear on an object, i.e. "*Home* in on that silo sitting on the right bank".
2. When a piece of gear has gone as far as it will go it is termed *homed*, i.e. "We *homed* the ratchet at the break coupling and will have to reset another wire".
3. The shore place where the crew of a tugboat or towboat wishes they were.
4. The actual place where the crew of a vessel works and probably spends more hours of time than anyplace else; so, the tug or towboat must really be their *home*.

HOME PORT
1. Sometimes used to refer to where the office of the operations department and where the Port Captain and/or Port Engineer are located. See: HAILING PORT.
2. Some companies assign crew members a place, city or port, from where they will pay travel expenses going to and from the vessel to which they may be assigned.

HOMELAND SECURITY
The term is defined as "a concerted national effort to prevent terrorist

attacks within the United States, reduce U.S. vulnerability to terrorism, and minimize the damage and recover from attacks that do occur". The U.S. Coast Guard is charged with spearheading this effort in the maritime domain and is now a part of the Department of *Homeland Security*.

HONEY BARGE

A barge that has a large holding tank to offload sewage and/or oily waste. It is usually a tank on the same barge that does MID-STREAM FUELING.

HOOD

1. A device that is fitted over a radar screen in order to clearly see the images displayed on the screen during periods of bright light. A person can then look at the radar through the small end of the *hood* to view the screen scope without the impairment of light.

2. A protective shelter over an opening in a tank or over a portion of the deck on a vessel.

HOOK

The term *hook* is used to describe a number of different devices; among them are:

1. Bale – A two pronged *hook* similar to ice tongs that is used to load and unload bales of cotton, or similar products.

2. Barrel – See: BARREL SLING.

3. Belt – Used to fasten the ends of a belt together.

4. Block – A *hook* attached to a block. It may have one on both top and bottom.

5. Boat – A curved prong at the end of a pole used to grab a boat coming alongside or to fish for a line or wire in the water or on shore.

6. Box – A sharp short-shanked *hook* with a right angled handle used by a roustabout or stevedore to assist in loading and stacking bales of material. Sometimes called a *longshoreman's hook*.

7. Can – Same as "barrel".

8. Cant – See.

9. Cargo – A strong short *hook* that is curved towards its base. Used in cargo loading and unloading to keep a sling from slipping off.

10. Grab – Used to grab or secure a link in a length of chain.

11. Peavey – See.

12. Pelican – See.

13. Rope – A *hook* in the end of a line used to assist in dragging a wire ashore.

14. Safety – A *hook* that has a hinged closure piece across its opening to keep the *hook* from slipping off from whatever it is attached.

15. Sister – Two *hooks* that match together when closed to keep anything attached from slipping off.

HOOKED UP

1. A term used to describe that the engines are running at full ahead, i.e. "We're clear of the lock and I've got 'er *hooked up*".

2. The action of fastening a wire in a ratchet's pelican hook.

3. The procedure of making the towboat up to a barge, i.e. "We'll drop down under the stern of BCB 1298 and get *hooked up*".

HOOP

See: HULA HOOP.

HOPPER

1. The cargo space of a *hopper* barge. See: BARGE.

2. The cargo space in a DECK BARGE that is fitted with a coaming. See: DREDGE.

3. Colloquial use for *hopper* barge, i.e., "We've got seven *hoppers* to pick up at ABC Dock".

HOPPER BARGE

See: BARGE.

HOPPER DREDGE

A vessel that is able to carry its load of dredged material to a disposal zone, and by a hinged mechanical bottom section is able to drop its load in the designated area. This type of dredge is seldom seen on the Western Rivers.

HORIZONTAL SECTORS

The degrees of visibility over which a vessel's navigation lights are required to be shown on their *horizontal* plane. The cut-off of a light's intensity will decrease slightly at the outside *sector* in which it is prescribed to be displayed. These values are found in Annex I of the INLAND RULES. See: VERTICAL SECTORS.

HORN

The ends or arms of a CAVEL or the ends of an H-BITT deck fitting that gives the appearance of *horns*. See: MEGAPHONE, TAKE THE HORNS and WHISTLE.

HORSE

The frame of a WICKET at a movable dam in which wooden boards are bolted together to stop the flow of water when the wicket is raised. The wicket is "thrown", or lowered to the riverbed, if there is sufficient water in the channel to provide for open river navigation. See: CHANOINE WEIR.

HORSE TREADMILL VESSEL

At one time back in the 1800s someone had the idea to put a paddlewheel on the side of a keelboat and propel it upriver by a *horse on a treadmill*. It didn't last too long as the rate of speed by the walking horse was not too good against the speed of the current, as well as tiring out the horse, feeding it, finding replacement horses, etc. However, there were a few ferries that applied the principle on the Ohio River. They were of the two HP principle. It is not believed that anyone measured the brake, effective, indicated, shaft, or thrust horsepower of the ferryboats. It was usually just simply called a *Horseboat* with horses trying to get to their oats.

HORSEPOWER

The rating of *horsepower* is a somewhat relative term that was devised by James Watt when working with steam engines in the late 1700s. Watt wanted to rate the abilities of different steam engines, so apparently he looked at what an average horse was capable of doing when working. There are various stories as to how he arrived at his conclusions, such as a horse walking at a grist mill or saw mill, a pony lifting a certain weight out of a coal mine, or perhaps other applications. However, a formula was devised that is still in use today that in essence says the amount of work to move one pound the distance of one foot is one foot-pound, and 550 foot-pounds of work per second, or 33,000 foot-pounds of work per minute equals one *horsepower*.

Today the same formula is used to evaluate steam power, diesel engines, electric motors, gasoline driven cars, plus a variety of other appliances. Some of the terms associated with James Watt's are as follows:

1. Horsepower (HP) – A measured unit of power that at one time was rated to be constant work of one horse.

2. Indicated (IHP) – The work produced by an engine cylinder during each stroke.

3. Brake (BHP) – Measured at the crankshaft coupling with a type of mechanical, hydraulic, or electric brake.

4. Shaft (SHP) – The power transmitted through the shaft to the propeller. It will vary depending on the draft of the vessel, water depth, and other factors.

5. Effective (EHP) – The measured power to propel a vessel.

6. Thrust (THP) – The power of the propeller in moving a vessel through the water.

7. Other terms used, especially by vendors touting the superior qualities of the engines they produce, are (among possibly others): Continuous, Input, Intermittent, Output, etc.

HORSESHOE DIKE
Another name for BULLNOSE DIKE.

HORSING or HAWSING IRON
A long caulking *iron* that was used by a caulker swinging a BEETLE to drive in and *horse-up* or harden, the caulking in joints and seams of a wooden hull. This was usually a two-man job, with one holding the iron and the other using the beetle.

HOSE
Various types of *hoses* are employed aboard towboats, tugs, and barges. There are cargo *hoses* used on vessels for taking on fuel, those for potable water, fire *hoses*, dewatering suction and discharge *hoses*, as well as a variety of different types for usage in the engine room and other places. The term apparently originates from the Dutch *hoos,* meaning "stockings", and the Germanic *hosen,* which means "trousers". The current meaning came into use when flexible piping or tubing was devised.

HOT OIL BARGE
A tank barge that moves products, such as asphalt, that are required to be heated to maintain their proper viscosity in order to properly flow when being discharged. The barge is equipped with heating equipment.

HOT WELL
A tank that receives water from the condenser on a steamboat. The water is then recycled and pumped by the feed water system back to the boilers.

HOT WORK
Any type of work, such as burning, welding, grinding, etc. that produces a degree of temperature that could ignite flammable gas vapors. Any tank that has such vapors should be tested and a permit issued authorizing *hot work* and the conditions under which it may be performed. A sign must be posted that says "Safe for Fire" prior to using any electrical-driven equipment, welding, or using a cutting torch when making a repair.

HOUSE
To stow equipment, gear, or mechanical devices in their proper place, i.e. "*House* the yawl boom in its cradle", or "*House* the lock lines under a tarp as an ice storm is coming". The term when used in this sense is most often pronounced "howze". The word appears to come from "hide" which is from the Old English *hydan,* meaning "to put out of sight".

HOUSE FLAG
The company flag or emblem that a tug or towboat may display. The emblem is usually painted on the outboard side of the stacks.

HOUSEBOAT
It used to be that a *houseboat* was a fairly good-sized comfortable floating home, much larger than a SHANTYBOAT. Then some entrepreneurial person designed a boat, not a yacht, put an outboard on it, later an inboard engine in it, so weekenders could tool around the inland lakes and rivers, and then called the thing a *houseboat*. A whole industry has grown up with the name.

HOUSTON SHIP CHANNEL
The city of Houston is located at the head Buffalo Bayou. In 1837 the first steamboat reached the city. Planters brought their cotton to the port to be loaded and taken to Galveston to be transshipped onto a seagoing vessel. In the 1870s the USACE surveyed the area and recommended that a channel be constructed with a depth of six feet, by 100 feet in width, however no funds

were appropriated. Finally, in the late 1890s, Congress authorized construction of a section of the waterway to where the turning basin is now located, at a depth of 25 feet, but by 1909 it had still only been dredged to 18½ feet. The city proposed a cost-sharing plan and the project was completed in 1914.

During WW II, the oil and chemical businesses had boomed in the area, and in 1945 Congress approved a plan to widen the channel to 300 feet to the turning basin. Then in 1957 the USACE recommended the entire channel have a depth of 40 feet. In the early 21st Century, authorization was given to widen the channel to 530 feet, with a depth of 45 feet, which was completed in 2005, as well as adding barge lanes to be constructed at a depth of 12 feet on either side of the deeper ship channel.

HOVERCRAFT

The trade name for a type of air-cushioned craft that when operating in the non-displacement mode is required to display, under Navigation Rule 23(b), an all-round flashing yellow light of 120 flashes per minute, or about twice the rate of the "special flashing light" displayed on the head of barge tows. These vessels are highly affected by winds. When in a crossing situation their line of travel may not be as their heading may indicate as they could be at a crabbing angle while moving forward.

HOWARD STEAMBOAT MUSEUM

The museum is located in Jeffersonville, IN, just across the street from Jeffboat Shipyard. It is a large old mansion built in the 1890s by Edmonds J. Howard, the son of James Howard, the founder of the Howard Shipyard, where Jeffboat is now located. The shipyard started in 1834 with the construction of the *HYPERION*, a packet of 65 tons (107' x 18' x 8'), and the yard was still in existence when it was acquired by the U.S. Navy in WW II. The last vessel built before the Navy took over in 1940 was a twin-screw diesel towboat, the *FRANK COSTANZO*, for a coal mine company in West Virginia. The museum opened in 1958 with Mrs. Loretta Howard still living on the third floor and acting as curator, but she has since passed away. The museum houses a large collection of steamboat models, pictures, books, and other memorabilia.

HUG

To run a towboat and/or tow as close as possible to a designated place, i.e., "*Hug* the shore above ABC Point as the water's slacker there," or "*Hug* the red buoys in the XYZ crossing since a tow bumped on the green buoy side".

HULA HOOP

A looped piece of wire rigging that is fitted with a swaged metal clamp and used as a sling which would usually be put over a fitting such as a TIMBERHEAD. Then a RATCHET with one end already attached to the eye splice in a barge wire would have its other end engaged in the *hula hoop*. Most times the *hoop* has a set of chain links attached in it. The name comes from the appearance of a child's *hula hoop* when new, before it is pulled out of shape under the stress that is placed on rigging.

HULK

An old, virtually abandoned, vessel that is unfit for use, no longer considered seaworthy, and is most often tied to the bank in a slip, off the channel with all useable equipment removed. The word as it is used today is not clear. In old English it meant a "fast ship", which has little in common with a vessel that is basically rotting away in a boneyard.

HULL

1. The main body of a tug, towboat, barge or other vessel, including the bottom, sides and deck, but not the deckhouses, machinery, rigging devices or other appendages.

2. A vessel under construction in a shipyard is given a *hull* number that is referred to when it is under construction.

3. The word derives from the Dutch *huls,* and the German *hulse* meaning "a husk or a covering of seeds", or from the German *hulle,* to mean "a covering" or "a box". So it is, a shell, or covering, to house the engine, the machinery, cargo, and the crew.

HULL AND MACHINERY POLICY

A marine insurance policy that covers the *hull* and the *machinery* of a vessel. It also includes the permanent fittings on the vessel, its stores and provisions for the crew, as well as the bunkers.

HULL INSPECTOR

A term that describes any large log, piling, rock, buoy, or any other object that strikes the hull and/or wheel with noticeable force that may cause damage. See: PLANTER, SAWYER, and STEAMBOAT HULL INSPECTOR.

HUMMOCK

Broken ice that is mounded or piled up haphazardly creating an uneven surface. It is not flowing and is often caused by a vessel breaking through a cover of ice, which then piles on top and freezes to the existing sheet ice or goes under the sheet ice, and exerts upward pressure to break it.

HUNDRED-YEAR FLOOD

Usually represents the height of the flood of record in the last 100 years at a given location. It represents a one-percent chance in the following one hundred years that its level will occur again; however, it does not mean that there won't be more than one or more floods exceeding the flood of record in any 100-year period.

HUNG UP

Unable to move, normally a term used when a tow is aground.

HUNGRY RIVER

Said by the river gods when the current in the river causes the shoreline banks to cave in and start to wash away in order to add soil to its delta.

HURDLE

Another name that is given for a wooden pile dike.

HURRICANE

A relatively simple definition is a cyclonic wind that moves in a circular counterclockwise movement with speeds in excess of 74 MPH. The season in the Gulf of Mexico region is from June through November. The term *hurricane* is used in the Atlantic area. In the Pacific area they are generally termed *typhoons*. Although most upriver towboats and barges will not be in the vicinity of the path of a hurricane, they can be affected from the heavy rains associated with them and the runoff that can cause flash flooding. Those tugs and towboats along the Gulf Coast area or anywhere in the Lower Mississippi Valley can be severely impacted by surge waves, dense rainfall, flooding well over the banks of canals, and extremely high winds.

There are two versions of where the name *hurricane* came from. Some say it originated with the Mayans of Central America who called their storm God, *Hunrakau*. Others say it comes from the Mayan word *Korotura,* meaning "whirlwind." Take your pick. Maybe the two were brothers or cousins.

Hurricane and Storm Warnings

Small Craft Warning
Winds up to 38 MPH

Gale Warning
39 to 54 MPH

Storm Warning
55 to 73 MPH

Hurricane Watch
Alert for a *hurricane* MAY threaten an area

Hurricane Warning
Alert for a *hurricane* is EXPECTED at a specified area

Hurricane
Category 1
74 to 95 MPH   4 to 5 foot surge

Category 2
96 to 110 MPH   6 to 8 foot surge

Category 3
111 to 130 MPH   9 to 12 foot surge

Category 4
131 to 150 MPH   13 to 18 foot surge

Category 5
Over 150 MPH   18 feet or greater

Some of the worst *hurricanes* along the Gulf Coast in the 20th and 21st centuries:

1900	Galveston, TX
1916	Mobile, AL
1933	Brownsville, TX
1947	New Orleans, LA
1957	Louisiana Coast - Audrey
1961	Texas Coast - Carla
1965	LA & Miss. River - Betsy
1969	Mississippi Coast - Camille
1970	Corpus Christi - Celia
1979	Mobile, AL - Frederic
1980	Brownsville, TX - Allen
1983	Texas Coast - Alicia
1985	Louisiana Coast - Juan
1985	FL and LA - Elena
1992	FL and LA - Andrew
1995	FL and AL - Opal
2005	MS, LA, TX - Katrina & Rita

Hurricane trackers originally named *hurricanes* by their latitude-longitude designation. To reduce confusion in 1953 they started using female names (one can only speculate as to why). Then in 1979 they started alternating names, using female one year and male the next, in alphabetical order. If they run out of names like they did in the 2005 season, the names of Greek alphabet letters are used. If a storm results in extreme damage with large loss of life, the name is retired.

HURRICANE DECK

The highest continuous deck from bow to stern of a steamboat. The deck above the boiler deck. Where its name comes from in anyone's guess. Some have opined that it was a deck where passengers could sit or stroll with gentle breezes blowing. Since it originally was long, wide, and clear of any objects, it is more likely that it may have looked like a hurricane had swept it clear of anything that wasn't nailed down; besides hurricanes don't blow "gentle breezes".

HURTER or HEURTER

A grooved, cast slide in the concrete foundation of a movable dam where a PROP pole for a WICKET rides or moves then locks in place when the wicket is raised at a movable dam. The term comes to us from the French *heurter*, meaning "to strike something without doing damage". Thus, the slide allows the prop to discharge so the wicket can fall to the bottom of the river without being harmed. See: CHANOINE WEIR.

HYBRID ELECTRONIC CHART

This type of chart is a combination of a RASTER CHART and vector technology into a chart display. Essentially it gathers only the most important navigational data in digital form from the navigational chart, which is then overlaid on a raster chart.

HYDRAULIC HEAD
The vertical distance between the upstream level of water at a dam and the tail water, and the pressure that is created.

HYDRAULIC RIVER STUDIES
The evaluation of flow characteristics and physical behavior of rivers, studying the transport of sediment, the current speed, stages of river levels, predictions, and final discharge from an area. All of these characteristics are evaluated for design and modeling of the environment, water quality, flood management, channels for navigation, and all structures built in the studied area.

HYDRAULICS
A machine or device that uses oil under pressure to produce a mechanical force. There are many pieces of equipment on tugs and towboats that use hydraulically operated equipment, such as steering rams, steering gear, marine drives, etc.

HYDROELECTRIC POWER
Electric power generated by the flow of water through turbines at some dams, particularly on the Tennessee and Cumberland rivers, and the flows of the Columbia-Snake system.

HYDROGRAPHIC CHART
The charts issued by NOAA. Navigation charts that show the coastal environment of bottom contours, depths, types of bottom bed, the channel, buoys, etc. They are presently different in their depiction from typical USACE maps of the rivers. Charts are issued for seaport areas, as well as for the GIWW.

HYDROGRAPHIC SURVEY
A scientific investigation mapping the contour of a river bottom and/or depth of water in a section of river, as well as a measurement of current velocity at a particular river gauge, determining bottom or bed sediment, structures in the river, and any other features of interest.

HYDROGRAPHY
The study, science, and survey of the physical aspects of waterways, including rivers, the bottom, where the channel lies, where navigational markers are placed, where bridges, pipelines, or high lines cross a river and anything else of interest to a mariner in need of information on a chart.

HYDROLOGY
The discipline of engineering that is the study of the flow of fluids, especially (as it concerns river people), the flow of water. The U.S. Corps of Engineers does an excellent job in this regard concerning flood management, navigation, and the environment. The term comes from the Latin *hydrologia,* meaning "the study or science of water".

HYDROSTATIC TEST
A test taken in a shipyard of a vessel's tank(s) or a compartment to determine its water tightness, and to see if they can successfully withstand the design pressure required. The space is filled with water and sealed. A pipestand, set at a height determined by the tank(s) designed pressure, is placed above the deck and is then filled to the top of the pipe. Approximately one foot of water height in the pipe equals 0.44 p.s.i.

ILLUSTRATIONS 217

TYPICAL HAND SIGNALS USED BY CREW MEMBERS ON THE TOW TO INDICATE TO A PILOT THE DIRECTIONAL MOVEMENT THAT MAY APPLY TO A GIVEN SITUATION

HEADLOGGING

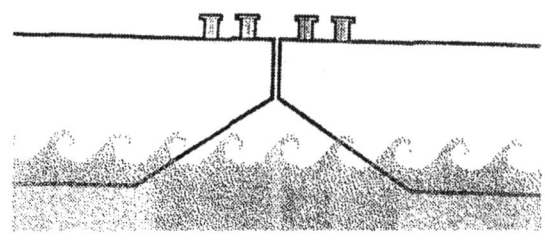

HEADLOG – ONE RAKE TO A SQUARE END BARGE

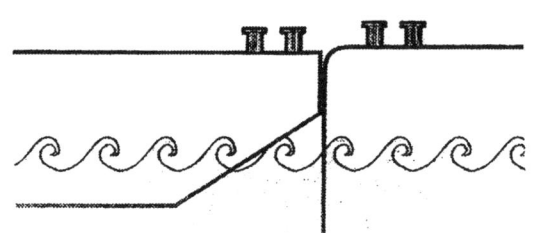

HEADLOG – ONE RAKE BARGE TO ANOTHER

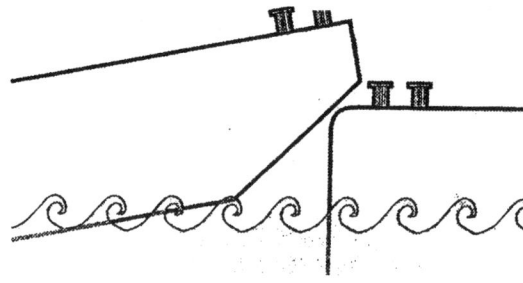

FAILURE TO HEADLOG

HIPPING A BARGE

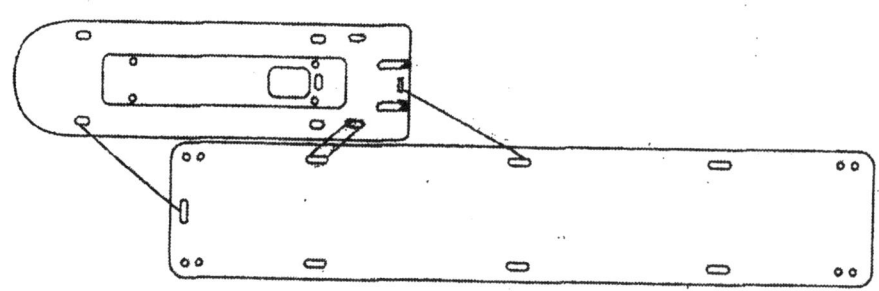

HOGGING - SAGGING - BUCKLING

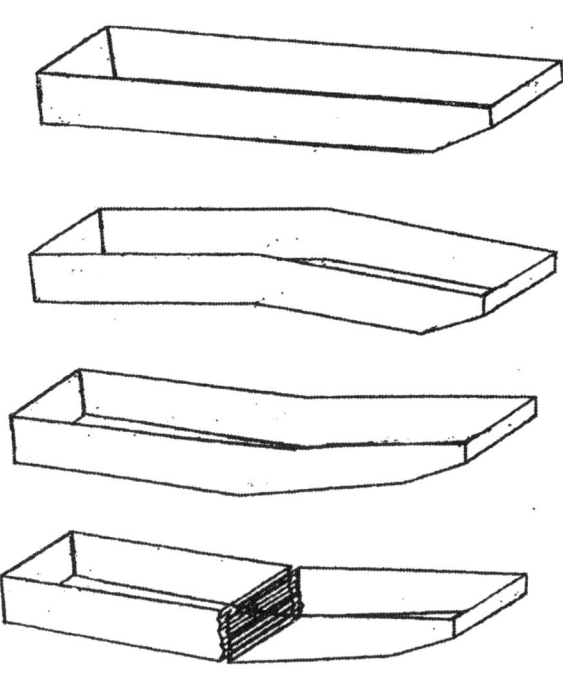

NORMAL - Outline of a barge as it would normally float in either an empty or loaded condition

HOGGING - When the center section of a barge is higher in the mid-section than its extremities (see)

SAGGING - When the ends of a barge are higher then at the mid-section (see)

BUCKLE - When extreme "sagging" of the barge occurs resulting in a rupture of plating and framing with a split in the hull (see)

HATCHES

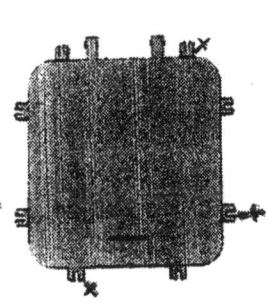

Square or rectangular raised off deck, hinged, has hold-down dogs

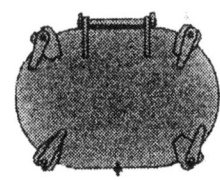

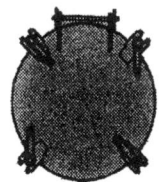

Oval raised off deck, hinged with hold-down dogs

Rotary locking type that sits flush with deck

Round shape, raised off deck, hinged, with hold-down dogs

I

IALA

An abbreviation for the INTERNATIONAL ASSOCIATION OF LIGHTHOUSE AUTHORITIES.

ICE

Frozen water. Fresh water starts freezing at 32 degrees F, or at 0 degrees Centigrade, and somewhat lower in salt or brackish water. Its word origin is from the German *eis,* which means "water". Apparently Latin and Greek people didn't see much of it. *Ice* can be an extremely destructive force on vessels that operated in the upper basin of the Western Rivers. See all terms below that refer to *ice.*

ICE CONDITIONS

1. Bottom Buildup – When ice forms on the bottoms of barges in a tow in extremely cold weather while running in deep water through ice covered channels. The condition becomes dangerous when going downstream into a lock with a loaded tow as when the chamber is dewatered the barges will settle on the lock floor with the possibility of tow rigging parting, as well as putting a stress on the barge hull. At old Lock #26 on the Upper Mississippi, Pilots were always warned to slack the tow's wires or put the tow couplings on fiber lines when lowering the lock water. At Lock #19, Keokuk, Iowa, it was reported one time that a tow of empty barges came across Keokuk Lake and entered the lock that has a submersible gate upstream. After the gate was raised the handrails on the gate were crushed or broken due to the thickness of bottom ice on the barges. The gate submerses about 17 feet below the water surface.

2. Brash – Broken floating ice. This type of ice can range from loose to heavy, or broken apart and refrozen.

3. Bridge – Ice across an area that does not restrict the flow of water.

4. Floe – A field of large sections of floating ice in a stream.

5. Free – When a river has no ice, or is practically free of ice, that could impede navigation.

6. Fresh ice – Defines ice that has not been broken through by a tow. It is also termed as a *natural cover of ice*.

7. Gorge, Gorged, or Gorging – The condition where ice which has become layered, piling ice upon ice, as it moves downstream with the current. When the flowing ice meets a restriction, such as a dam, lock entrance, a shallow area, or a restricted channel, it tends to pile up, eventually forming an almost impassable obstruction in the navigable channel, defining the term. In 1917 ice flows formed on the Ohio River between Warsaw, KY, and Rising Sun, IN, that held for 58 days. It was reported that ice 30 feet high backed up the river for 100 miles. *Gorging* also occurs where two converging streams meet and one is at a higher stage than the other, causing a back flow into the other stream. This frequently happens on the Upper Mississippi River before it joins the Ohio River at Cairo, Illinois, when the Ohio's flow and stage are high and the Upper's is low. As the Ohio backs up the Upper, it results in essentially a pooled-water situation. Floating ice on the Upper R. comes to a standstill and starts layering until at times huge *gorges* can result.

8. Jammed Ice – Occurs when large and small ice floes become frozen together, which can impede barge tow movement. Not as restrictive as a gorge.

9. Layering – When ice in a channel is broken by a barge tow, it mostly goes under the frozen ice to the sides where the tow has broken its path. The broken ice freezes to the non-broken ice, making, in effect, layers of ice.

10. Locking – When ice starts jamming in the upper forebay of a lock chamber, the Lockmaster will sometimes lock only ice through in order to keep it from blocking the lock gates.

11. Loose Floes – A condition where there are a lot of large floating floes of ice that are moving downstream and not freezing together. Usually seen when there is a rise in a stream's stage and the current is flowing faster.

12. Mule Train(ing) – (see) Towing barges astern in single file. This occurs when tows are unable to push or steer through heavy ice. Barges are then towed astern in single file. It is sometimes also called "railroading".

13. Packed Floes – When the ice cover of a stream consists of large floes that are in contact with one another, but not jammed or frozen together.

14. Open Water – A condition where the navigation channel has no ice that limits or constricts movement.

15. Run – The flowing of ice in a river. It can be light or heavy.

ICE PIER

A large heavily constructed *pier* in the river that protects a dock, bridge or other structure by causing ice flows to break up and sheer off when they hit. The piers are also used as a haven by tows when heavy ice starts flowing; however, they were more intended for use by the old wooden hulled-vessels than for the modern day steel-hulled vessels.

ICE SHEATHING

Metal plating put over the bow and sides of wooden-hulled vessels about a foot above and a foot below the waterline to protect vessels that had to work in rivers where ice was present. It not only protected the wood from eroding by ice floes, but also shielded the oakum between the side strakes of the hull from being cut out.

ICEBOUND

The situation that occurs when a vessel is stuck in ice and is unable to maneuver. These days on the river it rarely happens that a towboat itself is completely unmaneuverable; however, any tow in its care can become *icebound*. The act of a river freezing over, making navigation unfeasible, is also referred as *icebound*, i.e., "The Upper above Keokuk, IA is now *icebound*". The Upper Mississippi above its junction with the Illinois River becomes *icebound* to varying degrees in the winter season, starting at the Twin Cities' area and gradually working south. On the Illinois River, navigation at times is stopped due to ice conditions, causing the locks to be inoperable because of ice buildup. In the quarter century or more prior to the year 2007, the Ohio River had not experienced a stoppage of navigation due to ice.

In the steamboat days of wooden-hulled boats and barges, there were often disastrous results in icy conditions. Hulls were punctured and steamers broke in two if caught in a breakup and the run-out of flowing ice that might gorge. To combat some of the effects of icing conditions and render assistance to vessels caught when a quick freeze occurred, ICE PIERS were built where a vessel and tow could get some shelter.

ICEBREAKER

A vessel equipped to make a path through the ice to allow for navigation. The U.S. Coast Guard has *icebreakers* on the Great Lakes and coastal areas. At one time they outfitted one of their river buoy boats with a plow-like structure that was largely unsuccessful. There are none currently operating on the river systems.

IDIOT LIGHT

A light which blinks on as a warning that something is not within the normal readings regarding the engine(s) as to temperature, pressure, or some other cause.

IDLE SPEED

The slowest speed at which the engine(s) can operate, either when the gear is, or is not, engaged.

IENC

The abbreviation for Inland Electronic Navigation Chart. One of the hundreds of acronyms that are now used with electronic charting.

ILLINOIS AND MICHIGAN CANAL (I & M)

The first suggestion to link Lake Michigan to the Illinois River, and then to the Mississippi River came from Louis Joliet, the French explorer, in 1673. With starts of a land grant by the Federal government to raise money, and stops by financial difficulties, the *I & M Canal* was eventually completed in 1848. It ran 97 miles from Chicago to the LaSalle-Peru area at mile 223 on the Illinois Waterway. The canal contained a total of 16 locks (110' by 18' by 6') and was 60 feet wide at the surface, 36 feet wide at its bed, and six feet deep. It was a boon for farmers and merchants of the area since there were practically no roads or railroads in the area at the time. The first boat through had a cargo of sugar from New Orleans bound for Buffalo. However, within half-dozen years the railroads laid their tracks and took their toll. It later was more or less the drainage ditch for Chicago's effluent sewage discharges. The canal remained profitable up to 1900, and had a brief resurgence in WW I, but was in disrepair after that and went out of existence with the opening of the Illinois Waterway in 1933.

ILLINOIS AND MISSISSIPPI CANAL

See: HENNEPIN CANAL.

ILLINOIS RIVER

The river is formed by the meeting of the Kankakee and Des Plaines rivers almost 50 miles below Chicago. It flows in a southwesterly course for about 270 miles until it joins the Upper Mississippi River approximately 25 miles above St. Louis at Grafton, IL. The river actually follows an ancient riverbed that at one time was that of the Mississippi River. Eons ago in a glacial period the Mississippi was blocked and was diverted into its present course.

The name comes from a tribe of Indians, the Illiniwek, that were living in the area which the French traders called the *Illinois* so the name was given to the river. In 1675, a Jesuit Priest, Father Marquette, set up a mission, the first European settlement on the river, at Starved Rock. The river itself, and its upper reaches connecting to Lake Michigan, is part of the system called the ILLINOIS WATERWAY (see below).

ILLINOIS WATERWAY

The entire system is about 336 miles long and consists of the CHICAGO RIVER, its North Branch, South Branch, and Main Branch, the Sanitary Ship Canal, and the Cal-Sag Canal, and their entrances through locks to Lake Michigan, as well as where they join together to flow downstream through a series of locks starting at Lockport, IL. They join the Des Plaines River and then, in the pool of Marseilles L & D, join the Kankakee River at mile 273 to become the Illinois River.

Products had moved out of the Illinois River from the early 1700s, shipped by French traders on flatboats. The first steamboats arrived on the river in the Pekin and Peoria area in approximately 1828-9. In 1867 the USACE proposed a seven-foot channel and a series of locks and dams for the waterway, but funds appropriated for it were not sufficient. The State decided to make the improvements itself. They completed a lock and dam at Henry, IL, and later at Copperas Creek. The locks were 350 feet long by 75 feet wide, which allowed upstream traffic from Peoria with access to the I & M CANAL. State-Federal cooperation somewhat deteriorated, but some work continued. Locks and Dams at LaGrange were completed in the late 1880s, and at Kampsville in the early 1890s. The State then decided on the CHICAGO RIVER reversal to increase flow on the Illinois River by diverting water from Lake Michigan, which helped the channel depth on the lower part of the river.

The I & M Canal in the early 1900s was deemed inadequate to handle the commerce that was available to ship on it, so the State voted to improve and widen it, but the monies appropriated were not sufficient. In 1920 the State decided that a new series of locks and dams were needed. Then in 1921 the War Department, where the USACE was then located, approved a plan for five modern L & Ds, 600 feet long by 110 feet wide, with an eight-foot depth. In 1927 Congress authorized a nine-foot channel from Utica, mile 230, to the river's mouth at Grafton. During this period, in 1930, the Supreme Court limited the amount of water that could be diverted from Lake Michigan. Construction began and the upper five locks were completed in 1933, and the lower two, Peoria and LaGrange, finished in 1939. Improvements on the extreme upper end of the waterway were also undertaken, with all completed by 1965.

IMMERSION CHART or SCALE
See: DISPLACEMENT TONNAGE TABLE or SCALE.

IMO
An acronym for the INTERNATIONAL MARITIME ORGANIZATION (see).

IMPEDE
To hinder, delay, obstruct, or prevent another vessel from navigating on its intended course. The term is used in the Navigation Rules 8 and 9, with instructions to certain vessels "not to *impede*" the passage of other vessels in navigation. It comes from the Latin *impedire,* meaning "to shackle one's feet".

IMPELLER
The rotating and driving force of a centrifugal pump used for various dewatering functions on a towboat, tug, or barge.

IMPLIED WARRANTY
In marine insurance the *implied warranty* of a vessel means that at the commencement of a voyage the vessel shall be seaworthy for the trade and service for which it was intended to be employed, and reasonably fit in all respects to weather the ordinary perils that it might be expected to encounter on its journey to destination. Though river towboats do not go to sea, the term "seaworthy" is generic to all vessels.

IMPOUNDMENT
The waters that are confined behind a dam.

IN EXTREMIS
A legal term that applies to the condition where two or more vessels in navigation are approaching each other in such manner that a collision is inevitable unless some action is taken to prevent one. It is then that the vessels are deemed to be *in extremis.* In all vessel encounters there is the stand-on vessel and the give-way vessel. If *in extremis* is reached because the give-way vessel is not doing what is required, the stand-on vessel has a duty <u>not</u> to continue holding course and speed, but to take <u>some</u> action. As the court has said, "There is no right of way on which a vessel is entitled to insist when it is obvious that it will result in danger of collision". The term comes from the use of the "last illness" or "dying declaration" which is final.

IN LINE
1. When RANGE LIGHTS are seen exactly one over the other as a vessel is holding on them marking the centerline of a narrow channel.

2. Machinery shafting that is prop-

erly coupled and aligned one to another is said to be in *line* or properly lined up.

3. Said of a Pilot who is navigating a crossing or a bridge and all factors are in proper alignment to safely proceed without adjustment.

IN PERSONAM

A technical legal term that means an action or proceeding is taking place against a person, such as the master of a vessel, or the company that owns the vessel. The term comes from Roman law.

IN REM

A technical legal term that means an action or proceeding is taking place against property, such as a vessel. The term comes from Roman law.

IN SHAPE

Is used to describe when a Pilot has the tow properly lined up to navigate it through a narrow bridge, or into a lock chamber, or to start a flanking movement, or any other critical navigational maneuver.

IN THE MARKS

Describes when a Pilot has his vessel and/or tow well within the proper alignment crossing from one side of the river to the other, or to line up for a bridge, lock chamber, or navigating in accordance with a channel report.

INBOARD

1. To go, or take something toward the centerline of a vessel, i.e., "Bring that other lockline *inboard* from the port side".

2. The sides of barges coupled up in a tow or fleet, i.e., "When you take that gear out to the head of the tow, walk on the *inboard* side".

3. When a vessel is moored to a dock, or other structure, the *inboard* side is that which is closest to the shore.

4. The opposite of OUTBOARD.

INCHMAREE CLAUSE

A marine insurance term that covers all the hull and machinery of the vessel, including the permanent fittings, stores, provisions for the crew, and bunkers, from losses that might result from a latent defect in a vessel's hull or its machinery, or from errors in navigation, or of the management of a vessel by the master or its crew.

The clause is named after the steamer *INCHMAREE* which was lost in 1887 when, through the negligence of the crew, a pump on a donkey engine feeding water to a boiler burst. Since the losses involved were not deemed due to a peril of the sea, the insurance underwriters were not liable for the losses that were incurred. After that egregious claim by the insurance companies the clause became standard language in marine policies.

INCLINATION

1. The degree of transverse CAMBER from the centerline of a vessel to its sides.

2. The angle or degree of list in a deck, side to side, or fore and aft.

3. The slope or slant of a raked bow or stern.

INCLINING TEST or EXPERIMENT

A test using heavy weights such as concrete blocks, drums of water, etc., to determine a vessel's metacentric height by testing her initial stability. It is not done on barges or towboats unless someone submitted an unusual design for construction. Normal barge and towboat design for the waters in which they travel is not considered conducive to capsizing. It is, however, normal to undertake the test for passenger vessels navigating the Western River system.

INCLINOMETER

See: CLINOMETER.

INDEMNITY
The payment received by the assured from an insurance company for losses incurred under the terms of a policy.

INDICATED HORSEPOWER
See: HORSEPOWER.

INDUSTRIAL CANAL
The Industrial Canal is located in New Orleans. It runs east off the Mississippi River at about mile 92.5 where the entrance to the eastern section of the GIWW is located. Just inside the entrance to the Canal is the Industrial Canal Lock. From here it branches off its confluence with the GIWW and terminates at Lake Pontchartrain. It is also called the *Inner Harbor Navigation Canal*.

Originally the canal was proposed in the early 1800s where Canal Street in New Orleans is presently located, but since there were different levels of water between the Mississippi river and Lake Pontchartrain requiring a stable lock structure, the lock was never built. In 1914 the State of Louisiana authorized New Orleans to build a deep water canal south of the city. Dredging began in 1918 and construction was completed in 1921. A connection to the canal was added extending the GIWW east that enters the Mississippi Sound at the Rigolets, about 33 miles east from the Industrial Canal Lock. Later, in order to bring in ocean freight without requiring ships to navigate the Mississippi River from the Gulf of Mexico, a short-cut deep-water "outlet" channel was dug to connect the Gulf directly with the *Industrial Canal*. It was called the Mississippi River-Gulf Outlet, or MRGO for short. The deep-water channel was authorized to have a 36-foot depth with a 650-foot width; it is 66 miles long. Due to environmental and hurricane dangers it was finally decided in 2008 close it. The present Industrial Lock is being replaced due to capacity constraints. The new lock will be 1200' in length by 110' in width. A depth of 36' is authorized.

INERT GAS SYSTEM
The injection of an *inert gas* such as nitrogen or carbon dioxide into a tank barge, or any other tank that has explosive gases present, to replace the flammable fumes in order to reduce the chance of an explosion.

INEVITABLE ACCIDENT
A legal term used in maritime law for an accident that occurs between two vessels in which no negligence can be imputed to either vessel. The presumption is that both vessels are operating in a lawful manner, so that if no fault can be shown the accident can be said to be *inevitable* regardless if an irresistible force such as an ACT OF GOD is not present. However, in reality this is extremely hard to prove.

INFLAMMABLE
See: FLAMMABLE LIQUID.

INFRASTRUCTURE
On our Western Rivers, the term is associated with the basic organization of the U.S. Army Corps of Engineers, their structures, such as locks and dams, their other facilities, floating plants, buildings, and other capabilities that comprise the components to allow towboats, tugs, and barges to efficiently and safely operate on the river system.

INJECTOR
1. A nozzle unit in a diesel engine that meters the proper amount of fuel, atomizes it, and under high pressure injects it into the combustion chamber of the engine cylinder, allowing the engine to create horsepower.

2. A boiler feedwater device that forces water into the boiler.

INLAND AREA
Generally, the shoreward area of

water that is inward from the line of demarcation that governs inland waters from international waters.

INLAND NAVIGATION RULES
See: NAVIGATION RULES.

INLAND RIVER GUIDE
A guide published annually by the *Waterways Journal* regarding the businesses operating in the mid-continental waterways area. It covers: Barge and Towing Companies, Terminals, Fleeting and Harbor Services, Tankermen, Shipyards and Repair Facilities, Marine Contractors, Dredging Companies, Refuelers, Boat Stores, Brokers of Equipment and Freight, Marine Divers, Salvage Firms, Pollution Control Companies, Dis-tributors and Manufacturer Services, Government Agencies, Associations and Bureaus, and has Lock Statistics and Bridge Clearances.

INLAND RIVER RECORD
First published in 1945 by Capt. Fred Way, Jr., it is now revised annually by the *Waterways Journal* with a listing of all commercial and government vessels of the Mississippi River system, streams emptying into the Gulf of Mexico, and those on the Gulf Intracoastal Waterway. It includes the type of powered vessel, when built and where, whether it has been rebuilt and when, the size of the vessel, its type and make of engines and horsepower, whether or when it has been repowered, when its original name was changed if it has been renamed, if and when it was sold, and who owns or operates the vessel. Also contains much other pertinent information such as kort nozzles, retractable pilothouse, reduction gear, etc.

INLAND RULES
The *Inland Navigation Rules* are the statutory (became regulatory in 2004) rules along with a set of five regulatory Annexes that comprise the rules governing the proper conduct for mariners who are navigating vessels in order to reduce the risk of collision on the Inland Waters of the United States. These rules came into effect after passage of the Navigation Rules Act in 1980. They superseded and unified the various sets of Rules and Pilot Regulations that were in effect for the Great Lakes, Western Rivers, and Inland Waters. The *Inland Rules* closely parallel the International Rules; however, there are some major differences, as follows:

1. *Rule 3* – The *Inland Rules* do not contain a definition for a "vessel constrained by its draft" since the drafters were of the opinion that most of the time vessels operating on the inland waters of the U.S. were in constrained channel conditions and would possibly be constantly claiming the privileges in navigation that the International Rules provide.

2. *Rule 9(a)(ii)* – This *Inland Rule* gives the downbound vessel the right-of-way over an upbound vessel in a narrow channel.

3. *Rule 14* – Again, this *Inland Rule* gives the right-of-way to the downbound vessel over an upbound vessel in a Head-on Situation.

4. *Rule 34(a)* – Provides a major difference between the two sets of Rules. The International Rules provide for SIGNALS OF ACTION, whereas the *Inland Rules* provide for SIGNALS OF INTENT.

5. *Rule 34(c)* – The signals to be exchanged between vessels when overtaking were kept intact in the new unified *Inland Rules* from what they were previously. The drafters believed the old rules were well known and less confusing than those provided for in the new International Rules.

There are other less important differences that can be noted. It is the prudent mariner that reviews and studies the Navigation Rules which apply on a frequent basis to avoid the old maxim of seamen and rivermen, "The best place to know the rules and the worst place to study them is in a collision approach". See: NAVIGATION RULES and RULES OF THE ROAD.

INLAND WATERS

The Inland Navigation Rules define these waters in Rule 3(o) as follows: "Inland Waters means the navigable waters of the United States shoreward of the navigational demarcation lines dividing the high seas from harbors, rivers, and other inland waters of the United States and the waters of the Great Lakes on the United States side of the International Boundary".

INLAND WATERWAYS CORPORATION

The Inland Waterways Corporation was formed as a government entity by an Act of Congress in 1924 which provided for the creation of a company to operate vessels and terminals on the inland waters. Its purpose was to promote the use of waterborne commerce on the internal rivers. After WW II the corporation was sold to private interests in St. Louis (Pott Industries) and became FEDERAL BARGE LINE.

INLAND WATERWAYS REVENUE ACT
INLAND WATERWAYS TRUST FUND
INLAND WATERWAYS USER BOARD (IWUB)

See: USER TAX or CHARGE.

INNER BOTTOM

The void space between the outer shell plate of a vessel's bottom plate and the bottom plate of the compartment above it. All double-hulled vessels have an *inner bottom*. All tank barges now being constructed, and all river hopper barges, have double hulls therefore, all have an *inner bottom*.

INSERT PLATE

When the hull of a vessel has been holed in an incident, the damaged area is cropped out and a piece of plating is cut to size, put in the damaged section and welded in place. This is a required type of repair on vessels required to have a Certificate of Inspection.

INSPECTION

Various *inspections* take place on vessels. A Captain usually makes a cursory one every day, the deckhands check the voids of barges every watch, or engineers tour their spaces looking for anything out of place. The company that operates the boat sends out safety compliance personnel on occasion, and even insurance companies may send out an inspector. The official inspector of vessels, however, is the U.S. Coast Guard. They make *general inspections* for regulation compliance on towboats and tugs, and on tank barges they do a *material inspection* and issue a CERTIFICATE OF INSPECTION. The word is an adaptation from the Latin *inspicere,* meaning "to look into or examine".

Prior to the establishment of the STEAMBOAT INSPECTION SERVICE the only persons conducting any inspection of a vessel was the Captain or Chief Engineer. As described by Samuel Clemens in the 1890s in *Noah's Ark,* as to the procedure that Noah, in biblical times, would be faced with when the Inspector arrived; he would have been asked how it was built, of what material, its designer, the number of passengers aboard, their sex and ages, was there a surgeon aboard, size of crew, their training as seamen, experience at sea, animals aboard (which would require separate cages and the need for more keepers). Since the Ark only had two windows, electric lights would be required to be installed, also pumps. Since no motive power had been installed by Noah, the vessel would require sails or steam. When asked how the Ark was steered,

Noah had no rudder or the ability to maneuver. There were no anchors (six would be required), no lifeboats (25 required), no life preservers (2000 required), etc. And so the inspection went, as it sometimes does today when an Inspector who has never steered a tow comes aboard and issues citations.

INSPECTION PLATE

A steel plate that is bolted onto various sections of machinery, such as engines and gear boxes that can be readily removed if necessary to allow for inspection and repair.

INSPECTOR

An official who is charged with ensuring that rules and regulations are being adhered to in accordance with company orders, contractual obligations, bureau or association protocol, or governmental law or regulations. With regard to tugs, towboats, and tank barges, the term usually refers to an officer or petty officer of the U.S. Coast Guard. During the days of the Steamboat Inspection Service, the *Inspector* was a title given to the persons who inspected steamboats. They were *Hull Inspectors and Boiler Inspectors*.

INSULATED BARGE

Tank barges that have the tanks covered or sheathed with material to protect the cargo from either heat or cold (Cargoes of styrene have insulated coverings to keep the external heat, especially in Gulf-area summers, from polymerizing the cargo; cargoes of liquid sulfur or asphalt are insulated to retain internal heat and insure that they do not cool and solidify.

INSURANCE

See: MARINE INSURANCE, a necessary evil.

INTEGRAL TANK

A tank that is a structural member of a vessel, rather than a separate entity apart from the hull, i.e., a bunker tank or water tank that is a part of the hull of a towboat, or the cargo compartment of a tank barge.

INTEGRATED TOW

At one time most of the barges in commerce on the rivers had a raked bow and stern. These barges were not very efficient to push through the water due to the turbulence between the rake ends. Therefore, marine architects came up with the idea that a barge could have a raked bow and a square stern in order for two barges to be put together, stern to stern, allowing for a smoother hull line. This class of barges is known as semi-integrated. The first barges of this type on the river system were built by Socony-Vacuum (now Exxon-Mobile) in 1940.

Then it was decided to build barges with a square on both ends to put between the semi-integrated barges. These barges are known as box barges. A tow with all semi-integrated barges on the bow and stern of a tow, with all box barges between them, becomes an *integrated tow*. It is believed the first true fully *integrated tow* on the river was built in 1944 by Cargo Carriers, the river operations unit of Cargill, Inc. They built a towboat called the *M/V CARTASCA*, along with a set of barges that operated as a smooth-hull formed single unit in the haulage of grain. The entire unit was built 600' long to just fill a lock chamber on the Upper Mississippi River. See: UNIT TOW.

INTEGRATED TUG BARGE UNIT (ITB)

A tug with a curved bow structure that fits into a notched stern designed specifically for the tug, then marries up to it with a mechanical device. The tug of the unit is usually not designed to do other tug work, either towing astern, harbor handling, or push another barge not designed for its mechanical coupler. However, when the ITB operates as a unit it is very efficient, operating like a ship at sea does. See: COMPOSITE UNIT and TUG-BARGE UNIT.

INTENSITY OF LIGHTS

The *intensity of lights* is the minimum luminous power of navigation lights which vessels are required to display. The Inland Navigation Rules in Annex I lists the calculation formula with the amount of candelas (a measurement of light intensity) the lights are required to display.

INTENTION SIGNALS

The audible signals a tug or towboat will sound on its whistle in accordance with Inland Rule 34(a) and (b) when in sight of another vessel in a meeting or crossing situation of how they *intend* to pass one another; these are termed *Rules of Intention*. The International Rules require ACTION SIGNALS in this situation to indicate the action being immediately taken in directing the course of the vessel. Under Rule 34(c) (overtaking signals), both inland and seagoing vessels will sound *intention signals,* although the sounding requirements are different for the areas of operation.

INTERCHANGE POINT

The place where one towboat will drop barges or the entire tow and pick up other barges for another destination. Major *interchange points* on the river system are St. Louis, MO; Cairo, IL; Baton Rouge, LA; and New Orleans, LA. They are usually located at places of intersecting waterways or where significant tributaries enter a main river as well as at the end of a system like Pittsburgh, PA, St. Paul, MN, and Lemont, IL.

INTERCOSTALS

Short vertical plate stiffeners placed between floor frames.

INTERMEDIATE SHAFT

The drive shaft between the thrust bearing and the propeller shaft.

INTERMODAL TRAFFIC

Cargo that is moved to a point on one form of transportation and then further moved to destination by another form, i.e., when grain is moved from a storage bin on a farm by truck to a rail terminal. From there it is loaded into rail cars that transport it to a river grain terminal where it is loaded into a barge that moves in a tow to a seaport, where it is again transferred into a ship bound for a foreign country. That is *intermodal traffic*; however, in seaport areas it commonly means the interchange of cargo containers between modes of transport.

INTERNATIONAL ASSOCIATION OF LIGHTHOUSE AUTHORITIES (IALA)

The international group that sets the standards for aids to navigation to be displayed around the world. There are two regions, A and B. The United States is in Region B, which uses red buoys on the right and green buoys on the left when coming from the sea, as in "red, right, returning". Region A does just the opposite.

INTERNATIONAL CONVENTION FOR THE SAFETY OF LIFE AT SEA (SOLAS)

A treaty convention that is administered under IMO. Its members meet periodically to review and discuss safety issues. The U.S. Coast Guard represents the U.S. at the meetings. Although the standards that are set and agreed to usually apply only to vessels and seamen in international trade, the dictates handed down often become enacted into its member's state laws. Therefore, personnel involved in the operation of river vessels should always be cognizant of the discussions and recommendations of the various international groups that affect navigation issues.

INTERNATIONAL MARITIME ORGANIZATION (IMO)

This organization was established by the United Nations in 1948 as the Inter-Governmental Maritime Consultative Organization. The name was changed in 1982. The organization is made up of maritime experts from all member nations. It makes recommendations on maritime safety, environmental, operational and legal issues. The U.S. is represented at *IMO* by the U.S. Coast Guard. It is necessary to study the decisions made by IMO. They are often adopted by most nations, becoming International Law. They then may later become incorporated into national statutes. The International Navi-gation Rules are the basis for our domestic rules, however, there are a few important differences. Some originally wanted the IMO rules adopted without change for all U.S. waters. If that had occurred it would have resulted in a set of potentially disastrous and unsafe rules for navigastion on our Western Rivers.

INTERNATIONAL RULES

These *Navigation Rules* were formalized in the Convention on the International Regulations for Preventing Collisions at Sea, 1972, and became effective on July 15, 1977. They are commonly called the *72 COLREGS* although some amendments have been added since they were first adopted. The Rules are applicable on waters outside of the established navigational lines of demarcation in the United States. See: INLAND RULES and NAVIGATION RULES.

INTERPRETATIVE RULES

In the Navigation Rules, Annex V, 33 CFR 90, contains rules the USCG has deemed appropriate to better define how certain sections of the rules will be interpreted.

INTRACOASTAL WATERWAY

Intracoastal refers to the waterways along our Atlantic and Gulf Coast, as opposed to "inter-coastal" which refers to trade or voyages between the different coasts, i.e. the Atlantic, Gulf, and Pacific Coasts. See: GULF INTRACOASTAL WATERWAY.

INVASIVE SPECIE

Aquatic specie that are not indigenous to the inland waters of the U.S. and are a nuisance to the area, such as the zebra mussel.

IRISH PENNANT

A small piece of line tied to an object that is hanging loose or free and serving no purpose.

IRISH SPAGHETTI

Long sections of piping run out over coal barges in a fleet that looked like a mess of spaghetti. They removed accumulated leakage or rain water from the barge hulls by use of a STEAM SYPHON.

IRON CIRCLES

Iron or steel circular rings that are fitted on the outside and inside of a paddlewheel on its ARMS just below where the BUCKET PLANKS are attached. They hold in place the WOODEN CIRCLE, consisting of wooden blocks that are tightly fitted between the arms which are also further tightened by wooden wedges called KEY(S) and wooden GIB(S). The *iron circle* is then tightly bolted together as a main strength member of the paddlewheel.

IRON MIKE

A term sometimes used when referring to an auto-pilot system of steering.

IRONCLADS

Gun vessels of the Civil War on the Western Rivers that had their stern paddlewheel located almost amidships and encased in sloped armored plates, along with armored sides. The first designer was Samuel Pook, who was employed by James Eads, the great engineer and builder. The shape of the vessels led others to call them *Pook's*

Turtles. Some of the ironclads built and used on the rivers were named after cities on the Mississippi and Ohio rivers: the *CAIRO* (which was the first gunboat sunk by an electrically detonated mine), *CARONDELET, CINCINNATI, LOUISVILLE, MOUND CITY, PITTSBURGH,* and *ST. LOUIS*. See: CITY CLASS, COTTONCLADS and TINCLADS.

IRONS
See: CAULKING IRONS

ISLAND
Technically, an area of land surrounded by water. The term comes from the old English *egland,* or "watery land". There are many on the inland river system. When flatboat men first started navigating the rivers they gave the islands different names, either naming them after themselves, someone famous or someone they knew. Sometimes they were given fanciful titles, or their size or location provided inspiration. Others retained their Indian names. Floods destroyed some of them, others were created as the river cut through a meander loop, or a sand bar would build up and trees start growing on it. When Zadok Cramer first published his text and charts covering the navigation of the Lower Mississippi in 1801, he decided to number them, starting with Number One and proceeding downriver until there were over 100 numbered islands from Cairo to New Orleans. Some today still carry the number designation he gave them, a few new ones have built up, and some have disappeared, perhaps in the last high water.

ITB
See: INTEGRATED TUG BARGE UNIT.

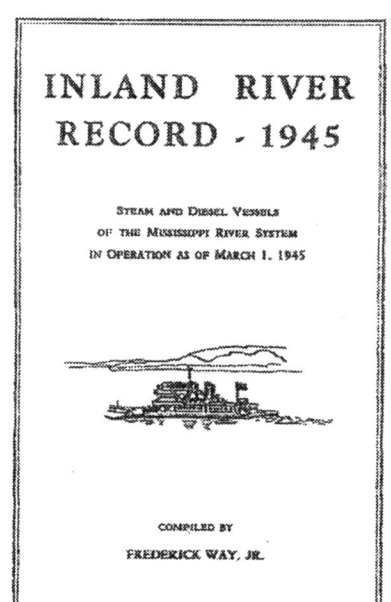

STEAMBOAT SECTION (sample)

SPRAGUE. Sternwheel towboat, steel hull. b. Dubuque, Iowa by Dubuque Boat and Boiler Works, 1902. 276x61x 7.4. Condensing engines, 28's 63's – 12 ft. stroke. Four water tube boilers Foster-Wheeler. 1600 h.p. Oil burner. Largest and most powerful sternwheel boat for inland River service. First owned by Monongahela River Consolidated Coal & Coke Co., Pittsburgh, Pa. and preformed several prodigious feats handling coalboats and 4 barges comprising 1,750,000 bushels of coal in a single unit and delivered it safely. Bought in summer of 1917 by Aluminum Ore Co., East St. Louis. In June, 1925, bought by Standard Oil Co. of La., and has been operated by this firm since. The paddlewheel of this boat, originally 40 by 40 feet, was altered to 36 ft. diameter while the boat was new. She has 21 buckets, each with 4-feet dip.

The RECORD listed 41 pages of steamboats and 48 pages for towboats in its diesel section. The current 2009 book has 423 pages of listings for diesel inland river vessels but no steamboats as none are currently moving freight.

INTEGRATED TOW

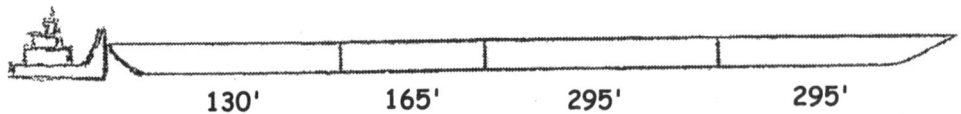

An efficiently designed unit of four barges being pushed by a towboat that will glide through a body of water with a minimum amount of water resistance. The total unit is constructed to be about 1190' long. The lead barge is approximately 295' long with a fairly long rake and a square stern. The second barge from the head or the tow is also 295' with a square bow and stern. The next barge is approximately 165' also with a square bow and stern. The fourth barge at the stern of the tow has a square stern that is coupled to the third barge. Its bow is raked, but it is more blunt than the bow lead barge. This allows for a less turbulent flow of water reaching the towboat that will be pushing the unit.

All barges are approximately 50' to 54' in width. The towboat pushing the tow is about 130' in length, making the total footage of the entire tow under 1200' or less than twice the distance of a 600' lock on many stretches of the river system.

This configuration allows a tow to enter a 600' x 110' lock chamber, tie off the two lead barges then knock loose the coupling wires between the second and third barges. The stern two barges and towboat will then go alongside the two lead barges and the whole tow can be locked at one time.

After the chamber is raised, or lowered, as the case may be, the tow will be slowly moved out of the chamber and the towboat with the two stern barges will drop behind the two lead barges. The deck crew will recouple the two sections of barges together with their holding wires and the total tow will again be underway to the next lock.

USS CAIRO - IRONCLAD GUNBOAT
From USACE publication

J

JACK

A device, usually screw or hydraulic, that is used to lift heavy weights. Also used to jockey large, heavy pieces of machinery into place, and often utilized to turn the shaft on an engine.

JACKASS

At one time *jackasses* were used on canals to pull vessels. On rivers they were employed to walk on a treadmill as the propelling power on some ferryboats. The only real *jackasses* on tugs and towboats today should possibly go back to walking that treadmill.

JACKKNIFE

The breaking of tow wires on one side of a tow causing a barge, or part of the tow, to swing around in the fashion of closing a pocket *jackknife*. This can happen by accident, such as hitting ground, a pier, or a wall; or it can be done deliberately while making up or rearranging tow, i.e., when a Pilot tells the crew, "*Jackknife* that lead starboard barge and let it slide down the tow and we'll let her slip into the notch on the stern". See below, JACKKNIFE LOCKAGE.

JACKKNIFE LOCKAGE

Rather than double-lock, a number of tows on short runs tow eight jumbo barges. The efficient way to run the tow this size is two wide and four long. For 600-foot long locks, this tow would be over 900 feet long, including the towboat, but only 70 feet wide. However, since the lock is 110 feet wide, the entire surface area of the lock can be utilized by *jackknifing* the tow and the boat as follows:

1. Tow enters lock.
2. Ties off three barges, the two bow barges and one aft of one of the bow barges. Tied off barges are 70 feet wide at bow with a notch under the two lead barges.
3. Towboat shifts remainder of five barges in tow up so the now spike barge goes alongside the two bow barges while the other four go up into the notch, leaving a space or notch on the stern.
4. The towboat breaks loose the FACE WIRES to the tow and maneuvers into the remaining space in the lock.
5. The lock tender lowers or raises, as the case may be, the lock chamber, then opens the gates.
6. The towboat slowly pushes the tow out through the chamber, then backs around as soon as there is room and replaces her face wires on the tow where they previously were attached.
7. As soon as the face wires between boat and tow are tight the Pilot backs down the *jackknifed* part of the tow and the deck crew uses a SWING LINE to bring the barges up in place with the three other barges, then quickly catches and hooks the coupling wires.

This is all done on the run and the tow is then finally on its way to the next lock. See: SET OVER SINGLE.

JACKSTAFF

A long upright pole rigged at the centerline bow of a tow, usually with a small company flag or just a white piece of material to show which way the wind is blowing. It often has a PEEP LIGHT attached to it, although some Pilots disdain its use. The pole and the peep light, sometimes called a swing light, assist the Pilot in easily holding the tow on course and watching the rate of swing against the background in front of the tow. The barge on which the *jackstaff* is rigged is commonly called the *jackstaff* barge.

JACOB'S LADDER

A portable flexible ladder usually made with rope sides and wooden steps that can be used to go into the hold of a barge. Not often seen in river trades. It is sometimes used by harbor Pilot to board or debark from a ship. The term refers to stairs rising to heaven as Jacob dreamed of in Genesis 28.

JAIL

A term for what is called a *brig* at sea or in the Navy. It is an informal place of confinement for miscreants or malcontents, mostly found on excursion boats for use by those who may have imbibed more alcoholic beverages in their digestive tracts than they could to handle. The last one known on a Western River vessel was a cage of iron bars about 4' by 4' that was on board the *BELLE OF LOUISVILLE* (ex-*AVALON*, ex-*IDLEWILD*), used to hold rambunctious or unruly persons. To reduce weight it was removed from the vessel at the turn of the 21st century. Apparently everyone has become more civil on the river and it was no longer needed?

J. BENNETT JOHNSTON WATERWAY

See: RED RIVER.

JAM

1. A line that was tied fast to a deck fitting that can not be loosened without cutting it with an axe is said to be *jammed*. See AXE KNOT.
2. If a line in a block becomes kinked or will not reeve through.
3. When a vessel is stuck in ice, it is said it is in an ice *jam*.
4. Log rafts that were stopped in a river due to an obstruction or low water.

JET DOWN

The act of using water pressure to force an anchor device into an alluvial riverbed in order to hold a navigation buoy. The anchor is called a PIE PLATE ANCHOR. This method of setting and holding buoys is the main way the Missouri River channel is marked.

JETSAM

Cargo or material cast overboard to lighten a vessel that is in distress and taking on water, or to make way through a vessel to fight a fire or other emergency. It is material that sinks under the water, or washes ashore. Value of the material so disposed is not generally recoverable under insurance terms unless the cargo was carried in a manner that was the "custom of the trade", which would then probably be decided in a court. See: FLOTSAM and LAGAN.

JETTISON

The act of throwing cargo overboard to lighten a vessel that is in danger of sinking, or which is aground and the crew is attempting to get it afloat, especially when the stage of the river is falling.

JETTY

1. A structure built out into the water but attached to land, such as a wharf, quay, large pier, or similar construction, sometimes also serving as a breakwater.
2. Structures similar to dikes that are used in the delta passes of the lower Mississippi River, constructed by James B. Eads in the 1870s to constrict the current in order for the flow of water to scour and deepen the channel. The building of *jetties* in the passes had been tried before and failed but the Eads plan worked, allowing New Orleans to become the world-class port that it is today.
3. Synonymous with subtle differences from terms such as DIKE, GROIN, and WEIR.

JEWELRY

All of the rigging on a tow used to couple barges together: the wires, ratchets, bull chains, shackles, chain links, slings, etc. The term came to refer to precious stones in the medieval days used for adornment on one's clothing. The word as utilized in river trades describes the ornamentation holding a tow together that makes it a thing of beauty in moving commerce.

JIGGER

A light luff tackle consisting of a single and a double block, both with hooks. It has a mechanical advantage of three or four, depending upon which block is the moving one. It is sometimes called a *handy-billy*.

JIGGER PUMP

A small portable pump used for pumping water from barges.

JINGLE BELL

One of the bells that sounded in the engine room when the Pilot of a steamboat wanted to change speed according to a set pattern of signals. It is also called a *chestnut bell*. See: ENGINE ROOM BELLS or SIGNALS.

JOCKEY BAR(S)

Steel bars or rods that are attached to join a vessel's rudder quadrants together, when there are two or more on a vessel, to ensure that the rudders work in tandem when the vessel is changing course. When the steering wheel or levers are moved, all steering rudders will move together as a unit at the same time and at the same rate of turn. The same is true for the flanking rudders. When the flanking levers are positioned either to port or starboard, the *jockey bar(s)* make certain the rudders will turn in unison.

JOCKEY WIRES or LINES

1. Crossed wires leading from the H-bitts on the head of a towboat to fittings on the stern of the tow to keep the towboat from sliding when it is faced up to its tow.
2. Leads of wires laid and fastened at an angle between strings of barges. One set will lead forward while another set will lead aft. Similar to SCISSOR WIRES.
3. Fore and aft *jockey wires* are used to couple barges end-on-end, with the wire made up to the timberheads on each side of the outside barge corners. They must be laid in pairs. The pulling ends lead off the end of one barge, cross over toward the center of the other barge, and hook into a ratchet fastened to a cavel or button. This arrangement keeps the barges from sliding at the coupling, which could cause a notch in the tow.
4. It is unknown as to the use of *jockey* in river terminology. It is sometimes employed when maneuvering gear into position, i.e. "I'll get a crowbar and see if I can get enough leverage to *jockey* the timber into place". This is in some sense the action of a *jockey* on a horse weaving and maneuvering the horse through a field to the finish line. However, the use of *jockey wires* on a tow is to keep barges from maneuvering from side to side. Therefore, it might be that the term was/is used in the sense to stop *jockeying,* or any type of sliding movement.

JOGGLE LAP or PLATE

A steel plate that is sharply crimped to fit over another plate. This allows a shipyard some small leeway when fitting up long lengths of plate and welding them together, instead of making a butt joint. When the internals of the vessel fitted with a watertight bulkhead a "waterstop weld" has to be made at the bulkhead in order to prevent water from flowing between compartments through the gap in the *joggle* since the *joggled plates* are not continuously welded on the inside of the hull.

JOHN BOAT

A flat-bottomed work boat, usually with a square bow and stern that is carried aboard towboats. It also may be called a yawl or a skiff. Some from the southland even call it a PIROGUE, but it really isn't.

JOINT(S)

A connection between two or more separated parts. There are many various types of joints that are employed on vessels, such as: ball, corrugated, expansion, flanged, flexible, as well as others. The following are a few of the more common types of *joints:*

1. *Butt* – A connection between two or more separated parts, such as the side-to-side *butting* (placing together) of two steel plates that are then joined by a welded seam.

2. *Joggle Lap* – See.

3. *Pipe* – The joining together of lengths of pipe with a fitting that either extends their over-all length, or allows them to branch off in various directions to join other pipelines.

JOLLY ROGER

Supposedly the pirate's black flag with a skull and cross bones; however, no one has seen one (at least not bona fide) on the river, at least not since the days of Jean Lafitte. However, there have been thugs and robbers in times past who might be considered pirates. See: CAVE IN ROCK.

JONES ACT

The so-called *Jones Act* is named after its chief sponsor, Senator Wesley L. Jones, of Washington. The legislation passed by voice vote in 1920 and there is no statutory history attached to it. The law contains many provisions, some of which have gone by the board, but two sections are of vital interest to persons on the river and general maritime industry. They are sections 20 and 27.

Section 20 deals with the actions that are available to a "seaman" or his estate in the case of injury or death. However, the Act did not define a "seaman", which has resulted in continuing interpretations by the Courts. The section, as originally passed, states:

"Any seaman who shall suffer personal injury in the course of his employment may, at his election, maintain an action for damages at law, with the right of trial by jury, and in such action all statutes of the United States modifying or extending the common-law right or remedy in cases of personal injury to railway employees shall apply; and in case of the death of any seaman as a result of any such personnel injury the personal representative of such seaman may maintain an action for damages at law with the right of trial by jury, and in such action all statutes of the United States conferring or regulating the right of action for death in the case of railway employees shall be applicable. Jurisdiction in such actions shall be under the court of the district in which the defendant employer resides or in which his principal office is located".

Section 27 clarified the cabotage provisions of vessel operations in U.S. coastwise, intercoastal, and noncontiguous trades, reserving them for U.S.-built vessels, manned by U.S. crews. We have had cabotage laws since 1817 in the U.S., but the *Jones Act* was more specific. It states:

"No merchandise shall be transported by water, or by land and water, on penalty of forfeiture thereof, between points in the United States, including Districts, Territories, and possessions thereof embraced within the coastwise laws, either directly or via a foreign port, or for any part of the transportation, in any other vessel than a vessel built in and documented under the laws of the United States and owned by persons who are citizens of the United States, or vessels to which the privilege of engaging in the coastwise trade is extended by sections 18 or 22 of this Act..."

There have, of course, been amendments and various interpretations to the language in these two statements by the courts, but the forgoing is what most mariners are talking about when the infamous *Jones Act* is mentioned. See: CABOTAGE.

JOURNAL

The part of a rotating shaft that rests in a bearing, usually called a *journal bearing*.

JUG BOAT
A small steamer that took jugs of whiskey up the shallow tributaries of the Missouri River and other streams to sell or trade for goods to bring downstream. On some streams, a cargo of jugs coming downriver was the major trade.

JUMBO BARGE
The most common-sized barge utilized on the Mississippi River and GIWW systems. They are either 195 or 200 feet long by 35 feet wide, designed to fit three wide (105 feet) and five long with a towboat pushing them (approximately a total of 1185 feet in length) in a lock that is 1200 feet long by 110 feet wide. At the turn of the 21st century this size of barge made up about 85 percent of the barging fleet on the Western River system. At a nine-foot draft the barges hold between 1400 and 1600 tons of cargo.

This type barge probably received the size designation when they were starting to be built since they each carried an average of about 500 tons more cargo than the commonly used STANDARD BARGE (175' by 26'). It was sort of like the baby elephant and the big adult one that was often called "Jumbo" in the circus. Presently the *jumbo barge* IS the "standard type" of barge being used; but there are many other sized barges on the river and canal system that are of greater length, width, and capacity than the *jumbo*, especially in the liquid trades.

JUMP SHIP or BOAT
To leave a towboat or tug without permission.

JUNCTION
1. The point where two navigable streams or rivers meet and join one another.
2. Where two or more channels intersect.
3. A type of buoy which is set to mark intersecting channels.

JUNE RISE
Traditionally, the large annual rise in the river stages, oftentimes on the Upper Mississippi and Missouri rivers when the spring rains come and snowmelt runoff occurs in the upper elevations of their valleys. Also, in the Ohio Basin tributaries start flowing to the mother stream and begin claiming old drift they had previously left behind and sending commerce on a new journey. See: SPRING RISE.

JUNK LINE
Worn out or heavily frayed lock line that is used for barge LEAVING LINE, or is made into BUMPERS. When caulking was performed on wooden hulled vessels the fibers of *junk line* were cut and pulled apart to become OAKUM.

JURISDICTION
As on land, there are various agencies that have control and authority over the river environment, including its vessels and the crews that who are employed on them, i.e. the U.S. Coast Guard, U.S. Army Corps of Engineers, Environmental Protection Agency, Public Health Agency, Occupational Safety and Health Agency, and many others. All have their *jurisdictional* area, sometimes overlapping one another. It is a price we pay for operating in the United States.

JURY RIG
A temporary or emergency makeshift type of repair to enable a piece of gear or a vessel to continue its work until a permanent repair can be made. The word probably derives from the Latin *adjutare*, meaning "to help".

JUSTICE
That, which one receives according to the law, be it favorable or unfavorable, for one's actions. In steamboat days, *justice* was usually what the Captain of the steamer decided was "just". Maybe it was not fair (in certain eyes), but nevertheless, final. The term derives from the Latin *justitia*, meaning "rightly".

JACKASS FERRY

Illustration from Steamboat Navigation (Croil)

In the 1800s there were numerous ferries that were powered by jackasses, or more often horses. The animals were usually in a narrow stall arrangement with the deck consisting of a treadmill. Although there were some with only one treadmill, usually there were two. When the ferry was ready to leave its landing a gear was released and as the jacks moved forward and the treadmill rotated a shaft that was geared to a sidewheel, sometimes one on each side, which would turn to provide propulsion to the ferry. After steam power became more readily available the jackasses returned to pull a plow or wagons.

JAIL

The pictured area of confinement was used on the Str. BELLE OF LOUISVILLE (and previous designations). It was the place that Capt. Doc Hawley and other Masters of the vessel would lock up persons who needed an attitude adjustment when they became overly rowdy. It has been reported that as many as six persons have been jammed into it at one time. Apparently the clientele from around the greater Louisville area have become much more genteel as the jail was removed in 2007 from its not too pleasant location near the bilge area of the engine room. It now can be observed at the Howard Steamboat Museum.

JIGGER PUMP

A portable pump used for numerous functions aboard towboats and barges, mainly to discharge water of hull leakage accumulated in the voids of a damaged barge

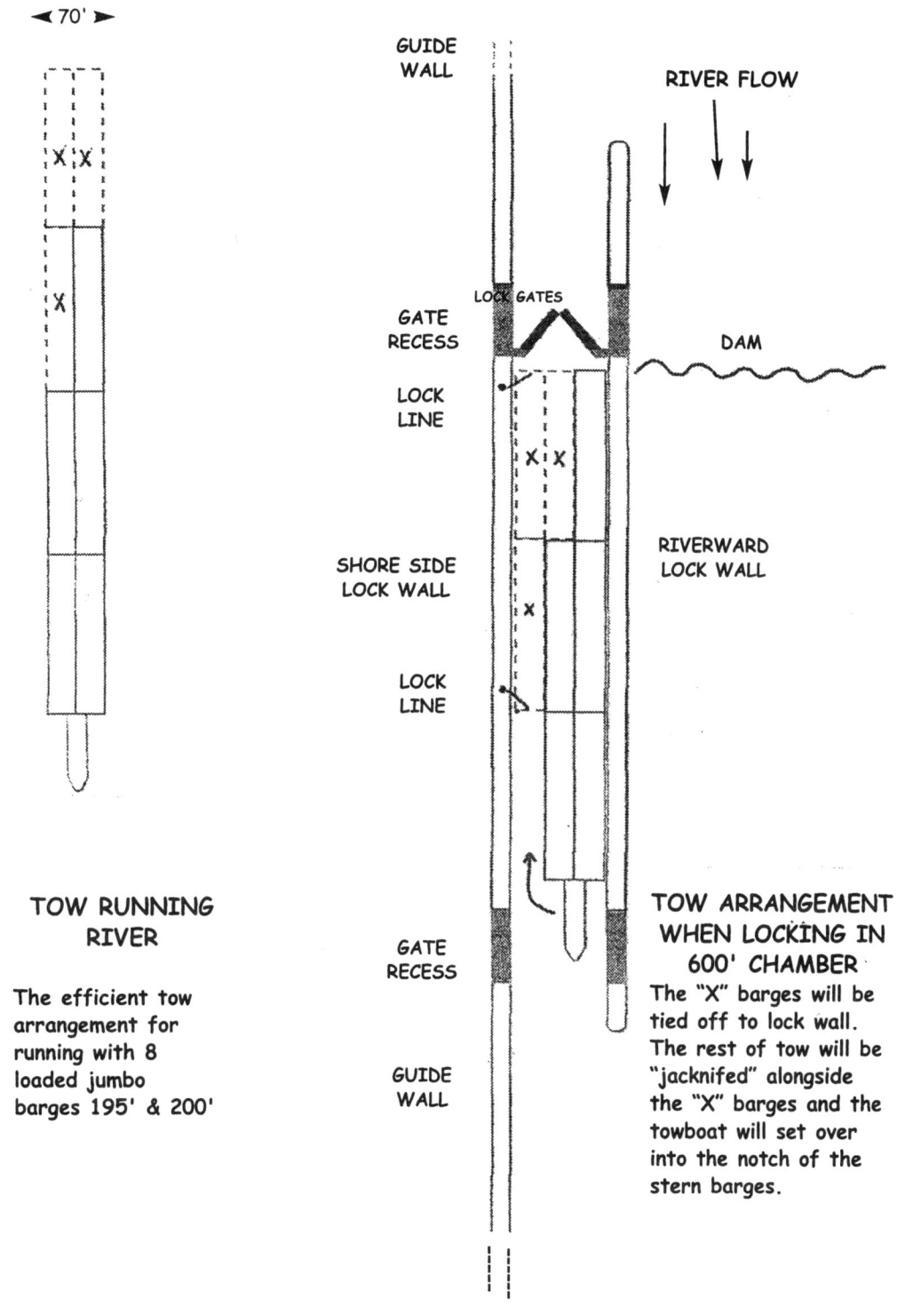

K

KANAWHA RIVER

The river is oftentimes referred to as the Great Kanawha. It is formed by the New River flowing out of North Carolina and the Gauley River formed in the mountains of West Virginia. They join together to form the State's largest navigable stream, the Kanawha. It was given numerous and various names by different Indian tribes who lived in the area. Early writers gave it some variations, terming it the Kenawah, the Kanonova, and others. Thomas Jefferson when writing of it called the river the Great Kanhaway, considering the New and Kanawha as one stream.

After the formation of the United States it was hoped to link the Kanawha with the James River in Virginia by a canal. It was highly advocated by George Washington. Work on building the canal was eventually done by the James River Company. However, floods, the Civil War and railroad competition never allowed the canal to be completed.

Early traffic on the Kanawha, like on most steams, was logging. Rafts were floated out about two-thirds of the year when there was enough water for them to clear the shoal areas. Salt became the main trade of flatboats built on the banks above Charleston. Later coal became the most important commodity shipped on the river which has continued to the present time along with extensive chemical production in the valley loaded into and from tank barges.

The first steamboat traffic on the river started about 1820 with a steamer making it up river to Charleston. Some basic improvements in the channel were made in an attempt to ensure a three foot depth to move coal out of the basin, but all work halted during the Civil War. The State of West Virginia was formed in 1863 and took over some waterway improvements and collected tolls to operate the system, but in 1881 it gave the federal government authority over the Kanawha River. The U.S. then undertook the building of a system of eleven locks and dams to improve navigability which was completed in 1898. It was the first stream in the U.S. to have movable wicket weir dams built. These improvements led to large movements of coal out of the Kanawha basin.

In the early 1930's the old system of eleven locks and dams was revamped and replaced with three fixed dams and locks. Presently the river is navigable in its lower reaches by the impoundment of water from the Robert C. Byrd dam (old Gallipolis L & D) on the Ohio River. Three other dams on the Kanawha River, Winfield, Marmet, and London, provide a nine foot project channel to the river's head of navigation above Montgomery, WV, at about mile 90. In the 1990's and into the new century these three locks are being replaced and enlarged to meet modern commercial needs.

KANAWHA RIVER RATCHET

See: CAJUN RATCHET.

KANKAKEE RIVER

The river was originally about 240 miles long starting its flow in northwestern Indiana and meandering through a great swamp of approximately 5300 square miles that was navigable by Indian canoe and later French fur traders. It was traveled by LaSalle and Father Hennepin in the late 1600's traveling between Lake Michigan and the Mississippi River. In later years as settlers moved in much of the wetlands were drained, the timber logged off and the land was cleared for agriculture. The river's course is now about 90 miles in length where it joins the Des Plains River south of Chicago at mile 273, just above the Dresden Island L & D, to form the ILLINOIS RIVER.

The name of the river apparently in the early times was called the River of the Miami for the Indian tribe who lived there. Later the Potawatomi tribe called it the Theakiki or Tian-kakeek (of various spellings) that Europeans translated to "wolf" for the name they called a different tribe, however some believed it meant "wonderful river", or "low land" (for it was mostly a swamp encompassing over 5300 square miles of territory). The French wrote the name as Qui-que-que or Quin-qui-qui.

The only early trade on the river was by canoe. Later when the drainage occurred there was some traffic by boat for a short time, but railroads soon took its place as the desired way to move freight, and when the I & M CANAL was completed in 1848 it carried the trade by water from Chicago to points south on the Illinois River and below.

KANSAS RIVER or KAW

The name of the river derives from various Indian tribes in the area who called it KeNze, meaning "south wind". It is also called the Kaw River by people in the area. Its name later also was given as the State of Kansas.

The river begins its journey from as far west as Colorado. Numerous rivers flowing out of the foothills and plains areas of the basin join in main force with the Smoky Hill River. Other tributaries join the Republican River flowing out of the State of Nebraska and, at its confluence with the Smoky Hill River, they form the *Kansas River*. The *Kansas* flows easterly about 180 miles to its mouth, joining the Missouri River at Kansas City, KS.

Canoes and BULL BOATS were the original means of transportation on the river by the Indians and the fur traders. The Chouteau trading company out of St. Louis maintained trade relations with the Indians for its business and started operating keelboats on the river in 1828. In 1854 steamboats arrived, with some going as far up as Fort Riley near where Junction City is located. Wheat and corn were the main commodities that came downstream. The end of steamboating occurred in about 1864 when railroaders convinced Kansas state legislators to declare the river non-navigable in order that they could build fixed bridges across the stream without an opening in them to allow navigational access for steamboats. Although later in the 1800s the USACE recommended navigation improvements to the river and bridge openings, which would have been beneficial to the region's citizens, the railroads continued to be in opposition and no improvements were undertaken.

KAPOK

A very buoyant water-resistant fiber that is used in life jackets and work vests.

KASKASKIA RIVER

The river is about 320 miles in length, being the second longest in the State of Illinois. It originates in the central-eastern section of the State of Illinois. Originally it terminated into the Upper (Middle) Mississippi at Chester, IL, but the Mississippi changed course in the late 19th century and the mouth of the Kaskaskia is now about 10 miles north of Chester. The name of the river is taken from that of the Indian tribe that lived in the area.

The French were the first Europeans to settle at the *Kaskaskia River* with an outpost in 1700 to minister to the local Indian tribes. After the establishment of the United States, settlers pushed west of the Allegheny range and staked claims all the way to the Mississippi River. The settlement of Kaskaskia became the first capitol of Illinois. In 1785, "the year of the great waters", a flood of record occurred on the Upper Mississippi River with waters rising 30 feet above the former highest known level. The flood waters virtually wiped out everything at Kaskaskia.

Little boat commerce occurred in the Kaskaskia basin due to shoal conditions. However, in 1962 the USACE was authorized to build a lock and dam project near the mouth of the *Kaskaskia River* to provide a nine foot navigable channel up to Fayetteville, IL, a distance of about 35 miles by straightening and making some cut-offs in the bends. The L & D effort was completed in 1973 to provide economic development and to transport coal from mines in the southern part of Illinois.

KECKLING

Chafing gear consisting of old line used on wire to protect it from excessive wear. Seldom used on the river for wire, but a form of it is being used for some of the extremely strong synthetic lines to prevent wear and prolong their life, a practice which could be termed *keckling*. See: CHAFE or CHAFING.

KEDGE

A lightweight anchor that was used by steamboats after having gone aground or were trying to go over a sandbar. The anchor with a long line attached was taken upriver, depending on the situation, by a john boat or yawl and dropped to make it fast, or bite into the riverbed. The steamboat, with its engine running full ahead, would take up the line on its capstan to pull, or *kedge* the steamer across the bar. The term comes from Old English, which signified a "brisk movement". Vessels in sea harbors gave the name to the small anchor that could be quickly and easily run out to move or warp a vessel to a different position in the anchorage. River steamboating not only used the name for the anchor, but also for the actual movement of warping.

KEEL (a)

On a tugboat with a V-shaped hull like most ships, the traditional *keel* is the main centerline structure running longitudinally from bow to stern, becoming the backbone of the vessel from which the framing rises. Since towboats and barges are flat-bottomed the *keel* is the bottom fore and aft plating on the centerline of a vessel first laid down during construction.

The main longitudinal bottom framing of a towboat is not usually on the centerline, nor does it necessarily run the full length of the vessel. It is used to support the engine(s) that drive the vessel and become the engine(s) bed, or engine KEELSON. These are the deepest and heaviest frames in the hull and provide the main longitudinal strength of the towboat.

Barges usually have transverse floor framing with the floor of the barge's cargo compartment attached to these frames. Their longitudinal strength is in the side plates of the hull and of the cargo box, with additional longitudinal framing in the voids and the deck plate. Like towboats, no typical *keel* is needed.

The old shallow-draft steamboats were very limber and received their stiffness and longitudinal strength from HOG CHAINS. Since they traveled in waters with very little depth, they could not have an extra protrusion on their bottoms that a typical *keel* would provide. It could also impair the type of steering necessary in a shallow, winding river. The term *keel* comes from the Norse *kjolr*, which meant "a ridge".

KEEL (b)

1. Blocks – The heavy blocked timbers in a drydock or on a hauling ways upon which a vessel rests while it is being repaired so that the bottom can be inspected and surveyed as necessary.

2. Cooler – A structure that is attached to the hull of a power-driven vessel that contains piping or a heat exchanger from the engine(s) of the vessel to cool its water temperature. The cooler may be inverted channels welded to the hull. See: SKIN COOLER.

3. Depth – The vertical distance from the waterline to the lowest or deepest part of the keel, sometimes called the keel line.

4. *Even* – A vessel is said to be "on an even keel" when the fore and aft, as well as the port and starboard, draft readings are the same.

5. *Laying* – The first stage of building a vessel, to which the rest of the vessel's structures are attached.

KEELBOAT

The *keelboat* of the Western Rivers had a pointed (model) bow and stern and was about 40 to 80 feet long by about 10 to 15 feet wide, with a draft of about two feet when loaded. The hull had a heavy timber keel with frames emanating upward from it that resulted in slightly rounded sides. They could carry about from 15 up to 50 tons of cargo, and were propelled downstream by the speed of the current, or rowed by the crew; sometimes they were helped by the wind if rigged with a sail. Upstream the *keelboat* would make 10 to 20 miles per day, depending upon the stretch of the river and the speed of the encountered current. When going upstream they would generally be poled by the crew planting their poles in the water and walking the length of the *keelboat's* narrow side deck, continually repeating the process. They would sometimes be CORDELLED or WARPED upriver. The downbound *keelboat* had a crew of about seven men but would increase the number to 10 or 12 when going upriver.

MIKE FINK was the legendary icon of the *keelboat* era. He could apparently, so the story goes, shoot straighter, fight harder, and drink more whiskey than any other boatman on the river. He was born in the late 1700s and was shot to death in 1822.

KEELER

1. One of the crew on board a KEELBOAT.
2. A nickname for a keelboat.

KEELHAUL

A practice of punishment for wrong-doing on sailing ships of the navies of the world between the 15th to 17th centuries. A line would be tied to the end of a yard on the mast on one side of the ship, then run under the ship and attached to the yard on the other side of the ship. The punished seaman would be hoisted to one yard, tied to the line and dropped into the sea. He would then be pulled under the ship and up the other side. A weight would be placed in the line so the seaman would not be severely cut up by the sharp barnacles attached to the hull. Usually he would be knocked out by bumping his head on the bottom and would drown. Few seamen survived. The practice was stopped by the end of the 1700s, as was BOWSPRITTING, in favor of the more humane (at the time) form of getting one's attention by using the Cat-o-nine tails. As far as is known, no *keelhauling* was done on the Western Rivers. It may be used, however, as an idle threat to a crewman who has made a mistake, i.e., "If you do that again I'll have you *keelhauled*". Since the art of *keelhauling* is said to have originated with the Dutch, the term derives from their word, *kielhalen*, which would mean "hauling under the boat".

KEELSON

Also spelled *Kelson* and pronounced that way, kel-son. Since towboats do not have the traditional KEEL, the *keelson* becomes the supporting heavy deep frames welded to the bottom plate that has become the "keel" of the towboat and that support the engine(s), running fore and aft as well as lending to the vessel's longitudinal strength.

KEEP HER

A command, an admonishment, or simply advice, in regard to the vessel or when doing work, i.e., "*Keep her* off the red buoy line, they're sitting in shallow water", or such as referring to a piece of rigging or line, i.e., "*Keep her* clear of the pump engine when you let her go, men".

KEEPER

A slip ring that slides over a locking device such as a PELICAN HOOK in a ratchet and secures the hook to the wire, chain, or sling to which the ratchet is attached.

KEEPER CHAIN or LINE

A small chain or length of line that is wrapped around a wire and secured to keep it taut when taking it off a windlass or other means of hauling in the slack. The wire is then secured to a fitting such as a cavel or set of timberheads and the *keeper chain* is released.

KEEPER PIN

See: DAGGER PIN

KENTUCKY RIVER

The source of the river falls out of the Appalachian Mountains near Kentucky's border with Virginia. Eventually three forks, the North Fork, Middle Fork, and South Fork come together at Beattyville, KY, to form the *Kentucky River*. It meanders in a northwesterly fashion past the State Capitol at Frankfort and finally discharges at Carrollton, KY, into the Ohio River, mile 546. The river had been given various names by early explorers. The origin of *Kentucky* for both the river and the Commonwealth is obscure. Various hypotheses have been put forth but none have been fully resolved. The most reasonable is that the name comes from the Iroquois Indian word *kentake*, which meant "prairie" or "meadow land".

Early travel on the river was by flatboat and keelboat. The main cargoes taken out were tobacco and bourbon whiskey. Small steamers first appeared in about 1816, mostly used for short periods of sufficiently high water and then only to Frankfort, about 65 miles above the mouth. However, there is evidence that steam-propelled craft were used on the *Kentucky River* before Fulton supposedly invented the steamboat. Also, John Fitch built working steamboats on the river but had problems with obtaining patents.

Surveys were made of the river by the Army Engineers in the late 1820s which recommended slack-water navigation and other improvements, but the federal government was not in favor of internal improvements which only affected a single state. Then the State decided to build a series of five dams with locks, 145' by 38', for year round navigation to above Frankfort. They were completed in 1842. Tolls were charged but the receipts were a disappointment. The Civil War stopped any further improvements and the structures fell into a state of disrepair. Various ventures were initiated to revitalize the lock and dam system to pre-war status but they all failed.

In 1880 the State gave jurisdiction of the river to the federal government. The U.S. repaired the five original locks and dams and built nine more up to Beattyville, the head of navigation, with the thought it would promote coal transport. The construction project was completed in 1917, but the river never became a commercial success. Some coal did move from the mines. Patrick Calhoun, who later founded American Commercial Barge Line which eventually became the largest barge line in the country, had his start in moving coal out of Beattyville to the Ohio River. Log rafting was one of the main cargoes on the river, but the last raft that floated down was in 1940. Eventually, as traffic died out, only Locks 1 and 2 (the oldest locks on the Western Rivers built in 1839) had any commercial lockage, which consisted of sand and gravel moving to Frankfort. The *TIMOTHY G* was the last commercial boat which travelled out in 2001. Therefore, the Corps of Engineers entered into an arrangement to return the structures and jurisdiction of the river back to the State of Kentucky.

KEVEL

On early steamboats it referred to a

carved wooden post with arms on the top of a timber. On old seagoing ships it was a term that referred to a holding device to secure halyards or other small lines. On recreational vessels and yachts a somewhat larger version is used to secure these vessels when mooring; however, it is not the size of the CAVEL (see) now used on towboats and barges. The term derives from the Old French *cheville*, meaning a "pin" or "leg".

KEVLAR LINE

A trade name for an extremely strong material that is used in some towboat fastenings where a strong, but light, line is desirable. It is very expensive compared to other lines or wires. It should be handled carefully since it will chafe or wear easily.

KEY(S) & KEYWAY

1. A *keyway* is a slot cut in a shaft or in a flanged fitting. When an appliance is fitted to the shaft, such as a gear or a propeller, a machined metal rectangular tapered *key* is inserted into the *keyway* in order to insure correct positioning and to keep the shaft from slipping on the appliance to which it is attached.

2. Wooden wedges that are used to tighten the wood blocks between the paddlewheel arms in the IRON CIRCLE. They are driven in between the ARM and the GIB.

KICK HER

A term used to get a vessel or tow turning, usually when moving at slow or moderate engine speed. The rudders are put hard over and the engine speed is increased to give more rudder power and turning movement. Also the Pilot may relay to a deck mate when moving very slowly ahead, "I'm going to *kick her* ahead a little", meaning he/she is going to increase the rate of travel through the water.

KICK LINE

The use of a line to hold the stern of a towboat fast while working the rudders and engine(s) in order to maneuver, or *kick*, the head of the tow out into the river before turning loose.

KICKER DIKE

A dike that is placed parallel to a channel, usually at the end of a revetment where the shoreline ends and recedes from the flow of the current. It is sometimes used as another name for a SPUR DIKE.

KILL OUT

The act of stopping the engine(s). Also, the act of backing down to stop all headway.

KILOGRAM (kg)

A metric unit of mass, but is used in measuring the weight of the mass. As such a *kilogram* is equal to 1000 grams, or approximately 2.205 pounds.

KILOMETER (km)

A metric unit of measurement that is equal to 1000 meters, or approximately 0.62 miles.

KILOWATT (kW)

A measure of electrical power equal to 1,000 watts, or approximately 1.34 horsepower.

KING POST

A short strong stanchion or post that is used to support a small cargo boom.

KING SPOKE

The *spoke* of the PILOTWHEEL of a steamboat that is straight up when the rudders are centered. It is distinctively marked, often with wrapped decorative cordage. It probably received the term because it was the highest *spoke* of those on the wheel when they were centered and for its ornamentation. It is sometimes called the midship *spoke*.

KINK

A twist or curl in a line. A line that

tends to *kink* usually has not been taken out of a coil properly when new. Since most all of the line used on tugs, riverboats, barges, and tows is "laid" right-handed when it is manufactured, it must be removed from the coil by taking the bitter end from the center of the coil in a left-handed, or counter-clockwise, fashion. A coil or line can be mounted in a sling with a bar through the center and unreeled from the outer bitter end, but most tugs and towboats do not easily have this capability. Then, after the line removed from the coil is being used, kinks can form if the line is not coiled down in the right direction. Since the line is of a right-hand lay it must always be coiled down in a right-handed, or clockwise fashion, or "with the sun". The word comes from the Norse *kika*, meaning "bend".

KITCHEN
See: COOKHOUSE and GALLEY.

KNEE WIRES
A wire(s) running from the H-BITTS in the center of the bow of a towboat (between the towknees) to the barge(s) being pushed, in order to keep the towboat from sliding or shifting when steering or backing down. Also called JOCKEY WIRES or ROCK AND ROLL WIRES by some.

KNEES
1. Short for TOWKNEES. The first *knees* used on riverboats were on the steamboats that hauled bales of cotton downriver. The *knees*, a triangular block, were installed on the sides of the main deck on some of the steamers to insure that the bales, piled as high as they would go to the next deck, would not fall overboard if the vessel took a list.
2. A triangular plate used to connect intersecting structural members in vessel construction to hold constant the desired plane or angle. The plates can be vertical or horizontal.
3. On wooden-hulled vessels, it was a natural angular curvature of a section of a tree used in the same manner as a steel plate *knee*. The word comes from the Old Saxon *knie*, meaning *knee*. The use of the term in shipyard construction was probably because a person's *knee* in a bent position forms a triangular shape.

KNIFE EDGE
The rim of a hatch that engages the gasket of a cover, lid, door, or other covering that will make a watertight fit.

KNIFE, RIGGING
A *knife* with a straight-edged folding blade about three inches long and fitted with a small folding spike, also about three inches long, that is used to separate the strands of small line when splicing it, or to use as leverage to tighten or loosen a screwed shackle pin.

KNIGHTHEAD
Heavy timbers on the bow of some of the old steamboats that supported a bowsprit. The term is said to come from the carved horns on the helmets worn on knight's heads, at least those of the Vikings.

KNOCK OFF
On the river the term means to quit doing what one is doing, or to stop working. The term is of nautical derivation, coming from the time of the old sailing and rowing galleys where slaves rowed to the beating of a mallet on a wood block by a drummer. When the drummer stopped his beat the slaves would stop rowing, or as they say, *knock off*. It is not used on the river meaning what Al Capone did to his rivals in Chicago.

KNOCKOUT
To release or separate the towboat or tug from its tow, or to release or separate a barge in tow to tie it off, shift it, or give it to a shift boat.

KNOCKOUT SINGLE
When locking, to move a tow into the lock and then release or separate the towboat from the tow when it exceeds the length of the lock chamber, and then lay alongside the tow while locking. When the lockage is complete the towboat slowly shoves the tow ahead after the gates are opened in the chamber. When there is sufficient room the towboat then backs down under the stern of the tow to again couple to it and continues out of the lock.

KNOT
1. To most landsmen a *knot* is something in a line or rope that is tied in, or to, something; however, there are many different configurations and detailed nomenclature of rope and line work used aboard vessels. The terminology consists of the variety of *knots, bends, hitches,* and *splices* (see all). Only a limited few of the most useful *knots* will be described in this text since *knots* themselves are a complete book subject. The term is believed to have Germanic roots and came down to the Old English *cnotta*, which meant "a lump or hard mass", probably more applied to a hard spot in timber.

2. A *knot* is tied into a piece of rope or line. It is the result of forming a loop in a line, putting a section of the line back through the loop, and possibly repeating the procedure in some intricate fashion. A BOWLINE is possibly the most useful *knot* utilized in the river trade.

3. A unit of distance equal to one nautical mile. Learned texts, however, seem to define this distance at varying lengths. Those noted have been: 6075.6 feet, 6076 feet, 6076.1 feet, 6080 feet, 6080.2 feet, 6080.27 feet, 6082.66 feet, and there are probably other "experts" who have different ideas. Since we do not use *knot* as a measurement on the inland rivers the debate will not be joined.

4. A unit of speed equal to a vessel making way through the water at a rate of one nautical mile per hour. The term derives from the old sailing ships dropping a piece of wood, called a chip log, over the side with a length of light cordage attached with *knots* tied in the line at stated lengths. The line was allowed to float away from the ship for a certain length of time, then the chip log was hauled in and the knots counted to figure the rate of speed the vessel was making. In various texts how this was done varies, probably because the Captain had a different or better way, he believed, in undertaking the measurement. Some examples of how it was done:
   a. In the earliest time it was simply a piece of wood thrown over the side from the extreme bow of the vessel and the time was set; as the piece of wood floated down the side of the vessel the person watching the time period would shout "mark", and it would be determined how far along the side of the vessel the wood had traveled which could then be translated into speed.
   b. When the chip log came into use, the line that was thrown over the stern had *knots* put in it every 47.3 feet, and a special sand glass was used that measured 28 seconds. At the end of this time the line was stopped, hauled in, and the number of *knots* that had run out was then counted, from which the speed could be determined. That is how the term *knot* came to be used in nautical terminology.

5. A type of protrusion from a tree log that can become an imperfection in a timber or planking that if knocked out would result in a leaking hull.

6. Other times where the term might be used in river verbiage might be: "His stomach was tied in *knots* when he was sliding towards the right hand pier of the Eads Bridge with the gauge at 30 feet", or "She had her tongue tied in a *knot* trying to explain how she made her gumbo", or "The Engineer had to get off the last trip because he had to tie the *knot* with his girlfriend or she was going to find someone else".

KNOTT'S RULE

Named after Michael A. Knott, an engineer in risk analysis of bridge design who hypothesized that the engineers who design bridges crossing navigable waterways with piers in the water must always consider the proposition that they will be struck sometime. His (Knott) Rule is: "If You Build It, It Will Be Hit". Hopefully, not often if it is designed properly. Properly is defined as having the supporting piers on the banks of the waterway.

KNOWLEDGE BOX

A name used in referring to the PILOTHOUSE. Also called the BRAIN BOX. There is an old adage that says, "A little knowledge can be a dangerous thing", with another follow up which states, "Incorrect knowledge can even be worse". Therefore, it behooves a Pilot to always have a learned comprehension of the RULES OF THE ROAD and other regulations governing the operation of vessels, as well as the following term, KNOW THE RIVER, whenever an unfortunate mishap may occur requiring one to appear before an Admiralty Court to explain the circumstances.

KNOW THE RIVER

It is one thing to know how to steer a vessel, how to handle a tow at a lock, or how to stay in the buoy line of a channel, but to be a Pilot you also have to *know the river*. As Captain Bixby told Sam Clemens when he was his cub Pilot, and related in Chapter 8 of *Life on the Mississippi*, (and then Clemens reflection on it):

"…My boy, you've got to remember it. You've got to remember the exact spot and the exact marks the boat lay in when we had the shoalest water, in every one of the five hundred shoal places between St. Louis and New Orleans, and you mustn't get the shoal soundings and marks of one trip mixed up with the shoal soundings and marks of another, either, for they're not often twice alike. You must keep them separate."

(Clemens) "…It turned out to be true. The face of the water, in time, became a wonderful book—book that was a dead language to the uneducated passenger, but which told its mind to me without reserve, delivering its most cherished secrets as clearly as if it uttered them with a voice. And it was not a book to be read once and thrown aside, for it had a new story to tell every day. Throughout the long twelve hundred miles there was never a page that was void of interest, never one that you could leave unread without loss, never one that you would want to skip, thinking you could find higher enjoyment in some other thing. There never was so wonderful a book written by man; never one whose interest was so absorbing, so unflagging, so sparklingly renewed with every re-perusal. The passenger who could not read it was charmed with a peculiar sort of faint dimple on its surface (on the rare occasions when he did not overlook it altogether); but to the pilot that was an italicized passage; indeed, it was more than that, it was a legend of the largest capitals, with a string of shouting exclamation points at the end of it; for it meant that a wreck or a rock was buried there that could tear the life out of the strongest vessel that ever floated. It is the faintest and simplest expression the water ever makes, and the most hideous to a pilot's eye. In truth, the passenger who could not read this book saw nothing but all manner of pretty pictures in it painted by the sun and shaded by the clouds, whereas to the trained eye these were not pictures at all, but the grimmest and most dead-earnest of reading matter."

KNOW THE ROPES

A crewman aboard a vessel that knows the business of good river seamanship, the use of the gear his vessel is equipped with, how to do his job safely, and what to do in an emergency is said to *know the ropes*. The term comes from the old sailing days when there were many masts with sails and numerous lines and halyards that had different names, in fact a book full of them. If the seaman became very conversant with all the different terms and what each referred to and what job it did, he *knew his ropes*.

KNUCKLE

A sharp bend or curvature in a steel plate, or a shape that forms the side and the bottom, or the deck of a vessel, and so defined as the bottom *knuckle*, bilge *knuckle*, or the deck *knuckle*. The term comes from the early English *knokel*, denoting the "bend" of an elbow, knee, or finger.

KNUCKLE CHAINS

Steel rods that ran from the FUTTOCKS at the turn of the bottom side knuckle to the RIDGEPOLE in a steamboat. They added support to the vessel sides.

KORT NOZZLE

The Kort nozzle was developed in Germany by an engineer, Dr. L. Kort, around 1930. The kort nozzle is a casing attached to the stern hull of a tug or towboat that enshrouds the propeller. It controls the direction and velocity of the water passing to, through, and away from the propeller to increase its efficiency and obtain additional ahead thrust. The Dravo Shipbuilding Company acquired the rights to use the application and in 1937 installed the first U.S. nozzle on the towboat PIONEER.

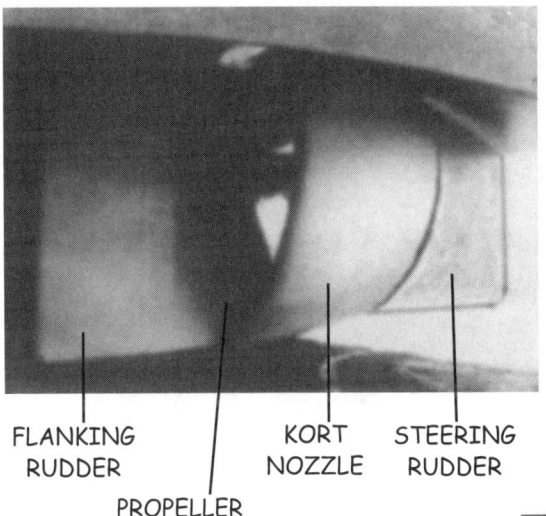

FLANKING RUDDER | PROPELLER | KORT NOZZLE | STEERING RUDDER

KORT NOZZLE

A kort nozzle localizes the thrust movement of a vessel through the water by the close fit of propeller blade tips to the inner skin of the kort. This tends to restrict the turbulent flow that normally occurs at the tip ends of the propeller on an open wheel vessel. The kort concentrates the motion of the water over the entire surface of the blade resulting in a much greater driving force through the water.

REPLACING KORT NOZZLE

Shows new kort nozzle being attached to a towboat in drydock

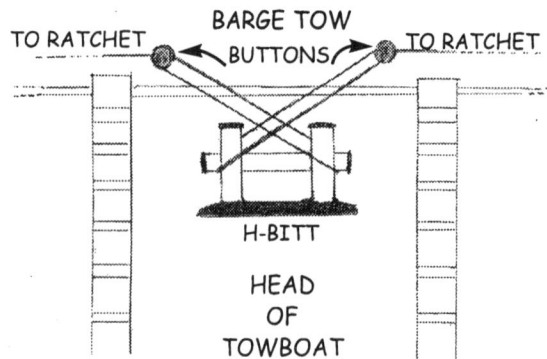

KNEE WIRES

After facing up towboat to a barge tow "knee wires" are sometimes placed between the H-bitt or other fittings on the head of the towboat with fittings that are on the facing barge(s). They are used on large tows not having rubber faced towknees. These wires make a stiff coupling preventing any possibility of a sliding motion when backing down full astern if the face wires are not extremely tight.

KEELBOAT

The picture depicts two keelboats and a flatboat. The keelboat along the shore shows the keelers are "setting" or "planting" their poles and walking astern to move the keelboat upstream. The other keelboat is being wind assisted by hoisting a sail.

KING SPOKE

A spoke of a steamboat's steering wheel that was sometimes painted white or other colors, or wrapped with white decorative rope work. When centered at the 12 o'clock position the rudders were in a straight fore and aft position.

L

LABOR
Said of a towboat or a paddlewheel boat that vibrates excessively while operating in very shallow water and the propeller(s) or paddlewheel becomes starved from lack of flow trying to reach them. It is a time a boat is working hard to do its duty. A vessel that is *laboring* loses much of its steering power. See: SQUAT.

LADDER
1. As on the shore, a device consisting of bars between two upright posts used to go to a greater height or descend from one. Used on the river when pushed into the bank to take out a mooring line, or on the tow to go from a loaded barge up to the deck of an empty one. The word comes from the German *leiter*, and has some relation to the unraveling of a stocking. How this relates to a device used for climbing is unknown.
2. Although some converts from ocean and naval service to a vocation on the river refer to a stairway as a *ladder*, most persons employed on the river say a stairway is simply called a stairway.
3. The boom on a LADDER DREDGE that carries the scoop buckets when dredging. Also see JACOB'S LADDER.

LADDER DREDGE
A *dredge* equipped with a series of chain-driven scoop buckets mounted on a crane-like structure called a *ladder*.

LADEN
The condition of a barge when it is loaded with cargo.

LAG
1. The time it takes a flood crest to move between two points, i.e. "The crest just reached Memphis and should hit Greenville about this time tomorrow".
2. The act of placing LAGGING on structures.

LAGAN
Goods that are cast into the river in an emergency and some way marked where thrown, such as by a buoy or float, in order that they may later be recovered. This practice is not recorded, at least in modern times, to find where it might have occurred on the river system, but it is a well known principle in maritime law. It is possible it could have occurred on the river by persons attempting to evade the federal authorities when transporting contraband. It is apparently of Germanic origin and is associated with the term "lay" which would follow that the cargo was marked where it "lay". See: FLOTSAM and JETSAM.

LAGGING
Insulating material that is wrapped around a structure or its piping that carries liquids or gases at elevated temperatures, which protects the material and persons who may come into contact with the structures. The term is also from the Germanic term *lay* and was probably derived from the use of laying wrappings around a heated container.

LAGNIAPPE
A Creole word, not really a river word, but used extensively in the South end of the Mississippi River and the Gulf Intracoastal Waterway, meaning a little something extra as a bonus for something done or for a favor, such as when a Pilot takes a pound of coffee over to a Lockman who has given extra help in pulling in a lock line when there was a running river with a strong outdraft. The word comes from the Spanish or Creole *la nada,* meaning "the nothing", and is pronounced as "Laen-yaep".

LAID UP
When a vessel is out of service, is

LAKE

Many sections of the river and canal system contain large wide expanses of water that are termed *lakes*. Some of the many examples would be Keokuk Lake on the Upper Mississippi, Peoria Lake on the Illinois River, and Kentucky Lake on the Tennessee River. The term comes from Latin *lacus,* meaning "lake or pool".

LAKE ITASCA

The source of the mighty Mississippi, it is a small glacial lake located in the hinterland of the state of Minnesota that had been given a lengthy native name describing the elk that roamed the area. In 1832, a geographer named Henry Schoolcraft became the so-called discoverer of the lake as the supposedly true source of the Mississippi's flow and called it *Itasca* which was taken in part from the Latin *veritas*, meaning "truth", and *caput*, meaning "head". The lake and the Mississippi's waters as well as those of the river's many tributaries traverse 2,340 miles before entering the Gulf of Mexico.

LAMPLIGHTER

A person employed by the government who tended to lighted navigation aids in isolated areas in order to provide for greater aid reliability. The *lamplighter* trimmed the wicks of the lantern, cleaned the globe, and added kerosene as required. The last *lamplighter* on the Mississippi River retired in 1982 when the kerosene lanterns became replaced by lights using battery power.

LAND

1. The shore above the height of the river, usually called the riverbank.
2. The act of bringing a towboat and/or tow into a fleet, dock, shore, or other place.
3. To put ashore cargo, gear, or people.
4. Where persons who do not work on vessels live.

LAND WALL

The shoreward wall structure of a lock, also called the GUIDE WALL.

LANDING

Any convenient place where a vessel can put into the shore to tie off, pick up or drop cargo or people. In the days of keelboats and packets, it was a designated locality in a town, a plantation, or any other place along a navigable river that a vessel could get to if signaled from the shore that transportation was needed for cargo or passengers. Later it also meant a company or public place (*landing*) where vessels tied up.

LANDING A TOW

The time when a towboat or tug brings a tow to the bank or a fleet, either to hold up for fog or other weather-related occurrence, to wait on a lock, or to drop barges, etc. A pilot might say to his head deckhand, "I'm going to *land the tow* on the upper fleet and tie off; we'll then take the port two stern barges and deliver them to ABC dock.........."

LANDING CRAFT
See: LST

LANDING WHISTLE

Landing signals by whistle or horn were first used on our Western Rivers when steam vessels started picking up freight or passengers at various landing points along the river. In the early days of U.S. river steamboat transportation, there was an absence of daily (or weekly, hourly, or by the minute) communication after a packet or steam towing vessel left its homeport on a trip. In order to call attention to someone at a landing, a boat would ring a distinctive bell signal on its roof bell. Later, when steam whistle signals came into use, a Pilot would sound his whistle when the vessel intended to make a landing. Those on shore would know which boat it was by the sound of its whistle and the number and type of blasts sounded. As companies of packets and steam riverboats developed their trade they would have all their boats sound the same signal whenever arriving at a landing.

Since the advent of constant communication via FM radio phone, mobile and cell phones, satellite service, fax machines, and computers, as well as the fact that few linehaul riverboats now make landings due to the use of fleet boats, helper boats, and midstream services, there seems to be little need for a *landing signal*. They are seldom sounded anymore except as a salute to kids or a friend on the bank, or when meeting another towboat (after or when passing so as not to be confused with required navigational signals). See: WHISTLE SALUTE.

A few of the standard company *Landing Whistle* signals are (were):

```
Ashland Oil              — • • — •
American Commercial Barge Line
                         — • • — •
Federal Barge Line       — • • — • •
Greene Line              — • —
Hillman Transportation — • — •
Mississippi Valley Barge Line
                         — — • • •
Ohio River Company — • — • •
Streckfus Steamers       — • • —
Union Barge Line         — — • •
Wheeling Steel Corp      — — — • •
```

LANDLUBBER
A person who is out of their element on the river, or who is more at peace with themselves on land than on the water, or is unfamiliar with the ways, customs, laws, and terminology of the river. In other words, a *landlubber* is a person who has not and will not read this book. The word *lubber* is from the Old French *lobeor*, which had the connotation of a "swindler" or other type of "useless person".

LANDMARK
Any conspicuous or prominent feature on the shore, such as a tall or unusual building, the tallest tree along the bank, a saddle or dip in tree line, smokestacks, a non-navigation light, or any other object which can be defined sufficiently to provide an assistance to navigation.

LANTERN
1. A portable lamp or light. Many fleets once used kerosene lanterns to mark the outward corners of the moored barges

2. The name given to the light aids that were placed on the shore in the old steamboat days.

3. The first navigation lights required by law were *lanterns* that were to be "so constructed as to show" their respective arcs of light to which the law applied.

4. The glass enclosure of on lighted buoys and shore lights placed by the USCG.

LANYARD or LANIARD
1. A small short rope used aboard a vessel to fasten down or tie to an object.

2. The small, usually decoratively woven line attached to the CLAPPER of the vessel's bell, used to ring it.

3. Also used in conjunction with an object, i.e. a knife *lanyard* that can be attached to a deckhand's belt loop and to the knife so the knife will not be lost overboard. In the Navy the boatswain's mate carried a pipe on which to blow signals to the crew. The pipe was attached to a *lanyard* which was usually artistically woven.

4. When cannon were carried aboard vessels, a *lanyard* was attached to the firing mechanism that was

pulled to fire the weapon. There have not been many of this type of *lanyard* on riverboats since Civil War days.

5. The term originally used on sailing ships for a line rove through a deadeye which was fastened to the shrouds or standing rigging of a vessel, which was then pulled taut and tied down. Apparently the word comes from the French *larniere,* which derived from a term meaning "loop or noose", possibly for use when the guillotine wasn't working.

LAP WELD

A joint where two plates are joggled to lap one over the other and welded together, rather than a butt joint where two plates are joined edge-to-edge and welded. A *lap weld* allows for a little error in fitting long plates for construction. However, when making this type of joint a STOP WELD has to be cut and completed at all watertight bulkheads to prevent leakage between compartments.

LARBOARD

The word formerly used to indicate PORT, or the left side of a vessel when facing forward. On ships, when giving the helmsman orders, the term could become confusing when using both STARBOARD and *larboard,* and the term was largely abandoned. Its origin comes from old English *laddebord,* meaning "loading side". In olden days most ships had their steering rudder on the right stern quarter of the vessel; therefore, the left side of the vessel would be tied off to a wharf to take on and discharge cargo.

LA SALLE, ROBERT

A French explorer, he was sent by his king, Louis XIV, to explore the Great Lakes and then to go from Canada down the Illinois River to the Mississippi River and to the Gulf of Mexico, in order to establish fur trading routes. This he did in the latter 1600s. He established a fort about where Memphis is today and when he arrived in New Orleans in the spring of 1682, he claimed all the land along the Mississippi River for France and named the territory Louisiana, in honor of the King. *LaSalle* was the first European to travel the length of the Mississippi.

LASH BARGE

LASH is an acronym for Lighter Aboard Ship. *LASH* barges are small, approximately 62 feet long by 32 feet in width with a hull depth of 12 feet. They have a capacity of about 450 net tons. The barges are designed to carry either bulk or packaged goods in the international trade. They may be loaded or unloaded at an inland river port, where they will be placed in a river tow destined for a deep draft port. There they are lifted onto and stacked on a specially built "mother ship". When reaching an overseas foreign port the barges are off loaded and then towed or pushed to an inland port area.

LASHING

1. A small piece of cordage used to tie things down or together.
2. A line, or wire, used between two barges to hold them together, or placed between barges in a tow as safety lines in case the wires part.
3. Sometimes refers to a short, but adequate, tie-off line used when securing a barge in a fleet. Also called a LEAVING LINE.

LATERAL SYSTEM

The system of buoyage used in the United States where the buoys follow and mark the sides of the channel, with red buoys on the starboard or right side when proceeding upriver, and green buoys on the port or left side of the vessel. See: BUOYAGE.

LATITUDE

The distance measured in degrees of arc north or south of the equator. Each degree has 60 minutes and each minute has 60 seconds. Also see LONGITUDE. In the past the term *latitude* was not used very much on the river except as a relative term by persons in the USACE who plotted the charts or maps of the river. However, with the advent of GPS both *latitude* and longitude will be more pertinent in river navigation usage. The word comes from the Latin *latitude*, meaning "breadth" or "broad".

LAUNCHING, LAUNCH-WAYS & LAUNCHING-WAYS

Launching is the act of putting a vessel that has been built or repaired on land into the water. There are a variety of ways this has been done on the river, from SIDE LAUNCHING, end-on *launches*, to simply just pushing the vessel into the water on SKIDS with a bulldozer from where it was built on the shore. However, at inland shipyards most *launchings* are accomplished by moving a vessel to the *launch-ways* (also called *slipways* or *ways*) which are a set of rails with heavy timbers attached (sometimes called SKIDS) that follows the sloping incline angle from the upper shore to a level below the low water line of the water's surface. The vessel is placed on CRADLES which is another name for *launching-ways*. The rail timbers and the bottom of the cradle are heavily lubricated. The cradles are held in place by lines or a mechanical device. At the proper signal the lines or device are let go and the vessel slides into the water by gravity.

LAW OF ARCHIMEDES

The principle of why vessels heavier than water float. Archimedes, who lived in the first century B.C., discovered that if an object (vessel) is immersed in a fluid (water) it is subject to an upward force equal to the weight of the water it displaces.

LAW OF TONNAGE

Not an official law that any vessel in navigation should or can rely upon for absolution in an altercation between two or more vessels in a collision situation. The thrust of the *law* implies that a larger vessel with the most tonnage and deeper draft should be given a greater degree of space or channel width in a navigating situation since it may be unable to maneuver as well as a vessel of lesser size and/or tonnage. The larger vessel will require more room to stop, to turn, or to accelerate if necessary. This informal guidance does not negate the actual reading and application of the RULES OF THE ROAD; however, actions taken, or not taken, by what should be a "reasonable prudent mariner" would dictate that avoidance of collision is more important than who has the so-called RIGHT OF WAY. Navigation Rule 9 recognizes this navigational situation in some circumstances when it refers to certain vessels that "shall not impede" another vessel.

LAWS OF OLERON

The first comprehensive set of written rules of seafarering customs which are the forerunner of modern Navigation Rules. The laws originated in the 12th century, when Eleanor of Aquitaine, on the Island of Oleron, took interest in the various customs that prevailed between those who went to sea under various flags. Of note, one should take heed in Rule 23 about Pilots failing to properly perform their duties:

"If a pilot undertakes the Conduct of a vessel…and fail of his Duty therein…and the Merchants Sustained Damage thereby, he shall be Obliged to make full satisfaction for same…and if not, lose his Head".

LAY

As used by on the river:
1. Describes the way a line or wire has its strands twisted together. On the river almost all line and wire is of a right-hand *lay*.

2. To go to, or take to, a certain area, i.e., *"Lay* that gear below".

3. To *lay* by is to stay in the place where the vessel is currently positioned.

4. To *lay* off is to stay away, or a distance away, from another vessel or object, i.e., "When you get to the next crossing *lay* off the green buoys as they are in shallow water".

5. To *lay* over, see: LAY OVER.

6. To *lay* to is to bring a vessel to a standstill, or almost motionless in the water.

7. To *lay* up is when a vessel is not going to be used for a period of time. All gear is stowed away and usually only a watchman or skeleton crew is aboard.

LAY DAY(S)

The contractual free time allowed for a barge to be loaded or unloaded once it is placed at a dock. See: DEMURRAGE.

LAY OVER

For vessels in the barging trades it usually meant the time waiting on a barge to be loaded or unloaded, or waiting for a connection with another towing vessel with barges needed for their tow destination. It could also mean to wait for a lock to open which might be down for repairs, or perhaps for repairs on the vessel itself waiting on parts or engineers to undertake the work.

In the steam packet days it could mean just about anything in addition to the time taken for loading or unloading. Schedules for packet boats didn't always work the way pushers of pencils expected them to occur. Perhaps a passenger train was late for a connection, or a boiler developed a bag prior to departure time, or possibly a Pilot quit and it became a problem to locate another, etc.

LAZY BENCH

A raised seat in the back of the pilothouse with room for two or three people to sit and watch the river go by, or kibitz about conditions, politics, people, etc. It is also sometimes called a *loafers bench* or a LIARS BENCH. The term *lazy* comes to us from the German *lasich*, meaning "idle or languid".

LAZY RUDDER

Refers to the steering ability of a vessel that responds slowly when executing a turning maneuver.

LEAD

1. When used in reference to barges in tow, it is those on the head of a tow, i.e., when the Pilot tells the Mate, "Check that *lead* barge in the port string. It seems to have a list."

2. When used in reference to a wire or line, it is the direction in which the wire or line runs, i.e., as when the Pilot tells the Mate, "Make sure we have both downstream and upstream *leads* when we tie that barge off".

3. If the *lead* of a line or wire is in one part it is termed a single *lead*. If the *lead* is doubled back to the vessel it is a two-part or doubled-up *lead*. In the above usage the word is pronounced "leed".

4. The weighted device at the end of a LEADLINE used to check the depth of water. When used for this purpose the word is pronounced "led".

LEAD DECKHAND

The senior or most learned deckhand on a watch who will direct the other deckhands as to their assignments if no Mate is on watch.

LEADER LINE

See: HANDY LINE, HEAVING LINE, and MESSENGER LINE.

LEADING EDGE

When a vessel has its engine engaged and is moving forward the *leading edge* of a propeller is the section that first cuts through the water to give the vessel propulsion ahead.

LEADLINE

In the 1800s and half of the 1900s, the

channels of most of the navigable river streams were not as stable as they are today, and not nearly so well marked with aids to navigation. Many times a Pilot would have to require the channel to be SOUNDED, or measured for its depth. This was done by use of a *leadline*, which consisted of a conical-shaped piece of lead (pronounced "led") that was hollow in the bed, in case the Pilot wanted to know the material that was on the river bottom. The hollowed-out portion would be filled with tallow that would pick up particles from the bed of the river. The *lead* was attached to the end of a marked line so that the leadsman could tell what the depth of the channel was and call back his reading to the Pilot. Oftentimes the calling of less than a "quarter less twain" was done in feet and inches. The *leadline* could be marked in various ways, but it was usually a variation of the following and the calls that were made thusly:

By the Mark One
6 feet (1 fathom)   Piece of leather
And A Quarter One
$7\frac{1}{2}$ feet   Piece of white cloth
And A Half One
9 feet   Piece of red cloth
Quarter Less Twain
$10\frac{1}{2}$ feet   Piece of black cloth
By the Mark Twain
12 feet (2 fathoms)   Leather split into 2 thongs
And a Quarter Twain
$13\frac{1}{2}$ feet   Piece of white cloth
And a Half Twain
15 feet   Piece of red cloth
Quarter Less Tyree
$16\frac{1}{2}$ feet   Piece of black cloth
By the Mark Tyree
18 feet (3 fathoms)   Leather split into 3 thongs
And a Quarter Tyree
$19\frac{1}{2}$ feet   Piece of white cloth
And a Half Tyree
21 feet   Piece of red cloth
Quarter Less Four
$22\frac{1}{2}$ feet   Piece of black cloth
By the Mark Four
24 feet (4 fathoms) Leather strip with a   hole in it
NO BOTTOM!!!
Over 24 feet

Currently when a sounding is needed by the Pilot, at least since the mid-twentieth century, it is done with a SOUNDING POLE, or by an electronic sounding device; however, the use of a *leadline* was one of the first navigation aids used by those who traveled on water and is said to have been used at least 2000 years B.C.

LEADSMAN
The Deckhand or Mate who heaves or casts the LEADLINE and calls out the sounding of the depth of the water. The term is pronounced "leds-man".

LEAK or LEAKER
A vessel that has some form of damage and is taking on water.

LEAVE
To depart from a place, i.e., "We will *leave* the Cairo Fleet at noon".

LEAVING LINE
A line that is left at a dock or fleet area used to tie off a barge. It is usually 25 to 40 feet long with an eye in one end. Most often it is a section of an old lock line or a line smaller in circumference, used specifically for mooring purposes.

LED LIGHT
An acronym for Light Emitting Diode. This type of light can be built in any color without a filter which would be required with an incandescent light. It can also focus all its power in the direction that is desired or required to show, unlike an incandescent light that will show 360 degrees. *Led lights* are now being used for some navigation lights.

LEE and LEEWARD
The side of a vessel that is away from, or protected from, the wind; or, the side opposite from which way the wind is blowing; opposite the WEATHER SIDE. The term comes from Old English *hleo,* referring to shelter(side).

LEEWAY

1. The somewhat angular lateral movement of a vessel and/or tow through the water due to wind and/or current in order to maintain a desired course. See: CRABBING THROUGH.

2. An amount of slack or movement in machinery.

LEFT BANK

The shoreline of a river on one's left hand when facing and proceeding downstream. It is also called the *left descending bank*. The light list for an area of the river will show navigational light aids to be on either the *left* or the RIGHT BANK. Red buoys mark the navigational limits of the channel on this side of a river, and usually show red or white reflective tape.

LEFT-HAND DRAFT

A cross current that is running more to the left side of the channel than being straight with it, i.e., "There is a strong *left hand draft* on the shoreward pier of the ABC Bridge". This verbal or written advice is given in relation to the left bank when a vessel is proceeding downstream.

LEFT-HAND PROPELLER

A propeller that has a rotation from starboard to port, or counter-clockwise, when going ahead, or forward.

LEFT RUDDER

The action of turning the steering levers, or wheel, to the left, or port side, in order for the vessel or its tow to move, or turn, toward the left side of the channel.

LEG

A particular reach of a twisting or crooked channel, i.e., as one Pilot to another, "The current in the first *leg* of the crossing is fairly straight, then there is a right-hand draft in the second *leg*, but as you come out of it before reaching the last buoy it straightens out again".

LENGTH OVERALL

The total distance from the forwardmost extremity of a vessel to the aftermost extremity of a vessel.

LENGTHENING

The infrequent practice of extending the length of a vessel. It is usually undertaken to accommodate a new type of propulsion unit of increased horsepower, and/or to increase the storage of fuel and water.

LENS

A mirror-like device is placed behind a light to enhance the projection candelas or light source to a much greater intensity. Used in searchlights of towboats and tugs as well as in navigational aids to navigation.

LEPROSY HOSPITAL (CARVILLE, LA)

The *hospital* for persons who had contracted Hansen's disease, or leprosy, was started in the late 1800s at Carville, LA, on the banks of the Mississippi River by the State of Louisiana. In 1921 it was taken over by the U.S. government. It was closed down in 1998, but there is now the National Hansen's Disease Museum located there. The hospital grounds are at Mile 191.5 on the left bank and are marked by a navigation beacon called *Hospital Light*. It was a tradition of river Pilots when they passed the grounds to sound three long blasts on their whistle as a salute to those who were patients, as well as to those who cared for them.

LET DOWN

A command to lower an object, such as a boom, or something attached to a hoist, or on a block and tackle rig.

LET GO

To take off, or cast off, all lines or wires to a place where a vessel or tow is moored; usually expressed as, "*Let 'er go*", and after all lines are free the response is, "All gone".

LEVEE

In the days of steamboats the *levee* meant most any gradient area where a steamer would land to load or discharge cargo, or to take on passengers. At present it refers to a built-up earth embankment or setback from the edge of the river that is designed to hold back floodwaters that may go over the edge of the riverbank and inundate low-lying areas. *Levees* are built to exceed a height of a flood event which might occur every so many years, such as a HUNDRED YEAR FLOOD, or a "fifty year flood" based on past historic heights of flooding. They are sometimes used in conjunction with a FLOODWALL protecting a city. The term is particular to the U.S. and comes from the French *leeve*, when referring to a "lever used to rise up".

LEWIS, CAPT. MERIWETHER

Partner (with William Clark) of the Lewis and Clark expedition which explored the Louisiana Purchase between 1804 and 1806, traveling from the mouth of the Missouri River upstream to the Pacific Northwest and return. They joined together when Lewis arrived at Louisville with a keelboat. After running the FALLS OF THE OHIO, they departed on their journey from below the Falls on 26 October 1803, which marks the beginning of their adventure together. After returning from their trip, Capt. Lewis was appointed Governor of the Louisiana Territory. While making a trip to Washington, DC, he is reported to have committed suicide while at an inn on the NATCHEZ TRACE. See: CLARK, CAPT. WILLIAM.

LEWIS & CLARK EXPEDITION

After the U.S. purchased the Louisiana Territories from France in 1803, President Jefferson summoned Captain Meriwether Lewis to his home in Monticello, VA to discuss leading an expedition into the newly acquired lands. Capt. Lewis went to the Pittsburgh area where he had a flatboat built. With a crew, at the end of August they started down the Ohio River arriving in mid-October at the FALLS OF THE OHIO. William Clark, whom Lewis had served under, joined the expedition and was made co-Captain although he did not officially have that rank. The group proceeded down the Ohio to the Mississippi where they keeled upstream to the Illinois side of the mouth of the Missouri River, spent the winter, and the following spring started their journey through the newly obtained territory. Up the Missouri, across the Rockies, down the Lower Snake and Columbia Rivers they went all the way to the Pacific. They then returned on a similar route arriving in St. Louis in September 1806. Their travels and story are commended to you. See: CLARK, CAPT. WILLIAM, LEWIS, CAPT. MERIWETHER, and LOUISIANA PURCHASE.

LIAR'S BENCH

Another word for LAZY BENCH. Sometimes this term is used since it has been said that some of the stories told by those who sat on the *bench* were somewhat off the mark in veracity, similar to the yarns that fishermen tell of the size fish they have caught. It seems at times that a 20-barge tow becomes a 30-barge tow, a light mist becomes a shut out fog, 30,000 tons becomes 50,000 tons, and pool water becomes the strongest outdraft ever seen at a lock, when a group of old and/or bold Pilots are sitting on the raised *bench* at the rear of the pilothouse conversing about their experiences.

LICENSE

1. All Pilots and other officers of river vessels must have a valid U.S. Coast Guard issued *license* in order to navigate a towboat and tow. They must pass a physical exam and take a written test, as well as have a certain length of service aboard towing vessels. See: PILOT LICENSE.

2. The certificate of ENROLLMENT issued to a towboat that allows it to operate between domestic ports in the United States.

LICKING RIVER

The river rises in the Cumberland Range in Eastern Kentucky and flows down for 320 miles, entering into the Ohio River at mile 470 between the cities of Newport and Covington, across the river from Cincinnati. It takes its name from the saline springs close to the river where animals would go to get their minerals.

It was an important transportation artery for Indians and early settlers to the region. Several attempts were made at making the river more commercially navigable up to and above Falmouth, KY, for a project with a total of seven locks and dams. The locks were to be 31 feet wide by 150 feet long, 6 feet over the sills, with an average lift of 17 feet each. Work started in 1837 but was suspended in 1840, and the project abandoned in 1842. Local citizens again requested Congress to make the river navigable in 1899. The Army Engineers investigated, but did not think it would be cost effective. It was estimated that 10 locks would be required between Falmouth and the Ohio River, and six locks and dams above Falmouth to assure a water supply during low water. Nothing was done. There are some terminals at the lower end of the river today.

LIE TO

The condition when a vessel with, or without, tow will be at the river bank because of wind, extremely high water, fog, or some other reason to disrupt safe navigation, i.e. "I'm going to *lie to* just below the lower dike and wait for the fog to lift".

LIFEBOAT STATION

See: LIFE SAVING SERVICE

LIFE BUOY or RING

A large *ring* of buoyant material, usually colored orange, that can be thrown from the vessel into the water in case someone has fallen overboard.

LIFE FLOATS or PLANKS

On steamboats, prior to the use of life jackets, packets and excursion vessels were equipped with what were called *life floats,* which were pieces of soft wooden boards such as pine or balsa that were about three feet long and about a foot wide with two hand-hold slots in them, to be used if disaster struck the vessel. Also the cabin doors and blinds on the vessels were hung on pintles to gudgeons. In the event of an accident they could be lifted off, thrown in the river, and used in the fashion of the *life planks*. A passenger could grab one or the other and hopefully paddle to shore.

LIFE JACKET or PRESERVER

Approved (by the USCG) *life jackets or preservers* are required to be carried aboard every towboat or tug for each person who may be aboard. At present they are termed PERSONAL FLOTATION DEVICES (PFD). Also see: WORK VESTS.

LIFELINES

Flexible lines that are strung along the outboard main deck for a person to grab if needed to keep from falling overboard. See: MAN-ROPES.

LIFESAVING SERVICE

The U.S. Lifesaving Service traces its origin to 1785 and the Massachusetts Humane Society which was a volunteer organization that maintained lifeboats and rescue stations along the Atlantic Coast to assist seafarers in trouble. Saving the lives of those in peril on water had, however, been undertaken by numerous keepers in lighthouses. In 1848, Congress appropriated money for the U.S. Revenue Marine Service to administer funds to go to stations which were mostly manned by volunteers. Thirty years later, in 1878, the network of *Lifesaving Stations* was organized as a separate agency. Then in 1915 both the Revenue-Cutter Service and the *Lifesaving Service* were merged together to form the U.S. Coast Guard.

In 1881 the *Life Saving Service* established the sole life-saving station that operated on the inland river system. It went into service as a floating barge, which housed its crew, and to which its rescue boats were tethered. It was located in Louisville, KY, at the landing above the canal leading to the locks. The station was placed there to warn and rescue persons from a craft which might go over the Falls of the Ohio. When the U.S. Coast Guard was established in 1915, it took over the operation of the station and it served as a base for the USCG mission on the river system. The station closed in 1972, but is credited with saving over 7000 lives while in operation. Its landing barge later became the wharfboat for the steamer *BELLE OF LOUISVILLE*. A navigation light and daymark on the vane dike at the head of the Louisville and Portland Canal at mile 604.3 was dedicated in 2004 to the work of the station and is now known as the U.S. Coast Guard Memorial Lifesaver Light.

LIFT

1. To raise a vessel to a different level, i.e. as in a lock, "The vessel was *lifted* 12 feet".

2. In regard to reduced visibility, i.e. "I hope this fog will soon *lift*".

LIFT BRIDGE

Any bridge spanning a channel which must be raised vertically to allow passage of vessels. See: BASCULE.

LIFT COVERS

Barge covers which do not roll and have to be lifted off to remove or load cargo. There are four strong lifting rings installed near the cover corners for a spreader sling from a crane to hook onto and engage when the covers are required to be lifted. These covers usually have doors built into the covers so that when they are spread over the cargo box of the barge, the doors allow the loading of certain types of bulk cargoes such as grains. When cargo does not have to be protected from the elements the covers can be stacked on each end of the cargo box of the barge.

LIFTING EYE

A triangular-shaped bar in a holder plate welded at one of four equally spaced places on a barge cover. Used by a crane with spreader hooks to lift and stack or remove covers from a covered hopper barge.

LIFTING WAYS

A set of inclined timbers with rails attached that extend from the top of a bank well down into the slope of the river shoreline. A sliding CRADLE is fitted to the rails. The cradles are lowered into the water at a depth just beyond the bottom of the hull of a vessel. The vessel is floated onto the cradles that are attached to a winch wire, which is then used to hoist the cradles up the slope in order for the bottom of the vessel to be inspected and/or repaired. The ways can also be used as a LAUNCH WAYS. Sometimes called a *marine railway*. See: DRYDOCK and SYNCROLIFT.

LIGHT(S)

Various types of *lights* are used along the interior river system to assist Pilots in navigating the channel. These *lights* have differing names, depending on the location of the *light* and/or its function. Some of these are:

1. *Bridge* – The *lights* required to mark the channel-span center and the bridge piers.

2. *Crossing* – Usually in pairs, one on each side of the river to indicate where the channel crosses the river from one bank to the other. Marks may be indicated by, "From 100 yards open

262 LIGHT BOAT

on ABC *Light* (RB) to 500 yards below XYZ *Light* (LB)".

3. *Dike* – A *light* placed on, or near the riverward end of a dike.

4. *Government* – An old name for a *light* maintained by the U.S. Government. The old Lighthouse Service, before 1939, maintained the *lights* and they were generally referred to as "government", but since the time when they were merged into the USCG the function has been a mission of the Coast Guard (which is also in the government).

5. *Lock* – See: LOCK SIGNAL LIGHTS.

6. *Private Aids* – See: PRIVATE AIDS TO NAVIGATION.

7. *Riding* – The required navigation *lights* to be displayed by a vessel at anchor or moored.

8. *Running* – The required navigation *lights* to be displayed by a vessel while underway. See: NAVIGATION LIGHTS.

9. *Shore* – Those non-navigation *lights* that in hazy or fog conditions can appear to be navigational in scope, such as a flashing traffic *light*, a blinking neon sign, etc.

10. *Traffic* – The *lights* maintained by the Corps of Engineers at the locks to indicate the readiness of the lock to receive traffic. Also, the warning *lights* used at Algiers Point in New Orleans harbor at the apex of an extremely sharp point of the river to indicate whether a northbound vessel should wait below the point for a southbound vessel to safely navigate around it.

11. *Wrecks* – See: WRECK MARKINGS.

LIGHT BOAT

When a towboat or tug is running without any barges in tow. It is also termed running *loose headed*.

LIGHT CHARACTERISTICS of AIDS TO NAVIGATION

1. *Color* – Lights on the river system are either Red (on the left descending bank only), or Green (on the right descending bank only), or White on either bank.

2. *Light Phases* – They may be "fixed", "group flashing", "occulting", "quick flashing", or "interrupted quick flashing".

3. *Visibility* – They will be 360 degrees, unless otherwise stated.

LIGHT DISPLACEMENT

The weight of a vessel without cargo, stores, fuel or crew.

LIGHT DRAFT

The depth of water a vessel draws without cargo. Usually refers to a barge on the inland river system when a surveyor or crew member will measure the barge's draft when it is empty of cargo, and then again after it is loaded to calculate the cargo tonnage the barge contains.

LIGHT LIST

A publication issued by the USCG for various regions around the country which lists all the *light* aids to navigation in their area. Volume V of the series is for the Mississippi River System. The volume contains all the official lights, lighted buoys, and many, but not all, of the daymarks maintained under the jurisdiction of the USCG on the Mississippi River and its major commercially navigable tributaries, as well as their mileage position and characteristics. It also lists cities, landings, locks and dams, river mouths, bridges, private aids, and a variety of other information of utmost interest to mariners. The first national *light list* was issued in 1869. They are now printed for different areas of the country, usually on an annual basis.

LIGHT(S), NAVIGATION

The USCG has two important *navigational lighting* functions. One is in prescribing the *lights* various vessels will display to indicate various attitudes of navigation which are enunciated in the Inland Navigation Rules,

Part C, which includes Rule 20, Application; Rule 21, Definitions; Rule 22, Visibility; Rules 23 through 31, that indicate which lights and where displayed on vessels engaged in different employments. Annex I of the Rules indicates the technical aspects of the *lights*; Annex II gives additional signals for certain fishing vessels; and Annex V list requirements for *lights* on moored barges and *lights* required on dredge pipelines.

The other lighting responsibility of the USCG is to maintain *lights*, and other marine aids, which are stationed throughout the inland waters of the United States. See: BEACON, GOVERNMENT LIGHT, LIGHT LIST, and NAVIGATION RULES.

LIGHT OFF

To start the engines or generators of a diesel-powered vessel, or to fire up the boilers of a steamboat.

LIGHT PERIOD

The time period for a flashing light to complete its flashing cycle until the next cycle begins.

LIGHT PLANT

Another name for a diesel-driven generator.

LIGHT SCREENS

Navigation lights on vessels are required to be visible in certain sectors and only in those sectors. For instance, a SIDELIGHT is required to show "... an unbroken light over an arc of the horizon of 112.5 degrees and so fixed as to show the light from right ahead to 22.5 degrees abaft the beam on its respective side". The Annex I to the Inland Rules, 89.09, states the lights, "...shall be fitted with mat black inboard *screens*..." (No length given).

The old Western River Rules stated that these lights "...shall be fitted with inboard *screens*, projecting at least three feet forward from the lights, so as to prevent them from being seen across the bow". No particular color for the *screens* was designated in early days. Later they were required to be glossy black, and later still flat black. See: SCREENS and SCREENING.

LIGHT SECTORS (NAVIGATION LIGHTS)

1. The arc of visibility of a *navigation light* shown from a vessel.

2. The *navigation lights* to be displayed by vessels must show at a prescribed intensity and be visible a certain distance through certain horizontal and vertical *sectors*. These ranges are contained in Annex I of the Navigation Rules.

3. Certain lighted aids to navigation have characteristics to only show through limited *sector* degrees of the compass, or to show different color in more than one *sector*. At present none are in use on the Western Rivers, but may show in some areas along the Gulf Coast.

LIGHT STANDARD

A stand or structure that is used on the head of barge tows to hold the running lights required to be shown. They are usually portable except on some unit tows.

LIGHT TOWER

See: SKELETON TOWER.

LIGHT WATERLINE

The draft of a barge that is empty of cargo. See: WATERLINE.

LIGHTED BUOY

A buoy that displays a light, either fixed or flashing. Not often seen on the Western Rivers except to mark an obstruction; but can be seen in certain coastal bays, sounds, and channels where deep draft vessels navigate. See: BUOY.

LIGHTENING HOLES

Holes that are cut out of structural pieces to reduce weight without any degree of strength loss. They are used in non-watertight bulkheads and can also serve as access *holes*. Also often cut out of the floor frames of double bottomed barges.

LIGHTER

1. The act of removing cargo from a vessel, usually a barge, when required due to a shallow channel, or damage to the vessel, or because a vessel is hard aground.

2. To remove fuel, water and possibly supplies prior to going on a small drydock.

3. A barge that is used to take on cargo from a deeply laden vessel, such as a tankship, and then used to transfer the cargo to a terminal or another vessel.

LIGHTER ABOARD SHIP BARGE

See: LASH BARGE

LIGHTHOUSE

There are no *lighthouses* on the river system. As a matter of interest, the first known *lighthouses* in the world apparently were in Egypt about 600 B.C. where priests lit fires to show smoke during the day and the fire glow at night to warn of danger. The first manned *lighthouse* in the United States was the Boston Light, established in Boston Harbor in 1716. It is said that a *lighthouse* was established at Natchez, MS in the 1800s by an influential Congressman from that area. It served no useful navigational purpose as it couldn't be distinguished from the lights of the city. Although *lighthouses* historically have been immensely helpful aids to navigation along our coastal and Great Lakes shores, perhaps Ambrose Bierce had this Natchez light in mind in his description of *lighthouse* as: "A tall building on the sea-shore in which the government maintains a lamp and the friend of a politician" (*DEVIL'S DICTIONARY,* late 1800s).

LIGHTHOUSE BOARD & SERVICE

When the United States was formed lighthouses were generally built and maintained by the States. In 1789 an Act of Congress provided for the U.S. government to support, maintain, and repair certain aids to navigation by the Treasury Department. The States over the early years ceded control of their lights to the federal government. Later the *Service* was under the jurisdiction of the Revenue-Marine Bureau. In 1852 a *Lighthouse Board* was established by Congress, composed of Army and Navy officers and scientists under the Treasury Department. In 1874 Congress extended the *Lighthouse Service* to include inland rivers when they called for the establishment of lights, day beacons, and buoys for use by vessels navigating those streams. In December of that year the first two lights were placed on the Upper Mississippi at Jefferson Barracks just south of St. Louis, and at Twin Hollow, MO, just above Cairo, IL. Later in the month a light was established at the foot of the Grand Chain on the Ohio River about 16 miles above Cairo, IL.

In 1903 the *Board* was transferred to the Department of Commerce and Labor. Then in 1910 the *Board* had its first single Commissioner appointed to supervise its duties and its name was changed to the *Bureau of Lighthouses*, but more appropriately known as the *Lighthouse Service*. In July 1939 the *Lighthouse Service* was amalgamated with the USCG. See: BEACON and GOVERNMENT LIGHT.

LIGHTHOUSE TENDER

Boat(s) operated by the Lighthouse Service. The first *Lighthouse Tender* on the Western Rivers was the sidewheel steamer *ALICE*. Each tender delivered kerosene, extra lanterns and spare lenses, wicks and other supplies to the Lightkeepers on their routes. At each keeper's landing the *tender* would blow a whistle signal to announce his arrival in case the keeper was in the fields or tending to animals. If a light was not burning when a steamboat passed, a steamboat would sound the same signal to alert the keeper to relight it. The signal was one long and three short, which was known as the lighthouse whistle. Generally, since 1865 it has been the custom of naming tenders after flowers, trees, or plants. See: BUOY TENDER.

LIGHTKEEPERS

Early lights that were displayed to assist in navigation of steamboats on the river system appeared in about 1874, although there were few of them. The Lighthouse Service hired commercial fishermen and sometimes farmers to attend to kerosene lights hung from poles or limbs of trees. Each *lightkeeper*, or as they were sometimes called *lamplighters*, would attend to a few lights every day, cleaning the lantern globe, trimming the wick and replenishing its fuel. It wasn't until the 1940s that all the old kerosene lanterns were converted to battery operation. See: LAMPLIGHTER.

LIGHTS REQUIRED FOR NAVIGATION

The *lights* prescribed to be shown by vessels are in Part C, of the Navigation Rules, and the definition of these various lights is in Rule 21.

LIMBER

The condition of wooden hulls in the olden steamboating days when they were built as light as practicable for the shallow rivers they had to navigate. A vessel's length and breadth to depth ratio made their hulls very flexible or *limber*. To overcome this condition they were fitted with CROSS CHAINS, HOG CHAINS, and KNUCKLE CHAINS.

LIMBER HOLES

Small holes cut in the bottom framing of a vessel to allow accumulated water in the hull to drain to a low area in order to be pumped. Although the background of *limber* is from the Latin *luminare*, meaning "light", the only connotation of the word to its use for the drainage of liquid products is the hole which would allow something to be seen between frames if a "light" was showing in the bilge of a vessel.

LIMITATION OF LIABILITY

Limitation statutes in the United States allows the owner of a vessel, including barges, to *limit the liability* for damages to not exceed the value or interest of the owner of the vessel if the actionable damage to the vessel was done without the privity or knowledge of the owner.

LINCOLN, ABRAHAM (Flat Boatman, Pilot, & Lawyer)

See: *EFFIE AFTON* (STEAMER) and SANGAMON RIVER.

LINE

The general term used for what non-maritime people call "rope" used aboard towboats and tugs, i.e. "Get that *line* over to the lock wall"; "Pay the *line* out slowly"; "Order two six-inch coils of *line*"; and other orders or remarks. Some use of the term "rope" is employed, however, such as "rope ladder", "rope yarn", "rope fender", "rope knife", but vocally by rivermen, cordage is mostly described as *line*. In reality *line* (or rope) is an assemblage of fibers twisted together to make threads or yarns. These are further woven or twisted into strands. The strands, when three or more are laid up, become a strong useful tool called *line* aboard vessels. See numerous references to types of *line* terms in this book that are further defined. The term derives from various roots, but all trace back to the Latin *linea*, with all having the same meaning as "rope".

In the old days of river usage *lines* were made of natural fiber, such as hemp, sisal and manila, however currently most *line* used aboard vessels is of a synthetic variety, or a mixture of them, including nylon, polypropylene, and polyethylene. Teflon, Kevlar, and other new trademarked types are being developed every year. All *lines* have different advantages and disadvantages, whether it is cost, elasticity, abrasion, absorption of water, stiffness, etc. All have to be determined by the owner as to what type best suits a vessel's operation.

At times the term *line* is used when referring to cable or wire, i.e. a command to "Turn loose the headline" may mean a wire and not a fiber-constructed line. However, most times a Pilot will use the term "headwire", but in any case the Mate will know what he is supposed to do.

LINE BOAT

A towboat that is not in a dedicated service, such as a UNIT TOW or the loading of a coal tow at the same dock each trip and delivering it to the same power plant; but rather a boat that picks up and drops barges at various and numerous docks along the river, usually handling large mixed cargo tows. The vessel may only work on a particular river, such as a length of the Ohio to Cairo where it might drop its tow and return upstream with another tow of different barge types and numerous destinations. Its original tow would be broken up to be placed in other *line boat* tows with perhaps some barges going up the Upper Mississippi while other barges would be placed in the tow of a larger horsepower towboat going down the Lower Mississippi to New Orleans. Also called a *Line Haul Boat*.

LINE DECK

The *deck* area of either the bow or stern of a barge and referred to by that name.

LINED UP

The term refers to when a Pilot is approaching a bridge or a lock and has the tow in shape to efficiently and safely navigate through the bridge, or into a lock chamber or along a lock wall.

LINES OF DEMARCATION

See: DEMARCATION LINE

LIQUID CARGO

Cargo that is transported in tank barges and can freely flow. The products range from food oils (soybean or palm oil), petroleum oils (diesel fuel, gasoline, heavy crude, etc.), sulphuric acid, molasses, alcohol, to all sorts of chemical products.

LIST

Occurs when a vessel is not on an even keel and draws more water on one side; a tilt or inclination to that side is apparent that appears to be more or less permanent. It is not known as to the origination use of the term in a nautical sense. Some believe it comes from the Old English *lystan*, which really meant "a desire or inclination" for someone, but a *list* isn't a desirable condition.

LOA

An abbreviation for *length over-all*. It is the length of a vessel, and/or tow, from its extreme forward end to the extremity of its stern.

LOAD

1. A barge that has been loaded with cargo and is in tow, or is at a fleet awaiting transit to an unloading dock destination. It remains a *load* until a consignee releases it after unloading the cargo when it is termed an EMPTY. The word is of Germanic origin and is related to "lead". At one time it meant a "way" or "journey". Its current nautical use of carrying cargo came into being about the 15th century.

2. The amount of power being supplied by an engine or a generator.

3. A crew member who has gone ashore and imbibed in too many liquid

spirits, i.e. "He came aboard carrying a heck of a load".

LOAD BINDERS
Different types of fastening devices that keep roll covers tightly fastened together when they are closed.

LOAD LINE CERTIFICATE
A *certificate* or document issued by the American Bureau of Shipping, or other officially recognized classification society, acting as agent for the USCG to assign a *load line* to a vessel that shows the minimum freeboard and maximum draft the vessel may be loaded to under specified conditions. It indicates where the PLIMSOL MARK shall be placed on the hull. Few barges on the river are assigned *Load Line Certificates* unless they make trips on certain parts of the Great Lakes or go into unprotected areas of the Gulf of Mexico.

LOADED DRAFT or WATERLINE
1. The deepest *draft* of any corner of a barge.
2. The average *draft* of all four corners of a barge. Used in determining the cargo tonnage of the barge by graduated draft tables or DISPLACEMENT TONNAGE TABLE.

LOADED TO THE GUNNELS
1. When a deck barge, usually in the sand and gravel trade, has water running over the edge of the deck. See: GUNWALE.
2. An exaggeration for a heavily loaded barge, i.e., "She's loaded to the *gunnels*".
3. Sometimes used to express a heavy tow, i.e., "We're loaded down to the *gunnels*".
4. A drunken crew member who tries to come on board.

LOADING DOCK
A terminal where cargo is loaded onto or into barges.

LOADING HEADER
The pipeline on a tank barge that is used to load or unload liquid cargo.

LOADING RATE
The *rate* at which cargo is loaded into a barge. Usually in the case of dry cargo it is tons per hour. In the case of liquids loading into a tank barge it will be in gallons per hour or barrels per hour.

LOADING SPOT
The place at a dock where a terminal operator requires a barge to be placed in order to load or unload it.

LOCAL KNOWLEDGE
A Pilot that is well POSTED in a river area and is one whose familiarity and experience, as well as frequency of transit through the waters, is more than that which appears on local area charts.

LOCAL NOTICE TO MARINERS
The USCG Commander of the Eighth Coast Guard District issues *notices* or bulletins on a periodic basis as necessary. These *notices* list any changes or discrepancies in the aids to navigation, any public events taking place which could restrict navigation, any warnings of danger such as a sunken craft in or near the channel, or any other occurrence which could affect the safety of navigation in the Eighth Coast Guard District. Up until 2005 these *notices* were sent out to the public upon request but are now placed on the internet and, in emergency situations, are broadcast on marine radio channels.

LOCK
1. An enclosed structure in a body of water that has a gate, or set of gates, at each end which by filling or emptying the chamber are used to raise or lower vessels as they pass from one level to another in a river or canal. The first *lock* believed to be constructed

was on a canal in Egypt in about 300 B.C. In the U.S. the first *locks* were in a canal at Little Falls, NY. They were 10 feet wide by 70 feet long, and had two feet over the sill. *Locks* have been built in various lengths and widths during the history of navigation in the United States; however, the most standard sized locks on the Mississippi system are either 600 feet or 1200 feet in length by 110 feet in width. See: DAVIS ISLAND LOCK and LOCK CHAMBER.

2. The act of making a passage through a *lock* chamber from one level to another. If the passage is from the lower end the process is to *lock up*. If the passage is from the upper pool to the lower pool it is called *lock down*.

LOCK ARRIVAL MARKS

A post or marker above and below a lock entrance when reached by a vessel desiring lockage is considered the time of arrival and which will determine its precedence for lockage if other vessels have arrived. Nearly all vessels at the present time establish lockage turn by use of the radio.

LOCK CHAMBER

The *chamber* of a *lock* is the functional part of the lock where the actual raising and lowering of vessels from one level to another takes place. If a vessel is on the upstream side of a dam it will enter the lock through the opened gates at the upper end and with the lower end gates closed. After the vessel is tied off in the lock, the lockmaster will close the upper gates and the filling valve. He will then open the drain valves allowing the water to leave the chamber by gravity flow. When the water in the chamber is at the level of the downstream side of the dam, or the lower level, the Lockmaster will open the lower lock gates and the vessel will leave the chamber. When a vessel is going upstream the process is reversed, with the drain valve closed and the fill valve opened.

The term *lock* comes to us from Old English *loc,* meaning "to secure an object", and the word *chamber* is from Greek *kamara,* which was "an object with an arched cover". Then that word evolved into the Latin *camera,* as "a vault with arched cover", then on to the French, becoming *chamber* and on to Middle English that described it as a "private room". So that means when a tow is in a *lock chamber* it is secured in a private room, like staying at the Waldorf Astoria.

LOCK DELAY

The time a vessel/tow arrives at a lock facility and cannot proceed to lockage because a queue of tows is already waiting, or perhaps there is an outage, or some other problem, to the time the vessel finally starts its approach to the lock chamber. It is also called *Lock Waiting Time*.

LOCK FLOOR

The bottom or bed of the lock chamber. The depth of the lock chamber is governed by the height of the lock sill which insures closure when the lock gates are closed.

LOCK GATE(S)

1. Miter – Double swinging gates which, at a mitered joint-type closure at the center of a lock chamber, when opened swing into a recessed area of a lock wall. Most of the lock gates on the Western Rivers system are currently of this type. The word comes from Greek *mitra,* meaning "turban", which was a headpiece curved to a point and worn by church authorities. Probably the term was/is used as the two gates in the closed position come to a horizontal apex or point.

2. Sliding or Rolling – This type of gate is recessed into a well on the land side of the lock. On the old low-lift dams on the Ohio River, many of the locks had this type of gate; however, the newer high-lift dams have miter gates.

3. Sumersible – Sometimes called a *Vertical Drop Gate*. A gate that is lowered to the riverbed when in the open position. These types of gates are only possible when the vertical distance between the upper pool and the lower pool is of sufficient depth to lower the gate to the bottom of the river, allowing a vessel with less than 12 feet of draft to enter the chamber from the upper side and to then raise the gate. The Keokuk Lock on the Upper Mississippi has this kind of gate on its upstream side. However, there have been times in the winter season when ice buildup on the bottom of barges was so bad that a downbound tow entering the chamber knocked off the handrails of the submerged lock gate.

LOCK RULES

The *rules* governing lockage are contained in the Code of Federal Regulations, Title 33, Section 207. The particular part governing Rules for the Ohio River, Mississippi River above Cairo, IL, and their tributaries are contained in subsection 300. They used to be printed in a small pamphlet which Pilots called the Blue Book. The Arkansas River had a Red Book and there may have been others.

LOCK SIGNAL

The Lock Rules require certain audio *signals* to be sounded to request entrance to the lock but nearly all lockages by commercial vessels are now arranged by radio communication. If unable to reach the lock by radio the following *signals* will be sounded on the vessel's whistle:

Single lockage required – One long blast, followed by one short blast.

Double lockage required – One long blast, followed by two short blasts.

When the lock is ready for the vessel to enter the lockmaster will sound the following *signals*:

To enter a single lock (or the landward lock if there are twin locks) – One long blast.

To enter the riverward lock (if there are twin locks) – Two long blasts.

If radio communication is out and the lock *signal* lights are inoperable, the lock will use the following audio *signals* as appropriate:

One long blast indicates permission to enter if a single lockage, or to enter the landward chamber of twin locks.

Two long blasts indicates permission to enter the riverward chamber if there are twin chambers.

One short blast for permission to leave the lock if a single lockage, or to leave the landward chamber in the case of twin locks.

Two short blasts for permission to leave the riverward chamber.

After the lockage is completed and the gates are opened, the Lockmaster shall sound on the whistle:

You may depart the chamber (or the landward one if there are twin locks) – One short blast.

You may depart the riverward chamber (if there are twin locks) – Two short blasts.

The si*g*nal of the lockmaster to attract attention, indicate caution, or to *signal* danger is the sounding of four or more short blasts.

LOCK SIGNAL LIGHT

Locks may supplement lockage readiness by use of flashing lights, as follows:

Red Light – Stand Clear, lock not ready to enter.

Amber Light – Lock being made ready, vessel may approach, under full control.

Green Light – Lock ready for entrance

Green and Amber – Lock ready for entrance but lock gates cannot be recessed fully.

It should be noted here that unlike the USCG, which has succumbed to international decision that "amber" is not a color but a resin, the USACE is still of the opinion that as "amber" can be stated as the color of the yellowish cast of the resin, and has decided that if the "amber waves of grain" have any validity, they can glow also on their warning lights.

LOCK SILL

The concrete threshold upon which the lock gate rests when it is in the closed position, allowing an almost watertight seal to keep water from entering or leaving the lock chamber. See: SILL.

LOCK VALVES

The *lock valves* control the flow of water into and out of the lock chamber. Various types of *valves* are used in different locking systems, i.e. gate *valves*, butterfly *valves*, etc. To drop the level of water in the lock, both the upper and the lower lock gates are closed. The dewatering or discharge *valves* are opened and the fill *valves* are closed. The water is evacuated by gravity flow from ports leading into a CULVERT and then to the river stream until the level in the chamber is the same as the tail water at the dam. When the dewatering of the lock is completed, the lower lock gates are opened to receive a vessel or allow one to depart from the chamber.

To fill the lock chamber the reverse occurs. After a vessel enters the lock chamber from the lower side of the dam the lower lock gates are closed. The fill *valves* are opened and the dewatering *valves* are closed. Water flows into the chamber through the ports from the culvert by gravity until the chamber's water level is the same as that of the upper pool level. The upper lock gates are opened and the vessel leaves the lock and continues its journey.

LOCK WALL

At the present time, a concrete structure that consists of a GUIDE WALL on the upstream and downstream ends which is also called the *long wall*, and the chamber, or *short wall* of the lock itself. There also may be a GUARD WALL on the riverward side of the lock. At one time the *walls* consisted of rock-filled cribs or of rock masonry.

LOCKAGE or LOCKING

The act or operation of *locking* a vessel(s). Types of *lockages*: DOUBLE, ICE (LOCKING), JACKKNIFE, KNOCKOUT SINGLE, OVERAGE TOW, RECREATIONAL BOAT, and SET OVER SINGLE.

LOCKING GUARDS

The act of two steamers racing extremely close to one another and then are sucked together, with neither one able to break loose from the other without losing speed and therefore allowing the other vessel to win the race to a lock, dock, or whatever. Since racing is not allowed by the USCG anymore because it is an unsafe practice, you no longer see this type of action.

LOCKING TIME

The time recorded by the lock tender to process a vessel/tow through the lock from the start of lockage to the end of the lockage.

LOCKMAN

Also called a *Lock Tender*. They are the persons who handle the deck crew's lines, work the barge haulage system if necessary, get the tow statistics, do routine maintenance at the lock, and probably cut the grass around the esplanade of the lock.

LOCKMASTER

The person in overall charge of the lock. Usually lives on the lock grounds and assigns the duties to the lockmen who operate under his/her direction. The *Lockmaster* has authority to issue all necessary orders and directions "to any and every person within the limits of the lock and the lock area, whether navigating the lock or not".

LOFT or LOFTING

The actual drafting of lines full scale in a MOLD LOFT of a shipyard to lay out drawings on construction templates for building a vessel.

LOG

1. The act of making an entry in the LOG BOOK.
2. A device used to measure speed through the water.
3. A large timber or tree floating in the water which can cause a great deal of damage to a paddlewheel or a propeller.

LOG BOOK

An "official" journal that records the basic events that take place aboard a vessel such as listing crew members, crew changes, mileages at given times, barges in tow, picking up and dropping off barges, groundings, lockages with times recorded, accidents, drills, and any other incidents or observations the Master or Pilot may record. The use of the word *log* in this sense for entries of a vessel's daily happenings comes from the use by ships years ago when they wanted to determine their speed. The Captain would have a piece of wood (log) dropped over the side of his vessel at the bow and then determine the time it took to reach the stern. By knowing the length of the ship he could estimate the vessel's speed. The event, along with the time, conditions, etc. was written down in a journal which became known as the *ship's log*. In the age of computers, the *log* entries for many companies are now recorded electronically on an official company form for rapid transmission to the headquarters where the company is based.

Some crew members, especially the Pilot may also keep unofficial *logs* of the happenings aboard the vessel, especially on their watch. See: BAR BOOK. Engineers also keep *logs* of happenings during their watches. In the steamboat days engineers recorded the changes in engine bell signals. See: BELL SIGNALS.

LOG JAM

Occurred most often when a *log* raft would hit a snag and hang up with the rest of the logs in the raft piling on top of one another. Originally the loggers would try to pry out the key log, the one that was first hung up, but if they were successful it sometimes became impossible for the raftsmen to get out of the way as the logs surged downstream. Many lost their lives, so they started carrying dynamite, setting the charge as close to the key log as possible and blowing apart the *jam*.

LOG OR LUMBER RAFT

Consisted of a mass of logs tied together and floated downriver to be cut up for finished lumber at a saw mill. A lot of commerce on the rivers before the steamboat consisted of timber floated in *log rafts*, especially out of the smaller streams. Europe denuded its coastal forests as well as those along their rivers systems for use in building ships and for heat energy, as was done in the U.S. When the population increased, lumber was used for building, and the land was needed for cultivation.

First the *rafts* only floated with the current. They were controlled, somewhat, by long sweep oars at the bow and stern, but current and wind did most of the navigating. Then small sidewheel steamers were used to help guide the rafts. Later sternwheelers were considered more efficient, and finally bow boats were also used for large *rafts*. They were lashed athwartship at the head of the *raft* to control its direction by backing or coming ahead on signals from the raft boat doing the pushing. The largest *log raft* floating down the Upper Mississippi to Rock Island was in 1896. It measured 270 feet wide by 1550 feet in length and contained about 2,250,000 board feet.

The business of log rafting on the Western Rivers pretty well died out in the very late 1800s and was almost extinct after WW I, with only an occasional small raft coming down the river. If you see one today, slow down and give them a salute on the whistle.

LOG STAMP

The end of each log in a log raft was *stamped* with a mark to designate the owner. It was similar to ranchers branding cattle and helped prevent theft, as well as identify logs that would break away in a mishap. After the raft arrived at a sawmill the logs could be identified by their *log stamp* and be properly accounted for when payment to their owners was made.

LOGISTICAL BALANCE or IMBALANCE

1. The coordination of a barging company to efficiently manage the movement of its barging equipment, including towboats, tugs, and barges, as well as crew members and supplies to their best advantage to benefit the company and its customers.

2. *Balance* is when a company's barges and the power to push them are in the proper and orderly ports in a river system, along with shipper demand for their service.

3. *Imbalance* occurs at such times as when there is a lock outage, channel blockage, extreme weather conditions of high water, low water, hurricanes, etc., when tows and barges stack up at one end of the transportation system, creating a backlog, while at the other end of the system there becomes a lack of available equipment to load cargo. When the barging pipeline is jammed it usually takes a period of time to get it back into *balance*.

4. The term comes from French *logistique,* which was in reference to the "movement and supplies" needed to support their army.

LONE STAR (steamer)

The last sternwheel steamboat in commercial cargo trade. It was laid up in 1967. In its last years it was pushing sand and gravel barges near Rock Island, IL, on the Upper Mississippi River.

LONG LINE

"Putting out the *long line*" usually refers to when the company is going to tie up the towboat or tug for a period of time and the crew will be laid off.

LONG SPLICE

When marrying two pieces of line or cordage together, it is a splice that is used to keep the spliced line almost the same diameter of the original line in order that it may readily be reeved through a set of blocks.

LONG TON

A weight of 2240 pounds. Also called a *metric ton*. Not used very much on the rivers since the standard measurement utilized for cargo is SHORT TON. See: TON.

LONGITUDE

The east-west measurement in degrees of points or places on a chart. The word comes from the Latin *longitudo,* meaning "length or long". See: GPS and LATITUDE.

LONGITUDINAL DIKES

A long continuous dike structure extending from a bank downstream in a generally parallel alignment with a desired channel line. It is often constructed in association with tie-in BAFFEL DIKES to the bank perpendicular to the *longitudinal dike*, which adds stability to the structure.

LONGITUDINAL FRAMING or BULKHEAD

The type of horizontal framing on the interior of a vessel's hull which provides strength to prevent sagging, hogging or buckling when exposed to rough water or loading stresses.

LONGSHORE WORKER

A person who is employed at a dock to load or unload vessels. Sometimes also called a STEVEDORE. In the days of steamboats, the persons who preformed the duties of placing cargo on or taking it off a steamboat were called ROUSTABOUTS.

LOOKOUT

Rule 5 of the Inland Navigation Rules requires that "Every vessel shall at all times maintain a proper *look-out* by sight and hearing as well as by all available means appropriate in the prevailing circumstances and conditions so as to make a full appraisal of the situation and of the risk of collision". Many court cases over the years have described the "five Ws" of a *lookout*, or the what, where, when, who, and why of *lookouts*.

The U.S. Congress in enacting the Inland Navigation Rules statute reported that, "On vessels where there is an unobstructed all-around view provided at the steering station, as on certain pleasure craft, fishing boats, and towing vessels…the watch officer or helmsman may safely serve as the *look-out*". The report goes on to say that certain conditions have to be taken into consideration, but it was not the intent of the rules to require additional personnel if none was required to enhance safety. In any official investigation of a navigational incident the first question will probably be, "Did you have a lookout?"

LOOM

The handle or the place one's hand is placed when manipulating an OAR.

LOOM OF LIGHT

A glow of light in the distance, around or across a bend, that is reflective in certain atmospheric conditions from city shore lights or another towing vessel's searchlight.

LOOP

A curvature in the bight of a line that crosses itself. It is the start of making one of the most useful knots to a riverman, the BOWLINE. However, if any *loop* is in a slack length of line it can be dangerous if a person steps in it; if the line becomes taut it could cause him/her to fall, go overboard, or be seriously injured.

LOOSE-HEADED

The act of a towboat or tug running without barges in tow. It is also called *light-headed*, or LIGHT BOAT.

LORAN-C

A radio-navigation system that can be used to plot a vessel's position. The term stands for *Long Range Navigation*. It is not used on river vessels since due to frequent changes in course on a river tow, plotting (other than visual awareness), is useless for river navigation. It is being supplanted by GPS positioning and AIS systems, with possible decommissioning of the LORAN system.

LOSE SEAL

Refers to the action when a towboat sucks air with its propeller in its tunnel and has erratic, or no, thrust.

LOSS

In the marine business, the term *loss* usually refers to some sort of casualty, such as the injury or death of a crewmember, or damage to a vessel, or harm to its cargo.

LOUISANA PURCHASE

Volumes have been written about the acquisition of much of the land west of the Mississippi to the Continental Divide that at the time was under the control of France which had recently acquired it from Spain when Napoleon through a treaty took possession of the area. He needed money to hold on to his military gains and did not understand the possible future value of the Louisiana Territory. The amount of land acquired about doubled the size of the United States at that time, 1803. Most important was the free access to the Mississippi and the port at New Orleans which had been a contentious issue when the area was previously under the control of Spain. Most of the rest of the land was an unknown. The acquisition that was obtained consisted of over 800,000 sq. miles for the price of $15 million, or about three cents per acre.

The following year, 1804, President Thomas Jefferson sent the so-called Corps of Discovery, under the leadership of Meriwether Lewis and William Clark who joined up at the FALLS OF THE OHIO, which marked the beginning of their expedition together to explore the new territory and report on their findings.

LOUISVILLE AND PORTLAND CANAL

The FALLS OF THE OHIO at approximately mile 604 on the Ohio River was a serious impediment to navigation during periods of low water. The falls were rock ledge barriers left from glacial times centuries ago causing a fall of approximately 22 feet over a length of about two miles. Early navigation on the river required cargo to be unloaded, carted to the opposite end of the falls and reloaded to another vessel for further transportation to destination. Many flatboats and other craft were lost trying to run the falls when there was scant available water depth.

With the advent of the steamboat, commercial interests in Kentucky, Indiana, and Ohio put forth ideas for a canal that would bypass the Falls, with fierce debate on which side of the river it should be built. Private funds for engineering were put forth, but insufficient funding caused them all to fail. However, various studies continued and it was believed the Kentucky route for canal improvement was the most practicable and economical. In 1825 the *Louisville and Portland Canal Company* was incorporated by the State of Kentucky with authority to raise money for acquisition of land and building a canal. Construction started the following year. After many financial crisis, as well as construction difficulties, the canal finally opened at the end of 1830 with tolls charged for usage. The canal on the upstream side was about two miles long and contained a set of three lifting locks, each 50 by 190 feet, and each with a lift of eight feet, eight inches. Many problems ensued, such as flood damage, sabotage, mud siltation, and over the years became inadequate to accommodate the size vessels being used on the river. It was reported a while after the canal opened that a barge was deliberately sunk at the entrance and kegs of gunpowder were set and exploded at one of the locks causing extensive damage. No culprits were apprehended, but it was believed that the perpetrators were probably the Falls Pilots that had lost a lot of their employment because of lockage operation or the teamster draymen that no longer were required to portage the cargo of vessels that could not run the Falls in low water.

In 1860 Congress authorized the *Canal Company* to borrow monies necessary to enlarge the canal and construct a set of two-tier locks with a total lift of 26 feet; the chambers being 80 by 350 feet. Work soon started, but funding for the Civil War and inflated costs brought construction to a halt. After the war, construction resumed and the new locks opened in 1872. Tolls for usage were still being collected. Finally in 1874 the U.S. assumed control of the Canal, and in 1880 Congress rescinded further collection of toll usage fees.

In the early 1900s canalization of the entire Ohio River began. At the *Louisville and Portland Canal* lock, now called Lock 41, it was decided to build a 110 by 600 foot lock and enlarge the canal width to 200 feet. Delays, because of WW I, accidents at the site, and floods hindered progress, but the new facility opened in 1921. As the Ohio River modernization project started after WW II in the 1950s, a new companion lock chamber 1200 feet long was built. Also undertaken was the deepening and widening of the channel and basin to reduce surge effect for the amount of water displaced when filling the large chamber. When completed the facility was named for William McAlpine who had been the dean of USACE Ohio River engineering.

Tonnage through the canal continued to grow. Congress authorized the building of a twin 1200 foot lock. Construction started with the demolition of the old 600 foot lock in 2001 and the new lock should be in service in 2008-9 time frame. See: FALLS OF THE OHIO and FALLS PILOT.

LOW HEAD

The vertical distance between the surface elevation of the water in the upper pool and the surface elevation of the water in the lower pool at a lock.

LOW PRESSURE

A system of weather patterns that usually brings cloudy and unsettled conditions. *Lows* rotate in a counter-clockwise direction. See: HIGH PRESSURE.

LOW WATER

A time when the gauges of a river, or a section of it, are at its lowest normal operating stages to maintain navigation. When it is *extreme low water* the navigable channel becomes restricted and barges may have to be lightloaded.

LOW-WATER DAM

A fixed weir placed in a back channel in order to divert its water flow to the main stem channel.

LOW-WATER DATUM

It is a point of reference used by the USACE to fix a gauge at a point of elevation in a river when determining rises and falls at that designated area.

LOW-WATER MARK

A point of reference to the lowest recorded level in a river at a given point.

LOWER

1. A shorthand term that Pilots use when referring to the LOWER MISSISSIPPI RIVER from Cairo Point to the Head of the Passes.
2. The main deck of a towboat is often referred to as the *lower deck*.
3. When used in referring to a point or section of a crossing or a bend, the term means further downstream, i.e. "Avoid the shallow water on the *lower* red", or "When you come out of the chute at the *lower* end, hold on the big old sycamore tree on the Kentucky shore".

LOWER GAUGE

In pooled channels with locks and dams the *lower gauge* is the downstream measurement of the river pool at the lock. It does not necessarily indicate the depth of the river at that point.

LOWER MISSISSIPPI RIVER

The *Lower Mississippi* is like the trunk of a huge tree, gathering the waters of an entire basin, only instead of growing upwards it drains most of the interior of the country between the Appalachians and the Rocky Mountains sending its fresh, and muddy, waters to the salty Gulf in a fruitless attempt to dilute it. Its trunk is anchored by its roots running east and west on the GIWW, and its tap root goes down past the HEAD OF THE PASSES to the Gulf of Mexico. Its lower branches are the RED RIVER system, the ARKANSAS and WHITE. It main mid-limbs include its largest, the OHIO with its many branches (tributaries), and then the limbs of the MISSOURI and the ILLINOIS, with its crown of the UPPER MISSISSIPPI that reaches all the way up to Lake ITASCA. The river's history in detail would take up a large amount of library space.

Although the entire length of the *Mississippi* is 2,348 miles, its distance from Cairo Point where the OHIO and the UPPER MISSISSIPPI joined together to form the *Lower Mississippi* and flow to the HEAD OF THE PASSES is measured by the USACE to be 964 miles. It was longer in the days when canoes, pirogues, and flatboats were first used in its navigation, but with natural and man-made cut-offs of bends, stabilization of its banks, and training works of various kinds have, at least for the present, fairly well harnessed the river into its existing course to the Gulf (unless another New Madrid earthquake occurs).

The Spanish explorer Hernando DeSoto, seeking to find gold, may have been, in 1541, the first European to travel through the Mississippi Valley. Though never finding the glitter of gold, and rebuffed by the natives, he was buried "at sea" in the waters of the mighty Mississippi in 1542. Other explorers followed to the river from the European powers of the 1600s, LaSalle and Father Hennepin also of Spain, Jolliet and Father Marquette from France, as well as the English coastal settlers that crossed the Appalachians and staked new claims in the lands.

President Jefferson's treaty with France in 1803 resulting in the acquisition of the Louisiana territories solidified the control of the *Mississippi River*, its banks, and its watershed to United States control. In not too long a time, its trading posts became cities, the lands became farms and homes to settlers, then steamboats had unimpeded access to the many reaches of the valley and the trading center of New Orleans located at the foot of the tree called *Mississippi* became one of the main seaports of the nation.

The romanticism of the river from the war of 1812, through the Civil War, flatboating, keelboating, steamboating, varnished truths, bald lies, and some veracity, by all who have lived, worked, traveled, and vagabonded their days and nights on the river have been written, sung, or faded away on a moonless night; but the river keeps rolling along, a ripple at a time, repeating itself one generation after another. What more can one say about our brief wisp of years here about a stream that existed before man laid eyes on it. May its trunk never be cut, its roots continue to reach out, it limbs be strengthened, and its branches bear bountiful fruit. Also see: MISSISSIPPI RIVER and UPPER MISSISSIPPI (as well as its branches).

L – SHAPED DIKES

Basically a SPUR DIKE with the river end like the foot of an "L" parallel to the flow of the current to reduce the turbulence and scouring effect at the end of the dike.

LST (LANDING SHIP TANK)

In World War II it was determined that to be successful in invading the islands in the Pacific held by Japan and the shores of Europe held by the Germans and other Axis powers that a new type of vessel was needed to land fighting men and equipment. Thus, the *LST* was designed. They were 327 feet long, 50 feet wide, and had a draft of 12 feet. Over 1000 of them were built. Of these, 724 were built at five shipyards on the inland river system. The first hull was built at Dravo Shipyard in Pittsburgh in 1942. Other yards doing construction were Ambridge, also in Pittsburgh, Jeffersonville Boat and Machinery Co. (later called Jeffboat) in Indiana, Evansville Shipyard in Indiana, and the Chicago Bridge and Iron Works at its yard in Seneca on the Illinois River.

Some 4000 vessels of different types were built for the war effort at these and other inland river yards in the early 1940s, including sub-chasers, minesweepers, destroyer escorts, other smaller landing craft, and yard tugs. Depending on one's perspective, *LSTs* were either affectionately or derisively known as "Large Slow Targets". *LST 325*, which was refurbished by a group of persons who sailed on *LSTs* in WW II, is now a museum located on the Ohio River at Evansville, IN. See: CATFISH NAVY.

LUBBER LINE

A fixed line on a compass exactly aligned with the fore and aft position of a vessel. The meaning of *lubber* is "a person who is lazy and clumsy". In some places it means deceitful or a swindler. One has to wonder how the word came to be tagged on to a description of something that is on the straight and narrow.

LUGGING

Refers to a diesel engine on a towboat or tug that is operating at an inefficient or low RPM or the engine is laboring under an excessive load. See: LABOR.

LULL

A temporary subsiding of wind force during a storm. Its origin is from Latin *lallare,* from which comes "lullaby", used to calm a baby to sleep, or maybe a Pilot.

LUMINOUS RANGE

The *luminous range* of navigation lights required to be displayed on vessels are measured in "candelas", which have a stated threshold factor, range of visibility, and a condition of transmissivity, all of which are set down by an International Commission on Illumination. These factors are listed in Annex I of the Inland Navigation Rules.

LWL

1. The loaded waterline of a vessel.
2. The low waterline along the shore.

LYING BY or LYING TO
See: LAY.

THE LAZY (OR LIAR'S) BENCH

USACE LOCK OPERATIONS

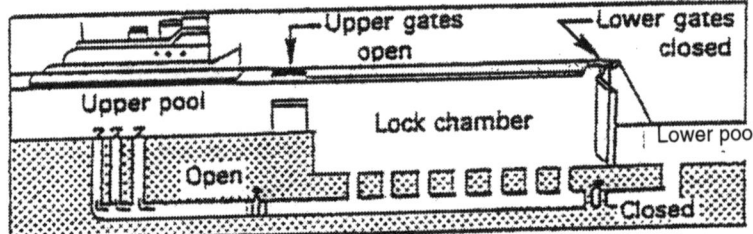

Filling valve open; emptying valve closed. Lock filled to upper pool level. Tow enters lock.

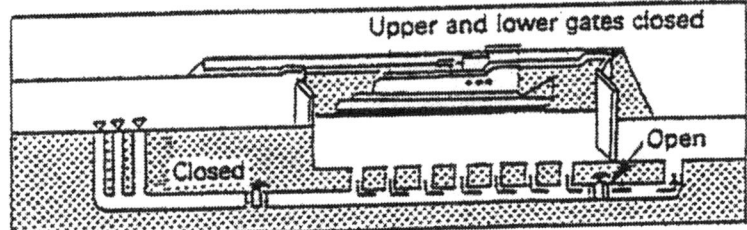

Filling valve closed; emptying valve open. Lock emptying to lower pool level.

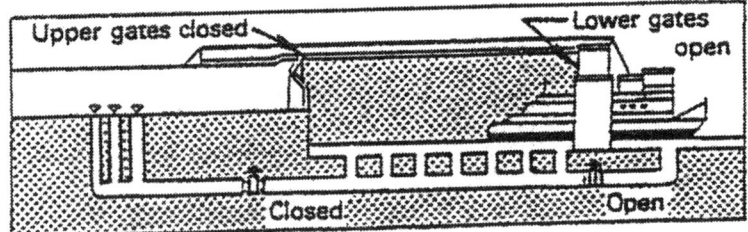

Filling valve closed, emptying valve open. Lock at lower pool level. Tow leaves lock.

DOUBLE LOCK OPERATIONS

Shown is a towboat and tow double locking southbound on the Upper Mississippi River at lock 11, Dubuque, IA. The first half of the tow, 9 loaded barges, has been pulled out of the chamber after lockage. The upper gates are opening to receive the second half of the tow, 6 barges and towboat. When it is locked down, the lower gates will open and the two parts of the tow will be wired together and the entire tow will continue down river.

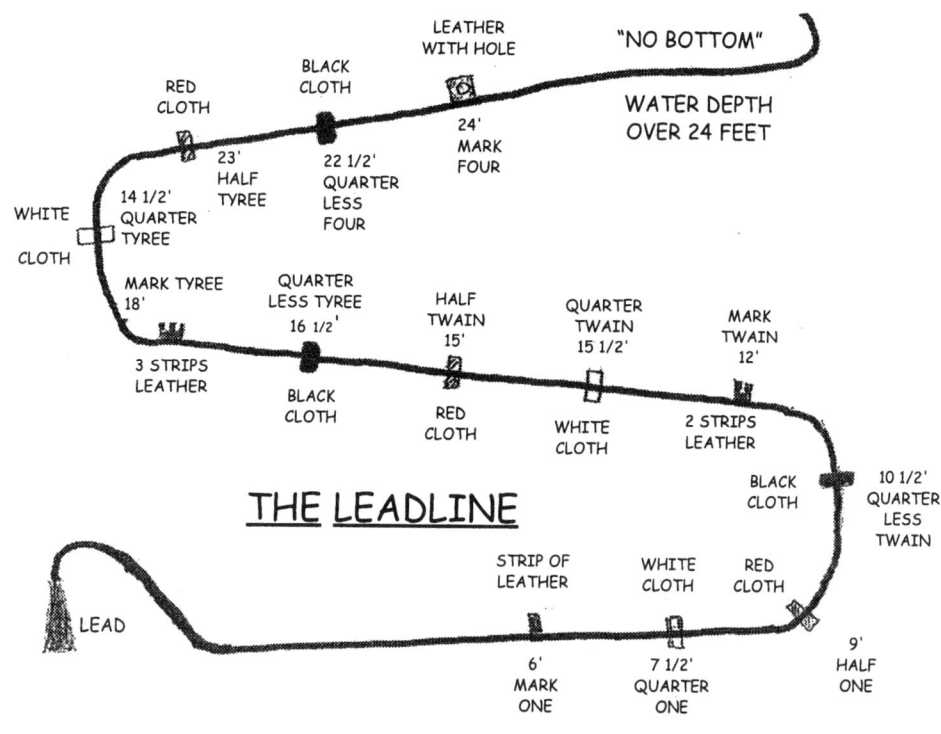

THE LEADLINE

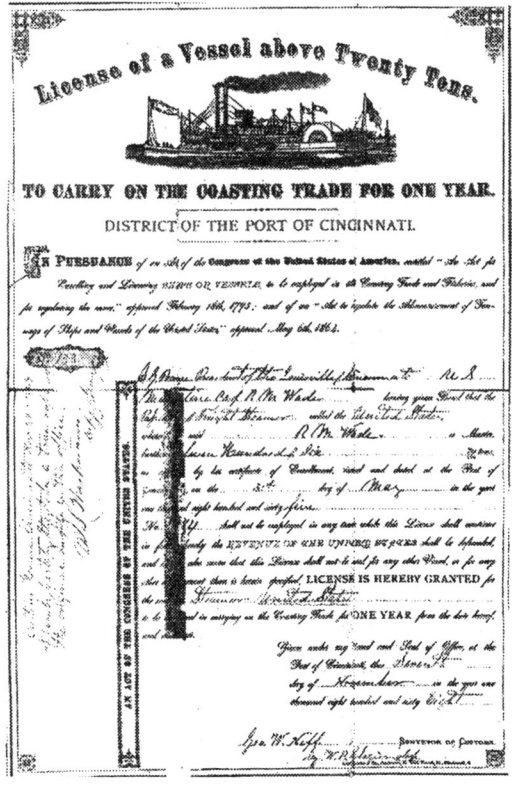

STEAMBOAT LICENSE

Copy of a steamboat licenseissued to the Str. UNITED STATES in 1865. On Dec. 4, 1868, she departed downbound for Cincinnati. At about the same time her company's sister vessel the Str. AMERICA left the Louisville wharf upbound. The boats were in passenger trade between the two cities, meeting near Warsaw, KY. On this night, however, there were complications as to the sounding of passing signals and the vessels came into a collision resulting in a great fire, a large loss of lives, and destruction of both vessels.

Courtesy of Life on the Ohio River History Museum Vevay, IN.

LIFEBOAT STATION

The only lifeboat station that was operated on the Western Rivers was locatd at Louisville, KY. just above the Falls of the Ohio

LANDING SHIP, TANK

Of the 1051 LST's built during WWII about two-thirds of them were constructed at inland "cornfield" shipyards located on the Western Rivers along with almost 3500 vessels built for naval service. They acquired the not so flattering nickname of "Large Slow Target" however, they were an extremely important component in winning the war.

FIBER LINE

The makeup of its component fiber parts as used on river and canal boats.

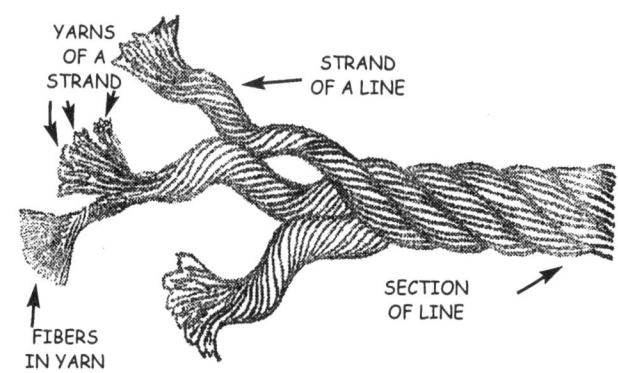

LAKE ITASCA FACTOID

It has been said and reported that on average a drop of rain that falls from the sky into Lake Itasca, the source of the Mississippi River, will take about 90 days before it will finally reach the Gulf of Mexico. It will then evaporate into the sky, enter a cloud and soon become a droplet of rain that again falls into Lake Itasca, starting a new journey.

M

MACHINERY SPACE
The area of a vessel where the main propulsion and auxiliary engines are located. It is more often referred to as the *engine room*.

MACKINAW BOAT
A flat or somewhat curved-bottomed boat with a pointed bow, built in various sizes, about five to 10 feet wide and up to 50 feet long, with a draft of less than 20 inches when loaded. It took its name from French fur traders who came from the Great Lakes area where the boats were commonly used. They loaded pelts and furs on the upper reaches of the Missouri River and took them down to St. Louis for sale.

MAGNETIC COMPASS
An instrument with a needle that is attracted to, and points to, the magnetic North Pole. Tugs may have one onboard, but they are seldom used on river towboats.

MAIDEN VOYAGE
After a boat is built, is accepted for service, and the shipyard turns it over to the new owner(s), it is the first trip, or voyage the vessel makes. Though not technically correct, it can also be the first trip made by a used boat that has been sold to a new owner. *Maiden* usually is a designation for a fair young lass who has not yet made her way in life but has been sheltered on the bank as SHE (see) grows up in a shipyard. So when she is launched and christened she goes on her first *voyage* as a *maiden* in her new nautical world.

MAILBOAT
From the earliest days of river commerce through the age of steamboats, mail was carried by river craft. The first *mailboats* were propelled by oars, similar to a whaleboat and were mainly used on the Ohio River. Later steamboats, both small and large, on main streams and their tributaries, regularly carried mail.

MAILBOX
Back in mid-1800s a Pilot Organization started placing *mailboxes* at various landings on the river system. Each member of the group had a key to the *box* in which they would place reports of their observations on channel conditions and changes over the previous stretch of river they had piloted, as well as pick up a report of another Pilot who had recently run the section of river that was ahead of them.

Later on, the survey boats of the USACE took over this duty and placed *mailboxes* on many of the rivers where there were frequently changing channel conditions. The last river to have the *boxes* was the Missouri River, but they were phased out of service in about 1970.

The channel inspector on each survey boat, dredge, or in the office would sometimes type or handwrite the conditions of the channel in his area with the marks to run, the buoys in the crossings, and any other pertinent information. The survey boat had a mimeograph machine where the Pilot would run off numerous copies and place them in the Corps *mailbox*. These *mailboxes* were not at docks or landings, but at some area on the bank of the river where a tow could nose in and a deckhand could readily climb the bank to the *mailbox* and procure a copy.

MAIN DECK
The first weather deck above the waterline that extends from the bow to the stern, as well as from the outer starboard side to the outer port side. *Main* when used in a nautical sense usually denotes a principle or largest in size or power type of structure or appliance, i.e. *main deck* (as noted), engines, channel or current, etc.

MAIN STEM or CHANNEL
1. A major river that receives its

flows from tributary streams, i.e., the Ohio River starts at the junction of the Allegheny and Monongahela rivers. These two rivers were in themselves *main stem* rivers in the basins they drained, but then became a part of the *main stem* Ohio River basin, which collects water from numerous creeks, ripples, other streams and rivers. Among the Ohio's tributaries are the Muskingum, Kanawha, Guyandot, Big Sandy, Scioto, Licking, Kentucky, Green, Wabash, Cumberland, and Tennessee rivers, all of which are considered *main stem* in their valleys. Eventually the Ohio River itself becomes a tributary flowing into the Mississippi River. So it becomes a matter of interpretation as to when and where a river is the *main* and which one is the *stem*.

2. Where more than one navigable channel is available in a stream, such as a channel behind an island, or off into a slough or between two or more spans of a bridge, the preferred channel to use is considered the *main channel*.

MAINLINE TOW

A towboat with tow that generally runs a fairly long river route over a lengthy section of it, i.e., most of the Lower Mississippi River or the Ohio River.

MAINTENANCE and CURE

A legal term under maritime law which generally says that a seaman, which includes those persons who are part of the crew of a river craft, who becomes ill or is injured when working on the vessel is entitled to a reasonable level of compensation to *maintain* himself/herself while off the vessel until he/she has reached a level of soundness from injury or any impairment from disease (the *cure*).

MAJOR REHABILITATION

A program undertaken by the USACE to restore capability of the infrastructure for which it is responsible. *Rehab* is undertaken on aging navigation structures due to outages and/or downtime just to keep a L & D in operation where frequent failures occur, or there is a possibility of this happening. The program is utilized when lack of reliability of the system and safety of personnel and users becomes apparent. *Rehab* is not just maintenance and repair at a lock or dam, but rather an overhaul of the structural components, including the lock chamber, its valves, the walls, fittings, hauling units, electrical motors, etc., as well as the lock gates, dam gates, and other integral parts of the L & D.

MAKE

To perform, or to execute, i.e. to *make* (navigate through) a bridge span, to *make* (navigate into) a lock chamber, to *make* (get to) Cairo Fleet, to *make* (steer) a bend, to *make* (transit) 36 miles of river on the last watch, to *make* (leak) water, etc.

MAKE FAST

To securely tie off a line or a wire.

MAKING IRON

A caulking iron, used to compress oakum caulking in the seams between the planking of a wooden hull prior to receiving the PITCH from the PAYPOT.

MAKING TOW

The gathering and assembling of barges, and wiring them tightly together into a tow to be pushed by a towboat or tug.

MAKING UP

The act of fastening barges, one to another, in assembling a tow. It is also the act of FACING UP a towboat to a barge or a tow.

MAKING WAY

The act of a vessel moving through the water. It can be *headway* or *sternway*.

MALE

The part of a fitting that is inserted

into a corresponding FEMALE part to make a connection.

MALLET

A type of wooden hammer, similar to a BEETLE, but with a larger striking head. Used for various purposes aboard a vessel. Sometimes, in place of the beetle, used with caulking irons to drive in caulking, or to apply extra force on a FID when splicing a stiff line. The term is from the Latin *malleus*, meaning "hammer".

MAN

1. The crewing of a vessel, whether it is a towboat, tug, or the yawl.
2. The act of doing a job, i.e. "*Man* the pump", "*man* the hose", "*man* the capstan", etc.

MANEUVER

The steering and handling of a tug or towboat, changing course or speed when underway or when operating at a dock or landing. The term comes from the Latin *manus*, meaning "hand or helper" and *operari*, meaning "to work", in essence meaning manual labor. It was adopted by the French in describing movements by its war ships, probably from the activities of sailors when manning the sails. It has come down to describing the art of Pilots skillfully navigating tows on our rivers and canals.

MANEUVER BOAT

A small barge equipped with a derrick on one end used to lower and to raise the wickets at movable dams. It is sometimes called a *wicket boat*.

MANEUVERABILITY

The capability and handling efficiency of a vessel in different situations. A Pilot may say of a towboat, "She steers well, but doesn't back worth a tinker's damn", or "She's slow to respond to the rudder, but when we put the throttle to her, she flies". But if the vessel is really not too good in responding in critical situations, the Pilot might declare with tongue in cheek, "She may not shove, but at least she won't handle at all".

MAN-HELPER

A pole of eight feet or so with a paintbrush attached to the end of it to assist a deckhand in painting inaccessible areas and avoid HOLIDAYS.

MANHOLE

A small opening, usually round or oblong, with a secure cover that allows a person entry into a tank or void space of a vessel.

MANIFEST

A document that lists the cargo, the amount, origin and destination, and other particulars. Most towing vessels do not carry *manifests* for all the cargoes in their barges, but often list their generic names in the deck logs. They do carry *manifests* for tank barge cargoes. Passenger vessels carry *manifests*, listing all persons aboard, including crew members. The term is from the Latin *manifestus*, which came to mean "a declaration".

MANIFOLD

1. The end of a piping system where a liquid cargo product is loaded, or where it is discharged from a vessel. The term comes from the German *manch*, meaning "many".
2. A grouping of pipe connections and valves on a vessel or at a terminal dock that collects or distributes liquid to various other pipes, tanks, or machinery.

MANILA LINE

A type of strong natural fiber from the leaves of the Abaca plant grown in the Philippines that is made into line. It was extensively used in all maritime trades prior to the development of synthetic line.

MAN-OVERBOARD

The unfortunate incident of a person falling off a vessel into a river or canal. Drills are conducted aboard manned vessels as to the best practices to be used to recover the person and to prevent a reoccurrence. The shouting of *MAN-OVERBOARD!* is to alert all in hearing distance that a person has fallen of the boat or barge and to render assistance.

MAN-ROPES

Lines, small wires, or chains used along the deck of a vessel to keep someone from falling overboard. Usually located on the main deck where fixed rails would tend to become damaged while the give of a line, wire, or chain-type railing would be flexible while still retaining its usefulness of protecting from slippage off a vessel. See: LIFELINES.

MANUAL

1. A device or thing that is operated by hand, not automatically or electronically.

2. The act of doing something by hand, and not by use of mechanical force.

3. One of the many instruction books aboard a towboat or tug with detailed directions as to what should/must be done, when, how, why, and whatever else might be required.

MARAD

An acronym for the U.S. MARITIME ADMINISTRATION.

MARINA

Refers to a harbor or docking facility where recreational boats are moored and/or are serviced. Usually these establishments provide fuel, supplies, pump-out facilities and other services to small craft. The source of the word is from the Latin *marinus*, to the Spanish *marino*, meaning "harbor".

MARINE

Anything that affects the water environment, whether an ocean, lake, river, or stream. Used extensively in the vocabulary of seamen and rivermen, along with "maritime," "mariner", and other derivatives. The term comes from the Latin *mare,* meaning "sea".

MARINE CASUALTY

See: CASUALTY (MARINE).

MARINE CHEMIST

A person who has been trained in the handling of hazardous and flammable products, who conducts tests on vessel tanks to see if they are "safe for fire" if repairs are needed to be made, and if they are "safe for men" if the spaces have to be entered. They also inspect tanks to determine if they are suitable to be loaded with product, then after loading may sample the product, test it and make a report. The vessel at destination may again be sampled, tested and reported to ensure quality.

MARINE DOCUMENT

See: ENROLLMENT, LICENSE, and MERCHANT MARINE DOCUMENT.

MARINE ENGINEER

The person on a towboat or tug who attends to the operation, maintenance and repair of the machinery and other equipment aboard a vessel. See: CHIEF (ENGINEER).

MARINE GEAR

See: GEAR and GEARBOX

MARINE HOSPITAL SERVICE

In 1798 President John Adams set up the *Marine Hospital Service* to assist destitute seamen. In 1912 it became the U.S. Public Health Service, but the *Marine Hospitals* retained the name until 1951. On the river system, the original hospitals were established at Pittsburgh, PA; Louisville, KY; Evansville, IN; LaCrosse, WS; Memphis, TN; and St. Louis (later Kirkwood), MO. The Kirkwood facility later became St. Joseph's Hospital and was where our daughter was born.

By 1981 all the federally run clinics and hospitals were closed. The hospital located in the Portland area of Louisville, KY, opened in 1852, but closed in 1933 due to the Depression. The city of Louisville bought and used it to care for the chronically ill. It was abandoned in 1976 and fell into disrepair, but in 2005 an effort was started to obtain funds to restore the building and turn it into a museum.

MARINE INSPECTION

An official *inspection* undertaken by the USCG of a vessel as to its suitability to continue in its trade. The inspecting officer will note deficiencies required by the regulations, if any, and give the attending owner's representative a list of requirements. Some may need immediate attention, some can be deferred for a period of time, such as 30 or 60 days, or to the next drydocking, or after the next gas-freeing. If the inspecting officer is satisfied with the vessel, he/she will endorse the existing Certificate of Inspection, or issue a new one.

MARINE INSURANCE

A policy whereby an operator of a vessel contracts with an insurance company to indemnify it against certain enumerated perils "of the sea (river)" to which his vessel may encounter, or the cargo in his vessel(s) that may be exposed.

MARINE RADIO OPERATOR

These were short-wave radio operators that vessels could contact to relay messages to their offices, or to patch through phone calls, either business or personal. There were stations located in various river cities. The most utilized ones were WCM Pittsburgh, WSM Memphis, and WFN St. Louis. All have gone out of existence. Computers, cell phones, and satellites now provide the communication of choice.

MARINE RAILWAYS

See: LAUNCH WAYS and LIFTING WAYS.

MARINE SAFETY OFFICE (MSO)

The USCG office where Marine Inspectors are located.

MARINE SANITATION DEVICE (MSD)

Equipment for a marine toilet that receives waste, treats it, and retains it in a holding tank, to be discharged into an approved collection facility at some later date.

MARINE SUPERINTENDENT

A fancier title than PORT CAPTAIN. Sometimes, in a large inland maritime company there may be two or more Port Captains, who will then report to a *Marine Superintendent*.

MARINE SURVEYOR

An experienced and knowledgeable person qualified to inspect vessels for condition or damage. While some marine surveyors are self employed, or independent, others may be in the employ of a vessel company or an insurance firm. The *surveyor* may be employed to negotiate terms with a shipyard for repair costs, or hired to conduct the oversight of a salvage operation or oil spill, or to testify as an expert witness in a collision case, or any variety of oversight examinations to which the *surveyor* has expertise. A *surveyor* may gauge barges to attest to their draft and estimate the tonnage on board, as well as examine vessels for cleanliness and cargo suitability.

MARINE TERMINAL

Any designated area of a waterway that has a permit to load, unload, transfer, or store cargo, or passengers, between land and vessels.

MARINE WAYS

The inclined timber rails at a shipyard that are fitted with triangular cradles, used to both launch vessels and sometimes to haul them out for repair.

MARITIME

Most often used as a preface to

other terms (see following entries) in a commercial or legal sense. The term is from the Latin *marinus,* which denotes "of the sea"; however, it also can refer to lakes, rivers and canals.

MARITIME ADMINISTRATION (MARAD)

Established in 1950 in the Commerce Department. Later, in 1981, it was transferred to the Department of Transportation. Its charter is to aid in the development, promotion, and operation of the U.S. Merchant Marine. It conducts technical studies, sometimes in concert with private marine companies. Other duties include overseeing the National Defense Reserve Fleet, as well as to operate the U.S. Merchant Marine Academy at Kings Point, NY.

MARITIME DAY

A day of remembrance for all mariners who have lost their lives in the service of their country. It is observed each year on 22 May to mark the anniversary of the first transatlantic voyage by a steamship, the *S.S. SAVANNAH* on 22 May 1819.

MARITIME LAW

A particular branch of law that deals with vessels, those who man them, those who take passage on them, and the cargoes that are carried on them. See: ADMIRALTY.

MARITIME LIEN

A lien, or privileged charge, against a vessel for services provided such as food, fuel, supplies, towage, repair, or other such necessaries; or of an injury caused by such vessel in navigable waters. The jurisdiction of complaint is in Admiralty Court.

MARITIME PERIL

A grouping of dangers and risks that are considered by insurance underwriters as unique to the navigation of vessels, including an inability to call a fire department, an inability to seek shelter in storms, or lacking the force to fight off pirates. These and other *perils* are often included in an insurance policy.

MARK TWAIN

1. A measure of the depth of water equaling two fathoms, or 12 feet.
2. The name *Mark Twain* was the "non de plume" of Capt. Isaiah Sellers, which he sometimes used when he wrote an article of practical and useful information on the river that would be published in the New Orleans newspaper, the *Times-Picayune.* Capt. Sellers started his river career as a keelboat Captain before steamboats were on the river, and had successfully piloted rivers that Samuel Clemens never ran. He introduced new innovations to safe navigation, such as signals to be used to indicate intent when vessels were meeting. He had a distinguished career as a river Pilot. Then in 1859, the cub (not yet Pilot) Samuel Clemens wrote a devastating parody of Capt. Sellers' articles that appeared in another New Orleans paper (the *Daily Crescent*) and signed his name, Sergeant Fathom. The good and proud Capt. Sellers never wrote another article. Therefore, when hearing the name *Mark Twain*, think about the honorable Capt. Isaiah Sellers (see), and think about Samuel Clemens as Sergeant Fathom, or six feet, which is half as much as "mark twain".

MARK(S)

1. The indication symbol on a LEADLINE that tells the depth of the water.
2. The call of the leadsman, "By the *mark* one", etc.
3. The navigational line a Pilot uses to safely navigate a crossing, a bridge, or a channel. A set of *marks* may be from a navigational aid (above or below it) to another point, such as another navigational aid, a building, a dike, a large tree, or any combination of factors, such as when one Pilot explains to another Pilot, "When I make that ABC Bridge at this stage, my *marks* are from

100 yards below the saddle in the trees below XYZ Point to the extreme west side of the span next to the channel span, then about half way over I start letting her fall down to the right-hand pier of the channel span until I can see the old white farmhouse below the bridge, then I pull down on the channel span lights and she'll just go right on through pretty as a picture". A Pilot's *marks* may be different as the stage of the river, the speed of the current, the size of the tow, and other forces of nature and circumstance change.

MARK UP

The term used when a vessel enters a shipyard to undergo inspection and repair. The operator representative of the vessel and the yard representative make a review of the vessel and *mark up* all noted repairs required. From that an estimate of cost is noted and agreed upon.

MARKINGS

The symbols, letters and numbers required by law to be placed on a vessel's hull, such as its name, hailing port, and bow and stern draft marks.

MARLIN-SPIKE

A spike-like tapered metal tool with a point on one end between 12 and 18 inches long that is used to part the strands when splicing wire. Over the years there have been various debates over the spelling and etymology of the word in various nautical journals. However, most river people call and spell it as it is shown, but if you spell it *marlinespike* or *marling spike,* the tool is still most useful when one has to splice wire. It appears to be traced to the Dutch *marlen,* meaning "to keep binding"; also from the Dutch *spiker.*

MARRY

1. When splicing lines together, the temporary placing of the lines end on and alternating the strands together prior to splicing.

2. To bend or splice two lines together.
3. The term comes from Latin *maritus,* meaning "married". That's why a deckhand says to his girlfriend when he gets off a towboat, "Let's get spliced".

MAST

On a towboat the *mast* is a vertical spar mounted on top of the pilothouse that usually carries the MASTHEAD LIGHTS with a WHISTLE LIGHT at its peak. The term is handed down to us from the Old English *maest,* which derived from the Dutch and Germanic *mast.*

MASTER

The person who is in overall command of a vessel. The term is not generally used as a title but rather a ranking in authority. As with a Pilot, the *Master* is called Captain, but sometimes referred to as the "old man" no matter what age he/she might be. The word made its way to us from the Latin *magis,* to mean "more, or more important". The requirements to obtain a license for *Master* are listed in 46 CFR 10.

MASTHEAD LIGHT

A white light placed over the fore and aft centerline of the vessel showing an unbroken light over an arc of the horizon of 225 degrees and so fixed as to show the light from right ahead to 22.5 degrees abaft the beam on either side of the vessel, displayed as required by the Navigation Rules. See: LIGHT(S), NAVIGATION.

MATE

The designated person in charge of the deck crew. On present-day towboats more often the person is called the head or lead deckhand. On steamboats, the *Mate* was under the direct supervision of the Captain in the management of the vessel as to its operations, and was in overall command of the deck crew and their duties. On excursion boats the *Mate* is the boss over all deck crew activities and janitorial services, except those relating to the engine room. In new 21st century regulations the USCG will designate a Pilot as a MATE (PILOT), and a STEERSMAN as an ASSISTANT MATE.

MATE (PILOT)

In the early years of the 21st century the USCG believed it had the infinite wisdom of bringing Western River PILOTS into the new era of their own educational background of seagoing terminology. Since the USCG hierarchy has a background in naval sea-type terms with its honorable traditions they apparently presumed they should eliminate the "inferior" background, traditions, terminology, and titles of river personnel. After all they believed "brown water" crews were only descendants of loggers, flatboatmen, keelers, steamboaters, tug boatmen, and diesel boat jockeys. So it came to pass that the USCG would remove the use of the title "Pilot" from riverboatman terminolgy and substitute it with "Mate", as this was term used at sea for those in command of a watch; however, command of a watch at sea is different from a person on watch in the pilothouse of a tow on the Lower Mississippi that can be 1400 feet in length and 245 feet in width, sometimes more, and taking up some 300,000 square feet of a river's surface. There are NO seagoing vessels, neither super tankers, aircraft carriers, nor container ships that occupy that amount of space in the sea; nor are there any deep sea trained personnel of the USCG that could take a tow like that and navigate it safely between two ports on the Lower Mississippi. However, after some protest to the USCG from rivermen the MATE title had (PILOT) added to it when the regulations were made official. Probably after the first decade or so of the new century as new sea-going trained New Londoners with only salt water training take over higher levels of command, the regulations will be changed to drop the (PILOT) in the MATE title as superfluous. The history and traditions of the Western Rivers be damned.

MAT-PLANT

A Corps of Engineers group of vessels and crew that are used to grade a riverbank and lay a MATTRESS of interwoven concrete blocks as a REVETMENT to prevent the bank from eroding in high flow conditions.

MATTRESS

A structure used to keep a riverbank from eroding. When the USACE started its program of bank stabilization, interwoven willow saplings, which were plentiful along the riverbank were used to form the *mattress*. These bundles of saplings were tied together and sometimes weighted down with rocks. Occasionally wire mesh was used to enclose the saplings and branches and other material which was laid off a barge in lengths of 85-90 feet. It was also weighted down with rocks, but these structures didn't last too long, especially in flooding conditions. A *mattress* now consists of large concrete blocks cast and tied together with heavy wire cables. The *mattress* is rolled off and laid by a MAT-PLANT well into the river below the low water line up to the top of the bank. This type of bank stabilization program has been exceedingly successful. See: MAT-PLANT, REVETMENTS and WILLOW MATTRESS.

MAYDAY

The international radio distress signal used as a voice communication to indicate a serious mishap, requesting urgent assistance. The call should be on VHF Channel 16 and be made three times, *MAYDAY-MAYDAY-MAYDAY*; the name of the vessel, the position of the vessel as close as possible, and the nature of the distress and the assistance which one needs should then be given. The term *MAYDAY* has its origin in the 1920s and comes to us from the French *m'aider,* a shortened version of the phrase *venez m'aider,* or "come and help me". See: PAN – PAN and SECURITY CALL.

McCLELLAN-KERR ARKANSAS RIVER NAVIGATION SYSTEM

In 1946 Senator McClellan of Arkansas and Senator Kerr of Oklahoma succeeded in having added to a Rivers and Harbor bill in Congress an authorization for the building the system now named for them. The plan called for hydropower, flood control, recreation and navigation from the Mississippi River up to Catoosa, OK, the port city for Tulsa. Money and specific construction for navigation projects did not come until 1957. Navigation up to Little Rock was opened in 1968. The project was basically completed at the end of 1970. It starts its journey at the mouth of the White River which enters the Mississippi River at mile 583, goes up the White for 10 miles to the Arkansas Post Canal that connects to the Arkansas waterway which continues in a gradual northwesterly direction across AR, into OK, until the Verdigris River meets it to be the final 50 miles of the system ending at the Port of Catoosa. The entire navigable waterway is 450 miles in length with a project depth of nine feet. It has 17 locks that are 600 by 110 feet. See: ARKANSAS RIVER.

MEAN DRAFT

The average draft of a barge after taking displacement readings at all of its four corners and averaging them in order to estimate the cargo tonnage from an immersion chart.

MEAN HIGH WATER (MHW)

When a river at a gauging point reaches its highest level in a given year.

MEAN LOW WATER (MLW)

When a river at a gauging point reaches its lowest level in a given year.

MEAN SEA LEVEL (MSL)

The height of a lock, city, bridge, or other place above the level of the sea. The following are representative heights above sea level at the following cities:

St. Paul, MN	684 feet
St. Louis, MO	380 feet
Peoria, IL	428 feet
Kansas City, MO	716 feet
Pittsburgh, PA	694 feet
Nashville, TN	368 feet
Cairo, IL	271 feet
Memphis	184 feet
New Orleans	0 feet

MEANDER LINES

The survey lines taken by a river survey vessel to delineate the curvature of the natural bank and the channel course. To *meander* means the curves in a river channel that deviate from a linear course. It takes its name from the Menderes River rising in southwestern Turkey that was an extremely winding one as it made its way to the Aegean Sea, to which the Greeks gave us, *Maiandros,* the original name of the river. Now you know "the rest of the story".

MEASUREMENT

See: ADMEASUREMENT, DISPLACMENT, GROSS TONNAGE, NET TONNAGE, REGISTERED TONNAGE, and TON.

MEET HER

When a vessel or tow is swinging in one direction, it is the application of moving the rudder in the opposite direction to either check or stop the swing.

MEETING VESSELS

From Inland Navigation Rule 14, it is when two power-driven vessels are meeting on reciprocal or nearly reciprocal courses so as to involve the risk of collision.

MEGAPHONE

A hand-held, funnel-like device that

is used to magnify and direct a person's voice to enable someone to converse with others at a greater distance. Used by a Pilot to give directions to persons out on a tow if the electronic BULLHORN is not working.

MEMBER
1. A part, piece or integral unit of the structure of a vessel, or a component of machinery in the vessel.
2. One of the CREW of a vessel.

MERCHANT MARINE
The commercial shipping of cargo tonnage in vessels by a country including ships, fishing vessels, passenger vessels, ferry boats, tugs, towboats, and barges, as well as the personnel who man the vessels.

MERCHANT MARINE DOCUMENT (MMD)
A document issued to all merchant seamen in ocean trades. It lists the skills that the mariner has been trained in and certified, such as lifeboatman, fire fighting, tankerman, etc. It is often called a *Z-card*. On the rivers and canals it is issued to persons who are certified to transfer certain liquid products in tank barges, and attests to the person's competency in their handling and so states on the MMD the type products that the person is allowed to transfer.

MERCHANT MARINE PERSONNEL ADVISORY COMMITTEE (MERPAC)
An advisory committee to the USCG made up of industry, union, marine school and safety personnel that basically undertake tasks to advise the Coast Guard on regulatory initiatives involving the training of maritime personnel.

MESSENGER
Another name for a small line that is thrown to the shore or a dock by a vessel's crew, or may be received from the shore. It is bent onto a larger line or wire which can be more easily handled by the crew until they can use the capstan or windlass to pull the heavy line aboard. See: HANDY LINE and HEAVING LINE. The term probably derives from the *messenger* who is the one who carries the message which will be the mooring line.

MESSROOM
Sometimes used in referring to where the crew eats, especially if their background is in the Navy, however, most people on the river use the term GALLEY, since it is the same area where the cook prepares food.

METRIC SYSTEM
A decimal system of measurement used internationally, especially in trade. It is used to measure lengths, weights, and capacity.

METRIC TON or TONNE
A measurement of weight equal to 2,204.6 pounds, or 1000 kilograms.

MIAMI AND ERIE CANAL
Start of building the *canal* began in 1825, the same time as the building of its cousin to the east, the OHIO AND ERIE CANAL, but this western route wasn't completed until 1845, some 12 years after the eastern route. The first part of the *Miami and Erie* ran from Cincinnati to Dayton, OH, a distance of 66 miles. When this section was completed in 1828 it took 54 locks and five aqueducts to operate the system. Work started to extend the *canal* (Miami Extension) the next 160 miles from Dayton to the Maumee Valley at the WABASH AND ERIE CANAL whose terminus was at the city of Toledo, OH. This section required an additional 103 locks, and also included many large reservoirs for water supply and feeder canals. It wasn't finally completed until 1845. The locks on the system were 90 feet long and 15 feet wide. See: CANALS.

MICKEY MOUSE
See: STEAMBOAT WILLIE.

MICRO-MODEL
A small-scale model based on a computer-generated response used to study a small section of a river or channel. It is of a lesser scale than that of a PHYSICAL MODEL, but it can be operational much more quickly and at much less expense. See: SIMULATED FLOW MODEL.

MID-BODY
The approximate mid-portion of a vessel's hull. The term is used most often on the river in reference to lines and rigging, i.e. "Make the line fast to the *mid-body* cavel on the port lead barge", or "Run those scissor wires on the starboard timberheads of XYZ barge back to the *mid-body* cavel on barge JL"; or when referring to damage or leakage, "She's taking water on the port *mid-body* tank". The term MIDSHIPS is also used.

MID-CHANNEL
The area of a navigable channel with the greatest depth of water. It does not necessarily have to be the centerline between two channel buoys.

MID-CHANNEL BUOY
See: JUNCTION.

MIDDLE BAR
A sandbar in the middle of the river with water on each side of it.

MIDDLE WALL
The center wall at a lock site that has two chambers.

MIDSHIPS
The approximate halfway point on a vessel between the bow and the stern, as well as the port and starboard side of a vessel. It is an abbreviation of AMIDSHIPS. Sometimes referred to as MID-BODY.

MIDSTREAM FUELER
A tank barge pushed by a small towboat that will meet a large towboat that is underway with a tow. With no need for the line towboat to stop the *midstream fueler* will refuel it, top off the potable water tanks, transfer barrels of lube oil, bring out line, rigging, groceries, laundry and various sundry items requested by the crew; some are equipped to take off holding tank wastes. This type of service has been in existence for over half a century, specifically to service diesel towboats. It was first started in Memphis by Jim Walden. However, back in the steamboat days of the 1800s there were some wood yards and, later, coaling yards, that would bring a flat out to the boats a loaded with supplies of fuel The flat would hang alongside until its cargo of wood or coal was off loaded, and then its crew would keel or float the flat back to their landing.

MIKE FINK
He was a true legendary character of the river, born in the 1770s near Fort Pitt, which was hostile Indian Territory at the time. He was a hunter (reported to be a crack shot), a scout for the militia, and a keelboat man. It was said that he could outrun, outshoot, throw down, drag out and lick any man in the country. If you desire to know more about him it's all written down in the book *Half Horse, Half Alligator* by Walter Blair and Franklin J. Meine.

MIL
A measurement equal to 1/1000 of an inch. It is usually referred to when determining the thickness of coatings on a vessel, i.e. "I want two mils of the primer, then two coats of PQR epoxy of three mils each". Engineers also use it in reference to wire diameter.

MILE
All distances on the river are measured in statute *miles* of 5,280 linear feet. The mileage marking of rivers is

different for each. For example, the beginning of mileage at 0 on the Lower Mississippi starts at the Head of the Passes below New Orleans, but this is a distance of about 20 miles inland from where it enters the Gulf of Mexico through its Southwest Pass and other passes to the Gulf. The Lower Mississippi River mileage then moves upstream until it reaches the junction of the Ohio and Upper Mississippi at *mile* 964 which is the end of its mileage journey. Then the Upper Mississippi starts over at *mile* 0 and continues upstream to the head of navigation at *mile* 853 in Minneapolis. The Ohio, meanwhile, starts its journey at *mile* 0 in Pittsburgh, where the Allegheny and Monongahela rivers join together to form its source and travels downriver to meet its junction with the Lower Mississippi at *mile* 981. And that's how it goes. Some river mileages start at the head of a stream, while others start counting mileage from their feet; but for most of them they go from their toe tips on up to where they get scalped and navigation ends. Even if canoes are able to continue navigating upstream or down, the "official mileage" does not.

The word *mile* is from the Latin *mille,* to mean 1000, as in *mille passus,* or "1000 paces" which the Roman Legions used to measure distances and estimate how long it would take (in paces) to move from one area to another. The Roman *mile* was 1620 yards, very close to our statute *mile* of 1760 yards (5280 feet), and not too far off a nautical *mile* of 2025 yards (6076 feet), which is based on the length of one minute of latitude as measured at the equator. Caesar's Legions ruled supreme in the century before Christ, but no towboats on the Western Rivers are recorded to have been named to honor him, only a gambling casino boat on the Ohio River that is thought to also do some gentle plundering of gold by its one-armed bandits. Also see: KNOT.

MILE BOARD or MARKER

A sign, approximately 12 inches wide by 36 inches long, painted white with black lettering, attached to a navigational light or daymark with its mileage of the particular river where the *mile board* is located.

MILE MARK

On river maps, usually shows a tiny circle following the channel line, with every five-mile increment listed.

MILK RUN

An easy towboating trade between two points, close to home, deep channel, temperate weather, on a comfortable well-maintained towboat, small tow for the horsepower, great food, good crew, plenty of time off, pay is fine, no bad bridges or locks, and ain't heaven great; in other words, the way life oughta be, an easy trip.

MILL SCALE

An oxide that forms on steel plates at the rolling mill where they are formed. Many shipyards now blast off the *mill scale* and coat the steel plates with a primer prior to forming them into boats and barges.

MILLER, CAPTAIN MARY MILLICENT

Reported to be the first woman in the United States to be granted a steamboat masters license, which she obtained in 1884. There is only sketchy information as to her career. Her husband owned various boats at different periods and she and their family traveled with him. It was rough financially for steamboating at the time she received her license. During that period they might not have been able to afford extra help. Since her husband was a licensed Pilot and could do the piloting duty, perhaps she then could have served as the required master. After an illness she died in 1894. She has been inducted into the American Merchant Marine Hall of Fame, as well as the National Rivers Hall of Fame.

MILLRACE

Extremely fast water, i.e. "They threw the dam up there the other day and that water was coming down like a *millrace*. Slowed our tow down to two miles per hour".

MINIMUM POOL LEVEL

The least depth level to which a pool is allowed to go and still maintain a project channel depth.

MINNESOTA RIVER

Its source is Big Stone Lake on the border of North Dakota and Minnesota flowing about 335 miles southeast to where it joins the Upper Mississippi River at mile point 844 about nine miles below the head of navigation and doubles the flow which emanates from Lake Itasca. The Indian tribes called the river *Minnesota*, meaning cloudy water, however others translated it as "sky blue (or tinted) water". A French explorer, Pierre Charles LeSueur, in 1700, named it after himself, and called it St. Pierre, which became anglicized to St. Peter when the Louisiana Purchase occurred. Later, the territorial governing body of the area asked that the name revert to its original native name, to which Congress assented in 1849.

The *Minnesota* drainage area comprises of approximately 17,000 square miles. Fur trapping and transport was the main focus of trade in early history. In 1850 the *Str. ANTHONY WAYNE* was the first steamboat to ascend the river, with many following when the river was ice free and had adequate depth. After about 1865 steamboat traffic subsided with the coming of railroad service. In the 1860s through the 1880s, inspections, surveys, proposals, and recommendations for improvements to navigation were made. None came to pass. A closure dam at the mouth with a small opening to allow passage of small craft was built to back up water about 28 miles, but problems with constant floods and repair resulted in it being removed in 1909. A sandbar buildup at the mouth constantly limited vessel traffic.

At the start of WW II, Cargill started a shipyard near Savage, MN, to build vessels for the U.S. Navy, with the proviso that the channel to its yard on the *Minnesota* would be maintained at a depth of nine feet. After the war other users of the river for delivery of coal to a power plant and companies shipping grain products for export sought assurance for a continued adequate channel for navigation. Congress authorized a nine foot channel depth on the river to mile 14.7.

MISSING AID

A navigational aid, such as a light or buoy, that is not in its assigned location or station.

MISSISSIPPI (the vessel)

Soon after the MISSISSIPPI RIVER COMMISSION (MRC) was created in 1879, the appointed members decided that not only did they need a vessel to undertake the duties of river project construction and repair, but one that could be used for inspection trips. The building of such a vessel was completed in 1882 and appropriately named the *MISSISSIPPI*, as have all the MRC vessels that succeeded the original one.

The first three boats were steam-powered, while the last two have been equipped with diesel engines. The fourth *MISSISSIPPI* was the first that was propeller-driven, replacing the sternwheel propulsion of the first three. It was built at Ingalls Shipbuilding Corporation in Pascagoula, MS, in 1961 and served until it was decommissioned in 1993, when it was replaced by the fifth and current vessel for the MRC. The new *MISSISSIPPI* was built by Bender Shipyard at Moss Point, MS. It is 241 feet long with a beam of 58 feet, making it the largest working towboat now operating. It has 6300 horsepower.

MISSISSIPPI RIVER

As designated by geographers, the

Mississippi River starts as a little stream emitting from small Lake Itasca in the north-central section of Minnesota from where it flows down to Minneapolis (the head of navigation), and then down to the Gulf of Mexico for a distance of 2,348 miles. The river, along with its tributaries, drains nearly all the land between the Appalachian and Rocky mountain ranges, or 41 percent or the continental U.S. Its entire basin includes all or part of 31 States and two provinces in Canada, or a total of 1,245,000 square miles. Its major contributing basins (besides smaller streams flowing into the Lower Miss) include the Upper Mississippi, the Missouri, the Ohio, the Arkansas/White, and the Red rivers. On an average annual basis it adds 612,000 cubic feet per second, or about 4,500,000 gallons, to the Gulf of Mexico. That is over a trillion and a half gallons of fresh water per year.

Many renditions of what the term "Mississippi" means, and where it came from, have been posited, but it is probably best to defer to George B. Merrick's learned description in 1909, "…so far as the northern tribes were concerned the Mississippi was in the Chippewa language, from which the name is derived: *Mee-zee* (great), *see'-bee* (river) – Great River. The Dakota called it *Wat-oag-tag'-ka* (big river). The Sauk, Foxes, and Potawatomi, related tribes, all called it: Mee-chaw-see'-poo (big river). The Winnebago called it *Ne-scas-hut'-ta-ra* (the bluff-walled river). Thus, six out of seven tribes peopling its banks united in terming it the "Great River".

It is also called the *Father of Waters*, and affectionately known as *Old Man River*. The explorers, French agent Louis Joliet, and Jesuit priest Father Jacques Marquette, are credited with finding (or at least letting the world know) of the Upper Mississippi in 1673. The Lower Mississippi had been discovered by Hernando de Soto in 1541. See: UPPER MISSISSIPPI RIVER and LOWER MISSISSIPPI RIVER.

MISSISSIPPI RIVER COMMISSION (MRC)

The *MRC* was established by the U.S. Congress in 1879 to address the importance of flood control and navigation in the Lower Mississippi valley. Besides meeting numerous times during the year, the Commissioners take a high-water trip over the course of their jurisdiction in the spring of each year, and a low-water inspection in the fall. They stop at various cities along their route to hold public hearings. All Commissioners are appointed by the President of the U.S. Two very prominent members of the first Commission were Benjamin Harrison who later became our 23rd President, and JAMES B. EADS (see), who was famous for many engineering feats on our river system. A history of the *Commission* was written in 2004 for its 125th anniversary entitled *Upon Their Shoulders,* by Charles Camillo ancxd Matthew Pearcy.

MISSISSIPPI RIVER – GULF OUTLET

See: INDUSTRIAL CANAL

MISSOURI RIVER

The river is formed in the Rocky Mountains of Montana where the forks of the Jefferson, Madison and Gallatin rivers come together. It then flows generally southeast for about 2547 miles until it joins the Mississippi River about 20 miles above the city front of St. Louis, MO. It is the longest river in the U.S.; its basin drains about 580,000 square miles and annually deposits over one-half million tons of silt into the Mississippi River, from which it gained the sobriquet *Big Muddy*.

In 1673, Marquette and Joliet were the first Europeans to discover the mouth of the *Missouri River*. After that French trappers appeared in the area, trading with the Indians. After the U.S. purchase of the Louisiana Territory, Captains Lewis and Clark commenced the second leg of their voyage of discovery up the *Missouri River* in 1804-1805.

Canoes, bullboats, mackinaws, and keelboats were the first non-mechanical means of transport on the *Missouri*. The first steamboat going up the river any distance was the *Str. INDEPENDENCE* which ascended about 228 miles in May 1819 before returning to St. Louis. A little later that year a government expedition of four steamboats and nine keelboats started up to the area of the Yellowstone River and to establish a fort. All vessels encountered difficulties on the trip and the only one that made it to the mouth of the Platte River below what is now Omaha, NB, was the *Str. WESTERN ENGINEER*.

Traffic by steamer continued and by the 1850s there were over 60 packets in regular trade. The development of railroading, however, resulted in a rapid decline of river commerce. In 1880 navigational improvements were limited to those below Sioux City, IA, and waterborne traffic continued to decline. During WW II two major floods occurred, in 1942 and 1943. Concerns by all persons in the basin resulted in the Flood Control Act of 1944, called the Pick-Sloan Plan of the USACE and the Bureau of Reclamation. It provided for six major dam reservoirs on the upper *Missouri* without locks, and a nine-foot maintained navigation system on the lower 732 miles of free-flowing river below Sioux City, IA, for about eight months a year.

MITER GATE(S)

Lock gates that are operated in pairs. They are each hinged on pins at a recess in the lock walls where they rest until they are opened to allow vessels to enter or leave the lock chamber. The gates, when closed, are pointed upstream and meet at a mitered angled seam, with the angle of *miter* on each gate exactly half the angle of the total meeting angle. The pressure of the water behind the meeting point tightens the seal at the closure. The term *miter* appears to come from the name of the tall pointed headdress worn by church officials, the origin of which is *mitra*, or "turban". See: LOCK GATES.

MITER SILL

The underwater concrete seat or threshold upon which the lock gate firmly rests when closed to seal out as much leakage of water from the chamber as possible. The *sill* is constructed several feet below the project channel depth of the river.

MIXED TOW

A barge tow (in olden days, a flatboat) that has many different commodities within its barging makeup, i.e. loads of coal, grain, steel, gasoline, etc. as opposed to a tow that is in a generally dedicated run with only one type product in its tow, i.e. exclusively coal or grain or chemicals, etc.

MODAL SHARE

The percentage of freight commodities that are transported by each mode of transportation, whether ocean, rail, truck, barge, pipeline or airlines.

MODE

One of the methods of transportation of freight, such as rail, highway, air, pipeline, or water.

MODEL BARGES

Barges that were built in the 1860s that were the progenitors of the modern cargo barge. They had a *model* (pointed) bow and stern, were 230 feet overall in length by 39 feet wide, and had a capacity of up to 1400 tons at a draft of seven feet. They were supported by HOG CHAINS which ran on the centerline of the barge. The first ones were built in the Pittsburgh area and were operated originally by Gray's Iron Line, which was the first common carrier barge line on inland waters. (S&D Reflector)

MODEL BOW

A shaped pointed bow as seen on most ships and tugs, the old steamboats, and on an occasional towboat.

MODEL TEST TANK

1. A physical mock-up to scale of a sectional course in the river to see what currents will do at different rates of flow, high water, low water, using dikes (both above water and underwater), flows at bridge piers, locks and dams, etc. to determine the effect on navigation and the environment. Many aspects of this testing are now done in computer models. See: WATERWAYS EXPERIMENTATION STATION (WES).

2. The building to scale of a towboat, tug, ship, or other vessel(s) to determine the most efficient hull structure to operate in its particular trade, including speed through the water, power needs, propeller design and pitch, steering, etc.

MODERATE SPEED

A term used in the pre-1980 Rules of the Road under Rule 16 of the International Rules, the Inland Rules and the Western River Rules, to indicate that a vessel navigating in fog or other reduced visibility conditions should go at a *moderate speed*. This was defined in court cases to reducing speed to be able to stop in half the distance of visibility. The current Navigation International and Inland Rules for vessels no longer uses the term, but under new Rule 6 admonishes vessels to "at all times proceed at a safe speed".

MOLD LOFT

A building where patterns of hull curvatures are laid out in templates or molds to be used in the shipyard to shape steel to the same design. Most of this work is done now by computer.

MOLDED BREADTH

It is the greatest breadth, or width, of a vessel measured from the outside of the frames or the inside of a vessel's skin or plating. Sometimes called the *molded beam*.

MOLDED DEPTH

The vertical distance measured amidships from the bottom frame, or the plate covering the keel, to the frame supporting the main deck.

MOM & POP OUTFIT

A small company with only one, or a couple of boats. It is a sort of referral to a time when the owner and his wife lived on the boat and ran it when they had business.

MONKEY

See: PILE DRIVER.

MONKEY FIST

A type of heavy knot, sometimes enclosing a weight such as a rock or a steel nut that is attached to the end of a HEAVING LINE or HANDY LINE, to enable to the line to be thrown further and more accurately. The thought was that the interwoven small stuff line encapsulating the weight looked like the clenched fingers of a monkey making a fist.

MONKEY LINE

See: HEAVING LINE or HANDY LINE. A name or term used on some rivers and at some locks for the line the lock tender lowers to the deck crew to haul up a LOCK LINE. It is sometimes fitted with a hook in the end of the line to receive the eye of a LOCK LINE.

MONKEY RUDDERS

These rudders were used on sternwheel steamboats and were mounted on a framework aft of the paddlewheel to give greater power in steering than that from the main rudders, which were located under the stern rake forward of the sternwheel. The *monkey rudders* were coupled to the steering rudders and moved when they did, not like the steering and flanking rudders on a modern towboat which are operated by separate steering mechanisms. The *monkey rudders* would often get knocked off in service when backing close to shore, by backing into drift or other debris, and sometimes by drift hitting them from the action or the sternwheel.

Without having a rudder aft of the thrust, the steering on a modern towboat would be similar to only steering a tow by just using the flanking rudders that are forward of the propeller(s). It is not known as to why the term *monkey rudder* was coined. Some have opined they are like the tail of a monkey that helps it in support when it changes direction. Others have speculated that since they are connected (acting in concert) with the main rudders it is the old adage of a mimic, "monkey see, monkey do".

MONONGAHELA RIVER

The river is formed where the Tygart and West Fork rivers join just above Fairmont, WV, with a course mostly directly north for 128 miles to where it meets the Allegheny River to form the Ohio River at Pittsburgh Point. It is there that all three rivers have zero (0) as their mileage location. The main tributaries of the *Monongahela* are the Cheat, entering at mile 89, and the Youghiogheny at mile 16. Its watershed basin covers over 7000 square miles.

The name, *Monongahela,* in its early days was spelled in variants of over two dozen ways on maps and in writings as phonetic descriptions of the pronouncements made by various Indian tribes. Generally, it was taken to mean "sliding banks", "many landslides", or similar representations. Early surveying of the river for navigation possibilities reported that caving banks constantly fell into the river that formed bars and obstructed the channel to boat traffic, so the local native name was aptly appropriate. Most locals and river Pilots simply refer to it as the *Mon.*

The traffic on the early use of the river was mainly whiskey made from rye which traveled downstream in flatboats. The Whiskey Rebellion which occurred in 1794 started in the Monongahela River Valley after Congress had imposed a liquor tax on distilled spirits. The river provided the area for the launching of the first successful steamboat when the *NEW ORLEANS* was built on its banks in 1811 and steamed all the way to New Orleans. The *Str. ENTRERPRISE* was built at Brownsville, PA, in 1840 and was the first steamboat to go to New Orleans and return upriver to its place of birth.

In order to make the river more efficient to navigate the first locks and dams built were by a private company, the Monongahela Navigation Company which built four dams by 1844 (158 by 50 feet). Later three more were added. After the Civil War the federal government built additional locks and dams on the upper reaches, making the total number 15 locks and dams by 1903. They also took over the private structures and eliminated their toll charges for lockage. Extensive replacement and modernization of the system started after WW II and continues in the new century. The main tonnage since the canalization of the river is coal. No one seems to know if whiskey is still transported in bulk on the river.

MONONGAHELA RIVER CONSOLIDATED COAL AND COKE COMPANY

See: COMBINE

MOON, FULL

Full moons were given different names by Indian Tribes before anyone discovered America. They have great meaning also to river people since Pilots spend at least some of their watches looking at them while they navigate their vessels. Since the lunar cycle of 29 days, varies the time frame for the *full moon* shifts somewhat, and they do not occur in the same month each year.

Wolf Moon – So-called since hungry wolves howled outside the Indian villages during the cold nights. Also called the *Old Moon.* Take heavier clothing when going to the boat.

Snow Moon – The heaviest snows

fall during this time, hence the name. It is a cold time to be on the river working wires, ratchets, and stiff lines.

Worm Moon – So named since it rose as the land began to thaw and earthworm casts appeared. Starting to warm up, not wearing the longies on deck anymore.

Pink Moon – The herb moss is pink at this time of year. It is also known as the *Sprouting Grass Moon*. Looks like Spring has sprung. Hope we don't have excessive high flooding this year.

Full Flower Moon – Flowers are abundant when this moon is in full bloom. Also called the *Corn Planting Moon*. The time when some rivermen want to be off for planting time.

Strawberry Moon – Full during the short time strawberries are in season. Hope the cook puts some out at dinner time.

Buck Moon – When the buck deer antlers push out, and rivermen are already thinking about the next fall hunting season.

Sturgeon Moon – When the sturgeon are biting in the Great Lakes. Also known as the *Corn Moon or Grain Moon*. Hope those fish in the Atchafalaya basin are also biting.

Fruit or Barley Moon – Reserved for the time when the Harvest Moon is full in very late September (sort of a stand-in for those 29 days in the lunar cycle). Beautiful, especially on the Upper Mississippi.

Harvest Moon – At its peak farmers can work late by its light to get the crops into storage and crew members need time off to help bring them in.

Hunter's Moon – Leaves falling, deer are fat, and IT'S hunting season. Crew members definitely need time off to fill the freezer for the family.

Beaver Moon – The beavers are gathering food for winter. Have to tell the wife to rummage around in the storage trunk and get out the heavy weather gear for next trip on the river.

Cold Moon or Long Nights Moon – Getting to the Yule Season. A lonely time to be on a towboat – need to get a relief.

MOOR
To tie off and make secure a vessel or tow to a dock, buoy, cell, or any other place for a period of time as opposed to a temporary situation, such as tied off on a lock wall or lock chamber. The term derives from the Dutch *maren*, meaning to tie or fasten.

MOORING BUOY
A large float with mooring rings or mooring posts that is secured by chains or heavy wires to one or more anchors in the riverbed. It is sometimes referred to as a *tie-off buoy*.

MOORING CELL
Large steel pile-driven and gravel or rock-filled cells at docks and other places that are used to secure tows. They are fitted with heavy steel rings set at various heights on the cell to be easily utilized for mooring at different stages of river levels.

MOORING LINE
A large strong line used to secure a tow.

MOORING PIN
Heavy steel pin in recesses in a lock wall used as extra security in tying off while in the lock chamber or on the lock guide wall waiting to lock.

MOSQUITOS
Swarms of small recreational boats that have little regard for navigational protocol that swarm around, flitting hither and yon, similar to the pesky flying insects that come on the river in the summer time seeking a meal of a riverman's blood.

MOTORBOAT
A power-driven recreational craft.

MOUNTAIN TRADE
When a Missouri River Pilot of a

steamboat left St. Louis with a destination of Fort Benton, Montana, a distance upriver of over 2300 miles, it was said, "He's going to the mountains".

MOUNTING A REEF

When an upbound tow comes to the head of a bend to make a crossing to the opposite side of the river, it may encounter a reef where the channel crossing is shallower than is the water in the bend. The Pilot must be careful to steer the tow very nearly head-on into the crossing to meet the current angle squarely and *mount the reef*. If not, the current running off the reef may cause the tow to veer out of the channel and top around, or worse, break up or go aground.

MOUSE (A HOOK)

The act of using a small piece of line wrapped across the jaw of a hook to ensure that the line, wire, ring, or object being hooked does not slip out and become unhooked.

MOUTH

The end or terminus of a river or stream when it enters another body of water.

MOVABLE BRIDGE

Any bridge that spans a navigable waterway channel that has to move in some fashion to allow vessels to pass through, such as a swing span, lift span, bascule, etc. See: BRIDGE.

MOVABLE DAM

A dam which has a series of WICKETS which are in the raised position to hold water in the upper pooled area; these can be lowered to the riverbed when the water rises to a certain level, allowing vessels to pass over the dam.

MUD

A sticky, slick substance consisting of water and earth. It has been referred to in many volumes written about our rivers, i.e. "big muddy", "muddy waters", etc. in sometimes affectionate tones and other times in a degrading fashion. Rivermen prefer the appropriate fondness type of terminology except when a tow gets stuck in its adhesive clutches.

MUD CLERK

An apprentice or assistant clerk employed aboard a packetboat who was required to keep tab on goods coming on or going off the steamer. Since nosing into a landing usually meant a muddy riverbank, the apprentice at times would be up to his ankles in mud, from whence he acquired his official title.

MUD DRUM

The purpose of the *mud drum* is to collect the sediment from the feedwater going into the boiler. It is located at the bottom of the boiler(s) and is required to be blown out several times a day when the boiler is in operation to prevent the buildup of sediment in the boilers. The act of defecation was called by the Engineer, "I'm blowing down my *mud drum*".

MULE TRAIN

In heavy ice a towboat may be able to push through, but is unable to steer a long tow in a twisting channel as breaking ice head on may be possible, however the side thrust of the steering action along the length of the tow against solid ice does not easily break it. Therefore, the Pilot will string out the tow behind the towboat in single file, with loose wires or lashings between each soft coupling. He will then usually put one barge on the head of the towboat, then attach a bridle at the stern to the strung-out tow behind him and begin towing the barges through the ice-covered channel.

There are times when three or four tows will tow in unison through an ice covered channel, one tow hooked to another's tow in single file with a length of a couple of miles. Care must be taken that a square end must be placed on the back of the towing vessel. If hard or gorged ice is encountered, and the tow is stopped, the momentum of the barges astern will run up on the stopped towboat. If a raked barge was immediately astern, it would ride over a towboat's stern causing damage and possibly sinking it.

Not very many towboats do any towing in the ice anymore. They are not built with enough stern space to rig an adequate towing bridle. Also, most line haul boats are fitted with kort nozzles that tend to get quickly clogged with ice, requiring the Pilot to back down to flush them out which stops the forward momentum of the tow each time it must be done. The term comes from the covered wagons carrying settlers that were strung out in single file and pulled by mules or oxen across the open land west of the Allegheny Mountains and prairies beyond the Mississippi River.

MULTIMODAL
See: INTERMODAL.

MULTIPLE ROUND POINT DIKE STRUCTURES
Circular piles of rock that are placed in the river out from a bank allowing a similar diversion as a dike with multiple notches. They are either laid in a line perpendicular to the shore or they can be laid in staggered fashion.

MULTI-PURPOSE WATER PROJECTS
The so-called navigation projects of the Western Rivers serve not only those shipping and those transporting cargoes through the many miles of rivers and canals of the interior of our country but, also provide many other benefits to the citizens who live there. Some can retain flood water and reduce crest heights as well as allow for low-flow augmentation during drought periods; others generate a tremendous amount of hydro-electric power; they provide cooling water for industry and drinking water to people; millions of Americans enjoy the recreational benefits they provide; environmental enhancement is always part of modern day planning of all water related surveys and studies; and, of course the economic and environmental benefits of barging products rather than shipping cargo on other modes of transport by using less fuel, and less BTUs per ton-mile, which also translates into less harmful emissions per ton-mile of products shipped from producer to consumer. Waterborne commerce reduces congestion, noise, possible accidents, and other unwanted social aspects that occur in congested cities. Therefore, *multi-purpose water projects* are a positive plus in this country.

MUSEUMS (RIVER)
There are quite a few museums in the area of the Western Rivers that are devoted solely to the history of the rivers, the river people, and river craft that have navigated them. There are also other exhibits in libraries, government visitor centers, etc. that display artifacts or pictures of river life. Listed here are some of the main exhibits available to the public.

National Mississippi River Museum – Dubuque, IA

George M. Verity Riverboat Museum – Keokuk, IA

National Great Rivers Museum (operated by USACE) – East Alton, IL

Mud Island River Park – Memphis, TN

USACE – Vicksburg, MS

Meriwether Lewis Dredge – Brownsville, NB

Sergeant Floyd River Museum – Sioux City, IA

Arabia Steamboat Museum – Kansas City, MO

Point Pleasant River Museum – Point Pleasant, WV

Ohio River Museum – Marietta, OH

Life on the Ohio River – Vevay, IN

Howard Steamboat Museum – Jeffersonville, IN

Falls of the Ohio Museum (operated by D.O.I.) – Jeffersonville, IN

USS LST 135 – Evansville, IN
River Heritage Museum – Paducah, KY
Smithsonian – Washington, DC

MUSKINGUM RIVER

Formed from the Walhonding and Tuscarawas rivers in east central Ohio, the *Muskingum River* flows 111 miles before entering the Ohio River (mile 172) below Marietta, Ohio. The river's name is attributed to an Indian expression for the "glare of an elk's eye". Early history indicated a local desire to link the river up to Lake Erie, but the Ohio and Erie Canal bypassed the *Muskingum*.

In 1836 the Ohio Legislature authorized improvement of the river for 91 miles. By 1841, dams, bypass canals, and 10 locks had been constructed to provide a channel of 4.5 feet. The locks were 175' x 36'. Some 40 years later the locks and dams were in serious need of repair. In 1886 the State of Ohio ceded the system to the federal government. The USACE made numerous repairs and improvements, basically restoring the existing system. In 1913, however, a devastating flood struck the area and it took five years to make the necessary repairs to put it back in operation. But by the end of WW I, railroads and trucks had taken most of the river-generated traffic. In 1948 the USACE ceased maintaining the system and turned it over to the State of Ohio in 1958. It is now used for recreational purposes. A most informative volume about the river and its navigation is *Steamboats on the Muskingum* by J. Mack Gamble, published in 1971. It gives all you need to know about the trials and tribulations along the river.

MUSSEL(S)

A freshwater aquatic mollusk with a hinged double shell, numerous in most Western River beds. At one time there was a great mussel-harvesting industry on the Upper Mississippi and the Tennessee rivers. See: ZEBRA MUSSEL.

MUSTER

To assemble part, or all of a crew, to enact drills, impart information, to insure all hands are accounted for in case of an accident, or any other important reason.

MUTINY

A rebellion against authority by a crew aboard a vessel refusing to obey lawful orders. It can be an attempt to seize control of a vessel. There hasn't been a recorded *mutiny* aboard any riverboats in the last half-century or so. If crewmen are dissatisfied now-days they just quit and get off the boat at the next lock or landing. The word is from the Latin *movere*, meaning "to move".

M/V

Used as a prefix, along with the name, of an internal combustion power-driven vessel. The term stands for *Motor Vessel*. Steamboats carry the prefix of Str.

M/V *MISSISSIPPI*

See: *MISSISSIPPI* (the vessel).

MARRY

The initial act of joining the ends of two lines together by entertwining their strands prior to splicing.

MONKEY FIST

The weighted end of a heaving line

302 ILLUSTRATIONS

MANEUVER BOAT

A work flat with an A-frame supporting a boom that was used at USACE locks and dams, mainly to raise and lower the wickets at a movable dam. The upper picture shows the boat as it was rigged. The lower picture is a maneuver boat at work tripping the wooden wickets at the pass of a dam on the Ohio River during a rising river. Swift running river.

http//www.steamboats.org/assets/images/steamboats/maneuverboat-35-jpg

ILLUSTRATIONS 303

MANIFOLD OF PIPELINES ON A TANK BARGE
(valves, blind flanges, P/V valves, drip pans, etc.)

**MARINE
HOSPITAL
LOUISVILLE**
(Now under restoration)

MARINE WAYS

Shown launching a barge on a marine ways. Some ways
also have the capability of hauling a vessel out of the water.

MAT-LAYING & MATTRESS SINKING PLANT

Articulated concrete mats devised by the USACE are used for revetting a shore line subject to erosion of the river current. They consist of concrete blocks made and stored at casting plants located along the Lower Mississippi River.
Each block is about 3" thick. They are wired together to allow flexibility to conform to the graded bank and the bottom of the river. A section of blocks is 4' x 20'. Sections are further cabled together as they are rolled off the sinking plant and laid in lengths exceeding 150'.

MOORING LINES

Typical types and names of mooring lines used to tie off tows to deadmen located at various places along a shore-line or when mooring at a dock

CURRENT

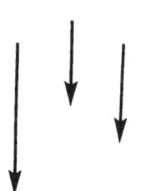

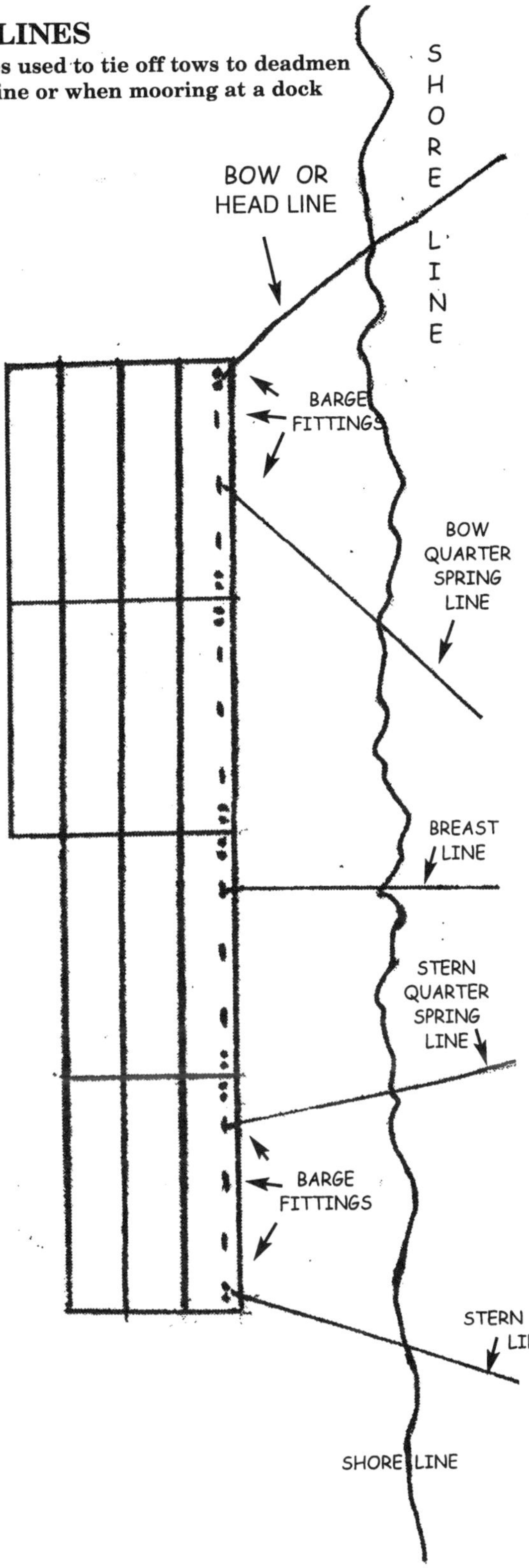

SHORE LINE

BOW OR HEAD LINE

BARGE FITTINGS

BOW QUARTER SPRING LINE

In most cases when mooring tows on the river the current will keep a strain against the bow or head line and the tow will stay perpendicular and close to the shore-line. If the current is strong and the tow is large and/or of heavy tonnage two lines with an even strain will be run out at the bow.

BREAST LINE

STERN QUARTER SPRING LINE

In slack water, wind, changing tidal conditions, or if the tow is of empty barges, etc., it is always necessary to have a stern line and perhaps other lines to securely moor the tow to keep it from moving ahead or for the stern to swing out into the channel, especially if it is left unattended.

BARGE FITTINGS

STERN LINE

SHORE LINE

MULE TRAINING
A towboat pulling a tow of barges through a heavy cover of ice on the channel.

MARLIN-SPIKE
When splicing wire it is a tool used to assist a person in interweaving the strands of each tuck. On the river when used it is between 12" and 18" in length with a fairly sharp point.

FID
A rounded piece of hardwood that tapers down to a blunt point. It is used to assist a person in separating the strands when splicing line (see: FID).

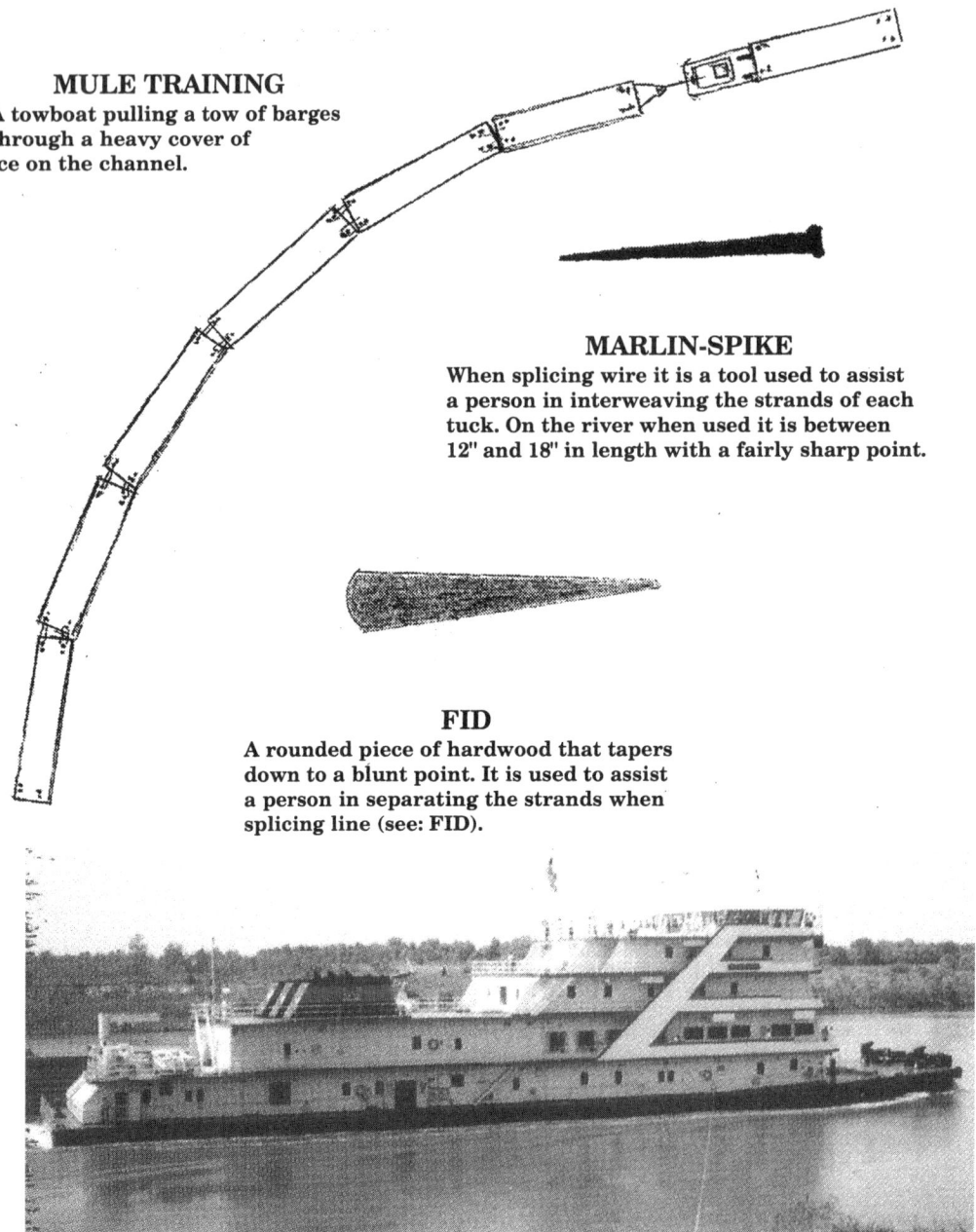

M/V MISSISSIPPI
The official high and low water survey vessel used by the Mississippi River Commission for public hearings on the Western Rivers. When not on official business for the MRC it is a work boat operating with mat-sinking plants, revetment crews, or construction workers.

N

NAKED LIGHTS
See: OPEN LIGHTS.

NAME BOARD
In the days of sidewheel packet steamers, the name of the vessel was displayed in large letters on the outside of the paddlewheel house; sternwheel steamboats generally displayed their names on the outside of the main deck cabin bulkhead in letters four or five feet high, usually near the after end of the cabin. The name of a vessel now is mostly applied to a not very wide board that is mounted on the railing outside the pilothouse. A vessel's name and its HAILING PORT is also required to be displayed on its stern.

NARROW CHANNEL
The term *narrow channel* is a subjective one. When two motorboats are meeting in a river they may believe they have all the room in the world to execute a safe meeting and passing. However, two towboats, each with 15 to 40 barges, may certainly consider the same channel area a place that is too narrow to conduct a safe meeting passage.

Therefore, in the Navigation Rules is Rule 9, the *Narrow Channel Rule*, which sets out the requirements for different actions to be taken by vessels that might be in what could be considered a *narrow channel*. The Rule gives the downbound power-driven vessel, proceeding with a following current, the right-of-way over the upbound vessel. So, in essence, it allows the downbound vessel to decide if the channel is too narrow to meet, and if, and where the upbound vessel shall hold up. If it decides that though the channel might be narrow the vessels will still be able to meet, the downbound vessel decides on which side of the channel each shall navigate their tows. If the meeting of the two tows is not successful and results in a collision, the courts will then decide if the channel was too narrow or not, and who was right, and who was wrong in their navigational decisions.

NATCHEZ TRACE
The trail that Ohio River flatboatmen took home after delivering their boats and cargoes to New Orleans. They made their way home over the *Trace* to build another boat, get another cargo, and take another trip. It was a dangerous journey. Not only was it long and rough, but it was home to robber outlaws and some groups of renegade Indians. It commenced at Natchez, Mississippi, went up through a corner of northwest Alabama, and wound up 444 miles later in Nashville, Tennessee.

NATIONAL ENSIGN or FLAG
"Old Glory" with 50 white stars on a field of blue, representing each of our individual United States, along with alternating 7 red and 6 white stripes signifying the 13 original colonies that set up our great nation.

NATIONAL MARITIME DAY
See: MARITIME DAY.

NATIONAL OCEANIC AND ATMOSPHERIC ADMINISTRATION (NOAA)
Formally known as the U.S. Coast and Geodetic Survey. It creates many of the charts used by mariners; however, the USACE works closely with *NOAA* and is still issuing charts for use on the inland rivers. A senior member of *NOAA* is designated to be on the MISSISSIPPI RIVER COMMISSION.

NATIONAL RESPONSE CENTER
The federal agency that is required to be notified in the event of an oil or chemical spill.

NATIONAL RIVERS HALL OF FAME
Located at the National Mississippi River Museum in Dubuque, IA. It hon-

ors individuals who have passed on who have contributed to the history, culture, development, learning and well-being of the inland rivers of the United States. Each year nominations are made in various categories for induction, including those who were river persons, builders, pathfinders, and those who contributed to the culture as artists, writers, and musicians. They also honor annually those individuals still living who have contributed greatly to the advancement of the river towing industry by presenting them with an Achievement Award.

NATIONAL WATERWAYS CONFERENCE

A national coalition in the U.S. that seeks to promote to the public and elected officials an understanding and the value of the inland waterways system. Its members include regional waterways associations, water carriers, shippers, public agencies, and those engaged in waterway services.

NAUTICAL CHART

A presentation of an area of waterways which includes water depths, types of bottom, navigational aids, obstructions, land topographical information, and any other information that might be of use to the mariner. Most of the printed descriptions or diagrams of the Western Rivers are maps, not *nautical charts* at the present time. They are being revamped and standardized as this is being written. In the not-to-distant future the printed *charts* may go out of existence as electronic ones take their place. The term *nautical* is from the Greek *nautikos*, with *nautes* to mean "sailor", and *naus* to mean "ship".

NAUTICAL MILE

The International *Nautical Mile*, adopted by the U.S., is 6076.11549 feet in distance, or 1852 meters. It equals one minute of arc on the earth's surface. It is not, however, used on the U.S. rivers system.

NAVAL ARCHITECT

A person who designs vessels by engineering in all the desirable features that will be pertinent to the marine trade in which it will be employed.

NAVIGABLE

Waterways that can be navigated by vessels. The word comes from the Latin *navigare,* meaning "to sail".

NAVIGABLE CHUTES and SLOPES

State legislatures required owners of mills along rivers to build into their dam *navigable chutes and slopes.* The *chutes* were openings in the dams that were some two feet lower than the rest of the dam's crest. They were closed with boards in low river stages to conserve water. When a vessel arrived above the dam the boards were removed and a flatboat would pass through the opening. If the water level at the dam's crest and that of the lower side of the dam was too great the mill owner was also required to build *slopes* at the base of the opening. These were rock-filled timber structures that sloped away from the dam chute to the riverbed at a very gentle angle of not more than four degrees.

NAVIGABLE PASS

A section of a movable dam that is lowered during periods of high water, allowing a vessel to navigate over the dam and not utilize the lock chamber. Although most of the locks and dams on the Ohio River when originally constructed had movable dams installed, they have all been replaced (except on the extreme lower end of the river above where it joins the Mississippi). Also there are two dams on the Illinois River still so equipped.

NAVIGABLE WATERS OF THE UNITED STATES

Precise definition of *navigable waters* is subject to judicial interpretation, however, the general definition used by most administrative agencies of the U.S. Government is: *Navigable waters of the United States* are those waters that are subject to the ebb and flow of the tide and are presently used, or have been used in the past, or may be susceptible for use to transport interstate or foreign commerce. A determination of navigability, once made, applies laterally over the entire surface of the body of water, and is not extinguished by later actions or events which impede or destroy navigable capacity.

NAVIGATION

The science, art, and ability to safely and efficiently conduct the movement of a vessel from one place to another. The term is from the Latin *navigare*, meaning "to travel in a ship".

NAVIGATION AID

See: AIDS TO NAVIGATON.

NAVIGATION CHANNEL

That part of a waterway in which vessels can be navigated. Generally, it is the deeper part of a waterway, one where aids to navigation have been installed. A small light-draft vessel may be able to navigate anywhere in a waterway outside of what would be termed a marked channel.

NAVIGATION CHANNEL (RADIO COMMUNICATIONS)

The marine industry has various audio *channels* assigned to it. The *VHF standby channel* is Channel 16, which is required to be monitored at all times when underway. The *VHF calling channel* is Channel 13, where a vessel will initiate a desire to communicate and request the other vessel to go to one of the other VHF working channels. Certain other VHF channels are assigned for use in a VESSEL TRAFFIC SYSTEM.

NAVIGATION LIGHTS

Those lights required to be displayed in accordance with the NAVIGATION RULES, Part C, Lights and Shapes, Rules 20 through 31, as well as the technical Annexes I and II. The rules define the types, where displayed, and their visibility characteristics.

NAVIGATION NOTICE (USACE)

Periodic advisements issued by the USACE regarding rules, regulations, and general information to navigation interests. The first *notice* each year lists rules for lockage, with special requirements in certain Districts or locks. It also lists a timeline for scheduled repair and maintenance to be undertaken on locks and dams. During the year changes to schedules, navigation outages, dike elevations, etc. will be issued or posted on the Corps and industry websites. See: NOTICE TO MARINERS for safety notices issued by the USCG.

NAVIGATION SAFETY ADVISORY COUNCIL (NAVSAC)

A statutory advisory council to the USCG made up of recognized experts and leaders in all navigational disciplines involved with the waterways, including owners and operators of vessels (both inland and deep sea), admiralty attorneys, professional mariners, recreational boaters, and State officials involved in vessel and port safety. The *Council* studies and makes recommendations on matters relating to maritime accidents, aids to navigation, regulations regarding navigational equipment, the navigation rules, and any other matter involving safety on the waterways.

NAVIGATION RULES

The *Navigation Rules* (COMDTINST M16672.2, revised as required) is the bible for every person navigating a vessel. The *Rules* set forth their applicability, the responsibility of the persons in different navigational situations, lights and shapes to be displayed, sound signals, and technical data that must be followed. This code is a revision of what were called the Rules of the Road, which in one form or another had been in use on the river system since 1852. It was more formalized in the late 1800s, and received update modifications over the years. In the 1970s numerous discussions took place, both internationally and in the U.S., to update and modify the existing rules, which resulted in what is termed 72 COLREGS, the current International Rules.

The U.S., as a signatory to the international treaty which brought the Rules into effect, agreed to Rule 1(b) wherein any special rules for national waterways would conform as closely as possible to the COLREGS. Our *Inland Navigation Rules* are the result of that effort. They went into effect on 24 December 1981. See: COLREGS and INLAND RULES.

NAVIGATION VESSEL INSPECTION CIRCULAR (NVIC)

A notice issued by the USCG to affected parties as to how they interpret certain provisions in vessel and personnel regulations as well as how they intend to carry out and put into effect their obligations for the programs under their jurisdiction.

NAVIGATOR

The person who lays out a safe course for a vessel to follow. The term is used in reference to a seagoing vessel. On riverboats and tugs the *navigator* is the person who is piloting the vessel who knows where the channel is, and how to safely navigate the vessel from one point to another.

NECESSARIES

A legal term, argued narrowly and broadly by courts, as to what outfitting, food, water, fuel, and other supplies are required, or should be on a vessel to render proper service.

NEEDLE

A long, slender piece of wood, three inches square, that is, and was, placed between raised wickets in a movable dam to slow down or stop the leakage during low-flow conditions on the river. In extreme low water weeds, straw, and other substances were added to the water just above the wickets that would be sucked into the needle cracks to further retard any leakage. The *needles* vary in length at different locks, depending upon the length of the wicket. See: WICKET. Also, it is a short piece of steel device used with thread by crewmen to sew up a rip in their trousers.

NEEDLE FLAT

A small shallow-draft deck barge used to transport needles across a wicket dam when inserting or removing needles between the wickets and then storing them for future use.

NEEDLE GUN

An air or electrically operated device which welders use to remove slag from around welds. It operates on a vibrating motion. Often also used by deck crews to remove old layers of paint and rust prior to repainting a vessel, especially in corners and hard-to-reach places.

NEGLIGENCE

Admiralty textbooks devote chapters to cite cases where one attorney is trying to prove *negligence* of a vessel or its command in an accident, while the attorney on the side of the vessel and/or its command is trying to prove their innocence in the matter. It is a subjective term. Basically, it is the failure to do something a reasonable person would do when confronted with similar circumstances, or conversely, do something that a reasonable person would not do when confronted with similar circumstances in the same situation. To keep yourself out of trouble and out of court always do the "prudent" thing.

NET TON MILE

The movement of each ton of freight in a barge the distance of one mile.

NET TONNAGE

The term *net tonnage*, or *net registered tonnage*, does not denote actual cargo weight capacity, but rather a measurement of the vessel's carrying capacity in cubic feet, whereby 100 cubic feet equals one *net ton*, regardless of the weight of the vessel or its cargo. The official undertaking the admeasuring first determines the GROSS TONNAGE cubic capacity. Then he/she takes certain measurements of those spaces that are useful and intended for earning revenue. Excluded from the admeasurement are certain working spaces, allowances for crew member living quarters, water ballast tanks, superstructure for any passengers, and a formula for engine room exclusions. Fuel bunkers are included in *net tonnage* as fuel could possibly be off-loaded and sold; therefore it is considered a cargo space. After a mish-mash of figures the *net tonnage* is officially recorded. In the experience of naval architects, engineers, mathematicians, masters, and probably even Einstein himself, no two supposedly sane persons doing an admeasurement of the same vessel could possibly arrive at the same gross or *net tonnage*.

NEW MADRID EARTHQUAKE

The worst earthquake on record in the U.S., and possibly in the world. It started on 16 December 1811 and is believed to have been about what would measure 8.0 on the Richter Scale. The tremors and quakes continued on into the New Year, with aftershocks occurring as late as the next summer. In early January 1812 an 8.4 quake occurred. Then on February 7, a quake of 8.8 occurred, by far the most violent. The quakes caused extensive damage, swallowed islands, and is said to have made the Mississippi River run backward for awhile. The earthquake created Reelfoot Lake in western Tennessee.

NEW ORLEANS (STEAMER)

The *Str. NEW ORLEANS* was not the first steamboat and not the first on the Western Rivers. It was, however, the first to make a lengthy successful journey from the banks of the Monongahela River to the seaport city for which it was named and opened the currents to new possibilities of travel and transport. Its trip started on 29 October 1811. It was delayed at Louisville due to the deepness of its hull and low water at the Falls of the Ohio making it too dangerous to run them. The delay allowed the *NEW ORLEANS* to go back upsteam to Cincinnati and prove its capability to stem a current. When sufficient water was available it ran the Falls and continued down the Ohio to where it met the Mississippi just in time to experience the shaken ground of the New Madrid earthquake. Some Indians believed the quake was the result of the belching fire of the steamboat. The Pilot lost his bearings as islands had disappeared in the Mississippi and channels had radically changed. They were able to navigate safely through the area and arrived at Natchez. At that port they took on bales of cotton and some passengers which would be the first cargo transported by steamboat on the Western Rivers. After reaching the city of New Orleans the steamer started making weekly trips between that city and the town of Natchez about 350 miles distant which were reported to be profitable. About two years later in Baton Rouge the vessel was impaled on a stump and sank.

Various speculations have been made as to size, shape, and the layout of the *Str. NEW ORLEANS*, but apparently no one is certain what she looked like. The length and breath have been reported to be 116 by 20 feet with a rounded hull which was said to have a depth of 12 feet. Some say she was a sternwheeler, others say a sidewheeler. Pictures have been drawn of a split cabin and others of a continuous one, and some show a small pilothouse forward. Most show two masts that could be used for sails when the wind was right. Even the engine has not been described. With a hull of 12 feet it may have been a beam type or a STEEPLE ENGINE which was set vertically, but no one knows, so only speculations are offered. What is certain, the *Str. NEW ORLEANS* was a prominent pioneer on the Western Rivers.

NEW ORLEANS TO BATON ROUGE PILOT (NOBRA)

A Pilot licensed by the State of Louisiana who generally pilots seagoing vessels on the Mississippi River between the ports of New Orleans and Baton Rouge, LA.

NEW YEAR'S DAY

An old maritime custom was to strike 16 bells instead of eight when the *New Year* was counted down. Also, on some vessels it was a custom to write the first day's log with all that happened on all watches in verse.

NIGGER

A term used in the past to describe a small auxiliary capstan or windlass used to haul in a small line or wire; also called a GYPSY. It was sometimes mounted on the side of a steamboat or towboat, and non-powered ones on rigging flats, derrick boats, log rafts, and other utility-type flats. The term appears in many of the tomes on river history, but it is not politically correct to verbalize it in current usage.

NIGGER BOILER

An auxiliary boiler for use when the main steam plant cooled down for cleaning, inspection or repairs. It was also sometimes called a DONKEY BOILER. Later when shore power could be supplied to vessels at docks or shipyards, this boiler was no longer needed. It is only referenced here for someone who reads of it in a book of the last two centuries.

NIGGER LINE

A line of about one inch or so, used with the NIGGER to shift barges when making up a tow, or to pull them tight. Used on log and lumber rafts to hold the booms together. Not politically correct to verbalize the term in current usage.

NIGHT HAWK

1. On steamboats it was an adjustable ornamentation that was painted a bright color on a vessel's jackstaff, located at about the Pilot's eye level. It was used to help gauge distances and the heights of objects.

2. Currently the term is sometimes used to mean a small flag, or piece of cloth, placed at the top of a jackstaff at the head of the tow to indicate which way the wind is blowing. The name probably originally derived from the ability of a hawk to see its prey at night. Now the term has been possibly carried over since the small flag flapping in a night wind could seem to resemble the wings of a hawk.

NIGHT VISION

The ability to see and navigate in very dim light to which eyes have become adapted. If a bright light is flashed, even that of a flashlight, in a Pilot's eyes, vision is temporarily hindered until the eyes again adjust.

NINE-FOOT CONTOUR LINE

A meandering line on some navigation charts that delineates the project depth of at least nine feet of water during a low-water reference plan.

NIP

A sharp bend or KINK in a line or wire that causes it to foul or jam in a block, a condition that will also weaken the line in that area. The term is also used when referring to an area where a line or wire is wearing in one particular area due to chafing. Changing the position by slacking or hauling in the line is termed "to change the *nip*".

NO BOTTOM

A section of the channel that has

more than adequate depth in which to navigate. In the days of packetboats it was considered four fathoms (24+ feet) or more on the LEADLINE. Today, the standard would be set by the Pilot on watch, but is usually between 18 and 20 feet when the person sounding cannot touch the bottom of the river with the SOUNDING POLE.

NO CURE, NO PAY

A contract term with a salvage firm in which the salvor contracts for a price certain to raise a vessel. If the salvage firm is successful in accomplishing what he contracted to do in a timely manner it is paid in full. If the salvage company cannot raise the vessel, it gets nothing, no matter how long it was on the job. At one time this type of salvage contract was common when the owner of the vessel and the salvor had total control of the operation and made all the decisions on how the salvage was to proceed. With the advent of many environmental laws this is no longer the case. The USCG will require a detailed salvage plan prior to the commencement of salvage and approve any change that may have to occur. Most salvage contracts that presently occur are usually let on a per diem basis. See: SALVAGE.

NOAH'S ARK

NOAH, of course, was the foremost mariner of Biblical fame who ensured that animals, including humans (and rivermen) would continue on earth. The *ARK* is the predecessor of all vessels that have evolved over the centuries due to his foresight, including the *USS RONALD REAGAN*, to steamboats, towboats, tugs, as well as canoes, skiffs, and yawls. So, always remember, those of you who enjoy working or floating on the water, that if it wasn't for *NOAH* and the *ARK* you would be up the creek without a paddle on a log.

In order to try to compare the size of what has been reported to be the measurement of the *ARK* with the size of some river craft that have plied the rivers we will attempt to lay out some estimates of measurements:

	Noah's Ark	Flatboat	Keeler	Jumbo Barge
Length in Feet	450	20–90	40–80	195
Width in Feet	75	10–25	10–15	35
Height in Feet	45	4–6	6–8	16 (w/coaming)
Vol. Cu. Ft.	4 million	800–1350	1920–7680	69,260
G.T	14,000	8–135	190–750	1400

NONCOMPLIANCE

A vessel, or its operation, that has failed to comply with a law, regulation, or standard.

NON-SELF PROPELLED

Vessels that do not contain a means to propel themselves, such as a dumb barge.

NON-SKID PAINT or COATING

A type of paint or coating that contains a grit that is applied to deck areas. When the coating dries it provides a surface that prevents or retards slipping or skidding when walking on it, especially when wet.

NON-SPARKING TOOLS

Tools that will not cause a spark, such as those made of brass. They are used to work around tanks and pipelines that contain flammable liquids.

NON-VESSEL OWNING CARRIER

A freight forwarder that consolidates freight from various shippers. The forwarder then contracts with a barge owner/operator for loading of cargo in a barge, with the delivery of the freight to one or more destinations.

NORMAL POOL

The stage of water depth maintained at a dam to meet its project impounded pool elevation that is provided for navigation.

NORMAL POOL ELEVATION

The height in feet above sea level of

NORMAL WEAR AND TEAR

A term used in the survey of a vessel. It denotes that the vessel has experienced an average or typical amount of wear and minor damages that a similar vessel of its age and type of service would have sustained during a comparative period of time.

NORMAN PIN

1. A pin that is sometimes horizontally in the side of a bollard, bitt, or post to keep a line or wire from slipping off if the lead is too acute.

2. A pair of bars at the stern of some older tugs to restrict the movement of a hawser to the side, keeping it centered off the stern. Sometimes the pins have a GOB LINE fastened across the top to keep the towing wire or hawser from jumping out. Now mostly replaced with a roller chock.

NORTHBOUND

Going upstream, it is the movement of a vessel against the prevailing current on the inland waterways, regardless of whether the directional progress of the vessel is north, south, east, or west. For instance, a tow leaving Paducah, KY, on the Tennessee River bound for Decatur, AL, would be considered going *northbound,* even though it would be traveling in a southerly compass direction. The opposite of SOUTHBOUND.

NOSE

1. A term sometimes used when referring to the forward extreme end of a towboat or its tow.

2. To ease the bow of a vessel into a bank or landing, as in: "We'll *nose* her in above that big Cottonwood, and see if you can get a line out".

NOTCH

1. A barge in tow that sticks out to the side further than the barge ahead of it. The resulting *notch* can catch in a lock recess or on a bridge fender works.

2. A section in the tow deliberately left open to accept another barge, as in: "We'll leave that *notch* on the starboard string at the bow, because we have to pick up ABC barge at the next landing and we'll just slip her in there".

3. When making a JACKKNIFE lockage, or a SET-OVER SINGLE lockage, the tow and/or towboat moves into *notches* it creates when breaking up the tow to accommodate the lock size.

NOTCHED DIKE

A stone dike with a *notch*, or depression. This permits a degree of flow through the dike, allowing for a diversity of vegetation and scour holes in the dike field that promotes the propagation of vegetative and fish species.

NOTICE OF PROPOSED RULE MAKING (NPRM)

A *notice* printed in the Federal Register by a federal agency (usually the USCG in regard to vessels and personnel) with an outline of a regulatory initiative that is being proposed. They give a date for comments to be made and submitted to the record, as well as note a list public hearing dates, where being held, etc.

NOTICE TO MARINERS

Information issued by the USCG to mariners on aids to navigation, channels, and other pertinent safety bulletins. It is usually available by radiotelephone or via the internet. See: NAVIGATION NOTICE (USACE) for rules, regulations, and information issued by the USACE.

NOT UNDER COMMAND

A vessel that is disabled in some way. Under the definitions in Rule 3 of the Navigation Rules it is described as a vessel which, through some exceptional circumstance, is unable to maneuver as required by the Rules and is therefore unable to keep out of the way of another vessel. At any rate, if you meet one, give it wide berth unless you are able to render assistance.

NOZZLE

A tapered reducer opening at the end of a pipe, hose, or a fitting that will increase the pressure of a fluid or gas in the line. The increased pressure is converted into velocity of the liquid or gas when expelled at its exit. This is what occurs at the end of a fire hose *nozzle* (or at other *nozzle* ejectors in steam or diesel engines), or at the expulsion of water from a KORT NOZZLE enclosing the thrust of a propeller.

NPRM

An acronym meaning NOTICE OF PROPOSED RULE MAKING. See: ANPRM.

NUN BUOY

A conical-shaped red buoy that marks the right-hand side of a channel when going upstream, or when entering our river system from seaward, so all seamanship courses in the Navigation Rules use the 3-R phrase, Red-Right-Returning. The term appears to come from an English garment for a child that was tapered at the ends, which gave it the appearance of a cone similar to the *buoys* used at the time. See: CAN BUOY.

NAVIGATION RULES
INTERNATIONAL—INLAND

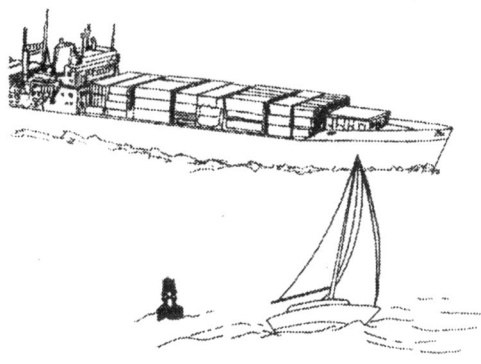

NAVIGATION LIGHTS

UNBROKEN VISIBILITY ARCS TO BE DISPLAYED BY EVERY VESSEL'S NAVIGATION LIGHTS FROM SUNSET TO SUNRISE AND IN RESTRICTED VISIBILITY

NAVIGATION RULES

The mariner's bible issued by the USCG. Named the Navigational Rules, it contains the Rules of the Road governing vessels in international waters as well as for those towboats and tugs that travel through our inland rivers and canals. Every person who navigates a vessel should be a student of its text. It has been profoundly stated,
"The best place is to know the rules and worst place to study them is in a collision-

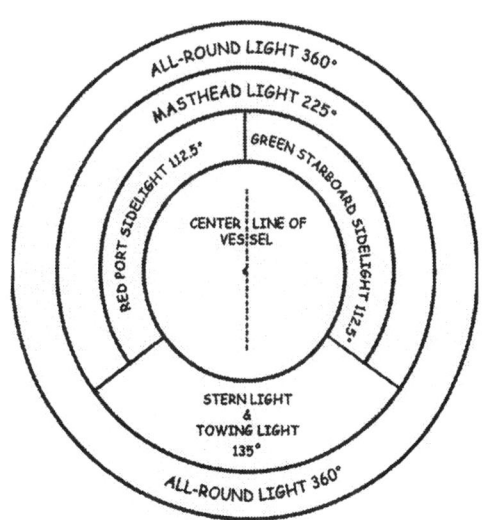

THE STEAMER NEW ORLEANS

From a wonderful painting of the first steamboat to successfully navigate the Western Rivers from Pittsburgh to New Orleans. Gary R. Lucy is the artist. He commissioned Glenn Hensley to build a model of what they thought the steamer NEW ORLEANS most likely would have looked like, which Gary then painted as it was moving down the river in 1811.

NOAH'S ARK

Noah, as most know, was the designated first pilot by the Almighty, so he is therefore the ancestor of all Western Rivers and Canal Boatmen. The picture depicts only one possibility out of millions as to what the ark might really have looked like. It's image has been drawn by thousands of inspired artists working in many different disciplines. Like the picture of the NEW ORLEANS on the previous page, since no one living knows the truth of the ark's size, shape, form, or draft, the cartoonish picture shown is probably as good a guess as any as to its operational image. Suffice to say that the good Captain Noah apparently ran a taut ark, or barging operation, and he brought his staunch craft safely through an all time record storm, then put his vessel into a safe port. So, now it can surely be said, "Well done, Captain."

NAME BOARDS

The sidewheeler SPREAD EAGLE with name painted on the wheel housing

The sternwheeler J.B. FINLEY displaying the name on the side lower deck and across stern of the vessel,. S & D photo

A modern diesel towboat, the CONTI – AFTON with small letters across an upper deck. At times the name is on a wooden board attached to the railing outside the pilot house. The name and port of documentation on the stern transom is mostly obscured.

O

OAKUM

A material made up from used strands of line such as hemp, sisal, or jute bagging. It is tarred and used as caulking in wood seams and around shingles to stop leaks in steel hulls. The fibers will swell to make a tight seal to stop or reduce water inflow. The term derives from the Old English *acumbe*, meaning "off-combings or shreds". The word as now applied came into general usage in the 15th century.

OAR

A long wooden shaft called a LOOM with a handle on one end for a person to pull on and a flattened area on the opposite end called a BLADE. It is usually fitted in an oarlock when used to row a small boat or yawl as opposed to a PADDLE which isn't used in an oarlock, however, an *oar* can also be used without oarlocks. Long *oars* used to steer LOG RAFTS are called SWEEPS. The derivative of the word appears to come from the Greek *eretmos*, on down to the Norse word *are*, and the Old English *ar*, which have the meaning of "directing movement or steering".

The lament of the old riverman of what he wants to do when he retires is an update of Odysseus's *Oar*, wherein the retiring riverman says, "When I get through with these boats and barges I'm going to put an *oar* on my shoulder and walk away from this river, and keep walking until someone asks me, what is that you're carrying? That's where I'm gonna build myself a house."

OARLOCK

A U-shaped fitting with a pin at its base that is placed in a small hole in the GUNWALE of a skiff or a yawl that receives the LOOM of an OAR and acts as a fulcrum when rowing. It is also called a *rowlock* or a THOLE PIN.

OBSCURED

The visibility sector area of a navigation light which cannot be seen by another vessel in a navigational situation.

OBSTRUCTION TO NAVIGATION

Any object that impedes, or could impede, the transit of vessels in the navigable channel, such as a sunken barge which is required to be marked with a SPECIAL PURPOSE BUOY. To rivermen, it is any bridge that has its support piers in the river and not on the river's banks.

OCCULTING LIGHT

Although it is sometimes described as a flashing light with the period of light being longer than the period of darkness, the USCG when using it as an aid to navigation states that it will, "Show light for 1 second, followed by eclipse for 1 second". It is not to be confused with a FLASHING LIGHT which is to show a single flash every two seconds. A quick flashing light will show a single flash every second. *Occulting lights* are not often seen on the river system; however, if the flashes of light do not appear to conform to that stated in the light list, it should be reported as an aid discrepancy.

OCCUPATIONAL SAFETY AND HEALTH ADMINISTRATION (OSHA)

The federal agency that promulgates and enforces safety and general health regulations for shipyards and terminal facilities, as well as some standards for vessels not under the jurisdiction of the USCG.

OCEAN-GOING

Any vessel that has been built to standards that can withstand the rigors of sea-operating conditions that allows it to operate outside the lines of demarcation. Not often seen on the Western Rivers above Baton Rouge, LA.

OFF

Used in the sense of "away from",

i.e. "The wind is blowing strong *off* the Arkansas shore", or "The current's setting me *off* the greens", or "I'm waiting on you just *off* the right shore below the bridge and we'll see you on one whistle", or "Keep *off* the reds in the next crossing, they're only sitting in six feet of water".

OFF-CHARTER SURVEY

The inspection of the condition of a vessel when it is being returned to an operator from whom it had been leased. The survey compares any noted damage that occurred during the charter which was not noted in the ON-CHARTER SURVEY.

OFF-LOAD

To unload or discharge cargo from a vessel.

OFF-STATION

Refers to an AID TO NAVIGATION that has moved away from its designated location, such as a buoy or a light.

OFF-WATCH

A period when a crew member has no assigned duties to perform and is basically at rest except in the case when there might be an all-hands emergency. See: ON WATCH.

OFFICER

On steamboats, *officers* consisted of the Master, the Pilots, the Mate, Engineers, and the Clerk(s). At the present time on towboats and tugs, the *officers* are the Captain (Master), the Pilot, now termed a MATE(PILOT), and sometimes called Watch Captain, and the Chief Engineer. The term comes from the Latin *officiatius*, meaning a place where work was done, then on down through the ages to a person who is in charge of those doing the work.

OFFICER IN CHARGE OF MARINE INSPECTION (OCMI)

The U.S. Coast Guard person designated by the Commandant, and under the supervision and direction of a USCG District Commander, who is in charge of a particular USCG inspection zone to oversee the administration and enforcement of the various statutes, regulations, and rules under his/her jurisdiction. Currently, all towboats and tugs operating on the Western Rivers are in the Eighth USCG District.

OFFICIAL NUMBER

The number that is assigned to each vessel that is documented by the USCG. The number is to be permanently marked on the forward beam of the vessel. On the river, documented barges usually have their numbers bead-welded on the bow rake void framing.

OFFSHORE SUPPLY VESSEL (OSV)

A cargo vessel that transports supplies, equipment, personnel, and goods to rigs involved in the exploration of energy products off the U.S. coast.

OFFSHORE WATERS

Generally, those waters and lands which lie seaward of the coastline. The term applies to the waters beyond the DEMARCATION LINE.

OFFSHORE WIND

A wind that is blowing from a shore toward the river, i.e. "There's a strong *offshore wind* coming from the right bank, so watch it when making the wagon bridge with these empties".

OHIO AND ERIE CANAL

Construction on the *canal* started in 1825 to connect Lake Eire at Cleveland to the city of Portsmouth on the Ohio River. It was built in sections with the first in the northern section opening in 1827 and the final section opening in 1832. Its total length was 308 miles and contained 151 locks, plus feeder canals and aqueducts. See: CANALS.

OHIO RIVER

The modern-day version states that

the *Ohio River* is formed at the confluence of the Allegheny and Monongahela rivers at Pittsburgh with the start of its mileage at zero. Some, including George Washington, believed that the Allegheny coming out of the mountains was really the headwaters of the *Ohio*. The river takes its name from some Iroquois Indian word that sounded like "Oyo" to the French, which they translated to mean "beautiful river", and often called it "la belle riviere". Others have stated that the name means "the bloody river", the stream of "great white water", or the "river of white foam". Probably all are accurate, depending upon where the particular tribe was located.

As now located, the river flows for 981 miles before it enters the Mississippi River at Cairo, IL. It drains the watersheds of 14 states in its basin and tributaries, consisting of about 204,000 square miles. Its bed drops gradually (except at the FALLS OF THE OHIO) from Pittsburgh to Cairo about 429 feet. It is opined that the first European to view the river was LaSalle in 1669 when he was trying to find a route to the Pacific. The river was certainly the route to what new settlers considered the West of the United States. It was a practical passage in a land of no roads, but only Indian trails. The basic means of transporting goods, and people, originated with the dugout canoe before evolving to flatboats and keelboats. The *NEW ORLEANS*, the first steamboat on the western waters, traveled down the *Ohio River* in 1811. The Ohio-Mississippi river system and its tributaries with their connecting waterways was the first "interstate" transportation system in the United States. Railroads had not been invented, nor trucks, nor airplanes. The rivers open up the vast lands to the west. So when people talk about taking the "interstate" when going to a distant city, ask them on which boat they will be traveling.

Federal involvement in river improvements started in 1824 with the removal of snags and some rocks from the Grand Chain on the lower section of the river. Some wing dams and dikes were also placed in service. After the Civil War the USACE conducted more detailed surveys and recommended a series of locks and dams to improve navigation. After much differing public opinion and funding problems, the DAVIS ISLAND LOCK and its movable WICKET DAM were completed in 1885 six miles below Pittsburgh. It was 600' by 110' and provided for a six-foot channel depth in the upper *Ohio River* reaches. In 1905 Congress authorized the extension of a slack water navigation channel of nine-foot depth to the *Ohio's* mouth. Not much was accomplished since coal tonnage, the major commodity from the area, was declining; however, WW I showed a greater need for river commerce and the L & D building commenced in earnest. The project of canalization was completed in 1929 with a total of 49 L & Ds.

After WW II as new industry moved into the Ohio Valley, it was determined that the structures from the 1920s were not accommodating the growth and needs of commerce. A modernization program for the river was undertaken to replace the existing navigation structures with longer, high-lift locks with deeper pools. This work started in 1954 and continues to the present day.

OIL

A mixture of hydrocarbons that usually exist in a liquid state in natural underground pools or reservoirs. Under 49 CFR, where listed as a pollutant, it is more broadly defined as "oil of any kind or in any form, including, and not limited to, petroleum, fuel oil, vegetable oil, animal oil, sludge, oil refuse, oil mixed with wastes other than dredged spoil". The origination of the term is from the Latin *oleum*, which meant olive oil.

OIL or HAZARDOUS MATERIAL PLACARD

A card or notice that is required on

OIL BOOM

A floating barrier that is placed around an oil spill to contain it or to divert it in another direction in order that it may be cleaned up with skimming devices or sorbent material.

OIL BURNER

Used in steamboat days to differentiate between vessels burning wood or coal to fire their boilers from one that used oil.

OIL SCREW

A vessel that is powered by one or more diesel engines and turns a propeller(s) as its means of propulsion.

OIL SKINS

See: SLICKER SUITS

OILER

A person who may work in the engine room assisting the engineer. Also called a STRIKER.

OIL-WATER SEPARATOR

Equipment aboard a vessel that can separate oily wastes, such as bilge slops, from water.

OL' MAN RIVER

The greatest moving lyrics written about our most important river were penned by Oscar Hammerstein II and set to the melodious composition of Jerome Kern for the Broadway musical *Show Boat* in 1927. The words were sung by "Joe", a roustabout on the docks, about the waters on which the showboat travelled. Since that original composition some of the words and phrases have often been changed to suit the singer performing or the times. The production was based on Edna Ferber's novel *Show Boat* written in 1926. The story depicted life, discord, and difficulties aboard the showboat *COTTON BLOSSOM* in the 1880s. The following is reported to be the first version as it was sung in 1927, (also see SHOWBOAT):

Dere's an ol' man called de Mississippi,
Dat's de ol' man dat I'd like to be,
What does he care if de world's got troubles?
What does he care if de land ain't free?

Ol' Man River.
Dat Ol' Man,
He mus' know sumpin',
But don' say nothin',
He jes' keeps rollin',
He keeps on rollin' along.

He don't plant taters,
He don't plant cotton,
An' dem tat plants 'em
Is soon forgotten,
But Ol' Man River,
He jes' keeps rollin' along.

You an' me, we sweat an' strain,
Body all achin' and racked with pain.
"Tote dat barge! Lift dat bale!"
Git a little drunk,
An' you lands in jail!

Ah gits weary,
An' sick o' tryin',
Ah'm tired of livin',
And skeered o' dyin',
ButOl' Man River,
He jes' keeps rollin' along!

OLD MAN

Has no particular reference to age. Sometimes used to describe the Master of a vessel, i.e. "The *Old Man* sure has been cranky this morning".

OLD RIVER CONTROL PROJECT

The project structure, authorized by Congress in 1954 and completed in 1962, was to control the flow of the Mississippi River through the Atchafalaya River basin, which had been capturing more and more of the Mississippi's river flow. A rock-filled dam was constructed to dam the Old River, and a canal with a lock was installed (1200' by 75') to allow navigation to and from the Mississippi River to the Atchafalaya and Red rivers. When built, the flow-control project was intended to prevent more than about 30 percent of the Mississippi to go down the Atchafalaya River. It was to also control the Red River flows, discharging them either into the Mississippi or allowing them to go down into the Atchafalaya Basin.

In 1973 a devastating flood on the Mississippi almost overwhelmed the Old River Project, causing extensive damage and undermining of its structural supports. An Auxiliary Structure was designed and constructed. It was completed in 1986 with the capacity to also provide hydroelectric power. See: ATCHAFALAYA RIVER.

OLERON
See: LAWS OF OLERON.

ON A STAND
A term used when a river has risen in height and has stopped rising, or had risen, started falling and stopped, with the gauge level staying stationary.

ON A STRING
A term used to describe a tug or towboat that is towing barges astern on a towline. See: MULE TRAIN.

ON BOARD
Used in the same sense as ABOARD. Anything that is on the vessel that is not stationary and permanently attached, including people.

ON CHARTER SURVEY
The inspection of a vessel when it is going to be chartered (leased) from an owner. The condition of the vessel is noted in detail in order that it may be compared to a survey that will be undertaken when the vessel goes OFF CHARTER.

ON DECK
Something that is placed outside on a weather deck. It usually refers to the main deck unless a specific deck is named where the object(s) were located.

ON SHORE WIND
A wind that is blowing either towards the right or left bank of a river. In this case it is not necessarily the "descending bank", but rather refers to the navigational situation, i.e. "A strong wind will be blowing on shore when you get to ABC Lock on your watch". If the tow is headed up-river and the lock is on the left descending bank, the wind would be across the tow from left to right; but if the tow is headed down-river the same wind would be considered blowing in the opposite direction, or across the tow from right to left. In other words, right or left depends upon which direction the tow is facing when looking towards the bow.

ON THE BANK
1. Anything that is on the shore.
2. A person ashore who is on days off from duty aboard a vessel.
3. Someone who has taken a shore job.

ON THE BEAM (PORT or STARBOARD)
Something that is in the general direction of 90 degrees from the heading of a vessel.

ON THE BOW or STERN
Something that is forward in the general direction of the heading of a vessel or something that is in the general direction aft of the vessel. Used with port or starboard, i.e. "port bow" or "starboard stern".

ON THE FLY
1. To make a maneuver of picking up or dropping a barge while still moving in the river and not tying off the tow; usually with the assistance of a FLEET BOAT.
2. To start a tow moving out of a

lock chamber in a JACKKNIFE or SET-OVER SINGLE lockage, and then dropping back under the stern to make the towboat up to the tow while it is still moving.

ON THE HIP
When a tug or towboat makes up to the port or starboard stern quarter of a barge or other vessel to tow it. See: HIP.

ON THE PORT or STARBOARD BOW QUARTER
In the general direction of 45 degrees between the bow and abeam.

ON THE PORT or STARBOARD STERN QUARTER
In the general direction of 45 degrees between the stern and abeam.

ON-WATCH
The period when a crewmember has an assigned duty and/or is ready to carry out his/her duties. See: OFF-WATCH.

ONE-ARMED BANDIT
A term sometimes used to describe a ratcheting lever-type chain hoist used to lift, or to pull in place, parts and machinery. It also describes a different type of machine on river gambling boats that take one's money.

ONE-LUNGER
In the early days of internal combustion engines, the term *one-lunger* specifically referred to single-cylinder gasboats. At the present time many use the term when referring to a tug or towboat with only one engine and one propeller.

ONE-TRIPPER
An old barge that has been patched so often that there are patches on patches. It usually only makes *one trip* in its trade, then has to go to a repair yard to be patched anew.

ONE-WHISTLE SIDE
When vessels are meeting head on, it is a port-to-port passing. See: TWO-WHISTLE SIDE.

ONSHORE WIND
A wind that is blowing from the river or canal to one shore or another, i.e. "When making the lock, look out for that strong *onshore wind* as it will want to set you into the bank before you get to the guide wall".

OPEN
1. To hold a vessel's course to the side of an object or place, i.e. "Hold your tow 100 yards *open* on Neverlit Light after you clear the point. That will keep you clear of the bar that is building on the left shore."
2. When holding on a set of RANGE lights, it is the condition where the lights are not in alignment indicating that the mariner steering a vessel is off-course.

OPEN CHOCK
A deck fitting used to guide the direction of a line or wire. It consists of a curved horn on each side as opposed to a closed chock, when the horns are joined at the top.

OPEN GAUGING
The SOUNDING of a tank of liquid cargo through a manhole or an ULLAGE HATCH or hole.

OPEN HOPPER
A barge whose cargo space is not covered.

OPEN LIGHTS
Any type of light or flame producing source that could be a possible cause of ignition on a tank vessel to either the cargo or its vapors. A prohibition of no *open lights* is posted on a sign on all non-gas free tank barges. Sometimes referred to as "naked lights".

OPEN RIVER
The condition of a river that has moveable dams with wickets (such as

the lower end of the Ohio River and two dams on the Illinois River) that allows the wickets to be lowered to the riverbed due to sufficient flows of water. This creates an *open river* and allows towboats to pass over the dam without requiring them to lock through the chamber. See: SCANT OPEN RIVER.

OPEN WATER

In periods of ice-covered channels, that section of a river or channel which is relatively free of heavy ice.

OPENING

A passage between two sections of the riverbank. It may, or may not, be navigable. It could lead to a harbor or just be a break in the shoreline leading to a backwater slough.

OPERATING COST

Those costs directly associated with operating a vessel (such as total crew costs, fuel, supplies, maintenance, and food), as opposed to FIXED COSTS.

OPERATING RATIO

The ratio of operating expenses to operating revenue.

OPERATING REVENUE

The amount of money (revenue) a carrier receives for its transportation services.

OPERATIONS & MAINTNANCE (O & M)

A budget term for the expenditures of the USACE, which is basically all the costs of operating and maintaining the navigational system of the inland waterways with which they are responsible. It does not include any capital costs.

OPERATOR

A person or company which has under its control a vessel or group of vessels that they provide with crews and the supplies necessary to run them, but which does not necessarily own the vessels.

OPERATOR OF UNINSPECTED TOWING VESSELS (OUTV)

An obsolete term used in regulations for a person who was a MASTER or PILOT of a tugboat or towboat on the inland waterways. See: MATE (PILOT).

ORDINARY HIGH WATER

In nature it generally refers to the boundary line of watercourses, and is the elevation to the limit of the recognized channel in rivers and reservoirs. It is the level of water that has been maintained for a period of time that leaves evidence on the shoreline at that height. This can be indicated by the destruction of, or lack of, terrestrial plants and the level below which aquatic vegetation appears. The term is used in determining the establishment of navigation pools.

ORIGIN

The place from which a journey starts. In the case of a barge, it may be a loading dock or some fleeting area. The *origin* may be one place to the shipper, but another to the vessel operator providing the transportation service for all, or only part of, the journey.

OUACHITA-BLACK RIVER

The river rises in Arkansas and flows about 500 miles in a southeasterly course until it meets with the Tensas and Little rivers to form the *Black River* which continues the journey until it enters the Red River. The *Ouachita* is named for an Indian Tribe called the Washita, which went out of existence after being absorbed into another tribe by about 1700. The name has been said to have various meanings, as the Cow People, Good Hunting Grounds, and Sparkling Silver Water. It is pronounced "*Whash* – a – taw".

In the early days of navigation the rafting trade was common. When the USACE first undertook making improvements on the *Ouachita River* steamboats were already active on it, going as far up as Camden, AR, when there was sufficient water. However, during low flow periods there was little traffic above its confluence with the *Black River*.

A survey was undertaken in 1872 which recommended dams with locks to create a four-foot depth in the channel year 'round, but the work was deemed too costly; however, snag removal was started. Then in 1877 the construction of dams commenced, but lagged in funding and the improvements fell into disrepair by 1882. At the beginning of the 20th Century, navigation lock and dam construction was undertaken and a $6\frac{1}{2}$-foot channel was completed in 1924 with six L & Ds. By WW II the size of the infrastructure was outdated. In 1950 Congress authorized a nine-foot channel, but not sufficient funds to build it. In 1964 construction was started on four L & Ds, which were completed in the 1970s. The locks are 600' by 84'.

OUT OF SHAPE

When a tow is not properly *shaped up*, or lined up, to make a bridge, a lock, a downstream landing, to enter a flank, or other navigational maneuver that could result in an accident. See: SHAPE.

OUT OF TRIM

A vessel that has a list to port or to starboard, or to the bow, or to the stern, or even a combination of lists when it might be considered catawampus. Not a desirable barge to have when trying to make it up in a tow.

OUTAGE

1. The failure of an aid to navigation to properly function as described, especially a lighted aid. It should be reported to the USCG.
2. The time a navigation lock is out of service for repairs.

OUTBOARD

1. Beyond, or away from the outside of the hull of a vessel, i.e. "Put the DEF barge on the *outboard* side of the OPQ barge".
2. To the side of the center line of a vessel or tow, i.e. "Place the barge running lights on the *outboard* sides at the head of the tow".
3. A portable motor that can be used to power a yawl or skiff.

OUTDRAFT

A lateral cross current that angles from the shore out toward the upstream spillway side of a dam in running water that pulls the head of a tow with it, at times making it difficult for a large tow to make a lock without the use of check lines.

Sometimes, it is also used to describe the current action of setting a tow away from the lower guide wall of a lock, but this is really the action of an eddy rather than the flow of current and is more often called a BACKLASH.

OUTER LOCK WALL

The wall of a lock on the riverward channel side of the structure or away from the shore.

OUTFALL

1. The heavy flow of a small stream or tributary into a mainstream river.
2. A discharge of a storm sewer, industrial plant, drainage ditch, or similar flows into the river.

OUTFIT

To place aboard a vessel all equipment and supplies necessary to safely navigate it on its intended voyage.

OVERAGE TOW

A tow that exceeds the normal area capacity of a lock and requires the assistance of a harbor or fleet boat to lock a portion of it through separately. The assistance boat then will wait for the linehaul boat above or below the lock, as the case may be, to reattach the *overage* section to the main tow when it completes its lockage.

OVERALL LENGTH

A measurement of the extreme fore

and aft length of a vessel or tow, from the forward extremity of the bow to the aft extremity of its stern.

OVERBOARD
Someone or something that falls, jumps, is put, thrown, or washed from a vessel into the surrounding water.

OVER-FILL
The act of putting more cargo in a tank than it can hold, causing it to overflow, or to load more cargo into the hold of a barge or tank, causing it to be at a heavier draft than is suitable for the channel.

OVER-FLANK
See: FLANKING

OVERFLOW
A tank that is spilling liquid product out of its hatch or vent because too much was loaded is said to be *overflowing*. Product that is spilling is referred to as *overflow*.

OVERHANG
On steamboats, *overhangs* were the GUARDS that extended outward from the hull of the vessel on the main deck in order to accommodate more cargo to be loaded, especially cotton. These decks had to be supported by CROSS CHAINS and KNUCKLE CHAINS, similar to HOG CHAINS, except they ran athwartship.

OVERHAUL
1. The act of one vessel OVERTAKING another vessel.
2. The dismantling of a vessel's engine, or other mechanical gear, to examine it and to repair and/or replace parts as necessary.

OVERHEAD
1. The top of a room or compartment. A landlubber would call it a *ceiling*. In old steamboat days it was called a ceiling, but after WWII as ex-sailors came to work on the river, the ceiling took on the more nautical terminology with most river people.
2. The general cost or expense of running a vessel.

OVERLOAD
1. Turning up all available RPMs on the engine.
2. Barges that are loaded to a greater draft than the navigable channel will allow, or dangerously reducing the amount of freeboard on a vessel, or other unsafe condition.

OVERRIDE
The action of co-opting a set mechanical function on a piece of machinery, such as that of a safety valve on a boiler, or that of an engine's governor.

OVER-STEER
The act of using too much rudder, causing the tow's bow to swing too far while entering a bend. This action results in the head of the tow being in the slackwater on the bar side of the channel, while the towboat would be in the stronger current in the bight of the bend. If the Pilot cannot break the swing by applying opposite rudder, the head of the tow may go aground on the shallow water of the sandbar, forcing the towboat's stern to hit the bank, or the tow may TOP AROUND. See: BILL HOOK.

OVER-THE-GROUND
The actual distance travelled or made good during a period of time, such as a measured number of hours, a watch period, a day, etc.

OVERTAKING RULE
Under Rule 13 of the Navigation Rules, when a vessel is gaining ground on another it will be, "deemed to be overtaking when coming up from a direction more than 22.5 degrees abaft her beam; that is, in such a position with reference to the vessel she is overtaking, that at night she would be able

to see only the sternlight of that vessel but neither of her sidelights".

OWNER

The corporation or entity that has a controlling interest in a vessel(s), but is not necessarily the operator of them.

OXBOW BEND

A long sweeping curvature of a river where the course of its flowing waters changes in a very fat "U" shape of almost 360 degrees.

OXBOW LAKES

Lakes and harbors that were once part of a main river channel that was cut off by the force of the current cutting a new channel, or by manmade forces that may have shut off a part of the river with dikes to realign the existing channel.

OXIDATION

The chemical reaction of oxygen with another substance, usually in conjunction with the presence of moisture, that causes damage. On the river it usually refers to the combination of oxygen and water that damages machinery and steel plates by corrosion or rusting.

OXBOW BEND

A long looping curvature in a river's course as it flows downstream that almost meets itself is known as an OXBOW BEND. The name derives from the U-shaped collar that is fitted to the neck of an oxen attached to the yoke. The bend depicted here is from the USACE Lower Mississippi River map book and is known as Slough Landing Bend, or more commonly called New Madrid Bend. The loop of river was studied and it was then suggested to make a cutoff across its neck from approximately mile 905 to mile 879. However, the idea was eventually abandoned. Many were of the opinion the shortening might have produced more unfavorable results than it would have solved. See: CUTOFF.

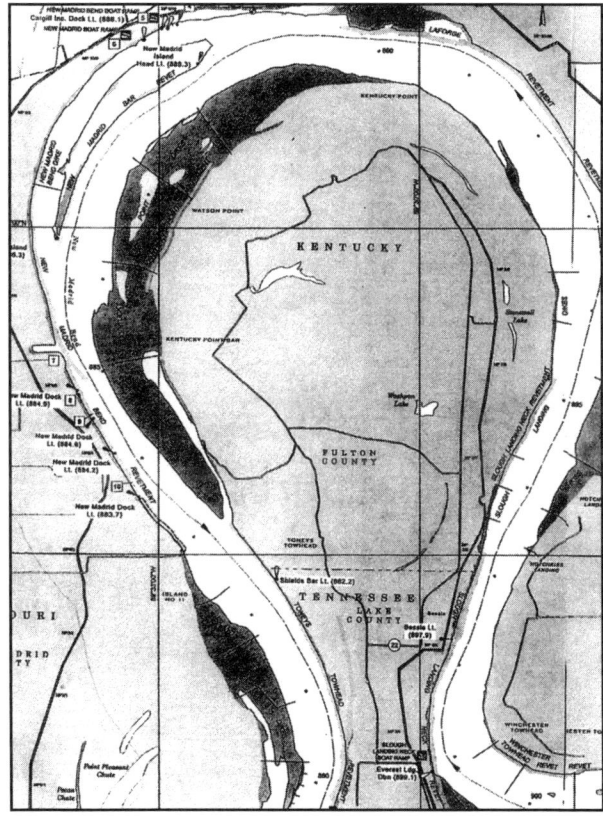

P

PACKETBOAT

A type of steamboat that, in the 1800s, opened the Western Rivers to the world. It carried cargo and mail, and was fitted with staterooms for passengers. It usually operated on a scheduled run between advertised ports. Most of the early vessels were sidewheelers with pictures and their name painted on the wheel housing of the paddlewheel. Later, the sternwheel steamboat became the norm. The *packetboat* trade nearly faded out during the Depression; some of the boats left the trade to become excursion vessels, and no longer carried freight. The term comes from the French word *paquet*. Originally, they were small fast boats to carry official dispatches, mail, and packages from port to port on a scheduled run, which denotes a *packet*.

PADDLE

A shortened oar that is used without an oarlock to propel a small boat, such as a skiff or a yawl, by use of manpower, and sometimes to direct its course in the current. The original use of the word in old English described a spade-like instrument. Its use as an "oar or part of a wheel" came into use in the 17th century.

PADDLEBOARD or BUCKET

One of the *boards* that provides the thrust or momentum for the PADDLEWHEEL.

PADDLEBOX

The wooden enclosure over the upper (above the water line) structure of the PADDLEWHEEL of a sidewheel packetboat. It was also called a *wheelhouse* by some.

PADDLEWHEEL

The propelling force of a sternwheel or sidewheel steamboat. It consisted of a heavy shaft that had a flange on each end with arms radiating out from it. To the end of the arms were attached wooden bucket planks or PADDLEBOARDS. See: DIP.

PADDLING ALONG

A term used to describe a vessel moving at slow speed, usually because whenever the vessel reaches its destination, it's going to have to wait for something or someone.

PADDY'S HEN AND CHICKENS

A group of islands with the largest one being the *Hen,* and the smaller ones the *Chickens*. They are located about seven miles above Memphis on the Arkansas side of the Mississippi River. It was the site of the worst maritime disaster in United States history. On 27 April 1865 the steamer *SULTANA* (see) had a boiler explosion, burned, and sank with great loss of life.

PADEYE

A plate (the pad) secured to the deck with a steel or cast fitting that has a circular opening (the eye), or may have a ring or a triangular bar attached to it, used to receive a ratchet, a shackle, or other piece of deck gear.

PAINT LOCKER

A small compartment on a towboat or tug where paint and paint supplies are stored.

PAINTER

A small line attached to the bow of a yawl, skiff, john boat, punt, dinghy, rowboat, or other small craft and used to tie it off or move it around. If a line is also attached in the stern it is called a *stern painter*. The word is not related to the use of "paint", but appears to come from the French *pentoir,* that meant an object from which "to hang things", perhaps a noose.

PALLET

A small portable platform, usually about 4' by 4', on which cargo of various sorts can be stored and moved by a forklift tractor to be easily loaded or unloaded from vessels. The word comes from French *pallet,* a small flat wooden blade with a handle. It came into its present use in the early 20th Century, probably when a French stevedore was loading cans of paint for shipment.

PALM
The smooth or inner side, of the fluke of a traditional anchor.

PAN—PAN
The radiotelephone signal to be verbally repeated three times in succession when one intends to give a message of some urgency, but not of crisis nature. The word is from the Greek *pan,* to mean "all". See: MAYDAY and SECURITY CALL.

PARCEL AND SERVE
To wrap a splice in wire or, a section of line with overlapping strips of canvas or other heavy material, then binding it tightly with closely wound small stuff to prevent chafing or the sparking of a wire on a steel deck. See: WORM, PARCEL AND SERVE.

PART
1. One of multi-sections of wire or line used to hold barges together or when used to tie a vessel off at a dock or other structure, i.e. "Put out a two-*part* line", or "Double up the wire in four-*parts* at the coupling".
2. One of the sections of line running in a TACKLE.
3. When a line or wire under severe strain finally breaks. The word in this sense comes from the Latin *partire,* meaning "to divide or share".

PARTNER
1. A term used in reference to a fellow Pilot standing the other watch on the same vessel.
2. A board fastened to the side of a wood beam at a joint to strengthen it. Sometimes called a "sister". In this meaning the word is an extension of "part" by "sharing or supporting".

PASS
1. The navigable opening in a movable dam when the wickets are down and there is sufficient water to go over the dam. See: OPEN RIVER.
2. Any one of the several outlets in the delta between the Head of the Passes at Mile 0 of the Mississippi River and the Gulf of Mexico.
3. A narrow channel leading into, or out of, a harbor or other waterway.
4. To heave, throw, or bend onto a handy line and give a mooring line to someone, as: "*Pass* me the line".
5. To lead a line through something, like a block or a chock.
6. To extend a directive or order to others, i.e. "*Pass* the word to the crew".

PASSAGEWAY
Another name for an interior corridor or hallway of a vessel. The term *passage* is from the Latin word *pace,* meaning "the distance between one's legs when taking a step". The word evolved into "passing through".

PASSENGER
1. A person who is riding a vessel certificated to carry a certain amount of *passengers*. The term originally was used to mean a person passing through a town or area either on foot or on an animal. It later took on the connotation of someone taking "passage" on a means of public or private transport.
2. Towboats and tugs are not (usually) certificated to carry *passengers*, however, people may be aboard as *passenger* guests if they have not contributed any monetary consideration directly or indirectly for carriage.

PASSENGER VESSEL
1. A vessel in ferry service that transports passengers from point to point.
2. An excursion vessel that takes people on short leisure trips, such as the *BELLE OF LOUISVILLE,* the *BELLE OF CINCINATTI,* the *NATCHEZ* and many others.

3. A vessel making overnight trips, such as the *DELTA QUEEN* or *RIVER EXPLORER*, which have ceased their operations, but there are still a few in existence on the rivers.

PASSING DAYMARK

Small boards with reflective tape, usually triangular or square, that are attached to navigation lights that denote a reference point only and are not usually to be steered on as marks in a crossing.

PAWL

A small, hinged steel bar that drops into a notch on a manual capstan base or winch to prevent the drum from moving backward. Also used on ratchets to tighten them; by flipping the *pawl* over a person can loosen or run out the ratchet. Sometimes the term "dog" is inappropriately used for this function.

PAY OUT

To ease out, render, or slack a line or wire in a controlled fashion, i.e. "After ya get the headline to the tree, let her *pay out* slowly until I flatten the tow parallel to the shore", or "Don't let that line *pay out*, snug her down!" The term comes from the Latin *pacare*, meaning "to appease" or in other words, to pacify or satisfy the strain on a line.

PAY POT

A type of can with a long spout in which PITCH was heated to a high fluid temperature and then poured (or PAYED) into and over wooden planking seams that had been caulked with oakum to protect and seal them. In this sense the use of the word *pay* is from the Latin *picare*, which later evolved into the use of material for sealing seams of vessels from the French word *peier*.

PAYED & PAYING

The act of applying hot PITCH from a PAY POT to a seam in a wooden hull after it has been caulked. After being *payed* a pitch mop was used to evenly spread the material.

PAYLOAD

A loaded barge or tow that adds substantial revenue to the bottom line, rather than one that simply covers the cost of operation, or the marginal cost.

P—CAN

On some vessels after drinking many cups of coffee, Pilots may feel the need to relieve themselves. There may not be anyone capable or available to provide relief for him at the time of need. That is where the essential *P—can*, usually an old coffee tin, comes in handy. Just make sure when disposing of its contents that it is on the lee side and that the Engineer isn't standing on the lower deck. There are various other names given to this useful device depending upon where a person was raised and the river or canal area where one might work.

PEA

A weight that was hung on a safety valve of a boiler in the early days of steamboating that tended to adjust the boiler's internal pressure. It could be placed in notches at various lengths of the lever similar to a scale weight. The further out on the safety lever the *pea* was placed, the higher was the pressure capable of being produced in the boiler.

PEA SOUP

The type of dense fog that makes it impossible to see beyond the bow of a towboat or tug. Fog that one can cut with a knife and serve for breakfast, but it isn't very tasty.

PEAK TANK

A ballast tank at the extreme forward end on the bow of a vessel.

PEAVY

Similar to a CANT HOOK, except that it also has a pike point at its end. Used in logging and on log rafts. It was named after the log rafter who designed it.

PEEP LIGHT

A very small dim light fastened to a jackstaff or swing pole on the centerline of the lead barges in a tow which acts as an aid for a Pilot in observing the swing of a tow. It is also called a *steering light* or a *swing light.*

PEG

See: PIN.

PELICAN HOOK

A type of quick-release holding device that consists of a curved piece of heavy metal that is attached to a link which is held in the closed position to the link by a ring or toggle. On the river and canal trades it is most often found at the end of a RATCHET and fastened to a barge holding wire which can be quickly released by knocking loose the holding ring.

The term comes from the Greek *pelekus,* meaning "axe" and *pelekan,* which is to "hew with an axe". Therefore, that is probably how the pelican bird got its name since its beak resembles the axe, and how we stole it from them since the shape of the ratchet hook somewhat resembles the bill or beak of the pelican bird.

PENNSYLVANIA RULE

An admiralty legal term that defines a situation where two vessels engage in a maritime collision, where one vessel is grossly negligent, and the other vessel (second vessel) committed a violation of a statutory duty during the accident, the court's judgment would render divided damages assessed to each, unless the second vessel could satisfy the court that its lack of compliance did not, and could not, have caused the accident. (This does not constitute legal advice.)

PERFESSOR

Slang title for the player of the CALLIOPE.

PERILS AT SEA (or on a Navigable Waterway)

An action in a navigable situation of such force that it is able to overcome the strength of a wellfounded vessel and the precautions exercised by prudent seamen.

PERIOD

The complete phase cycle of a navigational light aid's characteristics.

PERMANENT RIGGING

Ratchets, winches, chains, and wires that are installed on barges and cannot be easily removed without the use of a cutting torch. It is also referred to as *stationary rigging*. See: PORTABLE RIGGING.

PERMEABLE DIKE

A dike structure that allows most of the water flowing against it to pass through. It will however, slow the current sufficiently so that a large amount of it's bed load (silt) will settle out behind the dike barrier eventually creating a compact build-up of land, as opposed to a solid rock or stone dike that doesn't do much to slow the current, but simply guides it in a certain direction. Some stone dikes are now made with low spots or notches to make them more permeable in order to increase habitat diversity for fish species to propagate.

PERMIT

1. An authorization by the USCG in issuing a "*permit* to proceed" if an inspected vessel is damaged but is safe enough to move to be unloaded or to be repaired.

2. In order to build a dock on a navigable river, one must obtain a *permit* from the USACE for permission to construct it.

PERSONAL FLOTATION DEVICE (PFD)

There are a variety of devices that have been used for centuries to keep persons afloat to save their life if they inadvertently fall overboard from a vessel. They may have been an old keg or a piece of wood to more sophisticated affairs as needs became more apparent and technology changed. All the different terms came to mean something different to regulators and those using them. It was finally decided to call them *personal flotation devices* or *PFD's*. They include all of the following, from those used in the past to ones that may be yet developed in the future. Those in caps have some further description under their heading: Inflatable Portable Preserver, Life Belt, LIFE BUOY or RING, LIFE FLOATS or PLANKS, LIFE JACKET or PRESERVER, Ring Buoy, WORK VEST, and perhaps others.

PERSON-IN-CHARGE

A term given to the person who is trained in, and properly licensed or certified, to load or discharge a regulated liquid combustible, flammable, or hazardous cargo for a vessel, and is on duty to supervise the transfer.

PETROLEUM PRODUCTS

Products considered flammable, toxic, or corrosive obtained from the distilling and processing of crude oil, condensate, natural gas, and other hydrocarbon compounds. One of the main cargo tonnages moved on the inland waterways system.

PHAROLOGY

The art or science of lighthouses and signals. The name comes from the first lighthouse built on the island of Pharos near Alexandria, Egypt, in about 290 B.C. The lighthouse became known as the Pharos Light, which then became the root name for "lighthouse" in most of the ancient languages. And the science lives on the navigational lights along our riverbanks today. See: LIGHTHOUSE.

PHASE

1. Estimating the amount and timing of flows into rivers and gauge levels during the flooding as well as the falling stage rate.

2. The flash characteristics and timing of navigation lights.

PHONETIC LANGUAGE

The use of universal words instead of alphabetic letters when engaging in some means of electronic voice transmission. Although the language has changed over the years and some still use the words of the 1940's and 50's, i.e. Able, Baker, Charlie, are still in use:

A Alpha	J Juliet	S Sierra
B Bravo	K Kilo	T Tango
C Charlie	L Lima	U Uniform
D Delta	M Mike	V Victor
E Echo	N November	W Whiskey
F Foxtrot	O Oscar	X Xray
G Golf	P Papa	Y Yankee
H Hotel	Q Quebec	Z Zulu
I India	R Romeo	

PHYSICAL MODEL (of a river or structure)

An actual representation of an area of the river or a structure in it, such as a lock and/or a dam, or an actual cross-section of a river built to scale. *Physical models* are used to evaluate how river flows at various elevations will affect vessels, how sediment will react, if eddies will be created, and numerous other criteria which might be of concern prior to the design phase of a project. Most navigational *physical models* are constructed and tested at the U.S. CORPS OF ENGINEERS EXPERIMENT STATION located in Vicksburg, MS. See: MICROMODEL.

P.I.A.N.C.

An acronym for *Permanent International Association of Navigation Congresses*, a worldwide professional organization of 40 or more countries that meets and addresses a broad range of policy and technical issues dealing with navigation concerns, including all aspects of engineering, construction, and the environment. It includes individuals, corporations, and national governments. The U.S. Section is headed by the USACE.

PIASA BIRD

The *Piasa*, pronounced Pie – a – saw, comes to us from the legends of the Illini Indian Tribe. It was an extremely large fearsome-looking creature, part bird, part reptile, and part mammal that savored human flesh and brought terror to the people. Finally a Chief of the tribe had a vision of how it could be destroyed. Stationing his warriors in hiding in the brush around the cliffs, he offered himself as bait. When the *Piasa* saw him, it swooped down to attack but the warriors shot poisoned arrows at the bird, killing it.

The Indians, overjoyed at the death of the creature, then painted a large picture of it on the bluffs near Elsah, IL, mile 214 on the Upper Mississippi River. The first Europeans to see the painted image were Father Marquette and Louis Joliet in 1673. The painting was later destroyed by quarrying operations however, the depiction of the Piasa Bird has been reproduced from drawings and painted on different parts of the bluffs above Alton, IL, numerous times. The latest being about a mile above the city. It has been said that its name meant "the bird that devours men", but these and other interpretations seem to be fictitious renderings by latter-day storytellers.

PICKUP

An order to a towboat Pilot to add a barge at a dock or fleet.

PIECE

One barge of a tow. Tows may be described as a three *piece* unit or more, such as "the M/V *SALLY L* tow has 15 *pieces* in it", "the M/V *CHAZ* has a three piece unit chemical tow", etc.

PIER

1. Used to describe any construction that provides a mooring place for vessels, whether it is parallel or perpendicular to the shore. Sometimes referred to as a *wharf*, although on the river a "wharf" usually had an enclosed shed to store cargo.
2. A cell where a vessel can moor.
3. A means of structural support, such as a bridge *pier*.

PIGEON HOLES

Insert socket holes in the drumhead (top) of a CAPSTAN that are used to receive a CAPSTAN BAR to manually turn a capstan in order to tighten a line or a wire. Originally the holes were square, as was the end of the capstan bar, but all known holes now receive a rounded bar. Some boats will have a short wooden bar inserted in one of the *pigeon holes* that will extend three or four inches beyond the hole that is called a "capstan pin". It is used to secure a line by a half-hitch that has been wound in by use of the capstan. It is unknown as to where the name originated. Perhaps a pigeon or other bird made a nest in one of the apertures at one time and the crew started calling it a *pigeon hole*.

PIGTAIL

1. A frazzled loose end of a line.
2. Short pieces of unraveled old line used to tie an object, such as loose rigging, or to secure portable running lights on barges, etc. Also called COW'S TAIL.

P & I INSURANCE

A type of insurance policy that stands for *protection and indemnity*. Basically, it provides a vessel owner with insurance against claims for personal injury or wrongful death, as well as claims regarding non-collision damages and loss to other vessels and/or property.

PIKE POLE

A long round pole of about 20 feet in length, of wood or aluminum, fitted with a pointed steel end that has a hook. It is used to grab or hook a line or wire that is out of easy reach and pull it on board. It is sometimes painted with alternating red and white one-foot long bands that can be used to sound the depth of water. Sometimes it is referred to as a *spike pole*.

A similar type of pole, also called a *pike pole*, was used by log raftsmen to push and pull logs into place, but was only about 10 feet long. It was indispensable, not only in moving logs but also to help the raftsman keep his balance on the log raft. The term "pike" goes back to the 16th century when the knights of old used what the French called a *pique*, an infantry weapon that was a long slender pole with the pick or pike at the end used to impale enemy soldiers. See: PEAVY.

PILE or PILING(S)

A heavy wooden post (steel beams or pipe) or group of closely connected posts in a cluster, driven into the bed of a waterway, but extending above the water's surface. They are used for various purposes, such as mooring, protection of other structures, for dikes, etc. They are also driven into the bed of a waterway to provide a stable structure or foundation for a wharf, bridge pier, lock or dam structure, levee, etc. The term is from the Latin *pilum*, meaning "javelin", maybe because when first used it was a post with a pointed end to be more easily driven. Also for the ancients, the word was used to describe a "pillar".

PILE DIKES

Timber piles driven in small clusters either out from the shore to divert the current or along the bank as a TRAIL DIKE. The clusters have cross members between them. This type of dike still allows water to flow through, but collects debris, such as old tree logs and limbs, creating a favorable fish habitat. *Pile dikes* were once the primary type of river training dikes, but their maintenance cost is high. Since the 1960s they have been primarily replaced with other types of rock dike construction.

PILE DRIVER

A machine used to drive pilings. It consists of a frame that holds a piling and has a heavy weight in a slide, called a "monkey" or a "beetle-head" since it is similar to the action of a BEETLE mallet when striking a REAMING IRON, used to remove old oakum in wooden hull seams prior to recaulking. The weight of the *pile driver* is raised and dropped, or mechanically driven down on the end of the piling, sinking it into the riverbed. The driver is usually powered by steam or compressed air.

PILFERAGE

Things that come up missing on a vessel and no one seems to know what happened to them.

PILLOW BLOCK

A support for the bearings to equalize the pressure on the propeller shaft.

PILOT

1. It is the act of navigating a vessel. Various originations of the term *Pilot* have been given: From the Latin word *pilotus* that was based on the Greek *pedon*, meaning "oar" or "rudder". The term evolved into meaning "steersman", and the French used *pilate* as one who steers a ship, while the Dutch used *piloot*.

2. A person who is licensed and qualified to stand a navigation watch on a towboat or tug and is in charge of all vessel handling aspects of his/her watch, unless relieved of the duty by the Master of the vessel.

3. A *Pilot* on a towboat or tug is one who usually stands the after watch, whereas the Master, also a *Pilot*, who is in overall command of the vessel, stands the forward watch.

4. The proud term carried by those who navigate in restricted waters constantly using their expertise to safely

handle ships, tugs, towboats, and steamboats. The future usage of the term is in jeopardy, see: PILOT LICENSE and MATE (PILOT).

5. Sometimes referred to by the rest of the crew as "*Star Gazer*".

PILOT BOAT

A type of crew boat used by the various Pilot associations whose members hold State Licenses to navigate certain vessels (mostly ocean-going) over certain sectors of inland waters, such as the NOBRA, the CRESCENT RIVER PILOTS, and the BRANCH PILOTS of the Lower Mississippi. The boat ferries the Pilots out to the ships while underway, and then another one takes them off whenever required after the Pilot has navigated his/her stretch of river.

PILOT CANAL

When making a CUT-OFF, especially on the Lower Mississippi or Missouri rivers, a small canal was dug from the lower end of a narrow neck of a bend of the river during a period of low water. When high water with strong flows was indicated, the upstream end of the neck was opened and usually the river would quickly scour out a new channel, capturing the major flow of the river, while the old channel would silt in and create some oxbow lakes. This is no longer done, but was common in the 1800s.

PILOT LICENSE

When a license was issued to a person to pilot a steamboat and for many years after, including the diesel age, the person seeking it was required to take a copious written test and then draw an accurate map of the river section the license would cover. This consisted of showing the banks with their curvature; the navigational lights and other aids to navigation, along with their name and mileage point; all towns and cities; sandbars and other obstructions in the channel; all islands and their names; ferry landings; docks with name and description; all bridges, giving type along with support piers and vertical and horizontal clearances; all locks and dams, with the type of dam closure and regulation of its flows. If the newly drawn map did not comport to the official office copy of the licensing bureau, the *Pilot license* would be denied. If the drawing was acceptable to the inspector the person taking the test would be issued a First Class *Pilot License* over the river section that was depicted.

The licensing procedure has changed over the years, especially for those who pilot diesel towboats. The evolving procedure will change even more in the 21st Century. More testing with no requirement to make a drawing of the river will be required. There will be a lengthening of the time period (or as the USCG calls it "sea time"), to serve aboard a vessel with check-offs for learning certain procedures. It is estimated that it will take approximately five or more years of apprenticeship before a person will be able to stand a navigation watch without being under supervision. The term Pilot may go by the board as a person first becomes an APPRENTICE MATE instead of a STEERSMAN, and after service time and suitable learning skills are obtained, he/she becomes a MATE (PILOT). The applicants may never become a "Pilot" per se since the USCG, in its "infinite wisdom", attempts to change all river terms to conform to those used in the deep-sea trades. Perhaps it is because no one, or practically no one, in command at the USCG has the river experience necessary to maneuver a towboat with 30+ loaded barges down the Lower Mississippi River. However, those who are proud to be called PILOTS will continue to use the term, hopefully well into the following century.

PILOT RULES

Those additional U.S. Rules contained in Annex V of the Inland Navigation Rules, and listed in 33 CFR 88. They contain certain other requirements pertinent to U.S. waters, such as lights to be displayed on moored barges and on dredge pipelines.

PILOT WATCH

Usually described as the AFTER WATCH or the one from midnight to 6 a.m. or from noon to 6 p.m.; however, many vessels are experimenting with alternatives to this standard system and it may not always be the same in all cases.

PILOT WATERS

The navigable waters where a licensed Pilot is required.

PILOTAGE

A service mandated by a state that requires vessels to employ a licensed Pilot to assist by offering advice to the Master when navigating the waters of that state. In the State of Louisiana there are three Pilot associations on the Lower Mississippi. A ship coming into the passes of the delta of the river will take on a member of the Associated Branch Pilots, commonly called a Bar Pilot, at the sea buoy, who will guide the ship up to Pilottown. From that point the ship will be boarded by a member of the Crescent River Port Pilots Association, who will assist in giving navigational advice up to New Orleans. If the vessel intends to go up further toward Baton Rouge, a member of the New Orleans-Baton Rouge Steamship Pilots Association (NOBRA) will board and give guidance the remaining distance. Baton Rouge is the head of navigation for deep-draft ships.

PILOTHOUSE

The compartment or place on a riverboat that contains all the necessary equipment and controls to navigate the vessel and is usually the highest compartment of the boat. It is sometimes called a WHEELHOUSE since at the end of WW II a number of persons came to the river from the canal trade, where the wheelhouse term was more commonly used. Since nearly all towboats now have steering levers rather than a wheel with which to steer a vessel, perhaps it is time to return to the original terminology of *pilothouse* and not further evolve into a "lever house". The crews of steamboats sometimes referred to the *pilothouse* as the *Sky Parlor*.

The *pilothouse* on the old steamboats of the 1800s was basically open at its forward end until sometime in the early 20th century, when the use of window glass was perfected. A system of wooden boards closed much of the housing in inclement weather. At the front upper part was a hinged BROW BOARD, or visor that could be swung out and up to shield a pilot's eyes from sun glare and deflect some of the rain. The brow board had some half-moon cutouts for a Pilot to look through if it was absolutely necessary to close it in extremely inclement weather. The front bottom half was called a BREAST BOARD that could be hinged out and down.

PILOTHOUSE CONTROLS

Once the engines are running all controls for operating a towboat and tug are centered in the pilothouse to be used by the Pilot on watch, to go ahead or astern, to increase speed, slow down, or stop, without the necessity of communicating with any person in the engine room, as was required in the olden steamboat days.

PILOTING

The visual use of navigation marks, buoys, lights, and other aids to safely navigate a vessel or tow from one destination to another. Now, of course, radar and other electronic aids are also important in safe navigation. In 1909, George B. Merrick observed, "Every Pilot must of necessity be a steersman; but not every steersman is of necessity a Pilot". Merrick went on to describe what the "Art of Steering" and being a Pilot was all about.

PILOTWHEEL

On the old steamboats the *steering wheel* was a large-diameter device used to change the direction of the rudders. The wheel turned a drum with a tiller rope, or wire that was attached to it. The lines went through a series of pulleys and were further connected to the rudders. As the Pilot turned the wheel the tiller line would wind up, or tighten, in one direction while slacking off in the other.

PIN

1. The axle in a block upon which the sheave turns.
2. Sometimes referred to as the mooring post on the top of the lock wall.
3. A heavy steel holding device in a recessed cavity of the lock chamber wall that can be utilized to attach mooring lines while locking; sometimes referred to as a *peg*.
4. Sometimes refers to the holding bolt in a shackle.
5. A part of an articulated coupling system in the bow of a tug. The very heavy *pin* is engaged into a specially designed barge when the tug enters its notch to make a rigid connection but still allow some degree of movement.
6. A holding device to fasten timbers together. If steel they are termed "bolts", if wooden they are called TREE NAILS.

PINHOLE

A very slight or slow leakage from some area.

PINION

A small cogged wheel in a piece of machinery, such as a gear that engages a larger cogged wheel.

PINTLE

1. The vertical holding pin that fits in the rudder and the GUDGEON of the rudder post and allows the rudder to pivot.
2. The same term is used for the pin of a miter lock gate that fits into the gudgeon that is built into a recess in a lock wall. The term originally comes from the German *pint,* meaning "penis", but came to be used to describe a "pin" in the 15th century.

PINWHEEL

The action of turning a twin screw vessel in the shortest distance possible by coming ahead on one engine and backing on the other.

PIPELINE

1. The discharge line of a hydraulic dredge.
2. The loading and/or discharge line on a tank barge.
3. All parts of a pipeline on a tank farm including valves and associated gear.
4. See Annex V of the Inland Navigation Rules for lights to be displayed.

PIRATES

See: CAVE IN ROCK.

PIROGUE

A vessel of Cajun Country that is pronounced "pee-roe". Originally it was a dug-out log that evolved into a flat-bottomed wooden boat of various lengths and widths which is properly called a BATEAU.

PISTON

A circular disc which is closely fitted into a cylinder of an engine that receives pressure from steam, or the combustion of some type of fuel such as diesel, and transmits that force to the other moving parts of the engine. The term comes from the Latin *pistillum,* meaning "to ram or pound".

PIT and PITTING

A corrosive action on metal, especially steel, usually caused by ELECTROLYSIS. It can be retarded by ANODES, or special coatings on the hull of vessels. On certain inspected vessels, severely or deeply pitted plat-

PITCH

1. The distance a propeller would move through a solid in a single revolution if no slippage was involved.

2. The amount of the angle in a propeller blade to the axis of rotation. The amount of *pitch* to be put in a blade is a trade-off in efficiency for the trade in which a towboat might be employed. A vessel pushing a UNIT TOW would want to *pitch* the propeller for speed. Vessels pushing heavy loads would need a different *pitch,* as would those that need efficiency in backing astern if they would have to do a lot of FLANKING.

3. The fore and aft plunging action of a vessel in heavy seas. Not very frequent with towboats, but common with tugs in the open waters of an ocean.

4. A residue from the distillation process of certain viscous products, including the condensed sap of the pine tree that can be PAYED over wooden seams after being caulked with oakum. Besides its caulking use, *pitch* was at times used on steamboats to be added to fire the boilers when competing steamers were in a race "for the antlers", or to be first at a landing.

PITCH MOP

A stiff-bristled brush used to spread the PITCH from the PAY POT after a seam in a wooden-hulled vessel had been caulked.

PITMAN

A connecting rod on a paddlewheel boat from the crosshead on the engine to the crank of the vessel's wheel. Its name apparently comes from the time coal miners in Wales had to bail out the water that collected in the "pits". They were called *pitmen*. With the advent of steam power, the rod connected to the engine naturally took on the non de plume of the person who used to do the job. The "Pitman Roll" is said to be the rhythm of the paddlewheel as its buckets slap the water when they make their dip and the movement of the *pitman* gently rocks the boat.

PITTSBURGH POINT

The place in Pennsylvania where the Allegheny River and the Monongahela River meet to form the Ohio River at mile 0. It is also mile 0 to start the mileage up both the Allegheny and the Monongahela rivers.

PIVOT POINT

The point in the fore-and-aft line of a towboat and its tow where it turns or rotates when rudder action is applied. The *point* is usually about one-third of the distance from the head of the tow, but it will vary from tow to tow depending upon the length and width, on the different drafts of the barges, square ends dragging in the tow, and other factors.

PLACARD

A card required to be posted on tank barges containing certain liquid products, listing the product name, and hazards associated with it.

PLANK FLOAT

See: LIFE PLANK FLOAT

PLANKING

In a wooden-hulled vessel, *planks* are considered to be the boards used to sheath the exterior shell. If wooden *planks* are used in other areas they are so designated by name. All timbers from $1^1/_2$ to 4 inches in thickness are termed *planks*. The word *plank* comes from the Latin *planka,* meaning "board". Contrary to what anyone tells you there are no reported cases of anyone on the Western Rivers being required to "walk the *plank*", as sometimes demanded by pirates of their captives.

PLANK OWNER

Recognized by some to be those

members of the original crew of a vessel when it first went into service, or if the vessel changed ownership, the first crew operating it under the new management.

PLANTER

A large tree that has its roots caught on the bottom of the river, or "planted", with its trunk angled toward the downstream surface of the river. This type of snag has pierced through the wooden hulls of many upbound steamboats and sunk them. They usually could not be seen in higher than normal stages of the river. See: SAWYER and SNAG..

PLATING

In a steel-hulled vessel it is considered the exterior hull sheathing. Sometimes referred to as "shell *plating*". If steel plates are used in other areas they are so designated by name, i.e. cargo side *plates*, floor *plates*, tank top *plates*, etc.

PLIMSOLL LINE or MARK

A line, or mark, on the side of a vessel that enters the Great Lakes (with exceptions), the Gulf of Mexico, or other service beyond the DEMARCATION LINE, that denotes the depth of hull that the vessel is not to exceed. Also referred to as a LOADLINE, however, most river barges are not required to carry one as they do not go into open seas, or high wave conditions. The line, or mark, was named after Samuel Plimsoll (1824-1898), who fought against ship owners who overloaded ships in the name of greater profit to the detriment of merchantmen sailors who lost their lives when the vessels they were sailing were swamped and sunk in storms.

PLOT(TING)

To identify a position of a vessel and/or estimate a course on a chart or radar. On towboats and tugs it is accomplished in a visual sense constantly by river Pilots who always know where their vessel is at all times. The derivative of the word in a nautical sense is unrecorded. A *plot* is defined as a "piece of ground" that had to be marked off to establish where the boundaries may lie, which could be in the same intent of marking (*plotting*) the course of a vessel. In another implication the word means a "secret plan" to defeat a combatant, so the term may have evolved from this sense of marking a course of action to engage the enemy and came down in more technical usage to outwit the wiles of an approaching storm, to avoid crowded traffic lanes, or to engage favorable winds, etc. However, no one seem to know the actual origin except the Pilot as to why he is setting a particular course to follow.

PLUG

1. A rounded tapered piece of wood that fits into the bottom of a small boat that can be removed when the boat is out of the water in order to allow the boat to drain.
2. The act of stopping up a hole with shingles or a piece of wood and other material to stop leakage in a vessel's hull.
3. A type of weld where a hole(s) is drilled or burned in a plate that is lying on a frame member or another plate. The plate is then welded to the other part through the hole fastening them together and is termed a *plug* weld.
4. A *bleeder* or *drain plug* fitted in the lowest end of a hull compartment in a vessel. It may be removed when on drydock to drain any accumulated residue water. Also called *drydock plugs*.
5. A control structure in a FLOODWAY. See : FUSE PLUG. .

6. A boiler safety device. See: FUSIBLE PLUG.

7. The end of an electrical extension cord that makes a watertight connection.

8. A threaded stopper that screws over a length of pipe to prevent leakage.

PLUMB

The weight at the end of a line tapered to a point that is used when constructing a vessel to insure that the vertical framing is in proper alignment with the floor of the vessel. When used properly the framing is said to be *plumb*. It is similar to what a carpenter does in building houses.

PNEUMATIC

Air that is pressurized in an air compressor tank that is used to start engines, sound whistles, and drive tools such as drills, air hammers and descalers, etc.

POINT

1. The end of a sharp (more or less) tool, such as a knife, marlinspike, fid, etc.

2. One *point* of the 32 comprising the compass of 360 degrees, each of $11\tfrac{1}{4}$ degrees. In the past *points* were used to describe an arc of navigational light, as "from right ahead to two *points* abaft the beam"; the Navigation Rules now do not use *points* but, rather, give the actual amount of degrees as described under definitions in Rule 21. See: CARDINAL POINTS and COMPASS.

3. The lands at the foot or the end of a meandering navigable channel bend of a river where a crossing in the direction of the opposite shore is indicated.

4. Indentations along a shore bank protruding somewhat into the navigable channel such as revetment *points*.

5. Any protrusion of land that comes to an end with water on each side, such as at Cairo, IL (Upper Mississippi and Ohio rivers), or Pittsburgh, PA (Allegheny and Monongahela rivers).

6. Those things a Deckhand makes with the Captain when he/she completes a paint job with no holidays, or those that a good Cook earns from the crew at every meal.

POINT(S)

There are numerous *points* on the river (see #5 above), in fact, almost every bend has one. Radio conversations between Pilots might say, "I'll keep her under the *point* until you get clear and see you on two whistles", or "I believe I have time to clear the *point* and get high enough to see ya on one". However, there are two critical *points* on the Western Rivers that if anyone is in the vicinity will know what is being discussed when only mentioning *point*. The first is Pittsburgh *Point*, which was a hub as well as a bottleneck of activity in steamboat days. It was a place where log rafts congregated coming out of the Allegheny River flowing south, and those coming out of the Monongahela River, whose waters flowed north where they met and formed the Ohio River. Later, coal was king and coalboats and barges congregated at the *Point* waiting for a rising river that the steamboats could ride over the shallows to destinations more westerly, or even all the way down to New Orleans.

The other *point* of towboating is that of Cairo *Point*, where the waters of the Ohio and the Upper Mississippi join to form the Lower Mississippi River, whose basin drains most of the interior of the United States. It continues to be a hub of activity with barge fleets tied to wherever land is available with a sufficient depth to receive both barges and towboats. Barge tows are split up, some barges tied off to go in a different direction, others to be picked up and added to a tow, loose rigging is accumulated and returned to a towboat, or perhaps exchanged with the fleet operator, orders given, then changed, then changed again, and maybe a few more times as the dispatcher at the home office tries to straighten it all out, with Captains getting frustrated, and the deck crews becoming mad as they make tow, break tow, shift barge again, more shifting, and perhaps finally put the tow together and head out of the fleet. Additional *points* abound in localized usage, but the forgoing two have been the most important ones to the history of steamboating and continue to be in the world of towboating.

POINT BAR
A sandbar that forms by the erosion from the convex side of a channel bend, with the sediment carriage being deposited at the foot or *point* of the bend where the channel flow crosses the river to the other bank. Often vary in size and shape depending upon flow conditions.

POINT BARGE
See: CANOE BARGE.

POINT-BEND CUSTOM
The custom or practice of downbound Pilots on the Lower Mississippi River to navigate their tows in the *bend* side of the channel where the current was deeper and swifter while the upbound Pilots of tows would use the *point* or bar side of slacker water; however, the downbound vessel has the right-of-way under the Inland Navigation Rules and makes the decision of where and how the two vessels will meet or hold as necessary.

POINT SIDE
The shorter or convex side of a bend where the current is usually slower and the depth of its waters are shallower. Also called the *bar side*. It is the opposite of the BEND SIDE.

POINTWAY
A channel that is a cut-off from the main channel, sometimes located behind an island or behind a large sandbar in the middle of a river. It can be navigated at certain high stages of water if a Pilot has an up-to-date BAR BOOK and in some places can considerably shorten the distance a tow will travel and possibly avoid the swifter main channel current.

POLICE
1. To clean up a space or an area.
2. In some port areas there are law enforcement officers that have powered water craft that assist in keeping order as needed or required.

POLICY
1. Those written and verbal instructions that are to be adhered to in the operation of a vessel by its crew. It most often is in written form when issued by the operations department ashore, and is usually unwritten when it applies to how the Master conducts the day-to-day operations of the vessel.
2. The insurance terms described in a contract between the owner of a vessel and its insurer.

POLLUTION
Any substance emitted to the air or water environment that is deemed harmful. In the marine environs it has an ever-changing definition, basically as our laws are redefined by Congress and the courts reinterpret their meanings. The word derives from the Latin *pollure,* meaning "to soil or defile".

POLY LINE
A synthetic line that is made from fibers of polypropylene or polyethylene. It is fairly strong, does not absorb much water, floats, and is lightweight. It is mostly used in a circumference smaller than the lines used to lock large tows since it is not as strong as many of the other synthetic lines on the market. Used to tie off barges in fleets and as safety lines. See: LINE.

PONTOON
1. A small deck float, sometimes with its deck supported by tanks or drums. The term derives from the Latin, *pontis,* meaning "a bridge".
2. Used to support sections of the

discharge pipeline from a dredge.

3. Watertight compartments that hold up a seaplane when on the water.

PONTOON BRIDGE

Floating bridges that can swing open to allow for the passage of vessels. There were three on the Upper Mississippi River. All were constructed for the Chicago, Milwaukee, St. Paul and Pacific R.R. One was at Reads Landing, mile 762.7, which was built in 1882 with a navigable opening of 302.5 feet. It had a "machinery boat" that pulled the bridge open and pushed it back into place when closing it. The bridge was removed in the late 1940s.

The other two *pontoon bridges* were between Marquette, IA, and Prairie du Chien, WS, at mile 634.7. The first of these two was built in 1873 and rebuilt in 1912. It allowed for a channel opening of 160' in the east channel of the Wisconsin side of the river. Before it was built the C.M.ST.P.& P.R.R. used a ferry to take its rail cars up around Island 171 to the opposite side of the river when there was no ice. In the frozen winter they laid a rail bed across the iced-over river. The first bridge allowed access to the island with a short ferry transfer.

Later, in 1915, the main channel span on the Iowa side between Marquette and Island 171 was built, and rebuilt in 1927. It allowed for a horizontal draw opening of 238'. When disengaged, these two bridges let the current swing the pontoon section downstream on a hinge floating toward the Iowa shore to allow vessel passage. After a vessel passed through the span the pontoon section was winched back into the closed position. All of the *pontoon bridges* had a pulley system to adjust their rail tracks to the elevation of the height of the fixed section of the bridge when the river rose or fell. They were reported to have been the last adjustable-lift *pontoon bridges* in the world. In 1961 the bridges were closed and removed.

Another railroad *pontoon bridge* is reported to have been built on the Missouri River at Chamberlain, SD, by the C.M.ST.P.&P., but it has been long out of business. The bridge was probably dismantled during the construction of the Fort Randall Dam after WW II.

Additional *pontoon* bridges were built across navigable streams to ferry people and horse wagons. In the Civil War they were used to move troops. One notable one was built across the Missouri River at Nebraska City in 1888 that was over 1000 feet long and $24\frac{1}{2}$ feet wide. It had a draw that could swing open in the mid-section in shape of a "V" which provided a wide passage for boats or ice. Tolls for wagons, teams, animals and people were charged. High water, ice damage, repair requirements, and a train bridge that laid planks over its ties for over-the-water passage finally caused the *pontoon bridge* to cease operation in 1890. To See: FLOATING BRIDGE.

POOL

Most dictionaries define *pool* as a small body of water. It comes from the Germanic *pfuhl*. On the river it is that body of water that is contained by a dam, or between two dams, to provide navigation, and is much larger and deeper than what most landlubbers realize. Though the pooled waters of some dams are called lakes, such as Peoria Lake, Lake Cumberland, Keokuk Lake, Alton Lake, etc., they are still designated as the *pool* of Peoria Dam, or of Barkley Dam, or of Dam 19, or of Mel Price Dam.

POOL BOAT

A type of steamboat, and later towboat, designed for the coal trade on the Monongahela River and the upper reaches of the Ohio. Their upper superstructure was lower than the normal riverboats on the mainstream Ohio River in order to allow them to clear the low bridges in their area of operation.

POOL LINE
The waterline along the bank of a pool that is at the normal operating level of a dam.

POOL PILOT
A Pilot who normally only worked on a POOL BOAT in their normal area of trade.

POOL STAGE
1. In conversation when referring to a river that is at *pool stage,* it is basically at normal operating conditions. Where there are movable dams, it means that the dam is up (raised) and a tow will have to be locked through.
2. The gauge level of the river, both upper and lower.
3. `At dams that also have a power function of running turbines to produce electricity it is the minimum depth of the pool that can be maintained and still provide a project water depth to maintain navigation.

POOL WATER or RIVER
A normal condition of low flow with very little current.

POP RISE
A sudden increase in a river's level, usually from a rain storm in one of the hill areas of a river valley that causes an unexpected quick rise that is not too extreme and usually doesn't last too long.

POPEYE
The character appeared as a comic strip in 1929 and later in film, being celebrated as a sailorman. However, *Popeye* was really a riverman disguised as a sailor. He was born on the banks of the Upper Mississippi at Chester, IL where his creator, E.C. Segar, lived. *Popeye* learned his nautical trade from the descendents of Mike Fink and may have gone to sea a time or two, but his heritage is in the Western Rivers. Long may he live in our hearts.

PORT
1. An area where the loading and unloading of vessels takes place. It can be a single facility or it may be an area designated as a *port* of many miles in length comprising of numerous docks, sometimes under the direction of a PORT AUTHORITY. In the nautical sense, most words used in reference to *port* derive from the Latin *portus,* to mean "a haven".
2. The left side of a vessel looking forward. It was formally called the LARBOARD side which was the side that was put to a dock to load or discharge cargo as the right side (sterbord) was where the steering was conducted. The use of the term is from the Latin *porta,* meaning a "gate or door" which makes sense that if "larboard" meant loading side, or from an opening, that the term be changed to a word that also was an opening which could not be confused with STARBOARD. See: CAPTAIN OF THE PORT, HAILING PORT, and HOME PORT.
3. An opening, such as a door, or a circular opening to give light and/or air (porthole).
4. The opening of a cylinder in a steam engine for steam exhaust.
5. An opening in a bulwark to allow water to run out, called a "freeing *port*".

PORT AUTHORITY
An entity that may be local or state government-chartered which controls the operations of activities in a port area. It may operate or lease wharf space, or sell land to private operators.

PORT CAPTAIN
A person who most often was a former Master on a towboat or tug, who has been assigned to a shoreside position as a supervisor of the Captains and Pilots, as well as the rest of the crews on the fleet of boats a company may own or operate.

PORT ENGINEER
A shoreside engineering depart-

ment supervisor for all engineering personnel who oversees the maintenance of all machinery, including propulsion gear, and other mechanical or electrical equipment aboard a company's vessels.

PORTABLE RIGGING
Rigging that is not permanent or stationary to a barge. It is the rigging that is carried on the towboat or tug used to make up a tow of barges if they do not have sets of rigging attached to them in a more or less permanent manner. See: PERMANENT RIGGING.

PORTED GUARD WALL
Walls on the riverward side of navigation locks that allow the river to flow beneath or through the wall toward the dam.

POSITION
That geographic location where a vessel is located at any given time.

POSITION REPORT
A report that was given over short-wave radio transmissions for many years. Companies maintained scheduled times the reports were to be given. Currently, *positions* may be given by computer, cell phones, or some other electronic device, or may be determined by GPS tracking.

POSSUM
Pieces of knotted line bundled and tied together. Used by a deckhand to cushion a vessel when coming against a pier, cell, or lock wall. Also called the *poor man's bumper*. See: BUMPER.

POST
A name sometimes given to the tie-off pin, peg, or bollard on a lock wall.

POSTED PILOT
A Pilot who is up-to-date on all the changes that may have occurred in a channel that a vessel is going to navigate. At times Pilots who have not been over a section of river for a long time will make a run as an extra Pilot to get *posted* up.

POTABLE WATER
Water that is fit or safe to drink. The word is from the Latin *potare*, meaning "to drink".

POTAMOLOGY
The study, knowledge, geography, and science of rivers. It derives from the Greek *potamos*, meaning "the study of rivers". Those that pursue a career in this field are called Potamologists.

POUR ON THE COAL
A term used to mean "come ahead full speed".

POWER TRAIN
Sometimes used in reference to the main engine power plant, the gear box, and all associated shafting and bearings coupled to it.

POWER-DRIVEN VESSEL
The Inland Navigation Rules define these as, "any vessel propelled by machinery".

POWERHOUSE
The name of the building on the lock grounds that houses the machinery used to operate the lock and dam.

PRACTICAL CUT-OFF
Refers to the light intensity area of vessel navigation lights in their vertical and horizontal sectors as required in Annex I of the Inland Navigation Rules.

PRECAUTIONARY RULE
This term or rule is that of Inland Navigation Rule 2(a) which states: "Nothing in these Rules shall exonerate any vessel, or the owner, master, or crew thereof, from the consequences of any neglect to comply with these Rules or of the neglect of any *precaution* which may be required by the ordinary practice of seamen, or by the special circumstances of the case".

PRESSURE

A continuous force that is exerted above existing atmospheric *pressure*. In a tank it is an action of pushing out, the opposite of a VACUUM. If enough *pressure* is applied over a tank's tensile strength ability to withstand it, the tank will rupture or explode. The term is from the Latin *pressure,* to mean "being pressed". See: PV VALVE.

PRESSURE GAUGE

A measuring instrument that is attached to a compressor or hydraulic ram to indicate the amount of pressure in a tank or the force being applied to a ram.

PREVENTER

Any extra line, wire, sparring device, or other means used for extra safety in addition to the precautions normally taken to hold a vessel or tow at a landing or dock. The *preventer* might be employed during possible flood conditions, or when a sudden drop in a river stage is predicted, or when there is heavy ice flows or build-up situations, etc.

PRICKER

A small marlinspike with a handle used to splice small diameter wire.

PRIME

1. The act of displacing air in a pump with a fluid in order to allow the impeller of the pump to obtain the necessary suction action to discharge liquid from a tank.
2. The addition of fuel to a small engine's carburetor in order to start ignition.
3. The application of a barrier coating to steel after removing any oxidized material and prior to applying finish coatings.

PRIVATE AID TO NAVIGATION (PATON)

No person or other body may establish, erect, or maintain an aid to navigation in U.S. navigable waters unless it receives permission from the USCG; and once a permitted aid is established, it cannot be changed, moved or discontinued without permission from the USCG.

PRIVATE CARRIAGE

A vessel that carries cargo for hire by contract as negotiated between two parties. This is differentiated from a vessel that is in COMMON CARRIAGE that transports goods or cargo under the terms of published rate. Nearly all tonnage transported on the inland waterways today is of *private carriage*.

PRIVILEGED VESSEL

See: STAND-ON VESSEL.

PROCESS TIME

The time in minutes (or hours) it requires for a vessel or tow to lock through a navigation lock facility.

PROCTOR OF ADMIRALTY

An attorney who practices maritime law in an Admiralty Court.

PROFILE

An outline drawing of a vessel that indicates the location of decks, possibly showing some external gear such as capstans, fittings, etc., as well as the waterline of the vessel, and may show the lines of the compartmentation of the hull tanks.

PROJECT DEPTH (CHANNEL)

When a navigation waterways project on the Western Rivers is authorized or approved by Congress, its channel is usually to be constructed to a minimum *project depth* of nine to 12 feet and 12 feet on the GIWW. Other waterways or channels may have different project depths such as the Houston Ship Channel and the Lower Mississippi River from the Gulf up to Baton Rouge, LA.

PROLONGED BLAST

A sounding of a vessel's whistle

PROP

1. A long rod that provides support for a WICKET at a CHANOINE WEIR. The *prop* is attached to a wicket and slides in a HORSE at the base of the weir. When a movable dam is being raised, a MANEUVER BOAT pulls up the wicket. Its *prop* slides in the horse as the wicket rises. When in full upright position, the *prop* slips into a notch of the horse which secures it, keeping the wicket upright. When the wicket is lowered it is pulled slightly upsteam by the derrick on the maneuver boat and the *prop* is released from the notch in the groove and slides down as the wicket is lowered to the river bottom.

2. Slang, or short for PROPELLER.

PROPELLER

A mechanical screw-like device with blades attached to a hub (called a BOSS) that is mounted on a power-driven shaft that provides the propulsive power to move a vessel forward or aft, depending upon the way it is turning. It is also called a *screw*, *wheel*, or simply a *prop*. The blades of the *propeller*, usually three to five on towboats, are built with a certain PITCH. Some are constructed to turn right-handed (turning port to starboard), and some are left-handed, their motion being starboard to port. On twin-screw vessels, usually the starboard side is fitted with a right-handed *propeller* while a left-handed one is placed on the port side. Single-screw boats most often have a right-handed one. Most of the *propellers* on large towboats in service today are of stainless steel construction. The word derives from "propel", which comes to us from Latin *propellere,* meaning "to drive forward or ahead". Terms associated with a *propeller* are:

1. *Back* – the forward side of the *propeller blade* when observing from the stern of a vessel. It is the suction side when moving forward. The opposite side of the *propeller face..*

2. *Blade* – the driving force of the *propellers* which usually number 3, 4, or 5.

3. *Cavitation* –(SEE).

4. *Diameter* – the distance across the circle made by one complete turn of the *propeller*.

5. *Face* – the driving surface, or *pitch* side, of the *propeller* blade when it is in the forward movement position.

6. *Following Edge* – the opposite edge of the *blade* from the *leading edge*.

7. *Hub* – The heavy center axis of the *propeller* which is holed to allow it to slip over the drive shafting. Sometimes called a *boss*.

8. *Leading Edge* – the outer end of the blade that first cuts through the water when the *propeller* is in the forward movement position providing the thrust movement.

9. *Lock nut* – A large nut that secures the *propeller* to the drive shaft.

10. *Pitch* – the measured axial movement or advance during one complete revolution of the *propeller* if there was no resistance. Also see: PITCH.

11. *Radius* – The distance from the center of the *hub* to the *blade tip*.

12. *Rake* – The degree of the *blade* slant from the *root*.

13. *Root* – The center solid section of the *hub* where the *blades* transition in *pitch* to their *tip*.

14. *Rotation* – The directional revolving movement of a *propeller* when turning. *Propellers* are designed as to how they turn when they move a vessel forward. Right-hand *propellers* turn clockwise and left-hand *propellers* turn counter-clockwise.

15. *Shaft* – The aftermost section of the drive shaft, usually called the *tail shaft*, to which the *propeller* is attached.

16. *Slip* –(SEE).

17. *Tip* – the point of the *blade* that is furthest from its axis.

18. *Other* – there are many other variables when determining the proper *propeller* type to install on a vessel. A few are: number of *blades*, pitch angle, area of *face*, developed area, *pitch* ratio,

blade thickness, type of trade in which the vessel will be engaged, etc.

PROPELLER CLUB
An International organization that has local clubs in many of the ports around the U.S., including on the Western River system, as well as overseas. The organization takes positions on maritime policy and has a yearly national meeting. Local club units have monthly meetings with programs of interest to their members.

PROPULSION SHAFTING
All the shafting from the gear box to where the propeller is fitted on the end.

PROW
The portion of the pointed part of the bow of a packetboat that is above water. It is not used in reference to towboats. It comes from the Latin *prora*, meaning "before or in front".

PUBLIC VESSEL
A vessel owned by and being used in the public service of the United States.

PUDDING
1. The rounded decorative topping around a smokestack that adorned many steamers. They also gave some rigidity to the stack at the top and tended to muffle the sounds that were emitted along with the exhaust. Sometimes they were topped with "feathers" or FLUTES (see) to disburse hot sparks.
2. A type of fender made of cordage padding, rubber, or other soft material that is attached to the bow of a tug in order to provide a cushion when going alongside a vessel while engaging in support of docking or undocking, or other ship assistance.

PUMP
A device or machine that is used to remove or transfer liquid from one place to another. They can be fixed or portable depending upon their employment, and either manually or mechanically worked. Various types of *pumps* are employed on tugs, towboat, barges, and other vessels for a variety of purposes. See: BARGE PUMP, CENTRIFUGAL, POSITIVE DISPLACEMENT, and SPRING POLE.

PUMPBOAT
A small work flat or barge used in the coal fleets in the days of wooden barges that were equipped with a steam engine, lots of lengths of hose, and siphons. It did its duty of pumping out rain water and leakage from the many fleeted barges at a landing.

PUMP-OUT FACILITY
A place that receives waste from holding tanks and bilge slops.

PUNCH
When lined up for a bridge or other section of a river, and the vessel comes full ahead on the engine(s), a Pilot is said to *punch* her through.

PURCHASE
A mechanical advantage that is gained when hoisting and lowering or moving heavy gear or objects by various means, such as using a winch, capstan, chain hoist, a screw or hydraulic jack, a lever such as a crowbar, or other type of leverage. *Purchase* is most often applied to the use of TACKLE with BLOCKS. The word is from the Old French *pourchacier*, meaning "to seek, obtain, or gain an advantage".

PURGE
The act of forcing out the contaminated air in a tank or boiler and replacing it with fresh or non-contaminated air. The term is from the Latin *purgare*, meaning "to purify". See: GAS FREE.

348 PUSHER or PUSHBOAT

PUSHER OR PUSHBOAT
The European term for a towboat that moves barges by pushing them ahead. Across the pond they seldom ever use the term TOWBOAT.

PUSHKNEES
Sometimes used in reference to TOWKNEES.

P/V
Used as a prefix to the name of a passenger vessel.

PV VALVE
A pressure-vacuum relief valve installed on tank barges that prevents over- or under-pressurization of a cargo tank.

PACKET BOAT GORDON C. GREENE
From the *S & D Reflector*

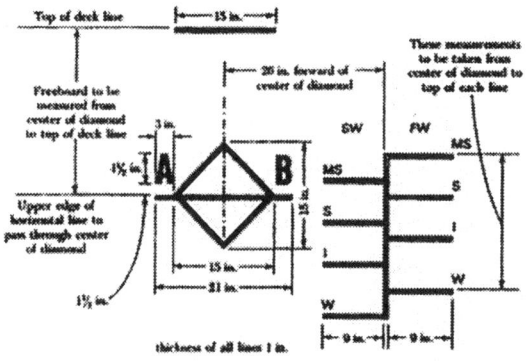

PLIMSOL MARK or LINE LOAD LINE

An ABS assigned mark for vessels navigating on the Great Lakes that shows the maximum draft to which they may load cargo. Similar marks are assigned to vessels going to sea.

PIASA BIRD
From the Illini Indian Tribe

PROPELLER

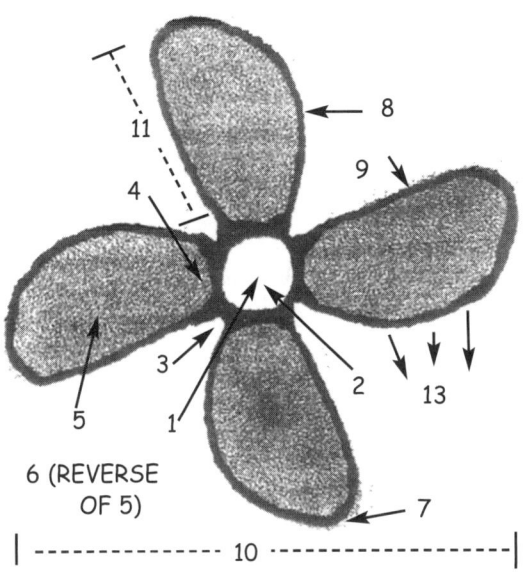

1. TAIL SHAFT END (where the lock nut or boss cap when fitted secures the propeller)
2. LOCK NUT or BOSS CAP (secures propeller to tail shaft)
3. HUB or BOSS (where propeller blades are attached)
4. FILLET (the thick base where the blades are cast or welded to hub)
5. FACE (the broad section propeller blade)
6. BACK (the aft part of the propeller blade)
7. TIP (furthest distance of blade from hub)
8. LEADING EDGE (forward edge of blade)
9. TRAILING or FOLLOWING EDGE (back edge of blade)
10. DIAMETER (distance across circular rotation of propeller)
11. RADIUS (distance of blade from hub to tip)
12. PITCH (measurement of movement the blade would make in a static environment of one revolution)
13. ROTATION (direction propeller turns moving ahead)

PIPELINE OF DREDGE

A dredge, which shows a "boobie house or hut" at the end of the pipeline where a person would sit to direct the discharge to different areas. Two theories are derived for its name. A boobie is considered a dullard, which comes from the boobie bird, which landed on a ship's rails and could easily be caught by a sailor for the crew's meal. The other is that in old sailing vessel days a wooden hatch near the bow of the vessel, which housed the anchor chain, was called the "boobie hatch" where malcontents, possible mutineers, or other sailors being disciplined would be thrown as punishment. Perhaps the job of manning the boobie house on a pipeline was for slow learners or a person who didn't jump when the mate had given an order. Don't pass this on to USACE crews that do a magnificent job in maintaining and keeping our channels open.

Q

QUADRANT
A metal structure about a quarter of a circle in circumference with a grooved rim that sits on the top of a rudder shaft to which the rudder cables are attached. On towboats and tugs it took the place of the *tiller*. The term is from the Latin *quadrans,* "one of four parts".

QUADRUPLE-SCREW
On large riverboats, most have twin or triple propellers, but a few have had four. The first was the *M/V LACHLAN MACLEAY* (built in 1955, open wheel, 3600hp), followed by the *M/V MISSOURI* (built in 1956, kort nozzles, 3600hp). Both boats were designed for shallow draft to run on the Missouri River. Then came the building of the *M/V UNITED STATES* in 1958, followed by the *M/V AMERICA* (built in 1960), both with kort nozzles, 9000hp. At the time these last two towboats were built they were the most powerful on the river system. All four vessels were built by St. Louis Shipbuilding Company and were originally run by Federal Barge Line.

QUALIFICATION or QUALIFIED
Verification that a person has completed the requisite time (so-called "sea time") on the job, has the necessary physical attributes for the position, and has the essential skills and knowledge to perform the duties of the position.

QUARANTINE
1. The isolation of persons on a vessel usually because of questions of health regards and the prevention of the spread of some type of disease. A vessel will fly a yellow flag if under *quarantine* and it will have its anchorage or mooring marked by a *quarantine buoy* (see below). The term comes from the Latin *quadraginta,* which meant a period of 40 days, the length of time to be isolated to determine if someone had an infectious disease; but now there is no time limit that someone, or vessel, may be in *quarantine*.

2. Sometimes used as a slang term to mean a person is restricted to a vessel because one has work duty to perform.

QUARANTINE BUOY
A yellow painted buoy of no special shape to indicate the area, or a vessel, that is under *quarantine*, or isolation from the general visitation of non-required personnel. All other vessels and personnel should keep clear of a vessel so marked.

QUARTER
1. The term used to designate a section of the side of a vessel that is half-way between the stern and mid-ship, or to denote half-way between the bow and midship. The term is from the Latin *quartarius*, meaning "the fourth part". Use of the term *quarter* on deep sea vessels usually only applies to the stern area of a vessel.

2. Used in reference to a LINE that leads from either the stern or bow *quarter*, as well as to a deck fitting such as a cavel, button, or timberhead.

3. Used to denote a direction, i.e. "There's a small boat on the port bow (or stern) *quarter*", or, "The wind is coming off the starboard stern (or bow) *quarter*".

QUARTER BOAT
Living accommodations for sleeping, cooking, eating, etc. for crews at construction sites, both private and government, that are away from towns and not easy to reach, such as during revetment construction, and when building locks and dams. The term *quarter* in this usage is from the old military meaning for a dwelling place and possibly derives from the quartermaster who was to provide supplies and lodging for the troops. It then evolved into some of the terms used in QUARTERS (below).

QUARTERS
1. The rooms on a vessel that are used by the crew for sleeping.

2. A station assignment for crew members in times of a drill or actual emergency such as fire, collision, etc.

3. On a vessel of war it means to man

one's battle station; the command for this action is "General *Quarters*". Although it was a term that may have been used in the river battles of the Civil War, it is not used on the river today.

4. When used as a call shouted out during a battle, it meant that the caller was surrendering and was asking for mercy.

QUAY

A stone or concrete dock area for mooring, as well as the loading or unloading of vessels. The term comes from the Celtic *kay,* meaning the same thing, and the way the term is pronounced, although some pronounce it as "key".

QUEUE

A backup of vessels and tows waiting at a lock that is undergoing repairs, or for a dredge to open a channel, or standing by for an ice gorge to break up, or any other mishap that is causing delay. The term is based on the Latin *cauda,* meaning "tail". Originally it was used to describe the tail on animals in heraldic symbols and wasn't used until the 1800s to mean "a waiting line"; probably because it looks like a long wagging tail.

QUICK-ACTING VALVE

A gate valve that can be opened or closed by lever action.

QUICK FLASHING

A navigational aid that shows a single flash every second.

QUOIN

A long triangular piece of wood like a wedge used to secure objects that may roll or shift. The term was a derivative or old English and French "coin" or "coign" to mean "a cornerstone" or "wedge". It was originally used on vessels of war to adjust the elevation level of cannon when firing.

QUOTE or QUOTATION

A rate offer that is given by a water carrier to a shipper to move their cargo from a point of origin to a destination, usually given at so much per ton mile. The term derives from the Latin *quot,* meaning "how many". Through the centuries it has come to mean a reference to a speaker, page or text of a book or document, etc.

QUARTERBOAT
The home away from home for USACE crews when laying and sinking revetment mats or other necessary construction improvements, as well as when they are called upon to respond to disasters and emergencies

R

RABBET
A groove, offset or recess, most often used at the end of a length of hull planking to receive another fitted into it. The *rabbet* joint would protect the planking ends and allow for a better caulking seal. There were various names for different places where *rabbet* joints were located. The term comes from the French *rabat,* meaning "a recess". It is different from, but see: REBATE.

RACE or RACING
1. A competition between two or more vessels to see which one is the fastest over a length of river (between cities or other destinations), or to beat another boat (to a landing, lock, or a given location). These *races* may be planned or may occur in happenstance fashion and are not sanctioned by anyone except the Masters or Pilots of the vessels involved. See: ANTLERS, STEAMBOAT RACE RULES, and STEAMBOAT RACING.
2. A sudden speeding up of an engine when CAVITATION takes place.
3. A term to describe a strong local current that is moving in, out, or around a pier, dike, or other object, especially in tidal areas.

RACK
1. The setting of the diesel engine that controls the speed.
2. Sometimes used to denote the bunk where a crewperson sleeps, i.e., "I'm going to hit the *rack*".
3. To SEIZE two pieces of line together with crisscross wrappings or figure eight turns between the line and then tied off in a square knot, rather than round turns, in order to keep the lines from slipping. Not often seen (on the river) except on the bitter end of a line employed through the end thimble of a block to more securely prevent the hauling line from running out of a block when under tension.

RACK HEAPS
A term used by Pilots in steamboat days for piles of twisted driftwood that accumulated on the riverbanks. giving the appearance of a jumble of deer antlers piled together. Also call *drift racks*. If enough driftwood massed together in a stream causing the cessation of navigation it was called a log raft stoppage. See: RED RIVER RAFT.

RACON
A contraction of RAdar and beCON. It is an acronym for RADAR BEACON (see).

RADAR
An acronym for *Radio Detection and Ranging*, an electronic device that was developed in WW II which sends out pulses of ultra high-frequency radio waves that are reflected off objects and are returned to a receiver, depicting a visual outline of the target on a screen. A highly useful piece of equipment on board vessels no matter what the weather conditions might be, but especially allowing them to safely operate in restricted visibility. The first *Radar* reported to be installed on a Western Rivers towboat was the M/V TRI-STATE in 1947, which was owned by the Ashland Oil Company.

RADAR BEACON (RACON)
An electronic transponder device that receives a signal from a vessel's radar pulse and responds by sending in return a distinctive type of signal that appears on the vessel's screen. It can be very helpful when navigating near lock and dam structures, bridge piers, certain docks and navigational aids.

RADAR BUOY
Buoys that are placed above and below the piers of the channel span of a bridge crossing a river. The buoys show up on a radar screen that better indicates to the Pilot where the piers are located and how his tow is aligned, especially during inclement weather or low visibility conditions.

RADAR RANGE

The distance an object is from a vessel's radar signal. Scope rings on the radar screen can measure exact distances from the vessel to the target.

RADAR REFLECTOR

Any type of device that may be attached to a small boat, buoy, float or other object that is capable of increasing the reflectability of a radar signal.

RADIO CALL SIGNAL

1. Each marine shore station has a lettered call sign which then is properly designated by name.
2. Each marine vessel has a lettered and numbered call sign, as well as being required to use its vessel name when initiating a call.
3. Calls of DISTRESS – use the word MAYDAY three times and start message.
4. Calls of URGENCY – use the words PAN – PAN and start message.
5. Calls of SAFETY – use the word SECURITY and start message.

RADIO DISTRESS FREQUENCIES

1. On single sideband radios it is channel 2182.
2. On VHF it is Channel 16.

RADIO SILENCE

The radio requirement if there is an immediate emergency where people or vessels are trying to alleviate a distress situation and need a clear radio channel; the use of the International *Seelonce Mayday* is used for all persons to stop their communications over the designated safety channel.

RADIOTELEPHONE

The rules for carriage and use of a *radiotelephone* are found in 33 CFR 26, and requires vessels to monitor as well as transmit on specified VHF channels. Basically, any power-driven navigating vessel over 20 meters in length, or any navigating towing vessel of 26 feet, must have *radiotelephone* capability. Vessels shall maintain a listening watch on designated safety channels and only transmit necessary information for safe navigation on these frequencies. Separate working channels may be used to relate other verbiage between vessels. Most towboats and tugs carry at least two and sometimes more working *radiotelephones* for not only their immediate use, but also for monitoring other channels.

RAFT

1. Timber or lumber that is fastened together and floated downriver. See: LOG OR LUMBER RAFT.
2. A structure of logs or lumber to be used as a flat-bottomed boat or floating platform. The term comes from the Norse *raptr*, meaning "rafter or beam", because a log was probably the main support of their dwelling.

RAFT BOATS

The name given to vessels that moved log and lumber rafts on the different river systems.

RAFTING

1. The act of tying off or mooring vessels alongside one another.
2. Floating ice that piles up one sheet on top of another.

RAFTING LOGS & LUMBER

The placing of BOOMS of logs or lumber together and floating them down the river to a lumber mill. The rafting business was one of the first main cargo industries on the river. Logs came out of tributary streams and were assembled into larger rafts on the main river. Originally the rafts floated with the current, sometimes with the help of a CORDELLE, especially where there was little or no current. Others were assisted with a yawl that went ahead with a line from the raft then anchoring it. The raft crew would then pull the timbers downstream. This was common in pooled areas of the river or when encountering headwinds.

Different areas of the river developed some of their own terminology for the tools they used and the actions they took that were at variance to other areas, so some may find a dissimilar meaning in how the expressions are explained.

RAFTSMAN
A member of the crew on a log raft.

RAG
A line that has become heavily frayed. It is then cut into serviceable sections and used to tie barges together in a barging fleet, or is scrapped or made into a BUMPER.

RAIL(s)
1. The top of a rounded BULWARK. Sometimes called a *cap rail*. The term *rail* comes from the Old French *reille*, meaning " an iron rod".
2. A pipe handrail on the outer edge of the weather deck of a vessel.
3. A pipe handrail found in the engine room main deck to protect personnel.
4. Small pieces of fancy jigsawed woodwork that was used in the gingerbread ornamentation of some of old packet boats. The finished product was termed "drapery".

RAILROAD
See: MULETRAIN.

RAILWAY
Another name for MARINE WAYS.

RAIN
Moisture that is condensed in the atmosphere and falls as solid droplets. It can range from a mist, to a drizzle, to a downpour that blocks out images on radar. It is a liquid from the sky that descends over the land and as it flows along off to a lower level it creates the rivers on which towboats and tugs navigate.

RAISE
1. Used interchangeably with RISE, i.e. "There has been a *raise* in the river since Monday", meaning the flow has increased; or "A *rise* in the gauge is expected by the end or the week". The word is from the Old Norse *reisa,* meaning "to bring up or to rise".
2. To bring a sunken vessel to the surface, i.e. to *raise* it.
3. The act of trying to call someone on the radio, i.e. "I'm trying to *raise* the vessel *DUMDUM* on the radio, but they don't answer".

RAISED TANK TOP
The raised top of a tank barge from the main cargo deck to accommodate more cubic capacity in the size hull form. This type of barge construction is typical for the double-skinned tankers used on the river and canals, since most petrochemicals are lighter per cubic foot of space than a cubic foot of water displacement.

RAKE
1. The sloped hull form for the end(s) of a barge or other vessel. It can be fairly straight back from the bow end (most barges) or have curvature (some tank barges) even to what is spoon shaped. See: SPOONBILL BOW.
2. The name given to barges that have a bow that is *raked*, i.e. "I have seven *rakes* and eight boxes in tow".
3. The name of a void space in the bow of a *rake* barge, i.e. "Better pump the *rake* of barge JKL 3456 since it appears to be leaking".
4. An inclination, or leaning, from the perpendicular, i.e. "His stack has a *rake* of about 15 degrees". It is believed to come to us from German *ragen,* "to project".

RAM
1. To hit with heavy force, such as to use the hull of a vessel to break ice. The term seems to be derived from the Germanic word for a male sheep, or *ram* with reference to its strong butting ability.

2. A type of vessel used on the river and in other waters in the Civil War that had a pointed bow that was heavily reinforced. It was used to run into and damage or sink enemy vessels. See: RAM FLEET (below).

3. The falling weight of a pile driving machine. Also called a *monkey* or a *beetlehead*.

4. A piston in a hydraulic cylinder, such as used in operating the steering gear.

RAM FLEET

A group of Civil War vessels that operated on the Western Rivers under the Union command of Charles Ellet, Jr., who believed a study of ancient history showed that using a vessel to ram one of an opponent's and destroying it was a valid tactic for steam warships. He was also the engineer who designed the Wheeling Suspension Bridge (see: WHEELING BRIDGE CASE). The *Ram Fleet* consisted mostly of lightly armored riverboats. They were not very well suited for ramming other vessels, even though their hulls and bows were strengthened. In his last battle with his rams against a Confederate fleet about 40 miles above Memphis his vessel, the *QUEEN OF THE WEST*, after having sunk the Confederate *LOVELL* by ramming, was damaged by a rebel vessel, the *BEAUREGARD*, and Ellet was badly wounded in the leg during the battle. He died a few weeks later.

RAMP

A structure from a wharf vessel that is used to accommodate the bringing aboard of cargo and passengers for further transfer to a riverboat or barge. It also sometimes serves as a spar to keep the wharfboat off the bank in rising and falling river stages.

RANGE

1. The distance to a vessel or other object on land or in the water.

2. The luminous minimum intensity *range* distance that vessel navigational lights are required to be seen as noted in Annex I of the Inland Navigation Rules.

3. The frequency and audible signal *range* of whistles used on vessels as provided for in Annex III of the Inland Navigation Rules.

4. The difference of a gauge reading between flood stage and pool stage, or a difference between the highest stage of water and the lowest.

5. The difference between a high tide and low tide on a given day.

6. Two separate navigation lights in a line on a shoreline, with the back one higher than the other, and when lined up indicates the centerline of a channel.

7. A vessel equipped with an anchor, such as a tugboat, that lets an anchor chain out to a sufficient length or *range* to assure an adequate holding. Also called SCOPE.

8. The appliance where the cook on a towboat or tug prepares hot meals for the crew. More often called a *stove* on the river.

RANGE MARKER

A ring that shows on a radar screen that can be adjusted to various lengths to measure distances. Most radar has the capability of showing multiple rings.

RAT GUARD

A large circular disc of aluminum or sheet metal with a small hole in the middle that can be fitted over a mooring line of a vessel or fleeting barge line to attempt to keep rats that are on shore from walking a line or wire to come aboard a vessel. Not seen very often in the river trade, but used frequently by ships in coastal areas.

RATCHET

A strong, heavy turnbuckle with threaded eyebolts in each end to which a PELICAN HOOK is attached. A handle is attached to the barrel of the turnbuckle that has a COGWHEEL in its center and a PAWL that engages the wheel's angled teeth. The rotating pawl only allows the barrel to move in one direction when it is being worked. The *ratchet* is used to tighten the wires between barges in a tow. A tow of 15 barges will usually have at least 60 *ratchets* and wires, or more, holding it together.

RATCHET STRAP
A steel plate welded to the deck of a vessel that has a steel triangular ring to which a ratchet can be readily attached.

RATE(s)
Basically, in river transportation it is the monetary quotation given by a carrier to a shipper to move cargo from a point of origin to a destination. The basis of the quote may be affected by many factors, including river conditions, opportunity for backhaul, the tonnage involved, type of equipment required, the cargo to be transported, the status of supply and demand, and other factors. See: QUOTE or QUOTATION.

RAVE HOOK
See: REAMING IRON.

REACH
1. The term is used in various ways to describe a particular section of a river channel. Some use it to describe a straight section of a river which can be seen between the points of two bends. Others use it in regards to a length of river between two points, such as between two gauging stations. Some pilots may use it to relate to a section of river which they are currently intimately familiar, i.e., "I'm currently posted (see: POSTED PILOT) on the *reach* (or STRETCH) between St. Louis and Cairo, but not below there".
2. The extent of a crane's radius to safely lift an amount of tonnage.

REACH ROD
A steel rod connected to a valve in a tank below a deck which extends through the deck in an oil-tight fitting to a valve handle used to open or close the valve.

READ THE WATER or RIVER
When a Pilot visually observes the surface of the water to sense where a reef might be building, to see sand boils on a cutting bank, to view eddies occurring under a point and all the other ripples and water colors that might indicate fast water or slack, or a sunken object, a sawyer, watching the flow of drift, estimating current speed in the bend and on the bar side of the channel, the shape of the bend and shorelines, etc. All these factors, and others, go into *reading the river*.

REAMING
1. The act of opening the seams in planking to remove old caulking in order that they may be properly recaulked. The iron used to accomplish this task was called a REAMING IRON. It was also called a ramming iron, a rave or raving hook, reefing iron, clearing or cleaning iron, jerry iron, meeking iron, raising iron, and probably other names as were all the different caulking tools depending upon the area and shipyard where one worked and what his boss called it.
2. The act of enlarging a hole to receive an object, such as a bolt or rivet.
3. What the Captain of a vessel does verbally if orders are not carried out promptly and correctly.

REAMING IRON
A tool used by CAULKERS to remove old caulking and to adequately open the seams of a wooden-planked hull prior to recaulking. It was a curved, steel round bar, about $1/4$" or so in diameter that had a sharpened point on the end to pull out the caulk. Also called a *hoe, rake,* or *rave hook*. See: CAULK and REAMING.

REAR ADMIRAL
The title comes from the English

when they sent their naval vessels out to engage the enemy. It is related that their different fleets were commanded by *Admirals*, with the highest-ranking *Admiral* taking the lead in attack, followed by fleet vessels led by lesser ranking *Admirals,* with the lowest ranking *Admiral* taking up the *rear.*

For awhile the USCG called one-star *Admirals* "Commodore", but when conferring with similarly ranked officers in the different U.S. services, or at foreign conferences, or when seating arrangements at official conferences or dinners were made, they were given a lesser status. So the USCG decided to call them *Admirals*, *Rear*, of course, although the newly ranked ones are referred to as the "Lower Half" and those more senior in service are called the "Upper Half". See: ADMIRAL and VICE ADMIRAL.

REARRANGE TOW

A term used when the Pilot has to move barges in the tow. It usually happens after going upriver or down and stopping at a port where a barge has to be picked up or dropped. It may be an empty barge that is being dropped and a load being picked up. The Pilot probably cannot put the load in the same place in the tow where the empty was located since it would unbalance the tow and likely make it unsafe when steering; therefore, some other barges will have to be shifted to make sure the tow can safely and efficiently continue its journey.

REBATE

1. A notched joint in the frame of a wooden-hulled vessel that fits into a sister notch of an adjoining structural piece. The word derives from the French *rabat,* to mean "a recess", but it is different from RABBET.

2. In the business of freight charges it may be a discount, deduction, allowance, or a kickback of the originally agreed to rate for transportation. It could be legal or illegal. Consult a legal dictionary or a lawyer if unsure.

REBUILT

1. A vessel that undergoes extensive refurbishment, possibly with replacement of machinery parts, including its engines.

2. A USCG aid to navigation that may have been extensively damaged which is repaired, repainted, etc., and returned to service.

RECESSED WHEEL STEAMER

A vessel that had the stern paddlewheel fully inside the hull of the vessel with the superstructure built around it. On some small tributary rivers with narrow channels it gave some added protection to the wheel from overhanging limbs when navigating close to the bank. It was also called a *bootjack* since the shape of the stern of the hull which housed the wheel resembled the device used when removing one's boots.

RECIPROCATING PUMP

A type of pump that works by the to and fro motion of a piston in a cylinder, moving product with each stroke of the piston.

RECREATIONAL BOAT

A vessel that is constructed and used primarily for noncommercial activity. There are usually a lot of them on the river in the summer months.

RECREATIONAL BOAT LOCKAGES

1. When a commercial tow that has no hazardous cargo is locking and has room to accommodate waiting recreational craft it may be allowed to simultaneously lock through with the tow if both parties agree.

2. If there is a queue of commercial and recreational craft waiting to lock, a separate lockage will be made for recreational craft after each three commercial lockages.

RED FLAG

The term used to describe a tank barge that is transporting flammable products and is required to show a *red flag* when loading or unloading its cargo, or is not in a gas free condition. Most tank barges have a permanent metal *red flag* showing on deck.

RED RIVER

Two small streams in northwest Texas come together near Amarillo to form the *Red River*. It then flows easterly and marks the entire southern border between Oklahoma and Texas. It continues its journey into Arkansas eventually heading south. After entering Louisiana the river travels southeasterly, where it receives flows from many tributaries before joining the Atchafalaya Basin, having traveled about 1300 miles. The *Red River* gets its name from the red clay soil areas of its bed and along its banks.

Early explorers had mostly neglected the navigable possibilities of the river due to the obstructive snags in it. See: *RED RIVER RAFT* below. The town of Natchitoches, LA, was the head of navigation. After Henry Shreve essentially cleared the log obstructions in the river, navigation was possible to the city of Shreveport, which was named after him. However, without maintenance of the channel the snagging impediments to navigation returned.

Eventually, in 1873 an open channel for steamers again was obtained, but a railroad line was built through the area and most cargo traffic into and out of Louisiana's *Red River* area was transported by rail and the interest in the waterway declined. Almost a century later, in 1964, the USACE, after conducting numerous studies and surveys, filed a report on the feasibility of navigation to the city of Shreveport by building five L & Ds. In 1968 Congress authorized the project, but the funds to build were slow in coming. In 1973 the first appropriations for construction were enacted. The navigable section of the waterway was renamed the *J. Bennett Johnson (Red) Waterway* in 1997 in honor of the Senator who was instrumental in obtaining federal funds for the project. The waterway has an authorized depth of nine feet with a channel width of 200 feet from the mouth of the Old River to mile 211.4 at the Caddo-Bossier Port, just above Shreveport. The waterway contains six locks and dams. The locks are 684' by 85'.

RED RIVER OF THE NORTH

The *Red River of the North* is different from the RED RIVER in the southern U.S. states of Texas, Oklahoma, Arkansas and Louisiana. The river was named by French trappers as *Riviere Rouge de Nord,* taking its title from the red clay soils of through which it flowed. It originally was formed as a part of a glacier lake which eventually disappeared. The river is formed by two smaller streams, the Bois de Sioux which forms the lower border of North Dakota and Minnesota; joined by the Otter Tail River at about the mid-point of MN and flows north into the province of Manitoba, Canada. Eventually it mouth empties into Lake Winnipeg after a journey of about 545 miles and draining an area of over 40,000 square miles.

In the mid-1800s trade developed between settlers in the Red River Valley and the trading center at St. Paul, MN, mainly by trail or road. Travel on the river was mostly by canoe and flatboat. In 1859 the first small steamboat was built for use on the Red. More steamers were built and trade on the river was fairly robust between Winnipeg to the north and Fargo, ND, to the south even though floods and then low water caused seasonal navigable problems. Eventually railroads were built between Winnipeg and St. Paul and finally also east-west rails were also laid.

Even though the *Red River of the*

North has no connection to the Missouri or Mississippi rivers, the rationale of it being in this Lexicon is that it was part of the definition of WESTERN RIVERS and remained so until the unification of the Inland Navigation Rules took place in 1980 and its niche was replaced by the RED RIVER (of the south).

RED RIVER RAFT

After Henry Shreve showed everyone how to clear the Mississippi River of snags with his snagboat *HELIOPOLIS*, the USACE requested him to work on the 140-mile log jam that clogged the *Red River*. He started in 1833. By 1838 he had opened a channel to Shreveport, LA, which was named to honor him. Even though Shreve warned that continual maintenance of the channel would be required, his advice was ignored. A flood soon toppled additional trees and new debris into the river causing blockages. Adequate funds were not available to accomplish the necessary support to prevent more clogging of the channel. The Civil War started and no maintenance work was done. A survey by the USACE in 1872 found that the *raft* had grown to approximately 32 miles. The following year a path was cleared through it again, but funds for maintenance of the channel were still in short supply. However, the channel was finally opened.

REDUCER

A short pipe fitting that is used when coupled to the end of a large section of piping that must receive at its other end a smaller diameter section of piping or a hose connection; i.e., an 8" pipeline of a terminal that must be fitted to a 6" diameter hose that then couples to a 6" barge pipeline.

REDUCTION GEAR

The gears that are located in a gear box which couples to the engine crankshaft and the propeller shafting. It reduces the most efficient high speed RPM of a diesel engine's drive into a more powerful thrust that is transmitted to the propeller shafting allowing the propeller to rotate at its optimum speed.

REEF

A ridge of low-lying rocks or sand that forms just below the surface of the water. It can also be a drop off in a crossing from shallow water into deeper water of a bend, as in MOUNTING A REEF. The term comes from the Old Dutch *ref,* or the Norse *rif,* meaning the same thing; a *reef*.

REEFER

A large walk-in cooler. Sometimes refers to the large refrigerator on a towboat.

REEVE

To pass a line or wire through a hole or an object, such as a closed chock, or a block. The term probably comes to us from the Dutch *reven,* meaning "to reef a sail".

REFLECTIVE MATERIAL

A type of material, usually in tape form, that shows bright luminous lighting when exposed to the rays of a searchlight. It is used on bridge piers, buoys, dayboards, locks, and other places where it might assist navigation and prevent an accident.

REFLECTOR

A type of device used by many small fishing or recreational boats to increase the ability of a radar signal to detect them and avoid the possibility of collision. Also used on some buoys for the same purpose of detection.

REFRIGERATED BARGE

A barge that is insulated and pressurized. It is outfitted with equipment to keep the cargo at very low temperatures, such as anhydrous ammonia. If the cargo heats up it will "boil" off and release toxic fumes.

REGATTA

A gathering of yachts or other pleasure craft that have races and/or parades in harbors or on the rivers. If conducted the organizers are required to get a permit if navigation is affected and the USCG will issue a permit and post a Notice to Mariners when the event is to occur. The term apparently derives from Italian and was originally used when gondolas raced on the canals of Venice, Italy.

REFUELING BARGE

See: MIDSTREAM FUELER

REGION B for buoyage systems

There are two regions of buoyage systems in the world; *Region B* consists of North and South America, Japan, Korea, and the Philippines. The rest of the world is in Region A. See: BUOYAGE for description.

REGISTERED BREADTH

The *breadth* of a vessel at its widest part measured from the outer side of its planking or plating on one side to the corresponding point on the opposite side.

REGISTERED DEPTH

The *depth* measured amidships from the underside of the tonnage deck to the bottom of the hold. If there is a double bottom the measurement is from the top of the plate forming the double bottom. This measurement does not reflect the draft of the vessel.

REGISTERED LENGTH

The *length* of the vessel measured from the rabbet of the stem on deck to the after side of the rudder stock. This measurement does not reflect the overall length of the vessel.

REGISTERED TONNAGE

The GROSS and NET TONNAGE shown on a vessel's official document. A *registered ton* is 100 cubic feet of cargo space regardless of the weight.

REGULATED NAVIGATION AREA (RNA)

A navigation area where the USCG posts special regulations regarding the conduct of vessels due to unusual conditions, such as an accident wherein there may be a blockage or partial blockage of the channel; during severe weather conditions such as floods, ice blockages, or extreme low water; during special public events in a city including regattas; when some construction or dredging is taking place; to prevent sabotage or other subversive or any other occasion that is regarded as appropriate to ensure public safety. *RNAs* are usually fairly short in duration, from one day to a few days' notice; however, certain operating conditions in either the area, or of the vessels transiting it, may be of much longer duration or of a permanent nature. These may be mandatory operational procedures and/or reporting requirements to reduce risk and enhance safety. See: SAFETY ZONE.

REGULATIONS

Rules issued by various government agencies that affect vessels and their crews. Many agencies issue *regulations* that impact vessels, but the main operating rules governing river towboats, tugs, and barges, as well as vessel personnel, are found in the Code of Federal Regulations, Parts 33 and 46.

REHABILITATION

The act of fixing, restoring, or rebuilding an object or structure that has become worn or deteriorated to the extent that it could be subject to a major shutdown or failure. See: MAJOR REHABILITATION.

REID VAPOR PRESSURE

The *vapor pressure* of a liquid at a temperature of 100 degrees Fahrenheit expressed in pounds per square inch absolute by an American Society for Testing Materials (ASTM) standard which measures the volatility, or its tendency to give off FLAMMABLE LIQUID vapors.

RELATIVE BEARING
The direction of another vessel or object in relation to the centerline of a vessel. It can be phrased in points, degrees, or location (port bow quarter, abeam to starboard, etc.).

RELIEF (CREW)
A replacement crew member, i.e., the Master leaves the vessel for earned time off and is replaced by the *Relief* Master, or a Cook gets off and is replaced by a *Relief* Cook. See: RELIEVE.

RELIEF VALVE
A *valve* that is set to open if a predetermined pressure is reached, thereby reducing the pressure on the line, in a boiler, or in a tank. Sometimes called a *safety valve*. See: PV VALVE, one that not only relieves pressure, but also provides relief if there is a vacuum in the tank.

RELIEVE
For one person to take over the duties of another. This usually happens at watch changing time, or when changing crews on a vessel.

RENDER
1. A line that passes freely through a block.
2. The act of slacking a line or wire. The term derives from the Latin *reddere*, meaning "give back". See: PAY OUT and SLACK.

REPAIR ESTIMATE
Undertaken by a company representative, surveyor, or shipyard when assessing damage to a vessel requiring repair. The cost of steel damage renewal is usually quoted on a per pound basis. The amount of steel that has to be cut out and replaced is estimated at so many pounds, as well as taking into consideration the area where the vessel was damaged. It includes the cost of the new steel, the labor man-hours, administrative costs, and profit. The shipyard will then quote a dollar figure per pound to do the repair work. Other types of repairs are usually quoted on the basis of time and material to do the work.

REPAIR FLEET
A central area where the USACE keeps its main force of repair vessels when it is not deployed to do channel maintenance or construction, i.e., working on a dam, building dikes, doing revetment mat laying, etc.

REPLACED
Notice by the USCG that an aid to navigation which was no longer on station has been restored to its former location with the same characteristics unless noted that they have changed.

REPORT(s)
Any required notification to a government agency, or to the operating company which the Master, Pilot or Engineer may be directed to submit for various diverse and changing reasons. There are many different *reports* required by various agencies for statistics, accidents, pollution, etc. that change by the year. Some must be made immediately by phone, but ultimately most will have to be submitted in written form.

REPORTABLE ACCIDENT
The USCG requires vessels to report all marine accidents, injuries or deaths. These are more detailed on their form CG 2692, Report of Vessel Casualty or Accident. They include groundings, loss of propulsion or steering, occurrences that affect a vessel's seaworthiness, loss of life, injury to a crew member requiring professional medical treatment, and property damage in excess of $25,000. See: SERIOUS MARINE INCIDENT.

RESERVOIR
A large holding area of water in the upper reaches of a river or a tributary stream secured by a fixed dam used for flood abatement and release to a navi-

gation channel during periods of extreme low flow conditions. It may also provide for power generation, water supply, and other uses.

RESET
Aids to navigation which have been replaced or moved to a new location, i.e., "The Coast Guard buoy boat *reset* the buoys in XYZ crossing and moved the dayboard downstream about 500 yards since the Corps dredged a new channel".

RESPONSIBLE CARRIER PROGRAM (RCP)
A total safety program developed by and for the towing industry under the auspices of its organization, the American Waterways Operators (AWO). The provisions of the *RCP* started in the 1990s and then in the early 21st century it became mandatory for companies to implement if they wished to retain their AWO membership. The program is a guide involving all aspects of a company's vessel operations, including its management, administration, and equipment, along with a periodic inspection by trained independent inspectors. The program also requires training of personnel in safety and security awareness.

RESPONSE PLAN
See: VESSEL RESPONSE PLAN.

RESTRICTED
See: REGULATED NAVIGATION AREA.

RESTRICTED VISIBILITY
The term is defined in the Inland Navigation Rules in Rule 3 (k) as "any condition in which visibility is restricted by fog, mist, falling snow, heavy rainstorms, sandstorms, or any other similar causes".

RETRACTABLE PILOTHOUSE
A type of pilothouse that that can be lowered into a recess so that it is no higher than the second deck level. The design of these towboats evolved because the bridges on the Illinois River above Lemont, IL (mile 300) are quite low and do not open for barge traffic. There are various slang names given to these vessels, i.e. *elevator* or *elevating pilothouse, hydraulic* (since they work on a large hydraulic shaft), *shotgun* (since they pop up), and others.

RETURN
When a sweep of a radar beam is made of an area it sends back, or *returns*, signals denoting objects or targets which it has detected, as well as their position. Sometimes these are called ECHOs. The radar infrequently will record false *returns* or echoes which the Pilot will have to scrutinize to determine their validity (such as highlines).

REVENUE CUTTER SERVICE
In 1790, Alexander Hamilton, the Secretary of the Treasury, formed a group of sailing *cutters* to insure that custom duties and tonnage tax charges for the new nation were collected. Congress authorized 10 *cutters* to be built and crewed. Since the Continental Navy was disbanded after the Revolutionary War, the only sea-going government vessels the U.S. had for a number of years were those of the *Revenue Service*. They participated with the Navy in the quasi-French war in 1798-1809 and again in the War of 1812. They have engaged in all subsequent wars where the U.S. has been involved however, sometimes only as observers. A *Revenue Cutter*, the *HARRIETT LANE*, was the first U.S. vessel to engage in naval activity in the Civil War, and the cutter *MIAMI* served as President Lincoln's personal transport.

When first formed the service had no official name for many years, except to be known as the *Revenue Cutters*. In 1843 it bore the name of the *Revenue Marine Division* of the Treasury Department. In 1894 the service was officially designated as the *Revenue*

Cutter Service. Then in 1915, Congress enacted a bill that was entitled, "An Act to Create the Coast Guard", which included the *Revenue Cutter Service* and the Lifesaving Service, whose names have since gone into the history books.

REVETMENT

A protection process to stop the erosion of riverbanks. The first protection of eroding shores was the use of woven willow mats, called FASCINE, weighted down by rocks in the 1880s. The use of reinforced concrete mats started about 1914. The application of asphalt along a graded bank was tried but it was difficult to be laid, and if holed, an eddy could undercut the asphalt and the revetment would fail.

New improvements in articulated concrete mattresses were made and it is now the mat of choice. Mat laying is now usually done by grading the bank at a slope and adding layers of heavy stone or a concrete mat on the slope from near the top of the bank down into the bed of the river. Each concrete block in a mat unit is 14 inches wide by four feet long by three inches thick. Twenty of these blocks bound together by stainless steel wire are called a "square", which is four feet wide by 25 feet long and is laid by a special USACE mat-laying barge.

Some bank protection is also done by what are called "Off Bank *Revetments*". This is a sort of a trail dike of rock laid on the outside of the existing bank and parallel to it to prevent further erosion by the river current without requiring the bank to be graded and a concrete *revetment* to be laid. See: MATTRESS, MAT-PLANT and WILLOW MATTRESS.

REVOLUTION INDICATOR

A device that indicates in the pilothouse the direction of the engine(s) and revolutions per minute (RPM) that it is turning.

RIB and RIBBING

The side framing of a vessel.

RIBBANDS

Support pieces used to temporarily hold in line the frames of a vessel when it is under construction or being repaired. The pieces are later removed.

RIDE AND GUIDE

A slang term for standing the pilot watch or AFTER WATCH on a towboat and simply having the responsibility for the navigation of the vessel while on watch; not like the Master who has the overall control, duty, accountability, and responsibility for the vessel, its tow, the cargo, and all crew members under his/her command, as well as its navigation when standing a piloting watch.

RIDE OVER

1. A crew member who elects to stay aboard and continue working when it is his/her usual time to get off the towboat or tug and take vacation time.

2. The misplacement of a line or wire over the bight of another that may cause it to jam or foul.

RIDE THE HEAD

Said of a lookout who is posted on the head of a tow when in restricted visibility, or when there might be a high amount or recreational boats or other vessels in or near the channel.

RIDGEPOLE

The centerline longitudinal steamer beam that adds support to the boiler deck and is attached to the STATIONARIES. The KNUCKLE CHAINS ran from the bilge knuckle to the *ridgepole* to add support to the sides of a steamboat.

RIDING LIGHTS

A name sometimes used for lights displayed by a vessel at anchor. See: RUNNING LIGHTS.

RIG

A term sometimes used when some special or unusual event is about to occur, i.e. "Move all the loose gear back to the boat and *rig* for a heavy storm", or "Get the stern cleaned off and *rig* it for towing astern as we are going to have to MULETRAIN through this ice". The term is from the Scandinavian *rigga*, meaning "to bind or wrap up" in the sense of preparing a vessel to go to sea.

RIGGING

A term that generally refers to all lines, wires, ratchets, slings, chains, shackles, and other gear that is used to connect barges in a tow, whether it is portable on the tow, or on the towboat or tug. All this gear, except line is sometimes referred to as *hard rigging*. It comes from the Norwegian *rigga,* meaning "to bind together or wrap up", as in making a group of barges into a tow. See: PERMANENT RIGGING and PORTABLE RIGGING.

RIGHT

1. To bring a vessel to an even keel after it has been listing.
2. The "right-hand", or the starboard side, of a vessel when facing forward.

RIGHT BANK, also RIGHT DESCENDING BANK

The shoreline of a river on one's right hand when facing and proceeding downstream. It is also called the *right descending bank*. The light list for an area of the river will show navigational light aids to be on either the *right* or the LEFT BANK. Green buoys mark the extent of the channel on the right side of the river when descending, usually with green or white reflective tape. It could be entitled, Green, Going, Gone (to sea). Do not confuse this with RED, RIGHT, RETURNING (from sea) when coming upstream.

RIGHT-HAND DRAFT

A cross current that is running more to the right side of the channel than being straight with it, i.e., "There is a strong *right-hand draft* on the shoreward pier of the XYZ Bridge". This verbal or written advice is given in relation to the right bank when a vessel is proceeding downsteam.

RIGHT HAND LAY

Where the yarns of a line are twisted from left to right, or clockwise. Nearly all line used on the river is *right-handed*. It should always be coiled from left to right, or with the sun.

RIGHT-HAND PROPELLER

A propeller that turns to the right, or clockwise, to move the vessel forward, when observing it from astern looking forward.

RIGHT-OF-WAY

Rule 9 and Rule 14 of the Inland Navigation Rules grants the *right-of-way* to a power-driven vessel operating in narrow channels or fairways and proceeding downbound with a following current over an upbound vessel. In Rule 15 a power-driven vessel crossing a river is required to keep out of the way of a power-driven vessel ascending or descending a river. In other navigational situations the Rules provide for the duties of the stand-on vessel and the give-way vessel. It is to be assumed that the stand-on vessel would have the *right-of-way* over the give-way vessel. However, always remember the old maxim, "No vessel has the *Right-of-Way* through another vessel".

RING BOLT

A large heavy ring that is fastened to a pier, cell, dock, or levee that can be used to attach a wire or line when mooring a vessel.

RING BUOY

A type of life preserver that is about three feet in diameter with a line attached, mounted at various places on the decks of a towboat to be thrown to a person who may have fallen overboard.

RING KNOCKER

A U.S. Coast Guard officer who

graduated from the U.S. Coast Guard Academy, or an officer in the U.S. Army Corps of Engineers who went to West Point.

RIPARIAN
Relating to the bank of a river or stream. Land that is lying beyond the natural watershed of a stream is not considered *riparian*. The term comes from the Latin *ripa,* meaning "bank", and *riparius,* meaning "belonging to the bank".

RIPARIAN RIGHTS
Generally defined as the right of a person whose land abuts a stream having the right of utilize of the land and the stream for useful purposes.

RIPPLE
1. A series of small waves on the water usually caused by the wind, or from the current action on some object just below the surface of the river, such as a snag or a sunken object.
2. What students of POTAMOLOGY call small bed forms that are of triangular shape.

RIPRAP
Large heavy stones placed on a bank to prevent erosion from the current of the river. The word is used by the USACE in revetment work. It probably comes from the words, *rip,* meaning "to tear apart", and *rap,* meaning "a severe or heavy blow" with some type of instrument. Since the stones used are broken pieces of large boulders that were hit by force and torn apart, the term seems to be quite apt for the purpose used.

RISER
A vertical pipe that rises above the deck, usually fitted with a flange to receive fuel or water, or ending in a screened gooseneck to vent air.

RISING RIVER
Said of a river where the gauge levels are raising hourly or daily.

RISK OF COLLISION
The Navigation Rules in Rule 7, *Risk of Collision*, outlines what a mariner should be doing, or avoid doing, prior to entering into risk or exposure to possible danger where two or more vessels are encountering one another. If a collision ensues from the encounter it is not just what each vessel did, but also what they failed to do. Each vessel is required to use all means appropriate to determine if a *risk of collision* exists. If one has any doubt as to whether a risk is present, it "shall be deemed to exist". Learn what the Rules say, study what they mean, and read them in totality for any given navigational situation.

RIVER
That place where Mike Fink ran log rafts and keelboats, about which Samuel Clemens wrote *Life on the Mississippi*, where steamboats opened the commerce of the mid-section of our nation, and towboats and barges of today keep it going efficiently, economically, and in an environmentally friendly manner. It is also the place where people enjoy the many benefits it provides, from its scenery, to recreation, fishing, water supply, electricity generation, and a host of other benefits. The term *river* comes from the Latin word *riparus,* which in turn came from *ripa,* meaning "the bank of a *river"*, and eventually evolved to denote the waters between the banks.

RIVER GAUGE
A *gauge* located at certain locations along rivers which indicates the height of the water surface above or below the low water datum of that location. Gauges are also located at locks and dams to measure the upper and lower pool levels.

RIVER GUIDES
Besides the local personal knowledge of flatboaters and keelers, there were no written *guides* for a person to

use in navigating the river until 1801, when Zadok Cramer, a bookstore owner in Pittsburgh, published the first edition of what was called *The Ohio Navigator* which gave guidance on the Ohio River. He later expanded it to the Lower Mississippi, calling it *The Ohio and Mississippi Navigator*. It also included directions and information on the Monongahela and Allegheny rivers. As different Pilots called some of the islands on the Lower by different names, Cramer decided to number them to reduce the confusion. Starting just below Cairo those depicted in his guide started with number "1". The numbered islands were in consecutive order downstream to number "126". In 1808 maps were added to the guide.

As steamboat traffic started on the rivers, others also published their maps and *guides*. The most important contributor was Capt. Samuel Cummings, who had piloted flatboats and steamboats, and drew his own maps of the river. His guide was called *The Western Pilot*. It included a lot of descriptive material of the towns along the river, as well as the various landings. There were others who published maps and instructions, but these were the best for the early years of travel on our Western Rivers. See: CHANNEL REPORT.

RIVER GULLS

Those birds that hover over water singing with a shrill, not very melodious voice, but are graceful fliers on wind currents and are pleasurable to observe while piloting a tow. Along coastal waters they are generally referred to as *sea gulls*, but since the Western Rivers are inland, to most rivermen they are *river gulls*.

The gulls (and terns) are of the Laridae bird family with numerous sub-species. They are long winged and have webbed feet to paddle along when floating on water. Most of the type *gulls* that rivermen observe are Herring Gulls and Ring Billed Gulls, which have white heads and underneath with grey wings, black tipped; or the Bonaparte Gulls, which have black heads with grey and white wings, but we refer to all of them as *river gulls*.

RIVER INDUSTRY BULLETIN BOARD (RIBB)

An important web site, www.ribb.com, that active rivermen use on a daily basis since it provides up-to-date weather information, including ice conditions; river gauges with forecasts and conditions; individual lock conditions, including delay times and number of vessels waiting; an ability to find the location of each river towboat; a list of links to federal governmental agencies; and other information pertinent to the river operators.

RIVER MILEAGE

See: MILE

RIVER STAGE

The height of the water level of a river at certain RIVER GAUGE stations which are published and broadcast on a daily basis along with the rate of rise or fall.

RIVER RAT

1. A person who enjoys being on, around, or involved in things that have to do with the river and river life. Not commonly used by a RIVERMAN to describe someone who works on towboats or tugs.

2. Used by loggers on the Great Lakes in a somewhat deprecatory manner to describe a RAFTSMAN who worked on the river. Also sometimes called a *river hog* or *river pig*.

3. Similarly used by deep-sea sailors to describe those who work on inland river towboats and barges. See: STEAMBOAT BUFF.

RIVER RAT

You might not know a *river rat*
Is certainly not really that.
They do not scamper from a cat,
They don't even know how to scat.

They seem to prowl the riverbanks,
About towboats they give their thanks.
If you think they can be a crank,
It's the mud coffee that they drank.

Their words are only river talk,
It's steamboats and towboats they stalk.
They talk cavels, bitts, oakum caulk,
Mention railroads and they balk.

If you stop them and want to chat,
It's only rivers, tit for tat.
So when meeting a *river rat*
Remember, it's not really that.

RIVER TRIALS
Running and testing the systems of a new towboat or tug prior to its acceptance by the new owner or operator. The vessel is taken out in the river and its performance is evaluated, with the engineer checking the engines and all other working machinery.

RIVER WALL
The *wall* of a lock chamber that is farthest from the shore, or the outermost lock wall.

RIVERBANK
All of the immediate shore surface that lines the course of a river's normal flow.

RIVERBANK BOAT
Said of a towboat or tug that spends more time tied to the bank or dock than it does running.

RIVERBED
The bottom of the land in which a river flows.

RIVERBOATS
Vessels capable or used in moving commerce on our many inland rivers, from packetboats, steamboats, towboats to tugboats. Other vessels involved in river trades will have their own specialized designations, such as ferryboats, excursion vessels, dinner boats, etc.

RIVERMAN
The person who makes, or who has made his, or her, livelihood working on steamboats, towboats, tugs and barges on the river.

RIVET
A steel pin that has one end finished with a flat head and the other end with a point that, after being intensely heated, is inserted in holes punched through two steel plates the "point" is then hammered flat, which fastens the plates together. This was the normal way steel hulls of towboats and barges were constructed until welding was perfected. There were various names for different types and places where *rivets* were used in construction. It is believed the word originated from the French *river*, meaning "to clinch together".

ROCK-AND-ROLL WIRES
Wires that are crossed between the H-bitts on the head of the towboat to fittings on the barge(s) the towboat is pushing against. Used in order that the towboat will not slide, especially if its towknees are steel (to steel). These wires are sometimes rigged from a loaded barge to an empty one for the same reason: to reduce sliding, since the fore and aft holding wire leads are so long. Called by various other names, i.e. *knee wires*, *head jockey wires*, *slide wires*, etc. Probably so-called after Elvis Presley for the rocking and rolling gyrating he did in Memphis in the late1950s and 60s.

ROCK BERM
Heavy rock that is laid at the foot of a place or a structure to protect it from erosion by the flow of current.

ROCK CUT
A section of channel where a bed of rock was dredged or blasted out to provide a navigable channel. Usually the navigable portion is fairly narrow and can be hazardous to the hulls of barges, towboats or tugs if they come too close to the edge of the *cut*.

ROCK ISLAND RAILROAD BRIDGE CASE
See: EFFIE AFTON

RODE
Refers to the chain, wire, or line attached to an anchor. Not much used on the river since towboats do not carry anchors; however, there are numerous anchor fleets that are used to hold, or moor barges.

ROLL
The side-to-side motion of a vessel off its longitudinal axis, or to roll back and forth from port and starboard. It has to be fairly rough water for a towboat to do much rolling when it is made up to a tow, but it is common in tug operations.

ROLL COVERS
Barge covers that are equipped with wheels (rollers) that ride on rails, which are mounted on the top of the hopper coaming of a dry cargo barge. These covers are normally telescoping, with the low covers rolling under the high covers to provide an opening to load and unload cargo.

ROLL ON/ROLL OFF (RO/RO)
A type of vessel that is designed to carry vehicles and wheeled containers, which can be driven on and off the vessel via a ramp.

ROLLER DAM & GATES
A type of GATED NON-NAVIGABLE SPILLWAY DAM in which the gates are long metal cylinders fitted with ring gears at each end that mesh with inclined metal racks supported by the concrete piers. The gate is raised and lowered by means of a chain or cable wrapped around one end of the cylinder and operated by a hoist permanently mounted in the pier. They have the capability when being raised to allow high flows of water to go underneath them, or to be lowered beneath the surface of an upper pool level to allow for the passage of drift, debris, or broken ice to pass over the top of them.

ROLLER CHOCK
A CHOCK that is fitted with *rollers* to prevent chafing of lines or wires when they are pulled in or payed out.

ROLLERS
Long rolling waves that come off the stern of a sternwheeler or the prop wash of a towboat or tugboat. Sometimes called a *rooster tail* when a fast-moving tow throws a high wave astern.

ROLLING A LINE
The action taken to free the eye of a line from its fastening on a mooring bitt, timberhead, or cavel when its lead is some distance away from the fitting. One must roll or throw a loose circular motion into the bight of the line to whip or snap it off the fitting to which it is attached. Sort of like a cowboy lassoing a calf, only he uses a line less than an inch in circumference while a deckhand uses one of four to six inches.

ROOF BELL
See: BELL

ROOF CAPTAIN
The Master of a steamboat who took care of the overall management of the vessel but did not stand a pilot watch. He was probably given that name since, when the steamboat was making a landing, the Master usually stood on the forward end of the upper deck, which was called the roof of the boiler deck. At this position he gave directions to the crew as necessary. However, the Master of the vessel never gave navigational orders to the Pilot on watch unless he relieved him of his piloting duties.

ROOSTER BRIDGE
A lift bridge that crossed the TOMBIGBEE RIVER at Demopolis,

Alabama. It is no longer in existence but was made famous on April 28, 1979 when the *M/V CAHABA* (named after the river) was using a river navigating practice with his tow called DROP 'EM THROUGH. When the bridge did not open, the towboat went sideways against the bridge pier, turned completely over, popped right side up, and then went about its business. A series of pictures taken of the accident made river history on the internet.

ROOT OF DIKE
The shoreward end of a river dike.

ROPE
Generally, a term for cordage over one inch in circumference; however, in most nautical usage, including on rivers and canals, the cordage is called LINE. The term *rope* is usually associated with things like bell *rope*, *rope* ladder, *rope* bumper, learning the *ropes*, give him enough *rope* and he'll hang himself, he's on the *ropes*, he was *roped* into staying on board, and he's at the end of his *rope*. The term derives from the Old Norse *reip,* or the Dutch *reep,* or the German *reif,* all meaning *rope*. So take your pick, but mostly what shoreside people call *rope*, those employed on tugs and towboats call LINE.

ROPE CLAMP
A device used to hold together the bight of a wire, usually to make an eye in the wire with a thimble inserted. The clamp consists of a U-bolt and a saddle. After a bight is formed in the wire, both parts of the wire are inserted through the U-bolt, the saddle is placed over the wires, and the bolts are tightened securely. Usually three or more clamps are used. Also called a CABLE CLAMP or WIRE CLAMP.

ROPE KNIFE
A knife with a single straight edge and a small folding spike that can be used when splicing small wire or line, as well as being useful in opening screw shackles.

ROPE WALK
Although "rope" is called "line" on the Western Rivers, at one time it was all fashioned by rope makers. The method used, with only some modifications, was basically the same by all peoples of every country going back to at least the Egyptians before B.C. utilizing only fairly simple tools until almost in the mid-twentieth century when mechanization of the entire process took place.

A building called a *rope walk* was the structure where rope was laid up. It was a long shed, or at least a covered area, with a length could be that of three football fields or more. The last one where rope was made finally shut down in 1970. Rope making consists of fiber yarns first stretched out on revolving hooks that rotate to twist the fibers in a right-hand manner to make yarn. The yarns then are further twisted together, but now in a left-handed way and made into strands. Finally the strands are then stretched tight by men on the *rope walk* to ensure that no kinks in the rope form when they insert a grooved "top" (looks like one) to keep the strands evenly spaced as they are twisted and the line is rotated into a final right hand lay. The result is a section of line that is called "hawser-laid". Line now used from materials both natural and synthetic, is mechanically produced from start to finish.

ROSE BOX
A round or square box at the lowest part of a compartment where all drainage will flow. It has perforations to keep out large material, but still allow water in. A suction hose of a pump is inserted into the box to remove the liquid. Sometimes called a *strainer box* or a *strum box*. Also, a smaller similar device that screws onto a pump suction hose used for the same purpose. The name was probably given to it when a deck crew member complained of the smell on the strainer when it had to be

cleaned, and the Mate said to him, "Sonny, don't worry me none about that, just clean it and think about roses".

ROTARY PUMP
A type of positive displacement pump that is operated with vanes attached to a rotor on a shaft in the pump housing that, when revolving, the vanes will push the liquid through a discharge line.

ROUND TO
To turn a vessel or tow around to go in the opposite direction.

ROUND TRIP
A vessel that is in a regular trade from a loading point to a discharge point. A *round trip* is from the start to destination and return.

ROUND TURN
When someone isn't checking down some movement of a barge smartly enough and letting line pay out, rather than holding it from slipping, they are usually instructed to, "Take another *round turn* on the timberhead".

ROUSTABOUT
A term coined in the early 1800s for a laborer who loaded and unloaded cargo, wood, or other freight on board a steamboat. The word comes from the word *roust* or *rouse,* meaning to "get up". As the *roustabouts* worked they sang songs called "coonjine" sort of like the shanties of sailors. An example would be:

 Mah job am hustling freight,
  On de packet *Minnie Snow*;
 Ah'm at de big fo'ard hatch,
  An' holler, "Look out below."

Oh, when Uncle Henry was a little boy,
 A-settin' on his daddy's knee,
  Says: "If ever I grow up to be a man,
  A steamboat man I wants to be."

ROW
To propel a small boat by means of oars. The term derives from various sources, the old English *rowan* and the Norse *roa,* as well as the Latin root *remus* and the Greek *eretmon,* meaning "oar" (relating to "rudder").

ROWLOCK
A U-shaped device with a leg or thole pin on the bottom that is loosely fitted into a hole in the gunnels of a small boat, such as a yawl or skiff. The "U" receives an oar fitted into it and acts as a fulcrum for a person rowing to efficiently apply power to an oar blade pushing against the water to propel the boat. See: OARLOCK.

R.P.M.
An acronym for *revolutions per minute.*

RUB BAR or RUB STRAKE
A heavy section of steel plate welded to certain portions on the sides of vessels, especially barges, to give additional protection against bumps and wear when scraping against docks, pilings, lock walls, etc.

RUDDER
In a traditional sense it is a blade-like device that is mounted in a vessel's hull in a vertical position at or near the stern used to direct a vessel's course. The direction is governed by the thrust of the water against the blade, either directly by a propeller or a paddlewheel, but it can be by the current as the vessel is moving through the water, causing the heading of the vessel to be diverted to either port or starboard, depending upon which way the steering levers or wheel is turned. For various types of rudders components used on the river see: BALANCED RUDDER, FLANKING RUDDER, JOCKEY BARS, JURY RUDDER, and MONKEY RUDDER.

It is said the term *rudder* derived from Old English *rother,* meaning "paddle or oar" which in turn came from a Germanic base related to rowing, or from the Teutonic *roder*, meaning "oar for steering". However, in Old English *sterbord* was used for "steering board", and since steering was done at the stern quarter on the right-hand side of a vessel, that term came down to us as "starboard" to indicate the right hand side of a vessel. The use of a steering device from the stern was first used by the Chinese centuries ago, but what it was called in their writings is unknown. The term "rutter" was a word for personal sailing directions drawn, written, and jealously kept by coastal pilots who guided ships along treacherous coastal areas and into harbors. A "rut" was the breaking of seas along a coastal area. It might have been that the use of the "bord" at a vessel's stern to direct its course and the use of the guidance of "rutter" knowledge to keep the vessel off the ruts, rocks and shoals that very possibly it may have evolved into becoming the term *rudder*.

Greek mythology indicates that the *rudder* was invented by Tiphys, who was the helmsman for the Argonauts, but it was not recorded how he did his steering. Therefore, when, how and why the apparatus for steering became called a *rudder* will have to be solved another day. As Leonardo da Vinci said, "He who loves practice without theory is like the sailor who boards ship without a *rudder* and compass and never knows where he may cast."

RUDDER ANGLE INDICATOR

A device that is located in the pilothouse of a towboat or tug that indicates to the Pilot the angle or position of the *rudder* to port or starboard off the centerline. Also called a *rudder telltale* or *tattle tale*.

RUDDER CHAIN

At one time many vessels had a small chain attached to their rudder since they often operated in areas where there was constant danger of it being knocked off by snags or sandbars, and only a few places where shipyards were located to make repairs. If the rudder was broken loose it could often be fished out by its chain and the crew could jury rig it until permanent repairs could be made.

RUDDER POWER

A Pilot may indicate that the towboat or tug they are on has a lot of *rudder power* or, conversely, doesn't answer very well to the rudder when steering. The rudder's ability to perform the function of directing a vessel's course depends on many factors, especially the underwater hull design including its appendages. It includes, first of all, the rudder design, size, and placement. Also playing a part in a rudder's ability is the efficiency of the engine that supplies power to the propeller, which is providing the thrust against the rudder.

The steering effect is different with a hull design that has KORT NOZZLES versus an open-wheel (propeller) boat, as well as a variety of other hull design considerations. The *rudder power* can be relative to the size of the tow and the vessel's horsepower that is required to handle the tonnage. It might be a change in employment of the vessel. Some towboats are originally designed for a high-speed unit tow but are later used for fully loaded coal or grain tows that have different barge hull configurations. Finally, it may be simply a difference of opinion between Pilots. One may say, "She doesn't steer worth a tinker's dam", while another Pilot might comment, "She handles and steers as good as my ole Austin Healey".

RUDDER QUADRANT

See: QUADRANT. Sometimes called a *rudder crosshead*.

RUDDER STOCK

The shank or post to which the rudder blade is attached that extends up through the hull and is fastened to the rudder quadrant.

RUDDER STOPS

Heavy lugs that are welded to the

sternpost that do not allow the rudder to turn more than its maximum design angle, about 40 degrees.

RUDDER TRUNK
The sleeve or bearing into which the rudder stock is fitted when it enters the hull of a vessel to the deck level.

RULE OF GOOD SEAMANSHIP
See: GOOD SEAMANSHIP RULE.

RULE OF SPECIAL CIRCUMSTANCE
See: GENERAL PRUDENTIAL RULE.

RULE OF TONNAGE
See: LAW OF TONNAGE.

RULEMAKING (REGULATORY)
The authority given or delegated by Congress to various governmental agencies with authority to promulgate rules or regulations governing the conduct of vessels and the people who work on them. On the river and canal system the main federal agencies that issue regulations which affect the management of vessels are the U.S. Coast Guard and the U.S. Army Corps of Engineers.

RULES OF ACTION
The rule requirements under the International Navigation Rules wherein vessels are meeting or crossing they only give whistle signals if they are taking some *action*, i.e., one short blast on the whistle means the vessel is altering its course to starboard, or two short blasts on the whistle means it is altering its course to port, while three short blasts mean it is operating astern propulsion. The vessel it is meeting does not sound its whistle in return if in agreement. It will only sound a whistle signal if it intends, and does, alter its course during the meeting or crossing situation.

RULES OF INTENT
The rule requirements under the Inland Navigation Rules when vessels are meeting or crossing require that they will give signals of how they *intend* to meet. One short blast on the whistle means "I *intend* to leave you on my port side", and two short blasts on the whistle means, "I *intend* to leave you on my starboard side". The recipient vessel in the navigational situation is required to answer with a like signal if it is in agreement, however, if not in agreement it will sound the danger signal.

RULES OF THE ROAD
The unofficial term for the International or Inland Navigation Rules. Prior to the adoption of the 72 COLREGS the rules for governing sound signals, lights, and conduct between vessels was called the International Regulations for Preventing Collisions at Sea, and the various Pilot Rules for Inland, Great Lakes, and Western Rivers in the United States. All were called the Rules of the Road for the waters that they governed.

The adoption of the 72 COLREGS and the unification of the various internal U.S. waters statutory and regulatory Pilot Rules resulted in the International Navigation Rules governing all vessels in international waters and the Inland Navigation Rules for all vessels in U.S. inland waters. Most mariners still refer to them as the Rules of the Road. Also see: UNIFIED RULES OF THE ROAD.

In the late 1800s Thomas Gray, of England, set out a group of rhymes as aids to memory regarding the Rules of the Road. Although not entirely correct today, we repeat them in order that the words of those who went before are not forgotten.

"When both side lights you see ahead
Port your helm, and show your Red.

Green to Green – or Red to Red
Perfect safety – go ahead!

If to your starboard Red appear,
It is your duty to keep clear;
To act as judgment says is proper;
To Port – or Starboard – Back – or,
Stop her!

But when upon your Port is seen
A Steamer's Starboard Light of Green
There's not so much for you to do,
For Green to Port keeps clear of you.

Both in safety and in doubt,
Always keep a good look-out;
In danger, with no room to turn,
Ease her! Stop her! Go astern."

RUN
The utilization of a vessel and its towing where it is normally employed, e.e. "We're in the Green River to Madison *run* moving coal", or "We usually *run* between New Orleans and Cairo, but once in awhile we go up the Ohio".

RUN AGROUND
The act of accidentally hitting the riverbed or a sandbar with a vessel; or the action of a Pilot to purposely ground a vessel to avert a greater calamity.

RUN OFF
Water that flows from higher elevations of a river valley that eventually discharges into the stream. The term is usually associated with storms or heavy rainfall resulting in an increased level at a river gauging station.

RUN OUT
1. To unscrew and loosen the ratchets and get them ready to use when putting barges together.
2. To put out a line or wire, i.e. "When the head line gets tight, *run out* a breast line".
3. A reading that is taken on rotating shafting to see if it is aligned in conformance to specifications, or how far out of alignment it may be.

RUNNING
1. A vessel that is underway.
2. A surge of water, i.e., "They're *running* 60 feet of dam".
3. Strong forward or aft movement of a tow in a lock when turbulence occurs when filling the chamber.

RUNNING BLOCK
A *block* that is attached to the object that is to be moved.

RUNNING FLANK
In some swift rivers with an excessively long sweeping bend and a narrow navigable channel it is extremely hard to maneuver through its length without landing on the shore when proceeding downstream with a fairly large tow for the size of the channel. Oftentimes the Pilot will execute the bend with what is termed a *running flank*.

This maneuver requires heading into the bend, backing full astern to allow the bend current to steer the head of the tow out from the shore without appreciably slowing the tow's speed through the water. At times in a long narrow bend this maneuver may have to be preformed two or three times through the course of the bend's length in order to keep the tow off the bank. This was a typical maneuver on the Missouri River before its course became more or less stabilized by use of rock dikes and other type training structures. See: FLANK for the entire discourse on flanking tactics involved.

The term is also used when in some places on the river when a Pilot wants to set up the tow when maneuvering around a bend above a landing or bridge by backing and starting a swing of the tow without causing an undue lateral sliding momentum.

RUNNING LIGHTS
Navigation lights required by the Inland Navigation Rules that shall be

displayed from sunset to sunrise and during restricted visibility. The term derives from the fact that these lights are to be shown when a vessel is underway, or *running*. See: RIDING LIGHTS.

RUNNING ON DUST

1. Used by steamboat engineers when the coal flat was low and they had to use the dusty fines of coal to fire their boilers.

2. When navigating an extremely shallow section of channel.

RUNNING ON FUMES

An expression used when running low on fuel.

RUNNING PART

The moving or hauling part of a fall in a tackle, not the fixed standing part.

RUNNING RIVER

Used when referring to a rising river that also has faster running current.

RUNNING THE FALLS

See: FALLS OF THE OHIO.

RUNNING THE MARKS

1. A set of navigational directions that used to be given in channel reports to indicate where the channel was located, especially if buoys were missing. As an example, "When 50 feet open on the third right bank dike, cross over to 100 feet below the ABC Light"; or "From 200 feet below the old fence line at the MNO Landing, head to where the FGH light used to sit on the left bank".

2. Pilots keep BAR BOOKS with their own marks, especially for high water when they can cut off mileage and note places where the water might be more slack when upbound. They also note where sandbars might be building or cutting away, or any other changes occurring in a channel which may affect their *running the marks.*

RUNNING THE WILLOWS

A phrase used in high water when navigating a tow upstream as close to the bank as possible to find the slackest water and make the best time.

RUNNING THROUGH THEMSELVES

A phrase said of a steamer that broke a PITMAN, or a crank pin or a wrist pin. If the break was on the aft stroke the pitman might go overboard, but if the stroke was forward the pitman would go through the deckhouse and severely damage the vessel.

RUN-OFF

The draining of the hills of a valley after a heavy rainfall, filling the small streams and tributaries with waters that flow into the main navigation channel.

RUST

The oxidation of iron and steel in the presence of oxygen and moisture, causing corrosion or wastage of the metal.

RUST BUCKET

Any old vessel that is run down and decrepit looking.

RUTTER

An archaic usage for sailing directions. See: RUDDER.

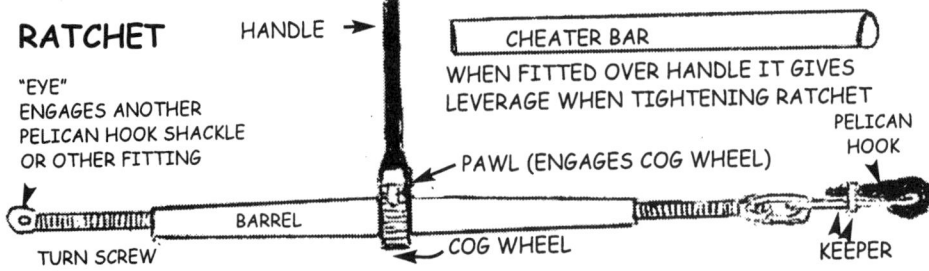

ILLUSTRATIONS 375

RAFTING LOG & LUMBER

At one time or another in the past a main commodity of most rivers were the log and lumber rafts free-floating in the current. Later, raft boats were used to assist. The picture is of one such boat and raft on the Upper Mississippi River.

RETRACTABLE PILOTHOUSE

Shown in the raised position. It can recess to be just above the second deck or lower all the way down to be flush with the main deck.

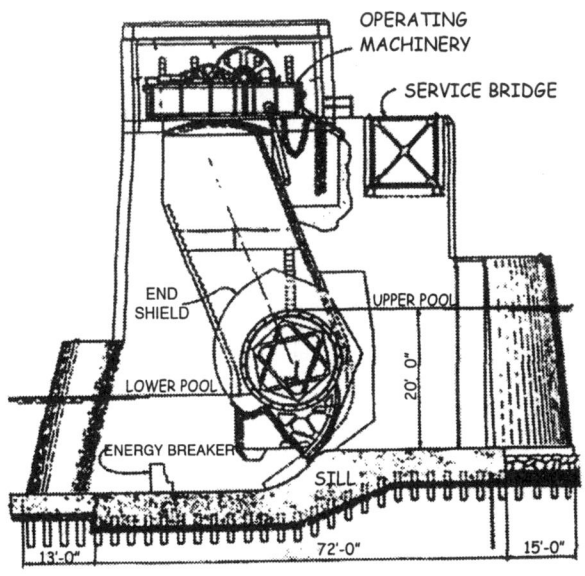

ROLLER GATE

A cross sectional diagram of a typical roller gate used at many navigational dams, which shows the principals of its operation. (From a USACE drawing)

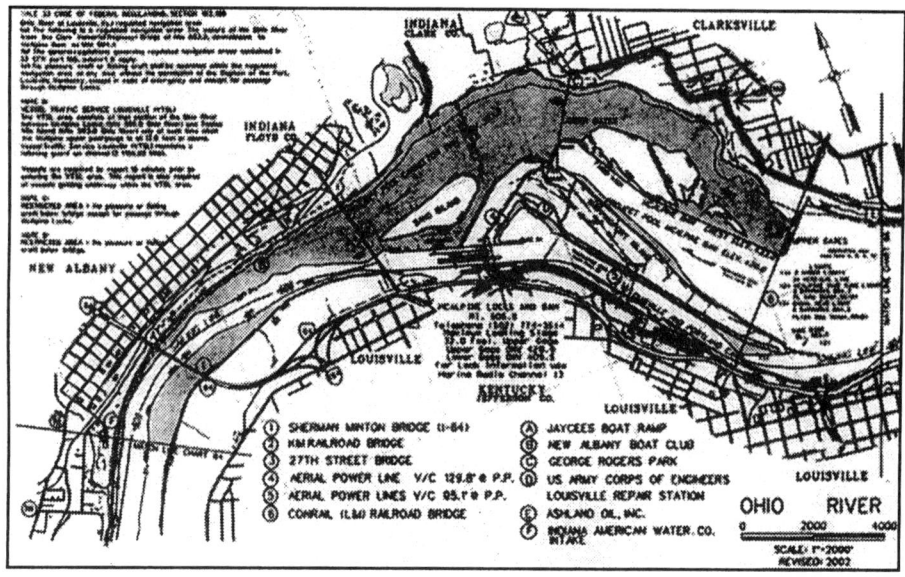

RIVER CHARTS OR MAPS

River chart or map of the Ohio River in the vicinity of Louisville, KY and Clarksville, IN (mile 604 to 609 showing the McAlpine Locks. The chart or map is reduced from an " x 11" booklet for the Ohio River. The charts are published by the USACE and are made for all Western Rivers. New technology is being developed to have them all digitized as shown on the map below of the Ohio and Upper Mississippi Rivers meeting to form the Lower Mississippi at Cairo Point.

These maps or charts are not used for actual navigation by river pilots, only for guidance of mile points, reference of docks, fleets, distances, obstructions, marking for observed high water marks, or other phenomenon, etc. How to navigate the bends in the river, knowing where the channel is located, how to line up the tow to safely run a bridge, and all the other quirks of a river are found in a good pilot's head, not in a book or computer print-out of a chart.

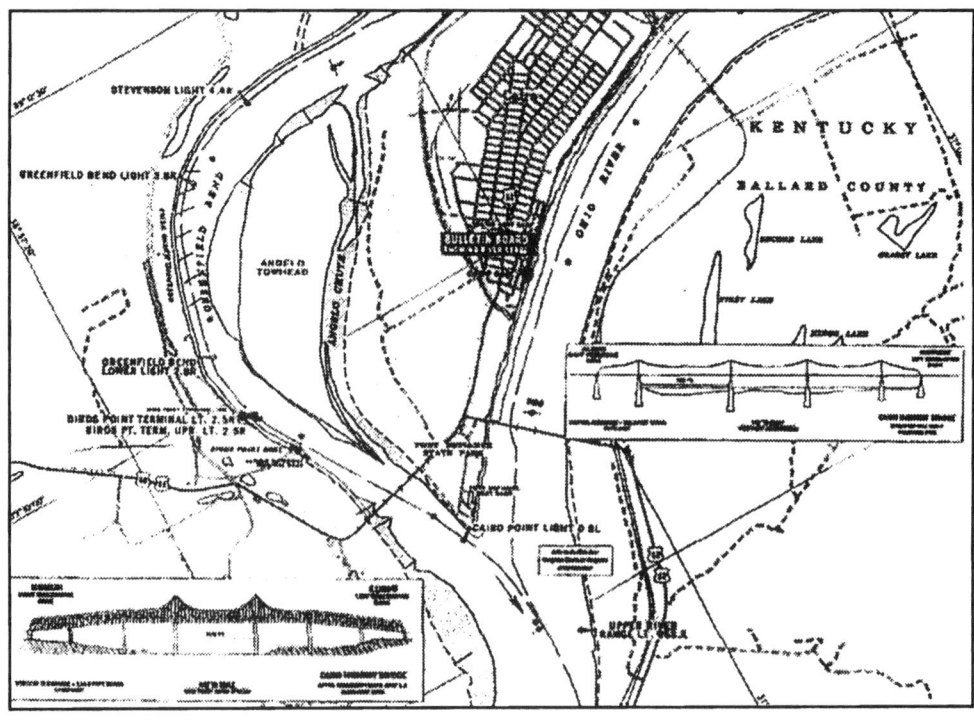

S

SABINE RIVER

Flows 555 miles from northeast Texas and at the lower end forms the boundary between the states of Louisiana and Texas until it is joined by the Neches River, eventually reaching the Gulf of Mexico near Port Arthur, Texas. Its name comes from the Spanish word meaning "cypress" due to a heavy growth of bald cypress in the lower parts of the river. The *Sabine* discharges more than any other river in Texas. Steamboats ran on the river in the mid-1800s, and in the late 1800s into the early 1900s extensive logging was conducted. The lower part between Orange and Port Arthur is the hub of the petro-chemical industry with extensive barging traffic.

SACK

1. A crewman's slang for his bunk or bed. Used when going to rest, i.e. "I'm going to *sack* out", or "I'm going to hit the *sack*". It is similar to using the term "rack".

2. The term also means "to plunder" as some of the Harpe's and Mason's did to flatboaters at CAVE IN ROCK in the early 1800s.

3. *Sack* may also be used when dismissing someone, i.e. "The Mate *sacked* me because I didn't SOOGEE the lower deck bulkheads when he told me to". Of course, that was probably better than being KEELHAULED.

SACRIFICIAL MATERIAL

Metal bars that are placed in strategic places on the hull of a vessel that will sacrifice themselves to protect the integrity of the steel hull and its appendages. See: ANODES and CATHODIC PROTECTION.

SADDLE

1. A structure with a rounded resting place to secure a boom when not in use. The term is originally rooted in the Latin *sella*, meaning "seat". It evolved into the Old English as *sadel, sadol,* or *sadul,* all having the meaning as we use *saddle.*

2. The resting place in a rack where a barrel is stored.

3. A low space or dip in a tree line that may be used as a navigation mark, especially on the Lower Mississippi and Missouri rivers.

4. Sometimes used to refer to the clip, or holder, that is tightened down when holding or securing wires in a U-bolt.

SADDLEBAG

In an accident where a barge hits a bridge pier or other object and becomes somewhat wrapped around it in a buckling or sagging position, it is said to be *saddlebagged,* like the *saddlebag* on the rump of a horse. Sometimes it happens with a barge tow, and with large log rafts. Also, the term is used when another vessel is collided with in the middle of a barge or tow, i.e. "That DBE tow *saddlebagged* us on the port side damaging barge #1232".

SAFE FOR FIRE

When the atmosphere of a tank or compartment has been tested and found free of flammable vapors, allowing burning or welding to take place.

SAFE FOR MEN

The atmosphere of a tank or compartment has been tested and found free of hazardous vapors and has a level of oxygen to safely let persons enter.

SAFETY HARBOR

Areas designated on the Tennessee River where small boats can seek shelter in high wind conditions on the lake areas above the dams. They are relatively free of stumps and other obstructions that could damage a hull or prop.

SAFETY HOOK

A hook on a boom line that has a hinged catch to prevent whatever the hook is attached to from slipping off.

SAFETY LINES

Lines that are put on top of wired barge couplings as a precaution to protect the integrity of the tow in case of bumping a bridge or going aground and the wire breaks.

Extra lines that are put out to hold a tow or fleet from breaking loose. It is highly recommended that, in case of strong storms, one reads the book *Home Is the Sailor,* by Jorge Amado, to find out how to properly moor a vessel.

SAFETY OF LIFE AT SEA

See: SOLAS

SAFETY SHOES

Heavy leather work shoes with a steel plate in the toe area that most crew members wear when working on barge tows to protect their feet in case of a dropped ratchet, chain links, or other heavy object.

SAFETY TREADS

A type of heavy material that has a very gritty surface. It is about six inches wide by 18 to 24 inches long and is glued to the steel decks on some walkways or stairs to help prevent a person from falling. See: NON-SKID COATINGS.

SAFETY VALVE

A relief valve on a steam boiler line that was set at a pre-determined pressure. It had a lever with an adjustable weight attached to it. If the boiler pressure exceeded the setting level, the valve opened (or "popped"), reducing the pressure in the boiler. Modern *safety valves* are now spring-loaded, eliminating any levers or weights. See: GAUGE COCKS and PV VALVE.

SAFETY ZONE

An area of a navigable waterway where the USCG imposes special operating procedures due to an immediate concern, such as an accident or a channel restriction. Similar to a REGULATED NAVIGATION AREA, but most often issued to inform vessels in the area of the occurrence of the instant importance of the event to insure navigation safety. It is usually imposed for a short duration.

SAGGING

The longitudinal deformation of a vessel's hull under stress when the bow and stern become higher than the midsection usually due to improper loading of cargo. If permanent distortion occurs it is called a BUCKLE, a term more commonly used on the river. It is the opposite of HOGGING. The word *sag* comes from the German *saken,* meaning "to subside".

SAIL EFFECT

The effect of wind on a long tow of empty barges when in a narrow channel such as the GIWW when a Pilot has to steer the tow at a pronounced angle heading as much as possible into the wind direction and crabbing his way down the Canal, or other channels, in order to not become WINDBOUND along the shore. It also affects empty barge tows when making locks, bridges, or attempting to go safely into a landing, as well as it did large packetboats with their high profile, closed in, superstructure.

SAILING LINE

A line on the printed map folios issued by the Corps of Engineers that generally marks where the channel was when the map was issued. Often times the channel may have changed, so the line is not too accurate and not to be blindly followed.

SAILOR

Not used in reference to people who work on the Western Rivers. All crew members are called "rivermen", and some "riverwomen". The term is, however, used with an adjective in a somewhat disparaging manner, such as *Sunday Sailors*, or *Weekend Sailors,* when some people do not follow the

Rules, customs, or safe practices when operating vessels on our river and canal systems.

SAILORMAN

The name given to the carpenter on a wooden-hulled steamboat. He was an important addition to the crew and highly regarded. Although not an officer, he usually ranked just below the Mate on the boat.

ST. CROIX RIVER

A river that forms a common boundary between Minnesota and Wisconsin for much of its length of about 164 miles, emptying into the Upper Mississippi River at Prescott, WS. The Ojibwe Indian tribe named it *gichi-ziibi,* meaning "big river". Later the French called it *Riviere Tombeaux,* which was anglicized into St. Croix.

The watershed of the river became a tremendous logging area producing millions of board feet of lumber. Log and lumber rafts were floated to the Mississippi and then joined together to float huge rafts to the St. Louis mills. The river now has no commercial traffic and is mainly used for recreation.

SALINITY

The term references the degree of salt in a body of water. On the Western Rivers it is not a problem, but on the Gulf Coast ports and the GIWW it is of concern since salty water leads to a greater degree of corrosion in steel hulls and the superstructure of vessels. Much of the GIWW's water is considered BRACKISH WATER due to tidal influences and the receipt of fresh water from inland sources. The root of the word is Latin *sal,* for "salt".

SALOON, MAIN

The central compartment on the boiler deck of a steamboat. It served as a dining hall and lounge for passengers who booked cabin travel. The cabin staterooms were to the side of the *saloon,* with those for ladies aft. It also usually contained a bar unless it was a TEMPERANCE BOAT. The term *saloon* comes from French *salon,* meaning "a large room or hall for receptions".

SALUTE

See: WHISTLE SALUTE

SALVAGE

1. The act of rescuing, saving, or raising a wrecked and sunk, or partially sunken, vessel and/or its cargo, then moving it to another facility for further disposal. A *salvage firm* is most often contracted on a per diem basis, or there may be an agreement to do the work on a NO CURE, NO PAY contract. The term comes from the Latin *salvare,* meaning "to save".

2. Used as an adjective with anything involved in *salvage,* i.e. award, barge, crew. team, tug, contract, loss, etc.

SALVAGE MASTER

The person who is in overall charge of a salvaging operation. He may be a representative of the vessel owner who confers with the person in charge of the salvage rig, but if the salvage was let on a NO CURE, NO PAY, basis the Master of the salvage rig is the *Salvage Master*. He is usually a person of extreme knowledge and experience in his field.

SALVAGE RIG

On the river system a salvage operation may only consist of a barge, with or without a crane or an A-FRAME, some large dewatering pumps, heavy winches, lots of wire, slings, the tools of the trade, and a towboat to push the barge and provide quarters for the salvage crew. However, it can also be more extensive, with heavy lift capability and powerful winches.

SAMPLING (CARGO)

1. On tank barges cargo surveyors often take *samples* of products in barges, both of petroleum and chemicals, at the loading dock and later at the facility where the cargo is unloaded in order to determine if any contamination has occurred. The *sampling* is usu-

ally taken through the ULLAGE HATCH or a special sampling pipe on the barge.

2. With grain cargoes a surveyor obtains *samples* at various locations in the cargo hold with a long tube that is capable of securing random *samples* at various levels of the loaded cargo. These are measured mostly for moisture content.

3. For *sampling* of the river bottom see: ARM (THE LEAD).

SAMSON POST

A large, long post that was on the centerline of a vessel and was a foundation timber for the CROSS CHAINS used to support the weight of the paddle housing of a sidewheel steamboat. It was found that as these vessels became larger, the strain of the heavy weight on a single post and the working of the wheel would often eventually punch a hole in the bottom of the hull. Later other support framing was used. The term apparently was given as an indication of the great strength that was expected of the post by using a sort of biblical reference. The *Samson Post* has also been described as a short stout support for a boom, but a more proper term for that usage is KING POST.

SAND and SANDBARS

A granular substance of mostly silica that is a product of erosion from rocks in the course of water flowing to the sea. It is technically defined by engineers as to its varying sizes, but all we know on the Western Rivers is that we have a lot of it that comes from the headwaters of the Appalachians Mountains in the East and those of the Rockies in the West, and their product makes a lot of *sandbars* and shallow water at times in once-navigable channels. The word comes from the Dutch word *zand*.

SAND BOIL

1. Sand boils are the result of hydraulic back-pressure during floods when high water against a levee face that is water-soaked causes under-seepage of the groundwater from natural aquifers by creating upward head pressure on the clay soil bottom of the levee. Small pinhole boils are normal, but if they are not corrected or contained they enlarge and can cause the weakened levee to breach.

2. A bubbling effect around a cutting bar that can indicate some deterioration and possible or potential collapse of the bar.

SAND DIGGER OR DREDGE

A dredge that obtains sand and gravel from the bed of a river. Often referred to as a *sand sucker*.

SAND FLAT

A small deck barge, usually built with a cargo box coaming, used in connection with a SAND DIGGER, to transport the cargo to a dock.

SAND WAVES

The bed (bottom) of a river can be extremely uneven or rough. The friction of water moving over its surface can affect the flow rate and the sediment transport rate. These rates are a function of the slope of bed, its depth, the size and the distribution of the material in the stream. A river's sediment travels in ripples along its bed, falling out at times to form sandbars which vary in size along its channel. Then as the river may rise it cuts into the bar, picking up its previous discarded sediment material with its new flow; as the river level falls it drops its sediment once again to form a new sandbar, lower down its channel route.

River Pilots are well aware of the phenomena as the depth of a channel, say 10 feet marked at a given gauge, with a standing rise of an additional 12 feet of water on the gauge may find that by the depth recorder over the same stretch of channel, only 19 feet of water is recorded rather than the 22 feet which would seem to be indicated. On a slowly declining river (to its original gauge), the 10 feet of water may still be there in the channel, but if the river fall is rapid there may only be eight feet or less since the flow did not keep moving the newly deposited silt fast enough to cut the channel.

However, not only are sandbars formed and cut away as the river continually carries the erosion of Iowa, Nebraska, Illinois, Missouri, and other states to the Gulf of Mexico in its journey to the sea, but it does so at times with what are termed *sand waves,* although the *wave* is not just composed of sand. It may have gravel, pebbles, clay, etc., in its composition. The *waves* travel at a rate much slower than the velocity of the steam itself. These are extremely large ripples of sand moving over the river's bed, which have been measured as high as 40 feet and several hundred feet in length (Corey, W.C. and Keller, M.D. in ASCE paper 1957), although this is not the general configuration of these *waves*. In flood stages this type of *sand wave* probably does not create a problem to navigation, especially to a vessel and tow moving downstream. However, they could cause some concern to an upbound tow since the encounter would be similar to the MOUNTING A REEF in a river crossing which, in certain stages of water, must be met by a tow almost perfectly perpendicular to the flow of the current or the tow will be set off its course.

These *sand waves* will rise up, roll along, and disappear, only to reform for awhile and again rapidly disappear depending upon the bed form variations which can change in a fairly short distance. The depth of water, the slope of the riverbed, the density of material load and its size, as well as other factors, all have an impact on the formation and disappearance of *sand waves* in a complex river channel. Also called *bed forms* by hydrologists. Small inconsequential dunes or waves are generally termed *ripples.*

SANGAMON RIVER

A river about 250 miles long that runs through central Illinois from an easterly direction to the west, reaching the Illinois River 10 miles to the north of Beardstown, IL. Its name comes from the Pottawatomie Indian word *Sainguee-mon,* meaning "where there is plenty to eat".

The river has a connection to Abraham Lincoln. As a young man Abe had ridden a flatboat down the Ohio River; when his family moved to Illinois he worked as a helper on another flatboat on the *Sangamon* and later rode and piloted a steamer for a trip on the river. There is an account that Lincoln received a patent (No. 6469) for a device to lift boats over shoal areas, but it was never manufactured. He was the only U.S. President to receive a patent. In the Illinois legislature he was active in promoting waterway improvements; however, he was the lawyer for the railroads against the steamboaters in the infamous *EFFIE AFTON* case at the Rock Island Railroad Bridge.

SANTA CLAUS

The name used for *Saint Nicholas* in the United States. Among other things, he is considered the patron Saint of seamen and, of course, rivermen. It is claimed that he may have been a sailor or fisherman at one time. Later, while on a trip at sea, they say he saved the life of a sailor who fell from a ship's rigging in a storm, a miracle which all seamen celebrate. This means at Christmas time on the river, he is the person in the red suit who comes down the stacks of tugboats and towboats and steamers, delivering presents to all the crews who have to work on that day. See: CHRISTMAS ON THE RIVER.

SAWYER

The SNAG of an old tree whose roots become embedded in the bottom of the river with its somewhat floating trunk pointing downriver. The bobbing up and down of the trunk in the river current in a sawing motion gave it the name. An extremely dangerous type of snag that caused much damage to packetboats, especially those that were upbound and could be impaled by the *sawyer.*

SCALE
1. Crusty deposits that buildup on the inside of a boiler from the injected water having impurities; these have to be periodically cleaned out for the boiler to efficiently heat the water.
2. Graduated range measurements of distances on a chart to determine course and evaluate periods of travel time to give estimates, times of arrival and other purposes. River Pilots do not use charts to determine courses, but rather only to estimate speed through the water by miles travelled over a given period of time indicated by river navigation light mile markers.

SCALING HAMMER
A hammer used to knock off or loosen the build up of oxidation or scale of lime deposits on the inside of a boiler. It is similar to a CHIPPING HAMMER.

SCAN
A sweep of 360 degrees on a radar scope.

SCANNER
1. The rotating radar antenna and its driver motor and housing. It is most often located on the top of a pilothouse.
2. Some vessels are equipped with a radio that can scan and monitor a number of frequencies.

SCANT OPEN RIVER
A condition when the wickets of a movable dam were down (sometimes only a portion of them) allowing for OPEN RIVER, however, with a water depth over the lowered wickets that was barely sufficient to maintain open river conditions. When this occurred Pilots were warned to slow down when making passage over the dam since a wicket could be sucked up into a propeller. Downbound vessels would usually stop their wheels just prior to going over where the lowered wickets were located, but as the current at the dam was swiftest at the restricted wicket area, upbound vessels often had to continue with most of their power to be able to stem the current and shove their tow through the navigational pass, and then hope for the best.

SCANTLINGS
The sizes and dimensions of the various structural parts that go into building a vessel, including, but not limited to, frames, beams, and plating. The term comes from the French word *escantillon,* meaning "sample".

'SCAPE PIPE
The term is shorthand for *escape*. On steamboats it is a pipe running from the engine through the deck above to vent steam. When handling a steamer at landings or other places and a quick response or extra power is required, the emission of steam relieves the back-pressure on the engine. A steamer that is moving at a high rate of speed is said to be *'scaping*.

SCARPH or SCARPHING
The act of making two shorter beams into one with no loss of strength. In wooden vessels it was done by either tapering off the ends or notching them and then bolting them together so as to make a timber of uniform size for its entire length. Often done where there might be a curvature in the hull line for timbers. On steel vessels the *scarph* is made by welding the pieces together. The term comes from our Scandinavian friends as *skarv* or *scarf,* meaning "seam or joint", and is also spelled *scarf* and *scarfing* in some tomes.

SCIOTO RIVER
A river that rises in central Ohio and flows to the Ohio River, terminating at Portsmouth, Ohio, at about mile 356. There is no commercial navigation on the river at present, but at one time

the river from Columbus to the mouth was the southern part of the OHIO AND EIRE CANAL, which ran to Lake Erie at Cleveland, Ohio.

SCISSOR WIRES

Barge-holding wires on a tow that are laid diagonally across barges, in pairs, i.e., on two barges laying side by side, one set of wires from the port barge would have a lead forward to the starboard barge while another set of wires would lead aft between deck fittings. This arrangement would prevent any movement between the two barges.

If the barges are end-on to one another the wires are laid fore and aft on the port timberheads and then the end of the wire lead crosses over the coupling toward the center and is fastened into a ratchet on the other barge to be tightened. On the starboard side the same wire arrangement would be laid in the same fashion and then crossed over toward the center and fitted into its ratchet. In other words, the two wires when fastened would appear from above to form a type of "V". This not only keeps the barges tightly fitted together, but also prevents any sliding from side to side. The type of arrangement is more often called fore and aft JOCKEY WIRES.

SCOOP

1. A bowl-shaped digging bucket used on a dredge or a crane. The term comes from the German *schope,* meaning "water bucket".

2. A small utensil about the size of the vertical half of a coffee can with a wooden handle that is used to bail water from a small work boat. However, on the river it is usually just a plain old pound or a two pound empty coffee can that does the job.

SCOPE

1. Generally, refers to the length of chain or wire let out when at anchor, and how much swing room is available; however, it is also sometimes used on the river to describe the length that is out for a mooring line. It comes from the Latin *skopein,* meaning "to look at". See: RANGE.

2. The term *scope* often is used on the river when referring to the images on the screen of a vessel's radar. It comes from *oscilloscope* which is in essence the electrical voltage emitting in a radar's cathode-ray tube.

SCOUR

The action of moving swift water that washes out a section of riverbed, or around a structure such as a bridge pier, an intake foundation, or a dike; or the action of eating away at a riverbank. It comes from the Latin *excure,* meaning "to clean off".

SCOW

1. A flat-bottomed vessel used for a variety of transportation needs, such as hauling sand or gravel, garbage, or rigging; some *scows* have a crane or pile driver mounted on them. A *scow* usually has a raked bow and stern with a flat transom across its width. The term is from the Dutch *schouw,* meaning "ferryboat".

2. A degrading term to describe an older vessel that has seen better days and is run down, not maintained and operated with a scrounge crew, i.e. "That old *scow* should have gone to the BONEYARD years ago".

SCOW BOW

Basically, a raked bow extending from a flat hull bottom to the headlog, along with a rounded or curvature of the knuckles up to the main deck.

SCRAPER

1. A tool which was used to scrape and smooth the seams in the sides of a wooden steamboat after caulking. The *scraper* usually had a triangular head that had been well-sharpened. Also a tool used to *scrape* off paint from wood or steel. The word comes from the Dutch *schrapen,* meaning "to scratch".

2. In the early 1800s navigation on Western rivers could be stopped in shal-

low reaches that had filled in with sand or gravel. *Scrapers* made of iron would be dragged across the shoal areas by teams of oxen or horses. In the mid-1800s, a barge equipped with a steam engine powering a winch would be anchored above the shallow area. A winch wire would be run out to a small boat that had a *scraper* which would then be winched through the obstructive area pulling the sand and gravel with it. *Scrapers* are still used to accomplish certain types of maintenance dredging at river docks. They are hinged on the end of a barge. The *scraper* blade is about four feet wide and 12 feet or more in length depending on the horsepower of the towboat employed. The blade is dropped to the river bed, the barge is backed away, and the material is moved from where it had silted in at the dock area.

SCRAPPING

The final event for old, worn-out, leaking barges when they are cut up for scrap to be recycled into new steel to make more barges.

SCREENS & SCREENING

For many years the SIDELIGHTS on towboats, tugs, and barges were required to have *screens*. These were to be three feet long so as to prevent their glare from being seen across the head, or centerline. Stern lights were to be *screened* so as to not be seen forward of the beam. No length was given. A steamboat towing astern was to carry two bright white lights in a vertical line to show from right ahead to two points abaft the beam on each side, but required no *screens*. A river steamboat with smokestacks was to show sidelights mounted on the stacks, showing forward, aft and abeam on their respective sides, but gave no requirement for *screens*.

Originally, these *screens* for sidelights were painted the color of their respective light, green on starboard and red on port, although there was no requirement to that effect. Later rules came out that required them to be painted black. When the unified Inland Navigation Rules went into effect in 1980, the Annex I to the rules states the sidelights shall be *screened* and painted mat black, but it gives no length for a *screen*.

SCREW

Another name for the propeller of a vessel, which is also called a *wheel*. It received this name because it advances through the water similar to the advance made by a *screw* when driven into a wood frame. If a vessel has two propellers, it is called a "twin-*screw* boat"; and if it has three propellers, it is called a "triple-*screw* boat"; etc, but we've never seen a five-propeller boat. The term is from the Latin *scrofa*, meaning "to sew". See: PROPELLER.

SCREW SHACKLE

The U-or pear-shaped shackle that is closed with a threaded pin through its eyes, one eye having threads to receive the threaded pin.

SCUBA DIVER

An underwater *diver* who inspects hulls for damage and can make temporary repairs if necessary, and also, assists in rigging for salvage work. On the river system most *divers* used to be of the "hard hat" type, but they are seldom seen anymore. The term *scuba* is an acronym for *self contained underwater breathing apparatus*.

SCULL

To move a small boat, yawl, or dinghy with the use of one oar or paddle from the stern or from one side. Also refers to a short oar, or *sculling paddle*, used to either propel or steer a small open boat.

SCUPPER

A small drain opening in a coaming or bulwark to allow water from the deck to run over the side of the vessel. The term comes from the old French *escopir*, meaning "to spit", and/or from the German word *speigatt*, meaning "spit hole".

SCUTTLE
The act of deliberately sinking, or causing to sink, one's own vessel. The term seems to come from the Spanish *escotilla*, meaning "hatchway", probably in the sense of leaving a hatch unsecured, allowing water to come in. Sometimes an opening much smaller than a hatch opening will be called a *scuttle*.

SCUTTLEBUTT
A term that migrated to the river from the Navy. The term came from the word "butt", the name for a cask of water the crew drank from that was located on deck. When a few crewmen gathered around drinking water it was a good time to exchange the latest rumor that each heard, whether true or not. It was the sort of talk that was deliberately passed, or "scuttled". So the loose talk became known as *scuttlebutt*.

SEA
A large body of salty water where towboats seldom venture to operate except for short places along the GIWW, but where tugs often earn their keep. From the Dutch, *zee*.

SEA CHEST
The intake of water at the side of a vessel's hull and its controlling sea valve.

SEA CLUTTER
False targets showing on a radar screen due to rough-breaking wave tops, heavy rain, or other weather anomalies.

SEA COCK
Any valve that provides an opening to the outside of the hull, either to provide for a discharge or for an inlet of water.

SEA LAWYER
A crew member who purports to know all the laws, rules, and regulations, and interprets them to his best advantage, always arguing about what he is required to do, citing dubious or wrong authorities in his/her arguments. On the river sometimes called a *Mess Deck* or *Galley Lawyer*, since most of the babble is undertaken in the galley.

SEA LEVEL
The half-way mark between high and low tides where the sea meets the shoreline. From that "zero" level as one moves inland upriver in the valleys whose waters flow to the sea, the elevations get higher. For instance, Pittsburgh, where the Ohio River begins, is about 715 feet above *sea level*; the head of navigation on the Mississippi at Minneapolis is about 730 feet above *sea level*.

SEA ROOM
Giving another vessel sufficient space in a channel to safely maneuver his tow, i.e. "Could you move a little more to the right-hand of the channel, Cap, so I can get by you?"

SEA SERVICE or SEA TIME
In regard to the licensing of personnel by the USCG, it also refers to those who are employed on vessels plying the rivers and canals. The term applies to actual service on a tug or towboat, not the time in the employ of a company; however, a "day of time" is regarded as an eight- hour day. If the watch time is a 12-hour day, the person will be credited with $1_{1/2}$ days of service.

SEA TRIALS
See: RIVER TRIALS.

SEA-BEE BARGE SYSTEM
A system of using barges that were half the size of a conventional jumbo box barge, or 100' x 35', which could be floated aboard a *See-bee* ship and then floated off in foreign ports to be unloaded. The venture was eventually phased out as commercially unprofitable. Most of the barges that were in the service were welded together, with

two *See-bee* barges making one jumbo hopper box barge for use in the river trade.

SEAGOING
A vessel that is capable of going to sea and fit to endure the strains that can be imposed in a sea environment. Few towboats are capable of going to sea, but most tugs can and some barges have seagoing capability.

SEAL
A wire device that is sometimes put on the hatch fittings and pipelines of liquid tank barges that is coupled to a soft metal that can only be removed by breaking the wire to open the hatch, or have access to the pipeline. It is sometimes used by shippers to detect if the tanks or lines have been tampered with. Also used on some bonded products.

SEAL (IN TUNNEL)
A positive flow of water to and through the propeller in a tunneled stern so that cavitation does not take place.

SEAM
1. The space or line between two timber planks of the hull in a wooden vessel. They are required to be CAULKED and PAYED.
2. Where two steel plates are welded together. This can be in a butt weld where the plates are welded edge to edge, or in a lap joint where the plates overlap one another, usually with one side being a solid weld while the other side is welded intermittently.

SEAMAN
1. Very generally, any person who is employed aboard a vessel in the legal vernacular is considered a *seaman*. On the river system these people are called *crew members*. They are persons trained in the duties required to safely and efficiently conduct the duties necessary on a towboat, tugboat, and barges.
2. The name of the Newfoundland dog that accompanied Lewis and Clark on their exploration journey up the Missouri River and on to the West Coast and back.

SEAMAN'S CHURCH INSTITUTE
An organization headquartered in New York, it also has facilities in other seaports and in two locations on the U.S. inland waterways at Paducah, KY and Houston, TX. The Institute was founded in the 1840s, providing a ministry for maritime crew members, as well as conducting educational courses for increasing the professionalism of those working in river, coastal, or sea services. Toward that end, pilothouse simulators have been constructed at both the Paducah and Houston facilities to assist in their continuing educational and training efforts.

SEAMANSHIP
The art and ability to conduct one's duties aboard any type of vessel where the person works, in a knowledgeable, skillful, safe, and efficient manner whether one is the Master of the vessel or a deckhand on watch.

SEAPLANE
A plane fitted with pontoons or floats which allows it to take off and land on water. When on water it is required to follow the Navigation Rules. At night Rule 31 states it shall show or exhibit lights as similar as possible as those of a vessel. Rule 18, Responsibilities Between Vessels, requires that a *seaplane* on the water, "shall, in general, keep well clear of all vessels and avoid impeding their navigation".

SEAPORT
A port that has access to the sea for oceangoing freight, but also can be served by inland barges. It is usually close to sea water, such as Houston and Mobile, however the Port of New Orleans is over 100 miles from the open sea, and the Port of Baton Rouge is over 250 miles up the Mississippi from the Gulf of Mexico.

SEARCH AND RESCUE

The exercise of looking for someone in distress on the river (or at sea) who may have fallen overboard or otherwise is believed to be missing in the water environment. It is one of the missions of the USCG as well as local government water patrols and other mariners that may be in the general area where the incident may have occurred to assist people who may be in distress.

SEARCHLIGHT

A powerful electric spotlight mounted on top of the pilothouse that a Pilot uses at night to see channel buoys, pick up reflecting tape on dayboards, navigate into lock chambers, see the set on bridge piers, and to visually assist in a multitude of other navigational and working situations. The first steamboat using electric *searchlights* was in about 1875. For many years, up until around 1980, most large towboats used a CARBON ARC LIGHT where two carbon electrodes, set tip to tip, burned, and the reflector then created an extremely bright beam. Most towboats and tugs now use XENON type lights.

SEAWALL

A concrete structure that protects a bank from the forces of waves coming from the open water of a sea, or on a river from waves or wakes. See: FLOOD WALL.

SEAWORTHY

A vessel's state of readiness attesting that it is properly constructed, maintained, has the necessary equipment and stores, and is properly crewed to undertake the intended service in which it is employed. It does not necessarily mean a capability to undergo the rigors of going to sea unless that is where it intends to travel, but includes all vessels that navigate on water, including the Western Rivers and the GIWW.

SECTORS

See: LIGHT SECTORS.

SECURE

1. To make a line or wire fast.
2. To insure that all hatch covers are tightly closed.
3. Making sure all loose gear and equipment are properly stowed.
4. To stop and shut down the vessel's engines, and/or generators and other operating machinery. The term comes from the Latin *securus*, meaning "without care or worry", from the *se* (without) and *cura* (care).

SECURITY

See: DEPARTMENT OF HOMELAND SECURITY

SECURITY CALL

When there is a need to transmit "safety messages" that might be a missing buoy, approaching foul weather conditions, or a change of channel conditions, etc., the person transmitting the message uses the international call of the French word "securite", and then conveys the message. The word is pronounced: *Say-cure-it-tay*.

SECURITY LEVELS

A national system to provide for *security* activities and planning, providing a scaled approach for possible escalating threat levels. It is an evolving program with various degrees, from a normal continuing awareness to the highest level of imminent attack possible.

SECURITY PLANS

All vessels and maritime facilities are required to have detailed plans in effect for the different security levels, as well as providing training for their employees in security. The entire "security concept" is changing rapidly since the turn of the century and will evolve and increase, as well as change, the definitions listed in this text. See: VESSEL SECURITY ASSESSMENT (VSA), VESSEL SECURITY PLAN (VSP) and VESSEL SECURITY OFFICER (VSO).

SEDIMENT

1. The material that comes from the run-off of the floodplain in the basin of a river valley or the erosion of the banks lining the river, consisting of silt, clays, sand, and gravel that eventually settles out of the flow and becomes a sandbar or part of the State of Louisiana. The term comes to us from the Latin *sedimentum,* meaning "settling".

2. A build up of loose scale in the inside of a boiler.

SEDIMENT FLOW STUDY

An evaluation of the transport of sediment in a section of river or a channel, that studies the dropping or depositing of sediment as water flows increase or decrease, and how sediment might be affected by dikes or other structures.

SEE YA ON THE ONE (or TWO)

A common transmission between two Pilots meeting on the river who have agreed to meet on a port-to-port passage (one whistle); or, conversely agree on a starboard-to-starboard passage, where they would each sound two whistles. In accordance with INLAND NAVIGATION RULE number 14 the vessel proceeding with a following current on the Western Rivers shall initiate the appropriate sound signal.

SEIZE

1. Said of working parts of an engine or other mechanical components that freeze up or stop working, usually due to lack of oil or grease.

2. The fastening together of two lines, or a line within itself in forming an eye, with small line taking numerous tight turns. The wrapping line is termed *seizing* and can be done in various ways. See: RACK.

SEIZURE

The act of taking possession of a vessel by a U.S. Marshal under a judicial order, usually for failure to satisfy payment of a legal monetary obligation. The Marshal will "post" the vessel, with no one allowed on board except for safety reasons.

SELF-HELP PROGRAM

A program that is initiated by the towing industry when there is a backup at a lock where many vessels are waiting to double-lock. First is an agreement as to how many tows will lock one way in a sequence, usually three to six tows at a time. Then tows near the end of the queue will tie off their tow and go to the lock to assist by taking the break cut of barges from other tows out of the lock, thus speeding up the lockage procedure.

SELF-PROPELLED BARGE

A barge that has propulsion. Although common in European waters, these type barges are very seldom seen on the Western Rivers of the U.S. except for very small vessels, such as rigging flats or pump flats used at fleets.

SELF-UNLOADING BARGE

A barge that has the capability to unload its own cargo, such as many tank barges and some cement barges that are equipped with pumping equipment and engines.

SELLERS, CAPT. ISAIAH

A noted steamboat Master on the Mississippi River who occasionally wrote articles regarding river conditions for a New Orleans newspaper and would sometimes use the pseudonym of "Mark Twain". Samuel Clemens, then a cub learning the river, wrote a biting parody of Capt. Sellers' articles and it was sent to a rival newspaper in 1859 for publication under the name of "Sergeant Fathom". Sellers never wrote another river article after that and never forgave Clemens.

Later, Clemens was looking for a catchy nickname to help sell his writings; he adopted the old name that Sellers had used of "Mark Twain". Clemens is reported to have remarked at the time that he would use it, "Now since Sellers is gone and he has no further use for it"; but actually Clemens "greatly exaggerated", as he was using the pen name a year before the death of Captain Isaiah Sellers, the first to use the sobriquet MARK TWAIN as a signature after, of course, the ancient leadsman who shouted out the signal of two fathoms when sounding a channel.

SEMI-INTEGRATED
A barge that has a raked bow and a square, or box stern.

SEMPER PARATUS
The motto of the U.S. Coast Guard, meaning "Always Ready".

SENSORS
Many towboats and tugs currently have a wide degree of *sensors* employed on board, especially in automated engine rooms as well as on a large number of other working machinery, electronic equipment, and electrical systems. The devices record temperatures, pressures, capacity, times, etc. If the vessel gear so equipped is out of the normal programmed parameters, the *sensor* will trigger a response, usually either a flashing light and/or sound an alarm.

SEPARATION SCHEME
See: TRAFFIC SEPARATION SCHEME.

SERIOUS MARINE INCIDENT
An incident aboard a commercial vessel in U.S. waters consisting of the following: Death, injury requiring more than first aid, property damage over $100,000, total loss of a vessel, discharge of oil in excess of 10,000 gallons, or a reportable quantity of a hazardous substance. Drug and alcohol testing of the crew is required if their vessel is involved.

SERVE
The act of tightly winding small stuff, or COWTAIL, around a wire splice after worming it, and wrapping or parceling it, to keep a wire with protruding wire strands from sparking on the deck of a tank barge, and to prevent FISHHOOKS from catching in the skin of people handling the wire. It is a part of the process of WORM, PARCEL AND SERVE. The term is from the Latin *servire*, meaning "keep or protect" and came from *servus*, meaning "slave".

SERVING MALLET
A wooden hammer-like device with a grooved head to fit the curvature of a wire cable. It is used to tightly and evenly distribute *serving* material around a wire. Seldom seen on the river since most *serving* is done by hand, when it is undertaken.

SET
The term has universal meanings of time, place or position, value, direction, construction, damage, groups, etc, that it is impossible to determine the background of the how and why the term *set* derives its meaning in all instances. Some of its usages in nautical terminology are:

1. A directional current or tidal movement running across the channel sailing line that tends to move an object, vessel or tow in an undesirable lateral slide.

2. An observation of channel flow, i.e. "There's a strong *set* on the lower red buoy", or "The flow through the open dam gates is going to *set* you off the upper lock wall".

3. An observation of wind action on a vessel or tow, i.e. "The wind is so strong out of the West, make sure you play it and don't get this empty tow *set* against the starboard channel pier of the DEF Bridge".

4. To place an object in a particular location. See: SET PILING and SETTING A BUOY.

5. To lay out, or *set*, a vessel's course.

6. The *set* of the sun, the moon, or other celestial bodies.

7. To determine, or *set*, the value of a vessel or service.

8. To schedule, or *set*, the time of departure.

SET IN

Damage to the hull of a vessel, i.e. "When the M/V *NEVERSAIL* collided with us, her bow barge *set in* the bow of our starboard lead barge over eight inches".

SET PILING

The act of a pile driving vessel driving piles into a river bed.

SET UP THE TOW or VESSEL

1. To navigate a vessel in a manner to be in position to safely steer through a bridge, or into a lock, or to meet another vessel in a narrow channel, or to FLANK a sharp bend, or any other close navigational situation requiring utmost care of being in proper shape.

2. To have the crew get the tow ready to lock, receive other barges in tow, to drop a barge, to exchange tows, or to moor the tow; meaning to have all lines, rigging, and other equipment ready for use.

SET-OVER

1. To move a towboat from one place to another when facing up to the tow.

2. The act of a towboat breaking out from the tow at a lock to make a SET-OVER SINGLE lockage.

3. Moving a barge in tow.

4. The act of a dredge moving over in the channel, or breaking a dredge pipeline to allow a vessel to proceed through a channel.

SET-OVER SINGLE

When making a lock with the tow total length exceeding the lock length, and there is a notched space in the tow whereby the towboat, after entering the lock, can disengage from the tow and move up into the notch to permit the unit to make a single lockage. After locking is completed the towboat starts the tow out of the lock, and when there is sufficient room between the stern of the tow and the lock gate, the towboat drops behind the tow and again faces up to the tow's stern and continues on its journey. See: JACKKNIFE SINGLE.

SETTING A BUOY

When a USCG buoy boat places a buoy in the river to mark the channel. See: BUOY.

SETTLE

A vessel being loaded with cargo or fuel is said to *settle* in the water, or to increase its draft. It also refers to a vessel which is holed from hitting a rock, object, or other vessel and is taking on water. If it *settles* too far it will be said to have sunk.

SHACKLE

A most useful forged device for holding and connecting wires, ratchets, other rigging, and when towing. *Shackles* come in a variety of sizes and shapes, including "chain", "bow", "anchor or pear", etc. On the river most of the *shackles* that are utilized are in the family of "chain", either with a straight pin or a screwed type. The term comes from the Dutch *schakel*, meaning "a link or coupling". The term also denotes a form of restraint, as a person whose movement is under control by use of *shackle*s (leg irons), but since the Civil War it isn't recorded that this use has occurred on riverboats.

The *shackle* consists of an oval rounded bar in a basic U-shape. Its somewhat flattened ends have holes in them called "eyes" that receives a round holding "pin" that spans the opening at the end which is designated the "mouth" or "throat". The "pin" can be smooth (with a head) that will have a small hole in its end to receive a cotter key to keep the "pin" in place, or one "eye" of the *shackle* may be threaded to receive a threaded "pin". When farm boys first come on board to learn the river trade they call the device a "clevis", but we learn 'em right.

SHAFT

There are various pieces of equipment in an engine where the term *shaft* is used, such as a "cam *shaft*", a "crank-*shaft*", or a "*shaft* coupling". The term is often misused when referring to other equipment, such as a rudder *shaft* (it is a "stock"), or calling the length of an anchor a *shaft* when it really is the "shank". The term comes to us from the Latin *scapus,* also meaning *shaft*, probably related to the length of a spear.

SHAFT ALLEY

The area along which the propulsion *shafting* runs.

SHAFT HORSEPOWER

The horsepower measured by a torsion meter at the *shaft*.

SHAFTING

A general term that describes the components that make up the propulsion *shaft*. The driving power of an engine is transmitted through the *shafting* to a vessel's propeller, turning it in order to make a vessel move. Generally *shafting* is made up of the following components:

1. The thrust *shaft*, or bull gear *shaft* from the reduction gear.
2. The line *shaft*.
3. The stern tube *shaft*.
4. The tail *shaft,* which is tapered down with threads on its end to receive the propeller.

All the different sections are coupled together by flanges at various joints and supported by bearings and the STRUT at the aft end of the *shafting* and where the propeller is held in place by a propeller lock nut.

SHAKE

Flaws that occur in timbers or planking. Sometimes called a *shan, shaken, or shaky.*

SHAKE UP A REEF

When a fast moving vessel, throws a long following wave across a wide area which gives the appearance of turbulence on a reef.

SHAKE-DOWN CRUISE

See: RIVER TRIALS.

SHAKINGS

The fibers of old line or cotton used in the making of OAKUM.

SHALLOW-DRAFT

A relative term; how shallow is shallow? The term is most often applied in reference to vessels of limited depth which ply the nation's inland waterways. It is sometimes used to describe vessels that can navigate on rivers that have lesser maintained depths, such as was the case on the Missouri up until the 1970s when six feet was the normal loading draft at a time when it was nine feet on other rivers. The term *shallow* is from the Old English *sceald*, meaning the same thing.

In steamboat days, *shallow-draft* vessels might be the only ones capable of navigating some rivers during any season. This was often the case on the Ohio River during the summer low-water season. On tributaries which had a minimum navigational depth all year, such as the Big Sandy River, necessity dictated the use or BATWING BOATS that drew little more than a foot of water. Some *shallow-draft* steamers that operated on the upper Missouri River were said to have been capable of running on spit.

SHANK

1. The proper name for the main support of an anchor betweens its "stock" and "arms" that carries the "flukes".
2. The straight part of a rivet or a bolt.
3. The part of a drill that holds and tightens the drill bit.

SHANTYBOAT

A non-powered barge-like flat with a house built on it, used by many families who lived along the river in the past. It has been given some notoriety by authors (and artists) Harlan and Anna Hubbard, and Lucian Ben Burman. *Shantyboaters* always claimed that by the grace of God the first three rows of the crops growing along the shoreline of a river belonged to them. Many farm owners took umbrage to that notion and a shotgun sometimes made the *shantyboat* owner cast off for easier pickings.

SHAPE

1. The manner, position, or condition of a tow being lined up to undertake a particular navigational maneuver, i.e. "He's getting in *shape* to run the bridge".

2. Not in the right or correct position of being lined up to properly undertake a navigational maneuver, i.e. "He's out of *shape* to run the bridge".

3. A channel report directive as to where to navigate, i.e. "After making the crossing from ABC light to ZXY light run down the *shape* of the shore....."

4. To a naval architect it usually means to give an area of a vessel some curvature.

SHAPED TIMBERS

When a wooden-hulled vessel required *shaped* or bent strakes, the timbers, 2 to $2^1/_2$ inches thick, were put into a large long tank filled with water. Heavy steel fire boxes were placed under the tank and set on fire to boil the water. After a sufficient time in the boiling water, usually four or five hours, men with grab hooks would fish out a timber from the tank and quickly form it up to the vessel hull frames while still hot to give it the necessary sheer, or somewhat twist the timber as needed, especially in the stern, when they spiked it into place.

SHAPES

1. Those visual aids referred to in Part C of the Inland Navigation Rules and its Annex I, consisting of balls, cones, and diamond *shapes* painted black which are required to be exhibited during certain navigational employments. See: DAY SIGNAL or SHAPE.

2. Steel structural lengths such as bars, angle irons, channels, T-bars, etc., used in vessel construction.

SHAVE

To run something extremely close, or to be involved in a near-miss situation, i.e., "In the next crossing, ya better *shave* that lower red or you'll get set down on the revetment with this tow", or "We had a close *shave* when we met the *NEVERSAIL* since the wind caught her and we almost came into collision".

"SHE"

Almost forever, at least on the Western Rivers, vessels have been said to be addressed in terms denoting the female gender, even those that might have the name of a male person. There has been a lot of hypothesis as to the origination, but no actual historical proof as to why. Some say that since most sailors were men, they thought of their ship as a maternal comforter and protector. Others say that vessels are like women: they are beautiful, very costly to maintain, and it takes skill to successfully handle them. However, in 2002, the London shipping news, Lloyd's List (which had used *she* and *her* since 1734) decided to start calling vessels an "it". We can only hope that this action from across the pond will not migrate to the river system.

"SHE TAKES THE HORNS"

See: ANTLERS.

SHEAR

1. A stress loading on plating or timbers that may cause them to break and/or overlap; or the strain on a part or pin that was holding something, such as a shaft in place, causing it to break.

2. Frictional stress on a river bot-

tom by the flow of water causing the movement of the bed material.

SHEATHING
A covering of thin boards, thin steel or sometimes copper sheets on the wooden hulls of steamboats in places of extreme wear due to ice or rubbing bottom. It is also sometimes called *double-plating* of old steel hulls that may frequently be leaking. See: DOUBLE-PLATE and ICE SHEATHING.

SHEAVE
The grooved wheel or roller in a BLOCK held in place by a pin. It is pronounced "shiv". The word is from the Germanic *sciba,* to mean "a disc" or "wheel".

SHEEN
The EPA defines the term as any amount of oil that causes a film or *sheen* upon, or discoloration of, the surface of the water.

SHEER
1. The longitudinal upward curvature of the main deck of a vessel. The term is related to "shear", meaning "to cut" (away).
2. A sudden movement of a vessel away from the course being steered, i.e. "She took an abrupt *sheer* away from the red buoys in the ZXY crossing. Guess there's a bar building out into the channel".

SHEER BARGE or BOOM
1. A *barge*, or floating *boom*, placed at the upper end of a fleet or dock, angled upriver into the shore at its bow, with the stern out in the river. Used to keep driftwood or ice from building up on a fleet of tied-off barges by allowing the debris to *sheer* off.
2. A floating structure used at some bridges to guide vessels into the bridge and also to protect the piers. See: SHEER FENCE (below).
3. Sometimes used at docks and wharfs to protect them from a vessel continually bumping against them due to wave action.

SHEER FENCE
A grouping of pilings with crossboarding attached that are placed above and below some narrow horizontal clearance bridges that are used to protect the bridge piers and the barges that may come in contact with them. These types of *fences* allow tows to lightly land on them and slide through a bridge without damage to the bridge or the tow.

SHEER OFF
To move away from, i.e., "In this shallow water she wants to *sheer off* the red buoy line".

SHEER PLAN
A side profile elevation drawing of a vessel.

SHEER STRAKE
The topmost STRAKE in a vessel's hull; in the case of a wooden vessel it is usually the thickest of the *strakes*, giving more longitudinal strength to the vessel.

SHEET PILING
Interlocking steel strips that are driven into a riverbed to construct mooring cells, build cofferdams, or fabricate dock structures.

SHELF
A ridge of rock making out into the river from the shore, which is at a lesser depth than the authorized channel. These can make for a bad day if not avoided.

SHELF TIMBER and CLAMP
Timbers that are laid longitudinally to support the deck beams. The main timber is called the *shelf,* and the supporting timbers are called *clamps*.

SHELL
The outside wooden planking or steel plating that form the bottom and

sides of a vessel's hull. The term comes from the Dutch *schel*, meaning "a covering of scale or shell".

SHELL BARGE
Basically the same thing as a SAND BARGE or flat, except that it transports sea shells. Mostly seen in the Gulf Coast area.

SHIFT
1. To move a barge from one position to another in a tow or in a fleet.
2. To transfer a barge from one dock to another, or from a fleet to a dock, or from a dock to a fleet or tow.
3. A change in the lateral direction of the current in a crossing.
4. A change in the direction of the wind.
5. A significant movement of cargo in a barge, causing a listing of the barge and the possibility of capsizing.

SHIFT BOAT
A small towboat that works at a fleet, dock, or harbor, moving barges into and out of tows, fleets, and terminals. Also called *day boats*, *dinner-bucket boats, fleet boats*, or *harbor boats*.

SHIFTING BAR
A sandbar that is cutting away and moving downriver, possibly causing channel changes. See: SAND WAVE.

SHIM
A piece of thin metal or wood, sometimes tapered, used to level or true up a piece of machinery or framing. It may also be applied to loose or slack places in fittings or machinery to tighten them.

SHINGLE
A wedged piece of wood similar to a type of narrow wooden house *shingle* that is indispensable when attempting to stop a leak in a vessel's hull. It is believed the term is from the Latin *scindula*, to mean "a split piece of wood". They are essential to be aboard vessels. *Shingles* were originally split from log timber sections called bolts with a "froe" which is a sharpened flat blade of metal a couple of inches wide, about a foot long with a loop on its end which was fitted with a wooden handle at a right angle to the blade. The blade was driven into the end of the timber with a mallet. The handle was then worked back and forth until it split off a piece of wood. Now, of course, a towboat or tug gets their *shingles* from a boat store who obtains them from a vendor who in turn gets them from a mill that pops them out by the thousands and wonders why a boat store would be buying them.

SHIP
1. Generally, on the inland waterways it is defined as a large vessel capable of navigating in the international sea-going trades.
2. In admiralty law just about anything floating falls within the jurisdiction of the admiralty court, including tugs, towboats, and barges.
3. To have cargo transported from one place to another by water.
4. To take on water through a crack or hole in the hull or an open hatch.
5. To place things in a correct position to work properly, i.e., *shipping* a rudder means to hang it after being repaired; to *ship* stores or gear is to place or stow them in their proper place; to *ship* cargo in a barge is to load it, etc.
6. The origin of the word is hazy. Does it predate Noah's Ark? However, it seems to come from the Germanic *schiff* and/or the Dutch *schip,* meaning the same thing as we spell and define *ship*. Others say it has a Teutonic origin.

SHIP CHANNEL
A fairway leading into a port that is used by deep-draft vessels, such as the Houston Ship Channel leading to the Port of Houston from the Gulf of Mexico.

SHIPBUILDING
1. The art or design of vessels.
2. The construction of vessels.

SHIPFITTER
A person who makes the templates, then properly marks, shapes and constructs or welds the plates for the hull of a vessel.

SHIPMATE
A person who has worked, or who is working, with another crew member aboard the same vessel. It is only used if the relationship was cordial. If not, it is usually phrased as, "Yeah, I was on a boat with him, but he wasn't any *shipmate*".

SHIPMENT
The cargo being shipped in a barge or on a packetboat.

SHIPPER
A company or person who ships cargo or goods on a vessel (barge) from one place to another at a specified price.

SHIPPING PAPERS or MANIFEST
A bill of lading listing the cargo, the amount, kinds, grades, and approximate quantity, its destination and consignee, as well as any other terms and agreements between the shipper and the carrier.

SHIPPING UP
1. The process of getting a tug or towboat ready to undertake the task for which it was designed, i.e., assemble the crew, make sure all the necessary gear is on board, take on fuel, fill the potable and wash water tanks, bring stores aboard, and make sure the vessel is well equipped to get underway.
2. The act of starting the engine of a tug or towboat, or the act of engaging the engine to start the vessel's movement, either in the ahead or reverse position.

SHIP'S BELL
See: BELL

SHIP'S PAPERS
See: DOCUMENTATION

SHIPSHAPE
A vessel that is clean, well kept, with all gear properly stowed in place, and a crew that is knowledgeable in its duties. The term is used on the rivers the same way it is understood for vessels that go to sea.

SHIP-UP JACK
The lever in the engine room of a steamer that sets the forward or astern direction a paddlewheel is to turn.

SHIPWRIGHT
A person who builds wooden vessels, or who repairs them.

SHIPYARD
A place where vessels are built or repaired.

S.H.I.T.
With the advent of the internet, wonderful information can be obtained, but sometimes the accounts given on the web do not increase one's knowledge. Such is the case of the Urban Legend created by the posting "the" definition of the word *SHIT*, as follows:

"In the 16th and 17th centuries manure, used for fertilizer, was transported in cloth bags by ship. In its dry form these bags were not particularly heavy, but when stored in lower parts of the hull in wooden ships they would tend to absorb water from condensation and the elements. This not only made the bags heavier, but the process of fermentation would begin, which would create methane gas. The methane would begin to build up below decks. If someone went into the hold to inspect the cargo with an oil lamp or a lighted pipe an explosion would occur. Several ships were

destroyed in this manner before the loss of the vessels was determined. After the problematic source of the disasters was found, bags of manure were required to be stamped with the term *S.H.I.T.* which, at the time was an acronym for "Ship High In Transit". This was to help insure that excessive moisture would not come in contact with the sacks."
A search of maritime tomes, legal glossaries, and laws of the era indicate there is no truth in the foregoing etymology of the word *shit*. Be that as it may, the word has been heard and used by a Pilot or two in the couple of centuries of Western River navigation. The word is usually preceded by an "Oh", and, when combined with *shit*, can stand alone or can be part of a comment used by a river Pilot while downbound with 35 loaded barges when an engine fails just above the Vicksburg, MS, bridge, or when a flank is held too long in a sharp bend on the Missouri River and the tow is set aground on a bar, or in other similar circumstances. The word, of course, is not obscene, or blasphemous, but is considered somewhat vulgar. So, in the future when one feels the need to use the "word" coming on, just say: "Oh, ship high in transit". We'll all know what you mean.

SHOAL(ING)

An area of the river that is extremely shallow; at times when river gauges are low a sandbar may be building up or already visible. The word comes from the Old English *sceald,* meaning "shallow".

SHOCK LINE

A heavy section of line, single, doubled, or tripled up, that is very strong, but elastic. It is used as a *shock absorber* on a towing wire when engaged in towing barges astern. Tugs may use it in rough seas when lines may become slack and then tighten suddenly. Towboats towing barges "on a string" while in ice encounter the same problems of sudden stoppage and sudden thrust ahead. On a string of barges behind a towboat, the couplings between them are loosely wired, with the eye of the wire and a fitting on the barge coupled together with numerous parts of soft line used to cushion the *shock*.

SHOLE or SOLE

A piece of planking placed under a timber or any other post or spar that is used for shoring, to give it more of a bearing surface in order to spread the point of direct force. The word derives from the Latin *solea,* in reference to "sandal or sill".

SHOOTING THE FALLS

See: RUNNING THE FALLS.

SHORE

1. The land that is adjacent to the river's waters. Technically, it is the land below the ordinary high-water mark. The term is derived from Low German *schore,* related to "shear" as "a division between land and sea".
2. The place where crew members go when they leave their vessel.
3. The act of putting a temporary brace on a structure to provide support, or to keep cargo, gear, or equipment from shifting.

SHORE BOSS

An office manager who is seldom, if ever, on a towboat or tug, but who thinks he/she has the divine knowledge of every navigational situation. Sometimes the counsel is good, and sometimes it defies rational reality and practicable applicability. But if you are on a tug or towboat, it's great if he/she listens and knows and understands the problems you may have, as well as offering some decent and constructive advice.

SHORE POWER

Electrical power that is supplied to a vessel that is on drydock, or tied to a dock or wharf and its generators are shut down. In ocean-going vessels when shore power is used it is referred to as AMP (alternative marine power) or the slang term "cold ironing".

SHORELINE
The imaginary line where the river's waters touch the land regardless of the gauge reading.

SHORING
The use of timbers and/or other material for bracing cargo that may be shifting, or to support a temporary repair in the hull of a vessel that has sustained damage in an accident.

SHORT BLAST
The sounding of a vessel's whistle for about one second's duration. See: WHISTLE SIGNALS.

SHORT SPLICE
The act of marrying two pieces of line together with usually three tucks on each side, though sometimes four are used. It is the most common line-joining *splice* used on the river. It is strong, but somewhat bulky; however, where used it doesn't have to reeve through anything. See: LONG SPLICE and SPLICE.

SHORT TON
A weight measurement of 2,000 pounds.

SHORT-HANDED
When a vessel is manned without a full complement of crew.

SHOT
A section of chain, usually 15 fathoms long, connected to another chain. Not seen now on the river, but ships measure the length or scope of chain (usually called cable) they have out by the number of *shots* that are deployed. It is unknown exactly where the term originated. Some say it has its roots in a version of "shoot". One has to wonder what a *shot* fired from a gun has to do with a section of chain, or even a small jigger of liquor.

SHOT BLASTING
A process employed by some shipyards that runs steel plates and structural shapes through a machine that blasts the steel with small steel *shot* to remove mill scale, blow it away, and then spray on a thin coat of primer prior to the steel going into the yard for construction.

SHOTGUN PILOTHOUSE
See: RETRACTABLE PILOTHOUSE

SHOVE
The act of moving a vessel or tow ahead, i.e., "I'm going to *shove* up just below the point and see you on two whistles", or "We can't *shove* this tow in this strong current so we're going to double-trip". The word comes from the Dutch *schuiven*, meaning "to push hard, or to thrust".

SHOVE OFF
To leave or depart a place, i.e., "We're going to *shove off* from the RST dock at 3:00 this afternoon".

SHOVE UNDER
When a tow is running in slack water or in an eddy and the bow end of the tow hits swift current, the head is likely to dive and the lead barge(s) may be swamped. Also, on some vessels with low freeboard, either a towboat without a tow or one that may be pushing its tow too fast may cause the bow of one of the barges to become submerged.

SHOWBOAT
A floating theater vessel. *Showboating* was first seen on the river when keelboats traveled along the Western Rivers where populations were growing and people craved for some entertainment in their lives. The first *showboat* is reported to be a keeler operated by Noah Ludlow in 1815

and named *NOAH'S ARK*. The first vessel built as a *showboat*, the *FLOATING THEATER*, was launched at Pittsburgh in 1831 by the Chapmans, a family of entertainers. Other *showboats* followed, but stopped their performances during the Civil War. However, they were reestablished soon after hostilities ceased. The owners produced melodramas and music for their patrons. By the 1940s and WW II, the traveling *showboats* that were still operating went to permanent locations at river cities that could provide the attendance needed to support them. The oldest *showboat* still operating as a theatre in 2006 is the *MAJESTIC,* located in Cincinnati, Ohio. There are numerous entertainment boats at present in various cities, but they do not travel from river to river, or city to city.

To learn more about the subject, read Philip Graham's *Showboats* and Betty Bryant's *Here Comes the Showboat,* which tell about the families who played and ran the boats, and their history. Then, of course, read the glamorized novel *Showboat* by Edna Ferber, written in 1926, which became a famous musical. See: OL' MAN RIVER.

SHREVE, CAPT. HENRY MILLER

One of the notable pioneers in river history. He was born in 1785 in New Jersey, but at age 22 he started keelboating. He built his first steamboat in 1814, which he operated successfully to New Orleans and back up the Ohio River. In 1816 he built the sidewheel steamer *WASHINGTON* that gained fame as breaking the FULTON-LIVINGSTON monopoly for the steamboat trade on the river. The steamer itself was innovative and was widely copied. Captain Shreve built the hull of the vessel with a shallow draft and a broad beam. The boiler and engines were mounted on the main deck horizontally instead of down in the hold.

In 1826 Shreve took the post of Superintendent of Western River Improvements. He designed the first steam-powered SNAGBOAT, the *HELIOPOLIS*, to clear sawyers, snags, and planters that played havoc with the hulls of steamboats. He cleared the RED RIVER RAFT that had prevented navigation on that river. Also, Shreve designed many channel improvements on the river, and was the developer of the CUT-OFF on the Lower Mississippi River in order to shorten the stream and speed up the river's flow in certain stretches. His name lives on in the 21st Century; the U.S. Corps of Engineers named a heavy-lift derrick barge after him, the *HENRY M. SHREVE*, with a capacity of 550 tons lift (350 tons @ 105 feet radius). That's more than his snagboats ever thought of lifting.

SHUT-OUT VISIBILITY

When visibility is reduced to being unable to see beyond the bow of one's vessel, due to fog, rain, snow, smoke, sand or dust storms, or other similar situations. It is worse than "restricted visibility".

SHUTTLE BOAT

A boat that makes a consistent round-turn run between two ports or docks on a regular basis.

SIDE

The flanks of the shell of a vessel and its superstructure, both down the port and starboard *sides* in a fore and aft direction. The *side* shell connects to the bottom structure at its lower juncture and to the deck structure at the upper end.

SIDE TANK

1. One of the tanks on the side shell of a towboat or tug. It will usually contain fuel to propel the vessel, or for water supply or it may be a void tank.

2. One of the *void tanks* on either the port or starboard side of a double-skinned barge.

SIDE-LAUNCHING

A shipyard that *launches* the vessels it builds on CRADLES that are placed at right angles, or athwartships, underneath the vessel being *launched* allowing it to slide down the launch-ways parallel to the shoreline. Often times these type ways can also be used to haul out vessels in order to drydock and repair them. See: LAUNCHING, LAUNCHWAYS & LAUNCHING WAYS and SKIDS.

SIDELIGHTS

The lights to be displayed on the sides of a tug or towboat, as well as at the outboard bow ends of a barge tow, with a red light on the port side and a green light on the starboard side, each to show from right ahead to 22.5 degrees abaft the beam on their respective sides.

SIDEWHEELER

A steamer that had a paddlewheel on each side of the vessel. Early designs showed the wheels slightly forward of amidships, but the design of the Str. *J.M. WHITE* with its paddlewheels about two-thirds aft of the bow became the norm after she made record-breaking trips.

SIGHT

The condition where "vessels shall be deemed to be in sight of one another only when one can be observed visually from the other" as defined under Rule 3 of the Navigation Rules, however the ability "to observe" other vessels has changed greatly over the years with the ability "to view" other vessels on a radar screen or an electronic chart. The ability for actual visual contact is most important however, in regard to only sounding maneuvering signals "when vessels are in sight of one another". Otherwise a vessel must continue sounding fog signals.

SIGHT GLASS

1. A heavy shatter-proof glass that is affixed to tank barges at each ullage hatch of cargo tanks equipped with a closed gauging system in order that the TANKERMAN who is loading or discharging the cargo from the barge can visually estimate the amount of cargo in the tank without opening the ullage hatch and chance the breathing of toxic vapors.

2. A glass tube mounted on a steam boiler at the median desired level of the boiler's water. Its designed intent is to indicate the level of water in the boiler, similar to the purpose of GAUGE COCKS.

SIGNALS, HAND

There is a semi-uniform set of signals that are used by crewmen to *signal* the Pilot when they are out on a tow and voice communication is not available. Some examples of giving direction or information by hand signals include to steer to starboard or port, to be clear of an object, to stop the engines, to back down, to come ahead, the degree or closeness to a lock wall or bridge pier, etc. Some pilots may desire different particular hand gestures, but generally the standard signals on most towboats and tugs are shown in the pictures at the end of the "H" section.

SIGNALS OF ACTION – SIGNALS OF INTENT

In accordance with the International Navigation Rules, when two vessels are meeting and neither vessel sees any need to alter its course, no sound signals are given. If one, or both, vessels believe they should take some action to insure a safe passage they sound a signal to the other vessel, one short blast to mean "I am altering my course to starboard", or two short blasts to mean "I am altering my course to port", or three short blasts to mean "I am operating astern propulsion". The other meeting vessel does not answer with a like signal, unless it is also taking some action. These are called *Signals of Action*.

On the internal waters of the United States, and in accordance with the Inland Navigation Rules, when two vessels are meeting one vessel will signal the side on which it wants to meet. If it sounds one short blast it means "I intend to leave you on my port side", or if it sounds two short blasts it means "I intend to leave you on my starboard side". The other vessel will sound a similar signal if in agreement, and if not, will sound the danger whistle. Then both vessels are required to take precautionary actions until an agreement is reached. On the Western Rivers the downbound vessel has the right-of-way and will sound the initial passing signal. These are called *Signals of Intent*.

SILL
The concrete base support at the entrance to a LOCK on which the lock gate(s) are sealed when closed to prevent the escape of water flow. Also, the same for gates that are used at the entrance to a GRAVING DOCK. The word is of Germanic origin *schwelle*, meaning "threshold".

SILT
Fines of sand, clay, topsoil, or other similar material carried in suspension in running river current that is eventually deposited as sediment on the river bed as it makes its way to the sea. The act of *silting in*, or *siltation*, means a water course has dropped its suspended load of sediment and an area has filled up with *silt*. It is an example of why the State of Louisiana exists. The word is of Scandinavian background relating to the marshes in coastal areas, coming from *sylt*, meaning "salt marsh". See: SAND WAVES.

SIMULATED FLOW MODEL
Computer models used by the USACE to generate hydrographic behavioral studies of river currents and their effects on a section of river or a structure. Studies are accomplished both in actual physical models for large complex evaluation of projects as well as by using computer modeling for smaller less involved studies.

SIMULATOR
A training device used to assist Pilots in decision-making. They are set up as fully equipped pilothouses and include radios, radar, electronic charts, alarms, etc., and look out at full visual imaging of a section of river or a canal. The imaging screen has changing weather conditions, interaction with other vessels, and emergency situations. At present the two most geared to inland river and canal operations are operated by the Seamen's Church Institute at Paducah, KY and Houston, TX.

SINGLE LOCKAGE
The locking of a towboat and its entire tow in one operation, not requiring a double lockage.

SINGLE SCREW
A vessel that has only one propeller.

SINGLE SET-OVER
See: SET-OVER SINGLE.

SINGLE SIDEBAND
An older technology of AM frequency radio communications which has been phased out in favor of VHF radio, computers, GPS, cell phones, and satellite communication.

SINGLE SKIN
Refers to a barge or other vessel where there is only one barrier between the water environment and the cargo, machinery spaces, and other sections of the vessel. Most tank barges used to be constructed in this manner with no inner bottom or side wing tanks. Now all barges, except deck barges, being built are of DOUBLE-HULL design and construction.

SINGLE-UP
1. To remove all extra lines and safety rigging from a tow, or part of a tow; usually when leaving the tow in a fleet, exchanging tows with another vessel, or when getting ready to drop barges at a dock.

2. An operation when getting ready to leave a fleet with a vessel, or a vessel

with a tow, to take in, remove, or cast off, and take aboard all but one mooring line.

SINK
1. To descend lower in the water, i.e., when the hull of a vessel is receiving fuel, or when it is leaking and is taking on water. If the leakage is severe, the vessel is said to be *sinking*. The word comes from the Dutch *ziken,* and the German *sinken.*
2. When a vessel's hull has taken on water beyond its ability to sustain buoyancy, the past tense is used indicating that the vessel *sank*. In describing where the vessel may be in relation to a navigational hazard, it may be said that "a *sunken* barge is located at the right descending pier of the JKL Bridge".

SINKER
A heavy concrete block with a steel eye ring that is used as a holding anchor for navigational buoys in many rivers and in coastal areas.

SISAL
A fiber made from the leaves of the Agave plant in Mexico that is used in making a type of rope line. It was extensively utilized when manila fiber was difficult to obtain, but is of less strength, is stiffer when it becomes water-soaked, and is seldom seen today on the river, especially with the introduction of the various synthetic fiber lines that are available.

SISTER HOOK
A type of holding device made of two matching parts that slip or marry over one another to form a closed fastening that will not slip off an object to which it is attached while under tension. Often used on a crane's lift line when raising and lowering small boats, heavy hoses, barrels, etc. Also called a *clip, clasp,* or *matching hook.*

SISTER KEELSON
Timbers that are SCARPHED and placed on the side of the main KEELSON to give additional strength to a wooden-hulled vessel.

SISTER SHIP or VESSEL
A term to describe towboats, tugs, or barges that are of basically the same design and construction. Sometimes called *copycat vessels.*

SITUATIONAL AWARENESS
A new term that is now used in investigations of accidents to determine if a person involved has, or had, lost their *situational awareness* of what was occurring and therefore is, or was, at a degree of fault in the occurrence. It appears to be the case where one has to prove they did not lose it when a catch-all charge of "loss of *situational* aware-n*ess*" is levied.

SKEG
1. A vertical fin (one or more) that extends downward from a vessel hull, either fixed or movable, and sometimes capable of being hoisted by a winch when not in use. Its purpose is to reduce YAW and assist in keeping a vessel on a straight course. Often used on barges when being towed astern. See: DAGGER BOARD. The word is from the Old Norse *skegg,* meaning "beard".
2. Not often seen currently on river barges. However, on sidewheel river steamers *skegs* were sometimes placed on the stern corners for assistance in maintaining a straight course.
3. A small fin placed on some buoys to give them direction in current and to retard their turning or spinning.

SKELETON CREW
A vessel that has the bare minimum number of crew members on board to operate it. This may occur when running LIGHT BOAT from one area to another; while standing by a fleet during high water; while making limited shifts at a dock or similar employment not requiring the full complement of a crew.

SKELETON TOWER

A *type of construction* that is common today that is being erected to hold aids to navigation along the banks of the river and canal system. Not too long ago fixed aids that were posted along the river system consisted of heavy lumber construction, or perhaps a light or dayboard was nailed to an available tree. With the revetting of riverbanks many trees close to shoreline are gone and the expense, weight and time to build structures has required the USCG Aids to Navigation branch to devise a better, faster and more efficient system of displaying aids. Generally, holding structures for lights and daymarks is a triangular metal latticework frame that can be efficiently erected in a minimal amount of time. It probably became known as a *skeleton tower* since it doesn't have much body, only bones.

SKIDS

To launch a vessel end-on or sideways on wooden runners, usually for a boat that is built in a small shipyard that doesn't have a permanent launchways. The term comes from when loggers used to *skid* their logs off the bank into a waterway. Itinerant loggers out of work were said to live where they were usually employed, or "skid-row". Originally, it is believed the word came from the Norse *skith,* meaning a "stick of wood", or "ski".

SKIFF

A small utility boat that is carried aboard a towboat or tug and used for a variety of purposes, usually with a pointed bow and square stern. It can be propelled by oars or an outboard motor. This is the name most often used by crewmen from the southern region of the Mississippi Basin. Also, called by numerous other names, i.e., yawl, jon or john boat, dinghy, pirogue, etc. See: YAWL. The *skiff* type of vessel apparently derives from the old German *schif,* meaning "ship".

SKIMMER

See: OIL SKIMMER

SKIN

The shell planking or steel plating of a vessel's hull. If in a wooden hull there are two layers of planking the outer layer is called "the case".

SKIN COOLER

A system of connecting channels welded to the outer skin of a vessel's hull, or a manufactured grid unit, through which the engine cooling water is piped and circulated, thereby reducing its temperature to approximately that of the surrounding river water.

SKIPPER

A term sometimes used in referring to the Master of a vessel.

SKY PILOT

An affectionate title or name given to a clergyman who appeals to a higher personage when navigating rough waters and stormy nights such as those of the Seaman's Church Institute who minister in behalf of, and to, seamen and rivermen.

SKYLIGHTS

Openings of a steamboat on the TEXAS DECK that allowed for *skylights* to be placed between it and the HURRICANE DECK, providing both light and air into the SALOON.

SLACK

1. A line or wire that is not under tension. If the tension needs to be increased one has to "take up the *slack*". The term derives from the Latin, *laxus,* to mean "loose", or "not drawn tightly".
2. The act of reducing the tension on a line or wire, i.e., "*Slack* off on the head line".
3. Granules of coal fines up to about $1/4$ inch in size, more than coal "dust", but of lesser size than coal "lumps".

SLACK WATER

1. Water where the current is very

slow. The place where Pilots like to run upbound in order to make more miles. On a river, upbound vessels mostly stay on the bar side where the current is less strong.

2. In tidal areas it is the time between the "flood" and the "ebb" flows.

3. The pooling of a river by the use of dams with locks to provide for what is sometimes termed "*slack water* navigation".

SLICK

1. When there is an oily surface on the river or canal. See: SHEEN.

2. A flat calm on the surface of the water.

SLICKER SUIT

Rain gear for crew to wear in inclement weather.

SLIDE

The sideways or lateral movement of a vessel or tow when steering a sharp bend. As the vessel moves deeper into the bend, the *slide* towards the bend side of the steering maneuver increases due to faster current in the bend than that on the bar side.

SLIDING or ROLLING LOCK GATES

See: LOCK GATES.

SLING

1. A short piece of wire about four to six feet in length with an eye in each end, or one eye in one end and a short length of heavy chain links attached to the other end. Used in wiring barges together with one eye placed over a deck fitting and the other coupled to a ratchet. See: HULA HOOP. Also called a *strap*.

2. A length of wire fitted with eyes or hooks that is used to hoist or lower cargo or gear when attached to a crane or boom.

SLIP

1. The difference between the PITCH of the propeller if it was turning one revolution in a solid mass from the actual forward thrust of a vessel moving through the water.

2. The difference between the mean circumference of a PADDLEWHEEL that turns one revolution in a solid mass and the actual advance the vessel would make through the water.

3. A place to moor a vessel, usually between two piers. Mostly used on the river in reference to small craft moorings, as in "boat *slip*".

SLIPWAYS

See: LAUNCHING, LAUNCH-WAYS, & LAUNCHING-WAYS and SKIDS.

SLOP TANK

A tank on board a vessel that receives and contains oily bilge waste until it can later be pumped off to an approved disposal facility.

SLOPE SHEET

The slanting internal incline of the end(s) of the cargo hopper of a raked barge.

SLOPES

A timber crib structure filled with rock on a sloped incline that was placed below a NAVIGABLE DAM CHUTE (see) to keep a vessel running the chute at a dam built for milling from submerging a flatboat if the upstream and downstream water level differential at the dam was too great.

SLOT

Refers to the position a vessel might have in a queue of tows waiting their turn to lock, or where there is a channel blockage waiting to be cleared.

SLOUGH

Generally, refers to a backwater shallow area that is not navigable by loaded tows. It is pronounced "sloo".

SLOW BELL

Running a vessel or tow at minimum RPM, i.e., "I'm just running *slow bell* to save fuel since we'll have to wait up at DEF Lock anyway".

SLUDGE
A buildup of sediment in fuel tanks, or in the bottoms of petroleum product barges.

SLUICE
A type of gate or valve that regulates the flow of water from one height to another.

SLUSH
Generally on the river it refers to ice that has been broken and churned up by numerous vessel propellers. If it refreezes it can cause channel blockages. When it first appears it means that sheet ice will be soon appearing. If it is free floating after an ice season it usually means the ice is disintegrating and perhaps boating can return to normal.

SMALL CRAFT ADVISORY
A notice issued by the National Weather Service (NWS) that indicates fairly strong winds of up to 38 mph are forecast that may result in dangerous conditions for small vessels, or those with low freeboard. At certain places the NWS will fly a single red pennant by day and display a red light over a white light by night. They discontinued these signals in 2006; however, due to public complaint they have reinstated the practice.

SMALL STUFF
Cordage that is less than one inch in diameter, used for tying things, or as bindings.

SMELLING THE BANK or REEF
In a narrow, shallow channel it is the tendency of the stern to be sucked toward the shore and the bow end of a vessel or tow to veer away from the shore. See: BANK CUSHION and BANK EFFECT.

SMELLING THE BOTTOM
When a vessel is in shallow water, the flow is constricted between the bed of the river or canal and the bottom of the vessel and its tow. In such conditions a vessel doesn't readily respond to rudder placement, its speed decreases and cavitation occurs, or perhaps the vessel sucks down and bumps the riverbed.

SMOKESTACK
The place where the exhaust of the emissions of a vessel from the burning of carbon is emitted to the atmosphere. Sometimes called a *chimney* on old steamers, a *funnel* on ships, and mostly on towboats and tugs it is simply the *stack*.

SMOKING IT UP
Said of the old steamboats when they were getting ready to leave a landing and the Engineer was getting up steam in the boilers so that the chimneys were churning out smoke from the firebox.

SNAG
A tree or log that has become planted on the river bottom but is visible above the surface of the water. It could cause damage to a wheel if hit. At times, *snags* could catch other driftwood and in effect act as a dike, changing the direction of the flow in a river and the channel line. The word *snag* is of Norse origin, meaning "a stump of a tree trunk", that became known as a timber or tree submerged in a body of water as an obstruction to navigation. Later it became something that obstructs, catches, or describes an impediment to an otherwise successful endeavor. See: PLANTER and SAWYER.

SNAG CHAMBER
A watertight compartment in the bow portion of steamboats to protect it from sinking in case they ran into a snag that might puncture the hull.

SNAGBOAT
A vessel designed to remove snags, sawyers, and planters out of the navigable

channel to prevent damage to vessel hulls. The first mechanized one was the steamer *HELIOPOLIS*, designed by Capt. Henry Shreve. Two hulls connected just aft of the pointed bows with a strong beam holding them together. The boat would ram up against a snag and catch it on the snag beam; chains would then be wound around it and, with the use of cranes and strong winches, the snag would be pulled up and cut up by steam-powered saws. The pieces were returned to the river. These boats became known as *Uncle Sam's Toothpullers*. A few years later Shreve, with another snagboat, cleared the RED RIVER RAFT on that stream. *Snagboats* were so successful that they no longer exist. If a few snags do hang up in a channel, a barge with a crane on it will remove them.

SNAKE
1. To put a line or wire into or through a small opening.
2. The proud name (at least to them) of a Kanawha River boatman.

SNAKE LINE
A line that is run from one diagonal position of a barge to that of another barge in order to check it into a position in the tow; or to check a towboats position in tow from one place to another, i.e., "Take a line to the port stern of the BBB barge and as we drop it back I'll *snake* it into the notch with the capstan".

SNAKE RIVER
Approximately 1,038 miles in length, this river is the major tributary of the Columbia River system. It rises in Yellowstone National Park and flows through the Grand Teton National Park. It is navigable for 140 miles from its mouth to the head of navigation at Lewiston, ID, by transiting four locks. The river has numerous dams on it to generate hydro-electric power and to provide irrigation. See: COLUMBIA-SNAKE RIVER SYSTEM.

SNAME
See: SOCIETY OF NAVAL ARCHITECTS AND MARINE ENGINEERS.

SNAP-BACK ZONE
The area where a line or wire could forcefully recoil upon breaking, somewhat like a rubber band, causing injury or damage to anything in its path. Some types of synthetic lines are especially dangerous in this regard.

SNAPE
In wooden vessels it is the beveling or tapering of the end of a beam.

SNATCH BLOCK
A block with one SHEAVE and a hinged shell, or cheek, that can be opened to allow it to be placed directly over a bight of a line or wire without having to reeve it through the end of the block.

SNEAK BOX
A small boat about 12 feet by four feet, drawing about a foot, but can be of varying sizes. It was developed along the coastal waters of the Atlantic for hunting. Its name comes from its ability in marsh grasses to sneak up on waterfowl. Although *sneak boxes* are not a familiar sight on the Western Rivers, the term became known when Nathaniel Bishop (in 1875) took a trip in one from Pittsburgh to the Gulf of Mexico, which he christened the *CENTENNIAL REPUBLIC* and wrote a book called *Four Months in a Sneak Box*.

SNOW
1. Used when referring to the clouding of a radar screen by flickering white spots caused by interference of the signal, or by precipitation giving the appearance of a mass of snow falling.
2. White stuff in the air that are frozen ice crystals of vapor seen as white flakes.
3. What someone from the office does when they tell the Captain why

they can't get a relief for some crew member, or why they have to reduce costs on the towboat or a tugboat.

SNUB IT
To smartly check or slow a running line leading from a deck fitting, but not so smartly as to increase its tension to the degree that causes it to part. If it is *snubbed* on a single timberhead it is called a "snubbing post" or a "checkpost".

SNY
In wooden boat building, it is a term used to describe the curvature of the wooden planks when fitted into the hull. See: SHAPED TIMBERS and SPILING.

SOCIETY OF NAVAL ARCHITECTS AND MARINE ENGINEERS (SNAME)
A professional organization for people who design vessels, the machinery on them, the dynamics and effects of the environment that surrounds them, and all technical aspects of navigation. Their members issue many knowledgeable marine science papers every year.

SOFT DIKES
A type of dike for channel flow control that has been used on the Mississippi River just below Baton Rouge, LA, in Red Eye Crossing to reduce the amount of dredging that was required yearly. Historically, modern dike construction is of piling and rock, but it was believed accidents could occur with hard dikes in this extremely busy section of river. It was decided to build the underwater dikes using strong bags made of geotextile material, fill them with sand, and place them on the river's bed. The bags ranged in size from 40 to 115 feet in length and were 45 feet in diameter.

SOFT LASHINGS
A small group of barges being pushed by a towboat that are connected together by lines rather than made up together with wires and ratchets (hard rigging). Most often this type of towing is for short distances in a harbor between fleets or docks.

SOFT LINE
Fiber line, either natural or synthetic, as opposed to wire line.

SOFT PATCH
A makeshift temporary repair that is used to stop leakage in a hull. Usually it is a piece of wood or steel plate with adequate gasket material on it that is placed over the holed area with a long bolt through its center. When covering the ruptured area, a bar with a hole in its center is placed over the bolt from the plate piece. The bar, sometimes called a STRONGBACK, is then bolted and tightened to secure the *patch* until permanent repair can be made.

SOLAS
An acronym for *Safety of Life at Sea*. It is an International Treaty that has been revised and added to ever since the first one was created in response to the sinking of the *RMS TITANTIC* in 1912. A conference was held and international agreement was reached and signed in 1914. At present the Conference meets every four years. Along with the first agreement on ice patrols, radio communication and life-saving equipment, the Conference also has set out protocols that have been adopted for ship structures, stability, propulsion, electrical systems, fire safety, navigation, dangerous cargoes, and other subjects. Although the vessels that navigate on the Western Rivers and our internal canals are not subject to the provisions of *SOLAS*, usually the thrust of its provisions are often adopted as regulatory initiatives by the USCG for inland vessels.

SOLE
See: SHOLE.

SOLSTICE

The two times a year when the sun reaches its maximum northward (about 21 June for summer) and southward (about 22 December for winter) declinations from the celestial equator. It is from the Latin *solstitium,* meaning *sol* for "sun" and *stitus* to "stand still", or for "the time that the sun stands still".

SOMERSAULTING

The sail area of packet and excursion vessels makes it difficult for them to get away from a landing if there is a strong onshore wind blowing. *Somersaulting* is a maneuver that is used to overcome the wind by first putting the vessel's rudders hard down toward the channel and ringing up the engineer to come full astern. When the vessel backs away and will no longer turn, the engines are stopped, the rudders fully toward the opposite direction, and "full astern" is again rung. As the boat whips around and heads into the wind, the engines are stopped, the order to come "full ahead" is given, and the steering rudders are used to maneuver as necessary. You're safely underway to the next port.

SONS & DAUGHTERS OF PIONEER RIVERMEN (S & D)

An organization first formed in 1939 to preserve and promote the history of steamboating and the heritage of our inland river system. A quarterly journal called the *S & D REFLECTOR* is published. One is not required to have a relative who was a *pioneer riverman* to join, but if you are interested in steamboats and riverboats you will enjoy the organization.

SOOGEE

To wash down a vessel or a section of it, i.e., "We are going to *soogee* the 2nd deck on the after watch". The term is a shortened version of a sea-going term, *soogee-moogee,* that was a solution of washing powder and/or caustic soda for cleaning paintwork. It has been spelled many different ways, such as: suegee, soogy, sewgee, suji, sujee, soojie, sugee, and probably others, but the word is always pronounced as *sue—jee*. Like its spelling, there are many versions as to the origination of the term, from Arabic sailors to those from Japan.

SOUND

1. A wide body of water between barriers, such as the Mississippi *Sound* on the Gulf Coast.
2. A term to indicate free of defects, suitable for use.
3. A signal given on a vessel's WHISTLE.
4. Measuring depth. See: SOUNDING.

SOUND SIGNALS

The audible whistle *signals* to be used by vessels in different navigational situations are described in Part D, *Sound and Light Signals*, Rules 32 through 38, as well as in technical Annexes III and IV of the NAVIGATION RULES. See: WHISTLE.

SOUNDING

1. The act of measuring the depth of water with a marked SOUNDING POLE, a LEAD LINE, or by an electronic *sounding* machine.
2. An indicated depth noted on a chart, or chart curve.
3. To measure the depth of cargo in a tank barge.
4. To take a measurement of the depth of any water in bunkers, or void spaces, especially barges.

SOUNDING POLE

A long wooden or aluminum *pole*, about 20-24 feet in length, that is painted in alternating foot-long contrasting colors, usually red and white with a black strip at the 10-foot mark, used to sound the depth of water in the channel or at landings. Most times it is the PIKE POLE doing double duty.

SOUNDING WELL or PIPE or TUBE

A pipe on the deck of a vessel that

extends into the bottom of a tank where measurements can be taken with a metal rod or sounding tape to determine how much fuel, or water, or dry, the tank may contain.

SOUP or SOUPY

Except when referring to what a cook may serve at dinnertime, the term is mostly used to refer to heavy weather that causes visibility problems for a Pilot when navigating in rain, snow, and especially in fog, i.e. "It sure is *soupy* out there tonight. Can't see more than a tow length ahead. If it keeps up we may have to choke a stump".

SOURCE

From whence a river or steam originates, i.e., the *source* of the Mississippi River is Lake Itasca in Minnesota, while the *source* of the Ohio River is its two tributaries where they join, the Allegheny River and the Monongahela River, etc.

SOUTHBOUND

The downbound direction (with the flow of a river) that a vessel is traveling on the inland waterways. For instance, a tow leaving Nashville, TN, on the Cumberland River, bound for the Ohio River would be *southbound,* even though it would be traveling in a northerly compass direction. The opposite of NORTHBOUND.

SOUTHWEST PASS

The main navigable artery of the Mississippi River to the Gulf of Mexico for seagoing vessels through the delta from the HEAD OF PASSES, where the river officially terminates.

SPALES

Sometimes termed *cross spales* or *spalls*. They are temporary planks or timbers used to hold the framing of wooden vessels at their proper spacing until they can be fastened in place.

SPAN

1. A measured length between support members of a vessel.

2. The distance between two or more places, such as a line between its extremities from where it starts to where it leads to a pulley, fastening, object, another line, etc.

3. A particular draw in a bridge that may have more than one *span* that is navigable, i.e., "I'm going to run the right-hand *span*", or "I'll run the shore *span* if you want to come down through the main *span*".

4. The length between the supports of a bridge that crosses a navigable waterway. The only practical way to build one is to have the bridge pier supports on each bank.

SPANISH WINDLASS

See: CAJUN RATCHET.

SPANNER (WRENCH)

A wrench that is used to tighten small hoses. The rotating female end fitting of a hose has two small pins attached, 180 degrees apart. The curved end of the *spanner wrench* has a hole in it that fits over the pin, allowing a person to easily and speedily tighten the hose. Generally used on potable water hoses and fire hoses.

SPAR

1. To keep vessels off, or away from, the shore, or other objects. *Spar* material usually consists of heavy timbers, pipes, or steel beams that are called *spar poles*. The word comes from the Old Norse *sperrask*, meaning "to kick out".

2. A general term used to describe a mast, boom, gaff, etc., and can refer to any pole used on a vessel.

SPAR BARGE

A barge, usually removed from active general cargo service that has been securely moored to the shore and is used in a fleet to tie off active barges. It will act as a *spar* to keep them off the shore and from becoming grounded in a falling river.

SPARE

Anything extra that is carried aboard a vessel in case of a failure to a working part or piece of gear. It does not include the daily working rigging, line, etc., but could include a propeller, engine parts, shafting, sternwheel buckets, etc. The origin of the term is old English *sparian,* meaning "to refrain from injury".

SPARK ARRESTER

Any device that has the capability to stop or quench sparks that may be emitted from a gas or diesel engine. Normally they are standard equipment on fixed or portable pumping engines used on tank barges.

SPARRING OFF

See: GRASSHOPPERING and SPAR.

SPEAKER BOX

A communication system run by wire from the pilothouse to the head of the tow to allow the Pilot to talk to the Deck Mate when entering a lock, going through a narrow bridge, when serving as a lookout in fog, etc. With the advent of handheld VHF phones and other communications devices, the speaker box is now seldom used. More often was called a *squawk box* by the crew.

SPEAKING TUBE

A tube leading from the pilothouse to the engine room, usually made of brass, to convey voice communication. Except on some older vessels, the system has been phased out.

SPECIAL FLASHING LIGHT

Described in the Inland Navigation Rules as: ".... a yellow light flashing at regular intervals at a frequency of 50 to 70 flashes per minute, placed as far forward and as nearly as practicable on the fore and aft centerline of the tow and showing an unbroken light over an arc of the horizon of not less than 180 degrees nor more than 225 degrees and so fixed as to show the light from right ahead to abeam and no more than 22.5 degrees abaft the beam on either side of the vessel."

The light was originally a fixed amber light to be shown at the centerline of tows, effective on 1/1/49. It was unique to the Western Rivers and was started because some people, especially those on small recreational vessels, had difficulty distinguishing tow lights from other background lighting in city areas. Then in 1972, in order to make it more distinct, the fixed amber light was required to be a flashing one. When the Inland Rules were codified and became effective in 1980, it was decided to abide by the International body of rules, in that "amber" was not a color but a resin, so the light then became termed "yellow". There is no *special flashing light* in the International Rules.

SPECIAL PURPOSE BUOY

In addition to the red and green buoys that mark the channel there are numerous other types of buoys to indicate notice of ongoing activities, i.e., anchorages, dredging, wrecks or dangers, quarantine of an area, temporary yacht race courses, etc. The *special purpose buoy* has no lateral significance.

SPECIFIC GRAVITY

The analysis taken with a hydrometer by a chemist to determine the ratio of the density of a liquid substance in a cargo tank at a given temperature against a standard, usually that of distilled water. A sample reading is taken when a liquid barge is loaded, and again at its destination when it is being unloaded.

SPEED OVER GROUND

The actual measured river miles traversed by a vessel or tow during a watch or over a given amount of time. The miles are measured from a river map or the LIGHT LIST. Some call it the *speed made good*.

SPEED THROUGH THE WATER

The speed that a vessel could make

in a body of water with no current. If, at a given RPM it would make 10 MPH, but the vessel was trying to stem a current of eight MPH it would only be making about two MPH through the water. Conversely, if the vessel was traveling with the current, it would be making about 18 miles per hour.

SPELL

To relieve a person from his/her primary duty while on watch, such as a LOOKOUT, or during inclement weather while on deck in order to get coffee or warm up for a period of time.

SPIDER

A three-way, sometimes more, electrical connection for hooking up the running lights on the head of a tow by an electric power source from the towing vessel.

SPIKE

Heavy, long, iron or steel pointed pins used to hold wooden timbers and planking in place. They were usually square in shape with a round or diamond-shaped head. Short *spikes* were called *spiles,* although when *spikes* of any length were withdrawn from planking the hole left would be filled with a tight-fitting wooden peg which was also termed a *spile.*

SPIKE BARGE

A single barge that is wired by itself to the head of a wider tow of barges.

SPILE

See: SPIKE.

SPILING

1. The measurements or template taken by a vessel builder to determine the shape of a curved structural part or section prior to cutting and fabrication of the material.
2. When building wooden-hulled vessels, the planking of the hull is fitted to the curvature of the hull in the bow and the stern by twisting and fastening it into place. See: SHAPED TIMBERS and SNY.
3. The use of wooden willow stakes woven together to hold banks to keep the current from eroding them.

SPILL

1. The act of accidentally discharging oil or hazardous cargo products into the waters of the United States.
2. Water going over a dam without going through turbines to produce electricity, if the dam is capable of generating power.
3. The seemingly somewhat innocent word *spill,* unless it's bad stuff, comes from the old English *spillian,* meaning "to kill or destroy" by causing the enemy to shed, or *spill* their blood.

SPILLWAY

A specially constructed section of a dam or levee to allow a dumping of surplus water to run over, through, or around the dammed area. It does not permit a navigable passage. If the water flow is controlled by a movable weir, it is a controlled *spillway.* If the elevation of the cresting water is only controlled by a fixed weir, it is called an *uncontrolled spillway.* Also see: FLOODWAY, which are *spillway* areas used to reduce the impact of devastating flood heights by providing an outlet of flood waters into an adjoining area that is not heavily populated.

SPINDLE

The vertical shafting that is keyed to a CAPSTAN on which it turns.

SPITTOON

An essential metal container, usually brass, in the pilothouse of nearly all steamboats. It is used to receive the expectorations of a Pilot and those who may be sitting on the LAZY or LIARS BENCH. The word comes from the old English *spittan,* meaning "to eject saliva".

SPLASHBOARD(S)

1. Boards that fit into grooves

between the TOWKNEES of a towboat, to minimize water from spilling over the bow when running LIGHTBOAT.

2. On the old wooden barges that had little or no sheer on their bow end, *splashboards* were often placed on the head of tows to keep water from coming over the bow and washing into the hoppers.

SPLICE

The act of joining, or marrying, one part of a line or wire with another line or wire by interweaving the strands to one another, or to itself in the case of an EYE-SPLICE. The term is believed to come from the Dutch *spissen,* with some saying the word is related to "split", which means "to divide". So, it seems strange that on the one hand we are joining together with a different thought of tearing asunder. Maybe that is why if a line parts, we take the two "bitter ends", perform the process of "marrying" them together, and carry out the act of uniting them by "*splicing*" the broken parts (or maybe hearts) as one. The term apparently has always had a nautical heritage, so when a deckhand says he wants to get off the boat to get *spliced,* tell him to make certain all the "tucks" are tight and make sure his line is "payed out" properly, not to "snub" it too abruptly, and make sure it never "parts". See: SHORT SPLICE, LONG SPLICE, MARRY, and TUCK.

SPLITTING ON THE HEADS

The term means to FACE-UP a towboat almost exactly between two barges breasted up side by side so that the TIMBERHEADS of each barge are an equal distance from the centerline of the towboat.

SPLITTING THE PIER

A term used by log rafters when they had a huge raft in the river and encountered the menace of all rivermen, a bridge not wide enough to accommodate the width of the raft. In Capt. Walter Blair's words in *A Raft Pilot's Log,* if the bridge had a pointed pivot pier with a long sheer boom or fence on one side to slide on, the maneuver involved moving both the towboat and the bow-boat over on the piece that was to run the span on the outside of the long sharp pointed draw pier. Holding on to both sections of the wide raft the rafters would float it close to the bridge and let loose the coupling lines of the half with no boats attached to float down the sheer fence or boom side of the bridge. The two boats, one at each end of the other piece, could back it out and over to the other side of the pivot section so it would slide along the outside of the long pier. With a little shoving by the towboat it was soon clear of the bridge and placed beside the loose floating piece and coupled up to it again. See: DOUBLE HEADER.

SPOIL

A term that formerly was used to describe what was dredged from a riverbed to deepen a channel since it was considered of no economic value. It has been found that what was termed a waste product can have many useful purposes, such as beach enrichment, levee building, fill, and for building products, so the term has been changed to *dredge material*. The term comes from the Latin *spolium*, referring to "the skin stripped off animals that had been killed". It evolved into a meaning of plunder or damage and eventually to despoiled material or waste.

SPOKES

The handles on a steering wheel that extend beyond its rim that are used to easily turn the wheel. The word is from Old English *spaca*, with a meaning of "spike".

SPONSON

1. A fore-and-aft beam that supports the outer bearing and paddlebox structure of a sidewheel steamer.

2. A watertight projection added to the side of a vessel in order to decrease

its displacement immersion in the water.

3. Sometimes used interchangeably with PONTOON, as on a SEAPLANE.

SPONSOR
The person who christens a vessel when it is launched, officially named, or accepted by the owner. It is usually a woman, because vessels, however named, are termed a "she"; in addition, it is considered bad luck for a boat to be christened by a man. The word is like a marriage vow; it comes to us from the Latin *spondere,* meaning "to promise solemnly".

SPONTANEOUS COMBUSTION
A condition that happens when some cargoes, such as coal, catch on fire by a chemical reaction and without an apparent outside cause. The fines in the product oxidize producing heat and causing the ignition.

SPOOK
A term for a false target appearing on a radar screen but isn't really there. It can sometimes be a reflection from a highline crossing, or an atmospheric condition. Also called a *ghost*.

SPOONBILL BOW
A rake with a degree of curvature to it somewhat resembling the rounding of a spoon. On steamboats this type of elongated bow was effective when used with a spar to work the vessel off ground, especially on the Missouri River. Its rounded design also added buoyancy to the vessel and reduced its draft. This bow type is still sometimes seen on the lead barge of a unit tow. The streamlining allows the barge to shed the water more easily and increase its efficiency and speed through the water. The modern-day usage of *spoonbill bows* on river barges is believed to have first been designed and incorporated into the bows of oil and chemical tank barge tows of the Chotin Company in the 1950s.

SPOT
The place to position a barge in a fleet or at a dock, i.e., "We'll *spot* the barge at the #4 cell above the two loads at the terminal".

SPOT MARKET
When a barge isn't committed to a particular trade and is surplus to a vessel owner's barge commitments, a company will use the barge to load a commodity for whoever is willing to pay the going freight rate at that time.

SPRAGUE (STEAMER)
The largest steamboat ever constructed for towing service on the Western Rivers. She was built in Dubuque, IA, in 1902. Her length exceeded the size of the locks on the Upper Mississippi, so her sternwheel had to be shipped by barge separately and added at St. Louis. She was 315 feet long by 62 feet wide. Her wheel was 37 feet in diameter. In one trip it was reported that she took 61 barges with 67,307 tons of coal to New Orleans, a record that still stands. She was known to steamboat buffs along the river as *Big Mama*. Books have been written of her, and songs sung.

SPREADER BAR
1. The frame aft of a sternwheel where MONKEY RUDDERS were mounted.

2. A *bar*(s) between the chimneys of some steamboats. They served as braces, along with guy wires or chains; see: STACK SUPPORTS. At times they became quite decorative, oftentimes showing a distinctive company logo.

3. A *bar*(s) used to hold apart a bridle used to load and unload cargo such as pallets, pipe, steel plates or rolls, etc.

SPRING
The opening of a seam in the planks of a wooden hull that starts to leak, or a cracked or damaged steel hull that allows for the ingress of water into a vessel or of liquid product out of its

tank. In the past tense one would exclaim, "We've *sprung* a leak".

SPRING LINE

A line leading diagonally from a towing vessel to a barge, the shore or a dock. It also can be a line leading to the shore, lock wall, etc. from a tow. Usually the lines are rigged in pairs, with one line leading forward and the other aft. This will tend to restrict the movement of the vessel or tow from either surging forward or aft. The name for each of the lines take on their positional location, i.e., *bow spring, forward spring, aft quarter spring,* etc.

SPRING POLE PUMP

A type of pump used in steamboat days to discharge water from coal barges that may leak or contain excess rain water. The pump was of wooden construction about four to six inches square and ten or so feet in length to reach over the gunwale, forming a type of well with a spill chute at the top to direct the discharge. The fore and aft well planks were an inch or two longer than the side planks to allow water to easily enter the bottom of the well. The seams of the well were caulked to make them as watertight as possible. About two inches above the bottom of the pumpbox well was a wooden closure plug with a hole in the center, or on two sides, covered with a flexible leather or rubber flap. Also in the well was a closely fitted block of wood that acted as a piston plunger. The plunger block had two holes drilled through it off center that were also fitted with flexible flaps. The block had a rod attached to it that was a little longer than the pump well. Fastened to the rod was a limber willow sapling.

The operation of removing water consisted of placing the pump box in the lowest corner of a barge. Water would come into the well by hydraulic pressure, it being higher outside in the barge than in the well. The water would work its way through the flaps in the well and at the top of the plunger block, gradually equalizing to the same level in the well as in the barge. When equalized the flaps on the piston block would close. A man would then take a flexible sapling about 15 feet long and affix it onto the plunger rod. A small post with a yoke at its top would be stuck in the coal of the barge. It would act as a fulcrum for the sapling attached to the pump. When pressing down on the sapling pole, the water that had accumulated in the well would be pulled up by the spring action in the sapling into a trough at the top of the well pump and ejected over the side of the barge while at the same time causing suction in the pump well, opening the flap on the well bottom closure and drawing more water into the well. The pole would spring back down when the man pumping let go of it. The flexible leather flap of the piston block would open, letting it ride to the bottom of the well to again be pushed down to pump more water from the well and sucking in more from the cargo box. As the well again filled with water the process would be repeated until there was only a minimum discharge.

SPRING RISE

Usually the onset of the spring season of the year brings rain, as well as snow melt runoff from the upper reaches of valleys, causing the rivers to increase their flows and the stages of water levels to increase. River people tend to talk about how much the rise will be, what precautions must be taken, and will the locks be put out of service, and so on. See: JUNE RISE.

SPUD

A heavy timber, pipe, or steel H-beam that is dropped through a well, or SPUD WELL, of a vessel, that when lowered to the bottom of a river will allow a vessel to become a stationary platform. Used extensively on dredges, some dock facilities, salvage barges, and scows. See: GRASSHOPPERING for use of a *spud* on getting over sandbars on steamboats. It is unknown as to how the term came into being. It certainly has no relation to "potato" that did not acquire the nickname until the 19th century. The original meaning of *spud* was that of a dagger, and perhaps the act of a timber sliding in a chamber or SPUD WELL related to a dagger or knife being inserted and withdrawn from a sheath.

SPUD BARGE

A deck barge that uses a SPUD to moor when performing its work function. It will have two to four SPUD WELLS where the spuds are placed. It is equipped with a winch to raise the spuds, and usually has a crane and any other equipment needed in its normal employment.

SPUD DOWN

The act of lowering a spud. A vessel is said to *spud down* when utilizing spuds to hold a vessel in a stationary position.

SPUD WELL

A square or round compartment watertight to the interior of a vessel, but open to the water on its bottom and to the atmosphere at its top, comprising the entire vertical height of the vessel's hull to an extension of three or four feet above the deck. It is used to contain the spud that is raised or lowered through the casing (well) to the river or canal's bottom to securely position a SPUD BARGE.

SPUR

1. Any beam that is interrupted in its support, such as an opening.
2. A structural part serving as a support.
3. Curved sections of timber used to support decks when entire lengths cannot be used.
4. The term apparently is handed down to us from the old English *spora*, or *spura*, which referred to a "spike device" worn on one's boot to urge a horse to greater speed. Since it was a "projection", it has come to mean a point of land, a sectional part of timber, etc.

SPUR BEAM

A timber fixed to the side of a vessel that supports each end of the SPONSON that in turn supports the paddlewheel box and the bearing of the paddlewheel.

SPUR DIKE

A structure that extends outward from the shoreline of a river to deflect the current away from the bank, protecting it from erosion and to help scour the channel as well as provide for aquatic habitat. They are usually built in a series along the shore.

SQUALL

A sudden severe storm with rain, snow, or hail, accompanied by strong gusty winds that may be changing directions. The word relates to "squeal" and refers to the howling of the wind and rain that may sound like a baby screaming or bawling.

SQUARE

1. *End* – A barge with one or both ends *squared* off, or in the shape of one end of a cube. If the barge has only one *square* end it is called a SEMI-INTEGRATED BARGE. If both ends are *squared* off it is called a BOX BARGE.
2. *Away* – to tidy up or properly stow all gear. Also to admonish someone, i.e., "If you don't get *squared* away, you better start looking for another job".
3. *Knot* – next to the BOWLINE probably the best knot used on a vessel. Sometimes called a *reef knot*.
4. *Wheel* – where the pitch of a propeller is equal to its diameter. On a paddlewheel it is when the width of the wheel equals its diameter.

SQUARE WATCH

Where one set of the crew stands

watch from 12 to 6 and the other half of the crew stands watch from 6 to 12, both a.m. and p.m. See: DOG WATCH and WATCH.

SQUARED AWAY

Having all gear and material in its proper order, or completing a task in a satisfactory and orderly manner.

SQUAT

The settling or lowering of a vessel's stern in a channel due to its speed though the water, especially when navigating in a narrow shallow channel. The vessel's engine tends to lug down, vibration is more pronounced, rudder response becomes uncertain, and maintaining steerage is difficult. To alleviate the condition the vessel must slow its engine speed allowing a boat or tow to probably make the same amount of timely distance through the channel, but without causing possible damage to the vessel or washing along the shore. In this situation water somewhat draws away from the river banks and rushes back ashore after the vessel or tow moves away. The term derives from the French *esquatir,* meaning "to flatten or push down".

STABILITY

The ability of a vessel to maintain its equilibrium position after heeling over from whatever causal factor and remain stable. The term is from the Latin *stabilis,* meaning "stable".

STABILIZED CHANNEL

A river or canal channel that stays in one position with relatively little or no maintenance.

STACK

1. A buildup of barges or tows waiting to lock, or stopped, because of a channel blockage, i.e. "We're *stacked* up here at mile 555 waiting for the dredge to open the channel".
2. To put in a neat pile, i.e. "Have the deckhands *stack* the rigging on the starboard stern of barge 898".
3. The structure where the engine gas is exhausted, sometimes called a SMOKESTACK, and in days gone by, a CHIMNEY.
4. To place barge covers on top of one another at the ends of a barge. The word in all these meanings comes from the Old Norse *stakkr,* meaning "haystack".

STACK EMBLEM

A company logo that is placed on the exhaust stack of a towboat or tug that denotes the owner or operator of the vessel.

STACK GASES

The emissions from the engine when leaving the stack.

STACK LANTERNS

Before the 1980 Navigation Rules became effective, Western River steamers with two chimneys or smokestacks were allowed to carry their sidelights, called *lanterns,* on the outboard side of their stacks, the red to port and the green to starboard, to show forward, abeam, and aft on their respective sides. There are only a couple of these steamers still operating that have been grandfathered in to allow them to continue showing these lights.

STACK SUPPORTS

Some steamers had massive smokestacks, or chimneys, both in height and diameter. They were supported from the effects of wind, and the shock of grounding, allisions, and collisions by CHAINS, that were in reality long rods, each section about 10 feet long, up to one inch in diameter, with an eye in one end and a hook in the other so they could be fastened together. The last connection anchored to a deck support beam had a turnbuckle that could be tightened to make certain there was no slack in the chain and that an even strain was applied in all directions.

STACKING KNEES

Small triangular braces that were placed along the sides of steamboats to keep bales of cotton from slipping overboard. They were the forerunner of TOWKNEES on towboats.

STAGE

1. A reference gauge from which the rise and fall of a river at a particular point or place is evaluated. The term derives from the Latin *stare,* meaning "to stand". In this sense it is where the level of the river is "standing" when the gauge is taken. See: FLOOD, GAUGE, HIGH WATER, LOW WATER, POOL, and RIVER.

2. A period of time in a process, such as in a race; or a certain point when building a vessel; or an evolutionary period of the courses of a river's flow through a continent, etc.

3. Any suspended platform is termed a *stage*, such as used by painters, construction workers, window washers, etc. As used on the river, a *stage* is a platform from a vessel to the shore. Also sometimes called a *browboard* and a *gangboard*. It has been said that this of type *stage* took its name from the showboats that used to go up and down the river playing at towns along the way. The performers would go out on the swinging platform and give the townspeople a sample of what the show would be like. Since the showboat had in its theater a *stage* where the actors did their acting, sang, and did tricks, the platform took on the name of *stage*. This, however, may be an Urban Legend as the term *stage* or *gangway* to go aboard and depart vessels was used before there were river showboats.

STAGGERED BUCKETS

A STERNWHEEL that has BUCKETS (planks) which are half the width of the wheel. The port side buckets are placed in a staggered position from the starboard buckets. Some believe this placement results in a more efficient wheel, allowing greater thrust and speed as well as a smoother running vessel with less humping from the motion of the pitman. Also see: HERRINGBONE WHEEL.

STAIRCASE LOCKS

In effect all locks on a river system act as a set of stairs from the mouth of a river to its head of navigation which is at a higher elevation; however, the term refers to locks that are immediately adjacent to one another, requiring a vessel to make two or more lock lifts (or lowering) to move into another navigation pool. When the locks at the Louisville and Portland Canal were first constructed in 1830, vessels had to go through three locks to make the transit. The old Wilson Lock on the Tennessee River had two locks in staircase fashion, with another just downstream that also had to be used in low water. At present there are no *staircase locks* on the Western Rivers, although they are still common on rivers and canals of Europe and Asia.

STANCHION

1. Upright posts placed to support the beams holding up a deck. See: STATIONARIES.

2. A vertical structural member used for support, such as a guardrail, or a fixed drip pan. The term is from the Old French *estanchon*, meaning "support".

STAND

1. The period of tidal flow between flood and ebb.

2. To maintain the same water level; a river that has risen in height but has not yet started to fall is said to be at a *stand*.

3. *By* – a command to get ready or prepare to perform some duty, i.e., "*Stand by* to catch a line", or "*Stand by* to receive the store boat to starboard".

4. *Clear* – An admonition to keep out of the way or move away from a possible

impending danger, i.e. "*Stand clear* of the swinging boom".

5. *In* – To move a vessel or tow closer to shore.

6. *Off* – To keep a vessel's course away from some possible hazard, i.e., "*Stand off* the lower green buoy since it's sitting in shallow water".

7. *On* – See: STAND ON VESSEL.

8. Out – A protrusion making riverward fairly far out from the shoreline such as a building bar, i.e. "Watch for a *stand* out at the lower end of the next bend, it's getting shoal there".

9. *Watch* – To be on duty for a period of time.

STANDARD

1. Referring to a practice or performance consistent with what is the normal method or safe procedure of the trade in which a vessel and crew are employed; the conformity to established good operating practices.

2. A banner or other object used as an emblem.

STANDARD BARGE

A barge with dimensions of 175 feet long by 26 feet wide that will carry approximately 900 tons of cargo at a draft of nine feet. Usually an open hopper type built basically to carry coal, but can also be of a covered type. It was originally designed this width since timber trunks were usually cut and made into lumber at a *standard* length of 26 feet. The original wooden barges used on the Monongahela River had bottoms of 24 to 26 feet wide, laid in transverse fashion; posts were attached and the sides were framed longitudinally. The first locks on the Mon were 190' by 50'. Then in 1851 the coal monopoly of the Monongahela Navigation Company privately built locks of 250' by 56' with the capability of being able to fit barges in two wide; therefore the *standard* width of the barge resulted in the *standard* width of the locks. Later when the DAVIS ISLAND LOCK & DAM was built 110 feet wide that was to accommodate the width of four *standard barges* which has become "the standard" for most locks on the river system. See: STUMBO.

STANDARD KNEE

A support brace that is inverted and placed above the deck rather than underneath it to add support.

STAND-BY VESSEL

A vessel that is positioned at a place where some danger may exist to warn or assist other vessels, such as at the location of a sunken barge, a fleet in a fast rising or falling river, assisting at a lock that has a strong outdraft, or other similar conditions.

STANDING PART

That part of a line or wire that is fixed, as to a BLOCK or other source, and is not the hauling or running part.

STANDING RIGGING

The wires, ratchets, slings, and other rigging that is used to couple barges together in a tow which is of a semi-permanent nature, not PERMANENT RIGGING.

STAND-ON VESSEL

In accordance with Inland Navigation Rule 17 it is the vessel that is to keep her course and speed, except under special circumstances, when encountering another vessel. In the old rules this term was called the *privileged vessel*. See: GIVE-WAY VESSEL.

STAR(S)

Those specks of little white lights up in the sky on a clear dark night that are seen by the crews on towboats and tugs. A very technical version that is assumed to be correct is only found in books on ASTRONOMY, a fascinating science. When rivermen gaze up at their beauty while cumulus cloud forms drift along to hide them, and then reluctantly allow them to peek through again in the black sky, their thoughts are probably also drifting along with a thought or two of being off the boat and at home.

STARBOARD
The right side of a vessel when looking forward. In the old Teutonic sailing days when they went on their raids, the oar used to steer their vessels was on the right-hand side. From this the sailors of old England called it a *sterbord,* or steering board (rudder), hence the term morphed into *starboard*. See: PORT and RUDDER.

START
1. The commencement of any activity, i.e., to *start* making tow, painting, soogeeing, etc.
2. The beginning of running an engine when the mechanical force is applied.
3. To begin pumping a vessel.
4. The loosening of a strake or a seam results in a vessel to commence leaking.

STATE BOATS
Vessels built after WW I for the U.S. government. They were four sternwheel light-draft steamboats (294 feet long by 50 feet wide) named for the states in which they would travel, the *Str. ILLINOIS, IOWA, MISSOURI,* and the *MINNESOTA*. They were converted to propeller drive in 1937-1938. The vessels went out of service in the early 1950s.

STATEROOM(S)
The cabins where passengers were housed on a packetboat. Early steamboats named their cabins after the different States of the union. Captain Henry Shreve has been reported to be the first to have adopted the practice. Other vessels continued the procedure with these spaces acquiring the generic name designation of *stateroom*. Now on towboats all living quarters are so named, even if a State is not labeled on the door. This, however, may be another Urban Legend since ships used the term *stateroom* long before there were steamboats on the Western Rivers. The term is listed in British Admiral Smyth's *The Sailor's Word-Book* of 1867. On ships of the olden days most crew members slept on deck or in a hammock and there were few cabins for officers. However, it became fashionable at times to carry personages of royalty or officials of the realm, in other words "heads or officials of state", which more likely gave title to the term *stateroom*.

STATIC DRAFT
The draft of a vessel taken while not moving, and in calm water. The opposite of DYNAMIC DRAFT.

STATIC ELECTRICITY
A dangerous condition that could cause a spark, which in turn could ignite the vapors of a flammable cargo on a tank barge. The movement of cargo when loading or discharging can generate *static electricity* which can be alleviated by properly BONDING it with a grounding wire. The term *static* derives from the Greek *statike,* which was a term for "weighing". The word *electric* is from the Greek *electron,* which has reference to "amber"; when rubbed with a dissimilar material this would produce an electric charge.

STATION
1. The duty *station*, or assigned position, of a crew member in an emergency.
2. The placement of an aid to navigation, such as a buoy or light. The aid is said to either be *on-station* or *off-station.*

STATION BILL
A posting of the duty and place where each crew member is assigned to report in case of any emergency or drill.

STATIONARIES
Heavy vertical posts on a steamboat that ran from the main deck up to support the boiler deck. The posts protruded somewhat above the boiler deck in order that heavy timber fenders could

be fastened by a line to them. The fenders would hang loosely over the side to allow some give while protecting the steamer when it was tied alongside another steamboat, or when in a lock, or when moored to a wharf.

STATUTE MILE
The distance measured as 5,280 feet, used when navigating on the rivers and canals of the U.S. and as shown on inland maps, charts, and light lists.

STATUTORY
A rule by law and any regulations promulgated under the statute which has the force of an enacted law.

STAUNCH
Well-built and of strong construction, watertight, not leaking. The base of the word comes to us from the old French *estanchier*, meaning "to stop the flow of water".

STAYS
Wires, and sometimes lines or steel rods that are used to support upright vertical appendages such as a swing pole, or the chimneys of a steamer. In this use the term comes from the Dutch, *stag*, in the sense "to be firm". They are also called *guys*, and in the case of steamer chimneys, CHAINS.

STEADY AS SHE GOES
To hold and continue on a precise course. If a vessel is making a course change and the vessel is swinging, to hold the swing and keep the vessel on a new heading. Of course, on a winding river, *steady as she goes* may mean keeping an easy distance off the shore as the vessel is steered down the bend, constantly changing its compass degree heading.

STEAM
Water when heated to its boiling point, 212 degrees Fahrenheit, turns into a gas called *steam* which, in the old English meant "vapor". When *steam* is in a container such as a boiler, it expands causing pressure. The excess pressure must be released or it will continue to build, or rise, until it becomes so great that the container (boiler) will explode. The boiler's pressure in a controlled release is what is used to develop the motion and the driving force in the engine of a steamer by forcing a piston in a cylinder of an engine to rise and fall; the piston is attached to a crank, or connecting rod, that goes to a crosshead connected to the shaft of a paddlewheel, and this is what rotates and propels a vessel. Sort of like "Dem Dry Bones," with the head bone connected to the neck bone, the neck bone connected to the back bone, etc., etc., all the way down to the toe bone, and then, "Oh hear the word of the Engineer". His name was Ezekiel.

STEAM COILS
A construction arrangement added to the cargo compartment of some tank barges to induce steam into a barge whose cargo needs to be heated in order to reach a viscosity whereby it can be pumped. These cargoes range from molasses, to asphalt, to liquid sulfur. The internal piping may be of serpentine nature or it may be of inverted large angles or channels welded to the deck of the cargo tank with a header at the end. This latter type makes it easier to clean the barge for a change of cargo.

STEAM FOG
A type of fog that occurs when very cool air passes over the surface of much warmer river or canal water, starting usually in the fall of the year. It looks like steam rising from the surface of the river and is especially prevalent in areas where there are discharges of warm water from electric generating plants. In some areas the only place where this fog is apparent is on the waterway or in very close vicinity to it. Although this type of fog is a hindrance to navigation, in the winter time on some sections of the Illinois Waterway

the *steam fog* rising to the trees continually and freezing on its branches gives a beautiful crystal setting.

STEAM GAUGES

1. A device to measure the pressure in a steam boiler.

2. Prior to the invention of mechanical gauges a boiler was fitted with three vertically positioned gauge cocks at low, normal, and full. When one was opened it would indicate the water level. By the hiss of the steam being released the Engineer then would estimate imprecisely the pressure in the boiler. A safety valve was also installed that started gurgling if the pressure exceeded the safe limits.

3. The dial *steam gauge* invented by Eugene Bourdon was used after the 1852 Steamboat Act. Now we have modern electronic devices. (S&D Reflector)

STEAM SIPHON or SYPHON

A device used on steamboats to remove water from vessels. *Siphons* came in various sizes, depending upon the job and the amount of pressure applied to eject the water. Some were built in permanently to a low part of the vessel. Most, however, were used on barges to remove rain water and any leakage, a common occurrence in the days of wooden barges. Steam to operate the *siphons* was supplied by the steamboat. Sections of pipe, called IRISH SPAGHETTI, would be run out on the barges in tow and by use of the *siphon*, the mate on watch would see that the water from any leaking barges was pumped overboard.

The *siphon* had three orifices; the largest was the suction part. Steam pressure was applied through a reducer at a right angle to the suction side, and the discharge side was opposite the pressure side. This type of pumping has gone by the wayside since the steamers have been phased out of service. The name comes from the Greek *siphon*, meaning "pipe".

STEAMBOAT

A vessel that is propelled by a steam engine. The first one used for any distance on the Western Rivers was the *Str. NEW ORLEANS* (see), when in 1811 she steamed from Pittsburgh to New Orleans.

STEAMBOAT BOILER INSPECTOR

A government inspector employed originally by the Treasury Department (later other government agencies) to inspect the safe working condition of the boilers and machinery on steamboats, as well as other safety conditions aboard the vessels. Worked in conjunction with the STEAMBOAT HULL INSPECTOR and sometimes did both jobs. See: STEAMBOAT INSPECTION SERVICE.

STEAMBOAT BUFFS

A person who follows the travels, and sometimes the travails, of steamboats, especially on the rivers where there are steamers still operating. They take pleasure in the history of the boats, the people who manned them, their building, books about them, etc. They have web sites, meetings, and generally turn out for any affair in their area that features anything about steamboating.

When an old steamer that huffs
and puffs
Comes up the river showing
her stuff,
Paddles turning, the river
is rough,
It is loved by every *Steamboat
Buff.*

Calliope, they can't get enough,
As they stand upon the river
bluff.
You may have to put on your
earmuffs,
But then you're not a real
Steamboat Buff.

You may think it's all a bunch of fluff,
But I'm here to tell you its no bluff,
If you don't like it, here's off the cuff,
Every *Steamboat Buff* will tell you, TOUGH!!

STEAMBOAT GOTHIC

As steamboat traffic became more competitive in the mid-1800s some vessels, to attract more customers, built more ornate and fancier accommodations which were termed "floating palaces". They were built with arches, trimmed with wooden scroll work, contained fine art pieces, lavish appointments, etc, which gave rise to the expression *Steamboat Gothic*. Whether it was for the elegance or the gaudiness of the steamer, beauty was in the eyes of the beholder.

STEAMBOAT HULL INSPECTOR

A Government inspector originally employed by the Department of the Treasury (later other government agencies) who inspected the hulls of steamboats for deterioration, and other deficiencies of safety rules for a vessel. Worked closely with the STEAMBOAT BOILER INSPECTOR and sometimes performed both jobs. See: STEAMBOAT INSPECTION SERVICE.

STEAMBOAT INSPECTION ACT OF 1838

Leading up to 1838, Congress and the public grew concerned with the growing amount of casualties on steamboats. In 1837 the *BEN SHERROD*, in a race with another steamboat, caught on fire and burned with more than 150 people losing their lives. In 1838 the steamer *ORONOCO* and the *MOSELLE* both had boiler explosions, with over 300 people dying. These accidents, and others, led to the passage of the *Steamboat Inspection Act of* 1838, which required steamboat owners to "provide better security of the lives of passengers on board of vessels propelled in whole or in part by steam". The *Act*, however, was weak and had little power.

STEAMBOAT INSPECTION SERVICE

In 1852, with the passage of the new Steamboat Inspection Act, a provision was included to establish a *Steamboat Inspection Service* in the Department of the Treasury that authorized the appointment of a Board of Supervising Inspectors who were assigned to specific districts. The inspectors were given authority to enforce laws relating to the construction, safety, operation, equipment, inspection and documentation of merchant vessels, to investigate marine casualties, enforce navigation laws, collect tonnage taxes and other fees, and examine, certify, and license merchant vessel personnel.

Over their years of service their mission was broadened, the name of their service changed, and they went into reorganized parts of the executive cabinet. During WW II they were temporarily assigned to the USCG. With a reorganization of the functions in the executive branch after the war, that change was made permanent.

STEAMBOAT INSPECTORS

Inspectors of steamboats have had a long history on the rivers:

1839, July 7 Steamboat Inspection Service established as part of Justice Dept.
1852, Aug 30 SIS transferred to Treasury Dept.
1903, Feb 14 SIS transferred to Labor and Commerce Dept.
1915, Jan 28 USCG created from Revenue Cutter Service and Life Saving Service
1932, June 30 SIS transferred to Commerce Dept.
1936, May 27 SIS renamed Bureau of Marine Inspection (BMI).
1942, Feb 28 BMI temporarily transferred to USCG (then temp. to the USN)
1946, July 16 BMI abolished, became part of USCG (now part Treasury Dept.)

1967, Apr 1   USCG transferred to Dept. of Transportation

2003, Mar 1   USCG transferred to Dept. of Homeland Security

STEAMBOAT JACK

A term for an extremely heavy RATCHET with an oversized barrel and turnbuckle screws with unwieldy PELICAN HOOKS. These ratchets have also been given some other old, and newly minted, adjectives by crew members that had to use them in making up tows. They have mostly been replaced by lighter, but equally strong, ratchets. Many of the old ones seem to have been accidentally been given the DEEP SIX treatment, but this can't be verified.

STEAMBOAT RACE RULES

The *rule* is that there are NO *rules*.

STEAMBOAT RACING

A practice sometimes indulged in by competitive Captains who believed their boat was better than that of some other Captain. In some regular trades the steamer that was able to arrive at a port first got to carry the mail and gained first call on the cargo that was available for shipping. So *racing* was often to their economic benefit.

Racing could become disastrous since Engineers, in order to get more pressure from their boilers, would hang a weight on the pressure lever allowing the boiler to exceed it safe limits. But if there was a weak spot in the boiler there might be a boiler explosion, with loss of life and probably loss of the boat. The 1852 Steamboat Act put some teeth into forbidding the excess pressure, but *racing* still went on. Even in the modern diesel trade races take place, such as in trying to beat another towboat to a lock, but the commercial aspects of *racing* no longer exist. There are, however, staged races such as the annual Derby Festival Race between steamers on the Ohio River at Louisville each May. See: ANTLERS.

STEAMBOAT WILLIE

The first cartoon movie character of Mickey Mouse by Walt Disney, appearing on 18 November 1928, which grew to become an empire (only because of the heritage of those reading this volume). All rivermen celebrate his birthday.

STEAMER

Another word for STEAMBOAT. A vessel propelled by steam.

STEEL TOWER

A skeleton-type of steel latticework that is used to display a light or other aid to navigation, replacing wooden structures. See: SKELETON TOWER.

STEEPLE ENGINE

A type of early low pressure steam engine with the piston set vertically between guides below the crank and attached to an iron cross beam on a large type of A-frame. It is believed this was the type used on the *NORTH RIVER* (Fulton's first successful boat) and possibly on the *Str. NEW ORLEANS*.

STEER

1. To guide and control the movement of a vessel in a desired direction by use of the rudder, or by engine controls on a multiple-screw vessel. The word comes from the German *steuern,* and the Dutch *sturen,* both meaning *steer.*

2. On log rafts one would *steer* by use of long SWEEPS. In the times after steamboats pushed the rafts, a BOWBOAT assisted in *steering* when the rafts were being pushed down river.

3. Long OARS were used for *steering* on KEELBOATS.

4. On a yawl or skiff *steering* is accomplished by use of an OAR.

STEER IT

Making a decision to steer a vessel or tow through a sharp bend rather than flank it, i.e., "When we get to Craighead I'm going to *steer it* rather than flank it".

STEERAGEWAY

A minimal rate of speed through the water that is sufficient to maintain effective rudder control to maneuver a vessel and keep it on course. The term *bare steerageway* is the lowest speed at which a vessel can maintain its effective maneuverability.

STEERING COUPLING

All barge tow couplings where barges are wired together in a tow receive a high degree of stress when the towboat pushing them applies rudder movement in order to steer the boat and the tow. The first barge-to-barge wired coupling out from the towboat or tug receives the most pressure, and is called the *steering coupling*. In a tow of more lengths of barges, each coupling further away from the boat has less stress. However, if the tow is of four or five lengths ahead of the towboat and one of the couplings between barges is of rakes made up to one another, two couplings away from the boat, it could be the coupling with the most stress if the other couplings are square-ended and bearing against one another.

STEERING LEVERS

Instead of a steering wheel, most modern towboats are equipped with *levers*, sometimes called STICKS, with which to control the rudders in order to steer the vessel. Most often there are two *levers* for steering the vessel when going ahead that work in tandem, and two *levers* to control the FLANKING RUDDERS when going astern that also work in tandem.

STEERING LIGHT

See: PEEP LIGHT.

STEERING OAR

Large long *oars* used on flatboats and log rafts at the stern, the bow, and the sides. They were usually called SWEEPS.

STEERING QUADRANT

A quarter of a circle steel casting attached to the top of the rudder stock or post to which steering cables are attached to direct the movement of the rudder.

STEERING RUDDER

See: RUDDER.

STEERSMAN

In most nautical language the term means the *helmsman*, the one who may be doing the steering of the vessel. It comes from an Old Norse word *styrmann*, meaning the "one who steers". However, the *steersman* on seagoing vessels was only given a compass course to hold, and all changes to the course were given him by the officer in charge of the watch. On log rafts and flatboats a *steersman* was the lead person on the stern that was manning the STEERING OAR. On riverboats the term has meant an apprentice who is learning the river to become a PILOT. It replaces the terminology of the days of Samuel Clemens when the learner of the river was called a "cub". Sometimes the person was designated a "striker" Pilot, but the term "striker" was more often used in conjunction with a person learning to become an Engineer. New terms for those learning to become a Pilot are being developed by the U.S. Coast Guard. The latest is APPRENTICE MATE.

STEM

1. The foremost part of a packetboat and refers to the upright timber when the side strakes are attached. It is not used with towboats since they are not pointed at the bow and basically, with towknees, have a somewhat flat surface at the bow, or head of the vessel.

2. The heavy vertical plating at the extreme forward end of a vessel with a model type bow, such as a tug. This use of *stem* is from the Old German *stefen*, meaning "a rising or ascending piece of timber".

3. To make headway, or hold one's own against a strong current, such as to

"*stem* the tide", or to "*stem* the flood" waters. The term comes from the Old Norse *stemma,* which meant "to stop" or "hold back".

STEMMING THE CURRENT
The act of holding one's own at the same mileage spot, not moving ahead or falling back from one's position in the channel, usually while waiting for lockage, or at a fleet holding up for a harbor boat to take barges from a tow or bring barges to the tow.

STEMSON
A section of compass (curved) timber on wooden-hulled steamboats which is scarphed into the KEELSON and to which the vessel strakes are attached.

STEP
1. To raise a mast or spar that is on a block or steel plate that places it in position.
2. One section of a stairway, with the horizontal face being the 'tread', and the vertical face being the "riser". The term comes from the Old English, *steppan.*

STERN
The extreme after end of a vessel. The term is from the Norse *stjorn,* meaning "where the steering took place".

STERN LIGHT(S)
Those lights that are required to be shown in accordance with part C of the Inland Navigation Rules. The lights to be shown will depend upon the employment of the vessel.

STERN LINE
A line that is led from the stern position of a vessel to the shore, another vessel, or to another object.

STERN RAKE
1. The keel on a towboat slopes upward at the stern to accommodate the flanking rudders, propellers, and steering rudders. This upward curvature is known as the *stern rake.*

2. The stern void compartment of a barge whether raked or square.

STERN TUBE
The watertight bushing which extends through the stern end of the vessel's hull carrying the propeller shafting to the STRUT bearing to receive the propeller.

STERN-END DECKHAND
When making a double locking, after the first cut (section) of a tow is tied off in the lock chamber the second half is backed out and tied off on the lock guidewall. The crewman who is with the backed-out section is usually the least experienced deckhand in the crew and does the tying off of the second cut. He is known as the *stern-end deckhand.*

STERNLINE (or TELEGRAPH) TALK
Gossip about what might be happening on the river, in the company, or about fellow crew members. When crews were larger the fantail at the stern was a good place to congregate, out of hearing of others to swap stories and feed one another a line. See: SCUTTLEBUTT.

STERNLOG
Heavy framing in the stern of a barge.

STERNPOST
A heavy timber in the aftermost part of the hull of a steamboat to which the rudder is attached.

STERNWAY
Having the motion of a vessel astern, or backward, through the water.

STERNWHEEL
A paddlewheel that provides the propelling power at the stern end of a vessel. The wheel consists of a shaft at its center, usually hexagonal, to which flanges are fitted on each end where wheel arms are attached in equidistant spaces. Holding

the arms in place are various wooden blockings closely wedged in between each ARM that makes up the WOOD CIRCLE. On each side of the "wood circle" holding the blocking in is an iron circular rim on each side of the arms called the IRON CIRCLE. Buckets are added to the ends of the wheel arms and held in place by STIRRUPS bolted to a BATTEN.

After propellers came into usage on towboats as a means of propulsion many owners continued to use paddlewheels simply because the facilities that were needed to drydock and change damaged propellers were few and far between in some areas of the river as well as being expensive to conduct the repair. Changing damaged planks on a *sternwheel* could usually be accomplished inexpensively by the crew on the steamer with very little time for the vessel being out of service. See: HERRINGBONE WHEEL, PADDLEWHEEL and STAGGERED WHEEL.

STERNWHEELER
A vessel equipped with a STERNWHEEL to propel it.

STEVEDORE
A person, or firm, who loads and unloads cargo from a barge or other vessel, or who operates the equipment to facilitate the loading or unloading. Sometimes called a LONGSHORE WORKER. In earlier times of the steamboat trades this person was called a ROUSTABOUT. The term of *stevedore* is from the Spanish *estibador*, meaning "loading and/or storing cargo".

STICK GAUGE
A long wooden stick, usually square, that is marked off in inches and is used to measure the amount of cargo in tank barge compartments. A shorter version is sometimes used by the Engineer of a towboat to measure fuel tanks, but presently on towboats the Engineer most often uses a metal tape gauge.

STICKS
A nickname for STEERING LEVERS and FLANKING RUDDER levers that control the rudder movement on most of the diesel-powered tugs and towboats now operating. They replaced the traditional steering wheel.

STIFF
Said of a vessel in regards to stability that it resists inclination from its upright position from external forces such as wind, waves, or other conditions which may make it prone to HEEL. See: TENDER (the opposite of *stiff*).

STIFFENER
Any steel angles, channels, T-bars, or shapes used to strengthen stress points in a vessel.

STIRRUPS
A U-bolt which is fitted around the wheel arm of a paddlewheel in order to attach a BUCKET (plank) and secured through the bucket by bolting to a BATTEN on the face side of the bucket. This allows damaged buckets to be replaced by the crew without going to a shipyard. The base of the word comes from the German, meaning "a climbing rope", probably to use in mounting a horse, which evolved into what a rider uses. For paddlewheel usage the holding device was probably given the name by a shipwright who raised horses, since it has the same shape as the implement equestrians use to place their feet in when mounting and riding.

STOCK
1. The cross piece secured to the upper part of the SHANK of a standard anchor and at a right angle to its flukes.

2. The shafting of a rudder that extends in a bearing through the hull of a towboat and is attached to the rudder quadrant or tiller which when turning steers the vessel. See: RUDDER STOCK.

3. Applies to supplies and stores carried aboard a vessel. See: STORES.

4. Refers to animals when they were transported on steamboats. See: CATTLE BARGE.

STOP

1. A protrusion that keeps a device from further movement such as RUDDER STOPS.
2. To check the movement of a line or wire that is rendering out.
3. The action of shutting down the propulsion action of the engine(s).

STOP VALVE

A valve in a pipeline that restricts or prevents the flow of liquid.

STOPPAGE

Any shutdown that causes navigation to cease, such as a lock that has some mechanical failure or due to maintenance, any weather incident such as a high flood stage or ice conditions, an accident, a security incident, or any other cause where vessels cannot move into or through an area.

STOPPER

1. A piece of line or chain, or a clamping device to hold the strain on a line or wire until the bight at the loose end can be taken off a winch or capstan and made fast to a deck fitting such as a cavel, timberheads, or an H-bitt.
2. A knot placed in a line so the bitter end won't reeve through a block.

STORE BOATS

Small steamers that ran on some rivers after the Civil War that supplied groceries and other goods to people along the river who had no access to towns, especially in the rural areas of the Tennessee River. They were called the *chicken wagons of the river*. They often bartered for the goods on board and sometimes would carry a few passengers. See: BOAT STORE for the modern version.

STORES

The supplies and gear necessary to efficiently and safely run a tugboat or towboat, including but not limited to food, line, tools, gear, and other supplies, etc.

STORM SIGNAL

Storm warnings that are issued by the Weather Bureau as necessary in coastal areas where visual aids are flown at certain strategic places. See: WEATHER WARNINGS.

STOVE IN

A place in the hull or superstructure that is severely indented, cracked, or broken, usually caused by some sort of accident. If below the waterline of the hull it will usually result in the ingress of water.

STOW

1. To arrange stores and supplies in their proper order. The term is a shortened version of "bestow" or "to give or put in place".
2. To make sure gear is secure and lashed down, if necessary, so it won't be washed overboard.

STOWAWAY

A person who has illegally hidden himself or herself aboard a vessel for whatever purpose, whether it is benevolent, or to do harm. In the past *stow* meant to "arrest and imprison", so in keeping with that it may be proper to say that the root of this word should be applied rather than the traditional meaning of something put in its proper place, especially in a security sense.

STRAIGHT SINGLE

When a vessel with a tow can enter a lock and complete the lockage without breaking any couplings between barges or disconnecting the towboat or tug from the tow.

STRAIN

The amount of tension on a line or wire with its resistance to the load on it. In physics it becomes the magnitude of deformation of a line or wire when it becomes somewhat deformed as it is pulled taut and alters into a narrower circumference. The word comes from the Latin *stringere,* meaning "to draw tight" or to "bind a person". See: STRESS since the two words are sometimes incorrectly interchanged.

STRAINER BOX
See: ROSE BOX.

STRAKE
A longitudinal run of hull boards or hull plates. The *strakes* are given various names depending on where they were placed, i.e., the "garboard *strake*" was the lowest one in a vessel's hull, while the highest was called the "wale" (although some call it the "sheer *strake*", but that *strake* is usually just below the "wale"). The term comes from the Old English *streccan*, meaning "to stretch". See: RUBBING BAR.

STRAND
1. In rope making, it is the various fibers, natural or synthetic, that are twisted together to make *strands* that are then laid up together to make a length of line. See: LINE and ROPE.
2. When under severe strain and a length of line or wire begins to reach its breaking point, it is said "to *strand*" and then to finally break or part.

STRANDED
1. To be aground in a more severe condition than GROUNDED to the extent that, if accidental, it will be difficult to get off ground, and if done intentionally it would be to save the vessel from sinking or a more serious condition. The term comes from the old English *strand,* meaning "to leave aground".
2. The parting or breaking of a line or wire.

STRAP
1. A type of fitting which consists of a plate that contains a steel triangular ring that is welded to the deck of a vessel. It is usually employed as a holding device in which to fasten a ratchet when wiring up tows of barges, or on the bow of a towing vessel when attaching to a tow.

2. A triangular lifting ring welded to barge covers (usually four rings) that are used to receive the hooks of a crane sling when removing or placing covers on a barge.
3. Another name for SLING (see).

STRAPPING
The measurement of shore and vessel tanks for the amount of liquid they may contain which is noted on a table calibrated for each tank.

STRAY
A navigational buoy that is off-station, or is floating free in the current, or is on the shore, or hung up on drift or a dike field.

STREAM
1. Any flowing body of water. Most often used when referring to a small creek or waterway that flows into a main channel, i.e., "Watch out for that *stream* about a mile above LMN Light since it's putting out a lot of water tonight, Cap". The word is from the Greek *rhein*, meaning "to flow".
2. The act of floating a line or object overboard in the current.
3. The movement of a vessel or object moving with the current, i.e. *downstream* or *upstream*.

STREAM LOAD or SUSPENDED LOAD
Light and/or small granular particles that are suspended most of the time in a river's flow. Where the river's current speed may slow down it may drop some of its load, only to pick up more where a section narrows and the flow gains strength. See: SAND WAVE.

STREAMER
A longitudinal beam that is attached to the vertical STATIONARIES to give support to decks and the roof of a steamboat.

STREAMING
1. To let flow with the current, such

as when letting out a line or wire as a vessel or tow is dropping down to another position; or to lengthen the scope of a towing wire or hawser; or when letting a flanking buoy freely float off the stern of a tow.

2. The charges a tugboat company assesses a vessel to assist it away from a dock or pier and out into the main channel.

STRESS

1. A vessel that is undergoing, or has undergone, some structural distortion of the hull in a grounding, collision, or weather-related incident. The word comes from "distress" such as a hardship or an exerted force upon a person, and comes from the Latin *strictus,* "to draw tight".

2. The pressure or tension exerted by a line or wire on a material object. Often incorrectly used with STRAIN. A line or wire with a high degree of tension is being "strained" and if increased it may part or break. A "strained" line or wire is applying *stress* on the object to which it is attached, i.e., a mooring pin on a lock wall or a cavel on a barge.

3. The emotion some Pilots feel if not properly lined up for a bridge, or lock, or correctly positioned for a flank.

4. The impending feeling of perdition by an engineer when he notes a steam boiler is way beyond safe working pressure.

STRETCH

1. Sometimes used to describe a length of river between two points, i.e., "Last week I drew the *stretch* from Green River to Cairo Point for the USCG to extend my license to include the entire Ohio River". See: REACH.

2. The time a crew member is working on a tug or towboat, i.e., "I did a 30 day *stretch* the last time out, but will put in 40 days or more this time. The old lady needs a new washing machine." However, a *stretch* on the river can mean a riverman's life work. See: TRIP.

3. Used to describe the elasticity of line that elongates when under strain. This is especially true of some types of synthetic line.

STRIKE

To take down, or to lower, such as *striking* the flag. This was the sense of the meaning of this word to this Lexicon, however, it is an interesting word having a whole host of meanings: to make a deal; to inflict pain (on a person); to create fire (from a match); a sudden thought coming to someone; to hit something (the ground or a pier); to discover (gold, silver, diamonds); an attack (on an enemy); a refusal to work; to make something (a coin); to miss a pitch (baseball); to hit all the pins (bowling); to take down (a tent or camp); and many more. The word apparently derives from Old English *strican,* meaning "to go, flow, and rub lightly". How this relates to any of the uses above can only be anyone's guess.

STRIKER

A name sometimes given to a person learning to become an engineer. The term formerly used was "Oiler", but now more often called, "Assistant Engineer".

STRING

Barges that are coupled together end-to-end in a tow, i.e., if there were 15 barges in a tow, three wide and five long, the tow would consist of three *strings*, the port *string*, the center *string*, and the starboard *string*. A Pilot might say, "Check the lead barge on the starboard *string* for water", or "That outside wire at the break coupling on the port *string* seems somewhat slack when I steer against it; better tighten it", or "Put the speaker on the center *string* when we go through the bridge".

STRING OUT

1. When pushing a tow of barges ahead in strong winds, becoming windbound, especially on the ICWW, a vessel may *string out* the barges and tow them

astern, or when being unable to push ahead or steer through heavy ice the tow may be *strung out* for astern towing. See: MULE TRAINING.

2. To reduce the width of a tow and make it more narrow in width and longer, thus reducing the current resistance to increase the speed over ground. See: STRUNG OUT.

STRINGER

An interior longitudinal framing member used to give the hull of a vessel increased longitudinal strength.

STRIP

1. When leaving a barge(s) at a dock or in a fleet, to remove all non-permanent portable rigging, all lines not necessary to safely moor the barge(s), and any other gear that may be on board the barge(s). The word is of Germanic origin, *streifen,* meaning "to take off, or unclothe".

2. To remove all non-permanent gear and supplies from a vessel that will be laid up for a period of time.

3. To dismantle a piece of machinery in order to overhaul and rebuild it.

4. To remove the last small amount of liquid cargo from a tank barge when pumping it off by choking down on the pump valve so the suction pipe will not suck air.

5. The pumping out of any condensate or seepage water in the void tank spaces of a barge.

STRIPPING LINE

Small lines in some tank barges that are utilized to remove the last possible amount of cargo from a tank when the regular cargo lines start to suck air and lose their ability to suction up the rest of the product in the tank. At times an auxiliary stripping pump is utilized.

STROKE

1. The entire distance that a piston in an engine moves.

2. The full movement of a ram in a hydraulic cylinder.

3. One entire pulling movement of an oar when rowing.

STRONGBACK

1. A bar across a small hatch closing with a bolt or toggle to securely tighten it.

2. A bar used with a SOFT PATCH to secure it when making temporary repairs.

3. One or more cross pieces over a small boat, yawl, or skiff, used to support a canvas to keep out rain water.

STRUM

A perforated plate that covers a water intake below the waterline of a vessel that will strain out most debris that might clog a pump. See: ROSE BOX for another type of straining mechanism.

STRUNG OUT

1. The placement of barges in tow end to end, i.e. "I want those 10 barges *strung out* side by side, five long. We'll make better time that way".

2. The position of barges on a towline of a tug or towboat towing them. See: STRING OUT.

STRUT

A strong steel support bracket, sometimes in a "V" shape, that extends from the bottom of the stern part of a hull. At its downward extremity it receives the propeller shafting after it has left the hull. The tail shaft goes through the *strut* bearing where it will receive the propeller, which will be securely locked in place with a propeller lock nut. It is sometimes termed a *shaft strut,* or a *shaft bracket.* On twin- or multiple-screw boats they may be called *spectacle frames* since they appear to look like a pair of eyeglasses. The term is from Old English *strutian*, meaning to protrude stiffly. See: SHAFTING.

STUDDING

Vertical framing that supports the decks to which exterior and internal covering may be attached.

STUFFING BOX

1. A tubular containment seal around the propeller shafting to prevent the ingress of water before the shaft leaves the hull of the vessel.

2. A fitting, gland, tube, or box that is placed at the termination of any shaft, rod, or other type of moving part that must be kept air-, water-, oil-, or steam-tight and not leak.

STUMBO BARGE

A barge that is 26 feet wide by 195 or 200 feet long. It is a contraction of "ST" for the STANDARD BARGE of 26 feet wide and the "UMBO" for the JUMBO BARGE of 195 to 200 feet in length. It is basically used in the upper reaches of the Ohio River Valley.

SUBMARINE CROSSING

A marked crossing on navigation maps and charts where a protected cable or a pipeline is dredged down in the riverbed. Signs on the shoreline also indicate the crossing.

SUBMERGED

Something that is beneath the water, such as a rock, a broken piling, a dock when there is high water, a river or canal bank, or an island.

SUBMERSIBILE LOCK GATE

See: LOCK GATES.

SUBMERSIBLE PUMP

A pump that can operate when completely immersed in water and is sometimes used to remove water from a flooded compartment.

SUCCESS (on the river)

It's reported that a cub learning to become a Pilot once asked his mentoring old Captain what was the secret to becoming a successful Pilot. It might have been Sam Clemens when he learned the river from Captain Bixby.

The Pilot answered the cub, "In two words you can achieve success if you follow them. They are, Right Decisions."

The cub took that in and then asked, "How do you make the right decisions?"

The old Pilot smiled and replied, "Experience."

To this the cub asked, "How does one like me obtain the necessary experience?"

The wise old Pilot, still smiling, responded, "Simple. The best way to gain experience and to learn doing things the right way is from two more very important words, Wrong Decisions."

SUCK AIR

1. When a cargo pump on a tank barge loses its ability to pump any more cargo from a tank and suction is lost.

2. A term used when CAVITATION of a propeller occurs.

SUCK DOWN

The tendency of a vessel in shallow water traveling at a fairly good speed to bump the bed of the river.

SUCKING MUD

A term meaning the towboat and tow are in extremely shallow water and mud boils are coming up around the vessel and its tow, especially when backing down.

SUCTION

1. The removal of something with a pumping device by creating a vacuum pressure. The term comes from the Latin *sugere,* meaning "suck".

2. The flow of water to a propeller by its screw-type action.

3. An action in shallow water which may draw a towboat stern in toward the bank, forcing the head of the tow away from it.

4. The CARGO LINE of a tank barge when cargo is being removed.

SUCTION BELL

A fitting at the end of a pipeline in a tank barge that is flared out like the mouth of a bell. It provides more immediate flow to the pipeline, both in dispersing cargo when loading, and to aid in stripping the barge when pumping cargo out of a tank.

SUCTION DREDGE
A vessel equipped with a large centrifugal pump that sucks up sand and sediment from a riverbed and pumps it through a pipeline to shore or to an out-of-the-channel place for deposit. This is a very efficient method and is used in most of the alluvial riverbeds of the Western Rivers. Also see: DREDGE, DUSTPAN DREDGE, and SAND DIGGER.

SUE AND LABOR
A marine insurance term that encourages a vessel's crew to expend all effort to save the vessel and its cargo. The policy agrees to pay for the extra expense of their efforts.

SUEGEE
See: SOOGEE

SULTANA (STEAMER)
A sidewheel steamer built in 1863 for the cotton trade on the Mississippi River. After the Civil War ended the vessel was in Vicksburg, MS, and the U.S. Army arranged for her to take on from 1800-2000 repatriated Union soldiers who had been prisoners of war and transport them upriver to their home areas. On 27 April 1865 just north of Memphis, near a group of small islands termed "Hens and Chickens", the boilers of the vessel blew up, resulting in the worst maritime disaster in U.S. history. Over 1700 persons lost their lives, and possibly more since others likely died later in hospitals that are not included in the official total. Numerous books have been written of the tragedy.

SUMP
A small well built into a double-skinned tank barge where the SUCTION BELL of a pipeline is placed to assist in stripping all possible cargo from a tank.

SUNK or SUNKEN
The past tense of SINK. To be submerged to the bed of the river. A bad day for anyone's vessel.

SUNRISE
The time when the sun appears or when full daylight is apparent.

SUNSET
The time in the afternoon or evening when the sun disappears or the light fades. It is a time when navigational lights on vessels are to be shown, unless the vessel is, or was, in RESTRICTED VISIBILITY when they are always required to be shown.

SUPERSTRUCTURE
All covered housing of a tug or towboat above the main deck, including the pilothouse.

SUPPORT MEMBERS
Any framing members that add support to a vessel's structure, such as beams, knees, stanchions, spurs, frames, posts, etc.

SURGE
1. The effect of a sudden slacking and then a tightening strain of a mooring line or wire. The term is from the Latin *surgere,* meaning "to rise".
2. A sudden forward, aft, up, or downward movement, such as a vessel at a pier, or in a lock when there is a sudden movement of wave wash, or when the swirling fill into the lock chamber causes a strain-slack-strain movement on a line by agitation of the water.
3. A wave on a river or canal bank coming off a vessel that is creating a bow wave that affects objects on the shore.
4. The effect of a large heavy tow in a shallow and narrow channel that displaces the water in the channel area. After the tow passes through the chan-

SURVEY

1. The thorough and detailed inspection and appraisal of a vessel when going on or off charter. The term comes from Latin *supervidere*, "to oversee".

2. An inspection determining the fair market value, or insured value, of a vessel or piece of equipment.

3. An inspection assessing damage to a vessel or its cargo.

4. The official appraisal of a vessel that was a party to a casualty in the attempt to evaluate responsibility.

5. An inspection to determine the suitability of a vessel and its equipment to safely and adequately perform the tasks it is to undertake; sometimes called a "trip and tow survey".

6. The examination of the cargo in a vessel to determine its condition.

7. Measurements taken of a section of the river or canal to determine factors to update navigation maps and charts, or the need for channel maintenance or structural improvement.

SURVEY BOAT

A small launch used by the USACE to make soundings of the channel to determine where certain dike structures should be located, take depth soundings to evaluate the necessity for dredging, and for other navigational condition purposes.

SURVEY REPORT

After the inspection or examination of a vessel or its cargo the person undertaking the *survey* will issue a written report of the findings and conclusions.

SURVEYOR (MARINE)

A person who carries out a SURVEY of vessels, cargo, gear, accidents, or any other inspections related to maritime interests and writes a report of his/her findings.

SUSPENSION AND REVOCATION

A proceeding against a mariner's license or document issued by the USCG. It is usually a fact finding hearing before an ADMINISTRATIVE LAW JUDGE who will render judgement.

SWAB

In the Navy and vessels going to sea, a *swab* is a mop. On the river a "mop" is still a mop.

SWAGE

A pressed metal fitting that is used as a clamp on a wire to create an "eye", or to secure a thimble with a set of chain links in the end of a wire. Except for emergency and special purposes very little wire splicing presently takes place on river vessels. Most wire rigging is precut to specification with eyes and fittings *swaged* as required.

SWAMP

A vessel that has filled with water and is in danger of sinking from the action of taking water over the side, and not from damage or holing.

SWASH PLATE

Any plate installed in a large cargo tank of liquid to reduce the free surface effect of rolling. Seldom used in river trades except when some open hopper barges might carry dredged material containing a lot of water, or products such as lime slurry. The conventional tank barges used on the inland waterways are compartmentalized, so any free surface effect is kept to a minimum.

SWEEP(S)

1. On a keelboat, a long oar used as a rudder.

2. Long oars used on flatboats on the stern, sides, and bow to assist in steering.

3. Very long oars used on log rafts on both the bow and the stern to assist in keeping the rafts in the channel. These oars could be 20 to 50 feet in length

depending on the size of the raft, and might have five or more sets on both the bow and stern. This was prior to the use of steamboats pushing the rafts with bowboats used across the head of the raft to assist in the steering.

4. The rotation of the flasher light line on the radar scope identifying land masses and targets.

SWELL

A long wave that moves continuously off the bow of a vessel or tow as it moves through the water. When the *swell* is high or prominent from a fast-moving tow it is said, "She's moving like a dog with a bone in her teeth".

SWING

To change the direction of a vessel to starboard or to port by turning the rudder while underway. A Pilot might say, "Better give her a little more rudder to get her *swinging* to port to shape up for the bridge", or "If you're going to stop that *swing*, you better give her more starboard rudder".

SWING ANCHORS

Anchors that are deployed to each side of a dredge, allowing it to *swing* from side to side on its *anchor* wires, which are attached through sheaves on the dredge ladder. The anchor wires are let out or shortened by winches on the dredge.

SWING BRIDGE

A *bridge* that is required to turn when opening to permit passage to vessels. When opening the *bridge* it rotates on a turnstile pivot, which may allow navigation through it to the left- or right- hand spans if the depth of water is navigable. The preferred channel side is marked on the chart. Also called a *wagon bridge*.

SWING CLEAR

When topping a tow around, or a barge in tow, when in a river or a limited area of water, making certain there is enough room that the action will be free, keeping the barge or tow from striking any structure or object.

SWING LIGHT
See: PEEP LIGHT

SWING MAN

A crew member who doesn't stand a designated watch, but works as needed to make lockages, pick up or drop barges, etc.

SWING METER

An electronic device that works on a gyro principle indicating the direction and rate of turn or swing of a vessel and its tow.

SWING OUT

The action of moving a fixed pivoting crane or davit outward from a vessel in order to lower or hoist a small boat or other gear such as barrels or a cargo hose.

SWING POLE

A long pole temporarily rigged on the centerline of the head of the tow that a Pilot can utilize to judge the rate of swing on the tow. It is also usually rigged with a small flag or piece of cloth to indicate the wind direction, as well as showing a PEEP LIGHT at night.

SWITCH BOAT
See: FLEET BOAT

SWITCH IN or OUT

Moving barges in or out of a tow, or from a fleeting area, or to and from a dock.

SWIVEL

The ability of a block, shackle, or other device that is able to turn freely in a circular motion when attached to something. The term derives from the old English *swifan*, meaning "to move in a course".

SYNCROLIFT

A trade name for a type of drydock platform or ship lift that sinks in the water; when a vessel is floated on, the platform is then raised by winches. When the platform is raised to a level even with the shoreline, the dollies on which the vessel rests can be rolled off to another position in a shipyard allow-

434 SYNTHETIC LINE

ing the *syncrolift* to be utilized for another drydocking.

SYNTHETIC LINE

Until shortly after WW II almost all line used on the river was of natural fiber, such as hemp, sisal, and manila. Since that time there have been many new and different lines made with new synthetic fibers, such as nylon, polypropylene, polyesters, and other extremely strong trademarked products like Dacron, and Kevlar. Each have their plus and minus points, depending upon their usage.

SYPHON or SIPHON

See: STEAM SIPHON or SYPHON.

TWO FAMOUS STEAMBOATS IN RIVER HISTORY

The above picture is of the Steamer Sprague—the largest steamboat built (1902) for towing on the Mississippi River. Note the "hog chains" arrangement above deck.

Below is a picture of the Steamer SULTANA. The first is of the sidewheeler at Helena, AR when loaded with Civil War veterans returning to their homes in the north. Note the decks loaded with soldiers. The other picture is a depiction from the *Harper's Weekly* in 1865 when the vessel burned with great loss of life.

STERN PADDLEWHEEL

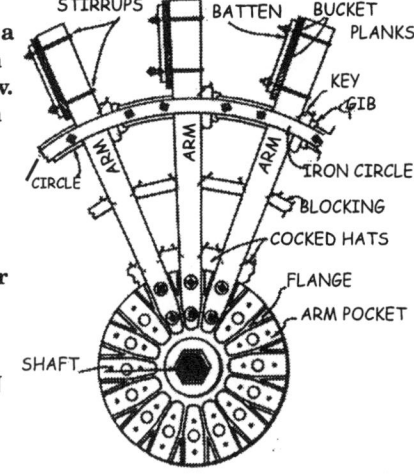

A sternwheel is a paddlewheel mounted at the stern of a vessel. SIDEWHEELERs had their paddlewheels on each side of their hull approximately 2/3 way back from the bow.

The image, as well as the explanation shown here is from "The Western Rivers Steamboat" by Alan Bate. A copy should be in every river person's library. The illustration depicts only a short section of the paddlewheel.

A FLANGE is attached to the SHAFT, which is usually hexagonal. ARMS are fitted into the ARM pockets and bolted into place. Sometimes they are braced by triangular blocks of wood called COCKED HATS. Further out on the ARMS are additional blockings of fitted wooden pieces.,

Just inside where the BUCKET PLANKS will then be attached is the principle wood blocking called a WOODEN CIRCLE consisting of more wooden blocks that will have their grain protected by wooden GIBS. All this is held in place by IRON CIRCLES on the inboard and outboard sides that are bolted together through the wooden blocks and also further tightened into place by wood KEYS, that are blunt type wedges driven in between the ARMS with STIRRUP bolts through wooden BATTENUS.

SPLICING

SHORT SPLICE — The act of splicing two sections of line together in a short splice is to unravel the ends of each section a short distance. Then MARRY them together by inter-joining the end strands of the sections being spliced. Next TUCK each strand through a section of the line, over and under each adjoining strand. At least three tucks should be made.

EYE SPLICE — Similar to the short splice, unravel a short section of the line and lay it back over itself to the desired measured size of the eye wanted. Then TUCK each strand into the body of the line, one over the other, until at least three tucks are made.

TACHOMETER

A mechanical device that measures the revolutions per minute (RPM) of a shaft to a propeller or a paddlewheel at any given time. The term comes from the Greek *tachos,* meaning "speed" and *meter,* a measuring device. The word is said to have originated by a European inventor in the early 1800s.

TACKLE

A purchase of two or more blocks rove with line or wire to give a mechanical advantage when lifting or hoisting something. The word is from the Dutch *tacken,* meaning "to lay hold of".

TAG or TAIL BOATS

Vessels that assist other vessels in controlling movement of a barge(s) on a towline, or as needed when in transit at a bridge or other close quarter work while navigating through a port.

TAG LINE

A small line used to control the swing of a boom, a load, or object that is on the boom line which is being lowered to another place.

TAIL GATE

A name sometimes given to the lower gate(s) of a lock since they are in the downstream *tail* water of the dam.

TAIL SHAFT

The end part of the propulsion shafting. The section of shafting that goes through the STRUT and to which the propeller is attached.

TAIL WATER

The gauge, or depth, of water immediately below a dam. Sometimes refers to the amount of water a dam may be discharging.

TAINTER GATE

Dam gates that can be pivoted and raised or lowered, constructed with enough built-in lift to allow for the highest flood waters of record to pass. The gate is named after a logger from Wisconsin who invented it in about 1880 for use in logging streams. The USACE bought the patents and first used the design on the Fox River in Illinois, and on the Illinois and Mississippi Canal. They were adopted for use on the Ohio River at some dams to be either raised for high water, or submerged to pass ice or drift. This type of gate is the most common on the Western rivers at present. It is basically a sectional type of cylinder mounted on radial arms that rotate on trunnion pins located in the dam piers. It is considered the most suitable and economical for navigable waterway usage.

TAKE A TURN or A STRAIN

To put another *turn* on a deck fitting, especially when a line or wire is under a degree of strain and is paying out, when a command is given, *"Take another turn* on the timberheads before it gets away from you", or "Don't let that line pay out, *take a strain* on it".

TAKE HER DOWN A NOTCH

To slow a vessel down, i.e., "I'm going to *take her down a notch* so you can get by before we get to the bridge".

TAKE IN

To pull aboard a line or wire, i.e., *"Take in* the stern line because we'll be turning her loose in a few minutes".

TAKE THE HORNS

See: ANTLERS.

TAKE UP

1. The act of shortening or tightening, i.e., *"Take up* the slack in that line", or "That wire is loose at the break coupling; *take up* on those ratchets".
2. The action of a seam between planks in a wooden hulled vessel that have dried up somewhat when taken out of the water on ways or a drydock which then swell together when again

immersed in water and make the hull watertight. The hull is said to *take up*.

TALL STACKS
A gathering of steamboats and sternwheel diesel-propelled vessels held every few years in Cincinnati in the fall. The first was in October 1988 to celebrate the city's 200th anniversary. The festival lasts nearly a week with boat rides, music, exhibits, etc.

TANK
A compartment on vessels, usually to carry liquids such as, fuel *tank*, water *tank*, cargo *tank*, etc.; however, they can also refer to a compartment that does not often carry anything, such a bow *tank*, void *tank*, wing *tank* of a barge, etc. It also can refer to a large *tank* on the shoreline, i.e., "Head for that *tank* above the point". The word goes back to the Latin *stagnum*, to mean "a pond".

TANK BARGE
A barge designed to transport liquid products. These barges carry all different kinds of petroleum products from diesel, gasoline, and asphalt, as well as numerous chemicals. Some carry food products such as soybean oil or molasses. Some are of special design to carry liquid sulfur, chlorine, or anhydrous ammonia. They come in various sizes, from small midstream fuel flats to general all-purpose jumbo barges of about 10,000 barrels to those of about 290' by 54' that carry 30,000 barrels or more of cargo.

TANK CLEANING
The stripping of clingage and residue product, or heel, from a tank barge after cargo discharge, and then either purging it of fumes, and/or washing it with either cold or hot water, sometimes with chemical solutions. See: BUTTERWORTH.

TANK FARM
A terminal that handles liquid products and contains numerous large storage tanks at its facility.

TANK TESTING
The study of a marine engineer's new hull design which is undertaken by building a model of the hull and having it evaluated in different conditions at a *tank testing* basin facility. Modification can then be made to the vessel design prior to actual plan approval and vessel construction. Some testing of designs are now preliminarily done by computer models, in regard to shoving ability with different size tows and tonnages, steering ability, backing and handling capabilities, as well as any other factors a future owner believes will be important to their operation.

TANKER
A large ship that transports liquid cargoes. Also called a *tank ship*. In the river industry tank barges are sometimes colloquially referred to as *tankers*, i.e., "The DEX barge fleet consists of over seventy-five percent *tankers*", or "I've got 12 grain barges and three *tankers*".

TANKERMAN
A person who is trained and qualified to load cargo in or out of tank barges and who has been issued a document by the USCG attesting to those cargo classes he/she is considered certified to properly handle.

TARIFF
A volume of general terms for movement of freight and specific rates for the cargo from one point to another. No cargo on the river now moves in accordance with a publicly issued *tariff*. The last general one published on the river system was about 1976. This benchmark of rates was established for most locations on the Mississippi and Ohio river systems. It is now used as a guide for quoting barge freight rates all over the system. From these base *tariff* rates shippers of commodities and their water carriers determine a percentage of that benchmark for what they are willing to pay to move their products, and the carrier decides if it is willing to

accept that rate. For example, if the *tariff* rate (1976) from a point on the Upper Mississippi was $5.00 per ton (2000 lbs.) to New Orleans, and the current agreed rate is at 250% of *tariff*, the price to move the cargo would be $12.50 per ton. If the barge contained 1600 tons of corn, then the delivered transportation cost to New Orleans would be $20,000.00.

The structure of rate quotes is fairly well known to barge operators, however, it is now a fluctuating number mostly affected by the supply of barges and a shipper's need for them to transport their cargo. There are different percentage quotes for different rivers and on different sections of the same river. The term as now used is of fairly modern origin. It originally referred to a table of numbers from an Arabic word "to notify". That apparently evolved down to the publishing of freight rate charges for the transportation of products.

TARP

An abbreviated name for *tarpaulin*, which is a heavy piece of treated canvas or a synthetic material that can repel water. Used in various places on towboats as a protective cover over line, gear, yawls, or whatever, to keep material from getting wet and/or freezing. It comes from the viscous liquid "tar" and the cloth that it covers, from the Latin *pallium*, meaning "a covering".

TATTLE-TALE

A follow up indicator in the pilothouse to show the angle of the rudder at any given time. Also sometimes called TELL-TAILS, however, that name more often refers to a different usage.

TAUT

1. A line or wire that is tight with no slack. There is some uncertainty as to the origin of the term. Some say it may be from the Old English *teon*, meaning to pull or drag. It apparently was spelled "tought" and had the meaning of being "distended", which would seem to mean "to pull apart" and would be well beyond any sense of "firmness". Others believe *taut* is a variant of *tough* which has the meaning of "strong or secure". Its usage as we apply it today came into being in the 17th Century. Just don't get to *taut* up as to the word's entomology, but make sure your verbiage is as *taut* as possible.

2. Said of a vessel that is well-kept, with a crew that is well-trained.

T-BONE COLLISION

A collision in which one vessel runs into the mid-ship section of another, more or less on a perpendicular angle.

TELEGRAPH

See: ENGINE ORDER TELEGRAPH.

TELEGRAPHING

The lowering of a steamboat's stacks to clear the spans of a low bridge. So named, since the *Str. TELEGRAPH* was reported to be the first steamer to be built with hinged stacks to allow the necessary clearance of them under a bridge.

TELL-TAILS

Small strips of light cloth tied at a high unobstructed protrusion visible to the Pilot in order that the direction and force of the wind might be gauged. See: TATTLE-TALE.

TEMPERANCE BOAT

A packet steamer that did not serve liquor.

TEMPLATE

A pattern of thin wood or heavy paper made full-sized to duplicate the same dimensions for construction or repair of a section of a vessel. It is used to mold or pattern an exact likeness in wood or steel, and then the new piece is fitted into the desired area.

TEMPORARY LIGHT or BUOY

An aid to navigation that is temporarily placed to mark a change in channel until permanent aids can be placed, or to mark some obstruction until it can be removed.

TEND

1. To take care of, i.e., "Stand by and *tend* to the bow line until the rest of the crew relieves the watch". In this sense the term is a shortened version of "attend".
2. A directional movement, i.e., "She *tends* to want to drag to port a bit". When used in this way the word took on the meaning "to be inclined" in the 16th Century.

TENDER

1. A small boat that is used in the service of another vessel, such as a dredge *tender* that shifts the pipeline around or sets dredge buoys; or other types of service such as ferrying persons or supplies to or from shore for a working vessel or plant.
2. Refers to both a small flat sometimes used by a diver, as well as to the person who may be attending to the diver's gear and needs.
3. Said of a vessel that is inclined to roll more than normal, usually because it too narrow and/or has a high superstructure. Not often said of a towboat, but can apply to a tug. See: HEEL and STIFF (the opposite of *tender*).
4. An offer to supply services for hire or a payment for services rendered.
5. A person who oversees the opening and closing of drawbridges is called a bridge *tender*.
6. Said of a Mate that speaks soft kindly words to those under his command, i.e. "Get your lazy tails busy splicing line, can't have you guys lollygagging on my watch."
7. Can be said of the steak served aboard towboats on Saturday, i.e. "The cooks sure has put out some *tender* steaks today".

TENNESSEE RIVER

Geologists say the *Tennessee River* has had various courses over its history with the upper section flowing into the Gulf of Mexico, while its middle meandering flows ran into the Mississippi and then changed course to dump its waters into Alabama. Its lower section went into what is the area of the Tombigbee River. When a new ice age occurred eons ago it ran through the continent and scoured out new valleys. The flow of the river then started its present northward journey to finally end up in the basin of the Ohio River. European explorers came to know the river as where the Little Tennessee River and the HOLSTON RIVER (see for history of change) merged together. However, the modern version, since the formation of the Tennessee Valley Authority (TVA), has the start of the river where the Holston and the French Broad meet. From this point the *Tennessee* now flows 652 miles in a northerly direction until it empties into the Ohio River at Paducah, KY.

Cartographers in early days drew it with various names with the French calling it Riviere des Cheraquis, or Cherokee, as that was the name of the Indian tribe that lived in the area. The Indians had a settlement on the river called "Tanase". This name was spelled with different variations and finally evolved into *Tennessee*. The river's basin drains about 40,500 square miles. Keelboats and flatboats were used for transport in the early settlement days. Various shoals caused obstructions to navigation with the worst apparently being the Muscle Shoals area, about 30 miles long between about river miles 250 and 280. Swift water between shoals also created difficulties as the elevation between Knoxville and Paducah drops 500 feet. With the success of steamboating on other river systems people in the valley saw their future in its development on the *Tennessee*. The *Str. OSAGE* in 1821 apparently made it up to Huntsville; in 1828 the small *Str. ATLAS* steamed up to Knoxville, the head of navigation.

Physical obstructions to navigation however, hindered the valley in reaping the benefits of steamboating; and as railroads extended their reach not many improvements were made on the river except for snag removal the clearing of a few sandbars. Efforts were made to build and maintain a canal in the Muscle Shoals area. Final plans had a design for a canal 14.5 miles long with 17 locks (120 by 32 feet) with five foot lifts. When opened in 1836 tolls were charged to recover costs. The project was not successful and was abandoned a year later. Near the end of the century and on into the new one in 1900 the USACE built a canal at Muscle Shoals and Colbert Shoals which was not very helpful to vessel traffic.

In 1933, Congress created the Tennessee Valley Authority (TVA) which was probably the first large multi-purpose water and economic project in the U.S. Its aim included water and flood control, development of navigation, electric power generation, assistance to agriculture and forestry, along with efficient use of the soil, and industry development to provide job opportunities to people suffering in the depression.

The improvement of river navigability for commercial traffic included nine high lift dams with locks. They were partially completed in 1945 and stabilization of channel width and depth was finished by the end of 1952. Some modernization of these structures along with the replacement of some has taken place on a continuing basis.

TENNESSEE-TOMBIGBEE WATERWAY (TENN-TOM)

Although the waterway between the Tennessee and the Tombigbee rivers is considered new, it was first recommended by the French explorers when they were active in settling there in the mid-1700s since rivers were the only practical way to move commerce. It was investigated by the Corps of Engineers in 1875 but found to be commercially impracticable. Again investigated prior to WW I, but still believed too costly. With the development of the TVA dams on the Tennessee River, other studies were made, and finally after WW II Congress authorized the project. Construction started in 1972 and it opened to commerce in 1985. Its construction involved the largest earth moving project in history with the excavation of over 300 million tons of rock and soil. The cost of the project was $2 billion and took 12 years to build with completion at the end of 1984. The project has a total of 10 locks and dams.

The *Tenn-Tom* starts at Yellow Creek (mile 215, Tennessee River), goes through the "Divide Cut" for 29 miles with two locks and dams, and down through five locks and dams of the canal section or the so-called "Chain of Lakes, then enters the *Tombigbee River* reach which includes three locks and dams. At Demopolis it joins with the Black Warrior River and they flow together until joined by the Alabama River to become the Mobile River which goes to the Port of Mobile and into the Gulf of Mexico. All locks are 600 by 110 feet. The total distance of the waterway is 234 miles.

TENNESSEE VALLEY AUTHORITY (TVA)

In 1933, President Franklin D. Roosevelt signed the Act to create the TVA, which was intended to improve navigability on the Tennessee River, provide flood control, assist in reforestation, help industrial development throughout the valley and promote agricultural programs. This they have done, enabling modern navigation to Knoxville from the Ohio River (a distance of about 650 miles) by the development of locks and dams, which also generate tremendous hydroelectric capability to provide economical power to the entire area. The project also provided a route to the Gulf Coast at Mobile, AL, via the TENN-TOM WATERWAY in the Pickwick Dam pool when the TENN-TOM was constructed.

TENSILE STRENGTH

The measurement of a piece of material put under stress until it deforms, breaks, or ruptures. It is most often used when referring to steel plates and frames; but can apply to line, wire, or other material parts in a vessel.

TERMINAL

Any facility on a river or canal where barges can be loaded with cargo or unloaded, or where there can be an exchange of passengers. The word comes from the Latin root *terminus,* meaning "the end", and originally was used when referring to the end of a person's life or when an action ended. In the 19th century it took on the meaning of the *terminus* of a journey on the road which, of course, was where cargo was destined by either wagon or vessel. Now however, the term can mean the start as well as an ending destination.

TERRITORIAL SEA

Generally, this was the open water three miles beyond the baseline of a nation's coast. In the time that the area was first established, the gunnery available could not fire a round at a greater distance, so it was decided if one was not able to protect the waters beyond the three-mile limit from the passage of a ship, and a ship was not able to attack those on shore from that distance, all the waters beyond that distance should be considered free water for anyone wishing to navigate through it. In 1982 an international treaty changed the distance a nation might claim to 12 miles. With intercontinental missiles one wonders where the next line might be.

TESTING

Various types of *testing* are undertaken on vessels during construction and throughout their lifetime of service. Some tests are required by the USCG and classification societies, while additional ones may be performed by the owners to insure the continuing safety and suitability of their vessels. These tests may be visual, hydrostatic, air pressure, ultrasonic, x-ray, or any other method appropriate to discover deficiencies that may require repair or replacement.

TEU

An acronym for a *twenty-foot equivalent unit*, the measurement of a trailer-type box used in the container trades. The TEU and the FEU (forty-foot equivalent unit) are the common units that move on barges and ships. Although some have moved on the rivers since the early 1960s they have become more frequent as trades have developed in the 21st century.

TEXAS CHICKEN

A maneuver in a narrow channel wherein two vessels that are in a meeting situation hold a course directly toward one another head-on and at the proper moment each vessel steers somewhat to starboard. As their bows pass one another they steer back to port leaving a cushion of water between them. When past and clear they each straighten up on course and go on their way. It looks scary to neophytes, but it is the only safe way to meet in some narrow and somewhat shallow channels with ships and large tows. The name *Texas Chicken* got its name from vessels that traverse the Houston Ship Channel, where ships have to routinely use the maneuver. If vessels tried to make a normal port-to-port passage in this type of situation, they would be sucked together and collide. The Channel is also not so humorlessly called the "Veer Ditch", since both vessels have to veer away from one another and then veer back to the channel line when they are abreast of one another.

TEXAS DECK

The deck above the hurricane deck on a steamboat. This deck was originally meant to provide living quarters for the boat's officers, but later designs enlarged it to accommodate more passengers. Different explanations have been given as to origination of the deck's name. Some versions state that the *Str. TEXAS* was the first vessel to have a stateroom built on the hurricane deck; another declares that the names of all the other states had been expended on all the other staterooms until the supply was exhausted. The only one they had left was *Texas*, and the deck on which it was on was so named. Yet another account stipulates that this deck was so named in honor of that time when the Texas came into the Union in 1845 as the 28th state. The term Texas comes from an Indian dialect called Caddo, *tecas,* which had the meaning of "friends or allies".

THALWEG

Theoretically, it is the lowest part of a river valley. However, on the Western Rivers it usually refers to the deepest part of a section of the channel and is most often used in reference to the deepest part of a bend in the river. It is not necessarily the center of the channel, but is usually where the swiftest water flows.

Where a navigable river constitutes the boundary line between foreign countries, international law construes the *thalweg* as the deepest section of the channel and denotes its centerline course as where the boundary between the countries shall be determined. Therefore, it allows both countries navigable access to the waterway. The word comes from the German *thal,* meaning "valley", and *weg,* meaning "way".

THANK YOU, MA'M

Said on almost every crossing on the Missouri River when you bumped (hit bottom) and didn't break up the tow during low-water periods. It was called a *Thank You, Ma'm* grounding, also referred to as a BUMP AND GO.

THANKSGIVING RISE

A term used mostly in the Ohio River trades; like the annual "Spring Rise" that occurs on most rivers, oftentimes a late fall run-off from the Appalachians occurs around Thanksgiving time. In early steamboat days when the Pittsburgh coal boats couldn't run because of low water during late summer and early fall, the *Thanksgiving rise* meant the fleets of coal barges could start their trips down to New Orleans.

THEN ON DOWN

A common phraseology of the old written channel reports. Crossing marks might indicate, "From 50 feet open on the last dike on the left bank to the big cottonwood; when halfway across, pull down on the daymark on the right bank, *then on down* the shape of the shore", or it might state, "After making the crossing, *then on down* the shape of the shore to Neverlit Light". It is one or those subjective terms that experienced Pilots all understand, meaning an easy distance off the shore, not too wide out towards the bar, but not too close to the shoreline that the current could set the tow in on the bank.

THICK WEATHER

Said of weather when the visibility is appreciably reduced, usually due to fog, a heavy rainstorm or driving snow. On towboats and tugs it makes it difficult to use a searchlight at night to pick up a navigational aid as the moisture, especially snow, will cause a reflection further reducing visibility. A strong rainstorm may also affect the radar images making targets unclear.

THIEVES PASTE

A *paste* put on a sounding rod or tape when measuring fuel tanks to determine if they have any water in them. The paste changes color when in contact with a liquid and it "always catches the *thief*". The act of taking the sounding for water determination is called *thieving*.

THIMBLE

An oval, somewhat closed U-shaped piece of metal usually galvanized. Its outer surface is grooved to fit the curvature of a wire, and inner surface smooth.

It is swaged into a wire with a set of chain links, with the other end of the wire having a swaged eye splice to make a barge tow makeup wire. Sometimes it is made up bare, with no chain links, in order to be able to receive an eye splice from a length of line. The *thimble* prevents chafing by the wire on the line. A *thimble* can also be spliced into a line where a shackle might be employed. As with a wire, it tends to protect against any chafing of the line at the bearing area. The word is from the Old English *thymel,* derived from "thumb" and meaning to protect the thumb when pushing a needle through fabric.

THOLE PIN
A *pin* shafting with a U-shaped upper section that is fitted into a receiving hole in the gunwale of a yawl or skiff that receives an oar. Most often used in pairs on each side of the boat's gunwale, serving as a fulcrum for the oars to apply power when rowing. The term is from the old English *thol,* meaning "peg or pin".

THOROUGHFOOT
When a length of line may have developed kinks, it is the process of coiling the line down against the lay to work the kinks out, then bringing the lower end of the line up through the coil, and recoiling the line with the lay. This procedure may have to be done more than once.

THREAD
1. A consistency of fibers of various materials such as sisal, hemp, manila, or synthetic materials that are spun together. The resulting *threads* are twisted together to become STRANDS, with the strands then twisted together to ultimately turn into what is called LINE.
2. The spiral part of a screw or bolt, as well as the female and male parts of a coupling that are joined or screwed together.

THREE SHEETS IN THE WIND
A condition no one on the river arrives at since we ain't got no sheets in the wind, except maybe when Mike Fink was operating a keeler.

THROTTLE
A device that is used to manage or control the speed of an engine by regulating its fuel or steam supply. The *throttle* can be set from full ahead to full astern, or any other position in between, or to stop. On towboats, if powered by more than one engine, each engine has a separate *throttle* control in the pilot house.

THROUGH THE HAWSEPIPE
Although riverboats do not have a *hawsepipe* (where an anchor chain runs at the bow), the term refers to an officer of a vessel who came up from the deck or oiler status to become a Pilot or Engineer, rather than receiving their river education from some type of maritime school. The term is sometimes, but seldom, used on the river. A Pilot is said to have come off the deck, or an Engineer has apprenticed in the engine room. Although presently to become a Pilot, and receive a license, now requires some degree of schooling, the actual art of piloting a towboat or tug, or of overhauling an engine, is only learned on the job. Knowledge of theory, the laws, rules, regulations, and proper safe methods can be enhanced greatly by taking courses at qualified schools, but seldom if ever the skillful application of the knowledge.

THROUGH WELL
See: SPUD WELL.

THROUGHPUT
A measure of productivity at a terminal. The amount of tonnage (such as of coal, grain, paper, logs, steel, etc.) loaded or unloaded, or the amount of containers handled or barrels of liquid that were loaded, unloaded, or transloaded, on an hourly, daily, monthly, or yearly basis. The term also refers to the total capacity of the terminal.

THROW OFF

1. To take off, or make loose, a line or a wire attached to a fitting on another vessel or to the shore.

2. The bow wave that may come off a fast-moving vessel, i.e.' "That ship is sure *throwing off* a heck of a wave, hope he doesn't break loose any barges at the KLM dock".

THRUST

The push or propulsion exerted by the turning movement of the propeller when it is set in motion by the engine shipping up. The origin of the word is from the Norse *thrysta,* which has some relationship to the Latin *trudere,* meaning "to press ahead suddenly, or *thrust*". Perhaps it was what an Roman soldier did suddenly with his sword since he didn't have a propeller.

THRUST BEARING

A propeller that is turning ahead is screwing itself forward with an extraordinary amount of force and could cause wreckage to the engine unless prevented from doing so. When the propeller is operating in astern propulsion it tends to pull the shafting out from the vessel. To prevent these actions from occurring a *thrust bearing* is installed on the line shaft immediately aft of the engine. This *bearing* absorbs the linear force of the shafting. In the motion ahead the prop pushes the shaft forward, however in effect the *thrust bearing* is then pushing the towboat or tugboat. The thrusting movement creates a tremendous friction building a great amount of heat so the *bearing* must be continually and adequately lubricated or it will freeze up.

THRUSTER

A propeller located in a tunnel that can direct a sideways lateral movement to a vessel or tow. Although there are bow and stern *thrusters*, on the rivers one is usually referring to BOW THRUSTERS that are placed in the bow of a lead barge in a unit tow. It assists in high wind conditions, especially in narrow channels and when making landings or entering lock chambers.

THWART

A seat in a small boat, such as a yawl or skiff, that runs between the sides of the boat at the gunwale, or athwartships, for persons to sit upon. The origin of the word is from *athwart,* meaning "across". Possibly the nautical use of the term of putting a board across the beam of a small boat upon which to sit seemed to fill the meaning of "across". However, the non-nautical meaning of *thwart* is "to oppose" or "cross" someone, but if you must do it, wait until the boat docks.

THWARTSHIP

Transverse, or at right angles, to the centerline of a vessel.

TIDAL WATER

Those waters along the Gulf Coast which are subject to the influence of tides. These effects can become critical to navigation in certain passes that may have strong cross-current flows to or from the Gulf of Mexico during *tidal* ranges.

TIDE

1. A rising and falling of the water levels along the Gulf Intercoastal Waterway subject to gravitational pull between the Earth, the Sun, and the Moon. It will result in inflows and outflows of interior waters that can result in severe cross currents at outlets through the GIWW. The term is from the old English *tid,* and is related to "time".

2. Sometimes referred to as a rising river, i.e., "The *tide* (river) is coming up".

TIDE TABLES

A tabulation of days giving the times of predicted high and low *tides*.

TIDEGATE

See: FLOODGATE

TIE OFF or UP

The act of making secure or mooring a towboat, tug, barge, or a tow to a dock, mooring pier, lock wall, fleet, or another vessel. To make a vessel FAST.

TIER

A group of barges in a tow or at a fleet. Usually refers to sections of a tow, i.e., "We'll be dropping the head *tier* of barges at the OPQ Fleet next watch", or "Our pickups at the OPQ Fleet are in the middle *tier*".

TIGHT or TITE

1. The same as TAUT; not loose or slack.
2. Sound, not leaking, i.e., "The boys sure did a good job of CAULKING; she's *tight* as a drum head, we've not shipped a drop of water since we left ol' Louieville".

TILLER, TILLER LINES and TILLER ROPE

1. Sometimes *tiller* is used when referring to the QUADRANT where the rudder head of the rudder stock is fitted to provide steerage. Wires (called *tiller wires* or *line*) are attached to the steering system controlled from the Pilothouse. At one time steamboats used fiber rope line on the *tiller*, but after many fires aboard vessels, in which the lines burned, causing the loss of ability to steer before a Pilot could run the burning vessel aground, the Government took action. The 1838 Steamboat Act called for iron rods or chains in place of tiller rope, but these were impracticable on Western Rivers. The law was ignored and later was ruled invalid to steamers in river trades. However, steel wire came into use and eventually all steamboats installed it for their steering systems.

2. *Tiller lines*, which are in reality wire cables, are attached to the *tiller* or quadrant and run through a series of pulleys to the steering controls in the pilothouse.

3. If a pilot wheel is the means of steering a vessel, a *tiller rope* is attached to a drum on the back side of the wheel which when turned the rudders will move in the direction of the turn of the steering wheel. The *tiller rope* is further attached to the *tiller lines*. Entomology traces the word *tiller* back to a "weavers beam" which was used when weaving threads in and out, or to "thread one's way" when making cloth. So in this sense the *tiller* makes the rudder move and allows a Pilot to change course, or "weave" a vessel through a narrow winding channel.

TIMBER

That which comes from trees in the forests that went into the building of wooden steamboats and mostly provided them with the fuel to fire their boilers when they first started moving people and commerce. Certain types of woods were prized for certain purposes in building steamers but, as ready supplies dwindled, some *timber* and lumber planks came from as far away as Oregon to build Western River vessels. In wooden steamboat construction, various parts were given prefixes to the word *timber,* depending upon where they were used, i.e., floor *timber*, cant *timber*, square *timber*, etc. The word comes from the old English meaning "building" or "building material".

TIMBER CRIB DAMS

Large timber box-like structures bolted together and filled with quarry stone used in the construction of dams and locks. Prior to 1895 all locks and dams were built in this fashion, or with the more expensive stone masonry. After a period of bad flooding in the river, extensive repairs were usually required.

TIMBER MAT or FENCE

Heavy wooden boards placed on the deck of a barge, sometimes in a frame, where machinery would run, especially a crane. Used to spread the weight of the crane and its load when the crane would travel, thus preventing indenting or WASHBOARDING of the barge deck.

TIMBER PILE
See: PILE

TIMBERCLADS
Gunboats of the Civil War on the Western Rivers that had been strengthened to carry heavy guns; their sides were covered with five-inch thick oak boards to withstand the attack of most rifle fire. See: COTTONCLADS, IRONCLADS and TINCLADS.

TIMBERHEAD
A vertical post or bitt about 24 inches high, placed either singly or in pairs, used for tying off barges with lines, or to couple barges together with hard rigging. When wooden barges were used in transportation, vertical timber supports or stanchions protruded up through the deck that served as posts to tie off the vessels. The extended top, or *head*, of the *timber* has continued to also be the term for the steel bitts in use today.

TIMBERHEAD TALK
Gossip or rumors with no actual or factual background by the crew while sitting on *timberheads*. See: SCUTTLEBUTT.

TIME CHARTER
An employment of a vessel to a charterer for a specific period of time at a daily, weekly, or monthly rate, with the owner furnishing the crew, supplies, provisions, etc.; however, fuel may be a separate item.

TIME OFF
The period of *time* when a person is *off* the vessel. In the old river days of flatboating, keelboating, and steamboating, a person would usually stay and live on the boat until they quit or by agreement take a few days or a trip off. Towboat crews today work a schedule of so many days on, and so many days off, with personnel on a regular rotation. For many years it was 40 on – 20 off, then came 30 – 30; now each company has its own policy with a lot of flexibility. If a person wants more time off he/she just doesn't get paid as much, but if crew members like to work they can stay on longer and sell back to the company their earned *off* time.

TIME ZONE
Most river vessels operate in the Eastern or Central *time zones*, usually reflecting where their home offices are located. Even if they travel between the different *times zones* periodically, they normally do not set the clocks ahead or back as they travel.

TINCLADS
The name given to lightly armored gunboats in the Civil War of both the Union and Confederate Navies on the Western Rivers and their shallow tributaries. These sacrificed the weight of the heavily clad IRONCLADS in order to reduce the amount of water they drew so they could navigate in shallow streams. Their draft was from something shy of two feet to a maximum of four feet. Some would only draw from eight inches to one foot of water. It was said that one such vessel had mounted a large sprinkling can on her jackstaff, bragging that it carried its own water supply on which to navigate. Another, so the story goes, had a Mate who could tap a keg of beer and run the *tinclad* for four miles on the suds. Most swore they could navigate on heavy dew. Abe Lincoln called them his "web feet". They were lightly armored to only withstand musket fire for the most part. Their firepower was minimal at best. See: COTTONCLADS, IRONCLADS and TIMBERCLADS.

TIP CLEARANCE
The amount of distance from the end, or *tip*, of a propeller and the hull, or the propeller's clearance when located in a KORT NOZZLE.

TIPPLE
A structure that extends out over a coal dock that directs the coal loading into a barge from a storage yard, or directly from rail or truck dumping.

TITLE XI

A government loan guarantee program under the Maritime Administration that allows borrowers wanting to build vessels, and shipyards to make improvements, to obtain a fixed rate of financing for up to 25 years. This allows the borrower to find a better, or a preferred, loan rate from a lending institution. The Maritime Administration oversees the program for the government and holds a first preferred mortgage on the vessel, or security interest in the shipyard, over the life of the loan.

TOE

1. The edge of a flange of a steel structural member.
2. The lower end or downstream part of an island.

TOE DIKE

A short dike sometimes built at the toe, or end, of a revetment and parallel to the current flow. It is also used to stop erosion in a bank line.

TOE RAIL

A bar or small piping, usually only an inch or so high. It is raised slightly off the deck surface and is sometimes added to the main deck of a towboat along the edge of most of its outboard sides to help prevent someone from slipping off a towboat.

TOGGLE

1. When tying off a vessel or a tow to the bank and wanting a quick release, the eye of a tie-off line is run out to a large tree, and brought around the trunk. The bight of the line is fed up through the eye sufficient to put a heavy piece of wood, called a *toggle*, through the loop that is formed. When turning loose, all one has to do is pull out the wooden *toggle*.
2. When steamboats were at paved cobblestone landings at city fronts, there were usually ringbolts in the landing used to secure vessels. The eye of a line was run through the ring and the bight of the line then put up through the eye. In this loop a wooden *toggle*, consisting of a three-foot long 3" by 3" piece of wood was inserted that could quickly and easily be pulled out when a vessel was ready to depart the landing.
3. In sea trades small *toggles* are used as quick releases for life rings, flag signals, and on some sails, but not on riverboats. The origin of the word is hazy, but was, and is, used as a fastener for a jacket or other garment, and probably was related to "tangle" as at sea it was used as a small piece of wood attached to a short small stuff line that had a BECKET or loop in the other end. The small line was used to secure furled sails of sailing ships to keep them from becoming entangled. Also see: SPANISH WINDLASS.

TOLLS

A charge for use of a lockage on a river. In the past there had been charges for lock usage when the facilities were in private hands. For example, when the Louisville and Portland Canal was built by private interests in 1830, vessels were charged 20 cents per ton to transit, which was soon raised. Eventually the government took over the firm. Also, another group formed a corporation and obtained a license from the State of Kentucky to operate the Green and Barren rivers after the Civil War and promptly exercised monopoly control over the river traffic by *toll* charges, driving competitors out of business. In 1886 the State ceded its ownership to the Federal Government which then bought the franchise and ended *tolls*. On the Kentucky River the State had built most of the lock and dam projects and charged *tolls*, but found it unprofitable to continue operation. Like on the Green and Barren, the facilities were in a state of disrepair after the Civil War and the State tried to divest themselves from their operation. After a study of the river, the State ceded control of it to the federal government in 1880. See: USER CHARGES.

TON

There are many measurements of *ton*. Among them are units of mass, force, volume, energy, power, and other somewhat slang usages. The term comes from the old English *tunne,* or *tun*, which was a large wine cask that held about 252 gallons and weighed about 2100 pounds. See: the following terms for a somewhat more descriptive difference: DEADWEIGHT TON, DISPLACEMENT TON, GROSS TON, METRIC TON, NET TON, LONG TON, and REGISTERED TON.

TON MILE

The measurement of one ton of cargo (short ton, 2000 pounds) moving the distance of one mile. Freight rates are based on *ton miles* traveled, sometimes with a minimum amount of tonnage required; i.e., if a shipper only loads a barge to 1000 tons and the contract calls for a minimum of 1400 tons at 5 mils per *ton mile*, and the voyage is 1200 miles, the shipper will pay the carrier $8400, rather than the $6000, as the shipper did not load to the minimum tonnage required.

TONNAGE

See TON above; however, be warned that when you get into Registered *Tonnage*, both Gross and Net, the description is somewhat like an artist's interpretation of what should go on the canvas. Two or three or more people doing the admeasurements of a vessel will probably come up with different renditions of what they determined the *tonnage* to be – some abstract, some classical, some pure folklore.

TONNE

Same as METRIC TON.

TONS PER INCH (TPI)

The weight in short tons (2000 pounds) of the cargo in a barge for each inch of immersion in the water from a draft table. In the field it is an approximation since it requires the vessel to be absolutely dry throughout its hull spaces, and the measurements of draft have to be taken sometimes in wavy waters from all four draft mark readings and then averaged. The proper way to arrive at an accurate tonnage figure is to measure the barge draft when empty and then after it is loaded and compensate from the table to figure the cargo tonnage.

TOO THICK TO DRINK, TOO THIN TO PLOW

A saying that has been attributed to many rivers. It has been used for the Platte River in Nebraska, as well as saying it was "a mile wide and an inch deep". It's been attributed to the Yukon, the French Broad, the Colorado, the Mississippi, and even the Yarra River in Australia, as well as others in probably many other lands. However, it best describes the Missouri River in all its majesty of the days before rock dikes and dams on its upper reaches. Its silt load would put a few inches in the bottom of a bucket when it settled out. It was said to cure whatever ailed one.

TOOTENANNY

A concert that occurs when a group of people (STEAMBOAT BUFFS) get together and bring an assemblage of old steamboat whistles, hook them up to a steam plant, pull the whistle cord, and then hear the moaning sounds that in days of yore drifted along the river valleys of passing vessels blowing their intentions when steam was king. A few recordings of them have been made.

TOOTHPICK

A short steel bar about 24" to 36" long placed in the link between the shackle and the turn screw of a ratchet to keep the screw and the wire from twisting when the barrel is being tightened, and sometimes used when loosening the ratchet.

TOOTHPULLER

See: SNAGBOAT.

TOP AROUND

The act of turning a towboat or tug, with or without a tow, completely around, such as after making up a tow in a fleet that has a southbound destination, one *tops the tow around* to continue its journey. Also, the action can occur inadvertently when coming up under a point and a strong eddy *tops the tow*, or when a swift cross current in a tidal range or other places is misjudged, or when encountering other misadventures in swift currents or strong winds. See: BILL HOOK.

TOP OFF

1. The act of slowing down the rate of cargo flow when loading tank barges so they do not overflow and cause a spill.
2. To add additional fuel to partially full fuel or water tanks of a towboat or tug.

TOPMARK

Distinctive marks on the top of buoys to more readily distinguish and identify its purpose to the mariner. It will also usually have some sort of reflective material applied to it.

TOPOGRAPHIC SURVEYS

The study and drawing of accurate descriptions of the physical features of a river valley. These were first undertaken by the USACE for locating forts in desirable and defensible locations and was continued when assigned the civil works functions of improving rivers. The Corps first had to study and depict the terrain of whole valleys for elevations and estimations of run-offs from the land and streams by making *topographic surveys* before construction of locks and dams and other watershed training works. The term comes from the Greek *topo*, meaning "place", and *graphic*, meaning "writing".

TOPPING LIFT
See: DERRICK

TOPSIDE

1. On or above the main deck, i.e., when a crew member is on a lower level in a vessel and goes to an upper level, i.e., "I'm going *topside* to see how the Captain wants to arrange tow when we get to Cairo".
2. Sometimes referred to as that part of a vessel's side hull plating above the waterline.

TORCH BASKET

In the 1800s steamboats had no electricity, so when they were at remote landings taking on or discharging cargo or passengers, a type of portable illumination was used to light the area. The *torch basket* was of iron mesh of about a foot in diameter that swung in a yoke at the end of long iron bar. The basket was filled with pine knots, other wood chips or shavings, and rosin. The rod of the basket was fitted to a socket and swung over the side of the vessel so that falling embers would go into the water. A crew member was assigned to keep the basket burning while others were working the landing and also to insure that no fire started on the vessel.

TORNADO

A mobile whirlwind of intense velocity rotating in a funnel shape with a tremendous destructive force. Seek shelter for your vessel and tow if possible. The word comes from the Spanish *tronada*, meaning "thunderstorm", derived from *tronar,* "thunder" and *tornar,* meaning "to turn".

TORQUE

The twisting force exerted by the engine on the shafting to turn the propeller. The term comes from the Latin *torquere,* meaning "twisting".

TOTAL LOSS

When a vessel has suffered so much damage from an accident or disaster that it is determined to be valueless, an insurer pays the full sum that was issued under its policy to the owner and then takes possession of the vessel.

TOUCH AND GO
See: BUMP AND GO

TOW
1. To take one or more barges or other vessels and transport them to another place by a towboat or tug. The term comes from the old English *togian*, meaning "to drag".

2. The act of pulling one or more vessels astern. See: MULE TRAIN.

3. One or more barges and/or other vessels wired together as a single unit and pushed ahead by a towboat or tug. See: TOWBOAT.

4. The act of placing one or more barges on the side (one or both sides) of a tug or towboat to transport them to another location. See: ON THE HIP. As seen by these definitions, towing on the rivers and canals means "to *tow*" behind, ahead, or alongside.

5. The length of a *tow* being pushed ahead is measured from the extreme head of the lead bow barge to the aftermost stern end of the stern barge or the stern end of the towboat or tug which may be pushing the *tow*. If a barge, or barges, are being towed astern the length usually only refers to the length of the towed vessels and does not include the length of the towline unless specifically mentioned, i.e. "I'm towing a 300' barge on the end of an 1800' wire towline".

TOW BITTS or TOWING BITTS
See: H-BITTS.

TOW HAULAGE SYSTEM
A mechanical system consisting of a winch on a lock wall with a small but strong wire that is used to assist in removing tow sections at locks that receive tows longer than the capacity of their chamber. A towboat shoves its tow into the lock chamber, breaks coupling wires for part of it (which stays in the lock chamber), then backs the other part out astern of the lock gates. The first cut of the tow then locks through. After the first cut is raised or lowered, as the case may be, and the lock gates are opened, a wire from the *tow haulage system* is placed on the barge tow cut which is then pulled out of the chamber and tied off on the lock wall. The chamber is reversed and the towboat with the rest of its tow enters the lock, is locked up (or down), shoves out of the lock, makes up to the first cut, the mooring lines are let go, and the towboat proceeds up/down river.

TOW LINE
1. A line or wire that leads from the stern of a tug or towboat to a barge or barges that are being towed astern. See: TOWING LINE.

2. A line or wire leading from a tug, towboat, or barge aft to another vessel that is under strain when moving ahead. The opposite of a BACKING LINE which would be under strain when going astern.

3. A length of line, usually 150-250 feet long, leading from the bow or bow quarter of a canal boat to the harness of one of the horses or mules that was doing the towing of the boat.

TOW PATH
The walking way or path along a canal where mule or horse driver would guide the towing animals when they were pulling a canal boat.

TOW SIGNALS
See: WHISTLE SIGNALS

TOWAGE
The act of providing a service of moving vessels from one place to another, to assist vessels in shifting barges in tow, of making up tows, of shifting barges in a fleet or to a dock, for a fee, such as by the hour, day, per mile, or any other agreement suitable to both parties.

TOWBOAT
A riverboat that is designed to move barges by pushing them ahead. It is

equipped with TOWKNEES on its bow to easily fasten to a tow which it controls. Then the begging question is asked, why are *towboats* called "tow" boats when in Europe they are called "pushers"? Then finally, doesn't "tow" mean "to pull"? In the old Western Rivers Pilot Rules of many years ago, in Rule Four it stated: "Steam vessels, when towing other vessels....." It would appear that packetboats may have had barges or other hulls tied alongside to make a "tow". It isn't probable that in river current vessels were very often towed astern, especially when moving downstream, since any mishap would have caused the astern barges in the current to overrun and seriously damage or possibly sink the towing vessel. However, the regulatory section of the Pilot Rules for the Western Rivers, in reference to the lights to be shown, utilized the words "towed ahead":

"Section 332.16 The lights for barges and canal boats when towed ahead....."

Later in the same section it states: 'When one barge is towed by a steamer. And such barge is towed ahead....."

The same section went on to address vessels towed by a hawser behind steam vessels, so it appears that the term "towed" was used in conjunction with the terms "ahead", "alongside", and "behind" or astern. Most maritime dictionaries define the term *towboat* as mariners of our Western Rivers do. However, many terms defined in this Lexicon are different from those used in other venues by people who have never worn out a pair of shoes working on the river or have knowledge of the terms as rivermen use them. The Western River heritage and tradition indicates that a *towboat* can tow barges astern, alongside, or ahead. Learn to live with it and not try to solve the "reason why" through classic etymology.

Each *towboat* has its own personality, whether in how it steers; flanks; shoves a tow; how it handles, or doesn't handle in making a downstream landing; how it vibrates, or doesn't; its quarters and their livability; and a dozen other things that give it a distinctive personality. Even boats built to the same design and specifications will be deemed different by the people who man them for any period of time.

TOWBOAT GREETING

1. A customary greeting, or notification, at a landing, or some other appropriate place, is to sound the whistle signal of the company in employ of the vessel. If the company does not have a distinctive signal, a common one used is one long blast – two short – one long – one short. See: LANDING WHISTLE.

2. If passing a towing vessel where one knows the Captain/Pilot of the other vessel, it is common for both to go out on the respective wings of their pilothouses and give a river wave: crossing the arms overhead, and then dropping them to the side in a spread-eagle fashion, sort of like an "all clear" or "all's well" signal.

TOWHEAD

A small island that may be formed around a sunken vessel or other obstruction in the river that causes a bar to build. As vegetation develops it traps more sand and may grow in size, however, a flood can cause it to disappear faster than it grew. The term is also sometimes used to refer to the upstream end of an island.

TOWING

1. On rivers, the term is used in reference to barges being pushed ahead, except when a towboat is MULE TRAINING.

2. With tugs in open or rough water, the term is used to mean *towing* astern.

TOWING LIGHTS

Those lights prescribed by the Inland Navigation Rules as outlined in Rule 24, whether towing by pushing ahead or by towing astern. They are different.

TOWING LINE or WIRE

When a towboat or a tug tows astern in narrow channels and close quarters, it is usually fairly close up without a long scope of line. Most towboats will use a BRIDLE made of wire and then either a wire or line leading from the FLOUNDER PLATE (or fishplate) to the towing vessel. Also see: TOW LINE which is used interchangeably.

TOWING OFFICER ASSESSMENT RECORD (TOAR)

A program of the USCG that evaluates the abilities and compentancy of a person seeking to become a Mate (Pilot) of towing vessels. The appraisal is performed by Masters that have sought and received approval of the USCG to be a DESIGNATED EXAMINER (DE). The TOAR contains a list of tasks and regulatory initiatives that a prospective candidate is required to satisfactorily undertake, learn, and complete in order to receive a license as a Mate (Pilot). A Designated Examiner must assess the performance of the candidate in the program and if satisfied that he/she has successfully fulfilled the requirements the DE will sign and date the TOAR. The *Record* will be presented to the USCG when the apprentice applies for a license. See APPRENTICE MATE.

TOWING SAFTY ADVISORY COMMITTEE (TSAC)

An advisory committee to the USCG made up of people from the towing industry, unions, and public representatives to give their best advice as to safety concerns and regulatory proposals to the USCG. They meet semi-annually or as needed.

TOWKNEES

Heavily constructed braces, usually two or four, across the bow end of a towboat. They are built like a right-angle triangle with one end flat against the deck, the other end vertical at the bow, and the hypotenuse side having a set of steps to use if needed to reach the deck of an empty barge being pushed ahead. This structure allows a towboat to HEADLOG against its barges, especially empty or light-loaded rake-end barges which might otherwise slide up onto its bow. See: HAGESTEPS.

TOWLINE

1. When a barge tow is being pushed ahead by a towboat, any barge "hung" (or placed) alongside that is on soft lines next to the tow will have a line from its bow fittings to the barge tow's fittings it is alongside; this is the *towline*. Then it will have a stern line that leads in the opposite direction that will be called a "backing line". This will keep the barge snug and not running ahead if the tow has to back down.

2. A hawser line or wire off the stern of a tug or towboat leading to the bow of a barge being towed astern.

TRACK

1. To follow the movement of another vessel on a radar scope or an electronic chart or to mark a target that might appear, such as a buoy.

2. A vessel or tow that maintains its course well without using much rudder is said to *track* well.

TRACTOR TUG

Defined in numerous ways by different people. Originally in the 1950s it was a tug with a cycloidal propulsion system, or a variable-pitch drive system of vertical rudder blades rotating on a drum under the hull between the mid-body and bow. Now Z-DRIVE units are considered *tractors* and some tugs are equipped with two units, although in Europe technically only vessels equipped with Voith Schneider (VSP) units are referred to as *tractors*. New technology on the move is resulting in improved efficiency.

TRADE

1. A general term for the type of cargo that a vessel normally has in its tow, such as the "coal *trade*", the "grain

trade", the "oil *trade*", or the "mixed cargo *trade*".

2. Used to indicate the route a vessel is engaged in, such as being a "pool boat" for the Upper Ohio River; or a vessel that is a Missouri River boat; or one that is in the Cairo to New Orleans *trade*, called a Lower River boat.

3. In packetboat days its *trade* usually referred to a vessel that was operating between two port cities, i.e., Pittsburgh to Wheeling; Cincinnati to Louisville; New Orleans to St. Louis; etc.

TRADE WINDS

Certain winds that blow in the tropics around the Indian Ocean. They were exceptionally beneficial to sailing vessels in days of yore. Although those winds do not affect riverboats, one of the finest small-powered, 1400 hp, vessels ever operated for river trade was christened the *M/V TRADE WINDS*. It was built in 1949 at Hillman Barge and Construction Company, later in its successful life was unfortunately renamed. It was sold or traded many times to different owners, operating in various trades in diverse areas of the Western Rivers. Finally the grand old lady met its match in the 2005 hurricanes of Katrina and Rita and sank in the New Orleans area.

TRAFFIC

1. The amount of vessel tows in an area, i.e., "The *traffic* is heavy in the Paducah area today", or "There isn't much *traffic* at the Mel Price Lock".

2. The reporting of a vessel's position and activity to the vessel's operations department.

3. The collective amount of vessels and tonnage moving through a port, lock, or a particular terminal.

TRAFFIC LIGHTS

Lights at Algiers Point in New Orleans that signal in high water if it is safe for a vessel to continue navigating downstream, and to signal an upbound vessel to hold until a downbound vessel can safely clear the bend. See: LOCK SIGNAL LIGHTS.

TRAFFIC SEPARATION SCHEME

A system of traffic lanes in some port entrances from sea to separate deep-draft vessels entering the port from those that are leaving. The separate lanes are marked with buoys. There are no such systems on the Western Rivers; however, there are some areas where shallow-draft vessels can navigate in shallower reaches of the channel, while deep-draft vessels must keep nearer to the centerline. See: LAW OF TONNAGE.

TRAIL DIKE

A pile dike that is driven along a shoreline to keep it from eroding. The piles are wired together with cross members. These dikes were extensively used on the Missouri River. Some are now constructed of rock and are called *off bank revetments*. See: REVETMENTS.

TRAINING DIKE

See: SPUR DIKE.

TRAMP TOWING or TRADE

1. A towboat that makes drops and pickups of barges with different commodities at numerous places, docks, and fleets along the river. It is the opposite of a "dedicated" tow or trade route.

2. A towing company that has few, if any, barges of its own, but picks up various barges for other barge owners as the opportunity presents itself and delivers them where requested.

TRANSDUCER

A device that is placed in the water, usually at the centerline of the lead barge in a tow, or if using two, on the outboard side of each head barge of the port and starboard strings. It emits an electrical signal to measure the depth of the water from the surface to the bed of a river or channel. The signal of depth

TRANSFER

The loading or unloading of cargo to or from a barge.

TRANSFER FERRY BOAT

Vessels that moved train cars across the river. They were fitted with tracks which ran the entire length of the vessel in order to roll the rail cars onto the ferry. After crossing, the tracks coupled up to the landing on the opposite side of the river. At one time there were many of these boats until railroad bridges were built to handle the traffic. The last two operating on the Western Rivers were the *Str. JAMES Y. LOCKWOOD*, running between Natchez, MS, and Vidalia, LA; and finally the *Str. GENEVIEVE*, based at St. Genevieve, on the Upper Mississippi, which made her last crossing and delivery in 1961.

TRANSFER PROCEDURES

1. Required information for the transfer of any oil or hazardous material product from a vessel. The *transfer procedures* must include the generic name of the product, as well as its appearance, odor, the hazards involved in handling it, what to do if a spill occurs, and firefighting procedures.

2. The procedures shall include a description of the transfer system piping and its valves, its containment system, and emergency situations, if applicable, while loading or discharging product, as well as the personnel required and their duties during cargo *transfer*.

TRANSFER SYSTEM

Includes the entire physical system on a tank barge to load or unload cargo, including the pump, piping, valves, containment, and whatever else is necessary to permit a safe transfer.

TRANSIT

To make a passage through or across a body of water, i.e., "We're leaving the Harvey Lock and will *transit* down to Algiers", or "We're about to *transit* the canal above McAlpine Lock".

TRANSMISSION LINE

Numerous aerial *transmission lines* cross the river system. They are marked on navigation maps and charts. They usually show a target reflection on the radar scope that is called a SPOOK or GHOST.

TRANSOM

The stern end plating, or wooden beams, and framing of the after section of a vessel. It can be a squared end or a raked end, but on the river it usually refers to the vertical squared stern. The term is from the French *traversing*, meaning something that is "across".

TRANSPONDER

An integral part of an AUTOMATIC IDENTIFICATION SYSTEM that sends out a radar signal from a vessel to a central location identifying the vessel, as well as the vessel being able to receive identifying signals from vessels in its area of operation.

TRANSPORT

1. The act of moving people or cargo from one place to another.

2. The bed load of a river that is *transported* by the current from one area to another.

TRANSPORTATION WORKER IDENTIFICATION CREDENTIAL (TWIC)

An identification card required by most of the personnel employed in the transportation chain, including crew members aboard tugs and towboats. It will be required by people applying for a license.

TRANSSHIP

The transfer of cargo from one vessel to another, or to another form of transport.

TRANSVERSE
Athwartship, or across the beam; lying at right angles to the fore and aft lines of the vessel. Used mostly when referring to the framing of a vessel, as opposed to LONGITITUDAL framing.

TRAP WATER
The term is/was used mainly in the pools where the dams had bear trap gates to regulate the river's flow. These gates were often in the middle of, or on the opposite side of, the river from where the lock chamber was located. When the *traps* were open it would cause a draw of current toward them, resulting in an OUTDRAFT at the upstream approach to the lock. A Pilot conversation might be, "How's it looking above the dam?" The reply might be, "They're running *trap water* so ya gotta hug that right shore on the approach".

TRAVELING CAVELS
On some upstream lock walls there is a rail on which rides a movable cavel on wheels. It is used when double-locking to keep the first cut of the tow tight against the wall with a line from the lead barge of the cut fastened securely to the *traveling cavel* as it is being pulled out by a winch.

TREAD
The horizontal surface or walking surface of a stair or step.

TREE NAILS
Long cylindrical wooden pins that were sometimes used to secure wooden hull planking on steamboats. They were usually oak and considered superior to iron nails and bolts since they would not rust out or loosen. They had to be as dry as possible and gummed when inserted, and driven in with a BEETLE so when immersed in water the pins would swell with no leakage. With some wood if the *tree nails* still had a degree of sap in them they were singed in a low fire to force the sap to the surface. When the *nails* were then driven in the sap acted as glue when it dried.

TRIANGULATION
A barge movement of cargo in a long term contract of a shipper and a barge owner or operator between two points on the river/canal system. The *triangulation* of the barge results in the contracted movement of cargo from its origination at a loading facility to a destination dock; the cargo is unloaded and the barge is cleaned. It is then reloaded in the same area with a different cargo and shipper and is destined to some other river location. That cargo is unloaded, and the barge is further reloaded in that vicinity with a new cargo that will be destined to, or near, the area where the prime contract movement is located. This makes for an efficient utilization of barging equipment; however, it requires a great deal of coordination to achieve efficiency while at the same time satisfying customer requirements.

There is probably some cost-effective futuristic thinking by river operators who are looking at "quadrupulation" or "squareupulation" of four movements, or even the "quintupulation" or the "pentaganation" of five movements to maximize their efficiency. It's a computer world.

TRIALS
The place no mariner wants to be, especially if one is a defendant. See: BOAT TRIALS.

TRIBUTARY
A small stream that flows into a larger one. The word derives from the Latin *tributum,* meaning "to make a payment" (to the main stream).

TRICE
To hoist or haul up and make fast. The word is from the Dutch *trisen,* meaning "to pull".

TRICK
Taking a turn at the wheel, or steering. Not much used on the river.

TRIM

1. A vessel that is floating level in the water, with the same draft both forward and aft, as well as to port and starboard. If a vessel is lower in the stern than the bow, it is "*trimmed* by the stern". If a vessel is lower in the bow than at the stern, it is "*trimmed* by the head". A vessel that is down by the head, or down by the stern, it is said to be "out of *trim*". Any vessel out of *trim* to port or to starboard, it is said to LIST. If all corners of a vessel are at different drafts, it is *trimmed* "catawampus".

2. The cargo hold of a barge, either with dry cargo or liquid, is *trimmed* within its cargo compartment(s) to insure the weight within the compartment(s) is fairly evenly distributed over the entire hold. This will prevent the possibility of HOGGING or SAGGING. The word *trim* apparently comes to us from the old English *trymian* or *trymman*, meaning "stable, strong, and to arrange in orderly fashion". Its nautical sense is of a vessel that is on an even keel or evenly loaded. In about the 16th century, the term was first applied to adjusting (or *trimming*) a vessel's sails.

TRIMMING

The act of shifting cargo, fuel or water in tanks, pumping, or any other corrective action to adjust or improve the distribution of displacement on the vessel and bring it back to trim.

TRIMMING HATCH

A small lift opening in a barge cover, used to add more cargo in order to trim out the barge, or to evenly load it.

TRIMMING THE BUSHES

When a vessel is running close to the bank in slacker water.

TRINITY HOUSE

Established in 1514 in Britain by Henry VIII, it was originally chartered to establish safety of shipping and control over Pilots. Later the maritime authority erected lighthouses and started buoyage systems in its waters. It was the forerunner of safe navigation rules as we know them today.

TRIP

1. To spend a period of time on a vessel, i.e., "I'm going to be on here for a 30 day *trip*", or "We've spent the last 20 days of my *trip* on the Lower, I hope we go to the Ohio for the rest of it". Also called a STRETCH.

2. The movement of a vessel from one port to another. See: DOUBLE TRIP.

3. The time it takes to get from one port to another.

4. To knock off the keeper on a pelican hook, i.e. to *trip* it.

5. For tugs with anchors the term can mean the use of a *trip* line that assists in loosening or breaking free an anchor from its bottom bed.

TRIP PILOT

A Pilot who isn't in the regular employ of a company, but who hires on for a trip, or a period of time. The Pilot is usually hired and paid by the day.

TRIPLE LOCKAGE

A lockage that has to be done in three cuts. On some locks that are restricted in size it may take three or more lockages to transit the lock. This was/is common on some of the locks on tributaries of the Ohio River. See: OVERAGE TOW.

TRIPLE-SCREW

A vessel propelled by three propellers.

TRIPPING

1. A Pilot that is not working regularly for a company. See: TRIP PILOT.

2. The act of lowering the WICKETS on a movable dam. See: TRIPPING BARS (below).

3. Sometimes used to describe a GIRDING (see) action when a tug or towboat is towing another and is unable

to keep control of the towline which can possibly cause the towing vessel to be capsized.

TRIPPING BARS
A long bar used at WICKET dams to trip or dislodge the props that held the wickets upright. These bars were sometimes fouled by gravel and drift, causing problems with the mechanism. With the adoption of the HURTER groove in the wicket slide, the *tripping bars* were eliminated.

TRUCKING ON
Said of a vessel that is moving at a good and steady speed.

TRUMAN-HOBBS
A statute enacted in 1940 that deemed all bridges across navigable waterways were obstructions to navigation. They are allowed to be tolerated to serve the needs of land transportation if they still allow for the reasonable needs of navigation. If a bridge is deemed an unreasonable obstruction by the USCG, they can order that it be altered, replaced, or removed. Procedures for determining the degree of obstruction, the benefits to the cost of making the necessary change, and the process for any modifications to a bridge are outlined in 33 CFR 116.

TRUSS
A support structure based on triangular framing. It is mostly used in reference to bridge structures, but is also used in the framing of vessel hulls, especially barges. The word comes from the old French *trusser,* meaning "to bind or hold together".

TRUST FUND
See: INLAND WATERWAYS TRUST FUND.

TRY COCK
A small valve on a boiler, usually arranged in a row of three, used to manually test and determine the amount of water in a boiler. This was the method used on the steamboats before they were required to have glass gauges and effective safety valves. Sometimes called *gauge cocks*.

TUCK
When splicing line, it is the interweaving of the strands of the bitter end of a line into the bight if making an eye splice; or, when splicing two lines together, it is the interweaving after marrying (see: MARRY) the two lines. It is from the Old Dutch *tucken,* meaning "to pull sharply". So when the line ends were interwoven the person doing the splicing will pull on each strand to make sure the splice is secure.

TUG or TUGBOAT
Usually described as a relatively small, sturdily built, but powerful vessel that primarily assists vessels at sea, in harbors, and when docking. It has a high ratio of power for its dimensions. A *tug* will also tow astern or push barges. Traditionally, it is described as having a pointed or slightly rounded bow. This is a misnomer in attempting to describe a *tug* with the variety of its usages and designs of the 21st Century. Currently *tugboats* perform in a never ending variety of tasks. Their designs are from the traditional to those that almost resemble a saucer with an inverted cup for its pilothouse. Their underwater propulsion systems allow them to travel under control forward, backward, or to either port or starboard with equal ease. They can tow astern, push ahead, or couple to a notch in a barge and act as a ship in high wave conditions. You name it and there is a *tug* that has been designed to do it, except so far, it is not able to act as a submarine. The term is related to tow, and its usage as towing or pulling other vessels started in the early 1800s.

TUG COMMANDS
When a tug is engaged in assisting a ship to dock in a harbor, the operation is usually directed by a Pilot on the ship being docked. In each harbor ship Pilots

who work with the tugs have a system of commands. They used to be by whistle since the Pilot could not see the tug from the bridge of the ship. Different Pilots used a variation of signals. There has been some effort to standardize them but it has not been able to be worked out. However, with the use of VHF radio communications between the tug and the bridge of the ship, the use of audio signals, and even perhaps hand signals, may be a thing of the past.

TUG-BARGE UNIT

Tugs that couple-up to a single large barge and basically operate as one unit. The tug usually fits into a deep notch in the stern of the barge. If it is wired to the barge it will operate as a towboat does in fairly calm water. If the tug is in open seas in rough water it will drop out of the notch and take its barge on a towline. If the unit is a fully integrated one it will be rigidly connected as a single vessel and will act the same as a ship. If it is an Articulated Tug-Barge unit it will have a hydraulic pin engaged into the hull of the barge that will allow some vertical movement of the tug in rough water. It will stay in the notch in almost all situations until it gets to its destination.

TUMBLE HOME

The inward curve or slant of a vessel's side above the bilge knuckle to the deck.

TUNNEL STERN

A somewhat half-moon indentation in the stern hull plating of a towboat's hull to allow a propeller blade of greater diameter to turn, with the upper part of its blade at the approximate surface of the water. This allows a larger wheel to be fitted to the shafting, increasing the vessel's thrust power while at the same time not extending below the depth of the vessel's hull.

TURBIDITY

Sediment suspended in water most often caused by the varying velocity of a river current on the riverbed. Turbulence can also occur from propeller action, dredging, or other causes that result in the disturbance of the sediment on the river bottom. The term is from the Latin *turbious*, which conveys "confusion", and is from *turba* that means "a crowd"; therefore, *turbidity* probably refers to muddy river current as a "crowd of sediment making its way downriver".

TURBINES

The use of hand (man) power was the norm at most locks to open and close the gates and for other mechanical needs; some used WATER POWER, while others had steam engines installed. About 1920 turbines were installed on some locks to provide local power. Currently, some of the dams on the Ohio River have electric-generating *turbines,* as do the dams on the TVA river systems that supply electricity to industry and the citizens of the area.

TURBOCHARGER

A compressor that is driven by an engine's own exhaust gas that forces more air (oxygen) into the engine, increasing its power output from each cylinder.

TURN (AT LOCK)

When a vessel approaches the ARRIVAL POINT at a LOCK it establishes its *turn* to lock by sounding its desire by the appropriate whistle signal. In reality, in modern times, all vessels call by radio to the lock and indicate they are ready to make a lockage. The lock tender will then tell the Pilot how many vessels may be ahead of her and which boat they will follow. With increased traffic on the river and some buildup of tows, normal lock procedures are not always followed. In order to speed up the processing of tows, at times the Lock Master will set up a procedure of three or more lockages up, followed by three or more lockages down.

TURN A TOW

When a downbound towboat meets an upbound tow of the same company, they may receive orders from their dispatchers to exchange tows. This often occurs with larger companies, perhaps because one of the boats is of a higher horsepower and would be more effective in the lower reach of a river, or because they may want to repair one of the vessels in a particular shipyard, or perhaps the piloting crew of the vessels is more familiar with the navigation of certain sections of the river.

TURN AROUND

The act of a towboat or tug reaching the end of its destination, dropping its tow, picking up or reloading, and heading back in the direction from whence it came, i.e. "We're going to Cairo, drop this tow at the fleet and *turn around* with 30 downbound loads".

TURN BOAT

As with TURN A TOW, sometimes in a very active shipping area such as New Orleans, a company will designate a towboat which will always be the boat that builds a tow and takes it up- or downriver, as the case may be, to meet another of its company's boats to exchange tows.

TURN BUOY

Usually considered the main buoy in a crossing that a vessel makes its initial turning maneuver on, and then goes on down the shore; or the buoy(s) in a crooked channel that a vessel steers on when negotiating through a crossing.

TURN IN

To knock off at the end of a watch and go to bed or one's bunk to rest (not to watch TV).

TURN TO

The act of starting work, usually to the humble command of the mate who kindly says, "Let's get your sorry rear ends up off those timberheads and get to making tow!"

TURN TURTLE

A vessel that capsizes, or turns over.

TURNBUCKLE

A device with a screw mechanism that is used to tighten or slacken wires. *Turnbuckles* also are used to tighten or loosen the CHAINS that provide rigidity or flexibility to the hull of a Western River steamboat and to support its CHIMNEYS. The RATCHET used on Western River towboats in tightening barge tow wires is basically a large *turnbuckle*. See: CROSS CHAINS, HOG CHAINS, and KNUCKLE CHAINS.

TURNED AROUND

The act of filling or dewatering a LOCK CHAMBER to prepare it for the entry of a vessel or tow, or to ready it for the second half of a DOUBLE LOCKAGE.

TURNING

The act of changing the direction of a vessel's course.

TURNING BASIN

A large area of sufficient water depth or a wide channel where vessels can safely turn their tows around.

TURNING BUOY

The major buoy in a crossing, or other channel, where a Pilot makes the main change of course to start steering in a new direction.

TURNING CIRCLE

The area or space it takes to turn a vessel's tow completely around. In slack water it is a measurement of rudder efficiency; however, on the river it becomes a degree of available distance between banks, or channel width, along with current speed and wind velocity conditions when handling a tow of barges.

TURNS

A measurement used by some com-

460 TVA

panies to evaluate the productivity of a barge, or group of barges, in a trade by the number of *turns*, or trips, they make from origin to destination on a monthly or yearly basis. Sometimes referred to as the *turn rate*.

TVA
See: TENNESSEE VALLEY AUTHORITY

TWIN-SCREW
A towboat propelled by two propellers.

TWIST
The act of turning a twin-screw towboat around by coming ahead on the outboard engine toward the direction of the way one wants to turn, and going astern on the other engine.

TWO-BLOCKED
When the PURCHASE of blocks has come together and can go no further in pulling or hoisting an object. Also the term is used on any hoist or pulley line that has reached the highest position of its lift ability.

TWO-WATCH SYSTEM
The normal routine for river towboat crews whereby they are divided into two watches. The regular hours have historically been the forward watch being from 6 to 12, both a.m. and p.m., and the after watch being from midnight to 6 a.m. and from noon to 6 p.m. However, some companies are using seven hours on with five off, then five on and seven off; and others are experimenting with eight hours on and four off, then four on and eight off. See: DOG WATCH.

TWO-WHISTLE SIDE
When two vessels meet and agree to pass one another starboard to starboard. See: ONE- WHISTLE SIDE.

TAINTER GATE
A cross sectional diagram of a typical Tainter gate, used at many navigational dams, that shows the principals of its operation
(From USACE drawing)

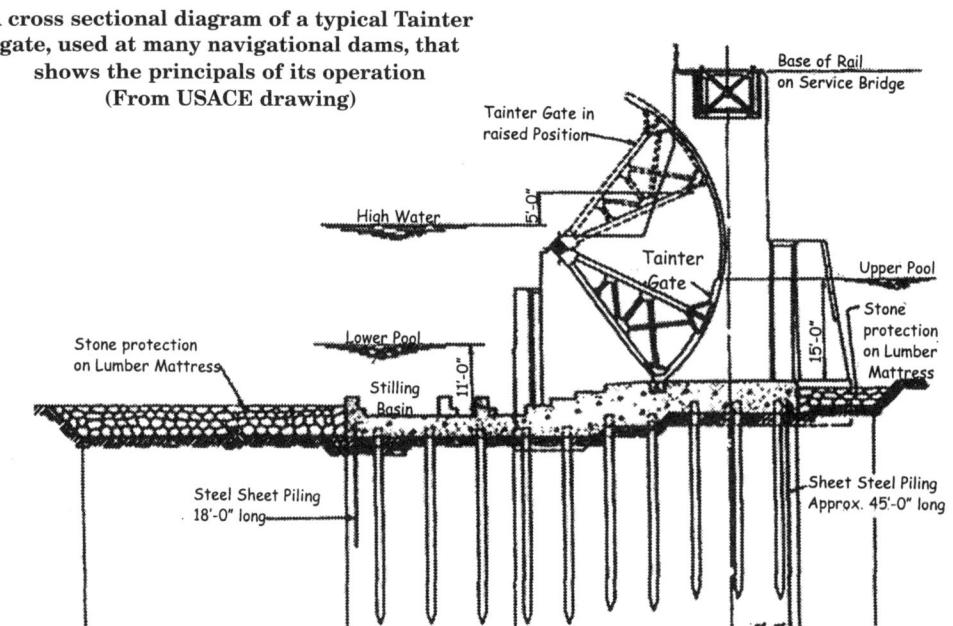

TENDER

A term used for many vessels, particularly in government service, that perform duties in varies efforts associated with the river such as servicing navigational aids, which is illustrated by the GOLDEN ROD, which was in service to the U.S. Lighthouse Service on the Missouri River until the service was merged into the USCG in 1939. After that it worked on the Illinois and Upper Mississippi. The KANKAKEE is the type buoy boat now used on the Western Rivers.

The USACE also uses a variety of vessels that are designated "tender", such as the small towboat that may push a crane barge, assist in placement of a dredge pipeline, move a spud barge, do survey work, etc., or the small personnel craft that might ferry persons from place to place, also do some variety of survey work, or engage in many other kinds of river employments, but which might more properly be entitled a "launch".

TEXAS CHICKEN MANEUVER

A meeting situation that takes place between vessels in a narrow channel such as the Houston Ship Channel where most vessels stay near the center of the waterway where the deepest water is located. Therefore, when meeting another vessel they approach head to head. When the vessels are close to one another, each steers to its right hand side of the channel.

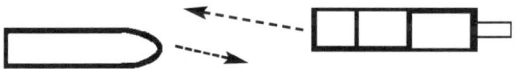

When the vessels are nearly abreast of one another they reverse course and steer towards the left-hand side of the channel. This action causes a cushion of water between the two vessels, which offsets any suction action that might occur between them.

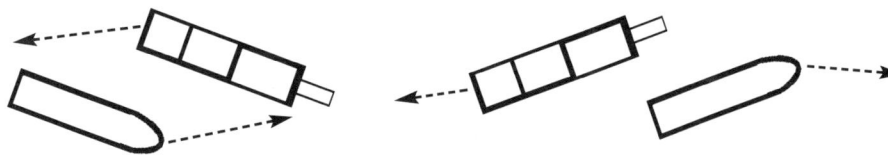

When almost clear of one another each vessel again straightens its course toward the center of the marked channel as they navigate toward their destinations.

462 ILLUSTRATIONS

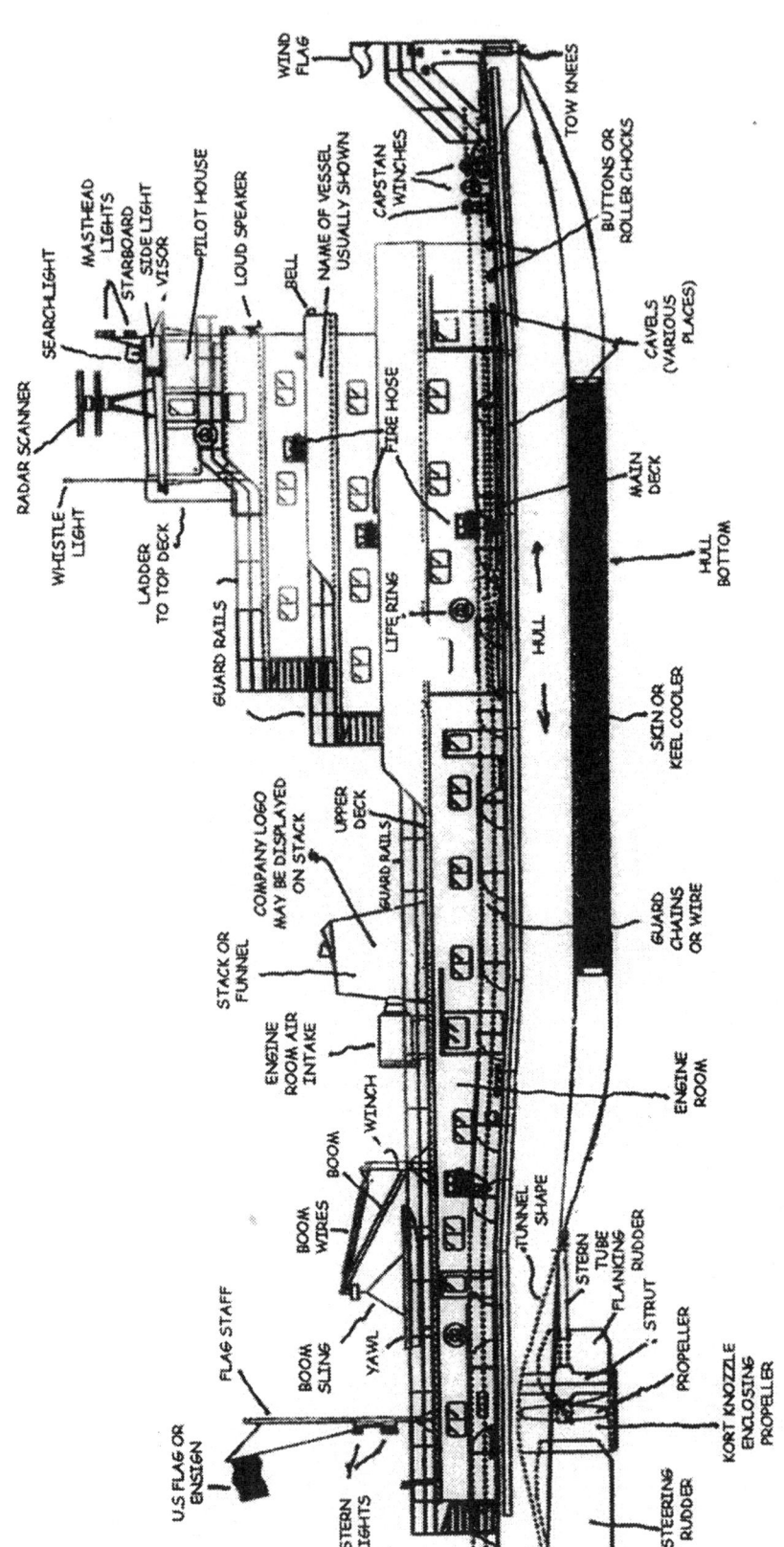

TOWBOAT PROFILE

A side view drawing of a typical towboat with a listing of the major outward components visual to the interested observer

U

ULLAGE
The amount of empty space in a tank containing liquid that hasn't been filled, or the amount of space from the top of the tank to the liquid level. The term derives from the old French *euillier*, meaning "to fill up".

ULLAGE HATCH
A small hatch, usually built into a larger cargo hatch or expansion hatch, through which the ullage can be taken. Also, used by a TANKERMAN to see into a tank as to the progress in loading product or of discharging it.

ULLAGE READING
To take a measurement of the amount of space left in a liquid cargo tank. Sometimes referred to as ullages.

ULLAGE TAPE
A small flexible steel tape with a non-sparking weight on its end. The tape is attached to a crank-operated reel and is used to measure the ullage in a tank, or to sound the tank for depth of liquid product or water.

ULTRASONIC DEPTH SOUNDER
See: DEPTH SOUNDER.

ULTRASONIC TESTING
A type of non-destructive electronic testing that is undertaken on older vessel hulls instead of drilling a hole in the steel plate to determine the thickness of the existing plate to measure the amount of wastage of a vessel's scantlings.

UNCLE SAM'S TOOTHPULLER
See: SNAGBOAT

UNCOIL
To pull out and straighten a new line from a coil. To avoid kinks forming in a length of line, one must always bring the bitter end of the line out from the center of the coil.

UNDER-KEEL CLEARANCE
The distance between the lowest point on a vessel and the highest point of the bed of a river or canal on which the vessel is navigating.

UNDER POWER
Refers to vessels that are propelled by machinery that must abide by the Navigation Rules that apply to it.

UNDER-POWERED
A vessel that does not have sufficient power to properly perform the task that has been given to her. Either the current is too swift or the amount of tonnage is more than the vessel can safely handle.

UNDER THE ARM
A term used sometimes by a Pilot referring to a barge in tow that is alongside the port or starboard sides of the towboat pushing a tow, i.e. "I've got one *under the arm* on my starboard side", or "I've got 'em *under both arms* this trip. Guess I'll have to put on a bit more deodorant before we get to Paducah".

UNDER THE POINT
A vessel or tow that is directly *under the point* of a bend. In relation to vessels it usually refers to the position of a northbound tow that is navigating in fairly slack water. When and if it starts around the point, the swifter current coming off the point will want to set the tow toward the outside of the channel above the point. That could result in a dangerous navigating condition if there is a downbound vessel above the point.

UNDER TOW
A vessel being towed by another vessel, i.e. "We have the M/V NEVERSAIL dead boat *under tow* with us, taking her to the shipyard to be dry-docked".

UNDERWAY
The time when all lines are turned loose from any object to which a vessel might have been moored; it is not at

anchor; and the vessel and/or its tow are not aground. It is considered *underway* whether or not the vessel is making way through the water.

UNDERWRITER

Generally a person, or entity who agrees and contracts to insure a vessel against certain risks and perils and agrees to reimburse the contract holder, or policy holder, for any loss or damages that may be incurred while the policy is in force.

UNDOCK

1. The act of removing a vessel from a drydock.
2. To turn a vessel or tow loose from a dock.

UNDOCUMENTED VESSEL

A vessel that is not required to obtain, and does not have, a vessel document issued by the U.S. Coast Guard.

UNIFIED RULES OF THE ROAD

See: INLAND NAVIGATION RULES.

UNINSPECTED VESSEL

Vessels that are not required to be inspected by the USCG and do not carry a CERTIFICATE OF INSPECTION (C.O.I.). At present, dry cargo barges and towboats are not considered *inspected vessels*; although towboats do undergo certain types of safety and security inspections by the USCG, they are not issued a C.O.I. As laws and regulations change it is probable that towboats and tugs will be inspected in the near future. Tank barges are inspected by the USCG and are required to have either a C.O.I. on board, a Permit to Proceed, or a gas-free certificate.

UNION

The bringing together of two parts to allow them to act as one, such as a coupling shaft between two pieces of machinery, or fittings to join sections of piping.

UNIT TOW

Refers to a tow, usually of liquid tank barges, that is made into a single, smooth hull form of a raked semi-integrated bow barge, two or three box barges, and a semi-integrated barge at the stern with the raked end made up to the towboat. With the proper horsepower it is a very fast and efficient *unit*. Two units coupled together side by side are termed a *double unit*.

UNITED STATES ARMY CORPS OF ENGINEERS (USACE)

The history of the Corps is too long and varied to record in a Riverman's Lexicon. To list all its accomplishments and the names of all the people who made them happen would be impossible, so this section will only enumerate a few of the actions affecting our mid-continent rivers. There are many fine books on the different Corps Districts that have been published that may be pursued by those with an interest in river history.

Engineers comes from the French who called these builders *genie,* which in old English became *enginator*, and represented the people who built fortifications for defense in war, as well as those who operated the weapons of attack on an opponent such as battering rams and catapults. Now they more often oversee the design and building of structures for peaceful purposes, but are always ready to respond to defending against, and attacking if necessary, those who might transgress our freedoms.

The Corps traces its history to 1775, when the Continental Congress needed engineers during the American Revolution to design and construct fortifications. Col. Richard Gridley was appointed Chief Engineer to Gen. George Washington. After our country became the U.S.A., the West Point Academy was built to train engineers in 1794, and then the Army took over its operation in 1802. Probably the first real involvement of the Army in the river system beyond the Appalachians was when Capt. Meriwether Lewis shook the hand of Capt. William Clark below the Falls of the Ohio and then began the trip to the mouth of the Missouri River and on up that waterway to see if a passage to the Pacific Ocean was possible.

The first commitment of the *USACE* to civil works on the river system was in 1824 when Congress passed the General Survey Act, which provided funds for improvements on the Ohio and Mississippi rivers. The Corps started removing snags and also commenced an attack on sandbars on the Ohio River. The involvement of the Corps was ongoing but waned in the mid-1800s when the Civil War took place; there were budget concerns, regional differences, and community opposition to some projects, which all took their toll on commitment.

In the latter part of the 1800s the DAVIS ISLAND LOCK and DAM was built near Pittsburgh and the Congress, impressed with its success, in 1888 authorized a six-foot project channel down the Ohio. In the early 1900s, before any of the six-foot project dams were built, the Corps was authorized to resurvey the entire Ohio River and came to the conclusion that a nine-foot channel with 600' by 110' locks would be more cost effective; this was authorized in 1910. The entire project was completed by 1929.

Other major projects for navigation progressed. The Upper Mississippi became canalized, as well as the Illinois Waterway, the McClellan-Kerr System, and the Tenn-Tom in more recent years. However, with rails crisscrossing the nation, some navigable rivers have waned and even shut down for commercial traffic, while others have had varying degrees of success; nonetheless, our rivers provide the most economical, safe, and environmentally friendly transportation system in the USA. The Corps continues to operate the locks and dams of our navigation system, to repair and oversee major rehabilitation when necessary, and design and build new structures as needed.

Besides civil works on our rivers, the Corps is the main builder of levees and flood wall safeguards against high water conditions. They are involved in hydropower production and environmental protection. Between 1831 and 1852 the Corps even supervised lighthouse construction in the country until the Congress set up a Lighthouse Board as a separate agency. They are builders of coastal defenses; are active in all the wars we fight as combat engineers; supervised the building of the Panama Canal; were directly involved in the WW II Manhattan Project; assist other nations in their civil works projects; design and supervise the construction of military bases and other facilities; you name it and the Corps of Engineers has been there.

Presently the Corps Directorate consists of about 35,000 employees, most of them civilian. They work in eight regional Divisions, consisting of 45 Districts that basically follow watershed basins. The Divisions are as follows, along with the rivers that mostly affect the towboating industry:

1. Great Lakes and Ohio River (LRD) – The Great Lakes, its harbors and the Ohio River and most of its tributaries.

2. Mississippi River (MVD) – The corridor of the Mississippi River from our border with Canada to the Gulf Coast.

3. North Atlantic (NAD)

4. Northwestern (NWD) – The Missouri River and the Columbia River.

5. South Atlantic (SAD) – The GIWW from Alabama east to Florida and the rivers that flow into the Gulf of Mexico in that area.

6. South Pacific (SPD)

7. Southwestern (SWD) – Those waters in Texas and the Arkansas River Basin.

UNITED STATES COAST GUARD (USCG)

The establishment of the *U.S. Coast*

Guard occured on 28 January 1915 when the REVENUE CUTTER SERVICE and the LIFE-SAVING SERVICE in the Department of Treasury were merged. In 1939 the LIGHTHOUSE SERVICE was also placed under the USCG's direction. In 1942, at the start of WW II, the USCG was operated as a part of the U.S. Navy and the BUREAU OF MARINE INSPECTION & NAVIGATION was temporarily assigned to the *USCG*. After the war, the *USCG* returned to the Treasury Department. Soon after that the BMIN was abolished and made an integral part of the *USCG*. In 1967, the Coast Guard was transferred to the new Department of Transportation. Then in March 2003, with another executive reorganization, the USCG became a unit of the Department of Homeland Security.

The *USCG* is multi-mission orientated and has broad responsibilities including aids to navigation, law enforcement, search and rescue, pollution response, marine inspection, licensing of mariners, and security in the marine environment. It celebrates their birthday every year on August 4, commemorating its establishment in 1790 when Congress created a "system of cutters" to collect revenue at U.S. ports.

The motto of the *USCG* is *Semper Paratus*. The historians at the Coast Guard do not seem to know exactly when and who coined it. It has been speculated that it may have been from the reports of a newspaper editor who wrote of the exploits of the Revenue cutters during the Civil War, saying in part, "Keeping always under steam and ever ready, in the event of extraordinary need, to render valuable service, the cutters can be made to form a coast guard whose value it is impossible at the present time to estimate." The "ever ready" phrase was made into Latin as *Semper Paratus,* which is now translated into "Always Ready". However, the words were apparently on the logo of the Revenue Cutters as early as 1860, which would be a year before the Civil War commenced. A marching tune with words was later composed by a Coast Guard Officer in the 1920s entitled, *Semper Paratus*.

The former Second Coast Guard District, located in St. Louis, MO, was the major Western Rivers presence encompassing most of the towboat operations in the United States. The USCG eliminated the district in the 1990s and now handles its duty functions regarding members of the towboat and barge industry through the Eighth District, headquartered in New Orleans, LA. The *USCG* provides the aids to navigation for our waterways, including the marking the channel with buoys, navigational lights, and daymarks. They license mariners, oversee pollution incidents and provide assistance as necessary, as well as inspect and insure that inspected vessels are properly maintained. They assist in search and rescue, and monitor security functions on vessels and in our ports, and assist in natural disasters, such as hurricanes and floods.

UNITED STATES COAST GUARD AUXILIARY

A voluntary civilian organization consisting of boat owners and others that promotes boating safety and security on waterways, education in operating small boats, and conducts safety checks of equipment of those who own recreational craft. It was officially established by Congress in 1939 and closely affiliated with the USCG. Although it has no official policing power it assists the Coast Guard in patrolling public boating events and regattas, and will render assistance to disabled vessels or those in distress.

UNITED STATES CODE (USC)

A series of volumes that are a codification of the laws of the United States. Most of the general laws governing the operations of vessels fall under Titles 33 and 46. See: CODE OF FEDERAL REGULATIONS.

UNITED STATES ENSIGN or FLAG

The national flag of the most wonderful nation in the world. It contains 50 white stars in a field of blue representing each of the States of the Union, and 13 alternating stripes of seven red and six white representing the original colonies that gave us a Declaration of Independence, fought for it, and finally adopted a Constitution to govern us along with a Bill of Rights to keep us free. It is to be flown proudly from morning hour to sunset. God Bless America.

UNITED STATES POWER SQUADRON

A national organization that promotes boating safety and offers classes in many of the ports where it is active. In cooperation with the U.S. Coast Guard Auxiliary it will conduct safety checks on vessels for recreational boat owners.

UNITIZED CARGO

Palletized or containerized cargo.

UNIVERSAL JOINT

A shaft fitted with a joint that is able to be coupled to another piece of machinery that is not in line with it. These are commonly used on pumping equipment as a connection between the motive power and a pump.

UNLAY

To take apart or untwist the bitter end of a line, usually in preparation to splice it.

UNLOAD

To discharge the cargo from a barge or tow.

UNREEVE

To take a line or wire out of a block. See: REEVE.

UNSCHEDULED CLOSURE

The unplanned shutdown of a waterway or lock and dam facility due to some unprecedented weather occurrence such as a hurricane, flood, levee break; an unforeseen event of mechanical or physical failure; or an accident.

UNSEAWORTHY

A vessel is deemed to be seaworthy unless it is proven that, due to some fault of the crew or a deficiency of the vessel or its equipment, it was unable to withstand the perils of the sea or river when in navigation.

UP

1. To *go up above* is going to a higher deck on a steamboat, towboat, or tug from the deck on the vessel where a person might be located.
2. To *heave up* is to pull in a line or cable.
3. To *haul up* is to take in an anchor.
4. To *lay up* means to tie up a vessel for a period of time, secure all machinery and gear, and discharge the crew, except perhaps leaving a watchman aboard.
5. To navigate against the current is to *go upstream*.
6. To go *up-the-hill* is the act of going ashore.
7. To *tie up* is to moor a vessel.
8. An interesting word that is from the Dutch *op,* and the German *auf.* If we didn't have the word, one would certainly have to invent another or be *up the creek.*

UP THE HILL

Any person or thing that is not on the towboat but on the shore, i.e., "The Captain has gone *up the hill* to make a phone call", or "Sam went *up the hill* to pick up some papers".

UPBOUND

A vessel that is navigating upstream on a river. The opposite of DOWNBOUND.

UPPER

When employed as a noun it is used by rivermen as a shortened term to refer to the *Upper* Mississippi River, i.e., "When we leave the Ohio we'll drop our tow at Cairo Point and pick up one for the *Upper*".

UPPER DECK

Any deck above the main deck on a towboat.

UPPER GAUGE

The gauge reading of the pool level at the upstream side of a lock and dam.

UPPER MISSISSIPPI RIVER

The source of the Mississippi River system is LAKE ITASCA, however, the start of navigation is at Minneapolis, mile 853. Its mouth is where it joins the Ohio River just below Cairo Point to form the LOWER MISSISSIPPI RIVER. The river is sometimes segmented into two parts, the *Upper* being that section above the mouth of the Missouri River, while south of it (or some say below the Chain of Rocks fixed dam and the canalized river), is termed the Middle Mississippi River to its junction with the Lower Mississippi and the Ohio Rivers.

Numerous tributaries feed the *Upper Mississippi* from its border states. One, the Illinois River, was at one time the bed of the Mississippi, but in ancient times a glacier shut off its flow and the Mississippi dug itself a new channel further west than we know it today. Its main tributary, the Missouri River, contributes more water to the Lower Mississippi on an annual basis than does the rest of the *Upper River* itself.

For what is termed the European world, the *Upper Mississippi* was discovered in 1673 by Louis Jolliet and Father Marquette, although other French trappers and explorers may have seen it earlier. The first vessels in commerce were those of the fur trade, consisting of birchbark canoes that were easily damaged in ice, and the dugout pirogue. Eventually the pirogue evolved into the mackinaw used on the Great Lakes. It was also called a bateau. Later, the keelboat was used; these ranged in size up to a length of 80 feet. Besides furs, shot made from the lead mines was an important cargo. Then logging became a dominant source of trade. This was first done by floating the rafts downstream in the current. When steamboats came to the river they provided power to push huge rafts of logs and lumber downriver to mills. They were often assisted by a bowboat. (See: RAFTING LOGS & LUMBER). This continued from the late 1800s up to World War I, by which time the commercially harvested timber had mostly disappeared. Also starting in the mid-1880s, immigrant farmers in the Midwest began planting, harvesting and shipping grain, which has become the dominant cargo transported on the river today.

Surveys to improve river navigation on the *Upper* were done as early as 1829 but nothing occurred. After the Civil War some channel work was accomplished by excavating rock from the Rock Island Rapids. At the Des Moines Rapids a lateral canal 7.6 miles long with three locks was constructed from Keokuk to Montrose, which was completed in 1877. Experiments with jetties and wing dams were carried out. In 1878 Congress authorized a $4\frac{1}{2}$-foot channel from St. Louis to St. Paul to be accomplished by use of wing and closure dams. After much of this work was completed, in 1907 Congress authorized a six-foot channel. In 1913, Keokuk L & D (400' by 90') opened, replacing the three locks in the Des Moines canal. Other improvements continued; in 1917, L & D #1 (400' by 56') was completed to make Minneapolis a river destination, but there were no river terminals located there. The Le Claire Canal L & D (350' by 80') project at the head of the Rock Island Rapids opened in 1924. The USACE had been committed to an open river navigation concept up until this time, when they started thinking about a nine-foot channel. After much controversy the Congress in

1930 authorized the nine-foot channel project. During the 1930s up to 1940 with the completion of L & D 24, the Upper River nine foot project with locks 600' by 110' was in place. Some modernization has occurred, such as the addition of L & D 27 in the Chain of Rocks Canal, the replacement of the small lock at Keokuk, and the replacement of old L & D 26 with increased capacity.

UPRIVER or UPSTREAM

1. The direction in which a vessel or tow is proceeding against the current. The opposite of DOWNSTREAM.

2. Some place or thing that is above in mileage from where one is located, i.e., "The dock at Quincy is about 200 miles *upriver* from us", or "The vessel NEVERSAIL is only about 12 miles *upstream* ahead of us".

UPTAKE

The ventilation flow of smoke from the boiler furnace of a steamboat, or the noxious combustion emissions of a diesel engine through the chimney or stack of a vessel. The discharge can be either natural or induced by forced ventilation.

USABLE WIDTH or LENGTH (OF A LOCK)

Although most locks on the Western Rivers system are 600' by 110' or 1200' by 110', those dimensions are not the official *usable lockage length and width*. The USACE wants to have some leeway for vessels entering the locks so that tows do not become wedged in them, which could cause damage to the structure as well as to the barging equipment. Lock walls are constructed vertically true, but on older facilities over a period of years can lean slightly inward. Therefore, most lockmasters do not want vessels or tows in excess of 108' in width. They do not know how many bumps and damage protrusions may be on the hull of a barge over its official width. Also, in the winter there can be a buildup of ice on the lock walls or on the sides of barges that can reduce the available *usable lockage width*.

Regarding the usable length of locks the USACE likes to have at least five feet on each end which would mean a 590' total length of tow in a 600' lock. However, in certain special circumstances, with requests made in advance, some locks are able to exceed a length of 600' due to the extra space when the miter gates are closed. Also, sometimes after tying off in the chamber, a towboat can loosen or take off its face wires and twist the boat sideways, creating extra space. This is, however, only for extremely special circumstances of specialized towing situations.

Considering the depth over the sill of a lock where the lower miter gates are sealed, there is usually a three- to five-foot clearance over it in low pool, but some older locks may have less. Lockmasters do not want damage to the sill and may refuse to lock vessels of excess draft during low water periods.

USER TAX or CHARGE

In 1978, Congress enacted the Inland Waterways Revenue Act, Public Law 95-502, that established a tax on the fuel that is consumed in the propulsion of towboats that operate on most of the commercially navigable U.S. rivers and the GIWW canal. The original fuel tax started at four cents per gallon in 1980, and increased incrementally to 10 cents per gallon in 1986. Then in 1986 Congress increased the fuel tax to incrementally rise to 20 cents per gallon. The monies collected from the tax go into an Inland Waterways Trust Fund, where they generate interest until they are dispersed to pay for 50% of construction costs of new locks and dams, and the rehabilitation of older ones.

Subsequent legislation in 1986, Public Law 99-662, set up an Inland Waterways Users Board comprising of 11 members to serve as a federal advisory committee. The members consist of

470 UTILITY CROSSINGS

commercial shippers and carriers representing different geographical sections of the country and different commodity movements. The Board usually meets two or three times each year to develop and make recommendations to the Secretary of the Army and the Congress. They prepare and send an annual report of the Board to Congress regarding the construction and major rehabilitation priorities, as well as the funding levels needed.

UTILITY CROSSINGS

Those crossings over and under the river and canal beds of the Western Rivers and the GIWW They are noted on the charts and maps of the navigable system and include submarine or submerged cables, aerial crossings, and pipelines.

U.S AGENCY EMBLEMS ASSOCIATED WITH THE RIVER SYSTEM

ULLAGE HATCH (or HOLE)

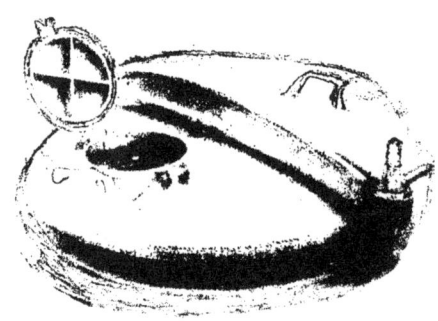

The image shows a typical ULLAGE HATCH in the open position inset in a tank hatch cover. The flame screen has been inserted. When closed a keeper dog in the ullage cover will be tightly dogged to secure the hatch. The small ullage opening is used to measure the "ullage" or the depth of cargo, to take samples of the product for testing, to check for water with a dipping or measuring tape, and for a tankerman to observe the progress rate when loading or discharging cargo. Sometimes, especially on double-skinned tank barges, the ullage hatch will be consteucted directly in the tank top.

V

VACUUM
A partial absence of air. This can occur in liquid product barges that operate in changing temperatures where the product expands on hot days, pushing out existing air or vapor in the tank space above the cargo, but fails to replace it when the product contracts during a cooling period. Also, if a cargo pump is engaged to discharge without opening a vent to allow air to enter, this would result in a *vacuum* in the tank. The presence of a *vacuum*, or the over-pressurization of a tank, is the reason PV VALVES (which are set to open if a pressure or vacuum exceed a preset level) are placed on tank barges. The term *vacuum* is from the Latin *vacuus,* meaning "empty".

VALVE
Devices used to control the flow of a liquid through a section of piping, either allowing the liquid to flow or to stop its flow. There are various types of *valves* used on tugs, towboats, barges, engines, etc. Some examples are: Gate, Check, Relief, Safety, Pressure, Globe, Butterfly, etc. Some of these *valves* also are given names for the function they perform within a piping system. The term goes back to the Latin *valva,* meaning the "leaf of a folding door".

VANE DIKE
A series of dikes placed at an angle of 10 to 15 degrees downstream of the shore to control sediment flow when aligning the channel. They are sometimes used in conjunction with a SPUR DIKE, in effect creating a type of L – SHAPED DIKE.

VAPOR
A substance that is suspended in the air. On tank barges crewmen should always be aware of the gaseous *vapors* emitted by some liquid cargoes, which could be toxic or flammable. See: VENT HEADER for a *vapor control system.* The term has the same meaning as the Latin *vapor,* meaning "steam".

VARIABLE COST
See: COST.

VARIABLE PITCH PROPELLER
A *propeller* in which the pitch can be changed to fit the most efficient thrust capability, depending on current, loaded tonnage, whether the vessel is moving with or against the current, etc. This propeller design has not found much favor on the river systems, mainly due to drift damage problems and with vessels oftentimes working in close proximity to the riverbed with resulting impairment of the propeller blades.

VARIABLE RANGE MARKER
A luminous ring on the radar that can be set to a distance desired by the Pilot. It can be decreased or increased as needed to mark the range from or to a target.

VARIATION
The degrees of difference between true north and that of a magnetic north course from wherever one is located.

VEER
1. To pay out, or allow a line to slacken. The word is from the Dutch *vieren,* meaning to slacken or let out.
2. To swing toward or away from something, i.e., "*Veer* to starboard, he's not changing his course!"

VEER DITCH
See: TEXAS CHICKEN.

VELOCITY
The speed of the current or of a wind in miles per hour.

VENT
1. Piping and/or valves that allow vapors to escape from a closed tank, as well as that allow air into the tank or space . See: PV VALVES.
2. To allow a tank or space to air out.

VENT HEADER
The collection pipe header on a tank barge where toxic vapors can be gathered and *vented* at a high place above the barge, or returned to a tank-loading terminal for recovery and disposal.

VENTILATOR
1. A fairly large goose-necked duct which can be rotated in order to catch the wind to provide air to the lower decks, especially the engine room. See: AIR SCOOP and COWL.

2. An opening to a space that provides natural ventilation fitted with a cover giving it the appearance of resembling a mushroom; therefore, it is called a mushroom *vent*.

VERGE
An old term for the aftermost mast on a steamboat. It probably comes from the Latin *virga,* meaning a "rod" which a religious man might carry, or from the Latin *vergere,* that meant "to bend or incline". It was both.

VERTICAL CLEARANCE
Distance measured from an upper to a lower point, generally in a line perpendicular to the horizon. Used particularly in determining AIR DRAFT and AIR GAP.

VERTICAL DROP GATE
See: LOCK GATES.

VERTICAL SECTORS
The required minimum intensities and ranges of visibility that electric navigational lights are required to show in accordance with Annex I of the Inland Navigation Rules.

VERY HIGH FREQUENCY (VHF) RADIO
In accordance with 33 CFR 26, all towboats and tugs over 26 feet in length, while navigating, are required to carry and be able to transmit on VHF radio from the pilothouse. Most vessels carry at least two radios to be able to monitor more than one channel.

VESSEL
Most general dictionaries define the word in the first sense as "a large ship". The Navigation Rules, however, are more definitive stating that a *vessel* "includes every description of water craft, including nondisplacement craft and seaplanes, used or capable of being used as a means of transportation on water". The word can be traced back to the Latin *vas,* which defines a "vase" as a receptacle to hold liquids. How the term to hold liquids became the definition of something that floats in liquids rather than holds them (unless it's a tanker) is hard to reconcile. Perhaps the first trading done by shipping was the carriage of "wine *vessels*".

VESSEL CONSTRAINED BY HER DRAFT
This term in the International Navigation Rules is in regard to power-driven vessels that, because of their draft, are severely restricted in their ability to deviate from the course they are following. It is not in the Inland Navigation Rules, since nearly all towboats and tugs that are on the rivers and canals are generally *constrained by draft* most of the time and no special privilege should be inferred or assumed.

VESSEL DATA RECORDER (VDR)
The "black box" of the aviation industry is available to the marine industry in the form of VDRs These have various capabilities to record voice, radio, radar, speed, rudder response, heading and course steered, depth of water, wind speed, all alarms, and even record if you sneezed.

VESSEL ENGAGED IN FISHING
As defined in the Navigation Rules it means "any vessel fishing with nets, lines, trawls, or other fishing apparatus which restricts maneuverability, but does not include a vessel fishing with trolling lines or other fishing apparatus which do not restrict maneuverability ".

VESSEL MANAGEMENT SYSTEMS (VMS)

The administration of vessel routines that are required by governmental regulations, supplemented by any company policy, rules, procedures, and/or directives. These include all vessel log data, drills, inspections, reportable incidents, security exercises, safety and occupational training, and any other activities that are deemed important. A *VMS* includes a review of the VOYAGE DATA RECORDER (if supplied).

VESSEL NOT UNDER COMMAND

A vessel which, through some exceptional circumstance, is unable to maneuver as required by the Inland Navigation Rules and is therefore unable to keep out of the way of another vessel. In most instances it means a vessel which has lost power or its ability to steer due to rudder failure. The term is a misnomer since there is still someone in command, unless the entire crew has left the *vessel* and no one is aboard. It is more the lack of ability to take prudent and normal navigational action when encountering another vessel. There is, in most instances, some action, that can be taken to reduce a hazard, such as dropping an anchor or something to act as a weight to reduce way through the water, rigging a temporary rudder, backing full astern, etc. However, to be able to do it in a timely and effective manner may not suffice to prevent a collision.

VESSEL RESPONSE PLAN

A regulation contained in 33 CFR 155 which require vessel owners and operators to have a detailed response plan for their *vessels* and crews in case of a spill of an oil or hazardous product. It includes notification of the spill, procedures for responding to the incident, training, drills, equipment needed, record keeping, and other requirements.

VESSEL RESTRICTED IN HER ABILITY TO MANEUVER

A vessel which, from the nature of her work, is *restricted in her ability to maneuver* as required by the Inland Navigation Rules, and is therefore unable to keep out of the way of another vessel. Rule 3 gives examples of the types of conditions that may restrict a vessel, such as various servicing actions of buoy setting, dredging, and others, as well as a towing operation that "severely" restricts a vessel from deviating from its course.

VESSEL SECURITY ASSESSMENT (VSA)

An analysis that examines and evaluates the vessel and its operations taking into account possible threats, vulnerabilities, consequences, and existing protective measures, procedures and operations.

VESSEL SECURITY PLAN (VSP)

The plan developed to ensure the application of security measures designed to protect the vessel and the facility that the vessel is servicing or interacting with, the vessel's cargoes, and persons on board at the respective MARSEC Levels.

VESSEL SECURITY OFFICER (VSO)

The person onboard the vessel, accountable to the Master, designated by the Company as responsible for security of the vessel, including implementation and maintenance of the Vessel Security Plan, and for liaison with the Facility Security Officer and the vessel's Company Security Officer.

VESSEL TRAFFIC SERVICE (VTS)

Systems established by the USCG in various ports which monitor and direct the movement of vessels in order to prevent accidents. Each VTS is specific to a port or area and varies in accordance with the particular needs of the region and the type of traffic involved. Vessels are directed from a Vessel Control Center. Some systems only go into effect when certain conditions occur, such as a degree of higher than normal water; while others control all movements with manned service centers and radar surveillance of the entire waterway that the VTS encompasses.

VIBRATION

A more or less continuous movement of machinery transmitted to the hull and superstructure of a vessel. These movements can be the result of a variety of causes, from machinery beds not properly dampened or secured, to the misalignment of connecting parts, internal machinery not operating properly, etc. The word derives from the Latin *vibrare,* meaning "to move to and fro".

VIBRATION ISOLATER

The use of pads or dampeners, usually rubber, to reduce vibration of operating machinery in a vessel and reduce noise levels; and/or the use of springs or other new devices and materials to more or less float the superstructure of a towboat independent of the machinery located in the hull. Sometimes when used on riverboats it is referred to as a *floating deckhouse.*

VICE ADMIRAL

The most senior admiral(s) in the USCG next to the Commandant and above the rank of Rear Admiral. In this meaning the word *Vice* is from Latin *vice,* meaning "in place of".

VISCOSITY

The measurement of liquid indicating its resistance to flow, i.e., neither molasses or asphalt flow very well unless they are heated, while gasoline flows like water. The term refers to a product that is thick and sticky with a semi-fluid consistency, and is given to us from the Latin *viscosus,* which in turn was from another Latin word that meant "bird lime". A *viscosity index* is a table that measures the flow rates of certain liquids at given temperatures.

Some tank barges in certain dedicated trades are equipped with heating equipment while others that change cargoes may have steam coils installed. When a barge so equipped arrives at a dock, the terminal, if necessary, will hook up a steam line to the barge's coil header to heat the cargo prior to unloading.

VISIBILITY

The ability of a person's eye to see horizontally and identify an object by day, and lights at night, at a certain distance in order to make appropriate safe navigational responses. A visibility code was developed giving the visibility ranges of weather. It should be noted that on inland waters there may be other pollutants mixed in the atmosphere to further restrict visibility distance.

VISIBILITY CODE	DISTANCE
0 Dense Fog	Less than 50 yards
1 Thick Fog	50 to 200 yards
2 Moderate Fog	200 to 500 yards
3 Light Fog	500 to 1000 yards
4 Thin Fog	$1/2$ to 1 mile
5 Haze	1 to 2 miles
6 Light Haze	2 to $5 1/2$ miles
7 Clear	$5 1/2$ to 11 miles

There are further levels of clarity, but if a Pilot on the river can see for 11 miles there isn't too much to worry about. Remember, *dense fog* ranges out from the pilothouse a distance to about half-way up the first barge of the tow. The word comes from the Latin *videre,* meaning "to see". See: RESTRICTED VISIBILITY.

VISOR

1. On a towboat or tug it is a short sloping metal awning forward and off the sides of the pilothouse that reduces glare from the sun and shield against rain. The word comes from the root of Old French *vis,* meaning "face", since it was the moveable protection of a knight's helmet protecting his face in battle.

2. On steamboats, prior to the advent of glass that one could properly see out of, it was a wooden hinged affair that offered scant protection from inclement weather. It was called a BROWBOARD which was met at the bottom by a BREAST BOARD when the pilothouse was closed.

VISUAL

The term means to be able to see another vessel by a person's sight and not by use of electronic means as noted in the Navigation Rule 3, "Vessels shall be deemed to be in sight of one another only when one can be observed visually from the other". The word is from the Latin root *videre*, meaning "to see", and its derivative *visus*, meaning "sight".

VISUAL AID TO NAVIGATION

Any aid that can be seen that assists a Pilot in navigating a vessel. It can be lighted or unlighted, such as an official USCG navigation light, daymark, or buoy, or any other mark, including a bridge, a farmhouse, a storage tank, or even a big cottonwood tree.

VOICE TUBE

A hollow tube that ran from the pilothouse to the engine room to render some means of communication between the Pilot and the Engineer on duty. Its need has gone by the board since there is now direct engine control from the pilothouse to the engine room on towboats and tugs, whose engine rooms are often untended.

VOID

A space in a vessel that is usually left completely empty. For instance, all the spaces surrounding the cargo compartment in a double-hulled barge are *void* spaces. The term is from the Latin *vacare*, meaning "to vacate", possibly short for *avoid*.

VOLUME

1. The capacity measure of a vessel, or a subdivision of it, either in dimensions of feet and inches, or of cubic capacity of space, i.e., tons, gallons, bushels, barrels, etc.
2. The audio sound signal intensity and range audibility of whistles installed on vessels as required by Annex III of the Inland Navigation Rules.
3. A publication such as this Lexicon that transmits knowledge as well as pleasure.

VOYAGE

The act of a vessel going from one place to another and returning to the original place of departure. It is not a term expressed very often by rivermen, who would usually indicate *voyage* as *a trip,* or *a round trip. Voyage* in river terminology is more often expressed in legal contractual language as below in VOYAGE CHARTER. The word comes from the Latin *viaticum,* which meant the necessary food and supplies for a journey. This usage then evolved into *voyage.*

VOYAGE CHARTER

Used to describe a charter agreement of a vessel for one origin and destination and return voyage. The term *voyage* comes from the Latin *viaticum,* to mean "provisions to take on a journey", while the term *charter* goes back to the Latin word *chartula,* referring to "paper".

VOYAGE DATA RECORDER

An instrument that records and stores vital operating information. A type of black box that can store at least 12 hours of data such as GPS position, radar scope readings, electronic chart data, communications in the pilothouse and transmissions over the radio, speed through the water, engine control placement and change, rudder positioning, heading, depth recording, possible wind speed and direction, any alarms that may occur, and possibly other data. It may be used to monitor performance, or utilized to implement educational training and efficiency procedures. The data processed will also be employed in accident investigations of allisions, collisions, fires, groundings, man overboard, possible security breaches, etc.

GATE VALVE

The most common of control valves used on river tank barges. It is so named as the sliding closure component, called wedge, controls the amount or degree of flow through the pipeline. Its name describes its function as a type of lift gate that allows the ingress and egress of product through the pipeline. It is also called a sluice valve by some.

BUTTERFLY VALVE

This type valve provides a quick action by only requiring a 90 degree movement of the control handle to turn the valve disc into a closing or an opening position. The closure discs of the valve are mounted on a common spindle that somewhat resembles butterfly wings.

P/V RELIEF VALVE (PRESSURE VACUUM)

These type valves are placed on all tank barges to prevent over-pressurization of each tank system, or in case the tank(s) are not properly vented they could be subjected to an untoward vacuum which could cause deformation of the collapse of the tank. Most of the new type P/V valves being placed on barges insure that personnel near the vent are not exposed to vented vapors. The valves are set to open at a preset pressure or vacuum.

CHECK VALVE

A check valve is a mechanical device that sllows liquid to flow only in one direction. It is sometimes called a non-return or one-way valve. It is like the flapper valve employed in a SPRING POLE PUMP (see) that was used on coal barge fleets in the steamboat days. Sometimes the valve is employed as a safety device to prevent back flow in a pipeline in case of failure. They may be swing, ball, or lift type.

W

WABASH AND ERIE CANAL

Originally, in the late 1700s and early 1800s there were ideas to connect the *Wabash River* to *Lake Eire* through a section between the Maumee River which flowed into Lake Erie and the Wabash which flowed into the Ohio River. Both rivers had some degree of navigability, but a portage between them in the vicinity of Fort Wayne, IN, would be required as a connecting link. The two rivers were accessible except when frozen in the winter and during the extremely low drought periods of summer.

By 1832 a decision to build the canal had been made and ground was broken. At the time roads were either non-existent with no bridges across streams or were mud holes when it rained. Railroads (which were considered) had started but no rails were being made in this country. Also the idea of the successful Erie Canal which had opened seven years prior stirred the local imagination. The canal was built in sections and was finally completed in 1853. The canal started in Toledo, OH, went up alongside the Maumee River to Fort Wayne. Then an excavated length to the Wabash River was made where the canal paralleled the river down to Terre Haute where another excavation was dug across to along the Eel River which ran into the White River where the canal ran alongside down to Evansville, IN, on the Ohio River at mile 792. The canal had a distance of 397 miles and was the longest canal built during the canal age. The *Wabash and Erie* had 73 sets of locks and 18 major aqueducts in its length.

Floods, costs of operation, and the building of railroads led to the *Wabash and Erie Canal's* gradual demise with some sections being shutdown each year. By 1874 the *Canal* was abandoned for commercial traffic.

WABASH RIVER

The *Wabash River* commences its journey at Grand Lake in the west-central area of the state of Ohio and flows in a northerly and westerly direction across much of Indiana until it reaches the city of Lafayette. Here it takes a southerly turn, eventually forming the border between the lower half of Indiana and Illinois. It finally enters the Ohio River at mile 848 after a journey of about 475 miles. Through the area of this long winding river various Indian tribes lived, but its name derives from the Miami Indian pronunciation of Wah-bah-shi-keh, meaning "pure white" as it flowed through its limestone bed. This name was written by the French fur traders as Ouabache, which then became anglicized to Wabash. Its basin drains over 33,000 miles. The river was a main trading route between Canada, the Great Lakes, and the Mississippi-Ohio corridor of connecting rivers.

Flatboats and keelboats were early regular travelers on the river as the territory became populated. Steamboats arrived on the river in 1823 traveling as far up as Loganport, IN, and the idea of building a canal to connect the *Wabash River* to Lake Erie was born. See: WABASH AND ERIE CANAL. In the 1960s and 70s there were proposal requests made to canalize the river from its mouth to Terre Haute, IN. Although the USACE made some preliminary feasibility studies at the request of a Congressional member they could never rationalize the benefits to the cost of building a system of locks and dams on the river.

WAGON BRIDGE

See: SWING BRIDGE

WAIST

The central or middle part, and usually the widest part, of a vessel. The word comes from the Old English *waest*, meaning "growth" coming from various Germanic and Gothic roots.

WAITING TIME

The time a vessel is standing by and not engaged in productive navigational activity, such as waiting for orders, waiting for tug assistance, waiting for crew to arrive, etc.; however, it is <u>not</u> activities such as waiting for fog to lift, which would be "holding up in fog", or "fogbound", nor would it be waiting for lockage, as this is more appropriately termed "waiting turn", or "lock delay".

WAITING TURN

The time after arriving at a lock to make a lockage and standing by until other vessels and tows are locked through.

WAKE

Turbulence in water as a result of a vessel moving through it. The wave thrown off the *wake* can vary depending on the depth of water, the speed of the vessel and/or its tow, the displacement of the vessel(s), the current velocity, and other factors. A *wake* can travel a long distance depending upon the body of water in which it is created and may only be seen or felt long after the vessel has passed the place where the *wake* reaches the shore. The word comes from the Old Norse *vaka,* which was "a hole or space in the ice".

WALE

1. The uppermost planking of a wooden hull, more often called the GUNWALE. In Old English the word was *walu*, and the general idea was of "a ridge". The term was used in the 1200s to denote horizontal planking in ships.
2. A piece of heavy timber bolted horizontally along a series of pilings or the concrete of a dock to act as a fender to a vessel landing there.

WALKING (the Boat)
See: GRASSHOPPERING

WALKING (the Towboat)

The Pilot of a multiple-screw towboat has the ability to walk it sideways, and sometimes with a barge(s), especially empties. Depending upon the desired sideways direction, either to port or to starboard, the Pilot puts the flanking rudders hard over in the direction wanted for the vessel to travel or *walk*, then backs astern on that engine (in direction of travel) while coming ahead on the opposite engine. The steering rudders are used to keep the vessel steady in the sideways movement. Engine speed may have to be adjusted on either or both engines to insure that there isn't undue headway or sternway.

WALKING AWAY

Said of a vessel that has overtaken and passed another as well as continuing to gain distance, i.e., "We passed that Valley boat in ABC Bend and just *walked away* from her".

WALKING BEAM
See: BEAM ENGINES.

WANIGAN

A storage compartment for cooking utensils and supplies, ranging in size from a small chest to a small shed. The term was used to describe a cookhouse and storage area for the belongings of log and lumber rafters on the raft. The word comes from the Ojibwa Indians, meaning "a storage pit".

WAR ZONE

An expression used to describe the section of the Lower Mississippi between Baton Rouge, the head of navigation for most deep-draft ocean vessels, to below the city of New Orleans. The *war zone* corridor is a navigational area filled with numerous docks, wharfs, fleets, landings, shipyards, outfalls, and even lock entrances. Its traffic consists of towboats, tugs, barge tows, offshore supply vessels, fishing boats, crew boats, harbor work boats, ferries, and excursion vessels, as well as freighters, tankers, and some craft that are not sure where they are going, all navigating along about 150 miles of waterway.

In the pilothouses of most of these vessels there is a constant stream of chatter from the two, three, or more radios which are giving official or non-official directives, navigational communications between meeting vessels,

USCG information on vessel or safety traffic, office-to-vessel traffic, and gobbledygook. Pilots must be able to attune their hearing to filter out the necessary transmissions from the unnecessary. It is indeed a combat domain where one must learn to avoid direct engagement that could result in a collision.

WARNING
See: DANGER SIGNAL.

WARNING SIGN
All tank barges carrying dangerous cargoes are required to display a *warning sign* stating: Warning – No Visitors – No Smoking – No Open Lights. Usually at the sign is a metal tube or box that contains the barge's Certificate of Inspection, shipping papers, and the last Declaration of Inspection. Also posted will be a cargo information card that has general safety information related to the cargo contained in the barge.

WARP
1. In order to propel a keelboat upriver, it was sometimes necessary to *warp* it. This procedure consisted of taking a long line upriver with a skiff. The line was then fastened to a tree or snag, and the crew would pull the keelboat upriver or, alternately, the line would be wound in by a hand-operated capstan. The origin is from old English *weorpan,* meaning "to throw", which later became a weaving term of twisted yarn, possibly to become rope used to pull, but it's only a guess. See: CORDELLE.
2. Similar to the keelboat *warping*, the process was also used by steamers on the shallows of the Missouri River, and others, where a long line was run out, and made fast, or a small anchor was set, to assist when the water was too shallow or swift; the line was then reeled in on a steam capstan while working full ahead on the engine.
3. To move a vessel or tow along a dock by use of a capstan or a winch.
4. The name of the line, a *warping line* that is used to *warp* a vessel.

WASH or WASHING AWAY
1. To carry something away by the force of water, i.e., "The current is *washing away* the sandbar that made out from ABC Point", or "When we hit the eddy the current came over the bow and *washed away* the lock line off the head". The term is related to the English *water*, and the movement of it "to cleanse". See: AWASH.
2. In a sense of dredging, i.e., "They're going to have to *wash out* that dock at the lower end if we're going to be able to tie off at that spot".
3. The movement of water away from a vessel by the action of a propeller or paddlewheel that is usually called *wheelwash*.

WASHBOARDING
The effect of older well-used steel-constructed equipment when the sides become indented between vertical frames from coming in contact with docks, other barges, or service in the ice.

WASHINGTON (steamer)
See: SHREVE, CAPT. HENRY MILLER.

WASTAGE
Corrosion or abrasion of steel plates that has reduced the thickness of a vessel's hull and may require some of it to be renewed. The word *waste* comes from the Latin *vastus,* meaning "a desert, or something devastated".

WATCH
The normal periods of time a portion of a towboat's crew is on duty to oversee the normal navigational operations of the vessel and its tow. Traditionally, towboat crews are divided into two segments: the forward *watch* stands the *watches* between 6 a.m. and noon, and the 6 p.m. to midnight shifts. The after *watch* is on duty between noon and 6 p.m. and also the midnight to 6 a.m. shifts. On a one-engineer vessel, the Chief Engineer stands an as-needed *watch*.

Some vessels are experimenting with different *watch* periods, i.e., seven hours on, and five hours off, then five hours on followed by seven hours off; others are looking at eight hours on, with four hours off, then four hours on followed by eight hours off. There may be other variations in the future. The term *watch* derives from wake, or a sense of wakefulness. It comes to us from old English *waecce,* "to be alert and keep guard".

WATCH THE BUMP!!!

A shouted warning when barges are being shifted in tow, possibly topping around, and whenever moving into a dock, lock wall, or other structure. It alerts all crew members on a tow to brace themselves as the vessels make a hard contact in order not to be thrown off-balance and possibly fall overboard or otherwise fall down and become hurt.

WATCHMAN

A person who keeps a lookout on a vessel that is tied off with the crew (if aboard) not standing a regular watch. The *watchman* makes rounds to see that unauthorized people do not board, looks for any danger such as smoke, fire, listing, and seeing that mooring lines are secure, etc. On an excursion vessel the *watchman* also looks for similar dangers, but also for any rowdiness or misbehavior as well as give answers to a barrel full of foolish questions.

WATER

Pure fresh *water* is made up of two parts of hydrogen and one part oxygen. River water consists of those elements plus lots of other things nature adds as the course of the river starts at its source on its journey to the sea. Man and other animals contribute additional impurities as it passes cities and farms. *Water* forms into ice at 32 degrees Fahrenheit or 0 degrees Centigrade. It weighs 8.3 pounds per gallon. One cubic foot of *water* equals 7.5 gallons and weighs 62.4 pounds. So when there is a lot of bilge *water* in a barge, it displaces some of its ability to carry cargo tonnage.

The density of fresh *water* is less than that of brackish or salt *water*, meaning a vessel loaded in the salt *water* of Galveston, TX, to the nine-foot level will have a deeper draft when it goes up the Mississippi River, with no increase in the cargo tonnage. This wonderful life-giving element's word origin is traced back to the Latin *unda,* meaning "wave", and to Greek *hudor,* meaning "water". It is our most precious commodity for drinking or floating on it.

WATER BALLAST

Water that is added to a void tank of a towboat to even its trim if light on fuel. Sometimes *water ballast* is pumped into void compartments of barges in order that barges in tow will properly HEADLOG. It may have to be added to barges in the Chicago area when barge covers are stacked on the ends of the barge making them too high to clear low level fixed bridges and their hulls have to be lowered or ballasted down in order to meet the height limits.

WATER FINDER

A type of paste that an engineer uses on his sounding rod or metal tape when gauging fuel tanks. If the paste changes color it indicates water is present in the tank. It is also called THIEVES PASTE.

WATER IMPELLED RATES

Since barging heavy bulk commodities is the only effective competition to the railroad for many industries, those located in the areas where barge transportation is available most often obtain rail rates that are cheaper than those industries that are situated far from water commerce. It is noted that often heavy users of coal or other products that are located on a river will build a dock with the intent of <u>not</u> using it, simply to force the rails to lower their pricing structure.

WATER INDICATOR
A type of gauging device that shows the level of water in a boiler.

WATER LIGHT
A light attached to a life buoy or jacket that will automatically energize when it comes in contact with water.

WATER PLANE
The horizontal line of a hull when it is to be immersed in water, as a naval architect (or someone claiming to be) has designed the vessel. There will be a *light plane* for a newly launched vessel without crew or stores; a *loaded plane* for a vessel wholly equipped, full of fuel and water; and other planes as may be determined by the designer or owner. See: WATERLINE.

WATER POLLUTION
See: POLLUTION.

WATER PRESSURE TEST
The testing of a fuel tank, or other liquid cargo tank, for leakage by filling it with water to its maximum working head pressure. Generally the working pressure is measured by a stand pipe fitted to the top deck level of the compartment, with each foot of water in the pipe equal to one-half pound of pressure. For raised compartments of tanks above the deck level other calculations have to be made by the design engineer.

WATER RESOURCE DEVELOPMENT
Programs for the *development of water resources* in the U.S. are impacted by a phalanx of government agencies, those that oversee agriculture, development uses, environment, power generation, flooding, and reclamation. The usage of varying water practices in the nation's first years was considered a responsibility of the various States or private interests; however, after the Louisiana Purchase the Senate asked the Secretary of Treasury, Albert Gallatin, to make a report on the internal needs of the country. It was issued in 1808 outlining the needs for roads, canals, harbors, and rivers. The report urged a strong federal concept of internal involvement and improvements, but Congress was of a mind that it was more than could be afforded; nevertheless, it became the cornerstone of *water resource development* for this country.

From the aspects of the Western Rivers, the USACE has always been the lead federal agency in surveying, planning, designing, construction, maintaining, and managing to our rivers and canals since 1824 when Congress passed the General Survey Act, and then the first Rivers and Harbor Act of 1826. Since that time our internal rivers have continued to be improved for multi-purposes throughout the land.

WATER TIE
Usually refers to tying a vessel off to something that is surrounded by water, such as a tree in a high stage of river. See: HIGH-WATER TIE and COME-BACK LINE.

WATER TUBE BOILER
A boiler that consists of pipes that are filled with water or steam and surrounded by flames and gases. See: FIRE-TUBE BOILER.

WATERBORNE
1. A vessel that is floating and not aground.
2. Said of a vessel that has just been launched and is floating in the water, or of a vessel that has just come off drydock.
3. Freight that is transported in vessels.
4. Refers to commercial statistics of cargoes, tonnages, origination points and destinations compiled by the government and published annually.

WATERFRONT
An area of a city or town that fronts on the water. At one time it was the busiest area of the community with docks, vessels loading or unloading

freight, supplies, and passengers. Now most of the *waterfronts* of cities are park areas. Also called *cityfronts*.

WATERLINE (WL)

1. The horizontal surface of the water that intersects the length of the hull of a vessel at its actual level to float when "light", or without fuel, water, or stores. There is also the *loaded waterline,* which is at the operational line she operates when on an even keel with all necessaries aboard. See: WATER PLANE.

2. On towboats, tugs and barges, it is usually the line referred to when taking draft measurements regarding where water intersects the draft mark, i.e., "The *waterline* is lapping at the top of the nine foot mark on barge 1776 so it's drawing $9\frac{1}{2}$ feet".

WATERLOGGED

Timbers in wooden-hulled vessels which were saturated with water caused it to have a sluggish movement. The term probably comes from the trees or logs that came off a caving bank and lay in the water for a long time, absorbing the moisture into the grain until a rise or flood took them away from the bank. As they floated along in the river they were barely visible on the surface of the water and have caused much damage to many an unsuspecting steamboat navigating the river that have the misfortune to run into or over them.

WATERS SPECIFIED BY THE SECRETARY

The Inland Navigation Rules generally include the inland waters of the United States, the Great Lakes, and the Western Rivers, as well as certain *waters specified by the Secretary*. The Secretary is the person-in-charge of the Department in which the Coast Guard is operating, currently the Department of Homeland Security. Most of the specified waters have to do with certain rivers that are not included in the provisions particular to vessels operating on the Western Rivers, especially as enumerated in Rule 9, 14 and 15. After being specified those provisions of the Rules pertaining to the Western Rivers become applicable to them.

WATERSHED

It is an area measured over a land mass of a particular waterway from the highest elevation of a stream and/or its tributaries downward flows of precipitation or springs to where it may join another stream. A *watershed* may be that of a localized creek or the drainage basin of a given river, or of a system of rivers, such as the Ohio River basin, or the Missouri River basin, etc., to one the size of the Mississippi River acting as a collective funnel of the runoff of the interior lands of the U.S. with its exit spout at the Gulf of Mexico.

WATERSTOP

When lapped or joggled side plates are employed on barge sides it is necessary at watertight bulkheads to cut into the joggle and weld it up at each side of the WT bulkhead. If not, water will seep from one compartment to another through the lap seam if flooded as the laps are generally only welded intermittently on the inside of the hull.

WATERTIGHT

1. A term used to denote that there is no leakage internally to the hull or between its designed watertight compartments.

2. A tank or compartment of a vessel that does not leak product into the marine environment.

WATERTIGHT DOOR

A strongly constructed steel hatch door that is fitted with a heavy seal material and with a number of DOGS as closure devices. When the dogs are tightened the door is able to withstand the pressure force against it without leakage.

WATERWAY

A river, stream, channel, or other

course navigable by vessels. See: GULF INTRACOASTAL WATERWAY, and types of water courses.

WATERWAYS EXPERIMENT STATION (WES)

Authorized by Congress after the devastating flood of 1927 on the Lower Mississippi River, the station was viewed to become a hydraulics laboratory for rivers. It is located in Vicksburg, MS, and has grown in scope and significance with its ability to tackle complex planning and design problems with practical engineering solutions for projects that benefit the whole of the U.S., as well as the rest of the world and even into space.

WATERWAYS JOURNAL

A news magazine of happenings on, to, or about the rivers and navigable canals of the internal navigation systems of the United States. It was first published in 1887 under the name *THE RIVER*, by a steamboat Captain from Evansville, IN, Abbott Veatch. In 1891 Veatch was in financial trouble and the publication was bought at auction by William Arste, who lived in St. Louis and started publishing it there. He changed its name to *THE WATERWAYS JOURNAL,* as it is known today. In 1921 Arste wanted to retire and he sold the weekly to Donald T. Wright, who continued publishing it in St. Louis. After Wright decided to retire he sold the WJ in 1965 to H. N. "Ray" Spencer, Jr. Since that time the paper has been under the editorial control of the Spencer family. It is affectionately known to river people as *THE RIVERMAN'S BIBLE*.

WAVE

1. A curling motion of water that rises and falls. It can be from natural causes such as the wind, especially on the Ohio River where the river flows mostly in an east-to-west pattern while the prevailing winds blow west to east. Also, during high wind times, *waves* occur in broad reaches on river lakes, such as Lake Pepin or Keokuk Lake on the Upper Mississippi, the various TVA lakes, and along the bays of the coastal areas. The word comes from the Old English *woeg*, meaning the "motion of the water".

2. *Waves* can also be the result of vessels moving through the water, especially at great speed. They can be generated by the thrust of a propeller or the turning of a paddlewheel. The height of a *wave* is measured vertically from its top, or crest, to its trough, or bottom between two crests. The length of a *wave* can be measured horizontally between two crests or two troughs. The period of a *wave* is the time between two successive crests at a given point. See: BOW WAVE and WAKE.

3. Movement signals by hand and/or arms to indicate directions or advice, i.e. a deckhand giving motion progress signals to the Pilot.

4. A motion indicating a friendly greeting. See: TOWBOAT GREETING.

5. The to and fro movement of the U.S. Flag as it flutters in the wind. Long may she *wave*.

WAY

1. The motion or progress of a vessel through the water. The term is from the Dutch and German *weg*, meaning "to carry or move".

2. A vessel is *underway* when it is not anchored or held fast to the bank in some fashion, but is not aground. A vessel *underway* may only be drifting and not making any *way* through the water. Also a vessel that is engaged in forward propulsion, but is not making any progress or *way* is simply *underway*.

3. A vessel making progress with forward propulsion is making *headway*.

4. When a vessel is in the process of moving forward but has not reached its desired speed, it is said to be *gathering way*.

5. If a vessel is coming full ahead on its throttle but is slowing down in speed over the riverbed, usually due to cur-

rent, the vessel is said to be *losing way*.

6. A vessel that is backing down with astern propulsion through the water is said to have *sternway*.

WAYS

The cradles or timbers on which a vessel is constructed or repaired. After building, the vessel will be slid on an inclined slope into the water on a LAUNCH-WAYS. If a vessel needs repair it may be hauled out on a LIFTING-WAYS, a DRYDOCK, or a SYNCROLIFT. Also see: LAUNCHING, LAUNCHING-WAYS, and SKIDS.

WEAR & TEAR

The gradual deterioration of a vessel over the years. Wood rots; steel corrodes and abrades; engines become worn simply by use in running; fatigue of other parts that leads to breakdowns, etc. The term is used often in charter surveys and charter contracts. One key phrase might say, "To be returned in like manner, normal *wear and tear* excepted". Depending on the length of charter the surveyor will expect certain indents, deterioration, and wastage to occur to a vessel even in the service of a responsible charterer.

WEATHER

1. The observation of the condition of the atmosphere at any one place at a certain time. The weather consists of air pressure and temperature, the the humidity in the air, the types of clouds that are present, the wind, any precipitation, and the visibility available. It is a term that can be applied to clear, cloudy, snow, rain, fog, hazy, windy, still, sunny and other conditions. There are books on weather sayings and superstitions, but we will not repeat them here. Some have a high degree of validity, some are accurate half the time, some only a tenth of the time. It is sufficient to say that all Pilots appreciate a full moon and cloudless night, and days that are sunny and bright with only a light breeze in temperate air for happy towboating.

2. The ability of a vessel to survive through heavy or serious storms with no, or minimal, damage, i.e., "When that storm blew up the other night and they had a tornado warning posted the barges were hemming and hawing but we weathered it and only broke three wires". See: BEAUFORT WIND SCALE.

WEATHER DECK

Any deck that is not covered, but is exposed to the elements. Some opine that it is the uppermost uncovered deck, others say it is the main deck. However, if one is exposed to the weather on a vessel, he/she must be on a *weather deck*.

WEATHER SHORE

The shore that is lying windward from the vessel or tow.

WEATHER SIDE

The side of a vessel toward which the wind and the other elements are blowing. Also known as the *windward side*. It is the opposite of the LEE or LEEWARD side of a vessel.

WEATHER WARNINGS

Warnings of impending weather conditions are issued by the National Weather Service both by radio alerts and by visual means, particularly along the coastal areas. The advisory conditions are as follows:

1. SMALL CRAFT ADVISORY — Winds up to 38 mph. Visual signal consists of a red triangular pennant shown by day, and a red light shown above a white light by night.

2. GALE WARNING — Winds from 39 to 54 mph. Visual signal consists of two red triangular pennants shown by day, and a white light shown above a red light by night.

3. STORM WARNING — Winds from 55 and above unless associated with a forecast of a hurricane, then it is winds up to 73 mph. Visual signal consists of square red flag with a smaller square black center by day, and two red lights by night.

4. HURRICANE WARNING— Winds which exceed 74 mph. Visual signal consists of two square red flags with a smaller square black center by day, and two red lights with a white light between them by night. If "hurricane winds" are blowing it is doubtful if the flags would last very long. See: BEAUFORT WIND SCALE.

WEATHERBOUND
Said of a vessel or tow that can not safely proceed because of adverse weather conditions, including high winds, wave conditions, blinding rain or snow, fog, etc.

WEATHERTIGHT
Usually on the river refers to the covers of a covered hopper barge which will shed rain and snow, but are not WATERTIGHT and would not keep out heavy sea flows of water or an extremely hard-driven rain.

WEB FRAMING
Usually refers to the transverse or athwartships framing on a vessel that provides strength. See: TRUSS.

WEDGE
A somewhat long piece of tapered wood that is in triangular shape. It is used mostly to secure things, such as preventing barrels from rolling, tightening down tarps, fitting keel blocks, or sometimes for stopping leakage from wide splits, etc. See: DAGGER PIN and GLUT.

WEDGE KEY
A somewhat tapered piece of wood that is used to tighten the WOOD CIRCLE of a paddlewheel. It is driven in, fitting between an ARM of the wheel and the GIB, which is used to protect the grain of the end of a wooden block in the wood circle.

WEEKEND CAPTAINS
Recreational boat owners who have just bought a new craft, read a book on "boating", stay in the middle of a channel when they have a draft of two feet, and are constantly on their new VHF radio telling everyone where they are (usually wrong).

WEEP or WEEPER
A barge that is leaking very slowly.

WEIGH
The act of raising or heaving an anchor from its hold on the bottom, but since there are few towboats equipped with anchors, we will leave it to our tugboat crews to call out "Anchor aweigh". The term apparently comes to us from the old English *wegam*, derived from the German *bewegam*, which had the sense of "conveying" or of "raising up".

WEIR
As used on the river the term describes a barrier that restrains, redirects, or holds back the flow of water. It can be a low dam or wall across a stream that raises the upstream water level. When it is uncontrolled it is called a fixed crest *weir*. The term comes from the old English *werian*, meaning "to dam up". See: DIKE.

WELD or WELDING
Essentially, *welding* is the glue that holds steel plates, shapes, and fittings to one another. There are various ways of *welding*, mostly by using intense heat and melting an electrode or wire where steel meets steel. Also there are various types of *welds*, i.e., *tack weld*, *butt weld*, *lap weld*, etc. that can be perused in tomes on vessel construction.

WELL
1. A built-in depression in the cargo tank bottom of a double-skinned tank barge where the SUCTION BELL of the tank piping will sit to allow for more efficient stripping of the cargo tank. More often called a SUMP.

2. A closed compartment of a tank barge which will house a centrifugal type pump.

3. Sometimes used for the watertight compartment that will house a DAGGER BOARD, a type of SKEG.

WELL OUT (IN THE RIVER)

A subjective term Pilots use to describe certain marks when navigating. Basically it means for one to keep their vessel a good distance away from an object or place, i.e., "Follow the shape of the bend, but stay *well out* from the lower dike since there is a bar building there".

WELL-FOUND

The description of a towboat or tugboat that is well-built, well-crewed, well-equipped, well- supplied, and well-maintained.

WEST OF HARVEY LOCK (WHL)

Harvey Lock on the ICWW is Mile 0. The mileage starts from this point going west from the Lock all the way to Brownsville, TX, at the border with Mexico. Also see: EAST OF HARVEY LOCK (EHL).

WESTERN RIVERS

The *Western Rivers* are described in the Inland Navigation Rules to mean the Mississippi River, its tributaries, South Pass, and Southwest Pass, to the navigational demarcation lines dividing the high seas from harbors, rivers, and other inland waters of the United States, and the Port Allen-Morgan City Alternate Route, and that part of the Atchafalaya River above its junction with the Port Allen-Morgan City Alternate Route including the Old River and the Red River.

Originally when the settlers started migrating from the East Coast, all the rivers flowing west of the Appalachians were considered *western rivers*. When the navigation rules were promulgated for these rivers they were simply called the *Western River* Rules for the Mississippi and its tributaries, and also included the Atchafalaya River, and the Red River of the North, which sources in Minnesota and ends up in Canada (and is no longer part of the *Western Rivers*. It is also not the Red River of Texas, Oklahoma, and Louisiana).

WET DOCK

Another name sometimes used for a GRAVING DOCK.

WET SIDE

Refers to the outside deck edges of a barge tow where crew members may have to walk. They are cautioned to always walk on the DRY SIDE (between two strings of barges) of any tow if possible, but if they have to be on the *wet side* to take extra precautions so as to not slip overboard.

WETTED SURFACE

Generally it refers to the external portion of the hull of a vessel that is submerged below the surface of the waterline.

WHARF

A place where cargo can be transferred or passengers embark or debark from a vessel. It is usually in the main area of a town and can simply be a paved sloping shoreline with heavy mooring rings securely anchored in the surface, or it can be a concrete quay or dock where a vessel can tie off. The word's origin appears to go back to the Germanic *werft,* to mean "a shipyard".

WHARFAGE

A fee charged to a vessel for use of wharf space for the transfer of cargo and/or people, either at a daily rate or per net ton. The fee may be assessed taking into account the size of the vessel.

WHARFBOAT

In the days of steamboats a *wharfboat* was a step up from a simple landing to pick up or drop cargo and/or passengers. *Wharfboats* were not used as transport vessels but, rather, served as floating warehouses, where goods could be stored until a steamer arrived to pick them up or where the steamer dropped off cargo to be held until a drayman could cart them to customers. There are few *wharfboats* left on the river system; those that remain are mostly used to service those in the excursion business.

WHARFINGER
The owner, operator, or manager of a wharf or wharfboat. More often presently called a *Wharf Superintendent*.

WHEEL
1. On a steamboat, it is the circular device fitted with spokes in the pilothouse which is attached to a drum that moves the tiller wires used to steer the steamer, and sometimes on a diesel engine vessel if an actual *wheel* is employed. It is more fomally termed a PILOT WHEEL. The origin of the word is traced to Sanskrit *cakra,* meaning "wheel circle", and the Greek word *kuklos,* meaning "circle".
2. The paddlewheel on a sternwheeler or a sidewheeler which propels the vessel.
3. The propeller on a towboat or tug. Also called a SCREW.
4. An attachment on a manual winch used to move and turn a drum to tighten or slack a wire leading from it.

WHEEL VALVE
A type of gate or stop valve that is opened and closed by means of a hand wheel. The wheel may be located at the valve or may be controlled by a reach rod if it is located on a line in a tank that would possibly be submerged in liquid.

WHEEL WASH
See: WASH

WHEELBOATS
A name given to paddlewheel boats that were powered by animals, mostly horses or mules, and occasionally by men, walking on a treadmill or a turnstile. Not very successful since the horses and mules would often have to be replaced as well as amply fed, on a lengthy voyage. They did have some success in the ferryboat trade.

WHEELHOUSE
1. The housing over a sidewheel of a steamboat.
2. A term sometimes inaccurately used for the PILOTHOUSE, which is the correct terminology on a towboat where steering of a vessel takes place. The use of *wheelhouse* appears to have migrated to the river after WW II when many people from the GIWW started working on the river. On the canal most people navigating a vessel were called "wheelmen" since the tugs and older small towboats did have steering wheels that were used to navigate from a *wheelhouse.* After WW II when ex-sailors, who had been aboard ships, first came to the river, they brought the term with them from the U.S. Navy. Often in the Navy the *wheelhouse* was a deck below the "bridge" where the Officer-of-the-Deck stands watch and directs the person doing the steering as to what course to steer.

WHEELING BRIDGE CASE
A classic case of rivalry between states, cities, and modes of transportation. A bridge was needed across the river at Wheeling, VA (before it was WV), to improve road transportation to the western territories. A suspension bridge was built and opened in 1849. Pittsburgh claimed it hindered its trade by restricting the clearance height under its span so that steamboat chimneys, or stacks, could not efficiently go to and from their port; therefore, the bridge was a hindrance to navigation. Wheeling interests said that steamers should put hinges on their stacks and lower them when they had to transit the bridge. Legal actions were brought. Then the *Str. HIBERNIA No. 2* ran down the river with stacks reaching 90 feet in height above the river level and struck the bridge, damaging the stacks. The Supreme Court said the bridge would have to be raised. This would effectively doom it. At the time it was

the longest suspension bridge in the world. Then Congress got into the act by passing a law in 1852 that declared the bridge was an official postal and military road, effectively putting it beyond court action. So, vessels started using stack hinges and A-frames to lower and raise their stacks.

Two years later, however, a storm with high winds blew through Wheeling and the Ohio River and the bridge came tumbling down. Wheeling interests started rebuilding the bridge using larger cables and heavier material. Pittsburgh obtained an injunction against rebuilding, which was granted, but Wheeling ignored it and continued rebuilding. When the Supreme Court was back in session, the injunction case was heard and the court decided that since Congress had given approval to the bridge, they found in unjustifiable to intervene and allowed the rebuilding to continue. The bridge still stands today.

WHELP

A longitudinal ridge on the barrel of a capstan, and sometimes on a winch. The *whelps* help to keep a line from slipping on the barrel or drum when a strain is placed on the line. The word is related to the Germanic *welf,* referring to "a young dog", so in a sense by tightening on the *whelps* it tended to "dog down" the line.

WHEN HALFWAY or WELL OVER

Terms that were used in the old channel reports and are used in the descriptive language of river Pilots to describe navigation or making crossings in the river, i.e., "*When halfway over*, pull down on the big old cottonwood tree, and then *when well over*, ease her down on Neverlit Light, and run an easy distance off the left bank".

WHIP or WHIPPING

The act of wrapping the bitter end of a line with small stuff called COWTAIL to keep it from unraveling, or to wrap the individual strands of a line prior to splicing it into another line or when making an eye splice. Keeping the strands tight makes it easier to insert them in each tuck of the splice.

WHISTLE

Under Rule 32 of the Inland Navigation Rules it is any sound signaling appliance capable of producing the prescribed blasts (see: WHISTLE SIGNALS) that comply with the specifications in Annex III of the Rules. The Annex gives frequencies and ranges of audibility, depending on length of vessel, directional properties, *whistle* positioning, and types of *whistles*.

On steamboats the *whistles* were sounded by steam power and had distinctive sounds. People said they could tell whatever boat was coming into a landing by the sound of its *whistle*. They could be elaborate affairs. The whistling device itself was called a "bell", and if the *whistle* had more than one "bell" it was called a "chime". The chimes were often three in number with different sized bells that gave off a harmonic sound when blasted. Steam *whistles*, as with bells, rotated to other steamers when the original one they were placed on might meet its demise.

It has been reported that the first steamboat to have a steam-powered *whistle* installed on board was the steamer *REVENUE* in 1840. The sweetest and most mellifluous sounds of the *whistle* have been attributed to various boats, depending on who heard them. The loudest *whistle* has been said to be the one on the steamer *SPRAGUE*, which had a deep rich tone, and was loud, and sonorous.

Most all diesel towboats and tugs today have air horns. On some of the older ones the Pilot could manipulate the air to a three-horn *whistle* to give it a rising and fading away moan when sounding; most new horns can only give a distinctive blast with no character, probably because Annex III technicalities might make the manufacturing companies nervous. See: WILDCAT WHISTLE.

WHISTLE BLOW

Every once in awhile steamboat aficionados get together, bring steam whistle*s* they have collected, get a steam boiler fired up, and sound off. A couple of records have been made of these *whistle blows*. The only problem, someone always complains that a whistle's tone doesn't seem the same as when it was sounded on the old vessel from which it came. The problem is that of boiler pressure, volume of steam, and maybe a variety of other factors, including one's aging ears and remembrance.

WHISTLE CORD or LANYARD

A cord or chain in the pilothouse affixed to the whistle to pull when sounding a signal. On most steamboats there was a foot pedal on the floor or deck of the pilothouse that the Pilot would step on to sound the whistle.

WHISTLE LIGHT

The *whistle light* is a distinctive feature of the Western Rivers. It is a white or yellow light that displays when the whistle is sounded. It originally came into effect on the river system when diesel boats became prominent and Pilots complained that sometimes they didn't hear the signal of a meeting vessel, but when meeting a steamboat they could see the puffing trail of steam of the number of blasts the steamer sounded. So it was decided that vessels would be fitted with an amber light to show when the whistle was blown. It only applied to the Western Rivers. Then when the new Inland Navigation Rules went into effect the "amber" changed to "white or yellow" and the signal became optional on all inland navigational waters. It is reported the *Str. SPRAGUE* was the first vessel to employ the light before it became required.

WHISTLE SALUTE

River companies devised different sound signals when coming into a landing to distinguish their vessels from those of other firms. The signals were a variety of short and long blasts on the vessel's whistle. Some of them are listed in LANDING WHISTLE. Many Pilots have ventured to posit various signals they deem suitable to hail someone on the bank or a fellow riverman as they are passing, so long as it <u>cannot</u> be deemed a navigational signal. Most often it is a long and two short blasts.

The two *salutes* that seem most appropriate to sound when honoring a river person who has crossed over the bar, or died, would be to sound the landing whistle of the company the person was mostly associated with, at his/her "final landing". A more generic one would be similar to that rendered to a fallen person of the military which consists of three rifle volleys over their grave. It is believed that three long blasts on the whistle of about ten seconds or so each (longer than the prolonged whistle) would be a proper tribute to one who has served his industry well. Can you hear it now? FAREWELL…FAREWELL…FAREWELL….This salute is also the one used by vessels when they passed the LEPROSY HOSPITAL near Carrsville, LA, on the Lower Mississippi.

HIS LAST TRIP

"Mate, get ready down on deck,
I'm heading for the shore;
I'll ring the bell, for I must land
This boat for evermore.

Say, Pilot, can you see that light—
I do – where angels stand?
Well, hold her jackstaff hard on that,
For there I'm going to land.

That looks like Death that's hailing me;
So ghastly, grim and pale;
I'll toll the bell – I must go in –
I never passed a hail.

Stop her! Let her come in slow!
There! That will do – no more!
The lines are fast and angels wait
To welcome me ashore.

> Say, Pilot, I am going with them
>   Up yonder through the gate;
> I'll not be back – you ring the bell
>   And back her out – don't wait.
>
> For I have made the trip of life,
>   And found my landing place;
> I'll take my soul and anchor that
>   Fast to the Throne of Grace."

The foregoing was written in memory of Capt. J.M. White. It first appeared in the Louisville Courier-Journal on Jan. 25, 1880. It is reprinted here from the S & D Reflector issued in December 1974.

WHISTLE SIGNALS (NAVIGATIONAL)

The requirements for when and where to sound whistle signals are found in the Navigation Rules, Part D, Rules 32 through 37, which provide for maneuvering and warning signals, what signals to sound in restricted visibility, signals to attract attention, and types of distress signals in addition to sound signals. See: BRIDGE SIGNALS and LOCK SIGNALS.

1. The Navigation Rules provide for two types of blasts on the whistle:
SHORT BLAST – A blast of about 1 second's duration.
2. PROLONGED BLAST – A blast of from 4 to 6 seconds duration.

WHISTLE TREADLE

When sounding a steamboat whistle many boats were fitted with a foot lever (the *treadle*) on the floor to the right of the pilotwheel, making it easier for a Pilot to use when actively steering and also sounding navigational signals.

WHITE RIVER

The *White River* starts its journey in the Boston Mountains of Arkansas spending most of it's over 700 miles in the state with a brief excursion into Missouri. It finally empties into the Mississippi River at mile 583. Keelboats in the early 1800s went to the upper reaches of the *White* and flatboats were regularly employed for the one-way trip downriver. Steamboats appeared in 1831 and started running to Batesville, AR, on a regular basis, about half the river's distance. In the 1840s steamers would go another 100 miles upstream to Forsythe, MO, and the mouth of the small James River during the "wet" season.

Before the turn of the 20th century surveys to improve the river's navigability had been made and a program was undertaken to build a series of 10 locks and dams on the river. The first was at Batesville which opened in 1904 with a plan to construct the rest at a rate of one per year. Only two others were built as rail lines started providing more regular service to the area. Although steamboat traffic held on until the 1930s their yearly numbers steadily decreased. The locks and dams that were built consisted of large timber crib structures that were put on a dredged leveled river bottom and filled with rocks and stones. The cribs had a concrete cap poured across the adjoining tops which held them in place. The dams were fixed with no control mechanism. When the river flows overtopped it became the channel for the vessels operating there. It was only in extremely low flow periods that the locks (175 by 36 feet) were used. After another study of the upper *White River* system in 1911 the decision was made that due to diminished river traffic no further dam construction would be undertaken. The three existing locks continued in operation until 1952 when they were sealed, but the dams remained.

After a serious flood in 1935 water resource concerns in the area were more for flood control than for navigation. The massive flood of 1937 caused the nation to call for additional structures to abate untamed water destructive forces. As a result the upper *White River* now contains a series of large reservoirs in northern Arkansas and southern Missouri, including Norfolk, Table Rock, Bull Shoals and others that provide water storage, flood abatement, electricity, and great tourism, including the town of Branson, but nothing in the way of commercial barge traffic. However, the lower 10 miles of the river provide the entrance to the McCLELLAN-KERR ARKANSAS RIVER Navigation System.

WHITECAPS

A frothing of water that crests and then breaks giving the appearance of having a white top. Often present on oceans and coastal areas, but also on large inland lakes and wide stretches of rivers when the wind velocities are strong. See: WIND SWELLS.

WICKET and WICKET DAM

The *wicket*, or Chanoine *wicket*, named after the French engineer who developed it in 1852, made possible a type of MOVABLE DAM that could be lowered to the bottom of the river when the water level was sufficient to navigate over a dammed area. The *wicket* was hinged to the concrete foundation of the dam crossing a section of the river. Each *wicket* was three feet wide. The length varied depending on the height of water to be held in a pool. Usually they were about 15 feet long. The *wicket* was made of wood boards bolted together in a steel frame called a HORSE. When first invented, the *wickets* were lowered by a tripping bar, but the USACE soon learned the French engineers had developed a grooved cast slide for the dam's foundation in which a steel prop could slide. Called a "heurter" by the French (and a "hurter" in the U.S.) this groove made raising and lowering the *wickets* into place much easier.

When raising a movable dam a MANEUVER BOAT used a grappling iron (see: GRAPNEL) to catch the top end of the lowered *wicket* and pull it to the surface by a crane on the maneuver boat, where the prop sliding in the hurter would catch and lock in place. The maneuver boat could lower the dam by pulling the *wicket* slightly upstream, the prop would release in the hurter, after which the current of the river would force the *wicket* to lie on the riverbed. The term derives from the Old Norse *vikja,* meaning "to turn or move", and evolved into describing a small door in a large one. So it probably pretty well describes one *wicket* as a small door with the large door being the entire dam. At one time most of the pre-WW II dams on the Ohio River were movable *wicket* dams which were replaced by high-lift structures since the old dams were high-maintenance and manpower-intensive. See: NEEDLE.

WIDE BERTH

1. An action to give more than sufficient space to another vessel when meeting or passing
2. To stay well clear of a shallow area, an obstruction, or any other type of hindrance to safe navigation.

WIDE OUT

Another state-of-the-art piece of advice given in channel reports or between Pilots, i.e., "When steering ABC Bend, stay *wide out* before you reach the foot of it since a bar is building in that area", or "Keep *wide out* off the shore at mile 614 because a mat-laying plant is working there".

WIGGLES

A curving stretch of channel that changes direction. The term is applied to numerous places on the GIWW where a series of curves or bends in the Canal occur, making it somewhat hazardous for two or more tows of fairly large size to meet one another. Customs between Pilots have been worked out as to which tow shall hold position until the other tow has passed through the section. It usually pertains to which tow has arrived at a certain canal mile point before a vessel heading in the opposite direction reaches its critical mile point as to who will do the holding and who will continue coming ahead.

WILDCAT

A drum on a windlass that is able to engage the links of an anchor chain. Since on the river few vessels have anchors or anchor chains, rivermen do not have to deal with *wildcats* although Mike Fink had been known to 'rassel a few in his time.

WILDCAT WHISTLE

As used on the Western Rivers it was described by Fred Way (S & D Reflector, Dec 1991) as: "A lengthy large single whistle is fitted at its tip with a squeally high-pitched little job which gets its action from what steam is left over in the big one. The result is a deep sonorous sound from the parent job, followed by an unearthly yowl from the little feller". It is said that some whistle collectors describe it in other terms, especially those of railroad buffs. See: WHISTLE.

WILLAMETTE RIVER

See: COLUMBIA – SNAKE RIVER SYSTEM.

WILLOW MATTRESS

The first efforts to protect riverbanks from eroding away by high water and constant current action was the placement of brush and small willow trees in bundles that were tied together in cross stacks of three or more feet. They were then assembled and combined into a large group resembling a giant *mattress* that was then floated into position along a bank that was to be protected. The *mattress* or *mat* was sunk by piling huge rocks on it that couldn't be washed away very easily. In some areas the *mats* were successful, but in others they sometimes failed in the first flood. As the willows that grew close to the shores were depleted, the limited use of lumber mats was tried. Later experiments were made with slabs of concrete which met with some success, but placing them properly was labor intensive. Around 1914 the first type of concrete blocks wired together seemed to be the best answer to bank erosion, and eventually evolved into the articulated concrete revetment mattresses that are used today. However, *willow mattresses* and other experimental products were still used up to the 1930s. See: MATTRESS, MAT-PLANT and REVETMENT.

WINCH

A hand-powered or machine-driven device used to wind in or tighten lines or wires on a drum which can be vertically or horizontally mounted. See: CAPSTAN. The term is from the old English *wince,* meaning "a pulley or reel".

1. A powered *winch* (sometimes manual) is used on towboats to tighten face wires when making up to a barge or tow.

2. A manually operated *winch* is used on some barge equipment, especially unit tows to tighten the wires connecting the barges together in the unit.

3. Used at locks to haul out a section of tow when double-locking is required.

4. Often used at docks to maneuver barges while loading or unloading them.

5. Used on dredges to maneuver on their anchors while making a dredge cut.

6. Tugs use the *winch* to manipulate the length of their towing wire or line.

7. Salvage rigs may be equipped with very powerful *winches* that are used when raising vessels that have sunk and for pulling vessels off banks, etc.

WINCH WIRE

1. The wire attached to the winch on a barge, or other vessel, with an "eye" at its bitter end that is affixed to a fitting on another barge, and is then tightened by the winch, either manually or mechanically.

2. The small haul-out wire located on the lock wall used to remove a barge cut from a lock.

3. Wires from the front of a towboat to its tow. See: FACE WIRES.

WIND

1. A movement of air from a particular direction. Pilots having empty

barges in tow have to pay particular attention to its direction and force when maneuvering at bridges, locks, landings, in narrow channels or other areas where the sail effect of the *wind* may affect the direction and steerage of one's tow. From the Dutch and German *wind,* meaning "to blow". See: BEAUFORT WIND SCALE.

2. To move, or take up, in a more or less spiral course, as to *wind in* or take up the wire on a winch. In this sense it is from the Old German *windan,* meaning "to take up".

WIND FLAG or SOCK

A small flag or pennant placed on a tow to assist the Pilot in determining the direction and strength of the wind. Depending on the circumstance there may be more than one flag in use, especially when running with a large tow of empty barges with a huge "sail" area.

WIND INDICATOR

A vane device that shows the direction of the wind. Sometimes it may be fitted to show the velocity of the wind. Also called, and see: ANEMOMETER.

WIND LINE

A line used to tie off a vessel or tow leading out from, and downstream from, a vessel or tow, or in the opposite direction of the headline, to keep the tow from blowing out into the channel, especially when it is a tow of empty barges.

WIND REEF

The action of the wind blowing against the current sometimes will give the false illusion by its rippling effect that there is a reef building immediately below.

WIND SCOOP

An inverted L-shaped type of funnel device made of sheet metal protruding above a weather deck and attached to an opening to a space below, especially the engine room of a towboat. It can rotate so that its open end is able to catch the wind from whichever direction it may be blowing and supply fresh air to a compartment.

WIND SWELLS

Waves, or large ripples, caused by the wind, usually when the wind is blowing against the current. The Ohio River, which generally is flowing East to West, oftentimes meets the prevailing winds that generally move from West to East which causes *wind swells* and "white caps", two common occurrences.

WIND VELOCITY

The speed of the wind in miles per hour. See: ANEMOMETER.

WINDAGE

The force of the wind and the effect it has on the resistance of an object to it, such as an empty tow, or large vessel with a great exposed sail area.

WINDBAG

On occasion, it can mean someone giving advice from a vessel's headquarters. At times they believe they know which way "the wind is blowing" when they "get wind" of a perceived problem from some "windy" person (blowhard). Instead of asking about the problem, they repeat the old adage, an "ill wind that blows no good". When confronted with the truth of the situation it "takes the wind out of their sails". So sail on Captain, and if their "ill wind" is of no use, "throw it to the winds". May you always have a "fair wind" at your back", and may you reap a "windfall" bonus in your paycheck so you can have smooth sailing ahead.

WINDBOUND

Most often becomes a problem when a towboat or tug with a long tow of empty barges in a narrow waterway such as the GIWW is unable to safely navigate, especially when meeting other tows, due to high wind velocities, and has to wait till the wind dies down to get away from the bank.

WINDLASS

A special type of winch that is used to hoist an anchor. The term seems to come from the Old Norse, *windass,* that meant "a winding pole", but since it was preceded in use by the WINCH it may have had some of its roots from there.

WINDWARD

The side facing the wind, or the direction from which the wind is blowing. A wind coming from the direction of the bow would be a *head wind*; a wind blowing on the side of a vessel would be a *wind from starboard* or a *starboard wind,* or a *wind from port* or a *port wind,* a wind from behind or astern of the vessel would be a *following wind*.

WING

1. An outside protrusion or appendage to the pilothouse, usually on both the port and starboard sides. The word comes from the Norse *vaengir,* meaning the "wing of a bird".

2. The outboard sides of the bulkheads in the cargo hold of a barge that is sometimes referred to as *wing* walls or bulkheads.

WING DAM or DIKE

A submerged dike used for training the channel. These were extensively used in the river prior to canalization of the river system to a nine-foot channel. *Wing dikes* are basically the same as SPUR DIKEs.

WING TANK

1. One of the side tanks of a towboat or tug. It may contain water or fuel, or it may be an empty void space that may be used in ballasting. Sometimes termed a SIDE TANK.

2. The empty void side tanks of double-skinned barges.

WING WALLS

The side walls of a DRYDOCK that are partially filled with water in order to sink down the dock in order to float in a vessel needing repair or inspection, or to pump out ballast water to float off a repaired and/or inspected vessel.

WING-IN-GROUND CRAFT (WIG)

Refers to a multimodal craft which, in its main operational mode, flies in close proximity to the surface (of water) by utilizing surface-effect action. In the early years of the 21st Century, none of these craft were operating on the Western Rivers. However, currently there is provision for them in the International Navigation Rules with certain responsibilities under Rule 18.

WINGWIRE

1. A wire leading at a greater angle from a tow to the towboat than the FACE WIRES. They are used to keep the towboat from heeling over in a hard steer and giving more leverage to steer.

2. A wire leading to the stern of a towboat from a barge being towed alongside.

WIRE or WIRE ROPE

Strands of twisted *wire* that form a cable. As used on towboats, the core will be of fiber or synthetic material to allow more flexibility. *Wire* is measured by its diameter. Most rigging *wire* ranges from 7/8", 1", 1 1/8" or 1 1/4" in diameter. Not much splicing of *wire* currently takes place aboard towboats. Wire of desired lengths and fittings is purchased by a vessel's operator. Winch *wires* will have an eye swaged in one end with a whipped bitter end to attach to the winch. Barge *wires* will be of various lengths with a swaged eye in one or both ends, or one end will have a thimble to receive a shackle and chain links, or the links will already be in the thimble.

WIRE CLIP or CLAMP

A threaded U-shaped bolting that goes around two sections of a wire cable and then into a device called the "jaws". The jaws are then bolted and tightened in the clip. *Wire clips* are used to secure thimbles in the ends of a wire, or to make an eye. Usually three to five clamps are used in heavy (3/4" on up) wire. The "U" part of the clamp is always placed on the bitter end portion of the wire. Also called a *cable clamp*.

WITHDRAWN

An aid to navigation that is permanently or temporarily taken out of service, either because of a channel change, it is no longer needed, or for the seasonal suspension of navigation.

WITHY

Meaning a place where willows grow, as well as describing a slender willow or a small twig from it. During logging and the movement of log rafts on our rivers, *withys* were sometimes used to hold the logs together. The word is sometimes spelled *withe*. The term comes from the Old Norse *vithir*, meaning "willow".

WITH THE SUN

The proper way to coil down a right-hand laid line to avoid getting kinks in it, going along with a Mate's admonishment, "Coil it clockwise, damn it, *with the sun*", to a new deckhand.

WOOD DECKING

1. Older standard barges in the coal trade had *wood floors* in their cargo boxes and a sump box in their corners in order to let rain water be pumped out and not add to the tonnage, or increased draft, of the barges. This practice is no longer utilized.

2. On some deck barges that have crawler cranes equipped with treads, *wood decking* will be laid in order to spread the weight of the crane and its load over a wider area of the barge's framing and plating as it is walking up and down the deck while working.

WOODBOAT

A somewhat flimsy boat cobbled together at a woodlot by a "woodhawk", loaded with cordwood that was then sold to passing steamboats, sometimes including the woodboat itself, which was then chopped up and used for additional firewood. See: WOODING UP.

WOODEN CIRCLE

The outward reinforcing circle of a paddlewheel that is attached on the ARMS just below where the bucket planks are fitted to the wheel. The circle consists of wooden blocks, gibs, and wedge keys that are enclosed and contained in the wheel by the IRON CIRCLE, one on each side of the arms, which hold the blocks in place by through-bolts between the circles, both wooden and iron.

WOODEN ISLANDS

In the early 1800s these were described as places in rivers where large quantities of driftwood had accumulated and blocked parts of the channel. One such *island* was probably the fore-runner to the great RED RIVER RAFT.

WOODING UP

The exercise of taking on a load of wood for fuel on a steamboat at a woodlot, or a woodyard, located along the river wherever there was a supply of cut timber. The woodlot was run by a person called a "woodhawk" and was sold by the cord (8'long x 4'high x 4'wide). At times a woodhawk would have a flat that was loaded with cordwood; the flat would be lashed alongside an upbound steamer and unloaded as the vessel made its way upstream. When unloaded the woodhawk and his flat would be cast off to drift back to his landing. This was probably the first type of mid-stream fueling operation conducted on the river system.

WORK or WORKING

1. A vessel whose timbers or plates have some movement, either from the limberness of the hull or from stresses to the hull in heavy weather. If the *working* movement is severe enough, some weakening of the hull may occur resulting in leakage through the seams.

2. What all crew members do aboard tugs, towboats and barges. The word evolved from the German and Dutch

werk, meaning an "action done or completed".

WORK BARGE or FLAT

1. A small barge, usually non-powered, that is used around fleets to distribute, or take off, rigging or lines, and may have dewatering pumps to pump out water from cargo boxes or voids.

2. A barge utilized by the USCG Buoy Tenders that carry all the equipment necessary to set and maintain aids to navigation.

WORK LIGHTS

Those lights used around the main deck, as well as some floodlights, of a towboat or tug while performing work or handling rigging during darkness.

WORK VEST

An approved type of LIFE JACKET worn by crew members on the inland waters that is not as bulky as the type worn in deep-sea trades, giving the crew members greater flexibility to work more efficiently and safely.

WORKBOAT

A small towboat used at fleets, shipyards, and dock facilities. Called by various names, i.e., *fleet boat, harbor boat, a mule, store boat, shift boat,* etc.

WORKING AHEAD

The act on a towboat or tug of engaging a vessel's engine in the ahead position to either depart a lock or landing; or to slowly work against a line to hold position, or to maneuver the vessel's stern away from where moored.

WORKING WITH NATURE

All good Pilots learn to use the vagaries of nature to their advantage rather than work against them. They learn how to judge the speed of the current, its set or angle, it's eddies, the location of slack water. They learn how and where to anticipate a reef in a crossing; how to determine the wind's direction (especially with regard to empty barges) and any changes in its direction or speed, particularly sudden gusts. In addition, a Pilot must learn how current and wind affect the tow's heading. All other weather variances, including rain, snow, fog, moonlight and sunshine and their resulting data are all entered into a computer called the Pilot's brain. Hopefully the results of the outcome are the best of all possibilities and computations.

WORKMANSHIP

The degree of skill and craftsmanship in which a vessel is designed, constructed, and outfitted.

WORM, PARCEL AND SERVE

The act of filling the contour grooves of a line or wire with small stuff, which is usually tarred to lubricate it and help prevent moisture from entering the interior of the line or wire (to WORM); the lines or wire are then wrapped with strips of canvas or similar material (to PARCEL) in the same direction, or with the lay; and finally binding (to SERVE) the cloth covering strips very tightly, closely, and continuously against the lay with small stuff, cowtail, or the like. As the old riverman's chant says:

"*Worm* and *parcel* with the lay,
Turn and *serve* the other way."

On the river it used to be done extensively on wire rigging that had eye splices to prevent crew members from getting snagged by FISH HOOKS of wire strands in the splice, and especially on tank barges to prevent sparks when dragging a wire across the deck. Since most wire fittings used on barges are now SWAGED rather than spliced, the practice is seldom undertaken today.

WRECK

Any vessel, towboat, tugboat, or barge that has been severely damaged or sunk, rendering it unable to navigate, or unsuitable for navigation. The term derives from the Anglo-French *wrec,* which meant "wreckage washed ashore". ADM Smyth's Word Book of

1867 indicated that the word came from a type of seaweed called "wrack" that the sea washes on shore, as at times does the debris from sunken vessels.

WRECK MARKINGS

When any vessel or other craft is in a sunken condition the USCG requires of the owner to suitably mark it by night and day to warn and prevent another vessel from striking the wreck. Most often a buoy is used and placed on the channel side of the obstruction at a suitable distance away from the wreck.

The banner heading of the Riverman's Bible, well into their second century of publishing to bring all the river news that's fit to print to those who work on our rivers and canals and those whose businesses benefit from the fruits of low-cost, environmentally friendly, and energy efficient mode of transportation. Hope to see you in the year 3000.

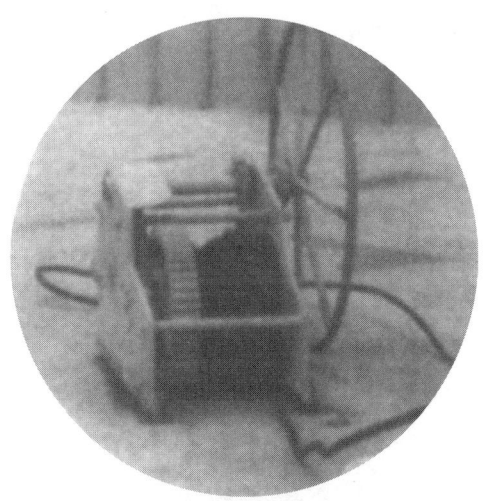

WINCH
Typical type winch used on towboats and barges

WARNING SIGN
Federal regulations, Title 46, requires tank barges with flammable or dangerous cargoes to display a warning sign visible to both port and starboard sides of the barge. The sign will have a holder for a cargo information card listing data of the cargo and safety precautions. At or near the warning sign will be a mail box or certificate holder for the barge's Certificate of Inspection, shipping papers, and other pertinent data. A painted red flag is also displayed on the barge.

WHEELS
Spare wheels stored at an inland shipyard to be used as replacement if required for vessels on drydock needing repair. See PROPELLER.

WHISTLES

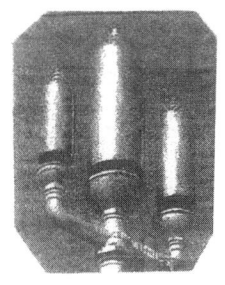 

**STEAMBOAT
3-CHIME WHISTLE**

**AIR HORN WHISTLE
USED ON MOST DIESEL
TUGS & TOWBOATS**

WICKET DAMS
The Chanoine wickets shown here are of the Davis Island Lock (see), the first lock constructed on the Ohio River a short distance below Pittsburgh, PA. It opened to river traffic in 1885.

TYPICAL WIRING USAGE ON BARGE TOWS

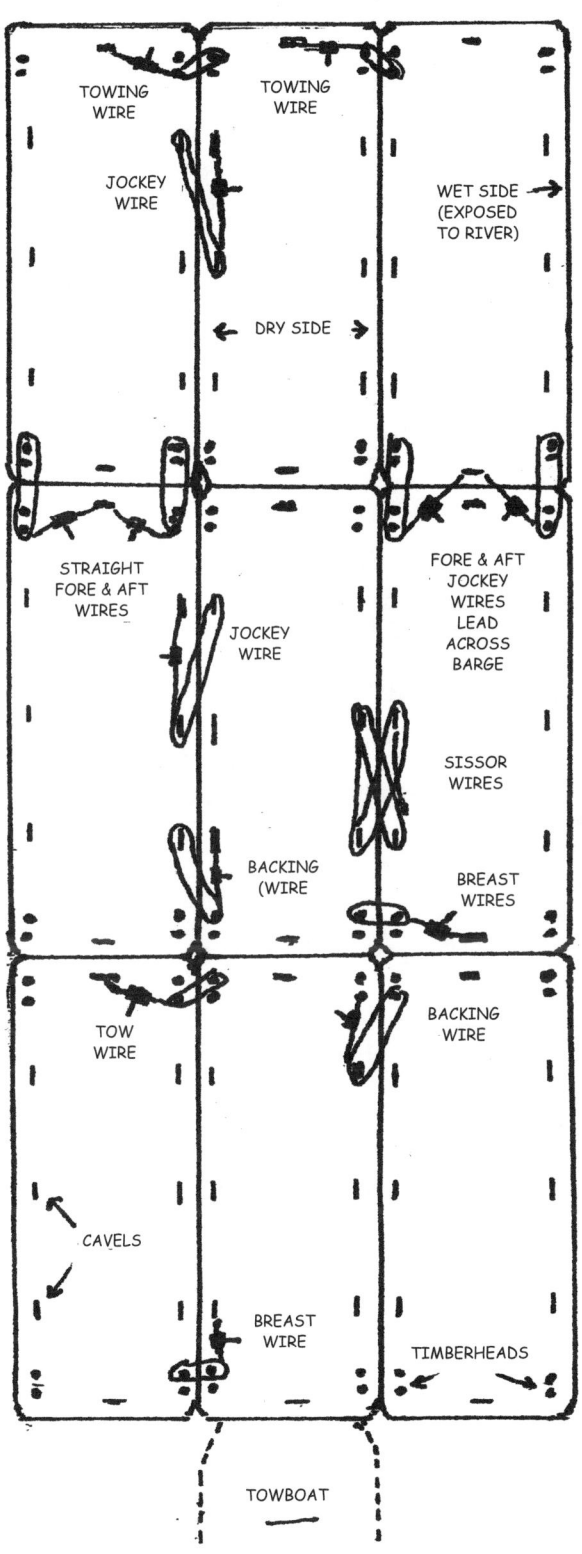

Many more sets of wires, ratchets, slings, and chain links are in use on a tow of barges than the examples shown in the diagram.

TOWING WIRE—a wire between a string of barges being pushed by the towboat leading aft to the strings on eithert side.

BACKING WIRE—a wire leading forward from a barge string being pushed to the strings on either side. It takes the main strain when the towboat is going astern.

JOCKEY WIRES—used in tandem between two strings of barges that insure the strings stay rigid whetherthe tow is going ahead or astern.

FORE & AFT WIRES—used when coupling two barges together end on end.

FORE & AFT JOCKEY WIRES—wires used together that cross at the coupling between the barges that keeps them totally rigid without any lateral sliding.

BREAST WIRE—a wire that holds barges or strings of them together.

WET SIDE—the river side or the outside walkway of tow strings.

DRY SIDE—the inside walkway between two or more strings of a barge tow where a person should walk when out on a tow.

X

XENON LIGHT

A projection-type searchlight powered with a bulb that is filled with a gas called xenon. The term comes from the Greek xenos, meaning "strange". The discoverer of the gas before the turn of the 20th century named it, apparently since he didn't know much about it. When a xenon light is turned on by what is called a "short arc", it produces a very bright light with a range of about five miles. It has basically replaced the CARBON ARC LIGHT that was used as a searchlight on towboats for many years.

**XENON LIGHT
(CARLISLE & FINCH COMPANY)**

This type light was the first great improvement to night vision for pilots since the carbon arc light was invented. In this new 21st Century mariners can look forward to further advanced technology to help them see in the dark by the use of thermanl imaging cameras.

Y

YACHT

The term is currently used to describe fairly large, fancy, and luxurious pleasure craft, either powered by sail or machinery. A *yacht* was originally referred to as a well appointed sailing vessel that was in the service of royalty, nobility, or officers and dignitaries of the realm. Nowadays it is the toy of anyone who can afford to own one. The word is brought to us from the Dutch *jaghte,* which in turn came from *jaghteschip,* which meant a "fast pirate ship". Noted in this volume to differentiate between vessels that are useful and pleasurable, and those that are simply pleasurable.

YARD

1. An abbreviated term for a SHIPYARD, and applies to much of the equipment employed there, i.e. *yard crane*, *yard paint shop*, *yard employees*, etc. This use comes from the Old English *gerd*, meaning an "enclosure or the land around a home."

2. A distance of three feet, or half a fathom. The term comes from the Dutch *gard*, meaning a rod or stick. The Old English used the term "rod" to be a measurement of distance which was the length of the measuring stick they used (about 16 feet). The length measurement of a *yard* being 3 feet didn't come into use until the 1800s.

YARDARM

A short spar from the mast from which the U.S. Flag is flown. See: VERGE.

YARN

1. Single threads of fiber are twisted together to make *yarn*; *yarns* are twisted to form strands, which in turn are twisted into LINE or rope.

2. Embellished stories which can often be heard emanating from one or more people sitting on the LAZY or LIAR'S BENCH.

YAW

A deviation from the desired course to port or starboard, or back and forth. It can be caused by weather conditions, but is usually the result of sloppy steering. A SKEG is sometimes used to reduce the *yaw* motion of a vessel. It is uncertain of the term's origination, but it may have come the Norse *jaga*, meaning "to fall off course".

YAWL

A small open boat about 14' to 16' long carried aboard a towboat or tug that is propelled by oars or a small outboard engine. Used as a utility boat for various purposes, i.e., to put a line ashore, to pick up or put off a crew member on shore, to paint the side of a vessel at the waterline, etc. Most often it is constructed with a pointed bow, square stern, and flat bottom. It is called by various names, see: SKIFF. It is believed that the name *yawl* first originated as a pulling or oared boat in Great Britain. Some have opined that it came from Scottish emigrants who came to America from near the town of Youghal, Scotland, which is pronounced "yawl", or as southerners would say, "ya'll come". Later masts were added to the vessel and it is described in various texts in various ways. However, when settlers came across the mountains to the Ohio Valley they brought the type of boat they called a *yawl* with them and it is still used today for numerous purposes.

YELLOW BUOY or FLAG

Not often seen on the river, but if encountered, keep well clear. The signal identifies a QUARANTINE BUOY area.

YOKE

An inverted U-shaped device that is attached to a valve bonnet supporting the valve nut fastened to the bonnet stud. A reach rod is fastened to the *yoke* that can be turned by a hand wheel to open and close the valve. The term

502 YOU HAVE TO

derives from the shape of a cross bar which was fitted and placed over the necks of oxen when they were working. The word is traced back to the Latin *iungere,* meaning "to join".

"YOU HAVE TO GO OUT......"

There was a saying in the old Life Saving Service that said, *"You have to go out, but you don't have to come back"*. It was attributed to the Skipper of a lifeboat at Cape Hatteras (Patrick Etheridge). As the crew shoved off to make a rescue of a vessel on the shoals, a crewman shouted out to Etheridge that they may make it to the ship, but they wouldn't be able to make it back to shore.

In 1915 the Life Saving Service and the Revenue Cutter Service were merged together, forming the U.S. Coast Guard. With that merger, the newly formed USCG kept Article VI of the Life Saving Service regulations intact in its Instruction for USCG Stations, as follows:

"In attempting a rescue the keeper will select either the boat, breeches buoy, or life car, as in his judgement is best suited to effectively cope with the existing conditions. If the device first selected fails after such trial as satisfies him that no further attempt with it is feasible, he will resort to one of the others, and if that fails, then to the remaining one, and he will not desist from his efforts until by actual trial the impossibility of effecting a rescue is demonstrated. The statement of the keeper that he did not try to use the boat because the sea or surf was too heavy will not be accepted unless attempts to launch it were actually made and failed, or unless the conformation of the coast – as bluffs, precipitous banks, etc. – is such as to unquestionably preclude the use of a boat."

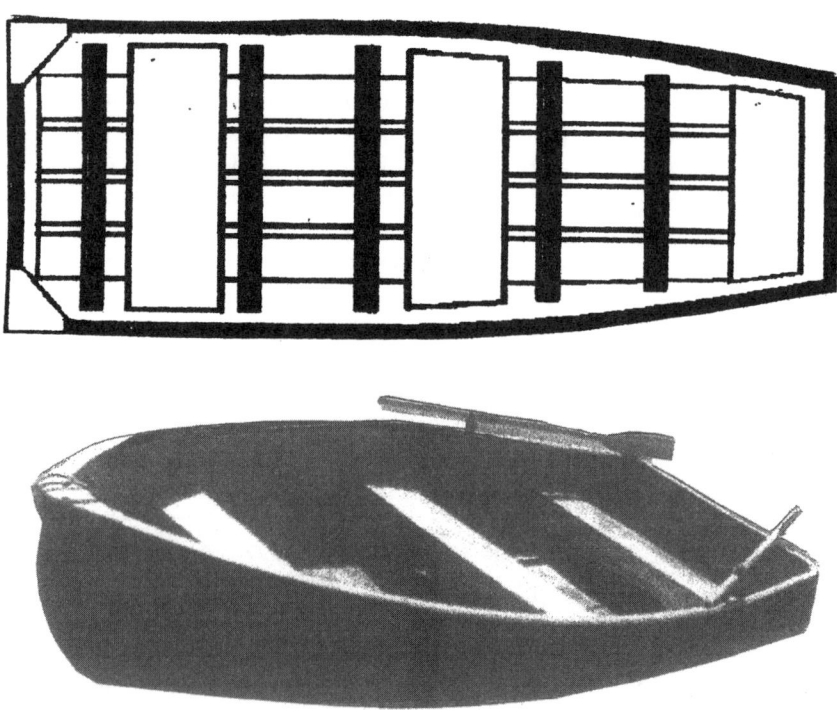

YAWL, SKIFF, DINGHEY, JON BOAT, Etc.
(also see: ZODIAC)

Z

Z-CARD
A short name for a card called a Merchant Mariners Document issued by the USCG to people attesting to their proficiency in certain maritime endeavors.

Z-DRIVE
A fairly modern innovation of propulsion in which propellers are mounted on pods emerging from the bottom of a vessel that have the ability to turn a full 360 degrees when directing their thrust. In this mode the vessel does not require a rudder. The operational thrust is first converted from a horizontal drive shafting from a vessel's engines to a vertical shaft in the propulsion unit and then again to a horizontal drive where the propeller is mounted.

Many *Z-drives* are now installed on tugs in coastal waters, especially those operating in ship assists at docks or anchorages. Up until 2008 the only units installed on a Western Rivers towboat is that of the *MISS NARI* which was converted from the hull of a conventional river towboat whose superstructure had been burned in an accident. The conversion occurred in 1982 when two Z-Pellor units were installed that operate in a kort nozzle. However, in 2008 and 9, Southern Towing of Memphis built four towboats employing this new technology to be used on the Western Rivers.

The name *Z-Drive* comes to us from "azimuth", which is a coordinate used by astronomers to denote an arc, or angle of an object's vertical position measured from a fixed reference point. It also can measure the horizontal angle or direction of a compass bearing. Therefore, the drive unit is capable of directing a vessel in any direction without forward or astern propulsion. The root of "azimuth" is Arabic *as sant*, meaning "the way", or, *as summut*, meaning "the direction". See: TRACTOR TUG.

ZEBRA MUSSEL
A species of invasive small, freshwater bivalve mollusk that was first discovered in the Great Lakes in 1988. It is believed to have been introduced to this country through the ballast water of an arriving freighter. They have spread throughout the river system of the U.S. from the Great Lakes into the Illinois Waterway and then to the Mississippi system. A nuisance, *zebra mussels* attach to hulls, increasing drag, causing higher fuel usage; clog water cooling intakes; and rapidly reproduce. They are to the hulls of inland vessels what barnacles are to our brethren of the ocean trades.

ZERO IN
To align a piece of machinery or a piece of equipment to a proper setting.

ZIG-ZAG CROSSING
A river crossing that requires a couple or more of course changes.

ZIG-ZAG PILOT
A Pilot who continually over-steers a vessel, requiring corrective rudder action, and then over-corrects their own steering action, resulting in excessive rudder action, waste of fuel, and a slower rate of speed.

ZINC ANODE
Sacrificial plates (anode) that are placed on propeller shafting, kort nozzles, hulls, etc. to prevent galvanic corrosive action on the propeller or hull itself.

ZINC COATING
A protective type of coating that goes on steel as a primer and is then over-coated with compatible top coats, such as epoxies or vinyl's.

ZODIAC
A trade name for a type of inflatable rubber boat that is used by some towboat companies to transport people and gear from and to the vessel.

ZONE

Used to denote a particular geographic area that is under the command of a USCG office.

ZONE TIME

The local time for the area in which a vessel is working.

ZZZ – ZZZ – ZZZ

An acronym for falling asleep when one is tired or bored or after absorbing all the foregoing terms. When you do, have pleasant dreams of the river, the vessels that have plied them from the dugouts, log rafts, flatboats, keelers, steamboats, to the present craft navigating our inland streams. And dream of the people that have preceded those making their livelihood in the river trades and pray for those that will follow that they may find as much enjoyment in being a riverman as it has meant to you and to me.

Z—DRIVE

The Z—Drive unit is located in a separate compartment, allowing it to be lifted out using a crane when repair is required for the propeller, the kort, or the machinery without requiring drydocking of the vessel.

Coupling to engine drive shaft

Housing for vertical shafting coupled to horizontal tail shaft

Zinc Anode

Kort nozzle enclosing the propeller

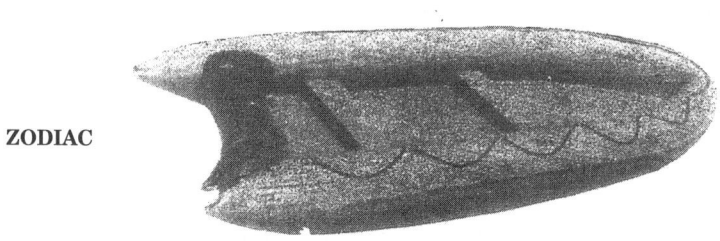

ZODIAC